GRAPHIC ARTISTS GUILD HANDBOOK

Pricing & Ethical Guidelines

SIXTEENTH EDITION

PUBLISHER & EDITOR

Graphic Artists Guild

NEW YORK, NY

DISTRIBUTOR

The MIT Press

CAMBRIDGE, MA

DEDICATED TO THE MEMORY OF
Milton Glaser (1929–2020)

The prolific life of graphic designer Milton Glaser came full circle on his 91st birthday, June 26, 2020. Yet his influence on design and American culture will live on. His famous Bob Dylan poster that was packaged with *Bob Dylan's Greatest Hits* album was one of the first of over 400 posters Glaser created throughout his career. Six million have been printed and distributed, and originals are collectibles worth hundreds of dollars.

His most iconic design was the I ❤ NY logo he created for New York State in 1976 as part of a campaign to promote tourism, especially in New York City, which was crime-ridden and on the brink of financial collapse. The logo, which he did *pro bono*, has been copied and modified thousands of times all over the world due to its universal appeal. It earns the state millions of dollars each year from licensing fees and merchandise.

The breadth of Glaser's work spans the entire design discipline— identity campaigns, book covers, packaging, signage, displays, film and TV advertising, and commercial environments. His redesign of the Windows on the World restaurant atop the World Trade Center included dinnerware, rugs, lighting fixtures, menus, and all its communication. His work also included illustration and even font design.

Push Pin Studios, which Milton co-founded with friends in 1954, was an international force in the 1960s and 70s, with a legacy that continues to inspire designers and illustrators today. He went on to influence popular culture with *New York Magazine*, co-founded with Clay Felker in 1968. Milton and designer William Bernard opened WBMG in 1983, where they designed or redesigned numerous publications, including *The Village Voice*, *The Washington Post*, and *Esquire*. Milton also mentored several generations of students, at Cooper Union and the School of Visual Arts.

In his work, Milton delighted in taking disparate influences from the past to create something entirely new and contemporary. Who could imagine that inspiration from a Marcel Duchamp self-portrait and Islamic art would result in the Bob Dylan poster that would become an icon of the psychedelic 1960s?

Milton is the only graphic designer to receive the National Medal of the Arts, and despite creating work for numerous prestigious clients, he was not impressed with fame or fortune. Early in his career he had to make a choice between pursuing fine art or commercial art. He said he chose commercial art because, "I wanted to do work that was public . . . work that was on the street . . .work that people saw." Although his design of interior spaces included such elegant places as the Rainbow Room at Rockefeller Center, the makeover he did for the struggling supermarket chain Grand Union appealed to him because it was anti-elitist.

His passion for design was coupled with his compassion. During New York's darkest hour, after the terrorist attacks of September 11, 2001, Milton designed a modified version of his iconic logo to help heal the city. I ❤ NY More Than Ever— with a dark bruise on the heart—was distributed as a poster throughout the city and reproduced on the front and back of *The Daily News*.

In an interview for *Surface* in 2018, Milton stated, "[Making the world a better place through art] is the highest attainment of the specialization. It is to recognize that it is not all about you, and that you have a communal function you can serve to help everyone get along." In his final days, Milton was working on another project for the people of his beloved city—a graphic titled *Together*—to help spread the message that "we are not alone" during the forced isolation of the Covid-19 pandemic. As he told *The New York Times*, "'We're all in this together' has been reiterated a thousand times, but you can create the symbolic equivalent of that phrase by just using the word 'together', and then making those letters [look] as though they are all different, but all related."

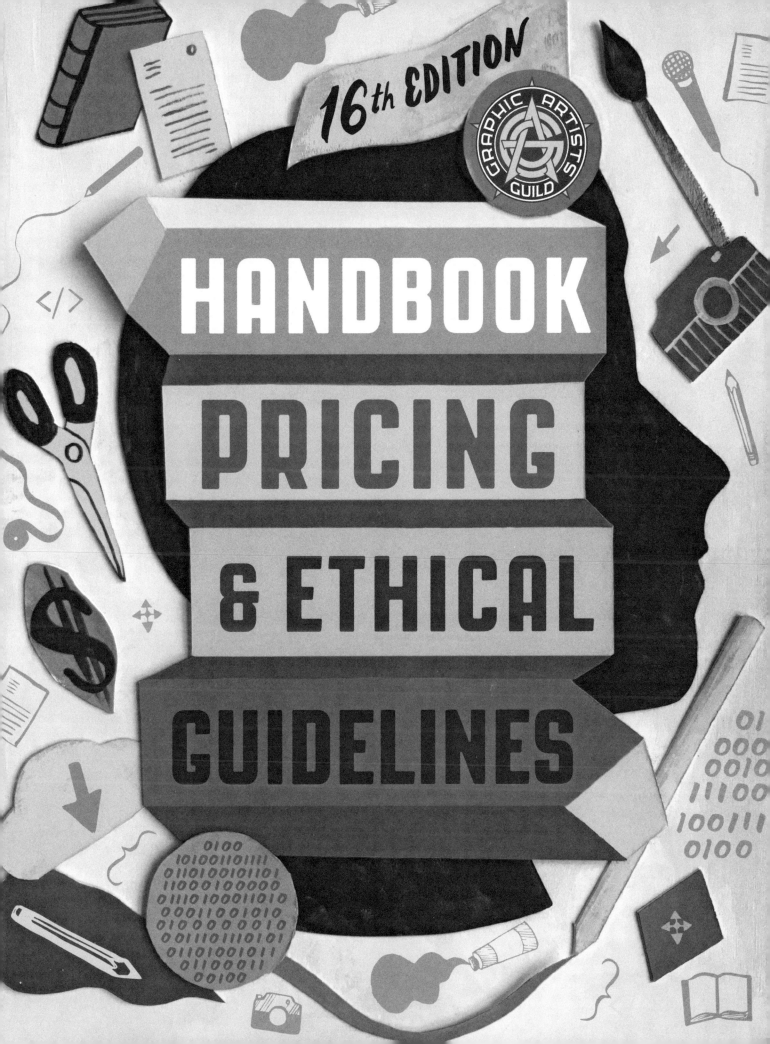

Published in the United States of America by the Graphic Artists Guild, Inc. 31 West 34th Street, 8th Fl. New York, NY 10001 USA Telephone: 212.791.3400 www.graphicartistsguild.org

Copyright ©2021, 2018, 2013, 2010, 2007, 2003, 2001, 1997, 1994, 1991, 1987 by the Graphic Artists Guild, Inc. except where noted. All rights reserved. No part of this book may be reproduced in any form or by electronic or mechanical means including information storage and retrieval systems without written permission from the Graphic Artists Guild, except reviewers who may quote brief passages to be published in a magazine, newspaper, or online publication.

LIBRARY OF CONGRESS CONTROL NUMBER: 2020938780

ISBN 978-0-262-54239-5

1 2 3 4 5 6 7 8 9

GUILD PRESIDENT
Lara J. Kisielewska
www.optimumdc.com

EXECUTIVE EDITOR
Patricia McKiernan

PROJECT MANAGER AND EDITOR
Deborah Kantor

ART DIRECTION AND
GUILD BOARD LIAISON
Linda Secondari
studiolosecondari.com

COVER DESIGN AND ILLUSTRATION
Kimberly Glyder
www.kimberlyglyder.com

BOOK DESIGN AND
PREPRESS PRODUCTION
Jill Shimabukuro

DESIGN SUPPORT
Jordan Wannemacher

PROOFREADER AND INDEXER
Heather Dubnick
www.hdubnick.com

PRINTING AND BINDING
Sheridan
A CJK Group Company

WORLDWIDE DISTRIBUTORS
The MIT Press
Massachusetts Institute of Technology
One Rogers Street
Cambridge, MA 02142

DIRECT-MAIL DISTRIBUTION
Graphic Artists Guild
212.791.3400
www.graphicartistsguild.org

Contents

1.

Running a Successful Graphic Arts Business

2.

Salaries, Pricing Guidelines, & Trade Practices

3.

Protecting Your Business & Intellectual Property

4.

Successfully Applying Practices

5.

Resources & References

About the Author

Serving artists and the graphic arts industry since 1967, the Graphic Artists Guild has established itself as the leading advocate for the rights of graphic artists on a wide range of economic and legislative issues, from copyright to tax law. Through this publication, *Graphic Artists Guild Handbook: Pricing & Ethical Guidelines*, the Guild has raised ethical standards in the industry and has provided an invaluable resource of industry information that is relied on by both artists and clients. The 16th edition represents 48 years of publication, with updated editions published about every three years.

The Graphic Artists Guild serves illustrators, designers, web creators, production artists, cartoonists, animators, surface pattern designers, and other graphic creators on a national basis. The Guild provides a wealth of services and benefits for its members, including professional educational programs, networking opportunities, discounts on a multitude of products and services, a legal referral network, and grievance handling. The Guild's website (www. graphicartistsguild.org) offers current information on Guild activities, updates on advocacy issues, members' portfolios, employment opportunities, and useful tools and resources for all graphic artists.

Foreword

My first "real" illustration job, in the mid-90s, came from Steve Heller at *The New York Times Book Review*. Of course it did. Steve is famous for giving new, untried illustrators a big break.

I had already been a scrappy cartoonist for several years, self-publishing minicomics by "borrowing" a photocopier at my friend's night job, and selling them through the mail to an underground network of fans for $2 a pop, but I'd never worked with a client before.

Working with Steve was easy. He was clear with his instructions, gave excellent feedback, didn't try for a crazy rights grab, and paid on time. None of which prepared me for the NEXT client. What to charge? How to make sure I get paid? How should I respond to this zillion-page contract? Wait, you want a contract from *me?* What the hell does that look like?

I am essentially self-taught. I didn't go to art school, and I had to figure out how to build an art career on my own. That felt scary. Fortunately, more experienced illustrators pointed me to the *Graphic Artists Guild Handbook: Pricing & Ethical Guidelines*. It was astonishing. Reading this hefty tome, full of the collected knowledge of thousands of professional graphic artists, I felt like I was donning a suit of armor.

What I've learned since then, as a professor in art school for the last 20 years, is that even going to art school is no guarantee you'll be taught anything at all about the demands and complexities of becoming successful as a professional artist working with clients.

In the last five years, I've moved into teaching and coaching mid-career professionals and aspiring pros as well. Learning to take charge of your creative life isn't something that happens by magic or osmosis, no matter how long you've been at it. The Muse doesn't grant you creative business acumen. Yet, that's the expectation I find most of us have—that artistic talent alone should be enough to build a career and that if you're an artist, there's something wrong with caring about building your business.

If you feel this way, it isn't your fault. The messages reinforcing that idea are everywhere. A friend talked about how "normals" see us as "purple unicorns" —amazing and magical yet utterly useless in any practical context.

I say, screw that.

The core underlying principle of everything I teach and do is that *you can take control of your life.* You *can* build a sustainable, resilient, creativity-centered career. I want to demystify the process and put tools in the hands of every person who wants to build a successful creative business.

And one of the most powerful tools I've ever encountered is this book. It's the only textbook I make my undergrads buy.

It's not only about pricing (the first thing anyone looks at, I'm sure).

It's about ETHICAL guidelines—the standards for how we should be treated as professionals and for how we should conduct business. It's a framework for seeing your own business as having the same legal rights and standing as the largest corporations. It's a tool to help you recognize the value of your work as intellectual property—how to protect it and how it can continue to support you.

It's the collected and compounded wisdom of our peers who came before us, generously sharing their knowledge, trying to save us from their missteps, in a kind of virtual mutual aid society.

It's eminently practical but embodies a subtly life-changing shift of perspective. When you hold this book in your hands, you hold the power to take control of your creative career.

JESSICA ABEL

Autonomous Creative and the Creative Focus Workshop

www.jessicaabel.com

Diversity, Equity, & Inclusion

Since its inception, the Graphic Artists Guild has fought for justice and equity for working graphic artists. In line with our mission statement and our origin as a labor organization, our advocacy work has focused on the economic realities of illustrators and designers. To that end, we have educated working artists on best business practices, advocated for fairness in the copyright system, supported legislation which benefits graphic artists, and communicated with policy makers on what our community needs to thrive.

However, our efforts are worth nothing if the economic rewards of artists' labor are not equally accessible to all our members. Inequity persists in the United States. This means that our members, and those in the larger community of graphic artists, do not all have equal access to financial resources, fair wages, and basic necessities such as quality health care.

In recognition of this, the Graphic Artists Guild is committed to pursuing a more diverse representation among our membership and on our board. We are working to promote social justice and diversity in all Guild activities, addressing issues related but not limited to race, ethnicity, gender, gender identity, sexual orientation, culture, religion, age, and ability. We are also committed to addressing the responsibility graphic artists have collectively, in creating and contributing to a fairer society. This extends to how we pursue our craft, how we conduct our business relationships, and how we add to the greater public good.

If our members cannot thrive equitably as graphic artists, based on the merits of their work, then we will have failed. We value inclusion as a core element of our mission. We firmly believe that together, we go farther in accomplishing that mission.

This work is ongoing. As we develop policy and best practices to support our members and the larger community of graphic artists, we will be adding them to www.graphicartistsguild.org/policy.

President's Prologue

We have definitely been cursed by living in interesting times. As I write this, at the close of a year no one will ever forget, the only constant in our lives has been change. We are each at a markedly different place than we were at the start of 2020, a place we could not have imagined—neither personally nor professionally. It's hard to count the ways that life is different now. And some things may never return to being the same as they always were.

We're all facing some measure of economic uncertainty brought on by the global pandemic. Some of us have lost jobs or opportunities, whereas others of us are busier than ever, as small businesses turn to digital communications for customer outreach. Some of us are adjusting to working from home, and others, who have always worked remotely, are relieved that the perceived stigma of working from home has been lifted.

One of this year's lessons is the importance of advocating for yourself—with policy makers to ask for pandemic assistance, with clients to express the value you deliver, and with potential clients to justify your worth. That is where our *Graphic Artists Guild Handbook: Pricing & Ethical Guidelines (PEGs)* remains a constant. The value *PEGs* offers is not in providing you with a cheat sheet on what to charge. It lies in the advice on how to work professionally, communicate effectively, and most importantly, convey the value of your work.

PEGs itself also teeters on the edge of change. Some of that change has already occurred in this 16th edition, as we've expanded content on pricing and income. But the most significant change is yet to come—the Guild is working toward replacing the printed handbook with an online version. We envision the 17th edition to be fully digital, with pricing survey data continually updated.

Another area of change is marked by our Diversity, Equity, and Inclusion statement (page xv) and the launch of the Guild's new Diversity Committee. We are committed to promoting diversity and inclusion within the Guild, and equity for all graphic artists. COVID-19 has exacerbated the inequities that already existed within our economy, including the graphic arts industry. The Guild recognizes this and is working to create a more diverse Board, develop a policy that supports more diversity, and engage with like-minded organizations that will expand our access to underserved areas.

The Graphic Artists Guild is dedicated to promoting and protecting the economic interests of graphic artists of all stripes—illustrators, graphic designers, cartoonists, animators, surface pattern designers, web/interactive designers, art directors, and more. In support of that mission, we have enhanced and expanded the *Handbook*'s focus on helping graphic artists achieve a sustainable living in this edition.

The Guild is built on three core principles, Advocacy, Community, and Business Resources. Producing *PEGs* fits squarely into that third category, along with monthly webinars and weekly podcasts. In fulfilling our Advocacy mission, the Guild represents the interests of graphic artists on Capitol Hill, at the Copyright Office, and internationally. And we build Community by offering a wide range of social and networking events to members and non-members alike. The Guild is first and foremost a membership organization. While we are immensely proud of *PEGs,* our most notable achievement, I invite all graphic artists who find this publication useful to visit www.graphicartistsguild.org and find out more about who we are and how we can help your career.

In this age of tremendous change and uncertainty, Guild members have each other's backs. Join us as a fellow member, or simply make use of the best practices for graphic artists outlined within this book and support our industry by being a model citizen. Either way, we're here for you, as a resource and as a champion in your corner fighting for positive change for all graphic artists.

LARA J. KISIELEWSKA
President, Graphic Artists Guild

Acknowledgments

Jessica Abel
Rocco Baviera
Jason W. Bay
Ilise Benun
Greg Betza
Rebecca Blake
Greg Britton
Eva Doman Bruck
Ellen Byrne
Kevin Callahan
Frederick H. Carlson
Joy Ting Charde
Echo Chernik
Angie Chua
John H. Clark
Becca Clason
Merril Cledera
Zachary Clemente
Stephanie Cooke
Ted Crawford, Esq.
Yanique DaCosta
Alan Daniels
Beau Daniels
Peggy Dean
Frank DeMarco
Meredith Desmond
Liz DiFiore
Martha DiMeo
Bil Donovan
Marion Y. Dorfer
Sophia Dowell
Alexandra Drosu
Ken Dutton
Meredith Elson
Sara Garson
Gayle Gaynin
Bethe Geller
Jeanetta Gonzales
Ilana Griffo

Jillian Hache
Lesley Ellen Harris, Esq.
Alison Hau
Nikki Hess
Paula Hinkle
Justine Lee Hirten
Lauren Hom
Danielle Hughes
Melissa Hyatt
Sue Jenkins
Julie Johnson
Sean Kane
Diane Kappa
Linda Joy Kattwinkel, Esq.
Caitlin Keegan
Blair Kelly
Joyce Ketterer
Ben Kiel
Jim Kopp
Ru Kuwahata
Lynne Lavelle
Veronica Lawlor
Caryn R. Leland, Esq.
Lou Leonardis
Ted Leonhardt
Rose Lowry
Karina Maas
Dan Mall
Nina May
Judith Mayer
Matthew McElligott
Erin McManness
Juliet Meeks
Nicole Mellor
Ted Michalowski
Jeremy Mickel
Janine Miller
Mark C. Miller
Gabriela Mirensky

Dawn Mitchell
Terrence Moline
Jeff Mottle
Jeanine Murch
Jess Murphy
Steven Noble
Colleen O'Hara
Elizabeth Olwen
Adam Osgood
Adrienne Palmiere
Shelli Paroline
Caitlin Pearce
Marc Phares
Max Porter
James Provost
Adam Questell
Nancy Ruzow
Cindy Salans Rosenheim
Steven Salerno
Colleen Sheehan
Jess Sheehan
James Sholly
Jon Sholly
Elizabeth Silver
Jamie Silverberg
Mark Simon
Mark Simonson
Eugene Smith
Eben Sorkin
Kristina Swarner
Jen Sweeney
Jon Valk
Luis Vargas
Christina Wald
Michael Waraksa
Theresa Whitehill
Kelly Wurster
Minjea Yoon
Christian William Zagarskas

American Society for Collective Rights Licensing (ASCRL)
Association of Registered Graphic Designers (RGD)
Creator Resource
Famous Frames, Inc.
Freelancers Union
Game Industry Career Guide
Lemonade Illustration Agency
Massachusetts Independent Comics Expo (MICE)
Morgan Gaynin, Inc.
Old Stone Press
One Club for Creativity
Society of Illustrators
Spark Design Professionals
The Animation Guild, Local 839, IATSE
The Creative Group
The Licensing Letter

Many thanks to the hundreds of graphic arts professionals—both Guild members and nonmembers—who
have contributed their expertise over the years to this
cooperative effort, including those who anonymously
completed the 2020 Pricing Surveys that are the basis for
the most current pricing data.

How To Use This Book

The 16th edition of the *Graphic Artists Guild Handbook: Pricing & Ethical Guidelines* continues to be a work in progress, evolving to meet the changing needs of graphic artists and their clients. It seeks to be as neutral and objective as possible and aims to promote the understanding that fees and terms are always negotiable between buyer and seller.

To some, the prices shown in the book will be too low; for others, too high. Still others may complain that prices do not reflect the current economy. The Guild recognizes that the level of expertise, years of experience, and reputation of the graphic artist will affect what is charged, as will the cost of living and size of the market where an artist works.

This book covers many different disciplines within the graphic arts; some specialties and niche markets within the industry are stronger than others, while some are affected more easily by changes in the economy. Rapid changes in technology have also had a major impact on pricing and the amount of work available in traditional print media. However, at the same time, advances in technology have created many new opportunities in digital media for graphic artists.

It is intended that the *Handbook* be what it says it is—*guidelines*, and only guidelines, for the seller and buyer to use to arrive at fair and equitable pricing for the work under consideration. The pricing charts, based on the latest feedback and reviewed by outstanding practitioners for each discipline, are not meant to be specific set prices. It is up to the individual graphic artist to determine how to price work—after taking into account all the factors related to the work.

So much information is packed into the *Handbook* that readers may miss valuable wisdom in their effort to quickly find a suitable contract or price. We suggest reading the book cover to cover and becoming familiar with issues that affect all disciplines. At the very least, read the chapter introductions; they will give you an overview and help direct you to specific information.

Part 1, Running a Successful Graphic Arts Business, is an introduction to the factors graphic artists need to consider if they want to be self-employed. They include essential business practices, such as pricing services, negotiating, and getting paid; professional relationships and ethical standards; and an in-depth look at professional and health and safety issues for both employees and the self-employed. The last chapter in this part covers the often-overlooked importance of marketing yourself to maintain a constant revenue stream, and ways to maximize your income in order to enjoy a sustainable livelihood.

Part 2, Salaries, Pricing Guidelines, & Trade Practices, is divided into six chapters, each featuring a major graphic art discipline that is further broken down by numerous sub-disciplines. The chapters cover, in depth, the many trade practices unique to the specific disciplines, enabling both art buyers and graphic artists to understand and appreciate the demands on time and talent reflected in the ranges of fees being paid.

Part 3, Protecting Your Business & Intellectual Property, includes two chapters. The first is an in-depth discussion of legal rights and issues, with a focus on copyright and related rights. The second explores the various types of contracts that graphic artists can use with a client to proactively protect their business and legal rights.

Part 4, Successfully Applying Practices, features interviews with 11 self-employed graphic arts professionals who have used many of the practices promoted in this handbook to create successful businesses and sustainable livelihoods.

Part 5, Resources & References, provides a list of numerous books, professional organizations, online course providers, websites, and other resources where you can learn more and find additional help.

The *Handbook* concludes with an Appendix of sample forms and contracts and a glossary of terms used in their development; every artist should make the effort to become familiar with these terms.

1

Running a Successful
Graphic Arts Business

{ 1 }

Essential Business Practices

This chapter discusses the fundamental business management issues common to all self-employed professionals in the graphic arts—from considering the complexities of pricing their services, bidding on jobs and preparing proposals, effectively negotiating with clients, keeping track of payment schedules, to getting paid and collection options when payment is not made in a timely manner.

SUCCESSFUL GRAPHIC ARTISTS *develop not just their creative skills but also the business skills necessary to market and maintain their careers so that they can make a sustainable living. As business people, graphic artists need to understand customary business practices, develop good client relationships, and become skilled at negotiating agreements that best protect their interests. As representatives of the graphic arts industry, they need to price their services to reflect their knowledge and expertise as well as the unique value they bring to clients. They also need to manage the record keeping necessary to assure prompt and accurate payment for their work. Securing these economic interests is the responsibility of graphic artists to themselves and their profession.*

The Nature of the Business

This handbook, which focuses on earning a living as a graphic artist, uses *graphic artist* as an umbrella term that includes graphic designers, web/interactive designers, surface pattern designers, illustrators, cartoonists, motion designers and illustrators, and animators. Graphic artists work in and do work for many different industries. Their work can be seen as corporate logos; in print, television, and web ads; in cartoons, books, magazines, and museums; on websites, phone apps, software, retail displays, retail products and packaging, clothing, textiles, movie posters, and TV titles; and as the centerpiece of animated movies.

Graphic artists may work on staff in both large and small businesses and organizations, such as corporate art departments and advertising agencies, communication companies and publishers, manufacturers, or design firms and studios.

A large percentage of graphic artists are self-employed, working as various types of freelancers: *temporary workers*, *independent contractors*, and *freelance business owners*. Some graphic artists have full-time staff jobs but also do freelancing as *moonlighters* outside of their regular work day. Others are *diversified workers*, with multiple sources of income from a mix of traditional employers and freelance work.

In the business world, graphic artists primarily sell a service to clients, not a commodity (although a creative product may be a byproduct of the service). Graphic artists are visual problem solvers, using their artistic skills to help their clients effectively communicate a message or tell a story, create a brand identity, enhance a product, or promote and sell a product or service. Therefore, the client is a key part of the graphic artist's business equation.

Clients

The graphic arts profession serves a wide variety of clients who need its services—from individuals and small business owners to educational institutions to multi-million-dollar international corporations. Potential clients can be found in every industry, market category, and media. See Figure 1–1 for the most common market categories and media in which graphic artists work.

Many graphic artists target their promotional efforts, based on the size of the client. Graphic artists just starting out may focus on small businesses, and as they create a body of commercial work and gain a reputation, attract larger and more prestigious clients. Even some well-established graphic artists may feel more comfortable working with small to medium-sized businesses or organizations.

Today, there is much more overlap between what designers and illustrators do than there was in the past. However, graphic artists still tend to specialize in doing work for clients in certain markets or industries, such as advertising, corporate, or publishing, who have needs that best match their artistic style and skills. Some artists even specialize within a specific discipline. For example, one package designer might create packaging for the entertainment industry, while another concentrates on retail products or food and beverages. On the other hand, even artists who are highly trained in a specific field, such

1–1 Examples of Market Categories & Media

The following are examples of market categories and typical media for which each market buys graphic art services. Within each category, there may be more media than space allows to be listed here.

Advertising
* Animation
* Client Presentation
  Preproduction, comps
* Collateral (brochures, mailers, flyers, handouts, catalogs)
* Displays & exhibits
* Interactive (mobile, tablets, etc.)
* Magazine/magazine supplements
* Newspaper/newspaper supplements/advertorials
* Online (websites, blogs, social media, digital publications)
* Outdoor (billboards, transit)
* Packaging (products, DVDs, videos, software, food & beverages)
* Point of sale (counter cards, shelf signs, displays)
* Posters (film, theater, concert, event)
* Presentations
* Television
* Other

Editorial
* Educational
* Audiovisual
* Encyclopedia
* Magazine
* Interactive media
* Newspaper
* Online / database
* Television
* Other

Institutional
* Annual Report
* Audiovisual (video, PowerPoint, etc.)
* Brochure
* Corporate / employee publication
* Presentation
* Other

Manufacturing
* Apparel
* Domestics
* Electronics
* Food & beverage
* Footwear
* Home furnishing
* Jewelry
* Novelty & retail goods (paper products, greeting cards, mugs, posters, calendars, giftware, other)
* Toys & games

Promotion
* Booklet
* Brochure
* Calendar
* Card
* Direct mail
* E-newsletter
* Poster
* Press Kit
* Sales literature
* Websites, social media
* Other

Book Publishing
* Anthology
* CDs / Online
* Educational text
* Mass market
* Trade
* E-books
* Other (hardcover or soft-cover edition, cover, jacket, interior, etc.)

as certified Medical Illustrators, can find other markets for their skills, such as the scientific and technical industries. Work such as web design and development, animation, and interactive media requires a more technical skill set, but all graphic artists need to keep up with rapidly changing technology, whether it's related to the software and hardware tools they use or the media for which they create work.

The Artist-Client Relationship

The artist-client relationship is one of the most important professional relationships a graphic artist will have. Graphic artists who understand this negotiate with clients to reach agreements that are mutually beneficial. Fair, honest, and straightforward business practices on both sides cultivate rewarding and lasting relationships—the key to success. For more about artist-client relationships, see Chapter 2, Professional Relationships.

Collaborative Relationships

Most projects that graphic artists work on require collaboration with other professionals in addition to clients and their representatives. A book designer, for example, may need to communicate with any of these professionals—an illustrator, photographer, writer, copy editor, proofreader, printer, and even other graphic designers. A web designer who is hired to create the aesthetic look of a website needs to collaborate with a coder and programmer to make the design functional. No one in the graphic arts business works in total isolation. Even a self-employed artist who is hired to create only the illustrations for a publication or an ad may need to work with an editor, art director, or marketing director.

A graphic artist employed on staff at an agency or in a corporate art department will be required to work as part of a team. Successful collaborations require a certain amount of give and take or compromise and mutual respect. The same communication and negotiation skills you need to work with clients can be applied to your working relationships with other professionals in the industry.

Developing positive relationships with other professionals in the graphic arts and related fields creates a network of people you can call on for advice and help throughout your career—your professional lifeline. These relationships also have economic benefits as they can lead to referrals for work. The best jobs often come by word of mouth from those who know you and your work.

Pricing Your Services

Graphic art is commissioned in highly competitive and specialized markets. Prices for each job or project are negotiated between the buyer and the seller. Each graphic artist sets his/her own prices, and no two jobs are exactly alike. The price for a job usually depends upon many factors, including how the buyer intends to make use of the art, the size and prominence of the client, the client's budget, the urgency of the deadline, the complexity of the art, and the graphic artist's reputation. Both historical and current practices reveal that the factors often considered in pricing decisions vary from discipline to discipline; the information in this chapter should be supplemented by reading corresponding sections within each discipline chapter.

In addition to the many factors to consider, pricing requires good artist-client communication, production management skills, and a careful periodic review of costs and time use.

How Much Income Do You Need?

If you want to make a sustainable living as a graphic artist, you need to treat your freelance graphic arts business like any other business. Before you even attempt to price jobs, you need to know how much annual income you need to pay your living expenses and to cover your business expenses (or overhead).

You also want to make a profit of at least 20–25%. A profit gives you the cash flow to keep running your business during times of unexpected expenses—your computer dies, a client has delayed payment, your landlord unexpectedly raises your rent, your car is involved in a collision and will be out for repairs for at least three weeks, you experience an injury that requires surgery and you can't work for a month, and the list goes on. A profit also helps give you the funds to reinvest in your business for such things as upgrading equipment, hiring an assistant, taking professional development courses to keep skills up to date, etc.

According to the Small Business Administration, 20% of small businesses fail in their first year, and 50% fail by the fifth year. Several studies that have analyzed the reasons why small businesses fail cite lack of cash flow and undercapitalization as two of the top reasons. You need to understand not only the cost of starting a business, but also of staying in business.

Once you know how much you need to earn yearly, you can divide that annual amount to arrive at an average amount you need to make per month, per week, per day, or per hour (see formulas for day and hour rates below).

These breakdowns are very helpful for understanding how much business you need to bring in and how much you should price your services. Breaking it down to shorter periods of time also helps you keep track of whether you are meeting your financial goals or falling behind.

There are various formulas for figuring out how much income you need to earn to keep your business sustainable, as well as variations of these formulas. Two of the more common ones are discussed below.

THE BASE MINIMUM REVENUE PLAN

This formula is based on starting with all your current annual expenses and adding a profit percentage to figure out how much revenue you must bring in. Annual expenses are used because if you try to use weekly or monthly expenses, it is easy to forget about expenses that are paid only quarterly or annually. This formula is good for most people, especially those just starting their own business, because it forces you to look at all your living and business expenses. It can be an eye-opener, but it really helps you become familiar with the reality of your financial situation.

LIVING EXPENSES

Besides the necessary living expenses of rent/mortgage, food, utilities, and transportation, you need to include health, life, and auto insurance; medical and education expenses; childcare; fitness and entertainment; travel and vacations; gifts and donations; and any existing debts, loans, leases etc. To make sure you don't forget anything, look at your bank and credit card statements. If you frequently use cash to pay for things, you will need to estimate those expenses.

Obviously, if you are single, your living expenses will be less than someone who has a family with children. And, if you live in a rural area or a small city, your expenses will most likely be less than someone who lives in a major metropolitan area. If you have a working spouse or partner who contributes to living expenses, then your expenses may be less than someone who has a non-working spouse or partner. The point is everyone's financial situation is different, so your income needs are different.

BUSINESS EXPENSES

A good way to make sure you have listed all your necessary annual business expenses is to use the IRS categories from Schedule C of the Income Tax Form 1040 (see Figure 1-2). If you are just starting your business, you will need to estimate these figures. Again, no two businesses will have the same expenses. Graphic artists who have an in-home studio or who are sole proprietors will

1–2 Annual Business Expenses

(Use actual figures from Schedule C of IRS Income Tax Form 1040 as a guide)

Advertising & promotion	_____
Car/Truck expenses	_____
Contract Labor	_____
Employee benefits	_____
Insurance	_____
Legal & professional services	_____
Office/studio expenses	_____
Rent or lease	_____
Repairs & maintenance	_____
Office & art supplies	_____
Business taxes & licenses	_____
Travel/meals/entertainment (not reimbursed)	_____
Utilities	_____
Wages	_____
Equipment	_____
Other Expenses (incl. copyright registration fees)	_____
TOTAL	_____

have less overhead than someone who must pay rent on studio space or who has employees. Depending on their discipline and services, some graphic artists will have greater equipment and material expenses. Others will have greater travel-related expenses. For a better understanding of self-employment taxes and sales tax and how to plan for them, refer to the section on Self-Employment Issues in Chapter 3.

PROFIT

As stated previously, a minimum of 20-25% profit is recommended for artists when starting their business. You will need a profit for unexpected expenses and for reinvesting back into your business (equipment and software upgrades, etc.). As your business grows and you are getting more jobs, increase your profit goal. You can adjust your profit goal every year or two, but remember that it will increase the amount of revenue you must bring in, and therefore, you will need to either bring in more work or raise your pricing to obtain a higher profit.

For the graphic artist in the example in Figure 1–3, who has annual expenses totaling $50,000 and wants

1–3 Calculating Your Annual Base Minimum

To arrive at your Annual Base Minimum, you would use the formula below, using your own figures (amounts listed are for illustrative purposes only):

1. Total Annual Living Expenses	$ 35,000
2. Total Annual Business Expenses (*total from Figure 1-2*)	$ 15,000
3. Total Annual Expenses (*add #1 & #2*)	$ 50,000
4. Profit (*multiply #3 by 20% or .20*)	$ 10,000
TOTAL ANNUAL BASE MINIMUM (*Add #3 & #4*)	**$ 60,000**

to make a profit of 20%, he/she would need to bring in $60,000 per year to sustain his/her business.

Using the Annual Base Minimum from the above example, you can then figure out monthly, day, and hourly rates. For a monthly average rate, you can simply divide the Annual Base Minimum by 12, so in this case, it would be $5,000 per month. However, realize that this is an average because some months you are going to work less than in other months, for example, December and whatever month you take a vacation. So, you have to be mindful that if you only bring in $3,000 one month, you are going to have to make up the remaining $2,000 in other months.

Because *per diem* (day) rates and hourly rates are used frequently in pricing jobs, they need to be based on actual number of days/hours you will be working, or you will come up short and not meet your Annual Base Minimum revenue.

CALCULATING *A PER DIEM* (DAY) RATE

You are obviously not going to be working 365 days per year. The work week should be based on 5 days, and you need to take into account other times you will not be working (vacations, holidays, sick days, etc.) It is recommended you subtract out 6 weeks for non-working days, so 52–6 = 46 weeks you will be working. Multiply 46 x 5 days per week to arrive at 230 working days. Now, divide your Annual Base Minimum by 230 days to get your Day Rate. Using the example above, $60,000 divided by 230 equals a day rate of approximately $260.

CALCULATING AN HOURLY RATE

To figure out your hourly rate, base it on working a 35-hour week. Then multiply 35 times 46 weeks for a total of 1,610 working hours per year. Then divide your Annual Base Minimum by 1,610 hours. For the example above, $60,000

divided by 1,610 hours equals an hourly rate of approximately $37 per hour.

However, most self-employed graphic artists recommend dividing the Annual Base Minimum by a much smaller number of working hours to allow for time spent on such non-billable work as writing proposals, billing, and self-promotion. A figure from 20 to 45% less, or roughly 900 to 1,300 hours, has been found to be more accurate and practical. For simplicity, if the Annual Minimum Base Rate above is divided by 1,000 hours instead of 1,610, the hourly rate becomes $60 (instead of $37). That's a big difference.

THE REVERSE REVENUE PLAN

For the Reverse Revenue Plan, you start with the amount of annual revenue you would ideally like to make and work backwards (see Figure 1–4). This method works best for graphic artists who have been in business for a few years and who have a good handle on their finances and understand how much work they are realistically capable of. It also requires good management skills.

Let's suppose that you are the artist in the scenario above, and now you want to increase your annual revenue goal to $80,000. To accomplish this and to put it into perspective, you would have to bring in (8) $10,000 projects, (4) $20,000 projects, (2) $40,000 projects, or some other combination totaling $80,000. If we subtract your business and living expenses (totaling $50,000) from your projected revenue of $80,000, you would earn $30,000 in profit (or 37.5%, instead of 20%). This is a simplistic example. In reality, profit will be less than $30,000 because the additional income will cause your income taxes to increase, which in turn will raise your business expenses.

In order to earn $80,000 in revenue, you would have to charge a day rate of at least $348 ($80,000 divided by 230

1–4 Reverse Revenue Plan

1. Annual Revenue Goal	$ 80,000
2. Annual Business Expenses (*total from Figure 1-2*)	$ 15,000
3. Net Business Income (*subtract #2 from #1*)	$ 65,000
4. Annual Living Expenses	$ 35,000
NET ANNUAL REVENUE (or profit) (*subtract #4 from #3*)	$ 30,000

days) or an hourly rate of $50–$80 per hour (depending on whether you divide $80,000 by 1,610 or 1,000 billable hours). Another option is to work more hours per year, which can be a recipe for burnout.

Pricing Jobs

Once you have figured out how much minimum income you need to make a sustainable living, then you can use this information as the basis for pricing jobs.

HOW TO CHARGE

You may wonder whether you should charge by the hour, the day, on a fee-per-use basis, or by the project. There are pros and cons of each, depending on the particular type of project.

BY THE HOUR

Regardless of the method of pricing you ultimately decide to use, as discussed above, you need to know what it costs you annually to live and conduct business, so you know whether the fee offered for a particular project amounts to profit, breaking even, or loss. Calculating the individual cost per hour of doing business enables you to evaluate your financial progress.

Industry professionals use a method similar to the one in the Calculating an Hourly Rate section above to establish an hourly rate. When considering a project, it is important to accurately estimate the number of work hours needed. Many graphic artists say that multiplying this estimate by your hourly rate demonstrates whether the client's fee for the project will at least cover costs. If it will not, negotiating with the client for more money, proposing a solution that will take less time, or searching with the client for another mutually agreeable alternative is recommended. Many large jobs, such as corporate design projects, require that the hours involved be used as a gauge to measure if the project is on budget.

Charging by the hour is an adequate method for relatively simple projects that require one or two services, have no additional costs such as materials, travel, etc., and no usage fees. If you prefer charging by the hour, you can charge your time at an hourly rate and list costs as additional line items for a total project cost. Avoid quoting projects—even simple ones—at an hourly rate until you've discussed all the parameters of the project.

One of the cons of charging by the hour cited by professionals is that clients do not want to be billed for activities they perceive as not being directly related to their project, such as preparing invoices, etc. This can be avoided by charging a high enough hourly rate that takes into account time spent on non-billable hours. See the Calculating an Hourly Rate section above.

Another disadvantage of pricing only by the hour is that although you are being compensated for your time, you are not being compensated for the value you bring to the client. As you become more and more skilled and experienced at what you do, you will be able to do jobs faster, so in essence, if you are charging by the hour, you actually are losing potential revenue because it is taking you less time to do a job. You should be compensated for your expertise and the value you bring to the client. By pricing by the project, instead of the hour, you can charge what you are worth (see the By the Project section below).

PER DIEM

Sometimes graphic artists are hired on a *per diem*, or day-rate, basis. Surveys of graphic artists and clients have found this to be a perfectly acceptable work arrangement and method of compensation, provided that it accurately reflects the work required and is agreed to in advance by both graphic artist and buyer.

A day rate, coupled with an estimate of the number of days needed to complete the work, art direction, consultation, and/or travel, gives both parties a starting point from which to calculate a rough estimate. A word of caution: some jobs look deceptively simple, and even the most experienced graphic artists and clients sometimes find that greater expenditures of time are needed than were anticipated. When negotiating an estimate, both parties often address questions concerning complexity, degree of finish, delivery time, expenses, and general responsibilities, and they agree that an estimate is just that and is not assumed to be precise.

See the Calculating a *Per Diem* (Day) Rate section above for an acceptable method of estimating an appropriate *per diem* rate.

The downside of charging *per diem* is the same as charging hourly: you are not being compensated for the value you bring to the client.

BY THE PROJECT (VALUE-BASED PRICING)

When you quote a job by the cost of the entire project versus hourly or *per diem,* you can quote whatever price you want, within reason. You are not revealing your hourly or day rate or the specific number of hours for which you are charging. For this reason, you can charge what you feel your value is to the client, and that value is going to change by the client and the project. For example, your value is going to be different when designing a Facebook page for a small local restaurant that has no online presence, compared to designing an e-commerce website for an international retailer with the expectation that it will increase its online purchases by 100%. This is often referred to as *value-based pricing.*

The idea of value-based pricing is to anchor your pricing against the value that you bring to the client. Sometimes you can quantify the value in numbers, for example, increase an organization's membership by 1,000 or increase sales revenue for a product by 50%; other times the benefits are intangible. If you can emphasize the value that you provide to the client (for example, "improve online presence which will increase sales," etc.) in your proposal process, then you will begin to see your income grow as a result. Clients are happy to pay for your expertise because in most cases, they don't know how to fix a problem or don't have the expertise to arrive at a solution themselves.

To help determine what your value is to the client and what their budget is, start by asking what the client's break-even point is for the project—in other words, when does the project pay for itself? If an organization with a budget of $12,000 for a website redesign says the project will pay for itself if they get 40 new members as a result of the redesign, then they will feel you are overcharging them if you price the project at $24,000. However, if you are confident that your redesign can bring them 80 new members, they are more likely to agree to the $24,000 because you are delivering twice what they are expecting—and the break-even point is the same.

If a client wants to see cost breakdowns in a proposal, you can break it down by project components (research, sketches, design, implementation, testing, training, etc.) instead of by time. Regardless of the size or type of project, if there are any materials, usage, or contracted services costs, they should be listed as separate line items.

While you should not charge clients more than the value they'll get in return, the price you charge for any project, no matter how small, should at least cover your time multiplied by your hourly or day rate as calculated from your Annual Base Minimum. You cannot afford to give your services away because a client is a small business or a not-for-profit organization. You need to make a living, just as they do. They have budgets for other expenses. If they say their budget is too small for what you quote, find less expensive ways to solve their problem, using less expensive materials, a simpler design, less features, fewer illustrations, etc., without giving anything away and without underselling your services.

Other Pricing Factors

There are additional factors that need to be considered when pricing jobs. They vary by disciplines and specialties. Sometimes these factors are dictated by the particular industry for which you are doing the work.

USAGE FACTORS

Setting prices for art involves *usage*, which depends on how, where, and for how long the art will be used (or reused).

USAGE RIGHTS

To encourage the free flow of ideas, U.S. Copyright Law vests the creator of every artistic or literary work with a bundle of rights that can be divided and sold in any number of ways. For visual ("pictorial") works, these include the rights

1. To copy (commonly known as "the right of reproduction")
2. To create a derivative work from an existing work
3. To publicly distribute
4. To publicly display
5. Audiovisual works also include the right to publicly perform

For more detailed descriptions of these rights, see Chapter 11, Legal Rights & Issues.

The price of graphic art is primarily determined by

the extent and value of its use, or "usage." Graphic artists, like photographers, writers, and other creators, customarily sell only specific rights to their creative work. The graphic artist specifies which rights of reproduction are being granted for the intended use, so learning how to define usage of work is critical for both illustrators and graphic designers.

Some inexperienced clients assume they are buying a product for a flat fee, with the right to reuse or manipulate the art or design without the permission of the graphic artist. Some purchase agreements are more like licensing agreements in that only the exclusive or nonexclusive right to use the work in a specific medium (such as magazine cover, point-of-purchase display, or billboard), for a limited time period, over a specific geographic area, is sold, or "granted."

The basic standard of sale for a commissioned work of art is "first reproduction rights" or "one-time reproduction rights." You should consider the value of the full potential of your work when estimating the value of "exclusive," "unlimited," or "all-rights" agreements. Current data indicate that reuse, more extensive use, use in additional markets, or international use receives additional compensation. Under copyright law, the sale of the original physical art or design (including digital media) is not included in the sale of reproduction rights and is more often a separate transaction.

In some cases (corporate logos, advertising, product identity), the buyer may prefer to acquire most or all rights for extended periods of time. Additional fees for such extensive grants of rights are usual and customary. In other cases, the buyer has no need for extensive rights. When negotiating transfers of rights, it is the graphic artist's responsibility to identify the buyer's needs and negotiate the appropriate usage.

Selling extensive or all rights, at prices usually paid for limited rights, is like giving the buyer unpaid inventory of stock art, thereby depriving yourself of income from additional uses and potential future assignments. Purchasing more rights than are needed deprives the public of access to the work and is expensive and unnecessary. If buyers ask for an all-rights or work-for-hire agreement to protect themselves from competitive or embarrassing uses of the work, you can easily draft a limited-rights contract with exclusivity provisions for the client, which will more appropriately meet the buyer's needs and budget and more adequately compensate you. Selling all rights at limited-rights rates also negatively influences the marketplace, keeping prices down and creating clients who expect something for nothing.

Grants of any rights should specify the category, the medium of intended use, and the title of the publication or product. Grants of rights may also specify, when appropriate, edition, number of appearances, and geographic or time limitations, for example, "advertising (market category) rights in a national (region) general-interest consumer magazine (medium) for a period of one year (time)." A common formula for editorial assignments is "one-time North American magazine or newspaper rights." Designers may choose to limit how their work will be used—for instance, in a particular brochure but not as the basis for the client's annual report.

INTERNATIONAL USES

Determining the value of work to be used outside the United States follows the same general guidelines as for other uses. In addition to the length of time, how and where the material will be used are important variables to consider. For example, selling rights to a French-language European print edition of a consumer magazine includes distribution in France, Belgium, and Switzerland. A country's economic condition also plays a role. A license for distribution in Japan might be considered more valuable than one for China because a higher percentage of the population would be reached.

ROYALTIES

In certain situations, a royalty arrangement is a good way to compensate the value an artist contributes to a project. A royalty is an accepted method of payment for most children's book illustration and all types of licensing. A *royalty* is the percentage of either the list (retail) or the wholesale price of the product that is paid to the graphic artist based on the product's sales. Royalty arrangements often include a nonrefundable *advance* payment to the artist in anticipation of royalties, which is paid before the product is produced and sold. Royalties are not appropriate in cases where the use of the art does not involve direct sales or where a direct sale is difficult to monitor. See more about royalties in the Licensing section of Chapter 4, Maximizing Income.

REUSE

In most cases, illustration is commissioned for specific usage. Rights that were not transferred to the client and were reserved by the artist can be sold elsewhere. Also, rights completed under a specified grant of rights or rights not exercised within a specified period of time return to the artist and may be sold again. Subsequent uses of commissioned art, some of which are called "reuse," "licensing," and "merchandising," have grown dramatically in recent years, creating additional sources of income for artists. While many artists are concerned about the resulting drop in new commissions, a significant number of artists have taken advantage of these new markets to enhance their income. Chapter 4, Maximizing Income, describes these opportunities.

ADVERTISING FACTORS

Some illustrators and designers who work in advertising and editorial print media markets check advertising page rates as another factor in gauging fees. Advertising page rates are an indicator of the resources and prestige of a publication. The higher the page rate, the more valuable a particular magazine or newspaper is to advertisers. Therefore, graphic artists who create ads or editorial art conclude that their skills are worth more to clients advertising in magazines with higher page rates and adjust their fees accordingly.

Advertising page rates vary according to the type and circulation of a magazine and therefore provide a standard for measuring the extent of usage and serve as a good barometer of a magazine's resources. For example, according to Agility PR Solutions, as of June 2019, *AARP, The Magazine* (published every two months) had the largest circulation of all U.S. magazines, at about 35 million. AARP publishes various versions of its publications based on the age of its readers and sells ad space accordingly. The 2019 ad rate for a four-color, full-page ad in the national edition of *AARP, The Magazine* for the 50+ age group (circulation 22,500,000) was $754,300. Obviously, AARP delivers a potential market to its advertisers that makes this cost worthwhile.

However, circulation numbers alone do not tell the entire story. The prestige of a magazine, often determined by the demographics of its readers, also affects its ad rates. Magazines with a majority of subscribers who are affluent, influential in their profession, or highly educated can charge higher ad rates. Examples of magazines with cachet include *Fast Company, New York* magazine, and *Scientific American.*

Print circulation figures and advertising rates for magazines no longer reflect a periodical's total resources. To be successful today, magazines must master both print and digital media across a variety of platforms. An example of an iconic print magazine that has done this successfully is *The New Yorker*, chosen by *Ad Age* as its 2016 "Magazine of the Year" for "raising up *New Yorker* content across a multitude of new platforms, for increasing web and video advertising by 31%, for increasing overall profit by 2% and for its savvy consumer marketing and successful paywall strategy." A 94-year-old weekly with 1.27 million subscribers, *The New Yorker* also is delivered digitally to tablets and smartphones. In addition, over 22.5 million unique visitors access its website monthly and 1.6 million

listeners tune in to its weekly radio show and podcast. *The New Yorker*'s annual three-day festival attracts 20,000 attendees. Content from *The New Yorker* can be found on Facebook, Twitter, Instagram, and Snapchat. Subscribers can download *The New Yorker Today* app, read it in an e-reader, or subscribe to an email newsletter that will deliver *New Yorker* stories right to their inbox.

Many magazine websites provide contact information for requesting media kits, which detail circulation figures, reader demographics, ad sizes and deadlines, and rates for the various types and styles of advertisements accepted.

COST-OF-LIVING FLUCTUATIONS

During periods of inflation, the change in the government's Consumer Price Index (CPI), which measures cost-of-living fluctuations, is another variable to be considered when calculating an appropriate fee. As the costs of printing, paper, distribution, advertising page and TV rates, and other items in the communications industry rise as time passes, so should prices paid for commissioned art. Such costs are generally reviewed annually, and any increases in the inflation rate are taken into consideration, say industry professionals. The CPI may also decrease, as we saw in 2008, which usually accounts for stagnant or declining fees.

BILLABLE EXPENSES

The cost of supplies and services that an artist needs to purchase or rent in order to complete a job needs to be budgeted for when determining the price of a job. These expenses vary by discipline and by project

Graphic designers traditionally bill clients for all expenses involved in executing an assignment, while textile designers and illustrators often absorb expenses for such things as art supplies because those costs tend to be modest. Necessary costs related to producing a job, such as model fees, prop rental, research time, production or printing, shipping, and travel expenses, are usually billed to the client separately. These expenses, even as estimates, are generally agreed upon and set down in the original written agreement. Often a maximum amount is itemized beyond which a designer may not incur costs without the client's authorization.

When graphic artists are required to advance sums on behalf of their clients, it is customary to charge a markup as a percentage of the expense to cover overhead and provide adequate cash flow. Dimensional illustration, for example, often requires substantial outlays for rental or purchase of materials and photography needed for a reproducible final. Refer to individual pricing charts in Chapters 5 and 7 for markup percentages.

Those who rent or lease equipment or use out-of-house services must maintain strict records of all expenses in order to bill the client. Billable expenses usually include rental or leasing fees, transportation to and from the equipment, and any costs incurred in recording work as hard copy or on film or digital media. Fees paid for technical assistants and the cost of research, reference, and preparing raw art (from photos or line art) for digitizing camera input are also billed as expenses.

Graphic artists also usually follow the markup conventions outlined above for equipment rental, particularly when they have spent time negotiating for rental time or purchasing supplies and services. Any graphic artist working with video animation systems should consider the revision cycles for technology and software updates as part of a regular review of expenses and charges.

Expenses such as purchases of equipment or technology to meet specific demands of the job are usually considered to be the artist's assets rather than expenses billable to a client.

Other Contractual Considerations

Graphic artists should consider a variety of other items, including cancellation and rejection fees, credit lines, samples, and liability for portfolios and artwork, when preparing to negotiate a contract.

CANCELLATION & REJECTION FEES

Traditionally, freelance graphic artists are entitled to remuneration if a job is canceled or rejected.

Whether they are paid, and where on the spectrum a particular cancellation or rejection fee is set, depends upon the specific circumstances of each case and upon the artist's determination to require such fees to be paid in an amount commensurate with the effort invested. For example, if preliminary work is unusually complex or the assignment requires completion on a very short deadline, artists may demand higher cancellation or rejection fees. Another consideration often taken into account is whether the graphic artist declined rewarding assignments from other clients in order to complete the canceled assignment in a timely manner.

CANCELLATION PROVISION ("KILL FEE")

Clients usually pay the artist a cancellation fee, sometimes referred to as a "kill fee" (a term borrowed from magazine and newspaper publishing), if the assignment

is canceled for reasons beyond the artist's control. The amount of the fee, based on a percentage of the original project fee, varies widely, depending upon the degree of the work's completion:

* If cancellation occurred prior to the completion of the concept or sketch phase, current data indicates the cancellation fee is most commonly between 25 and 50% of the original fee.
* If cancellation occurred after the completion of preliminary work and prior to the completion of finished work, current data indicates the cancellation fee is between 30 and 75%.
* If cancellation occurred after the completion of finished work, cancellation fees currently range between 100 and 150% of the original fee for graphic designers and illustrators and between 50 and 100% for animators and web/interactive designers.

Cancellation fees vary somewhat by subdiscipline. See Chapters 5, 6, 7, 9 and 10 for specific cancellation percentage rates.

Current data indicates that for most subdisciplines, all necessary and related expenses incurred by the artist at the time of cancellation (such as model fees, materials, or overnight shipping fees) are paid in full.

In the event of cancellation of a **flat-fee project**, all rights to the artwork as well as the possession of the original art revert to the artist.

Under a **royalty arrangement**, however, the client may demand all the originally agreed-upon rights to use the artwork upon payment of the cancellation fee. Even though the client chooses not to exercise a particular reproduction right at the time, that right is transferred to the client when the purchase is completed with payment. Depending upon the understanding between the parties, the specified right may revert back to the artist if not exercised within a specific period of time.

When determining an appropriate cancellation fee for royalty arrangements, many artists take into account a project's advance and any anticipated royalties. For example, suppose an illustrator completes the work for a 32-page children's picture book for which the artist received a $5,000 advance against a 5% royalty, and then the job is killed. If the initial print run were to have been 10,000 copies, with each book listing at $12.95, then the anticipated royalty would have been $6,475 (10,000 x $12.95 x 5%). After the $5,000 advance is subtracted, the anticipated royalty would have been $1,475. That would be the appropriate cancellation fee.

If preliminary or incomplete work is canceled and later used as finished art, the client usually is contractually obligated to pay the unpaid balance of the original usage fee.

Cancellation terms should be stipulated in writing, in contracts, and on confirmation forms and purchase orders. Otherwise, artists report that negotiating these fees at the time cancellation occurs makes it more difficult to protect their investment of time and resources. Artists also have found that contract language that makes payment of fees contingent upon the buyer's receipt of the artwork, not upon publication, anticipates the possibility of cancellation after acceptance and has helped ensure timely payment.

Graphic artists and clients may agree to submit any dispute regarding cancellation fees to mediation.

Examples of Cancellation provisions can be found on the Invoice forms in the Appendix: Contracts & Forms.

REJECTION PROVISION

According to current and historical data, clients may agree to pay the artist a rejection fee if the preliminary or finished artwork is found not to be reasonably satisfactory and the assignment is terminated. The amount of the fee varies widely, depending upon the degree of the work's completion:

* If rejection occurred prior to the completion of the concept or sketch phase, current data indicates the rejection fee ranges between 25 and 50% of the original fee.
* If rejection occurred after the completion of preliminary work and prior to the completion of finished art, current data indicates the rejection fee to be between 50 and 75%.
* If rejection occurred after the completion of finished art, current rejection fees are commonly 100% of the original fee.

All necessary and related expenses are customarily paid in full.

In the event of rejection, the client has chosen to forfeit any rights to the use of the artwork. Therefore, many artists refuse to permit rejected work to be used for reproduction by the client without a separate fee.

Like cancellation fees, rejection fees should be stated in any contracts or written agreements.

Artists and clients may agree to submit any dispute regarding rejection fees for mediation.

Rejection fees also vary somewhat by subdiscipline. See Chapters 5, 6, 7, 9, and 10 for specific rejection percentage rates.

CREDIT LINES

Illustrators usually incorporate their signatures into their artwork, and they are typically reproduced as part of the piece. For important pieces, especially when a letter of agreement spells out the terms of usage and payment, artists may request specific credit lines as part of the agreement. For some, this may mean a printed credit line with copyright notice; for others, merely the reproduction of the signature in the artwork. In some cases, as is traditional in magazines, both forms of credit may be agreed upon.

A copyright notice can be added to the credit line simply by adding "Copyright," the symbol ©, or "Copr." and the year of publication before the artist's name—for example, © 2017 Jane Artist. Such a copyright notice benefits the artist without harming the client.

SAMPLES OF WORK

It is a courtesy for clients to provide artists with samples of a finished print piece as it was reproduced. This piece, often called a *tear sheet*, shows the project in its completed form and can be displayed in an artist's portfolio. Even if clients purchase the copyright to artwork, artists' use of their original art in their portfolios is permissible as fair use (if it is not competitive with the copyright owner's uses), except in cases of work-made-for-hire, when the client's permission must be obtained.

LIABILITY FOR PORTFOLIOS & ORIGINAL ART

Although not as much of an issue as in the past because portfolios today are often transmitted electronically, if an artist's portfolio is lost by an art buyer, the law of *bailments* (the holding of another's property) makes the buyer liable for the "reasonable value" of that portfolio, if the loss arose from the buyer's carelessness. If the portfolio contained original art such as drawings, paintings, or original transparencies, the amount in question could be substantial. The same potential liability exists with commissioned artwork that a client has agreed to return to the artist. A model Holding Form for use by surface and textile designers, which can be modified for use by other disciplines, is provided in the Appendix: Contracts & Forms.

You can verify the value or appraisal of originals, transparencies, and other lost items by obtaining simple written assessments from a number of your clients, art directors, or vendors and then by presenting the figures to the party who lost the work or to a court. The full value of the work may be nearly impossible to calculate, since no one can be certain what the work will be worth over the life of the copyright, which is currently the artist's lifetime plus 70 years (see the Copyright Extension section in Chapter 11, Legal Rights & Issues). One factor that can affect a work's value is whether it is generic or specific. Generic works (a bald eagle soaring in flight) may have more potential for economic exploitation than specific works (a brand of laundry detergent). You may also need to prove that your work has generated additional income through transfers of rights.

The risk of losing original work can be minimized. First, whenever possible, avoid letting original art out of your possession. Instead of submitting portfolios of finished work, it is preferable to provide transparencies, color copies, or digital files. Second, you should have "valuable paper" insurance that protects against the loss or damage of valuable artwork in your studio, in transit, or while in the client's possession. That, however, is still not enough protection, since, as with any insurance, deductibles must be met, and claims may lead to prohibitive premiums or a complete loss of coverage.

Buyers need effective systems for tracking and storing original art in their offices. They should provide a record of receipt of every portfolio and maintain a tracking system within the organization. There should also be a system in place that logs original art when it comes into the studio and when it is sent to a supplier such as a printer. The risk of damage or loss to original art or portfolios is minimized if buyers avoid keeping portfolios overnight and on weekends. Finally, suppliers and vendors should understand that they might be held liable for any losses they cause as a result of damage to, or disappearance of, any original art.

In addition to record-keeping and tracking systems, buyers should minimize their legal risks by purchasing suitable insurance, since absolute guarantees of protection or original art are impossible.

Negotiating & Evaluating the Terms of an Offer

The project cycle is a process that graphic artists will experience hundreds of times in their careers. It starts with negotiating the terms for a new project with a potential client. The artist then decides how to price the work based on the parameters determined in the initial negotiation with the buyer. Usually, there are additional discussions about the terms of the project, which might include such parameters as schedule, credits, and usage. The terms are determined prior to signing an agreement and beginning the work. Throughout the project, certain bookkeeping and tracking functions must be performed in order to be assured of compensation, or to have recourse for other collection options in the end.

Successfully repeating this process over and over not only builds client loyalty and trust; it fosters financial well-being throughout a career.

All graphic artists must be able to analyze and evaluate the terms of an offer when potential clients want to purchase their talents. Understanding the scope of work and the terms of a contractual agreement is crucial. Only then can one skillfully negotiate mutually beneficial terms to reach financial and personal goals.

Negotiation can be learned and mastered. In negotiations each party seeks to accommodate its own needs. Many people think that they have to negotiate towards a "win-win" agreement. However, according to professional negotiators, win-win is admirable in spirit but is not good in practice. Entering into negotiations with the thought of win-win in the back of your mind sets you up to give up too much. In any negotiation you must protect yourself at all times, keeping in mind that the goal is to get as much as you can and realizing that the other person is doing the same. Remember, if either party pushes too hard, the negotiation will break off. Be empathetic, thoughtful, and kind to the other party to develop the mutual professional respect necessary for long-standing relationships and repeat business, but always remember that the sole purpose of bargaining is to get as much as you can. Win-win sets you up to make too many concessions.

Throughout the negotiation process, finding compromises that are necessary to reach a workable agreement can be taxing for both parties. Compromise is attained more readily if the two parties approach negotiations with a professional attitude and manner that sincerely conveys the willingness to develop solutions that meet their respective needs.

A common source of complaints is the failure by both sides to communicate effectively before work is started. Both graphic artists and clients must know and articulate their needs to each other in a straightforward, clear manner. Such frankness will reduce the chances of a misunderstanding or conflict later. It also helps to be mindful of your own feelings. Recognize that they are in response to something. Use them to guide your thoughts, questions, and next steps in the process. Putting the agreement in writing will further reduce potential headaches down the road when memories of what was said begin to fade.

Both graphic artists and clients have their own goals when entering negotiations. Most clients need to stay within an established budget for obtaining appropriate artwork or graphic design, while a graphic artist needs to find work that will earn enough to cover overhead expenses and make a reasonable profit. The graphic artist must determine if the client's budget is sufficient for the requested work. Remembering that value is not measured solely in dollars, graphic artists need to carefully consider all the benefits of a job, not just the fee. The more information each party has about the other, the more effective the negotiation.

Graphic artists need to know the budget and many other factors to accurately price a given job. They also need to have a good sense of current market forces, which is one of many reasons why this book was developed. Similarly, clients who use this book to keep abreast of current standards and contract terms are better equipped to establish more accurate budgets and to determine what rights to buy. The Guild encourages graphic artists and clients to adhere in all negotiations to the standards of the Joint Ethics Committee's Code of Fair Practice (see Chapter 2, Professional Relationships). Of course, in the end, if either graphic artists or clients find that the other party prevents them from achieving their essential goals, then the negotiation breaks down and the parties seek to fulfill their needs elsewhere.

Some graphic artists may be reluctant to ask questions or raise objections to a client's demands for fear of appearing to be difficult or argumentative. Successful professionals report, however, that as long as discussions are carried out in an appropriately professional manner, clients appreciate graphic artists who articulate their needs, since it prevents future misunderstandings. Above all, graphic artists need to remember that a client is not "the enemy" and that client relationships need to be cultivated.

Positioning Yourself as an Expert

There is a tendency among graphic artists to make too many concessions during negotiations, leaving money on the table because either they don't present themselves as experts or they are not perceived as experts by potential clients. Expertise is the most basic form of leverage. You have a skill that the client needs but does not have. When you are perceived as an expert in your field, your fees are non-negotiable. For example, no one questions the fees of a doctor, lawyer, plumber, or car mechanic because they are already perceived to be experts in their fields and skilled in the services they offer.

So, how do you position yourself as an expert? Ted Leonhardt, who is a management consultant for creative businesses, recommends creating your own "virtuous cycle." In economics, a virtuous cycle is a series of events that result in a favorable outcome, over and over again. For creatives, it means using your work, and the insights you've gained from doing it, to gain the interest and attention of future clients on a continuous basis. If potential clients are interested in you, then they have accepted you as an expert. When that occurs, they view your fees as non-negotiable, negating the need to negotiate. In fact, if you do respond to pressure to reduce your fees, you will lose some of your expertise power in the relationship.

To gain interest and attention, create "stories" about work you've done that illustrate your problem-solving skills and how you've achieved positive outcomes for your clients. You can write these stories on your website, on your blog or others' blogs, and in articles for professional publications. You can tell your stories in workshops, conferences, or at meetings of local professional organizations. To keep your virtuous cycle in motion, think of the completion of a creative project as only half of the job. The other half is using the completed project—your company's "product"— as a case study to prove and promote your expertise.

Media coverage and public speaking provide third-party endorsements that validate your value. Promotion generates inbound calls or prequalified leads—potential clients who identify themselves as needing the services your expertise can provide. The fact that they are calling you reinforces the value your services hold for them. When they hire you for a project, the virtuous cycle starts all over again.

Preparing to Negotiate

The very thought of having to negotiate the terms of a contract can bring on a feeling of dread. The process itself can cause severe physical and mental reactions— a churning stomach, sweats, nervousness, and memory loss. Why do these feelings get in the way of negotiating? First, we don't live in a bargaining culture; we live in a stated-price culture. Second, although effective negotiating skills are crucial for design firms and creatives working as independent contractors to be successful in their businesses, those skills are not taught in colleges and art schools. The good news is that negotiating skills can be learned.

Since negotiation can be stressful, preparation is extremely important. Knowing you have an understanding of the client's needs and the expertise required for the job, as well as knowing the parameters of what to ask for, will give you the confidence needed to be successful. Being objective helps you respond with agility so that the opportunity to negotiate the right job at the right price will not slip away. Though the deal at hand may seem crucial for success, it is usually not the case. Most graphic art careers are built upon hundreds of projects, not just one.

Learning as much as you can about a potential client prior to negotiating will make it easier. It helps to have a general understanding of the client's market and typical media for which that market buys art. See Figure 1-1 for examples of market categories and media. You can often find very specific information about a client, such as its products, services, key personnel, philosophy, and business culture, by doing an Internet search, which should include visiting the client's website. In addition to the wealth of information available on the Internet, business libraries contain valuable information about the marketplace. Directories for corporations and advertising agencies, such as those published by Standard Rate & Data Service, Inc., show revenue, circulation, media buys, officers, and so on. Publication directories list information about magazines: circulation, advertising rates, key staff, and other important data. Subscribing to major trade magazines may also be helpful. Consulting with professionals other than graphic artists who have worked with the client may also provide valuable background information.

ASK THE RIGHT QUESTIONS

Prior to every negotiation, be prepared to get the information necessary to evaluate the project. In order to do this, draw up a standard agenda or checklist that outlines the topics to be covered, and fill it out while having preliminary discussions (sometimes by telephone or e-mail) with

---

1–5 Preliminary Checklist for Negotiations

❑ Client info (company name, address, website)
❑ Primary client contact person (name, phone, fax, e-mail)
❑ Project description
❑ Creative services needed
❑ Subcontracted services (that are artist's responsibility)
❑ Deliverables (including quantities, print runs, etc.)
❑ Existing branding, products, media, etc., that deliverables need to coordinate with
❑ Deadline(s)
❑ Usage rights (media, market, time period, geographic area)
❑ Reproduction rights
❑ Projected expenses (equipment, supplies, rentals, travel, etc.)

---

the potential client. Include a job description, due dates, fees, expenses, and other pertinent notes (see Figure 1–5). Writing down such information as a standard business practice will reduce stress and will affect positively what you agree to in negotiations.

Beyond the basic information needed, the most crucial information will be gleaned by talking to the client and asking lots of questions. The most important things you need to know are why the client needs you now; what is driving their need; and why they have selected you to talk with. Do not assume what the client needs. You need to keep asking questions. Clues behind a client's need often will tell you how you should approach the job.

Figure 1-6 provides a list of questions you should ask. Notice that they not only ask about the company's goals and the need for the project that will involve your services, but also what the impact on the company, the competition, and the market will be; the key players and decision makers involved within the organization; the company's prior experience with a project of this type; and company politics, which can make or break a new initiative.

Note that not all the questions will apply to or be appropriate for every situation. You will need to modify the list as necessary.

DETERMINE YOUR REQUIREMENTS

Prior to negotiations, graphic artists need to know and make a list of what their highest expectations are for a project as well as their minimum requirements, such as no work made for hire and a reasonable deadline. What are you willing to compromise on; what are you not? What is the lowest fee you will work for? Think about this carefully—maybe you should be asking yourself, "What is the lowest fee I can work for and still make a living?" Undercutting yourself on price also may make it difficult to get a reasonable fee on future jobs, plus it devalues the entire industry. Creating this list sets the parameters for negotiation and prepares you to walk away from a job if the client cannot meet your minimum requirements.

DETERMINE THE CLIENT'S NEEDS

Both sides begin a negotiation by stating a set of requirements based on their needs. These requirements should not be confused with underlying needs, which a skilled negotiator strives to discern. For example, when the problem stated is, "My company is looking for a first-class brochure that we can produce for under $10,000," several underlying needs are not being directly articulated. The client may actually be saying, "I want top-quality work at an economical price. Can you accommodate me and

1–6 Questions to Ask Client Prior to Negotiation

Note: Not all questions will apply to every situation. Modify as needed.

* Why is the company (organization) doing this project at this time?
* What are the company goals? What are your goals?
* What effect will the project have on the company, the division, you, the world?
* What effect will it have on the market? On competitors?
* What are competitors doing that will impact our efforts?
* How do you envision the project moving forward?
* Who will be on your project team?
* Who will we report to? Why?
* Who will we need to get approvals from? Why?
* What's the model for success? Failure?
* Have you undertaken anything like this in the past? What was your experience?
* How is this effort viewed within the company?
* Are there groups who will be advanced by the project?
* Are there groups who will feel threatened?

List provided by Ted Leonhardt, www.tedleonhardt.com.

---

1. Know what past similar projects cost:
   a. What did they cost you?
   b. Are those fees acceptable in the current marketplace?
2. Know how long similar projects usually take to complete.
3. Know what the typical deliverables are.

Once you have a good sense of what the client's needs are, you can present your rules of thumb and follow up with, "How does that sound?"

Dealing with Common Tactics

Tactics are used during every negotiation, and it is important to understand them and not take them personally. Separating emotional responses from calm, detached observations of an opposing party's tactics can help defuse their effectiveness. Consider the following examples:

INTIMIDATION

It's easy to be intimidated by a powerful company. Clients know this and use symbols of their corporate power—the expensive lunch, the lavishly appointed office with original art hanging on the walls, the 20-foot mahogany conference table, imperious executives and assistants, etc., to make you feel vulnerable. But, if you are sitting at that conference table, you are there for a reason. You need to remind yourself that you have something that the company needs, something that is not widely available. Use that knowledge to your advantage. It's your leverage.

LIMITED AUTHORITY

A client's negotiator claims to lack the authority to make decisions. That enables the client to make rigid demands, forcing the graphic artist to offer concessions in the interests of moving forward. One possible solution is to treat the project under discussion as a joint venture and recruit the other person as a "partner." By emphasizing terms that create a partnership and sharing a stake in decisions, the client's negotiator is encouraged to represent the graphic artist's needs and goals.

PHONY LEGITIMACY

The negotiator states that the offer is a "standard contract" and cannot be changed. In such cases it helps to remember that contracts are working documents designed to protect both parties in an agreement. You

---

make me look good, or do I have to worry that what you do may not please my boss?" Knowledgeable and skillful questioning helps determine not only what kind of brochure is required to effectively meet the client's needs, but also whether some other solution might better solve the client's problem within the established parameters.

The answer to a stated problem is not always obvious. That's why it is critical to try to figure out the other person's true needs and expectations. A skilled negotiator responds positively to the underlying meaning of what the client is saying and shows a personal interest and regard for solving problems. It is important to remember that most clients' needs extend well beyond the purely visual solution. Sometimes their own success rides on the success of a project.

ESTABLISH YOUR RULES OF THUMB

All creative professionals need to go into negotiations knowing what their rules of thumb are regarding pricing, based on past experience:

should not feel pressured to sign standardized contracts if the terms are not favorable for you. Unfavorable sections or terms can be struck out. If necessary, you can make alterations using the explanation that "my attorney has instructed me not to sign contracts with these conditions" (see Chapter 12, Standard Contracts & Business Tools). Simply cross out and initial sections or language in the contract that are objectionable to you. The client may not agree with all your changes, but revising the contract serves to raise your issues and open them for discussion. The opportunity to raise your concerns is lost once you sign the contract.

CARROT ON A STICK

A client promises lots of future work if you just do this one job for a low price. This situation calls for some educating of the client. You will need to emphasize that, like any professional service business, your fees are based on the complexity of the job and the expertise, time, and materials involved. For example, a dentist charges a lower price for simply extracting a broken tooth compared to replacing it with an implant, which is a much more complex procedure, requiring additional equipment and more skill and time on the dentist's part. It's important that the client understand that a lower fee equals less services—fewer sketches or comps, a less complicated design, a smaller print run, fewer ink colors, etc. An artist's fees are based on making a sustainable living. The promise of future work (which may never materialize) will not pay today's bills. There is also the likelihood that if you give a client a reduced price on one job, it will be expected on future jobs.

THE WIMPY PROMISE

Beware of a potential client who tells you to "play around with it awhile, and if you come up with some-thing I like, I'll pay you." Like the Popeye character who would "gladly pay you Tuesday for a hamburger today," this type of client is likely to pay you nothing or definitely not what your time and effort are worth. Why? A person with that attitude either does not value your skills or is on a fishing expedition to get some ideas without paying for them. Even if the client's intentions are legitimate, an open-ended offer like this with no parameters or written agreement regarding what services you are being paid for leaves you vulnerable. Everything about it is vague and open to misinterpretation and dispute.

Once again, you need to make the client understand that you are a skilled professional offering a valuable service. Would the client ask an accountant to play around with his tax returns for a while, and if he likes the results, the accountant will get paid? If the client's concern is your skill level, offer to show samples of similar work from your portfolio, but make it clear that you do not do work on speculation (or "spec"), which is what the client is asking you to do. Also explain that "playing around with it" is an important part of the creative process, which may take longer than executing the finished piece. Let the client know that the process would benefit from his/her input.

EMOTIONS

Anger, threats, derisive laughter, tears, or insults may seem convincing and may, in fact, be genuine, but they are also tactical maneuvers. Listen carefully to the point of the message and separate it from the style of delivery. Never escalate an emotional situation.

Special Issues with Phone Calls, E-Mails, & Meetings

It is important to master the special skills needed to negotiate both on the phone and in face-to-face meetings. Each type of negotiation has advantages and disadvantages. Phone meetings allow the opportunity to refer to written materials for support, and being in your own environment may bolster your confidence. It is always easier to refuse someone over the phone.

Negotiating by phone also has disadvantages. If a difficult demand has to be made, it may be easier to do it in person. It's not easy to judge the reaction to what you've said without seeing the other person's face. And it can be hard for both parties to maintain focus on what is being said, making it more difficult to establish the rapport and partnership so important to any successful negotiation. If circumstances prevent you from meeting face-to-face, the next best thing is to use a video conferencing software or service so you can see each other during the phone negotiation.

E-MAIL

While negotiating by e-mail may seem easier and less intimidating, it is not advisable. It is even less personal than a phone call and can be open to misinterpretation. If an offer is extended by e-mail, follow it up with a phone call or meeting to confirm the details.

PHONE CALLS

As recommended above, a simple agenda or checklist should be used, outlining all the points to be covered. This helps keep the conversation centered on the important matters at hand and prevents the problem of omitting important details. Some individuals go as far as to prepare scripts for particularly difficult situations in which performing under pressure may cause confusion.

Taking notes during phone conversations is recommended. Graphic artists must simultaneously understand the aesthetic requirements of a project, agree on the business arrangements, and establish rapport with the client. Written notes of the project details provide valuable reference points and alleviate misunderstandings during the project.

If a discussion becomes difficult or gets bogged down, you should end the call and plan another call for after you've had a chance to consider the project. This gives you additional time in which to make a decision. In fact, many graphic artists make a practice of not accepting a job during an initial call. They take time to thoroughly evaluate all terms before accepting the work.

MEETINGS

Create environments for meetings that are comfortable and relaxed, whether in one party's office or in a neutral space. Always arrive on time, well rested, and prepared to make a thoughtful presentation. Planning goes a long way, and an unusual, thoughtful, and creative presentation establishes your expertise—and makes a sale.

In addition to planning, you need to be aware of how your behavior impacts the negotiation process. Below are some suggestions about behaviors—those to avoid and those to practice—that will result in more successful face-to-face negotiations:

Avoid showing your insecurity. As creatives, our "product" is personal, and we need praise and affirmation for who we are and what we do. In competitive situations many talented people concentrate on their weaknesses, not their strengths. They discount their own accomplishments and fear that their credentials are lacking. Know that whatever your insecurity is—and where the accompanying fear comes from—it's a vulnerability that can be used against you.

Refrain from talking too much. Nervousness can lead to talking too much, a sign of discomfort and insecurity that a trained negotiator can exploit. Avoid small talk unless the content relates to the business at hand. A well-placed word here and there helps establish credibility, but chatter also can be perceived as a lack of respect for the client's time.

Observe. A lot about the client's personality can be learned from physical clues, such as the office environment (wallpaper, furniture, desktops, artwork, and photographs). Body language also provides information about the client. Notice whether a seat is offered and whether the client consults a watch constantly and is not focused on the discussion. Understanding behavioral clues may give the graphic artist information that is advantageous for negotiating.

Listen. People appreciate someone who is alert, attentive, and understands what is being said. Listening actively, with nods of agreement, encourages the other party to communicate. Listening is a powerful tool. You will learn what the client really wants, and needs, and how it will shape the future of the company, as well as the client personally. Listen, take notes, read back what you wrote, and ask for clarification. It may be useful to use active listening techniques, such as, "Let me see if I understand corrcctly: You are saying that..." The more you know, the more accurately you'll be able to define your response to the client's needs.

Discuss Money Last

Money should be the last item on the agenda in a negotiation, for several reasons. It is the area where most disagreements occur. In the early stages of a negotiation, it is important to focus on areas in which it is easiest to reach agreement, such as the job description, difficulty of execution, usage and reproduction rights, deadlines, and expenses. These factors all define the value a job holds for the client. Delaying a discussion of money until later in the negotiation process also provides more time for an understanding, or even a feeling of partnership, to develop between the two parties. Negotiating about money before reaching agreement on other terms of the project is premature and could prove to be costly.

When the discussion appropriately turns to money, it is advisable to first outline or summarize all the variables that will go into the project, then try to get the client to make the first offer. It is advantageous to get the client to make the first offer, or better, to tell you the budget. Depending on how it is presented, a first offer is rarely a final offer and should be looked at realistically in terms of what the client expects in terms of services, deliverables, and usage. You are negotiating at this point and should already know what your "bottom line" is.

Sometimes, if the client refuses to meet your minimum requirements, you can negotiate an accommodation that has value to you, such as reducing a usage license from three to two years, requesting 500 samples to mail out as your next promotion, or bartering for in-kind services such as use of computer equipment or ad space. A client might say they don't have enough money in the budget to pay your design or illustration fees. However, they might have funds in another line item or in a different budget that could be used for the project. For example, if you are designing something that falls under advertising, maybe they could use their advertising budget to offset the cost. Or if the project requires you to travel, perhaps there is money in their travel budget that could be used for your travel expenses, which would leave more money for the graphic art services.

When discussing money, avoid common pitfalls by adhering to the following practices:

Don't accept the client's first offer. In business, some attempt to negotiate the fee is expected. Clients who present an initial budget are prepared to move up some on the fee. There is always a larger budget available, but they hold back to protect themselves. They'll expect you to ask for more. If you don't ask, they will lose some of the respect they initially had for you and your expertise. To maintain your expert position, you must define the scope required to meet the client's need. Since the scope affects the budget, you must be involved in setting the budget, too.

Don't be deterred by arbitrary figures. Sometimes parties set a limit from which they say they will not deviate, such as, "I will not pay more than $25,000," or "I will not accept less than $3,000." These figures or conditions are often set arbitrarily. Do not allow the price quotation to become a focal point that inhibits negotiating to terms that are agreeable and beneficial to both parties. Also, do not feel obligated to respond right away if someone starts a negotiation with the statement, "I only have $500, but I think you'd be great for the job." One can acknowledge the statement and still discuss the fee later when there is more of a foundation for a working relationship and more facts on which to base requests for more money.

Don't give away anything for free. Always get something in return for everything you provide. In the world we live in, everything that's valuable is measured in money. If you don't get compensation for what you provide, the client will not value it.

Never cut deliverables to meet the client's budget. Cutting deliverables has become the industry standard for dealing with price pressure, especially in the economic crisis of the past few years. However, cutting deliverables completely undermines your expert status. You spend valuable time building the exact combination of activities and deliverables to provide the best possible solution to the client's need. Then, if you cut services under the pressure

of bargaining, you negate your expert judgment and lose credibility; in effect, you're saying that the deliverables aren't really necessary after all.

Never rush to close. Often, we are so uncomfortable negotiating that we just want to get through with the bargaining, so we can do the work. Think of the negotiating stage as part of the creative process. It is. Take all the time you need to consider every step, every detail of the process. Rushing to close is another classic sign of weakness and insecurity. Time can be a source of leverage for you, especially if you know the client has a short deadline to meet.

ESTIMATES

At any time during negotiations, a potential client might ask the graphic artist for an estimate—even before all the details of the project have been discussed. When asked for an estimate, you should not feel pressured to give a figure immediately. The wiser tactic is to say, "I'll call you later with a quote." This will give you time to weigh your needs against the terms and scope of the project. It is good business for both parties if you estimate costs accurately, but also make sure that you will be adequately compensated if unforeseen circumstances arise. Never offer an estimate made up of a range of figures that brackets the desired price in the middle because many clients will hear only the lower figure.

TO BID OR NOT TO BID

Graphic artists are asked sometimes to bid on jobs, a practice often used for design and government-funded projects. It is important to clarify the nature of the bid and to find out with whom you will be competing. Ask who the other bidders are to determine if they are of comparable talent. If the client refuses to disclose the name of the competition, at least explain why it is to the client's advantage to choose you despite your price. Awarding work based solely on price rarely results in the best quality.

A client sometimes requests a bid in order to establish a budget and should say so when making the request. This gives you an opportunity to build a relationship with the client for future work. It should be understood that the information is for budget purposes only and that the terms and pricing for the project will be negotiated when the project actually happens. Often the parameters and the scope of work change significantly from the time a project is conceived to when it becomes a reality. (For information on bidding, refer to the section, Bidding on a Project, later in this chapter.)

An alarming practice, called "crowdsourcing," has become rampant on the Internet, and unfortunately for graphic artists, is becoming more widely accepted. Crowdsourcing websites offer freelance opportunities to graphic artists (and other professionals) by requiring them to bid against each other on jobs posted by prospective clients. The client tends to choose the lowest bidder to do the work, with little or no regard for the artist's skill level or the quality of the artist's work.

Some sites are run like art contests, requiring that artists submit sketches or concepts for the project, which are then voted on by the client. The "winning" artist gets the job. To add insult to injury, the "losing" artists have not only wasted time creating art they will never get paid for; they also lose all claim to their art. This type of crowdsourcing is nothing more than work on speculation (or "spec"), which industry professional organizations, such as AIGA and the Graphic Artists Guild, strongly discourage. (Read more about crowdsourcing in Chapter 3, under the section on Contests & Competition.)

If you are tempted to use such a site to get work, do so at your own risk and understand that crowdsourcing is negatively affecting the graphic arts profession. It perpetuates the misperception that artists are merely selling a commodity, not a professional service developed and honed through years of experience. In these situations, designers and illustrators lose their most important form of negotiating leverage—their expertise.

The way these sites operate also removes the all-important artist-client relationship from the equation, so there is very little or no collaboration. Without true collaboration, both the artist and the client lose in the long run.

Crowdsourcing also undermines U.S. artists' ability to make a living because they are competing unfairly with artists from countries with much lower standards of living, who can afford to underbid their prices to levels that are not economically feasible by U.S. standards. It further dilutes the profession by attracting amateurs who are competing with professionals with low prices and substandard design.

An essential element in every successful negotiation is knowing when to stop. Getting greedy when things start to go well or pushing for unreasonable concessions could lead the other party to abandon the process. Fair and equitable negotiating will help you win repeat business and reap the monetary rewards you seek.

When Negotiation Fails

Negotiation cannot guarantee favorable terms. Sometimes one party must either yield to unfavorable conditions or give up the opportunity. After you have evaluated the situation objectively, you may decide to protect yourself from an agreement that may be detrimental by walking away from it. Sometimes, no matter how hard you try, you just cannot make it work. It is an ill-founded notion to assume that a deal must be made at any cost.

Both parties should determine what their courses of action will be if the negotiation ends without agreement. Each party should make a realistic assessment of how much leverage they have in negotiation. Assessing the alternatives always clarifies a negotiating position.

Remember that not every negotiation will end in a deal. Two parties can "agree to disagree" amicably and part ways, with the hope of trying to negotiate again at a later date. Power is also knowing when to say "no."

For a summary of strategies to use for successful negotiation, see Figure 1–7, Ten Strategies for Negotiating Success for Creatives.

Bidding on a Project

Designers are chosen to work on projects in two ways. They either respond to a Request for Proposal (RFP) or, most often, prepare their own proposal in competition with other design firms.

Responding to an RFP or Design Brief

Often when a client needs a designer for a major project, the client prepares a Request for Proposal or a design brief that contains all the background information, objectives, and specifications for the project that a design firm needs in order to create and submit a proposal. The RFP is a great tool for client and designer alike because it focuses on all aspects of a future project. It helps the client get bids that are based on the same specifications, so the client is able to compare "apples to apples." And it gives the designer all the information needed to formulate an accurate proposal without endlessly questioning a prospective client.

There are drawbacks to responding to an RFP. One is that designers generally do not know who they are competing against. Did the potential client send the RFP to 50 firms, or did the client do some research and offer the RFP to a preselected group of three firms? (This can easily be resolved by asking the client who received RFPs.) Another drawback is that sometimes a highly developed RFP leaves the designer out of the critical phase of

1–7 Ten Strategies for Negotiating Success for Creatives

1. Build Your Own Virtuous Cycle

A virtuous cycle is a series of events that results in a favorable outcome, over and over again. For creatives, it is using your work and the insights you've gained from doing it to gain the interest and attention of future clients on a continuous basis. Their interest in you means that they have accepted you as an expert. When that occurs, your fees become non-negotiable in their minds. A well-managed virtuous cycle negates the need to negotiate.

2. Behave Like the Expert That You Are

Experts determine how to best meet a client's needs. Experts ask questions and create plans. Experts develop lists of the deliverables required to achieve success. Experts produce the budgets and schedules necessary to create the agreed scope of work. Experts don't cut fees to meet a client's demand because only the plan created by the expert will achieve success. Cutting fees undermines the potential for success and the power of the expert in the relationship.

3. Ask Questions and Really Listen to Their Answers

Listen, take notes, read back what you wrote, and ask for clarification. Listening is a powerful tool. You'll learn what clients really want, need, and how it will shape their future personally and the future of their company. The more you know, the more precisely you'll be able to define your response. Being really listened to is immensely flattering and endearing. So, not only do you learn about the opportunity, you also build a bond with the client.

4. Avoid Talking Too Much

Talking too much is a natural way to relieve nervous tension. Don't do it. It's a sign of discomfort and neediness that a trained negotiator can exploit. It's always a sign of insecurity when you're at the bargaining table.

5. Separate Yourself from Your Services

This is difficult for creative people. We are the product. As a result, we automatically care too much. When we care too much at the bargaining table, we lose perspective, and sometimes the insecurities that we all have rise to the surface and take over. If that happens, you must find an excuse to leave the bargaining table.

6. Don't Accept the Client's Initial Offer

In business, some attempt to negotiate the fee is expected. Clients who present an initial budget are prepared to move up some on the fee, but they hold back to protect themselves. Their initial budget is never the real budget—there is always a larger budget available. They'll expect you to ask for more. If you don't ask, they will lose some of the respect they initially had for you and your expertise. To maintain your expert position, you must define the scope required to meet the client's need. That means you must set the budget, too.

7. Do Not Give Clients Anything for Free

Always get something in return for everything you provide. If you don't get your fee for what you provide, clients will not value your expertise or your services.

8. Never Cut Deliverables to Meet the Client's Budget

Cutting deliverables completely undermines your expert status. You have built the exact combination of activities and deliverables to provide the best possible solution to the client's need. Then, under the pressure of bargaining, you cut services; what does that say about your expert judgment? It says you're just like everyone else—desperate for the work. Don't do it.

9. Never Rush to Close

Discomfort with negotiating often causes us to close the deal hastily and cave into the client's demands. Instead, think of the negotiating stage as part of the creative process. Take all the time you need to consider every step, every detail of the process. Remember the phrase, "I have all the time in the world." Rushing to close is another classic sign of weakness and insecurity. Don't do it.

10. Never Tell What You Would Have Done It For

Never, never, never tell. Often in a misguided attempt to connect personally with the client, one feels the need to reveal more than required. You never want clients to know how you compiled your costs or what your real bottom line was. If you do, rest assured that they will use it against you in the future. Or worse, they will feel taken advantage of.

These strategies were adapted from Ted Leonhardt's "Ten Steps to Negotiating Success for Creatives," 2012. Used with permission.

advising and helping to plan the client's marketing strategy. On the other hand, receiving a well-developed RFP is usually a positive indication of an organized client and is a time-saver for the designer.

Writing proposals is a very time-consuming process, and it is often difficult to assess the prospective client. Designers need to determine, using whatever criteria they find appropriate, whether or not the project is interesting or lucrative enough to spend hours preparing a proposal. A typical RFP or design brief includes:

Background. Information about the company or organization, including its size and primary services or products.

Audience. General information about the target audience. This helps convey the general scope of the project.

Objectives. Objectives can be as broad and general as "keeping the audience informed about our company," or they can be as specific as "get registered users of our product to order the upgrade."

Vehicle. What is the piece to be created? A brochure, newsletter, website, identity program, packaging, or other item?

Look & Feel. General direction about company positioning and its target market: for example, "a cutting-edge design that appeals to tech-savvy millennials who surf the Internet daily," or "a down-to-earth style that appeals to college-educated women over 50."

Specifications. Rights needed. Print: finished size, folds, colors, paper weight, quantity, etc. Also packaging, mailing/shipping requirements, etc. Digital: file format, resolution, page count (websites), user interface requirements (e.g., forms, animations, interactive features, etc.).

Time Frame. Goal date for final deliverable. Is a specific event or mailing distribution date being targeted?

Preliminary Schedule. Date when client-provided materials are due to designer. Dates for initial concepts, revisions, final art.

Other Questions. Will the designer handle printing? Are there other services that the designer must provide, such as finding writers, photographers, and illustrators? What is the final deliverable—a PDF file, an editable native file, or a printed piece?

Proposal Review Criteria. How will the client choose the designer? Will there be an interview? Should the designer include work samples with the proposal or provide the URL of an online portfolio for review?

Developing a Design Proposal

Often when bidding on a project, graphic designers develop their own proposals. They use initial meetings and research to understand the client's objectives and conceptualize possible directions. They also determine the target audience, desired response, and the overall effect to be achieved. Responsible clients communicate limitations clearly at the beginning of a project, such as budget and deadlines, and all the elements they will provide, such as text, photographs, artwork, or charts.

It is important for both client and designer to discuss specific directions about what is being bid upon. Being specific ensures that both parties will be able to avoid surprises in the scope and estimates of the project once the proposal is accepted.

Based on these initial discussions, designers establish their fees, often taking a combination of factors into consideration, including scope of services (what they will provide), project value, usage, market conditions, schedule, client budget (what can be accomplished for the money allotted to the project), hours expended, and gut instinct. The value the client expects to derive from the work is an increasingly important factor. For example, a company desiring top talent to develop a new identity program may be willing to pay a substantially higher fee than one calculated solely on expended time. Conversely, a designer may create a company greeting card for a long-term client as a client accommodation for substantially less than the market rates. While it may help a designer to walk through a project step-by-step, calculating the time needed for every activity and multiplying that time by the appropriate rate(s), the designer should view that information as a material guideline and not discuss projected hours with the client. As a rule, a designer's work should be judged for its value, as are the services of an experienced consultant or advisor, rather than by the time expended, as is the work of a vendor.

Once designers assess all these variables, they write a design proposal that spells out the scope of services, the client's responsibilities, and the estimated fees, expenses, and schedules.

WHAT TO INCLUDE

The proposal includes many of the following factors: an overview of the client's market; objectives and requirements of the project; research, art, and other components that will be developed or commissioned by the designer; typography, programming and other production services; printing requirements; intended use of the printed piece; and a schedule. In addition, designers frequently prepare documents explaining relationships with subcontractors (illustrators, photographers, etc.), billing procedures, and contract terms.

A proposal begins with an overview—a clear, concise description of the project. It includes a disclaimer that says that any prices and fees quoted are based on rough specifications of the items listed; if the items change, fees will change accordingly.

Proposals, like the projects they reflect, are divided into parts. These include a description of design and production; a description of fees; a payment schedule for the phases of work involved; usage rights, terms, and conditions; and collateral material to help sell the designer's abilities to the client.

Defining and describing the project phases helps facilitate the billing process and ensures the work will not proceed to the next phase until payment is received, according to the agreed-upon schedule. These checkpoints also give clients clear, tangible input at appropriate times as the project develops. (See Figure 1-8 for parts and phases of a design proposal.)

TARGETING THE PROPOSAL

The information supplied in the proposal is only for the design direction already discussed, specified, and agreed upon by the client and designer at their initial meetings. Since clients often compare a number of proposals before choosing a designer for the job, a proposal needs to be clear and thorough enough to be reviewed without the designer present.

The organization and appearance of a design proposal can be crucial in winning a job, especially when a design firm is competing against others. A proposal's appearance reflects a designer's ability and expertise as much as the information contained within it. Consequently, proposals should be organized logically, well written, well designed, and professionally presented.

When preparing a proposal for a new client, it helps to include collateral material such as promotion pieces, reprints of published work, links to websites, examples of similar projects produced by the designer, biographies of the designer and subcontractors involved in the project, and so on.

It is customary for project descriptions and cost proposals to be submitted to clients as a complimentary service. On the other hand, if a creative proposal—one that entails solutions to a client's objective—is submitted, any

fees and expenses incurred on a client's behalf and with the client's consent are billable.

If the client accepts the proposal, the terms and conditions are expressed in writing and are signed by authorized representatives of both the client and the designer or design firm. Always make at least two copies of the proposal for both client and designer to retain as original signed copies if the commission is accepted. When signed by both client and designer, a proposal is as legally binding as a contract.

It is important to note that any changes requested by the client beyond the scope outlined in the design proposal are considered *author's alterations* (AAs) and are billable. Additional services may include changes in the extent of the work, in the scheduling, and in the complexity of elements, and/or changes after client approval has been given for a specific stage, including concept, design, composition, and file production. AAs can become expensive to the client because changes are usually billed at an hourly rate. They may also increase the difficulty of completing the project within the time scheduled, causing overtime charges. It is the designer's responsibility to keep the client informed of any additional services that may be required by issuing timely change orders outlining the changes, and to obtain the client's approval, also in writing, of related additional costs before any changes are implemented and additional fees incurred.

Standard contracts, like those in the Appendix, do not provide the detailed explanatory material required in proposals for complex, multiphase projects. Those proposals are much more comprehensive than the contracts provided in this book. However, these contracts can be used as outlines or models.

Getting Started

Once the agreement is signed, the designer begins researching the project in greater depth. Before exploring any design directions, the designer reviews his/her findings with the client to make sure they agree. Then, with various design concepts in mind, the designer prepares a presentation showing general directions and formats for the project. Depending on the client's needs and the understanding between the client and the designer, the presentation may be "tight" or "loose." Preliminary renderings, or *comps* (an abbreviation for *comprehensives*), show the layout of the piece and are presented to the client for approval. Once approved, or revised and approved, the designer begins assembling the elements and services necessary to carry out the project within the client's agreed-on budget and time frame.

With the client's approval and/or involvement, the

1–8 Parts of a Design Proposal

Part 1: Design & Production Process

Design and production can be divided into three phases. Some designers prefer to divide their process into five phases: orientation; design development; design execution; prepress/production; and on press or in development (for website/app design). Feel free to devise a system that is easiest and most workable for you.

Phase 1: Describes the **design phase** of the project, including what form the design presentation will take, how many versions will be presented, the client approval process, and the time frame.

Phase 2: Explains the **production process**, which occurs after client approval of the design phase. It includes assigning illustration, photography, web design, etc.; copywriting; proofreading; supervision of those components; print/production time estimates; and client approval schedules.

Phase 3: Final production: After client approval of the previous phases, final production begins. Depending on the end product(s) a design firm has been commissioned to produce, this phase may be a matter of going on press and/or supervising the fabrication or manufacturing of products within a prescribed schedule. The quantity and specifications of any deliverables should be stated. If designers are involved with developing PowerPoint presentations, websites, and multimedia presentations, programming them is part of this phase.

Part 2: Fees

Fees and expenses may be handled in a number of ways. During the first phase, the design office may arrange to bill on a project basis. If clients prefer to be billed on a project basis, they usually establish an acceptable cap on the total amount billed. The project is outlined in briefer form than for Part 1, including the fees required for design, copywriting, photography, illustration, and so on.

It is important to explain what these fees include (design, layout, type specification, preliminary proofreading, production, and so on) and, more importantly, what they do not include (out-of-pocket expenses, author's alterations, overtime charges, photographic art direction, long-distance travel, etc.). The latter expenses, including percentage markups for account handling and supervision, should be stated and estimates of charges should be included if possible.

When supplying production prices for printing, be sure to state that these estimates are based on rough specifications and are budget estimates only. More exact quotations can be furnished at the time the final design mechanicals or comprehensives are reviewed by the printer.

Part 3: Payment Schedule

Many design projects are quoted and billed by phase, with an initial fee representing 30% of the total estimated fee and reimbursable expenses. An outline of the payment schedule should be provided.

Another method of payment is a monthly breakdown of the fee in equal increments (often called a *retainer*). This method allows the designer to predict income over a long project and discourages the client from attaching a value to each phase that may be misleading, since few projects follow the phase development in a strictly sequential way.

Part 4: Rights, Usage, & Credit

Discuss usage, ownership of rights and artwork, credit lines, approvals, interest charged for late payments, and any other terms (such as sales tax, confidentiality, or termination) deemed necessary. For clarification of these items, see the standard contracts in Chapter 12, Standard Contracts & Business Tools.

Signature lines for both client and designer and the date that the agreement is signed should follow. Both parties should retain a signed original and a copy.

---

designer makes key decisions on the specific look of the work, including the use of illustration or photography. Since few clients buy art on a regular basis, the designer negotiates with individual artists on the client's behalf and within the scope of the client's approved art budget. In this regard, designers often assume the responsibility for educating the client on the intent, content, and ethics of trade customs and copyright law.

Designers must also remember their own responsibility to the artists whose work they are considering. The continuing practice of using images from artists' portfolios, talent sourcebooks, or websites at the presentation or comp stage—without permission—prompted the Graphic Artists Guild to initiate the "Ask First" campaign to educate designers, art directors, and other art buyers to respect private intellectual property and the copyright laws that govern it. Art or photography should not be copied or borrowed for any use, including client presentations or comping, without the creator's permission. In addition, portfolios must be returned intact and in good condition (an unfortunate side effect of misusing sample work without permission has been damaged artwork and portfolios).

Scheduling Jobs

Pricing is not the only factor to consider when deciding whether to accept a job. You will need to determine if it's feasible with regards to your current schedule. It's not just a matter of the time frame or deadline being reasonable or not.

In order to make a sustainable living, most successful self-employed graphic artists work on multiple projects at any given time. Concurrent and overlapping projects ensure that you always have work. Otherwise, once a project ends, you will need to look for more work. This could take some time—even weeks—which means you are spending a sizeable chunk of time and effort that is not income-producing. Yet you still have expenses and bills that are due every month.

Some artists take on a combination of several small to medium-size projects. Even if you are working on a very large or long-term project, it's a good idea to take on a couple of smaller projects to fill downtime when you are waiting for someone else to finish their part of the project or when the client is reviewing the work and you are awaiting approval to proceed.

Sometimes, the expected start date for a project is delayed by the client for any number of reasons, such as waiting for budget approval, change in personnel, lack of client preparedness, etc. You don't want to be in the position of waiting around for the project to start with no billable hours. Smaller projects can fill in those breaks in time so that you have no income gaps. Taking on multiple projects helps to even out the feast or famine nature of the freelance economic life.

The size of the jobs is just one way to combine projects so that you have a manageable work schedule. Another way to combine them is by how labor intensive they are. If the various services you offer differ by how much time they take, then balance your work load with a combination of projects that require labor-intensive services with a couple that require less labor-intensive services.

If you are offered a new opportunity when you already are working on multiple jobs, you need to figure out if you can fit it in your schedule without sacrificing the quality of your work. There are only so many hours in a day. You cannot make the day any longer without sacrificing your work/life balance or your health.

You also need to schedule in time devoted to non-billable activities, such as promotion, preparing agreements or contracts, billing, professional development, etc. With the hours remaining, you can schedule in the income-producing projects. Therefore, when considering whether the client's time frame and deadline for a project are realistic or not, you cannot estimate based on 100% of your time. For example, if you work an average of 7.5 hours per day, and you've allocated 20% (or 1.5 hours) of your time to non-billable activities, then you have 6 hours left per day for income-producing projects. If at least 60% of your day (or 4.5 hours) is taken up working on a long-term project, then you only have 20% of your day (or 1.5 hours) to spend on a second project. If the client has a deadline for the work to be completed in 4 weeks, and you estimate that it will take 75 hours to do the work, then it is not reasonable to accept the project because in that time period, you only have 30 hours to devote to it (20 days x 1.5 hours per day = 30 hours). You need a time frame of 8 weeks to be able to meet the deadline. Before you decline the job, you could try to renegotiate the deadline. The less attractive alternative is to plan on working longer days or all day for 6 weekend days (6 x 7.5 hours = 45 hours).

An exception to this advice is bidding on projects. Unless you are tied down with a very long-term, labor-intensive project, you should probably go ahead and submit a bid even if you're not sure you will have enough time to do the work. Sometimes, there is a long wait between the time you submit the bid and when it is awarded. Or, as mentioned above, the client may end up changing the deadline. In the meantime, your situation may change—you may have finished some projects, or a large project was cancelled, freeing up your available time. By bidding, you have the option of accepting it or not, depending on what your workload looks like when the bid is finally awarded.

Some graphic artists chunk their work by days per week, rather than by hours per day. Using the same example as above, 1 day per week (or 20%) would be devoted to non-billable activities, 3 days (or 60%) would be spent on the major project, and 1 day (or 20%) could be allocated to a smaller job.

Seldom do multiple projects have the same start and end dates. Instead, they overlap or are staggered. Therefore, working on multiple projects requires excellent management and monitoring as well as skillful scheduling.

To learn more about scheduling and project management, see the section, Challenges Faced by Freelancers, in Chapter 3.

Keeping Track

Maintaining a system for documenting each project from start to finish will benefit the artist in a number of ways.

Written Agreements

A letter of agreement or a contract should be kept on file for each work assignment. Graphic artists assume certain risks if they start to work on an assignment prior to having a signed, written agreement. While an oral agreement may be enforceable, a written agreement protects both the client and the graphic artist by confirming the terms before memory fades or a misunderstanding arises.

A written agreement also demonstrates that both parties are professionals who treat their resources with care. When used properly, it can be a valuable tool that helps both parties clarify their needs and reflect their concerns and can specifically address any issues raised in negotiations. Should a client refuse to pay, a written agreement protects the graphic artist's rights and offers various types of recourse, including negotiation, collection services, arbitration, and, as a last resort, a lawsuit.

The document can be as simple or as complicated as the situation requires—from an informal letter of agreement, purchase order, or invoice to a comprehensive contract requiring the signatures of all parties.

WHAT TO INCLUDE IN AN AGREEMENT

The information included in a written agreement is very similar to what is included in a Design Proposal. Regardless of the discipline or the type of agreement used, the following items should be included:

* **Names of the graphic artist and client** (including the name of the client's authorized buyer or commissioning party).
* **Complete description** of the assignment or project.
* **Usage rights that are being transferred** (described in specific terms, normally naming a specific market category, medium, time period, and geographic region).
* **Fee arrangement** (including fees for usage, consultations, alterations, travel time, cancellation, and expense estimates and/or maximums).
* **Payment terms** (including a schedule for advances, reimbursement for billable expenses, royalty percentages and terms, where applicable, and monthly service charges for late payment).

* **Specifications regarding when and how the original work will be returned** (if hard copies or physical media have been delivered).
* **Copyright notice requirements and placement of the credit line.**
* **Assignment of responsibility for obtaining releases** for the use of people's names and/or images for advertising or trade purposes.

Formulating letters and contracts, or analyzing contracts offered by clients, requires a thorough working knowledge of copyright, business law, and related terminology. Graphic artists can become more familiar with these areas by carefully studying Chapter 11, Legal Rights & Issues, for copyright information; Chapter 12, Standard Contracts & Business Tools, for all types of standard contracts; and Part 5, Resources & References, for additional resources.

OBJECTIONABLE CONTRACT TERMS

When a client uses a work-made-for-hire clause in a design contract or demands all rights to artwork, every effort should be made to determine the client's real needs. Often such terms have been added to the contract by a lawyer trying to anticipate every possible contingency, but such terms are usually excessive and, if priced accordingly by the graphic artist, make the work too expensive for the client. Through study and practice, you can learn how to rephrase contractual terms to meet their requirements and negotiate to win the client's agreement. Knowing how to do that is a valuable asset for every graphic artist. (For definitions of common terms found in contracts used for graphic arts projects, refer to the Glossary at the end of this book.)

CHANGES TO THE ORIGINAL AGREEMENT

Getting paid on time and in full is the entitlement of any businessperson, and having a signed, written agreement; a complete understanding of the negotiated terms of that agreement; and accurate records help ensure timely and proper payment of fees. It is particularly important to confirm in writing any changes that alter the original agreement, and to record additional fees resulting from them. The Guild's model business forms, found in the Appendix, incorporate a number of these measures and can aid graphic artists in securing their rights.

Record Keeping

A standard record-keeping system helps facilitate accurate billing, bill tracking, fee collection, and tax liabilities. Being able to track invoices allows the graphic artist to remind buyers of outstanding obligations and to take whatever follow-up steps are necessary to obtain payment. It also provides a paper trail in the event that a disagreement or misunderstanding interferes with completing a project or receiving payment.

You may find it helpful to set up electronic job files for managing and keeping track of individual assignments, and accounting software for tracking the financial aspects of all assignments within a given time period.

JOB MANAGEMENT

A simple method of record keeping for self-employed individuals is to set up an electronic folder for each assignment, including identifying information (job number, the title of the project, the client's name, the delivery date, etc.). All information pertaining to the job is kept in this file. Subfolders can be set up for such things as contracts and written agreements, correspondence and notes about phone calls or meetings, invoices, memos, sketches, layouts, scans of expense receipts and outside vendor invoices, itemized hours spent on the job, etc. This information will prove very helpful as reminders or clarification to you or your client about the facts if there are misunderstandings or disagreements at any point in the project. Scans can be made of any pertinent documents that are in printed form. It is very important that information is filed in a timely way to maintain accuracy. The file then provides a single, complete record of the entire project. Job files should be backed up with an external hard drive, flash drive, or Cloud storage.

If the job is complex, the job file should be subdivided into sections to permit easy access to information. All sketches and drawings should be retained at least until after payment is received.

Cloud-based job management and tracking software is also available for the self-employed. It is especially helpful for small businesses with employees and subcontractors or for numerous and large projects. Features can include job setup; scheduling; tracking time (actual vs. estimated and by employee), milestones, and deadlines; and reporting insights. Custom quotes and invoices can be generated, with data flowing seamlessly from quote to job to invoice, and all project-related documents can be stored.

ACCOUNTING SOFTWARE

Graphic artists can keep track of the financial aspects of their entire business with software that simplifies bookkeeping and accounting chores, such as invoicing, tracking payments, and logging deductible expenses. These software solutions free up valuable creative time and greatly reduce preparation time for filing income tax. One popular freelance accounting software automatically transfers data to TurboTax. Mobile app features, such as being able to automatically track mileage, add to the convenience of these programs. Zapier.com has identified the 11 best accounting software specifically for freelancers and lists them by compatible platforms and the needs of various types of freelancers. There is even one for those who need to invoice in multiple currencies.

Billing Procedures

When signing a contractual arrangement, the buyer promises to make a specific payment in return for the graphic artist's grant of usage rights or sale of work. The graphic artist's invoices serve as formal notice to the buyer that payment is due; in many businesses an invoice is mandatory for the buyer to authorize a check and see that it is issued. Whenever possible, an invoice should accompany delivery of the finished art or design. A copy of the invoice may also be sent to the accounting department, if the business is large enough to have one, to facilitate prompt processing.

To encourage timely payment, graphic artists often incorporate payment terms into their billing process. One common procedure is to charge penalties for accounts that are past due as a percentage of the total, as allowed by law. Another procedure is to withhold rights of usage until full payment is received (see the section on Extension of Payment Time under Strategies for Dealing with Nonpayment section later in this chapter).

If the parties have not specified a payment due date, the generally accepted practice is payment within 30 days of delivery of the art or design. When a partial payment is due, or costs are to be billed during the job, the invoice or statement should be delivered as needed. Oral requests for payment do not substitute for invoices but serve as reminders in the collection process. If cancellation or rejection of the job occurs, the buyer should be billed immediately, according to the terms of the agreement, or if such a provision is absent, according to the standards discussed earlier in this chapter in the section, Cancellation & Rejection Fees.

Wording of invoices should be accurate and complete to avoid payment delays. The graphic artists' information should include their mailing address and their tax ID or Social Security number. Billing may be expedited by including such instructions as "Make check payable to Jan Artist or J. Artist Associates."

Sample invoices for Graphic Designers, Digital Media,

Illustrators, and Surface Pattern Designers can be found in the Appendix: Contracts & Forms.

Sales & Use Taxes

States have varying policies regarding sales and use taxes (for detailed information on sales taxes by state, especially in California and New York, see Chapter 3, Professional Issues, or refer to the website www.tax-rates.org). In the 45 states that have a statewide sales tax, the state rate in 2020 ranged from 2.9% (Colorado) to 7.25% (California), and it is levied on the sale or use of physical property within the state. A number of exemptions exist, including special rules for the sale of reproduction rights. Some local jurisdictions charge a sales tax in addition to the state tax (for example, in New York City in 2020, the sales and use tax rate was 8.88%, comprising the state sales tax of 4% and a local sales tax of 4.88%).

Generally, services—including the service of transferring reproduction rights—are not subject to sales tax. Transfers of physical property to a client (original art or mechanicals) should not be taxed if they are part of a project that will later be billed to a client by an illustrator or design firm. Sales tax is usually applicable for end sales or retail costs only, not for intermediate subcontracting, so an artist may have to retain forms showing that materials were intermediate and thus not taxable.

Many tax laws are unclear in relation to the graphic communications industry. In any case where graphic artists are unsure whether to collect tax, it is safest to collect and remit it to the state sales tax bureau. Graphic artists as well as their clients are liable for uncollected sales tax, and it may be difficult, if not impossible, to collect such taxes from clients whose final bills have been invoiced without including sales tax.

Because the laws governing sales and use taxes, as well as the interpretation of those laws, vary by state, it is in artists' best interest to contact the tax department in the state(s) in which they do business to find out how the law applies to their business and the specific services they offer and the products they sell. An accountant or tax attorney can also help interpret the law as it applies to an artist's particular circumstances.

Checks with Conditions

Some clients attempt to add terms to the contract or to change terms after the work is completed by listing conditions on the check, for example, claiming that endorsement of the check transfers all reproduction rights and/or ownership of the original art to the payer. A 1995 U.S. Supreme Court decision (*Playboy Enterprises, Inc. v. Dumas*) let stand a lower court decision giving creators mixed rights when faced with additional contract terms after the work is completed (see discussion in Chapter 3, Professional Issues and Chapter 11, Legal Rights & Issues). It has always been the Graphic Artists Guild's opinion that endorsement of such a check does not constitute a legal contract, especially if it conflicts with the previous contract. However, if you neglected to get a signed contract in place and you sign a check with conditions, you don't have the legal proof to fall back on. This is one more example of why it's extremely important to have a signed contract in place before you start a job.

When confronted with checks with conditions, you have at least three options:

Return the check and request that a new check be issued without conditions. If the conditions on the check violate a prior contract, refusal to issue a check without conditions will be a breach of contract.

Strike out the conditions on the check and deposit it if you signed a contract or sent an invoice that restricts the client's rights of use and if the artwork has been used already. In this case you should probably not sign the back of the check, but instead use a bank endorsement stamp, which eliminates the need for a signature. If the artwork has not yet been used, you should notify the client in writing that you are striking out the conditions on the check. If the client does not respond within two weeks, the check can be safely deposited.

The check should be returned in order to protect all rights if you have neither signed a contract with the client nor sent an invoice restricting use. Along with the check you should include an appropriate invoice restricting usage. Of course, this can be avoided by specifying in writing which rights will be transferred *before* beginning the assignment.

Tracking Invoices

Once an invoice has been sent to the client, you should track the outstanding invoice through your record-keeping system until it is paid. Copies of all invoices sent to clients, which should include your job number and the billing date, should be kept in an electronic "accounts receivable" folder (or in a comparable section in accounting software) in order of the payment due date. This folder should be reviewed at least once a month.

Whether you use your own system or accounting software, you can determine at a glance which payments remain outstanding by referring to the "payment due date." When payment is received, the date is entered under "payment received date."

Accurate, timely information on cash flow should trigger follow-up steps to collect past-due fees or other outstanding obligations.

Getting Paid

Once a project that meets the client's specifications has been completed and delivered, it is natural to expect that payment will be made as agreed to in the contract. Taking routine precautions in advance, such as clearly detailing payment and related terms in the written agreement, is the artist's best insurance against payment problems.

In addition to including your payment terms in the written agreement, there are other ways to encourage clients to pay you in a timely manner, improving your cash flow. They include

* Setting up a merchant account, so clients can pay you electronically
* Offering a discount for early payments
* Shortening your payment-due cycle (from 30 days to 21 days, for example)
* Assessing finance charges for tardy payments. This policy should also be included in your payment terms in the written agreement, so it comes as no surprise to clients.

You may feel awkward assessing a finance charge, especially if the client is a valued one, but you are not in the business of lending money, which is what you are doing when clients don't pay you promptly.

However, if you do not receive timely payment, you will want to implement appropriate and efficient collection strategies to avoid loss of income and time. Invoices become more difficult to collect as they get older, so prompt action is important. Figure 1–9, Step-by-Step Collection Strategy, details the actions graphic artists can take to collect outstanding fees. Note that this strategy does not represent legal advice; actions with legal ramifications should not be undertaken without consulting a qualified attorney (a list of Volunteer Lawyers for the Arts groups, by location, is provided in Part 5, Resources & References).

Prevention

The first step in any collection strategy is prevention. When dealing with a new client, be sure to ask for and check credit references. Then call the Better Business Bureau and credit-reporting agencies such as Dun & Bradstreet to verify the firm's worthiness.

The next logical step is direct communication with the client to determine why payment has not been made. Subsequent steps depend on the client's response and the nature of the problem. In most cases, the client will explain that the reason is a cash-flow problem. In other cases, the client may dispute whether monies are owed or how much. A direct discussion may clarify the problem and lead to a solution. If one discussion is not sufficient to resolve a delay, misunderstanding, or dispute, the client may be willing to try mediation.

If you encounter an unreasonable or evasive client, however, more forceful measures may be required, such as engaging a collection agency, suing in small-claims court, or initiating a lawsuit.

You should be aware that there are statutes of limitations on debt collection. The time limit varies by state and by the type of debt, and it may be as short as three years in some states for written agreements. So, it is in your best interest to go after debts in a timely manner, or you risk not being able to legally collect.

Common Causes of Nonpayment

Graphic artists usually learn why the payment has not been made during the first contact with the client. Following are some of the more common causes and basic strategies for responding to them. A more detailed explanation of strategies for dealing with nonpayment is covered in the next section.

GRAPHIC ARTIST'S ERROR

Perhaps an invoice was not provided, was sent to the attention of the wrong person, was incomplete or illegible, or did not document reimbursable expenses. You must correct the error to expedite the payment process.

BUYER'S ERROR

Once a project is delivered, the client may be involved in the next project and forget to process the check. One purpose of an invoice is to serve as a physical reminder; the client should not be expected to send the check automatically, without an invoice, and oral requests for payment are not sufficient.

If the cause of nonpayment is oversight, a new due date should be established with the client requested to follow up personally. You should send a letter or e-mail confirming when payment is expected to be made.

1–9 Step-by-Step Collection Strategy

Caution and restraint should be exercised in all communications with clients so that there is no question of harassment, which is a violation of the federal Fair Debt Collection Practices Law.

STEP 1. At the completion of the project, the artist should send an invoice to the client clearly stating the amount owed by the agreed-upon due date. If appropriate, the artist can include a notation that a late payment penalty fee will be applied to all overdue balances. (Many businesses assess a late fee of 1.5 to 2% of outstanding balances due.)

STEP 2. If the client does not make timely payment, the artist should send a follow-up invoice. A handwritten or stamped message to the effect of "Have you forgotten to send your payment?" or "Payment overdue—Please remit promptly" may help speed payment. If appropriate, the artist should include on the follow-up invoice any applicable late-payment penalty fee incurred to date as part of the balance due. To help expedite payment, the artist may include a self-addressed stamped envelope or his/her express mail account number for the client to use in mailing back the payment.

STEP 3. If the client does not make payment within 10 days of the follow-up invoice, the artist should call the client as a reminder that payment is due.

SAMPLE "PHONE SCRIPT"

Hello, [Client]:

This is Joe Talent at Ads & Such, and I'm calling to remind you that payment for the [name of project] that was delivered to you on [date] is now over [X] days past due. When can I expect to have payment in my hands?

At this point the client will probably give the artist a reason for the delay, which should be listened to patiently. It could have been simply an oversight, and the client will agree to send payment immediately.

STEP 4. If payment is not received within 10 days of the phone call, the artist should send a "Second Notice" that payment is overdue and expected within 10 days of this notice. The Second Notice allows for possible human error or "red tape" that may

have caused the delay and presents the client with another copy of the overdue invoice and a self-addressed envelope to simplify and speed payment.

SAMPLE "SECOND NOTICE" LETTER

Dear [Client]:

Ten days ago, I spoke with you about the outstanding balance of $[amount] owed for the [project] Ads & Such, delivered to you on [date]. You agreed to make payment within 30 days of acceptance, and now, [X] days later, you have still not settled your account.

This may be merely an oversight, or your payment has crossed this letter in the mail. If there are other reasons payment has not arrived that I should be aware of, I hope you will call me immediately.

Please do not jeopardize your credit record by failing to respond to this request. If payment has been sent, accept my thanks. If not, please send a check or money order for $[amount] in the enclosed return envelope no later than [date—usually 10 days from the receipt of the letter].

Sincerely yours,
Joe Talent
President, Ads & Such

Enc: copy of original invoice [marked "Second Notice"], return envelope for payment

STEP 5. If the client does not make payment within 10 days of the Second Notice, the artist can send the client a "Final Notice" letter. It should state that if payment is not made within three days, the debt will be turned over to either a collection agency or an attorney (see sections later in this chapter for more information on these options). See Figure 1–10 for sample wording for a Final Notice Letter.

Up to this point, a number of reasonable efforts have been made and sufficient time has elapsed to allow the buyer to respond or pay the debt. The artist has established a "paper trail" of documentation verifying the continued indebtedness and the artist's attempts to collect. If the buyer still fails to respond or pay, or acts evasively, the artist may reasonably assume that the buyer is avoiding payment intentionally. More severe courses of action are discussed in the Strategies for Dealing with Nonpayment.

DISPUTES & MISUNDERSTANDINGS

Some disputes are caused by unintentional actions or ignorance about professional standards and practices. For example, a client may make an incorrect assumption (such as assuming it is fine to delay payment when experiencing cash-flow problems) or may be unaware of appropriate professional conduct in a particular situation. You should instruct the client in the proper procedure, agree on a new payment date, and write a letter or e-mail confirming the new schedule.

BANKRUPTCY

If a client files for bankruptcy, there may be little a graphic artist can do except join the list of unsecured creditors. If the client is forced to liquidate assets to pay creditors, a percentage of the fee may ultimately be paid to the graphic artist.

Another problem in a bankruptcy may be getting original artwork or design returned, especially if the trustee or court assumes that everything in the client's possession is an asset. You must state that the work belongs to you and cannot, therefore, be considered an asset of the bankrupt party. While New York State has passed legislation that protects the work of gallery artists if a gallery files for bankruptcy, those protections are not extended to graphic artists unless their work is similarly on exhibit.

Strategies for Dealing with Nonpayment

The following represent a progression of strategies to use in cases of nonpayment, from simple remedies for client oversight to more drastic measures when a client refuses to pay.

DIRECT NEGOTIATION

Unless complex legal matters or large amounts of money are at issue, direct negotiation is usually the most appropriate approach. A phone call or a personal visit may be the most effective way to resolve a payment problem. It is important in this kind of negotiation to remain objective and realistic at all times. It is in the graphic artist's best interest to behave professionally when dealing with the client or anyone in the client's firm.

Always refer to the written agreement when contacting the client. Well-negotiated agreements usually foresee possible areas of dispute and specify the client's obligations and the graphic artist's rights. If necessary, remind the client of provisions in the agreement providing alternatives or penalties; they are there to provide negotiating leverage. If the reason for the payment failure violates the agreement or professional standards, the graphic artist should inform the client of the correct procedure.

Alternatively, you could send a brief, businesslike letter with a copy of the original invoice attached and marked "Second Notice." Remind the client of the overdue payment and request that he/she handle it immediately. All correspondence (letters and invoices) should be sent by certified mail, return receipt requested. Copies of all correspondence and memos of discussions between you and the client should be kept in the job file. Establishing a paper trail with the proper documentation may be crucial later.

At this stage, you can assume that human error, or red tape, was involved and that the call or letter will clear things up. These reminders often prove sufficient and forestall the need for stronger measures—until it becomes clear that nonpayment is deliberate.

EXTENSION OF PAYMENT TIME

Clients may claim a cash-flow problem (not having sufficient funds on hand to pay). It may be difficult to verify whether this is legitimate or an evasive maneuver. It is not unusual for the client to blame a late payment on the company's computer; however, long intervals between programmed payments are unlikely. Exceptions to automatic payments are made all the time. In this case, insist that a handwritten check be authorized immediately and paid within a week.

If the cause of the delay appears to be legitimate and future payment will clearly be made, you may wish to accommodate the client and grant a reasonable extension, with the new payment deadline confirmed in writing. Granting extensions should be viewed as the discretion of the graphic artist, not the client's right. Some graphic artists may require a service fee, often a percentage of the outstanding balance, as compensation for the delayed payment. Graphic artists who employ this practice should make sure to stipulate it in the written agreement. This practice should be used particularly when longer extensions are granted.

FINAL NOTICE LETTER

After direct negotiation has been attempted, a client may still refuse to make payment. The client may fail to respond to the graphic artist's letters and calls, give unreasonable explanations, not address the issue at hand, or not make payment according to the newly negotiated terms.

As a last effort before turning to stronger alternatives, the graphic artist should send a final notice letter

1–10 Sample Final Notice Letter

Dear [Client]:

Your account is now [X] months overdue. Unless your check or money order in the amount of $[amount] is received within [usually three days] from receipt of this letter, I will be forced to pursue other methods of collection.

You can preserve your credit rating by calling me today to discuss payment of this invoice.

If I do not hear from you within [three days], I will be forced to turn your account over to a collection agency [or attorney or the Graphic Artists Guild Grievance Committee].*

Very truly yours,
Joe Talent
President, Ads & Such

Enc: copy of Invoice [marked "Final Notice"], return envelope for payment

*The Guild's Grievance Committee handles disputes for members only.

(Figure 1–10). The basis of the graphic artist's claim should be stated briefly, with a demand for immediate payment of any outstanding balance. The final notice letter should apprise the client that the graphic artist is determined to pursue his/her legal rights and further legal action will be taken unless payment is received.

THE GRAPHIC ARTISTS GUILD GRIEVANCE COMMITTEE

The Graphic Artists Guild Grievance Committee provides guidance and assistance to its members in good standing who need to resolve differences with clients. Guild members in need of this service should contact the National Office.

Members may not claim the support of the Grievance Committee until the committee has reviewed the case and notified the member that the case has been accepted. The Grievance Committee may refuse a case if the member has begun formal litigation.

The committee reviews grievances at its earliest opportunity. If it determines that the grievance is justified, the committee contacts the member. It then recommends a plan of action and provides appropriate support, ranging from direct communication with the client, to testimony in court supporting the member in any follow-up litigation. It is crucial that the member participate fully and keep the committee advised of subsequent developments.

The Grievance Committee will not offer assistance in a dispute involving questionable professional conduct on a member's part, such as misrepresentation of talent, plagiarism, or any violation of the Joint Ethics Committee's Code of Fair Practice (see Chapter 2, Professional Relationships).

MEDIATION

Mediation, based on the services of an impartial outside party, is a long-established process for settling disputes privately and expeditiously. A mediator, acting as an umpire, does everything possible to bring the parties to agreement, but he/she cannot impose a decision upon them. If the parties cannot reach an agreement, they must proceed to resolve the dispute.

Submitting to mediation is voluntary, although signing a contract with such provisions establishes the client's consent to this procedure.

Mediation is speedier and far less expensive than suing in court. The conciliatory and private atmosphere may be more appropriate for parties who have had, or would like to have, a long business relationship. This service may also be relevant if your monetary claim exceeds the monetary limit of small-claims court.

Mediation may also be sponsored by some volunteer arts-related lawyer groups, including Volunteer Lawyers for the Arts in New York (www.vlany.org) and California Lawyers for the Arts (www.calawyersforthearts.org). For a complete list, refer to Part 5, Resources & References.

COLLECTION SERVICES

If voluntary dispute resolution such as mediation is not available or has not produced the outstanding check, commercial collection agencies will seek payment on the graphic artist's behalf. Collection agencies make escalated demands on the client through letters, phone calls, visits, and/or legal services.

Collection agency fees, in addition to routine expenses, generally range from 20 to 50% of the monies actually recovered, depending on the amount of money involved and how much time has lapsed since the work was first invoiced (older invoices are more difficult to collect). If the agency engages a lawyer, his/her fee is included, which can raise the percentage up to 50%. The highest rate is also charged for the smallest debts because it takes as much effort to collect a small debt as a large one. So, if the debt is under $1,000, you are better off going to Small Claims Court.

Before signing an agreement with a collection agency, you should review it carefully to determine the actions the agency will take and what it will charge. Of particular concern is dealing with an agency that may use practices that could be deemed unprofessional, since they may reflect unfavorably on you.

LEGAL RECOURSE

When all else fails, the legal system may offer a way to remedy the problem.

SMALL-CLAIMS COURT

Small-claims courts give a grievant access to the legal system while avoiding the usual encumbrances, costs, and length of a formal court proceeding. In contrast, the small-claims procedure is streamlined, speedy, and available for a nominal fee. Many small-claims court cases are heard by arbitrators rather than judges. This does not prejudice one's case and may even expedite a decision.

Graphic artists may bring claims seeking a monetary judgment to small-claims court. Besides nonpayment for a completed assignment or project, other claims may include nonpayment for canceled artwork, for purchase of original art, for unauthorized reuses, or for unreturned or damaged art.

Graphic artists can handle their own cases in small-claims court with a little preparation. Information is readily available from flyers prepared by the court, how-to publications, and, perhaps best, local rules books. The court clerk, or in some localities a legal advisor, is often available to help with preparation. Small-claims forms are also known as "trespass and assumpsit" claims forms.

Each state's small-claims court has a dollar limit for what it considers a small claim. Currently the dollar limit varies widely, from $1,500 (Kentucky) to $25,000 (Tennessee). Check your state's website for current limits and any special rules or exclusions. Amounts in excess of the limit require litigation in civil court.

Considering the high cost of pursuing a claim through civil court, you may decide it is more economical in the long run to reduce the claim to an amount that qualifies as a "small claim," especially if the amount in dispute is only slightly higher than the court's limit. The claim, however, must be made with the understanding that the balance above the court's limit is forfeited permanently. One possible way to avoid this is to split a larger amount into several small claims to be pursued individually—for example, if a client owes a large sum made up of payments due from several assignments.

FREELANCE ISN'T FREE ACT (NEW YORK CITY)

Freelancers in New York City have additional recourse for late and nonpayment under the Freelance Isn't Free Act, passed in 2016. The law requires clients to enter into written contracts with their freelancers, and provides extra penalties when clients fail to pay their freelancers on time, including statutory damages that essentially double the amount owed under the contract. Freelancers may file claims with the New York Department of Labor Standards as well as in small claims court.

COLLECTING AFTER A JUDGMENT

Should a client fail to pay after the court has rendered its decision or affirmed an arbitration award, the law authorizes a number of collection remedies. The graphic artist gains the right, within limitations, to place a lien on the client's funds and assets. Available funds, such as bank accounts or a portion of an individual's salary, may be seized by a sheriff or marshal and turned over to the graphic artist. Similarly, the proceeds of property, such as a car sold at public auction, may be used to settle the debt.

CONSULTING OR HIRING A LAWYER

A lawyer can assist in a number of ways and at different stages in the collection process. A lawyer may initially be able to provide enough information and advice so the graphic artist can pursue his/her own collection efforts. An initial consultation, whether in person or by phone, can confirm what the relevant law is and whether the graphic artist's position is supportable under the law. The lawyer may be able to advise about available resources, chances for successful resolution, and other legal matters.

For simple payment-due problems, a general practitioner or a collection lawyer can be hired to perform services similar to those of a collection agency. The psychological effect of receiving a lawyer's letter or call often produces a quick resolution to a dispute.

When a dispute must be cleared up before payment can be made, engaging a lawyer to negotiate with the client might be helpful. The lawyer may be able to take a more forceful role on your behalf and may bring about a fairer and quicker settlement. A lawyer's presence and negotiation skills may also result in avoiding a lawsuit. When the problem is resolved, and if it proves advisable, a lawyer can provide a written agreement to bring complex issues to a final and binding close.

If the dispute involves the question of who owns the legal rights to the work and who has economic control over it, a lawyer specializing in art-related law should be consulted. It is important that the lawyer be familiar with applicable copyright laws and trade practices, as well as the business aspects of your profession. In addition, an attorney's expertise in a specific area should be verified through direct questioning and by checking references. If you think your case might actually go to trial, do not hire an attorney who has no litigation experience, no matter how great he/she may be at negotiating contracts.

Lawyers' fees and structures vary. Some charge a flat fee; others charge a percentage of the monies recovered. Initial one-time consultation fees may be low. You should discuss fees with the attorney before requesting and/or accepting advice or assistance. Graphic artists with limited income may want to take advantage of volunteer arts-related lawyer groups. Most Volunteer Lawyers for the Arts (VLA) organizations place limitations on income for assistance eligibility (see Part 5 for a list of organizations).

SUING IN CIVIL COURT

Suing in civil court, or federal district court, is not usually necessary to resolve a payment or other dispute. Court should be considered a last resort, to be used only if all other options for resolving the problem have been exhausted. If big guns are brought out in a lawsuit early in a dispute, there's nothing to fall back to, but if other options have been exhausted, the only remaining choice is a court case, with an attorney's help.

Other cases that must be brought to civil court include monetary claims that exceed the small-claims court limit. Nonmonetary issues, such as suing for the return of original artwork or other contractual breaches, also must be taken to civil court.

Violation of copyright laws can be resolved only in federal court; current law requires that a work's copyright be registered with the U.S. Copyright Office before a federal case for copyright infringement can be initiated. It is also in your best interest to register your work in a "timely" manner so that if you win the case, you can get the maximum amount allowable under the law, which includes statutory damages and attorney's fees. Otherwise, you will only be eligible to receive actual damages and profits. The specific requirements for a timely registration are spelled out in the U.S. Copyright Office's circular, "Copyright Basics," available on its website at www.copyright.gov.

You do not necessarily have to hire a lawyer in order to sue. The law allows a person to appear as his/her own lawyer; in disputes where the issue is clear, graphic artists will usually not be at a disadvantage if they represent themselves. For disputes that do not involve large sums of money, a lawyer may be hired to advise the graphic artist on how to prepare the case, rather than for formal representation, which will help keep legal costs down.

When a lot of money or complex legal issues are involved, it is prudent to hire a lawyer. In such cases, the fee structure and expenses should be discussed with the lawyer at the outset. An attorney usually will bill time either by the hour or work for a contingency fee. Attorneys who accept a contingency (generally one third of an award or judgment, plus expenses) feel confident that they have a good chance of winning and are willing to risk their time to pursue it. If an attorney will accept a case only by billing time, it may be a signal for you to re-evaluate the chances of winning the case or to review the amount that can realistically be recovered.

Only the Beginning...

This first chapter has introduced you to the basic essentials of starting and running a graphic arts business. But, this is only the beginning. You will find much more in-depth information in Chapters 2 through 12 about professional relationships and issues, how to make your business sustainable, the specifics of pricing for various disciplines, legal rights and copyright issues, and standard contracts and business tools. Then in Part 4 you will be introduced to several working graphic artists who have successfully applied many of these practices to their own businesses—some in very unique ways. Part 5 provides an abundance of resources and references to supplement the information found in this handbook.

{2}

Professional Relationships

This chapter provides an overview of how graphic artists conduct business, and it examines many professional relationships they may encounter during their careers. Ethical standards for doing business with graphic artists are stressed.

VIRTUALLY ALL AREAS OF *commerce and communications use graphic arts. Graphic artists often specialize, focusing their talents to serve specific markets within the communications industry, such as magazine or book publishing or social media. They may work for corporations, manufacturers, retailers, advertising agencies, media companies, or for profit and nonprofit institutions. Clients may be individuals, small companies, or conglomerates. Some clients purchase art and design on a regular basis, while many are first-time, one-time, or infrequent buyers. Regardless of the type of client, the graphic artist should present a professional face to all buyers.*

Today, the role of the visual communicator is both simpler and more complicated. Much of the newer media blurs the distinctions among disciplines; visual artists, increasingly, must be adept at multiple disciplines. In general, illustrators and graphic designers differ in that illustrators create commercial artwork that conveys an idea pictorially for a specific purpose, while designers are professional visual problem solvers who work with the elements of typography, color, illustration, and photography to create all types of commercial visual communication tools. Illustrators and graphic designers may work in both print and digital media.

Because these lines have gotten fuzzy, employers may be uncertain about exactly who they need, and/or they try to get two for the price of one. Artists need to be clear on the various components of a project and why they're being hired. Artists also must ensure that clients are clear about the skill set required and who the appropriate artist is for the work.

Establishing and maintaining good working relationships between graphic artists and clients is vital to the health and prosperity of the profession.

Illustrator Professional Relationships

A client may commission artwork from an illustrator directly or indirectly, through an artist's representative or other agent. Clients occasionally contract with an art director, design firm or studio, advertising agency, or packager to hire illustrators for a particular project. The Guild recommends that both parties sign a written agreement prior to starting work. For more information about contracts, refer to Chapter 1, Essential Business Practices and Chapter 12, Standard Contracts & Business Tools.

Client

As experts in their fields, clients communicate their needs and objectives to graphic artists regarding the product and the market. Using their particular style and expertise, illustrators offer solutions to the client for the visual communications problems posed. Ethical professional practices, as well as the ability to describe problems effectively and envision winning solutions, form the practical basis of a successful partnership between client and illustrator.

During initial meetings, the illustrator and client discuss the problem in terms of the client's objectives and possible solutions, fees, usage, and contract terms. These discussions should create an agreement that addresses the concerns of both parties.

Regular art buyers usually have staff specifically responsible for all purchasing; these are art directors or other employees with expertise in commissioning art assignments. In a large corporation, for example, the art director, art buyer, or stylist probably has some experience in professional practices and pricing.

Art Director

In many organizations, art directors manage multiple projects or accounts simultaneously. They are responsible for finding the illustrators, negotiating the terms of the jobs, and supervising assignments to ensure their proper execution within prescribed budgeting and time constraints. Art directors base their choices of talent on their knowledge of the client's concerns and on the diverse styles of the artists available. To find illustrators, an art director consults talent sourcebooks, advertising directories, and major trade publications. In addition, an art director may review artists' websites, place ads in publications or with professional organizations, or contact employment services.

When speaking with illustrators, art directors need to be familiar with the project's schedule, the budget, how the artwork will be used, and a variety of other factors. Illustrators then negotiate appropriate rights, terms, and fees with the art director. The art director may then send the artist a confirming purchase order, or the artist may send the art director a proposal or contract and later, when turning in the artwork, an invoice and delivery memo. The factors used to determine the terms of agreement are thoroughly described throughout this book.

Design Firm or Studio

Design firm and *design studio* are often used interchangeably depending on the image the business wants to project. Therefore, the distinction between the two is blurred. However, a design firm is often thought of as a larger organization with more employees on staff, offering a full range of graphic art services, while a studio may be a sole proprietorship consisting of only the designer/owner or a small organization of two to three partners. However, this does not mean that a studio cannot be a full-service business. Established studios often have arrangements with other independent contractors, such as illustrators, web designers, photographers, editors, etc., that they can call on to provide specialty or complementary services when the need arises. A larger design firm might have one or more illustrators on staff, or it may also subcontract illustrators when needed.

Studio can also refer to the workplace of a self-employed illustrator or fine artist. In this situation, the client would hire and work directly with the illustrator.

Advertising Agency

Artwork for advertising agencies is usually purchased by an art director and an art buyer, who work together to select the illustrator to be used on a job. An art buyer is responsible for calling in a selection of artists' work for review by the creative group, who choose an illustrator based on the style of art needed and the work submitted. After an illustrator is selected, the art buyer and the illustrator are mutually responsible for negotiating the purchase of usage rights from the illustrator as well as the budget, schedule, trafficking, and invoicing of each assignment.

At the time of assignment, most agencies provide illustrators with a purchase order that details the rights purchased, ownership of the art, delivery dates for sketches and finished art, prices for the completed assignment, the cancellation fee at sketch and finish stages, and any additional expenses that will be covered, such as

2–1 Limited Rights

The following are categories for the purchase of limited rights, which may range from one-time to extensive use. All rights granted should be clearly detailed in the purchase order, including a specific market, medium, time period, and geographic region: for example, national (region), consumer magazine (medium), advertising (market), rights for a period of one year (time). Exclusivity within the markets purchased is usually guaranteed. Noncompeting rights may be sold elsewhere, unless the purchase order stipulates otherwise. Sale of the original artwork or sale of the copyright (which is sometimes erroneously called a buyout) is a separate transaction.

In-house presentation & research: Usage is generally purchased at the lowest rates in the advertising market, since the material will be used only in-house for presentation or in front of small groups. Agreements permitting more extensive uses generally require that additional fees be paid.

Test market: Artwork is historically purchased at low rates for use in a limited number of markets, and an artist's agreement should stipulate additional fees if use is expanded.

Displays, trade shows, public relations.

Point-of-purchase: Usage includes all point-of-sale materials such as signs, leaflets, shopping cart posters, catalogs, brochures, counter displays, and so on.

Outdoor: All posters that are not point-of-sale, including those used for billboards, painted bulletins, transit, and bus shelters, are in this category.

Publication: Usage includes newspapers, magazines, Sunday supplements, in-house publications, and any material included as part of a publication, such as freestanding inserts or advertorials.

Digital media: This use is increasing as Internet and mobile device usage continues to evolve. Digital rights may be purchased in addition to other rights and should include additional charges (for instance, a percentage of the publication fee).

TV use: Only television rights.

2–2 Multiple Rights

Many clients who use artwork for high-exposure products and services may seek to purchase multiple rights involving longer periods and more media, regions, and markets. Fees should be adjusted accordingly.

Unlimited rights: The purchase of all rights connected with the product for all media in all markets for an unlimited time. Longstanding trade custom provides that the artwork may be reproduced by the artist for self-promotion, and the artist may display the work. The artist also retains the copyright.

Exclusive unlimited rights: The artist may not sell any use to anyone else. The artist retains authorship rights and may reclaim these rights after thirty-five years. The artist may display the work or use it for self-promotion. Sale of the original art is a separate transaction.

Buyout: This vague term, though widely used, means different things to different people. It is an imprecise term that can lead to misunderstandings—most often to an artist's disadvantage. It often refers to sale of the copyright to a work of art, which should be avoided at all cost. (For a thorough discussion of this point, see the Copyright section in Chapter 11: Legal Rights & Issues.) The Guild recommends that specific usage rights sold and the status of ownership of the original art be explicitly stated in any agreement.

---

delivery charges or shipping. All terms in a purchase order or contract are open to negotiation until both parties reach agreement.

An understanding or contract has been reached when both parties sign the purchase order. As independent contractors, illustrators are responsible for sending a contract that describes the terms of the understanding. A letter of agreement does this nicely; for a sample form, see the Appendix. Rights purchased may be in any or all of a number of categories, which should be spelled out in the purchase order. (See Figure 2–1, Limited Rights, and Figure 2–2, Multiple Rights.) Each illustrator decides independently how to price each use of his/her work.

Packager

Packagers, who work predominantly in book publishing, coordinate all the components of a project and either present the finished concept to publishers for execution or manufacture the books themselves and deliver bound volumes to the publisher. Like publishers, packagers contract with illustrators, designers, and writers, and all negotiations are handled as if the packager were the publisher. Because of the relatively small size and weak financial strength of packagers compared with publishers, the importance of a written agreement cannot be overemphasized.

Artist's Representative/Agent

Illustrators, animators, textile and surface pattern designers, and other artists need to connect effectively with their markets. Some artists are as equally adept at solving visual problems as soliciting business, researching new markets, utilizing social media, designing and following up on promotions, and negotiating contracts and rights. But others are more skilled at solving visual problems than at marketing or promoting their own talent.

In an ideal world, artists would concentrate solely on creating their art. In order for this to happen, the best solution is to have a representative or agent who spends time, energy, and resources seeking work for artists. Professional representatives, skilled at representing artists' interests, are often more adept at negotiations than the artists themselves, resulting in better terms and higher fees than artists could secure on their own. For artists who are comfortable delegating business tasks, a professional agent can contribute thousands of dollars in additional revenue and hours of additional creative time. This arrangement is very cost-effective for the artist because representatives are compensated only when they find work for their clients; it is therefore in their interest to find the best outlets for their artists. The best artist-agent relationships are mutually beneficial partnerships, with the rep handling the business side of the artist's business.

But not every situation is ideal. If an artist feels that he/she is just another portfolio, or if a representative continually fails to secure work for an artist while insisting on receiving commissions for work secured by the artist, such relationships should be critically evaluated. Some agents will offer lower fees to ensure a good personal relationship with a buyer at the expense of the artist whose interests they have pledged to protect. Obviously, relationships with representatives who engage in questionable practices should be avoided.

For artists whose careers have reached the point at which they think they might benefit from professional representation, see Figure 2–3 for things to consider before partnering with a rep.

Representatives who handle a number of artists often concentrate on a particular style or market. For example, one rep may represent artists with highly realistic, painterly styles, while another may concentrate on humorous work. Some representatives have cultivated strong contacts in advertising, while others have extensive networks in the editorial or children's book market. Illustrators need to research which representatives are best able to serve their needs.

RESEARCH

To research reps, artists can start by doing an online search for "Artists Representatives," "Illustration Reps," or "Illustration Agents" to find a source where reps advertise. All the source books have online platforms where artists can get a sense of the type of talent an agent represents. Do not waste your time by submitting to the wrong type of group. Reps will know instantly if you are a good fit for their agency (for further information, see the Sources of Illustration & Design Talent section later in this chapter). The *Directory of Illustration, Workbook*, and others display many pages of advertising that are placed, in whole or in part, by artists' representatives. Interested illustrators can easily determine which representative is the best fit. Similarly, agents seeking additional talent often use these directories to locate suitable unrepresented artists.

Artists also should check SEO rankings for interested agencies and artist reps. Do these companies have their own websites? How do they look and rank? Are they updated on a regular basis?

CONTACT

Artists should check the websites of likely representatives to learn more about the reps and their submission policies. Some rep sites state whether they are currently accepting work or not. If you don't find their policies online, send an e-mail with (3) images of your best work in JPEG format, along with a link to your online presence, whether it is your own website or a third-party site. Address your e-mail to a specific rep by name; if the reps in a group are all female, do not make the mistake of addressing your e-mail to "Dear Sir." While it would be wonderful if reps could respond to every submission, they receive so many that it's not always possible. Do not take a lack of response personally.

Artists should always trust their own first impressions of a representative; as the rep impresses the artist, so he/she will impress prospective clients. If an artist feels compatible with a representative and the rep is interested in setting up a partnership, references should be checked.

2–3 Considerations before Partnering with an Artist's Rep

When an artist thinks his/her career has reached the point where it would benefit from professional representation, the following should be considered:

Be objective about your talent & stature. A reputable agent is interested in representing highly marketable talent—successful artists who no longer have time to cold-call new clients or follow up with existing clients. Although an entry-level artist could benefit from the services of a representative, most agents do not take on someone who is untried and unknown.

There are exceptions if the artist has a style that will sell or if the artist is exceptionally talented. The artist might be offered lower-paying assignments that veteran artists refuse. Once the artist's skills are honed, he/she is offered better paying assignments with more established clients. This practice benefits both the artist and the rep.

Identify & target your market. A frank appraisal of one's work and target market is necessary to make the best match with a rep. An artist with a sketchy, humorous style would not be suitable for an agent who represents predominantly painterly styles. Similarly, if one's work is best suited for the editorial or book cover market, pursuing a representative with a strong advertising clientele would not be very productive, though reps will, on occasion, seek out artists with strong potential to cross over into other markets. For example, a rep with only one fashion illustrator will push for that artist, should opportunities arise, but the fashion illustrator needs to make sure the rep has contacts in the fashion market. Opportunities will rarely come up for a fashion illustrator among children's book artists. Having a clear vision of your work and the direction in which you want to go is essential. You need a rep who shares that vision and wants to pursue that direction.

Seek aesthetic compatibility. An artist needs to know that his/her work fits well with the work of other artists represented. It is essential to be familiar with the work of the other artists in a rep's group because it is to the artist's advantage to dovetail smoothly with other artists while not competing with them. Each group is usually a reflection of the eye and aesthetic of the rep. It helps art directors to know the look of the agency where they are shopping for talent.

The best place to start is by talking with artists currently with the rep, as well as with those formerly represented. Talking to other artists is the best way to separate the good from mediocre agents working in the industry.

Among the questions to ask are: How much work did the representative generate over the year? Does the agent promote artists individually or as a group? Was the relationship productive for both parties? Were payments received promptly? Did the representative share in advertising and promotional expenses? What financial responsibility for yearly promotional costs did the artist carry? How were disputes, if any, resolved? If the relationship was terminated, why was it, and on what terms?

Talking with clients who have worked with the rep is another approach. You can visit the rep's website to see what clients it has worked with.

REACHING AN AGREEMENT

Artists' representatives have the authority to act on behalf of the artists they represent. They can commit the artist legally, but only in matters agreed upon in the artist-representative contract. Therefore, all terms and conditions of artist-representative arrangements should be discussed in detail, negotiated as needed, and confirmed in writing. Artists should have a lawyer read any contract and make certain the terms are clearly understood before signing. The Guild's Artist-Agent Agreement and Surface/Textile Designer-Agent Agreement can be found in the Appendix. If a more casual relationship is preferred, the Guild recommends that both parties, at the least, sign a memo that describes each person's responsibilities.

The following sections discuss the most important issues to be considered when negotiating an artist-agent agreement.

COMMISSIONS & FEES

Most artists pay reps a commission of 25–33% for jobs executed, excluding expenses. Higher commissions may be paid in surface/textile design and to agents who specialize in licensing. A lower commission of 15 to 20% is paid for union (and often non-union) film and production assignments, which tend to be longer and are paid at a lower day rate. Expenses not billable to the client are generally subtracted from a flat fee before the commission is computed. Expenses billed to the client as line items on an invoice are normally reimbursed to the person who incurred the expenses and are paid separately from any commission.

Policies and commissions concerning stock and reuse sales should be discussed and negotiated in detail. (See more about who should handle stock and reuse sales in Chapter 4, Maximizing Income.)

HOUSE ACCOUNTS

Clients that the artist contacted and developed before signing with a rep are called *house accounts*. Most artists do not pay commissions on house accounts that they service themselves. They generally pay a lower commission on house accounts that the rep services—from 10 to 20%, depending on the industry and how involved the rep's service are. A problem may occur when the artist initiates contact with a client, but no jobs begin until after a rep agreement is signed. Artists may become dissatisfied with a rep if they have to pay commissions on accounts that they feel they cultivated. To avoid this problem, the artist and the rep should negotiate prior to signing an agreement how work that materializes from such clients will be handled.

Artists need to ask themselves if they will realistically pursue these clients with promotions, calls, etc. It does the artist little good financially to call a client a "house account" if the artist is not going to pursue work as frequently as the rep will.

EXCLUSIVITY

Historically, reps usually expected an exclusive arrangement with an artist for at least North American markets, but they often agreed that the artist may continue to work directly with any previously established house accounts.

Since the recession in 2008, it is reported that there is an increasing trend of agencies allowing nonexclusive representation—meaning the artist can be listed with multiple reps. This is not an advantageous arrangement for agencies, as it reduces them to little more than a listing service. Exclusive agencies feel that it creates a situation in which agencies are competing against themselves. Some agencies allow nonexclusivity on a case-by-case basis, especially for highly specialized artists, such as medical illustrators, because request for their work is rare, so one agency cannot keep them working full-time.

There are other kinds of nonexclusive relationships. In one type, artists are free to promote their work in all markets, even those handled by the representative. In another nonexclusive arrangement, representatives handle only certain markets, such as advertising or publishing, and artists retain the right to promote their work in other areas. In considering this type of agreement, artists

should take into account the situation that occurs when an art director who changes jobs has a personal relationship with one rep and does not want to call another one. The Internet has created a more global marketplace, so some artists might have different reps in different countries. It makes sense to have an agent who understands the language, market, and business practices of a certain country or region.

From the rep's perspective, nonexclusive representation can also create a scheduling nightmare in an industry that often puts artists on "hold" or on a "right of first refusal" basis. To book an assignment with a nonexclusive artist, the rep has to check the artist's available schedule with multiple competing reps. Another potential problem is artists taking on too many assignments at the same time (unbeknownst to their various representatives), and as a result delivering subpar work or failing to meet deadlines. This practice is detrimental to the rep's reputation and to their client relationships.

While nonexclusive arrangements may seem beneficial to artists, in reality, they may be cutting themselves out of work instead of getting more work. Reps will consider artists who have exclusive arrangement with them first for jobs over nonexclusive artists.

Exclusivity is a crucial issue in any contract, since artists should feel that all their work will be marketed in the best possible manner. Representatives who ask for exclusive contracts should be willing to identify the other artists they represent, so artists can ascertain that they will not be competing against other artists in the group or lose jobs that might otherwise go to them. Artists who accept a rep's request for exclusivity may wish to consider negotiating exclusivity for their particular style or genre within a group. Any artist-rep arrangement can be negotiated if it offers the potential for mutual benefit for both parties.

EXPENSES

While all expenses are negotiable, artists are generally responsible for expenses related to their art. The rep provides the portfolio, but the artist retains ownership of the material in it. Any agreement should state that these pieces remain the property of the artist and that they will be returned to the artist upon termination of the relationship.

Reps are generally responsible for their selling expenses, such as phone calls, Internet charges/access, overnight deliveries, insurance, and entertaining clients.

Advertising in print and online source books and direct-mail promotion expenses are generally split between the artist and the rep in the same ratio as commissions. Agents often receive discounted group advertising rates in directories on a per-page basis. Artists should expect that their percentage of advertising costs will be based on any discounted page rates (or any other discounted expenses), not on published rates.

Reps should obtain the artist's authorization ahead of time for any expenses the artist is obligated to pay, such as costs for directories, websites, and promotional mailings. These expenses should be itemized and are deducted from the artist's fees.

BILLING PROCEDURES

In most cases the agent's firm handles billing, but this depends on the negotiated agreement. The party responsible for billing is obligated to send the other party copies of all purchase orders and invoices for the artist's work. The invoice should reflect exact terms.

Receiving copies of the invoices that show what clients are being billed is essential to ensure that the artist is being paid according to the commissions negotiated. There are reps who charge clients a markup, which is way beyond the agreed commission. Artists should also know at what rate their work is being billed to clients. They should not be paid at a time rate (hourly, *per diem*) if the rep is billing them at a higher per piece or frame rate. Also, a time rate does not take into account usage fees, which should be passed on to the artist. Another practical benefit of receiving billed invoices is that if the person handling the billing dies, declares bankruptcy, or reorganizes, the other party has proof of what is owed.

If the rep's firm handles billing, it is their job to maintain an up-to-date record-keeping and reporting system to inform artists about their finances. As important as the rep is, the office manager who does the actual invoicing, collecting, and disbursing of funds is just as valuable to the artist. It does an artist no good to perform excellent work only to have difficulties collecting payment. Before entering into an agreement with an artist's rep or agent, the artist should ask the following questions:

* Who manages invoicing, collecting, and payment for the art rep/agent?
* How are delinquent clients handled?
* Does the rep offer advances based on unpaid funds?

The artists also might consider running a commercial credit check (Dun & Bradstreet Report) on a prospective rep. The report will indicate the firm's financial position and current condition, including among other things, the firm's ability to pay its debts over the past two years, the likelihood that it will default on its payments in the next 12 months, and the likelihood that it will fail over the next 12 months.

If a rep fails to keep an artist regularly informed about all billing and payment transactions, there is a problem, and the artist should move quickly to terminate the relationship.

It should be noted that accurate record keeping is not just the rep's responsibility. The Guild recommends that artists maintain complete records of all documents, whether paper or electronic, and log any oral agreements. Monitoring finances and making sure payments are timely will benefit the artist's business.

TIMELY PAYMENT

If an artist believes that payments are taking too long, he/she may request that all client payments go to him/her directly.

FINDER'S FEE

Occasionally, a special opportunity is presented to an artist by an agent or broker, even though a formal relationship does not exist between them. Traditionally, in such special circumstances, the agent receives a finder's fee of 10 to 25% of the negotiated fee or advance. Because no formal relationship exists, this is usually a one-time fee, and if that client assigns more work, no additional commissions would be due. Occasionally, an artist will ask a rep to negotiate a difficult deal that the artist has secured, paying 10% or more, on a one-time basis.

DIFFERENCES

Even in the best relationships, differences may arise between artists and reps. Reps may become dissatisfied with artists who refuse what seem to be good jobs. Artists may become dissatisfied or discontented paying commissions to reps who they feel are not doing enough to generate more work. The rep and the artist must clearly express their concerns and explore why new work is not coming in. Perhaps the rep needs to try a new marketing approach, or the artist needs to develop a new style. If the relationship cannot be improved, the artist may need a different rep. In that case, they need to terminate their agreement amicably.

TERMINATION

This is a sensitive area for both artist and agent. Each party should be allowed to terminate with 30 days' written notice. After termination of services, an agent may continue to receive commissions for an agreed-upon period of time—usually three months after the termination date—on work that was generated from accounts developed by the agent. If an agent has represented an artist for more than six months, the right to receive commissions after termination is often increased by one month for each additional six months of representation. For example, after two years of representation, the agent would receive commissions for six months after termination. Royalty compensation on assignments contracted during the association continues until the client ceases payment on those projects.

Although circumstances can vary, artists rarely agree to give reps commissions on assignments obtained more than six months after the effective termination date. Of course, if an agent is entitled to receive a commission on an assignment obtained within the agreed-upon time, even if it started after the end of the termination period, it is due if the client's payment arrives after that time. This right, however, should not apply to house accounts. If an artist does not want to continue to pay commissions to a former rep, a lump sum settlement may be preferable and may be negotiated based on the previous year's earnings.

All termination terms should be negotiated at the beginning of a relationship. Most agents do not show artists' work during termination periods unless an artist specifically requests it, and agents should forward all inquiries about the artist to the artist. Agents should return to the artist all artwork (including digital images/files), portfolios, tear sheets, promotions, and any other images created solely by the artist at the end of the 30-day termination period, if not sooner.

BANKRUPTCY

Very rarely, a rep has been known to declare bankruptcy and fail to pay the artist's fees. The best way for artists to financially protect payment owed them is to be sure the artist-agent contract contains a clause that prohibits the agent from commingling the artist's fees with the agent's income and expenses. If a rep were to declare bankruptcy, you should consult your attorney to see what your rights are under bankruptcy laws.

THE IMPORTANCE OF SELF-EVALUATION

Legally, the rep works on the artist's behalf and is obligated to protect and promote the artist's interests. Legalities aside, the most practical, win-win model is that the artist and the rep are two independent businesses working together to improve both businesses. The best relationship is between a rep and an artist who work symbiotically so that each of their businesses grow, with both willing to put in the same investment of time, money, and communication. It is in the rep's best interest to see an artist succeed. It is in the artist's interest to help establish his/her rep's reputation in the field.

Some artists discover after having representation that they miss the control over their business that they had when they were working on their own. This is a personal choice, and if you like to control your business totally, you should consider this while deciding whether to pursue representation or not. Some artists love the partnership of having someone to bounce ideas off of for the purpose of getting the best terms and fees for their work. These are very individual considerations each person must make. Self-evaluation is extremely important when deciding how you want to run your business.

Graphic Designer Professional Relationships

Graphic designers are hired to communicate ideas. Whether they design books or billboards, movie posters or television graphics, corporate identity programs or websites, designers select and arrange a combination of type, color, imagery, and texture to transform a client's message into an informative, persuasive piece of visual communication.

To be effective, graphic designers need to combine aesthetic and strategic judgment with project management skills to create effective, timely marketing strategies for their clients. Designers usually execute projects at the client's request, taking the client's need and formulating an effective selling tool, product, promotion piece, or strategy to meet a specific objective. Sometimes they collaborate with market researchers and public relations specialists to help formulate design concepts. Often, they are called upon to advise clients on what they should be doing, diverting them from a comfortable approach to a more daring one.

Graphic designers play a multitude of roles when working with clients, including acting as consultants, teachers, and even shepherds. Often clients' questions provide opportunities for designers to help the clients understand how best to present and promote themselves, which is the purpose of a consistent, imaginative corporate identity program, for example.

Today's designers often must consider how their design solutions will work on the Internet or in three dimensions, as well as in print, while anticipating future needs. Such design considerations are essential today when multiple applications are in demand. (For further discussion of designing for digital media, see Chapter 6, Web/Interactive Design.)

Client Relationships

Because graphic design exerts such a tremendous influence on a company's image, service, or product, most businesses consider it a necessary component of their overall business strategy. Clients hire graphic designers to develop and provide a marketing approach and a creative direction for their visual communication needs and then to coordinate all production details through final delivery. In providing this service, designers often coordinate their art direction and design services with copywriters, illustrators, photographers, and printers, and bill the client for the entire package. As professional consultants, they assess the feasibility of a project based on their experience, knowledge of the market, and available resources. There are many advantages and disadvantages to this all-inclusive practice, and designers may choose instead to have all vendors bill the client directly.

Sometimes, though, clients choose to develop a project and then bring in a designer. This is usually inefficient. Many decisions will already have been made about matters requiring a designer's input, which may lead to unnecessary delays, additional costs, and inadequate solutions. The earlier a designer is called in to consult on a project, the more efficient it is for them to help develop the most effective solution for a design objective. The designer can contribute a fresh perspective, strategy, and aesthetic viewpoint that influence the project's impact, cost-effectiveness, and success.

A client may seek a long-term relationship with a graphic designer or design firm, particularly when planning a series of projects that need design continuity. When such a relationship is envisioned, a designer may be retained as a consultant during the early stages of a project to help strategize, plan, schedule, and budget.

Subcontractor Relationships

Design firms, art directors, or other art buyers who assume creative control of a project for a client often subcontract with independent contractors for work or services they cannot provide themselves, such as illustration, photography, web design, copyediting, and proofreading. Payment is due to these contractors in a timely manner, no matter when designers receive payment from the client. The designer and the independent contractor should sign separate subcontractor agreements.

Web Designer & Developer Professional Relationships

Compared to graphic designers and illustrators, a web professional is more likely to collaborate with other professionals on a project or work as part of a team. The terms *web designer* and *web developer* are often used interchangeably, but they have different job functions in the building of a website, and they require unique skill sets.

Web design refers to both the aesthetic portion of the website and its usability. Web designers use design software to create the layout and other visual elements of the site.

Web development refers to the functionality of the site. Web developers, sometimes called programmers, take the website design and bring it to life, using programming language, so that it is fully functional. The developer is the one who makes a site dynamic by using interactive elements.

There are some web professionals who can perform the functions of both the designer and the developer, but more often, they are two separate jobs. A client will most commonly interact with the web designer, since the designer's job will be needed at the beginning of the project.

Client Relationships

As in any graphic arts project, good communication and mutual respect between the graphic artist—in this case, the web professional—and the client are key to the success of the project. In web design projects, a healthy working relationship can be established if all parties view the client as the subject expert (regarding his/her business and industry) and the web professional as the technical expert.

EDUCATE CLIENTS

If you are the designer, one of the first steps you can take to ensure a good working relationship is to educate the client about the web design process and your role in it. If you will be doing only the design and another person will be doing the development, explain that role, too. Technology changes rapidly, and there is no way a lay person can keep up with these changes, much less understand the technical process. In fact, many clients have a misperception of what it takes to design a website. They may think anyone can design a website just by using some kind of software. Explain the creative process to them and all the thought that goes into finding the best web solutions for their specific business and goals.

There is also a common misconception that web and print media are very similar. It's important to take the time to explain to clients that web is very different from print and that the rules are different, too.

It is recommended that you educate potential clients *before* you sign a contract, so that they understand what is involved, the professional skills and expertise you bring to the project, how you work, and what you need (and don't need) from them. This way you can set some expectations and your working relationship will be clear from the beginning.

Freelancers, especially, are often viewed by clients as not being professionals. Establish boundaries early on, such as the hours and days you are available for business, including answering phone calls and e-mails. Do not feel compelled to answer after-hour phone calls or comply with requests to make changes outside of your usual business hours.

Be sure to educate clients about what it takes to make revisions and include a clause in your contract about revisions and the extra fees involved. Clients are notorious for asking for "one small final change." They need to understand that a revision, especially at the end of the process, right before the deadline, is never simple, and may affect the entire process.

Establish that you are the expert regarding web design and that while you will listen to their suggestions and consider them, in the end, you will make the final decision about whether a request follows best web design practices.

UNDERSTAND THE CLIENT'S BUSINESS

Just as you want clients to view you as a creative professional with technical expertise in web design, you need to recognize that clients are the experts in their specific business and industry. Your web design solutions need to be compatible with their business's strategies and goals.

In order to get a thorough understanding of the brand and its position in the industry, you'll need to gather assets and basic information and any user and customer research the client can provide, as well as interview the business's leaders. Researching the potential client's business prior to meeting to discuss the project will help establish you as a professional in the client's eyes. It shows your initiative and your interest in the client's business.

LISTEN CAREFULLY & BE EMPATHETIC

Listen carefully to your client's goals. Why do they want a website or a redesigned one? How do they perceive it helping their business? What specific features do they want it to have, etc.? They may have preconceived ideas of what they want but be unaware of all the options that are available. Thoroughly explain various options and platforms and why certain solutions better match their goals and budget. Throughout the process, pay attention to any concerns or reservations they may have.

KEEP CLIENT UPDATED

Keeping your clients in the loop throughout the web design process will not only ensure that their expectations are met but will also help them feel like they are part of the process. Creating a feeling of collaboration will go a long way in establishing a good working relationship and hopefully, a repeat client.

Team Relationships

Some large design firms may have both web designers and developers on staff, along with other web professionals. More often than not, both designer and developer are freelancers who may be located in different parts of the country. In some situations, the developer is hired by the designer to provide services, so as far as the developer is concerned, the designer is the immediate client. The differences between the two roles, coupled with the lack of physical proximity, can make it difficult to collaborate on a project

RESPECT OTHERS & THEIR EXPERTISE

Whether you are working on a team that is physically present or working remotely with other web professionals, the most important advice from industry professionals is to know your place, understand exactly your role in the project, and respect the other members of the web team and the expertise that they bring to the project. This includes remembering that everyone is working towards a common goal—to create the best outcome for the project.

CREATE A TEAM MENTALITY AT THE BEGINNING

It's important to think of yourself as part of a team from the very beginning of the project, even if you are not in close proximity with each other. Each professional working on the web project needs to feel valued and have input throughout the project. When primary players are freelancers working remotely, there can be a tendency for a designer to work in isolation and then hand the project off to a developer. Not collaborating from the very beginning of the project often leads to frustration on both sides. The designer wonders why the developer keeps asking so many questions and why design features aren't always built the way they envisioned. The developer might be faced with a design that is not possible to build so that it is optimally functional within the constraints of the schedule and budget. This lack of collaboration can be a waste of time for both the designer and the developer and can drive up costs. It is also not conducive for arriving at the best outcome.

Successful collaboration begins with good communication, which can be more difficult when working remotely. Experienced web professionals suggest the following for improving communication between designers and developers who are not in the same physical space:

* Include time for feedback from both sides.
* Add face-to-face time to communication.
* Work openly.
* Learn each other's language.

When discussing the project with the client, explain how a collaborative approach from the beginning between the design and development sides will result in a more productive use of time and personnel and ultimately, a better end-product. Then build several rounds of design and development in the schedule with time for feedback from each side at critical junctures.

Communication among team members working remotely tends to be a lot of written back and forth—in the form of e-mails or through messages on a collaboration hub or project management platform. This can take a lot of time and does little to build relationships among team members. It is recommended that you include periodic "face-to-face" meetings through video conferencing calls in your avenues of communication, especially at the beginning of a project. All team members will be able to "meet" each other and have faces to go with the names. Any concerns or questions about the project and each person's role will be able to be addressed in an initial meeting. Everyone on the team gets the same message. Video conferencing is a good way to discuss problems when they arise, and often leads to quicker solutions as everyone is involved.

Another way to aid collaboration is to keep work open by frequently sharing work in progress. Doing this keeps everyone up to date and part of the project. There are a number of collaboration tools designers can use to share work with a developer. The developer can then catch any design features that might become problematic. Developers often share by moving parts of a project to a staging server that everyone on the team has access to view. The developer can then ask for feedback on specific items.

Designers don't need to be able to write code and be programmers, and likewise, developers don't need to be designers to work together successfully, but it helps immensely with team communication if both groups understand the skills and priorities of the other group. Having a basic understanding of the other group's language will facilitate both communication and understanding and save a lot of time. If you are a designer, you want to be able to communicate your ideas effectively to the person who can make them happen.

Sources of Illustration & Design

Several resources are available to clients and graphic artists to find and/or promote talent.

Employment & Recruitment Agencies

Specialized employment agencies in various cities around the country refer graphic artists to clients for a fee, paid by the employer. They operate in the same way that most employment agencies do but specialize in visual communications markets. These agencies can be found by doing an Internet search for "creative staffing agencies." Most will fill temporary, freelance, part-time, and full-time assignments. Sometimes a temporary assignment may lead to an offer of permanent employment. Recruitment and search agencies (often referred to as "headhunters") are a unique talent resource for a firm in need of specialized employees. To the person seeking a position, they represent an employment resource that might not be readily available through other channels. These agencies are actually variations of employment agencies. Recruitment agencies receive the job description from the client, and their task is to find the proper person. Client relationships are confidential, and job descriptions need not be made public. They are, nonetheless, subject to equal opportunity employment laws.

Recruiters often utilize online job boards to advertise positions. Because the recruiting agency's fees are paid by the client seeking an artist and not by the artist who is placed in the position, the term "fee paid" in the advertisement indicates that the job candidate has no financial obligation to the agency. (For more about employment, see the Employment Issues section in Chapter 3, Professional Issues.)

Advertising Directories & Magazine Annuals

Advertising directories are widely known and used sources of talent. These directories generally showcase a specific type of work, such as illustration or graphic design. Artists purchase space in a directory where they display representative work and list a contact address for either the artist or the artist's representative. Most of these directories have online versions. Other annual publications are compilations of juried shows. Directories and annuals also provide references for the types and styles of work being done in the field.

Among the best-known national directories for illustration are The *Alternative Pick* (Altpick.com), the *Directory of Illustration* (www.directoryofillustration. com), and *Workbook Print* (www.workbook.com), which includes animation, motion, CGI, and photography as well. Directories of juried shows for illustration include *American Illustration* (AI-AP.com) and the *Society of Illustrators Annual* (www.societyofillustrators.org).

Directories for design include The *Alternative Pick* (Altpick.com), *Communication Arts Design Annual* (www.commarts.com/), *Graphis* (www.graphis.com), *PRINT Regional Design Annual* (www.printmag.com), and *Workbook Print* (www.workbook.com).

The work of the winners of the ADC Annual Awards, the oldest continuously running industry award show in the world, are featured on ADC's website (www.adcglobal. org/awards/). The awards celebrate the best in advertising, digital media, graphic and publication design, packaging, motion, photography, and illustration.

All the graphic design magazines hold yearly competitions and feature the winners in special annual issues. Many publications sponsor juried shows in areas of special interest such as dimensional illustration, humorous illustration, international design and illustration, photography, advertising, typography, and interactive. Print versions of directories and magazine annuals can be purchased directly from the publishers, online, or at most art supply stores and well-stocked bookstores.

The Internet

The Internet has become the primary resource for artists and clients alike. Illustrators and graphic designers can showcase and market their work on their own websites or on portfolio sites devoted to the work of many artists. Online directories exist side by side with print directories, and in some instances, they have replaced their print counterparts. For example, animation, design, illustration, photography, type, and web design talent can be found at Altpick.com (http://altpick.com/), the online version of The *Alternative Pick*. Clients can search for talent by name or artistic specialty.

Guild Resources

The Find an Artist section of the Graphic Artists Guild's website enables prospective clients to search online for artists by specialty and artistic style and to preview their work before making contact (www.graphicartistsguild.org).

The Graphic Artists Guild is a partner in the larger Design Employment Network. Through this collaboration, the Guild maintains for its members a listing of staff and freelance job opportunities on its website (https:// graphicartistsguild.org/member-benefits/career-listing/). Members and employers who are looking for talent can also post jobs for a fee. Jobs are instantly distributed across the prestigious and targeted design websites that make up the Network. They are also sent to a partner's e-mail list of over 30,000 members and promoted on social media channels.

Ethical Standards

The Graphic Artists Guild, established by graphic artists, is mandated by its constitution to monitor, support, and foster ethical standards in all dealings between graphic artists and art buyers. This is accomplished through Guild programs for members, through cooperation with related organizations, and through legislative activity on local, state, and federal levels.

The Code of Fair Practice for the Graphic Communications Industry

In 1948, the former Joint Ethics Committee published a Code of Fair Practices for the graphic communications field in response to the concerns of artists and art directors regarding growing abuses and misunderstandings and an increasing disregard of uniform standards of conduct.

The intention of the Code of Fair Practice, which was revised in 1989, was to uphold existing laws and traditions and to help define an ethical standard for business practices and professional conduct in the industry. Designed to promote equity for those engaged in creating, selling, buying, and using graphics, the Code has been used successfully by thousands of industry professionals to create equitable business relationships and to educate those entering the profession about accepted codes of behavior. It is also the foundation for the professional and ethical customs and practices which are promoted in this handbook. See Figure 2–4 for the full text of the Code of Fair Practice.

Although the Code provides guidelines for the voluntary conduct of people in the industry, which may be modified by written agreement between the parties, each artist should individually decide, for instance, whether to enter art contests or design competitions, provide free services, work on speculation, or work on a contingent basis. Each artist should independently decide how to price work.

As used in the Code, the word *artist* should be understood to include creative people and their representatives in such fields of visual communications as illustration, graphic design, interactive design, photography, film, and television.

2–4 The Code of Fair Practice

ARTICLE 1
Negotiations between an artist or the artist's representative and a client shall be conducted only through an authorized buyer.

ARTICLE 2
Orders or agreements between an artist or artist's representative and buyer should be in writing and shall include the specific rights which are being transferred, the specific fee arrangement agreed to by the parties, delivery date, and a summarized description of the work.

ARTICLE 3
All changes or additions not due to the fault of the artist or artist's representative should be billed to the buyer as an additional and separate charge.

ARTICLE 4
There should be no charges to the buyer for revisions or retakes made necessary by errors on the part of the artist or the artist's representative.

ARTICLE 5
If work commissioned by a buyer is postponed or canceled, a "kill fee" should be negotiated based on time allotted, effort expended, and expenses incurred. In addition, other lost work shall be considered.

ARTICLE 6
Completed work shall be promptly paid for in full and the artwork shall be returned promptly to the artist. Payment due the artist shall not be contingent upon third-party approval or payment.

ARTICLE 7
Alterations shall not be made without consulting the artist. Where alterations or retakes are necessary, the artist shall be given the opportunity of making such changes.

ARTICLE 8
The artist shall notify the buyer of any anticipated delay in delivery. Should the artist fail to keep the contract through unreasonable delay or nonconformance with agreed specifications, it will be considered a breach of contract by the artist. Should the agreed timetable be delayed due to the buyer's failure, the artist should endeavor to adhere as closely as possible to the original schedule as other commitments permit.

ARTICLE 9
Whenever practical, the buyer of artwork shall provide the artist with samples of the reproduced artwork for self-promotion purposes.

ARTICLE 10
There shall be no undisclosed rebates, discounts, gifts, or bonuses requested by or given to buyers by the artist or representative.

ARTICLE 11
Artwork and copyright ownership are vested in the hands of the artist unless agreed to in writing. No works shall be duplicated, archived, or scanned without the artist's prior authorization.

ARTICLE 12
Original artwork, and any material object used to store a computer file containing original artwork, remains the property of the artist unless it is specifically purchased. It is distinct from the purchase of any reproduction rights. All transactions shall be in writing.*

ARTICLE 13
In case of copyright transfers, only specified rights are transferred. All unspecified rights remain vested with the artist. All transactions shall be in writing.

ARTICLE 14
Commissioned artwork is not to be considered as "work made for hire" unless agreed to in writing before work begins.

ARTICLE 15
When the price of work is based on limited use and later such work is used more extensively, the artist shall receive additional payment.

2–4 The Code of Fair Practice (cont'd)

ARTICLE 16

Art or photography should not be copied for any use, including client presentation or "comping," without the artist's prior authorization. If exploratory work, comprehensives, or preliminary photographs from an assignment are subsequently chosen for reproduction, the artist's permission shall be secured, and the artist shall receive fair additional payment.

ARTICLE 17

If exploratory work, comprehensives, or photographs are bought from an artist with the intention or possibility that another artist will be assigned to do the finished work, this shall be in writing at the time of placing the order.

ARTICLE 18

Electronic rights are separate from traditional media and shall be separately negotiated. In the absence of a total copyright transfer or a work-made-for-hire agreement, the right to reproduce artwork in media not yet discovered is subject to negotiation.

ARTICLE 19

All published illustrations and photographs should be accompanied by a line crediting the artist by name, unless otherwise agreed to in writing.

ARTICLE 20

The right of an illustrator to sign work and to have the signature appear in all reproductions should remain intact.

ARTICLE 21

There shall be no plagiarism of any artwork.

ARTICLE 22

If an artist is specifically requested to produce any artwork during unreasonable working hours, fair additional remuneration shall be paid.

ARTICLE 23

All artwork or photography submitted as samples to a buyer should bear the name of the artist or artists responsible for the work. An artist shall not claim authorship of another's work.

ARTICLE 24

All companies that receive artist portfolios, samples, etc., shall be responsible for the return of the portfolio to the artist in the same condition as received.

ARTICLE 25

An artist entering into an agreement with a representative for exclusive representation shall not accept an order from, nor permit work to be shown by, any other representative. Any agreement that is not intended to be exclusive should set forth the exact restrictions agreed upon between the parties.

ARTICLE 26

Severance of an association between artist and representative should be agreed to in writing. The agreement should take into consideration the length of time the parties have worked together as well as the representative's financial contribution to any ongoing advertising or promotion. No representative should continue to show an artist's samples after the termination of an association.

ARTICLE 27

Examples of an artist's work furnished to a representative or submitted to a prospective buyer shall remain the property of the artist, should not be duplicated without the artist's authorization, and shall be returned promptly to the artist in good condition.

ARTICLE 28

Interpretation of the Code for the purposes of arbitration shall be in the hands of a body designated to resolve the dispute, and is subject to changes and additions at the discretion of the parent organizations through their appointed representatives on the Committee. Arbitration by a designated body shall be binding among the parties, and decisions may be entered for judgment and execution.

ARTICLE 29

Work on speculation/contests: Artists and designers who accept speculative assignments (whether directly from a client or by entering a contest or competition) risk losing anticipated fees, expenses, and the potential opportunity to pursue other, rewarding assignments. Each artist shall decide individually whether to enter art contests or design competitions, provide free services, work on speculation, or work on a contingency basis.

*Artwork ownership, copyright ownership, and ownership and rights transferred after January 1, 1978, are to be in compliance with the Federal Copyright Revision Act of 1976.

{3}

Professional Issues

This chapter provides a summary of important business issues affecting both staff and self-employed graphic artists, including employment status, taxation, working on speculation, entering contests and competitions, and health and safety in the workplace. It is designed to aid both buyers and sellers of graphic art.

PROFESSIONAL ISSUES *involve a variety of factors affecting the way graphic artists work and do business. Changes in business practices, technology, taxation, and copyright or other laws can dramatically impact a creator's business and livelihood. So too can emerging trends or practices that vary from accepted customs. While some of the following factors mainly concern the self-employed and entrepreneurs, others, such as health and safety in the workplace, technology, and entering contests, impact the entire profession.*

Employment Issues

While this section pertains primarily to staff employees, the subsection on Hiring Practices will be of interest to freelancers as well. The subsection, Employee Status, should be read by employees and independent contractors alike, as it shows how worker classification impacts both groups.

Hiring Trends

The global pandemic is disrupting industries and changing customer habits and preferences. According to the *2021 Salary Guide* by The Creative Group, a specialized staffing firm, this business upheaval is creating opportunities for creative and marketing professionals with the right skill set. They "are playing a key role helping firms navigate this environment by promoting new and revamped offerings, improving customer experiences, and expanding digital services for companies that were largely brick-and-mortar before the COVID-19 pandemic."

Despite the slow economy, The Creative Group found there is still competition for creative, digital, and marketing talent, especially in healthcare, manufacturing, technology, insurance, finance, and education. Those in high demand have experience using marketing automation and demand generation software, customer relationship management systems, search engine optimization (SEO) and search engine marketing (SEM) tools, and other e-commerce platforms. Creative professionals with expertise in user experience (UX) and user interface (UI) design and front-end web development will also be needed.

Companies are also recognizing inclusion and diversity as essential considerations when hiring. Professionals with varied perspectives and experiences are needed to come up with creative business solutions and to attract and retain top talent. "Creative and marketing teams are in a unique position to help a company showcase its overall inclusion and diversity efforts internally and externally."

Hiring Practices

USE OF FREELANCE & CONTRACT WORKERS

Generally, larger companies, particularly those that produce a significant amount of in-house graphic art for advertising, catalogs, corporate graphics, newsletters, websites, social media, and packaging, hire a full-time art staff and use freelance talent to supplement it. When there is no in-house staff or when the company chooses to subcontract a specific project or an area of a large project, such as a special advertising campaign, corporate identity program, or annual and quarterly reports, then independent agencies or design firms may be hired to work on retainer.

Whenever agencies and corporations downsize their art departments, hiring freelancers is favored over staff. These companies sometimes hire back the same individuals to work as full-time freelancers on the same projects but at a lower rate and without benefits. Even if the fee paid is greater than the salary previously earned, the loss of benefits—and the cost of replacing them—is significant, frequently resulting in a lower total income. This cost-cutting business practice has serious tax implications for both the employer and the graphic artist. For further discussion, refer to the Self-Employment Issues section later in this chapter.

Agencies and corporations are not the only businesses hiring freelancers. A current trend, according to "The Top 6 Freelancing Trends in 2019" at www.chunkofchange.com, is freelancers hiring each other.

Peer-to-peer hiring involves a freelancer ("prime") hiring other freelancers ("subcontractors") to secure larger projects and to diversify or add value to the services they offer. It can also free the prime freelancer's time up to develop more expertise and establish him/herself as an authority in the field, eventually leading to being able to command higher fees.

TEMPORARY EMPLOYMENT AGENCIES

For a variety of reasons, some skilled graphic artists opt to be temporary workers, hired by a temp agency that works on behalf of an employer, for the duration of a specific project, which could be days, weeks, or months. Some like the flexibility of temp work. Temp work can be a good option for graphic artists just entering the job market because it gives them job experience before they apply for permanent full-time employment. In fact, some temp jobs can lead to full-time employment at the company where the assignment is if the employer finds the temp worker meets their needs and is a good fit. Another advantage for working temp jobs is that the graphic artist can explore different types of jobs in a variety of settings to get a better idea of what they want in permanent employment.

For most temp jobs, the hourly rate paid to the temp worker is commensurate with industry hourly rates. If the graphic artist feels it is not commensurate with the skills required, the artist has the option of negotiating with the agency for a higher rate before accepting the job. The biggest difference in compensation between being a temp worker and a permanent employee is often the lack of benefits. If you are considering temp work, research the agencies thoroughly before you apply for work to see what benefits they offer, if any. Most of the major creative staffing agencies in the graphics arts sector—Aquent, Creative Circle, The Creative Group, and Paladin—offer benefits such as health insurance and 401K plans after a qualifying period, and they may handle taxes as well.

Read the fine print in any contracts you are asked to sign. Artists are often required to sign blanket contracts that ask them to release more rights of privacy and personal financial information than is relevant to the scope of their job. Some of these contracts would be considered extreme even by regular employees. This practice may have originated because companies request extremely protective contracts from other types of temporary workers, such as software developers, systems analysts, and computer consultants who have access to important corporate information and financial data. Such conditions rarely apply to a temporary graphic artist, and the same contracts should not be used.

Salaries

GENERAL TRENDS

Due to an economy challenged by the pandemic, many companies have been forced to slow hiring for creative and marketing positions, but it is expected that they will need to bring in additional talent for initiatives that will strengthen their online presence. Hiring must be done in a cost-effective way, requiring an adjustable mix of full-time and temporary employees.

According to The Creative Group's research, U.S. salaries continue to vary widely by city, due to several reasons, including cost of living and availability of talent. The highest salaries can be found in San Francisco, New York City, San Jose, Boston, Oakland, and Washington, DC. Salary adjustments for many other cities can be found in The Creative Group's *2021 Salary Guide* (http://creativegroup.com/salary-center), which includes a salary calculator.

For specific salary ranges by job title for each of the major graphic arts disciplines, refer to Chapters 5–10.

SALARY RESOURCES

There are several salary resources available to graphic artists. Some of them are updated and published annually, so check to see if there are more recent editions than the ones listed below.

SALARY GUIDES FROM CREATIVE STAFFING AGENCIES

The Creative Group. *2021 Salary Guide.* Current compensation data for creative and marketing professionals and emerging employment trends. Includes market variance factors to adjust salaries for specific cities throughout the United States and Canada. Download at www.roberthalf.com/salary-guide/creative-and-marketing.

Onward Search. *2020 Digital Creative Salary Guide.* Salary data for over 80 digital, creative, and marketing professionals. Available at www.onwardsearch.com/digital-creative-salary-guide-2020/.

24 Seven. *2020 Job Market Report.* Compensation data and hiring expectations for the digital marketing, creative services, development & tech, e-commerce, fashion, retail, and beauty industries. Download at http://info.24seventalent.com/24-seven-job-market-report-2020.

Vitamin T (Aquent). *Flexibility Fuels the Future: 2020 Salary Guide.* Salaries for over 45 creative, digital, and marking positions with location-based market adjustments. Download at https://go.vitamintalent.com/salary-guide.

Paladin. *2020 Creative & Marketing Salary Guide.* Localized salary data for creative and marketing professionals with detailed job descriptions and industry insights. Download at www.paladinstaff.com/recruiting/salary-guide/.

COROFLOT REAL-TIME DESIGN SALARY GUIDE

Coroflot is the longest-running career community focused on the design and creative professions online. Their mission is to connect designers with meaningful and creative opportunities at companies around the world. Coroflot offers a free online portfolio hosting solution, and their job board is the largest and most active site specifically targeted at hiring designers and other creative professionals. Coroflot also collects and reports current salary information from tens of thousands of design and creative professionals worldwide in real time, giving graphic artists a tool for salary negotiations. Graphic artists can get access to the detailed results of the Salary Guide for various job titles, including salary ranges and an average hourly rate for freelancers, when they add their own information.

Coroflot's Job Board can be accessed from the Graphic Artists Guild's website at https://graphicartistsguild.org/membership_benefits/career.

O'REILLY MEDIA 2017 DESIGN SALARY SURVEY

O'Reilly Media conducted an anonymous online survey of the salaries of designers, UX specialists, and others in the design space. From the 1,085 responses collected (from 48 countries), an in-depth report was developed that presents complete survey results, demonstrating how variables such as job title, location, use of specific tools, and the types of tasks performed affect salary and other compensation. Results can be accessed at www.oreilly.com/ideas/2017-design-salary-survey.

UXPA INTERNATIONAL 2018 UX SALARY SURVEY

Median salaries and ranges for 17 job titles, including Information Architect, Interaction Designer, User Experience Architect/Engineer, Graphic/Visual Designer, and Interface Designer. Salary differences by U.S. regions given. Read the report at https://uxpa.org/wp-content/uploads/2017/10/UXPA_SalarySurvey_2018v4.pdf.

INSTITUTIONS OF HIGHER LEARNING WEBSITES

Postsecondary schools that offer courses and degree programs in the creative fields often provide prospective students with information on their websites regarding details about various occupations, including job descriptions, skills needed, hiring outlook, and salary ranges.

BUREAU OF LABOR STATISTICS

The Bureau of Labor Statistics, through its Occupational Employment Statistics (OES) program produces employment and wage estimates annually for over 800 occupations. These estimates are available for the nation as a whole, for individual states, and for metropolitan and nonmetropolitan areas; national occupational estimates for specific industries are also available. Included in the data are the mean hourly wage and the mean annual wage for each of these occupations. This data can be accessed at www.bls.gov/Oes/current/oes_nat.htm.

ONLINE EMPLOYMENT SITES

There are several online employment sites that give median salaries for design and illustration job titles. Some also provide salary figures for specific companies. These sites include Glassdoor.com, Indeed.com, PayScale.com, and Salary.com.

Conditions of Employment

Graphic artists should consider conditions of employment as well as salary when applying for a salaried position. Some of the conditions for full-time workers to consider include policies, benefits, job description, and the performance review process.

POLICIES

Many employers have written staff policies outlining how a company relates to its employees. New York State companies, for example, are required by law to notify employees "in writing or by publicly posting" about their policies on sick leave, vacations, personal leave, holidays, and hours. Other items that may be included are employee grievance procedures, causes for discipline (up to and including discharge), criteria for salary increases and promotions, and parental leave. A written staff policy reveals much about the working environment and the potential employer's attitude toward the staff.

BENEFITS

All companies are required to offer such basics as minimum wage, unemployment insurance, workers compensation, and short-term disability insurance. Most companies also offer a benefit package to their full-time employees that may include health, long-term disability, and/or life or dental insurance plans. Such benefits are at the discretion of the employer and are not currently required by law. Benefits are often related to company size, with smaller companies offering fewer benefits. Larger companies and corporations often offer pension, profit-sharing, and stock option plans, and sometimes daycare facilities or childcare subsidies. An employee may qualify for a company pension depending on the plan specifications and the number of hours he/she works. Staff artists should check with their employer for details.

JOB DESCRIPTION

Just as a contract between a client and a freelance artist reflects their understanding of their relationship, a written job description can define what is expected of artists during the term of their employment. The Graphic Artists Guild strongly recommends that all artists taking a salaried position request a written job description, since it will help both employer and employee avoid assumptions and expectations not shared by the other party. A written description is also useful in the event a job changes significantly during the term of employment. Such changes may reflect greater responsibilities or functions, justifying a new title or greater compensation. If such changes are made, the job description should be rewritten to reflect the new title, duties, salary, benefits, and start date. It is also useful for the artist to obtain an official "offer letter" on company letterhead. This letter should state the salary, title, start date, and benefits, and be signed by the hiring authority.

PERFORMANCE REVIEW

A periodic (semiannual or annual) evaluation of job performance is helpful to both employer and employee. A formal review gives the employer the opportunity to discuss job performance and changes in job description and allows employees to gauge their performance and raise questions about their job expectations. Performance reviews also allow employer and employee to suggest ways to improve the "product" or the employee's function. When handled well, job performance reviews can pinpoint potential problems and help maintain good and productive relationships between employer and employee. The results of the job performance review should be kept on file, and employees should be allowed access to their file.

While many of the above conditions of employment are not mandatory, they help both employer and employee develop and maintain good relationships during the term of employment.

Workplace Issues

WORKPLACE STRESS

Closely following salary in importance are issues of workplace stress, including long hours of work, unrealistic deadlines, and repeated changes to projects in progress. These conditions lead to high levels of burnout and injury.

The learning curve required of graphic artists due to continually evolving technology is another stress. Keeping up with new software programs or frequent updates may necessitate expensive training programs, and constant professional development. One benefit of an in-house position is that many employers provide on-the-job training, especially if an assignment requires special competence.

CHALLENGES TO COLLABORATION

The Creative Team of the Future is an ongoing research project that explores trends affecting the role of the design team and the creative professional. Its 2016 report, *Collaboration in the Workplace: How to Overcome 7 Challenges*, was developed by The Creative Group (TCG), a leader among creative and marketing staffing agencies, and AIGA, the professional association for design, with a media partnership provided by Graphic Design USA, the news and information source for graphic designers and other creative professionals.

As part of the 2016 research, 800 in-house design professionals were surveyed, and creative veterans from leading organizations were interviewed to get their opinions on the state of the industry and where it's going. A recurring theme was the need for greater collaboration in the workplace, especially between creative and technology teams, in order to achieve better outcomes for the business. For example, as organizations kick off strategic initiatives, in-house designers are finding themselves involved more often in the early planning; however, they continue to face challenges communicating and clarifying expectations with and earning respect from colleagues outside their department.

According to the study, the seven most common complaints from in-house designers regarding the challenges that thwart true collaboration are "they don't understand our role and capabilities, they regard us as order-takers, poor communication is crippling productivity, no one can make a decision, approval processes drag on for days—or weeks, no one has time to meet, and we don't have a shared workflow."

The report provides many solutions to the above complaints for both employees and employers. As lines between departments (and sometimes jobs) continue to blur, creating an atmosphere where constant collaboration is encouraged will become a bigger priority for businesses. To be successful in a collaborative business environment, creatives will need to show what it takes to be a multi-team player by addressing common collaboration challenges head on and being proactive in bringing colleagues together to share ideas and information. (The full report can be downloaded at https://www.roberthalf.com/sites/default/files/documents/collaboration-in-the-workplace-tcg-01-2016.pdf).

Employment Status

Clients should be aware that the Internal Revenue Service takes a dim view of independent contractor relationships. From the government's perspective, employers use so-called independent contractors to evade employment taxes. If independent contractors are hired, the employer should be able to justify this designation in the event of an audit. If the IRS successfully reclassifies independent contractors, the very existence of a firm can be threatened. (For a complete discussion of work made for hire, consult the Work-Made-for-Hire section in Chapter 11, Legal Rights & Issues.)

In recent years, the Internal Revenue Service has cracked down on advertising agencies, design firms, publishers, and others by examining whether artists providing graphic design, illustration, or production services are actually freelancers or employees. In audit after audit, the IRS has determined that so-called freelancers are, in fact, employees based upon their analysis of the actual working relationship between the client and the graphic artist (see Determining Employee Status below). Especially vulnerable to IRS scrutiny, and a significant risk to the hiring party, are artists who work as full-time freelancers. One West Coast comic-book publisher, for example, went out of business after six-figure penalties were imposed by the IRS for misclassifying its employees as independent contractors.

There are advantages and disadvantages of each classification for both the artist and the hiring party. Independent contractors are paid a flat fee, simplifying the employer's bookkeeping; and depending on the freelancer's fee structure, the employer may realize significant savings on taxes, insurance, and other fringe benefits. Independents retain some control over their copyrights, time, and business tax deductions for materials, overhead on private workspace, and so on. But independents always risk loss of payment when work is rejected or canceled or when they work on speculation, while employees are guaranteed at least the legal minimum wage.

The IRS has a 20-factor control test (Revenue Ruling 87-41, 1897-1CB296) that it uses to clarify the distinction between employees and independent contractors. The control test is easy. Is the person subject to the control of or by the firm?

The guidelines, however, are too general to resolve every situation. Often some factors suggest employee status, while others suggest independent contractor status. Key factors that the IRS looks at include the following:

1. **Instructions:** Is the worker required to obey the firm's instructions about when, where, and how work is to be performed? If the firm has the right to require compliance with such instructions, the worker is likely to be an employee.

2. **Training:** Training a worker suggests that the worker is an employee. Training may consist only of having a more experienced employee fill in the newcomer on office procedures, or he/she might be required to attend meetings or read files and/or correspondence.

3. **Integration:** If a worker's services are part of a firm's operations, this suggests that the worker is subject to the firm's control. This is especially true if the success or continuation of the firm's business depends in a significant way upon those services.

4. **Personal services:** If the firm requires that the services be performed in person, this suggests control over an employee.

5. **Use of assistants:** If the firm hires, directs, and pays for the worker's assistants, this indicates employee status. On the other hand, if the worker hires, directs, and pays for his/her assistants; supplies materials; and works under a contract providing that he/she is responsible only to achieve certain results, that is consistent with independent contractor status.

6. **Ongoing relationship:** If the relationship is ongoing, even if frequent work is done on irregular cycles, the worker is likely to be an employee.

7. **Fixed hours of work:** Working fixed hours suggests the worker is an employee controlled by the firm.

8. **Full-time work:** If the worker is with the firm full time, that suggests the firm controls the time of work and restricts the worker from taking other jobs, and thus shows employee status.

9. **Work location:** If the firm requires that the worker be located on the firm's premises, that suggests employment. That the worker performs the services off-premises implies being an independent

contractor, especially if an employee normally has to perform similar services at an employer's premises.

10. **Workflow:** A worker required to conform to the routines, schedules, and patterns established by the firm is consistent with being an employee.

11. **Reports:** A requirement that reports be submitted, whether oral or written, suggests employee status.

12. **Manner of payment:** Payment by the hour, week, or month suggests an employee, while payment of an agreed-upon lump sum for a job suggests an independent contractor.

13. **Expenses:** Payment of expenses by the firm implies the right to control company expenses, and thus suggests employment status.

14. **Tools and equipment:** If the firm provides tools and equipment, it suggests the worker is an employee.

15. **Investment:** A significant investment by a worker in his/her own equipment implies being an independent contractor.

16. **Profit or loss:** Showing a profit or loss (due to overhead, project costs, and investment in equipment) is consistent with being an independent contractor.

17. **Multiple clients:** Working for many clients suggests independent contractor status. However, the worker could be an employee of each of the businesses, if there is one service arrangement for all clients.

18. **Marketing:** The marketing of services by a worker to the public on a regular basis indicates independent contractor status.

19. **Right to discharge:** If the firm can discharge the worker at any time, this suggests employment. An independent contractor cannot be dismissed without legal liability unless contract specifications are not met.

20. **Right to quit:** An employee may quit at any time without liability, but an independent contractor may be liable for failure to perform, depending on the contractual terms.

A MATTER OF INTENTION

The IRS may argue that workers with a very peripheral connection to the firm—for example, mechanical artists or illustrators—are employees. The penalties for unintentional misclassification of an employee are serious, but not nearly as serious as the penalties for intentional misclassification. Regardless of whether the misclassification is unintentional or intentional, the employer's minimum liability is $50 for each Form W-2 that the employer failed to file due to misclassification plus penalties of 1.5% of the employee's wages plus 40% of the FICA taxes that were not withheld and 100% of matching FICA the employer should

have paid. The employer has no right to recover from the employee any amounts determined to be due to the IRS. Interest and penalties may be assessed by the IRS, but only on the amount of the employer's liability.

On the other hand, if the misclassification is proved intentional, the governing agencies involved can impose additional fines and penalties, including criminal penalties of up to $1,000 per misclassified worker, the full amount of taxes not withheld, or even time in prison.

Employee misclassification is becoming an increasingly large problem for employers, workers, and the government. Many labor economists believe that within a decade, freelancers will outnumber full-time employees. A federal study estimates that approximately 3.4 million employees are classified as independent contractors when they should be reported as employees. Misclassification of employees costs the United States billions of dollars annually in underpayment of employment taxes and unpaid FICA and unemployment taxes.

Not only is the federal government cracking down, but so are state governments—by imposing severe civil penalties on employers who willfully misclassify independent contractors. For example, in 2011 California passed a law (which went into effect in 2012) that fines employers $5,000 to $15,000 per violation. Furthermore, if it is found that an employer has a pattern and practice of misclassifying independent contractors, the fine is increased to a minimum of $10,000 to $25,000 per violation.

PRECAUTIONS & SAFEGUARDS

After conducting a careful review of how their workers should be classified under the IRS's 20-factor control test, a client or firm may remain uncertain of what is correct. A wise approach is to err on the side of caution and, when in doubt, classify workers as employees.

If the firm believes a worker is an independent contractor, the two parties should negotiate a carefully worded contract that accurately sets forth the parties' agreement and is legally binding. To be most effective, in the event of an IRS or state challenge, the contract should state that the worker is an independent contractor according to the 20-factor test. The parties must then adhere to the contract. If a firm already has such a contract in place, it should be reviewed with the IRS test in mind and to confirm whether the parties are in fact following its terms.

To protect themselves from an IRS or state audit and any potential penalties, many clients treat every artist as an employee, even those who are clearly independent. In such cases, clients withhold appropriate taxes from creative fees and issue end-of-year W-2 forms rather than a Form 1099. To counter the potential loss of copyright (since works created by employees are considered works made for hire unless otherwise negotiated), artists should clearly establish themselves as independent contractors, preserving authorship and copyrights, and attempt to reclaim the rights to their works from the hiring party through negotiation.

IMPACT OF EMPLOYMENT STATUS

Worker classification can make a big difference to employees in several areas of employment.

JOB SECURITY

Employees do not enjoy the freedom of working for whomever they want, as independent contractors do, but they do enjoy the security of a regular paycheck. Another advantage that many employees have is the legal right to organize for the purposes of collective bargaining, a right denied to independent contractors.

MINIMUM WAGE & OVERTIME

The Fair Labor Standards Act, the federal law that guarantees a worker be paid fairly, establishes the federal minimum wage, sets requirements for overtime pay, and defines the 40-hour work week. These guarantees, however, only apply to employees. Independent contractors are not covered by the law.

BENEFITS & INSURANCE

The majority of employees in the United States are entitled to receive unemployment, disability, and workers' compensation insurance coverage; however, each state's eligibility requirements and specifics vary significantly. Depending upon individual company policy, employers may also provide optional fringe benefits such as paid vacations, comprehensive medical and hospitalization insurance, employer-funded pension plans, or profit sharing to full-time employees. Independent contractors must purchase their own disability coverage and have no access to unemployment insurance or workers' compensation. Furthermore, independent contractors must provide their own vacations, medical coverage, and retirement plans.

WORK MADE FOR HIRE

All work created by employees, unless otherwise negotiated, is done as work made for hire, which gives authorship and all attendant rights to the employer. Negotiating those rights back, while possible, is not easy. In contrast, independent contractors are recognized as the authors of their work and control the copyright, unless they sign a contract that specifically states the work is a "work made for hire." For a more detailed definition and discussion of work made for hire, see Chapter 11, Legal Rights & Issues.

TAXES

FICA Taxes vs. Self-Employment Tax. In 2020, the Social Security tax was 12.4% of an employee's gross income (up to $137,700). A graphic artist classified as an employee has only half of the Social Security tax (or 6.2%) withheld from his/her paycheck; the employer pays the other half. Likewise, the employer pays half of the 2.9% Medicare tax, or 1.45%, which has no income limit. Together these two taxes make up the 7.65% FICA taxes withheld from an employee's paycheck.

Instead of FICA, self-employed individuals pay the Self-Employment tax. The Self-Employment tax rate for 2020 is 15.3% (which includes the entire Social Security tax plus the entire 2.9% Medicare portion) on net self-employment income up to $137,700. If an artist's net earnings exceed $137,700, he/she continues to pay only the Medicare portion (2.9%) of the Self-Employment tax on the rest of his/her earnings.

There are two income tax deductions that reduce the tax liability of self-employed artists. The deductions are intended to make sure self-employed people are treated in much the same way as employers and employees for Social Security and income tax purposes.

First, net earnings from self-employment are reduced by an amount equal to half of the total Social Security tax. This is similar to the way employees are treated under the tax laws in that the employer's share of the Social Security tax is not considered income to the employee.

Second, self-employed artists can deduct half of their Social Security tax on the IRS Form 1040 (line 29). This means the deduction is taken from their gross income in determining adjusted gross income. It cannot be an itemized deduction and must not be listed on their Schedule C.

Tax Deductions. Independent contractors can reduce their taxable income significantly by deducting legitimate business expenses. Beginning with the tax year 2018, employees no longer may deduct unreimbursed business expenses.

Self-Employment Issues

The freelancing workforce has grown to 57 million Americans. According to 6,001 workers surveyed in the study, "Freelancing in America: 2019," commissioned by Upwork, the largest global freelancing website, and the Freelancers Union, a labor organization representing the independent workforce, 35% of the workforce freelanced in 2019. Of the freelancers surveyed, 60% said they started freelancing by choice. Of those who freelance full-time, the most common reason for freelancing was the flexibility it afforded. For the first time since the annual survey has been conducted, starting in 2014, as many respondents view freelancing as a long-term career choice as those who view it as a temporary way to make money (50% each). Nine out of 10 were optimistic about the future of freelancing, 71% said perceptions of freelancing as a career are becoming more positive, and 51% said there is no amount of money that would entice them to definitely take a traditional job. For more results from this study, go to https://www.upwork.com/i/freelancing-in-america/2019/.

Despite the optimism of the self-employed, there still remain challenges to the freelancing lifestyle.

Challenges Faced by Freelancers

Many employees dream of being self-employed so they can be their own boss and work on their own terms and schedule. Not having someone tell you what to do all the time sounds very liberating. Once the jump is made from being an employee to being your own boss, reality begins to set in. Being self-employed may offer you more flexibility in how and when you work, but with independence comes more responsibility.

If you were a salaried employee, you may have taken for granted what your employer offered you in addition to the weekly or bi-weekly paycheck—health insurance, a retirement plan, paid days off for holidays and when you were sick or needed to attend to family matters, and a paid vacation. Your salary and all of those benefits cost the employer money, which you are now responsible for financing yourself. To do that, you need clients and projects to produce income. Finding clients rests on your shoulders, too, and yours alone. You have no co-workers for discussing ideas or strategies. And, if you grow your business enough to hire employees, you are responsible for them, too.

For these reasons, the freelance life is not for everyone. Self-employed individuals often cite the following factors as challenges to overcome. Other issues of concern to the self-employed are discussed throughout this handbook.

ISOLATION

Freelancers often complain that working alone is isolating, especially those who work from home. They may have been attracted to the freedom of self-employment, but after a while they discover working in solitude for hours on end is not that appealing. They miss the camaraderie and support of co-workers. The freelance life can be not only lonely, but uninspiring as well. Graphic artists are creative problem solvers, so they need other people to discuss problems and brainstorm ideas with and to get inspiration from.

There are several things you can do to alleviate the isolation of freelancing.

INCREASE FACE TIME

Plan to meet at least once a week with other freelancers to work together or to socialize. If you can't meet in person, at least call a colleague or friend to discuss work problems. Conduct important meetings with local clients in person at their offices instead of over the phone. For long-distance clients, hold meetings using Skype or some other video conferencing software instead of the phone, so you can at least see their faces.

JOIN PROFESSIONAL ORGANIZATIONS

Join your local Chamber of Commerce and take part in some of their events and workshops geared to small businesses and the self-employed. Many offer monthly networking events. It is an excellent way to socialize with other professionals, gain business knowledge, access business resources, promote your business, and meet potential clients.

Join professional organizations that serve your discipline or that advocate for graphic artists or freelancers, such as the Graphic Artists Guild and the Freelancers Union. Some have local chapters in the larger cities that provide socializing, networking, and professional development opportunities. Even if there isn't a chapter near you, these organizations have websites with resources and a wealth of information you can access, including member directories so you can connect with other professionals in your field. Some have blogs that provide creative inspiration and helpful business and technical advice.

Many organizations offer workshops and webinars on business and industry-related topics. Some of the larger organizations sponsor annual or biannual national conferences with speakers and workshop presenters who are top experts in their field. You should try to attend a national conference every year or two to keep your skills up to date and to recharge your creative engine. They are also a way to network and make new contacts.

Lists of professional organizations, as well as some of the larger conferences and workshops, of interest to graphic artists can be found in Part 5: Resources & References.

CONSIDER A CO-WORKING SPACE

If isolation becomes a major problem for you, consider joining a co-working space. These are membership-based workspaces where diverse groups of freelancers, remote workers, startups, and other independent professionals work together in a shared communal setting. They are less expensive than renting traditional office or studio space, making them an affordable alternative. According to DeskMag (www.deskmag.com), the average monthly base price in the United States ranges from $195 for a hot desk (an open spot in a common area) to $387 for a dedicated (permanent) desk in an enclosed shared space. Private offices (closed, lockable spaces) are also available at slightly higher prices.

Prices vary by city and by the amenities they offer. Most dedicated spaces include a desk, chair, file cabinet, trash can, and high-speed Wi-Fi. Some include mail and package handling and conference rooms in the base price. Additional amenities may include kitchenettes, restaurants, showers, reception, cleaning services, etc. Many are open 24/7, an attractive option for freelancers who want flexible working hours.

The Harvard Business Review studied co-working spaces in 2015 (https://hbr.org/2015/05/why-people-thrive-in-coworking-spaces) and found that people thrive in the co-working environment for several reasons. Because members are from diverse industries, ventures, and projects, there is little competition or internal politics, creating a strong sense of work identity. Co-working spaces cultivate a culture of helping others. Co-workers have diverse skill sets that they can provide to other community members. Members reported that having a community to work in helps them create structures and disciplines that motivate them. Connection with others was a big reason why they chose co-working spaces over home offices.

SHARE RESOURCES OR GOALS WITH OTHER ARTISTS

Graphic artists and other creatives who provide services or produce and sell art have found that sharing resources or goals with other artists is another solution to combating isolation and its negative effects. These arrangements can range from formal, legal entities or informal agreements between two or more artists.

An **artist cooperative** is one of the more formal entities. Artist cooperatives provide benefits that are specific to their members, but can function similarly to other types of cooperatives, such as a worker cooperative, an organization that is owned and democratically governed by its members. Each member owns one voting share and has one vote on major decisions as outlined in the organization's bylaws.

While artist cooperatives are most commonly created for marketing purposes, which may include sharing retail or gallery space, marketing over the Internet, or publishing and distributing a catalog, they can also be formed to purchase expensive equipment that can be shared, to rent studio space, or to obtain discounts on materials that can be purchased in bulk.

Artist cooperatives are legal entities, generally established in the state in which they will operate and therefore are subject to that state's business statutes. While some states have cooperative-specific statutes, they may be specific to certain types of cooperatives other than artist cooperatives. If an artist cooperative does not fit within your state's cooperative statutes, a cooperative may be formed using other structures such as the corporation, limited liability company (LLCs), or nonprofit, but may be subject to some limitations and may require more creative drafting of related documents establishing the entity. LLCs, however, are a common choice because of their flexibility. To read more about artist cooperatives, go to www.co-oplaw.org/co-op-basics/types/artist-cooperatives/.

An **artist collective** is a specific type of cooperative in which a group of artists work together to achieve a common goal that defines the collective. The goal can be anything from sharing studio space, the cost of materials, marketing and promotional efforts, and advocacy to working collectively to inspire socio-political awareness in the community through exhibits. Everyone who is part of the collective jointly shares ownership, status, costs, benefits, and risks. Members work together to promote and support the work of every member of the collective.

A collective may be comprised of members with diverse, complementary, or common skills and talents. For example, Studio 1482 is an illustration collective located in New York City that offers a wide variety of illustration services for numerous markets. Each of the four members works independently to bring their unique point of view and personal style to an assignment, or they work together collaboratively to create a larger vision for their clients.

In contrast, the four female members of the Pencil Parade Art Collective do not share office or studio space—they are located in far-flung areas of the United States, but they share a common website that promotes their artwork to manufacturers and art directors in all markets. They are illustrators and surface pattern designers, but each has her own specialty within the industry or additional skill sets, such as web design, photography, and licensing. Like Studio 1482, they operate both as individuals and together.

The primary goal of the Crush Illustration Collective

is to support and challenge each other. The seven members, who live in five different time zones, share a common website where they display their work, but each has her own website as well. They do themed group challenges to critique each other's work, push their illustrations into new areas, and connect with and build their audience. They also work together on social media strategy and provide support and advice to each other on everything from communicating better with clients to offering strategies for working from home.

Informal arrangements may occur between graphic artists simply for the purpose of sharing physical office or studio space, with each maintaining their own freelance business and their own clients. In some shared arrangements, graphic artists may use their complimentary skills to form a team to work jointly on a project.

Even for informal arrangements, participating graphic artists should have a legal agreement drawn up that spells out who is financially responsible for such things as rent, utilities, and other expenses, especially if one of the group decides to leave the arrangement.

PROCRASTINATION & LACK OF MOTIVATION

The isolation of being self-employed often translates to procrastination and lack of motivation. There are several things you can do to avoid these time killers.

Build time in your schedule for breaks and doing something unrelated to work—get outside in the fresh air and take a walk or go for a run. Go to the gym or work out at home. Not only do physical activities break up the monotony of work, but they get you moving, which helps alleviate the ill effects of a sedentary job. Try meditation or yoga to relieve stress. Make sure you eat lunch every day. All of these things also serve to keep you healthy.

To keep your creative juices flowing, establish an online presence other than your website. Share your expertise by participating in forums and discussion boards. Doing this on a regular basis may have the added benefit of attracting new clients. For a change of pace, view the work of creatives in other disciplines—you never know where inspiration will come from. Periodically check out the portfolios of the very best in the industry.

Successful self-employed professionals say that adhering to a strict schedule is essential to avoiding procrastination.

SCHEDULING & TIME MANAGEMENT

One of the lures of the freelance life is that you can work when you feel like it. Does this mean sleeping in until noon most days, taking off to go sailing whenever it's a nice day, binge watching old TV shows all day? No, it means having the flexibility to create a work schedule that works for you and your lifestyle, but you still need a schedule. And, you need to manage your time wisely. Otherwise, you will soon find that procrastination and lack of motivation become a way of life, you do not have enough clients to produce enough billable hours, or you are missing meetings and deadlines with the clients you do have.

CREATE A SCHEDULE THAT WORKS FOR YOU & YOUR CLIENTS

All businesses have set hours. Can you imagine how frustrating it would be trying to go to a restaurant or to seek professional services that have no set hours? This does not mean your hours have to be 9 to 5, Monday through Friday. You can take your lifestyle and circumstances into account. Perhaps you have a working spouse that does not get the traditional Saturday/Sunday "weekend." Maybe you have young school-aged children and you have to work around their school schedule. Or, your schedule needs to take into account the two mornings per week you are taking a course. That is the flexibility of being self-employed—you can create a schedule that works around all those situations, and takes into account the time of day when you are most productive.

There are many variations on the traditional work week, which include the following:

Choosing Your Own Weekend. This schedule allows you to have the same weekend off as a spouse or partner whose days off fall on days other than Saturday and Sunday. Or, there may be an activity or class that only happens during the week that you'd like to participate in on a regular basis.

Split Shift or Late-Day Shift. Working a split shift (mornings and evenings) frees up your afternoons for other activities, socializing, etc. It's also a good choice if you have to pick up children from school and take them to afterschool activities, and it saves on the cost of afterschool childcare. An alternative is the late-day shift (working afternoons and evenings), which frees up your mornings for other activities and appointments. If you live on the East Coast, you will still be able to serve clients on the West Coast with the split shift and late-day shift. However, if you live on the West Coast and have East Coast corporate clients, the late-day shift is less desirable, as it would leave only two to three business hours for communicating.

Front-Loaded Week. Instead of spreading the 40-hour work week (35 working hours and 5 hours for lunch and breaks) over five days, it is spread over four days, meaning you work a 10-hour day Monday through Thursday, instead of an 8-hour day. This creates the three-day weekend, which may be highly desirable in the summer or if you like to travel. If you choose this schedule, build in additional breaks to prevent fatigue which will undermine your productivity.

POST YOUR SCHEDULE

Once you have determined your schedule, post it on your website(s) and any social media along with your contact information, in all business e-mails, and in any agreements and contracts you have with clients. This is for both your clients' and your benefit, especially if you choose a schedule that does not conform to the traditional business day and week. Clients will know when they can expect to reach you, and it will save you from being contacted by clients during your non-working hours.

Let your clients know about any upcoming changes to your schedule, such as travel, holidays, vacations, etc. when you will be unavailable. Create an automatic reply for your e-mail accounts to let contacts and potential clients know when you will be out of the office and when you expect to return.

START EACH DAY AS IF YOU ARE GOING TO THE OFFICE

Even if you work from home, you need to have a going-to-work mindset when you start your workday. Doing so helps avoid procrastination and makes you more professional. You should have a designated work area, preferably a separate room, in your home that is free from distractions. Make sure your roommates or family know your work schedule and let them know that you are not to be disturbed while you are in your "office" during those hours. That goes for family and friends who don't live with you as well. Discourage them from phoning or texting you during your business hours for nonemergency and social reasons.

In addition to your scheduled hours of business, plan a daily schedule, dividing the day up into blocks of time for working on client projects (billable hours), activities such as reading e-mails, making phone calls, self-promotion, invoicing, etc. (non-billable hours), and lunch and breaks. A daily schedule does not have to be the same each day. Perhaps you notice Fridays are generally slower. Then that would be a good day to spend more time on self-promotion. The schedule will also vary by the number of clients you have at a given time and how large their projects are.

Learn to compartmentalize your work, allocating a part of your day and/or parts of your week to each client, plus non-billable activities. Don't let one client take over your entire schedule. You do not need to be at a client's beck and call. If you've scheduled two hours of the day to work on Client B's project, don't let phone calls and e-mails from Client A or anyone else sideline you during that time. Responding to calls and e-mails not only takes time away from Client B's project, but it also interrupts your workflow, concentration, and productivity. Taking two hours or even a half day to get back to Client A is not unreasonable.

Manage your time wisely each day and set daily goals and tasks for yourself ahead of time, then stick to your schedule; otherwise, your projects and deadlines will soon get away from you. If you have a lull in client business, don't be tempted to do the laundry or clean your house instead. Use the time to search for new clients, prepare self-promotional materials, or learn a new software program—all things that are investing in your business.

There is time-management and scheduling software that can help you keep your business on track.

UNPREDICTABILITY OF INCOME

If you are used to receiving a regular paycheck, the financial unpredictability of the freelance life may come as a shock. You must have paying clients to earn income. Unless you have a domestic partner with steady income to support you while you start your business, you shouldn't plan on becoming self-employed until you have saved enough to cover your living expenses for the first year. Even established freelancers need to plan ahead for the lean times when business is slow and for unexpected expenses.

Because there are few full-time staff positions for illustrators, they are more apt to be freelancers than other types of graphic artists. Yet, illustrators in particular find it difficult to make a sustainable living freelancing. In the online 2nd Annual Illustrator's Survey of 1,443 illustrators conducted in 2018–19, 73% said they could not live comfortably off illustration alone. Only 45% said that illustration was their full-time job: 29% supplement their illustration work with a full-time creative job and 14% supplement illustration work with a full-time noncreative job. More findings from the 2nd Annual Illustrator's Survey can be found at https://bentheillustrator.com/illustrators-survey.

PLAN AHEAD

Before you become self-employed, figure out not only what your start-up costs will be but also what your monthly expenses will be to keep your business operating. If you will be working from your home, your expenses will most likely be less than someone who is renting office or studio space. Depending on your discipline, you may have to invest in expensive equipment. Typical business expense categories are listed under the section, The Base Minimum Revenue Plan, in Chapter 1.

You will also be responsible for paying taxes at the end of the year, including self-employment and income taxes. Self-employment taxes include Social Security and Medicare, which your former employers paid 50% of and which was deducted from every paycheck. Now you will be paying 100% at the end of the year. Likewise, your income tax bill will be steep because you no longer have withholding from a paycheck. It is advisable to set aside a portion of your revenue and save it in preparation for paying your tax bill at the end of the year.

If you sell art or products based on your art, you will also need to pay sales tax. In some states, sales tax is also levied against certain services.

It is recommended that you hire a Certified Public Accountant (CPA) who provides services for small businesses and the self-employed to not only do your taxes but also to help you set up your business. A CPA can be a valuable resource throughout your first year of business.

More detailed information about taxes can be found in the section, Taxes, later in this chapter.

PLAN FOR THE LEAN TIMES
Receiving self-employment income will be like riding a roller coaster—there will be ups and downs. Some months you have no revenue coming in and other months you will finally get paid for one or more projects. The lean times can be attributed to three factors:

* Slow business
* Deferred payment schedule
* Late client payments

Slow business can be caused by a lack of enough projects, but it can also be caused by the time of year. Seasonal slowdowns usually occur at the end-of-the-year holiday season between Thanksgiving and the New Year. Clients often prefer to start new projects after the first of the year. You may also notice a slowdown during the summer months when many people take vacations or travel. If you notice seasonal slowdowns in your business, plan to take advantage of the down time to work on non-billable activities that will benefit your business. Or, take your own vacation during these times.

You can be extremely busy but have no revenue coming in. This happens when you have lengthy projects that are not paid until the work is finished. To avoid this situation, whenever possible, include more frequent payment options in your contracts, such as a down payment, deposit, or payments at specific junctures in the project, or ask to be paid on a monthly retainer basis.

In the Illustrator's Survey 2018–19, 50% of illustrators admit they don't even ask for a deposit on a commission, while 32% say they ask and get one for most commissions. So, it doesn't hurt to ask.

Late-paying clients can be a real drain on your income, especially if their projects are large or time-consuming. To avoid chasing clients for payment, employ the strategies discussed in Chapter 1 under the sections, Keeping Track and Getting Paid.

To help even out the highs and lows of your income, set aside a certain percentage of revenue when you do get paid, for the lean months. Building a profit into your pricing formula will also help you plan for the lean times (see Pricing Your Services in Chapter 1).

Access to Health Insurance

Results from the study "Freelancing in America 2019" cited access to affordable health care as the number one factor politicians should most focus on to encourage more freelancers to move to their city or state. Compounding the issue of accessibility to affordable health care is the unpredictability of the future of health insurance as it continues to be the subject of intense policy debate. While the mandatory requirement to be covered by health insurance or face financial penalties has been rescinded at the federal level, it remains a requirement in certain states. Check with your state's taxation department to find out if it still has the mandate and what the penalties are.

SOURCES OF COVERAGE

In general, the cost of buying private health insurance for individuals and their families can be exorbitant. Yet, the alternative of not having health insurance can destroy you financially. All it takes is one serious injury or life-threatening illness. Or, perhaps you already suffer from a chronic health condition that requires frequent medical care and expensive medications.

COVERAGE ON SOMEONE ELSE'S POLICY
If your spouse or domestic partner has a health insurance policy through their employer, it is most likely less expensive for you to be covered by that policy than getting one of your own. Likewise, if you are in your early 20s and are covered by a parent's employer's policy, it pays to stay on that policy until you age off. However, it is very important that you pay close attention to the date when you will no longer be eligible to be on that plan and how long of a period you have to get on another policy.

If you miss the deadline, you will have to wait until

open enrollment in the Health Insurance Marketplace to enroll in a plan, which could mean several months without insurance coverage.

Finding affordable coverage for your or your family's situation is complicated. Plans differ by insurance provider, by state and locality, by the benefits they offer, and by cost. In general, the higher the deductible, the lower the monthly premium and the lower the deductible, the higher the premium, and family coverage is more expensive than individual coverage.

HEALTH INSURANCE MARKETPLACE

Ever since the Affordable Care Act (ACA) went into effect, the self-employed have been able to shop in the Health Insurance Marketplace for health insurance, either as an individual, or in some cases as a small business. You should be aware that the policies offered differ greatly by the state you live in. The open enrollment period is usually from November 1st through mid-December, with policies going into effect the following January. Certain life changes and circumstances allow you to enroll outside of the open enrollment period. You can also get health insurance if you qualify for Medicaid. As of this writing, parts of the ACA are still in effect, due to the inability of lawmakers to agree on a new health insurance program; however, this situation could change at any time. Therefore, you should check the health insurance marketplace frequently to stay current with any changes (www.healthcare.gov).

If you are a freelancer, consultant, independent contractor, or other self-employed worker who doesn't have any employees, you can use the individual Health Insurance Marketplace to enroll in flexible, high-quality coverage that works well for people who run their own businesses.

If your business has even one employee (other than yourself, a spouse, family member, or owner), you may be able to use the SHOP Marketplace for small businesses (www.healthcare.gov/small-businesses/provide-shop-coverage/) to offer coverage to yourself and your employees.

COBRA COVERAGE

If you are already employed and receiving health insurance through your employer but are considering leaving to go it alone as a freelancer, you may be eligible for Cobra coverage. Cobra is a stop-gap option that allows you to convert your group policy into an individual policy for a limited length of time. Your employer's plan administrator can tell you if you are eligible for Cobra coverage. If you are leaving your job, you may also qualify for the special enrollment period. However, both options have time

limits for making a choice, then you lose your eligibility. Be aware that if you are used to paying only a percentage of your health insurance costs (your employer subsidizes the remainder of the cost), you will pay 100% of the cost if you convert to a Cobra plan.

FREELANCERS UNION

The Freelancers Union offers excellent health insurance plans in some states, as well as supplemental plans, such as dental. Members are grouped together to keep costs lower than individual plans (approximately 30% lower in New York State). Membership in the Union is free. To find out if there are plans for your location and the costs, simply enter your zip code on their website at www.freelancersunion.org/insurance/health/.

GROUP MEMBERSHIP, TRADE, & PROFESSIONAL ORGANIZATIONS

Some group membership and professional organizations offer health insurance at group rates like those offered by an employer because they can band members together as a group of self-employed workers. Check out organizations in which you are a member to see if they offer this benefit.

You should be aware that some insurance policies offered through member organizations are not considered ACA-compliant. Although this is no longer an issue in most cases because the Federal penalty for not being compliant was removed in the 2019 tax year, some states still have a penalty for being noncompliant (New Jersey, Massachusetts, Vermont, and the District of Columbia) and the penalty can be quite costly.

NATIONAL ASSOCIATION FOR THE SELF-EMPLOYED (NASE)

NASE is an organization that provides day-to-day support for the self-employed. Annual membership rates range from $25 for students to $99 for veterans, and $120 for a general membership. Veteran and general membership benefits include access to insurance plans to fit your needs and budgets, including health, dental, life, and many more. You can also choose a Gold Membership for $45 per month, which includes many top-tier benefits, such as the cost of the premium for Critical Illness Insurance, which pays up to $5,000 in each of three categories (cancer, heart, and certain other conditions). For more details, go to www.nase.org.

HELPFUL RESOURCES

There are several resources that self-employed individuals can access to help them find affordable health insurance coverage:

FEDERAL HEALTH INSURANCE MARKETPLACE (HEALTHCARE.GOV)

The federal website of the Health Insurance Marketplace has two sections which specifically address the needs of the self-employed:

Health Coverage if You're Self-Employed (www.healthcare.gov/self-employed/coverage/) explains coverage options, answers specific questions freelancers might have, and gives link to additional information.

Reporting Self-Employment Income to the Marketplace (www.healthcare.gov/self-employed/income/) gives detailed advice on how to estimate net self-employment income. When you fill out a Health Insurance Marketplace application, you'll have to estimate your net self-employment income for the year you're getting coverage, not the previous year's income. It also gives advice on how to update your projections during the year if your actual income varies widely from what you estimated.

STATE HEALTH-CARE WEBSITES

Some states, such as New York (www.nystateofhealth.ny.gov), have excellent websites for searching the Health Insurance Marketplace. New York, for example, provides links to Brokers for small businesses with employees and Navigators, experts who will help individuals apply for health insurance coverage, understand their coverage options, and enroll in a plan that is right for them.

THE NATIONAL ASSOCIATION OF HEALTH UNDERWRITERS (NAHU)

The National Association of Health Underwriters represents more than 100,000 licensed health insurance agents, brokers, general agents, consultants, and benefit professionals through more than 200 chapters across America. NAHU members service the health insurance needs of large and small employers as well as people seeking individual health insurance coverage. One of NAHU's primary goals is to do everything possible to promote access to affordable health insurance coverage. Their website includes a Find an Agent feature. For more information, go to www.nahu.org.

Taxes

As mentioned in previous sections, self-employed graphic artists are responsible for paying several types of taxes: self-employment taxes (Social Security and Medicare), income taxes, and in some situations, sales tax. There are strategies that can be employed to make tax season less painful.

TAX STRATEGIES FOR FREELANCERS

CONSULT AN ACCOUNTANT SOONER, NOT LATER

Consult an accountant when you first set up your business. Even if you use accounting software, an accountant can help you structure your record keeping with tax reporting in mind, so when tax season rolls around, your income and deductions are already in the correct categories, saving you hours of time. Every freelancer's situation is different—there is no one-method-fits-all scenario. Avoid waiting to consult an accountant during tax season when they are already working long hours and focusing on existing clients.

SAVE ENOUGH TO PAY YOUR TAXES

To avoid not having the funds to pay that big tax bill at the end of the year, accountants and tax professionals recommend that for every dollar of revenue you earn, put aside 30% in a business savings account to cover Federal taxes and up to another 10% for state taxes if your state has an income tax. Once you are established, you can elect to pay your income tax quarterly. Your accountant can help you figure how much you should prepay, based on past and projected income.

KEEP ACCURATE RECORDS

The self-employed often keep inadequate or incomplete records. Not keeping accurate records of income and expenses may cause you to pay more taxes than you need to, or send up red flags to the IRS, resulting in an audit. One solution is to invest in cloud-based accounting software. It can be synced to your business bank account so that all your transactions feed into it. Then you can categorize them by the appropriate revenue or expense categories.

KEEP PERSONAL & BUSINESS RECORDS SEPARATE

Avoid commingling your personal and business finances. Open a checking account and a credit card that are used only for business transactions. Otherwise, keeping track of your business income and expenses becomes too complicated. If you should be audited, the IRS will look more favorably on you if you have separate records. It shows that you are a professional business, not a hobby, and there will be fewer questions regarding whether your deductions are legitimate business expenses or not. Do not pay personal bills directly from the business account. If you need funds to pay personal bills, pay yourself with a check from the business account that you then deposit in your personal account (or transfer funds electronically). Then pay your household and personal bills from the personal account.

KNOW WHAT EXPENSES YOU CAN DEDUCT

As a self-employed person, you can deduct or "write off" many business expenses that an employee cannot. These deductions help to lower your tax bill, but freelancers make mistakes by not being aware of what they can deduct. For example, you can deduct a percentage of your home office, a portion of Internet services and your cell phone bill, miles driven for business, and your health insurance premiums if you pay for your own insurance. Typical business expense categories used on Federal Tax Form 1040-C are provided in Figure 1–2 in Chapter 1.

You can also deduct the fees involved in registering your copyrights as a legitimate business expense.

Don't forget technology expenses. The rate at which technology changes is exponential and upgrades are frequent, creating a need for constant professional development. To ensure that the cost of technology is factored into your cost of doing business, include any of the following technology-related expenses that apply to your business under Annual Business Expenses (refer to Figure 1–2 in Chapter 1):

* **Office (Studio) Expenses:** website services, Internet access and hosting fees, domain names, monthly costs/subscriptions for apps, web-based software, merchant account fees, software, and hardware under $2,500 (printers, laptops, tablets, smartphones, and other smaller electronics). Also include the cost of setting up equipment.
* **Repairs & Maintenance:** computer equipment and peripherals.
* **Office (Art) Supplies:** thumb drives, printer ink cartridges, photo paper, as well as computer furniture under $2,500.
* **Travel/Meals:** related to technology professional development, conferences, workshops.
* **Equipment:** computer equipment over $2,500.
* **Other Expenses:** Technology-related educational expenses (course fees, books, software, etc.); hardware and software training costs, fees for professional conferences, periodical subscriptions, dues for professional organizations.

If you are not sure which expenses you can deduct, consult your accountant so you can keep accurate records and receipts throughout the year.

TAX DEDUCTIONS FOR DONATED ARTWORK

There is a popular misconception that artists donating their art to a charitable organization may deduct the "fair market value" of the work. Current law, in fact, distinguishes between "personal property" and "inventory."

While anyone may donate personal goods to any charity and deduct the fair market value, businesses may deduct only the actual cost of producing the item. Artists, therefore, may deduct only the cost of producing the work: the price of the canvas, paint, and other materials. If an artist sells an original work, the buyer of that work may donate the piece as personal property and be eligible for the tax deduction of the amount paid for it. As a result, historically, artists have either withheld their valuable originals or sold them to private collectors.

In the past two decades, there have been several bills introduced in Congress that would amend the Internal Revenue Code to allow artists to deduct the fair market value of qualified artistic charitable contributions. However, none of these bills were passed. The most recent was the reintroduction of the Artist-Museum Partnership Act (HR 1830) by Rep. John Lewis (D-GA) in 2017. It was referred to the House Ways and Means Committee for consideration.

SALES TAX

If you sell art or art-related products directly to customers, you will have to collect and pay sales tax. Some services are also taxable. This is another area for which you want to consult an accountant.

STATE SALES TAX

States have widely different policies regarding sales tax. In those that have a sales tax, the rate (as of July 2020) ranges from 2.9 to 7.25%, and it is levied on the sale or use of physical property within the state. A number of exemptions exist, including special rules for the sale of reproduction rights.

Generally, sales tax is applicable for end sales or retail costs only, not for intermediate subcontracting. An artist may have to file *tax-exempt forms* showing that materials were intermediate and thus not taxable. Services, including the services of transferring reproduction rights, are not subject to sales tax. Transfers of physical property to a client (original art or designer's mechanicals) are generally not subject to sales tax if they are part of a project that will later be billed to a client by a design firm or other agent.

Many tax laws are unclear in relation to the graphic communications industry, though efforts have been made to clarify them (see the New York State section later in this chapter). If artists are doubtful about whether to collect sales tax, it is safest, of course, to collect and remit it to the state sales tax bureau. Note, however, that one accountant advised that if you do charge sales tax, and it is found during an audit that you should not have, you are liable to repay that amount to the client. If artists are required to collect the tax but do not, they, as well as their clients, remain liable, and it may be difficult to try to collect the tax from clients for past assignments if an audit or another review determines that sales tax is owed.

Consulting an experienced accountant to determine your specific responsibilities for your state is the best course of action. If you are required to collect sales tax, most states require you to register as a vendor and as a collector of taxes on the state's behalf. You will be issued what is known as a resale number, enabling you to purchase certain materials, free of tax, for the creation of products to be resold to your clients.

The following examples of California, Minnesota, New York, and Wisconsin illustrate the great variation in state sales tax regulations.

California

In reaction to widespread inconsistency and errors in applying California's sales tax laws to graphic artists, as well as a high percentage of artist audits, the Graphic Artists Guild spearheaded advocacy efforts to change California's tax law to include provisions that set uniform conditions, cut the tax burden on graphic artists, and reduced exposure to audits.

The following provisions, affecting the advertising industry, were approved by the California Board of Equalization (BOE) and went into effect on January 5, 2000:

* Reduced the taxable portion of graphic design and illustration jobs based on the fact that part of the fees paid are for "conceptual services" rendered. The regulation presumes that 75% represents a reasonable allocation for these nontaxable services.
* Excluded website design and hosting from taxation, as well as transfers of artwork by remote communications (modem).
* Limited taxability of reuse and royalties to one year from the time of contract.
* Excluded the design of environmental signage from taxation.
* Applied changes to the advertising regulation uniformly to other industries where artists and designers are affected.

It is important to note that artists who take advantage of any of these exemptions must be sure to separate taxable and nontaxable charges on all invoices and must carefully document the exemptions.

On February 7, 2002, in a long-awaited victory for the California arts community, the California BOE voted to clarify the sales tax regulations affecting illustrators, photographers, cartoonists, and designers. The change benefits graphic artists in four ways:

* It virtually exempts sales tax on all reproduction rights (including royalties) on the artwork of graphic artists.
* It exempts sales tax on artwork delivered on computer disc if returned on disc.
* It exempts sales tax on print design when the designer buys printing.
* It clearly specifies that commercial photographers working in the advertising and publishing fields are considered graphic artists.

All artists and designers engaged in business in California are required to obtain a California seller's permit and to comply with applicable sales and use tax regulations. Businesses that do not have these permits are exposed to more extensive audits and face additional penalties than those that comply.

While it is not required, the Guild strongly recommends that artists working in California take advantage of a provision in the California Taxpayers Bill of Rights and obtain binding information by filing a document called a "Section 6596 Query." This is a personal letter from you to the BOE requesting information on how sales tax regulations specifically apply to your individual business. Answers given over the telephone are nonbinding and frequently inaccurate, but a written response from the BOE provides protection from contrary interpretations by an auditor during an audit.

Minnesota

In Minnesota, the sale of an advertising brochure is not considered the sale of "tangible personal property" (a physical product rather than a service or intellectual property such as reproduction rights); it is considered part of the sale of a "nontaxable advertising service." Since an ad agency sells a nontaxable service, it must pay tax on all taxable "inputs" (all the components of an advertising product provided by outside vendors such as illustration, photography, or copywriting) used to create the brochure, including commissioned artwork. In most cases, inputs cannot be purchased tax free, so illustrators may have to collect sales tax when selling work used in advertising brochures.

New York State

The New York State Tax Department has guidelines that answer the two questions asked most frequently by graphic artists about sales tax:

* When are graphic designers and illustrators expected to charge sales tax on their services, and when are their sales exempt from tax?
* When are graphic designers and illustrators expected to pay sales tax on the materials, equipment, and services they buy, and when are those purchases exempt from tax?

Charging Sales Tax. New York State sales tax law imposes a tax on the sale of tangible personal property. Many local authorities add their own sales tax to that imposed by the state. The resulting sales tax must be charged in addition to other charges, stated as a separate item on any invoice, and paid by the purchaser. Payment of sales tax by the seller (in this case the graphic designer or illustrator) or failure to itemize it on an invoice is prohibited. Mixing taxable with nontaxable items on an invoice makes the entire invoice subject to sales tax.

Exemptions from Charging Sales Tax. Six areas of exemption are relevant to graphic designers and illustrators working in New York State:

1. **Terms for resale:** When tangible personal property passes through intermediate owners, taxes are deferred until it reaches the final purchaser. An example is any item purchased in a store. Sales tax is paid by the end customer at the over-the-counter sale; the retailer does not pay tax when purchasing from the wholesaler; the wholesaler does not pay it when purchasing from the manufacturer. Consequently, any item purchased for resale may be purchased tax-exempt if the purchaser has a properly completed resale certificate. The responsibility for collecting the tax then falls on the seller when the item is sold to the final purchaser.

2. **Exempt use:** If the final sale is for an exempt use—for instance, promotional materials delivered to a client in New York that will be distributed out of New York State—the vendor must verify the tax-exempt status by obtaining an exempt use certificate from the purchaser.

3. **Sales to exempt organizations:** Nonprofit and educational institutions and most federal and New York State governmental agencies have tax-exempt status. In this instance, the vendor must verify the tax-exempt status by obtaining an exempt organization certificate or government purchase order from the purchaser.

4. **Grants of reproduction rights:** At the end of a creative process, if only specified restricted rights are transferred, but there is no transfer of ownership of tangible personal property (for example, the original, physical artwork or 50,000 brochures), the transaction is not taxable. Grants of rights are not subject to sales tax.

5. **Tax-exempt services:** Purchases of certain services that do not result in the transfer of tangible personal property are, by their nature, not taxable. Likewise, services provided by writers, copy editors, and proofreaders are also exempt if there is no transfer of tangible personal property. However, if a writer writes an article and then sells it to a magazine, that transaction is taxable.

6. **Out-of-New-York-State sales:** The sale of work to out-of-state clients, delivered out-of-state, is not subject to sales tax, but there must be evidence of out-of-state delivery.

Payment & Collection of Sales Tax. Whether a graphic designer's or illustrator's services are taxable in New York State depends upon whether there is a final transfer of tangible personal property. If there is, the entire contract is taxable, including all consultations, designs, preparation of artwork, and so on. If the graphic designer or illustrator sells to the client the rights to comps, mechanicals, computer data, printed materials, or fabricated materials such as exhibits or signs, the graphic artist's services are considered to be transferable personal property.

The results of graphic designers' or illustrators' services are not considered transferable personal property if the artists do not provide printing or fabrication services, if they grant reproduction rights only, or if they retain ownership of all the designs, comps, mechanicals, or computer data and transfer them only temporarily for reproduction, to be returned—unretouched, unaltered, and undisplayed.

In most cases, graphic designers and illustrators may discover that some of their projects are taxable and some are not. The importance of setting up taxable and nontaxable work in separate contracts cannot be stressed enough. Graphic designers and illustrators must remember that the onus is always on them to prove that a project is nontaxable. Therefore, all agreements, invoices, and digital layouts or illustrations should have very clear language stating that ownership remains with the graphic artist; that only rights for reproduction are being granted; and that any graphic representations or artwork are being transferred temporarily and solely for the purpose of reproduction, after which they are to be returned—unretouched, unaltered, and undisplayed—to the graphic designer or illustrator.

Corporate identity and logo programs are a special case. Conceivably, one could state in a contract that only specific, limited reproduction rights are being granted. In practice, however, the prospect of a client not having complete rights to their own logo or corporate identity system is not credible. Therefore, such a project is considered a taxable sale.

If a graphic artist or illustrator is required to charge sales tax, he/she should consult an experienced accountant to determine specific responsibilities. The artist will have to register as a vendor and, as a collector of taxes on the state's behalf, will be issued a resale number that will enable the artist to purchase certain materials, free of tax, for the creation of products to be resold to clients.

Exemption Documents Needed. Graphic artists in New York State need two exemption documents when making tax-exempt purchases: the *resale certificate* and the *exempt use certificate*. The resale certificate is only for items or services that are part of the item being sold—for example, the card stock used to make hand-crafted greeting cards. The exempt use certificate is for items used in the production of the final product that do not become an actual part of it—for example, watercolors used to create an illustration that will be scanned into a computer and sent to the client electronically. Resale certificates cannot be used to purchase anything that does not substantially result in the tangible property being created.

Graphic artists are required to keep accurate records of (1) all items purchased and (2) projects for which they were used. They are also required to retain the subsequent invoice that indicates that sales tax has been charged on that item directly or on the item into which it has been incorporated. It is essential that graphic designers and illustrators keep clear, thorough records of all projects, including all purchases for each project, so that in the event of an audit they can accurately show that they paid sales tax on purchases that required sales tax to be paid.

A graphic artist is entitled to purchase services or materials for resale or production without paying tax, even if sale of the final product will be exempt from tax—for example, to an exempt client or if the final product will be shipped out of New York State.

The resale certificate may not be used if the services do not result in a sale, such as when unrestricted reproduction rights are granted or if the contract is for consultation alone, with no tangible end result. On such projects, the designer must pay tax on all equipment, supplies, and services used.

Equipment, such as computers and printers, that is used predominantly for the production of work for sale (more than 50% of the time) may also be purchased exempt from sales tax by submitting an exempt use certificate to the vendor. This means that if only half the artist's work results in taxable sales and this equipment is used only half the time on design work, then the equipment is actually being used only 25% of the time to produce work for sale. It is therefore subject to full tax when purchased.

Wisconsin

Wisconsin law imposes state and county sales taxes on "the sale, lease, license, or rental of specified digital goods and additional digital goods at retail for the right to use the specified digital goods or additional digital goods on a permanent or less than permanent basis and regardless of whether the purchaser is required to make continued payment for such rights." The law defines "additional digital goods" as the following, if they are transferred electronically: 1) greeting cards; 2) finished artwork; 3) periodicals; and 4) video or electronic games.

"Finished artwork" means the final art used for actual reproduction by photomechanical or other processes or for display purposes. It also includes drawings, paintings, designs, photographs, lettering, paste-ups, mechanicals, assemblies, charts, graphs, and illustrative material, regardless of whether such items are reproduced.

Consequently, graphic artists in Wisconsin must charge sales tax on final projects delivered via e-mail and the Internet or on CD and DVD. The tax should be applied to only the final purchased product, not on communications, sketches, or proofs delivered electronically.

LOCAL SALES TAX

Sales tax is not limited to states; many local municipalities (counties and cities) also charge sales tax on products and/or services—in 2020, local sales tax was collected in 38 states, comprising a total of 11,000 tax jurisdictions. Alaska, one of the five states with no statewide sales tax, allows localities to collect a local sales tax. Major cities with the highest combined state and local sales tax rates are Chicago, IL; Long Beach and Glendale, CA; Tacoma and Seattle, WA; and Birmingham, AL. In some localities, the sales tax rate is equal to or exceeds the state sales tax rate. To make matters even more complicated, the laws governing what is taxable may differ between the state and the local municipality. This is the case in New York City: on certain purchases, only New York City sales tax is payable; New York State sales tax is not.

A contract cannot include some items that are taxable and some that are not. Therefore, where projects may result in a taxable sale or service, it is advisable to divide the project into two entirely separate contracts—one that is taxable and one that is not. It is essential to keep the two contracts entirely separate: separate proposals, separate agreements, and separate invoices. If any part of a contract is taxable, the entire project is taxable.

SALES TAX HELP

The Graphic Artists Guild strongly recommends that graphic artists consult experienced accountants or tax lawyers to determine tax liabilities for your specific state and locality. Because of their familiarity with an artist's business, these professionals are best suited to answer questions. An alternative is to contact your state's tax department. Its website usually offers contact info, either by mail, phone, or e-mail depending on your specific need. If a graphic artist finds that any ruling is contrary to these guidelines, notify the Graphic Artists Guild.

Another excellent source for information about sales tax, including pending legislation and changes in tax laws, is the Tax Foundation website (www.taxfoundation. org). To quickly look up current sales tax rates for all states, go to www.salestaxinstitute.com. Specific information is given for each state, as well as links to the state's tax department.

TAXABLE FREELANCE SERVICES

It is important for freelance graphic artists to understand that services they use, such as those of other freelancers (web designers, photographers, copywriters, etc.), may be taxable. Each state makes its own laws in order to stimulate a certain type of business or service. Artists should contact an accountant in the state or locality in which their business is located or performed to find out exactly what services are taxable.

In New York State, for example, freelancers must charge sales tax on their services to the graphic designer or illustrator, unless the exemptions outlined previously apply. When the graphic designer or illustrator's services result in a taxable sale, he/she may issue a resale certificate to the freelancer for the work.

In certain circumstances, artists who use freelance services should, for their own protection, pay any tax due directly to the state—for example, if the freelancer is a student and not registered as a vendor or if the freelance supplier does not bill and collect the tax. A specific fill-in section on the sales tax reporting form, entitled "Purchases Subject to Use Tax," is provided for this purpose.

When a freelancer works on a project that does not result in a taxable sale for the artist—where reproduction rights only are being granted to the client—then the artist must pay full tax on the freelancer's fee.

As part of routine record keeping, graphic designers and illustrators should keep carefully receipted invoices from freelancers showing that, where appropriate, sales tax has been charged and paid. If the evidence is not clear-cut, sales tax authorities will expect the artist to pay the taxes.

Threats to the Profession

The same advances in technology that have created labor-saving devices and instant global communication have also spawned a proliferation of electronic and online businesses that threaten the graphic arts profession.

DIGITAL CLIP ART

Some entrepreneurs have set themselves up in the business of supplying ready-made digital art. They hire illustrators to create "clip art" for rights-free online downloads, or as collections on CDs and DVDs, that provide some up-front income, minimal or no royalties, and wide exposure of an artist's work. Buyers of the clip art are then free to copy or alter the art without further compensation to the illustrator.

Stock house sales of specific rights to an artist's work provide some additional income from existing work without loss of rights and give some measure of protection, though they generally yield lower fees. Many veteran artists believe that these efforts are driving creators out of the illustration business as salaries and/or prices fall, inexpensive art proliferates, and sources of future income are diminished.

LOGO MILLS

Graphic designers face similar assaults on their profession by companies that devalue professional design services by competing unfairly on price with shoddy design, substandard services, unfair labor practices, and with no regard to copyright ownership. So-called "logo mills" are online operations that hire "designers" at ridiculously low rates to pump out off-the-shelf logos that are marketed to consumers at cut-rate prices. Most of these premade logos are simply pieced together clip art with mundane type treatment. The same logos are sold over and over again. Buyers can pay higher prices to get a "unique" logo, which means the company promises not to resell the design and the buyer simply owns the copyright as part of the package. "Customization" may consist of little more than providing the same logo in a different color scheme or with adjustments to the font.

A second type of logo mill offers "original" logos. The price of their services is based on the number of concepts, rounds of revisions, and designers working on the project (the greater the number, the higher the price), yet their prices are still below the prevailing market rates for professional design services.

In some situations, designers are made to "compete" to have their design accepted by the client. Successful designers are awarded points as well as a monetary bonus. Designers are required to critique each other's work with points being deducted from those whose work is panned. A loss of points means that the designer's fee will be lowered on future projects. The digital sweatshops of the design world, logo mills treat designers as just another expendable commodity instead of as highly trained professionals.

Logo mills have an insidious impact on the perception among business owners regarding copyrights. By simply ignoring the existence of copyrights in their pricing structure, logo mills devalue copyrights. The result is a business community that increasingly is unaware of the existence or value of copyright and unwilling to pay what to them seems to be an unfair or unnecessary fee tacked onto a job.

What clients don't realize is that often the logos they are buying have been stolen from a legitimate designer and are being passed off as "original." Since many of these offending "designers" working for logo mills are from other countries, U.S. copyright law isn't always easy to enforce. The client, however, who may be in the United States, is liable for copyright infringement. Clients also are unaware that these sites add indemnity clauses that put the onus for any infringement on the buyer. It remains up to designers to confront this perception and educate clients. If you are unsure whether a site is a logo mill or not, reading its terms and conditions will tell you what you need to know.

ONLINE FREELANCING SITES (GIG SITES)

Another type of business proliferating in cyberspace is online freelancing websites. There are many different business models for online gig sites and their terms differ widely, so you should research their terms very carefully before using them to search for work. Even some of the better sites charge fees for their services. These fees range from a nominal, very affordable annual fee to a percentage amount, or commission, deducted from the revenue you earn for each job. On some sites, the pricing is tiered: the more you pay, the more jobs you can apply for each month or the more services you receive.

The better features of some of these platforms include being paid very promptly, as soon as 10 days after the billing period ends, with billing done weekly and the site intervening on your behalf in payment disputes with clients. You may also be able to set filters, such as the minimum hourly rate for which you will accept a job. You also get exposure to more potential employers or clients than you would from your own site.

The worst of these sites prey on graphic artists eager to find work. They seldom allow artists to retain the rights to their work. They also denigrate the graphic arts profession by marketing themselves to potential clients as full-service creative businesses offering services at a fraction of the cost of a traditional ad agency or design firm and having a community of thousands of graphic artists at their disposal. However, in reality, the thousands of artists are actually freelancers who "bid" on posted jobs.

In the worst cases, the average job only pays $5–10—per job, not hourly. If an employer offered you a job at this compensation, they would be breaking the law—the Federal minimum wage is $7.25 per hour, and in 32 states, the minimum wage is much higher, and in the District of Columbia it is $14.00 per hour. No professional job pays such low wages. The bottom line, though, is that this is not a living wage in the United States. You would have to take on hundreds of these jobs to make a month's worth of income. You are not only demeaning your profession but also yourself by working for such a low wage.

The low wages offered by these sites denigrate the profession and remove the professional aspects from the work of a graphic artist. There is no interaction and relationship-building with clients to find the best solution to their problems or needs. At the low level of payment being offered, there is no time for the artist to use the normal creative thought processes to come up with possible solutions or for refining a design.

In one worst-case scenario, artists are lured into working for free under the guise of a contest; they must do all of the work up front at their own expense to be considered as a contestant. The online business negotiates the "award," keeping a percentage for itself, as well as all work submitted (even from those who lose the contest), and the "winners" and "losers" alike have no rights to the work they created.

The good news is there are other online alternatives to finding freelance work, such as job boards. Job boards work more like print classifieds. Jobs from various employers seeking graphic art services are posted with a short description and contact info. Job seekers apply directly to the employer and negotiate directly with the employer if a job is offered. Some professional organizations maintain job boards on their websites for their members; other job boards can be accessed by non-members as well. The Graphic Artists Guild posts jobs on its site as part of the Design Employment Network. Behance.net is another online site for finding creative work. The platform is also a portfolio site where creative professionals across disciplines can post work for free.

Technology will continue to exert a powerful influence on the graphic arts industry. The best way graphic artists can protect themselves from technology's often overwhelming effects is by staying informed about such issues as professional practices, pricing considerations, and ethical and legal concerns (especially copyright).

Entrepreneurial Issues

Speculative Ventures

Speculative ventures, whether in financial markets or visual communications industries, are fraught with risk. Individuals who choose this course risk loss of capital and incur expenses. Artists and designers who accept speculative assignments, whether directly from a client or by entering a contest or competition, risk not being paid for the work, take valuable time from pursuing other paying assignments, and may incur expenses out of pocket. In some circumstances, all the risks are placed on the artist, with the client or contest-holder assuming none.

SPECULATIVE ASSIGNMENTS

An example of a speculative assignment is when a buyer decides only upon completion of finished art whether or not to compensate the artist. This situation occurs in agreements where payment depends on "buyer's satisfaction" or "on publication." Typically, when a prospective client requests that work be created on speculation, there is too little information available to the artist to create a truly successful work because a true partnership has not been created due to the tentative nature of the speculative project.

Avoid speculative assignments by insisting on signed agreements or contracts between you and the client that outline the scope and timeline of the project, the deliverables, and costs, etc., *before* you start any of the work. If the prospective client wants to see a "sample" of your work, show examples of work from your portfolio that are most closely related to what the client wants.

CROWDSOURCING

A competitive form of speculative work that is of particular concern to the graphic arts profession is crowdsourcing—the practice of obtaining needed services, ideas, or content by soliciting contributions from a large group of people, especially the online community, rather than from traditional employees or suppliers. As an organization, the Graphic Artists Guild does not support spec work. In her address at IcoD's Professional Platform Meeting in 2014, Patricia McKiernan, the Guild's Executive Director at the time, had this to say about crowdsourcing:

Crowdsourcing may be legal as a business model, but it is another form of spec work taken to an extreme, and far from ethical from the Guild's perspective. We're talking about devaluing the work of an entire profession in an incredibly public fashion. Crowdsourcing sites encourage below-market rates and treat graphic artists as an expendable commodity, instead of highly trained professionals providing a genuine service.

...The below-market rates... ignore the value of copyright and create a perception within the business community that copyright doesn't exist, has little value, or that a business hiring a graphic arts service owns everything the graphic artist produces.

Furthermore, there is little chance of being awarded the actual project, and artists are required to give up rights on all submissions, even those that don't "win" or aren't used. These unscrupulous practices are not limited to businesses. There have been instances in recent years of political campaigns, and even government agencies, crowdsourcing design projects.

NONCOMMISSIONED WORK

There are a few disciplines in which it is customary for graphic artists to create noncommissioned work and try to find a buyer for it after completion. It is most common in licensing situations in which the client doesn't actually buy the art but leases (or rents) it for a specific purpose and period of time. Disciplines in which graphic artists commonly create noncommissioned work are surface pattern design; greeting card, novelty, and retail product design and illustration; and typeface design.

CREATING ART & PRODUCTS TO SELL

Many individual artists and designers, acting as entrepreneurs, create their own work and use those works in a variety of ways, including consumer-oriented products, such as a book showcasing their work, limited-edition prints, calendars, computer mouse pads, and T-shirts, to name a few. This work can be sold directly to the consumer through various channels, including craft shows, artists' own websites, and online platforms for selling art. This is also one way truly innovative work is produced.

In a more speculative arrangement, an artist may choose to put together a book of his/her work and submit the book to a publisher, who agrees to pay an advance against a royalty on sales. The artist and the publisher share the risks on their mutual investment, and the compensation to both parties is speculative, meaning both depend on the market response to the product.

For more about selling art online, see Chapter 4, Maximizing Income.

Contests & Competitions

Contests and competitions are a form of speculation that deserve their own section. Although contests are not a form of work *per se*, artists often enter them in the hopes of either winning prize money or getting promotion for their work.

GUIDELINES FOR FAIR COMPETITION

The Graphic Artists Guild has done extensive research on the fairness of competitions, including a nationwide survey of art and design competition holders and polls of jurors and competition entrants. This research resulted in the establishment of a list of guidelines for fair competition for three types of art contests or competitions:

* Competitions held by art-related organizations or associations to award excellence in the field
* Contests where all entries are created specifically for the contest and where the winning entries are used for commercial purposes
* Contests held by nonprofit organizations or where the winning entries are used for nonprofit purposes

The principal purpose of the guidelines is to enable competition or contest holders and entrants to make their own independent judgments concerning the way fair contests and competitions should be run and whether and on what terms to participate in them.

AWARDS FOR EXCELLENCE IN THE FIELD

1. The call for entry shall clearly define all rules governing competition entries, specifications for work entered, any and all fees for entry, and any and all rights to be transferred by any entrants to the competition holder.
2. Jurors for the competition and their affiliations shall be listed on the call for entry. No juror or employee of the organization holding the competition shall be eligible to enter the competition.
3. Criteria for judging the entries and specifications for the artwork to be submitted in all rounds shall be defined clearly in the call for entry as a guide to both entrants and jurors.
4. Deadlines and process for notification of acceptance or rejection of all entries shall be listed in the call for entry.
5. Any and all uses for any and all entries shall be listed clearly in the call for entries, with terms for any rights to be transferred.
6. For the first round, tear sheets, slides, photographs, or other reproductions of existing work shall be requested in order to judge the appropriateness of style, technique, and proficiency of the entrants. This round shall result in the choice of finalists. If samples from this round will not be returned to the entrants, that fact shall be clearly listed in the call for entries.
7. If the competition ends in an exhibition, hanging or exhibition fees paid for by the entrants shall be listed in the call for entries.
8. After the first round, the jury may request original art for review. The competition holder shall insure all works against damage or loss until the work is returned to the artist. All original artwork shall be returned to the artist. Any fees charged to the artists for the return of artwork shall be clearly listed in the call for entry.
9. Artwork shall not be altered in any way without the express permission of the artist.
10. All entries and rights to the artwork remain the property of the artist unless a separate written transfer and payment for the original have been negotiated.
11. If work exhibited by the competition is for sale, any commission taken by the competition holder shall be listed in the call for entries.

CONTESTS FOR COMMERCIAL PURPOSES

1. The call for entry shall clearly define all rules governing contest entries, specifications for work entered, any and all fees for entry, and any and all rights to be transferred by any entrants to the contest holder.
2. Jurors for the contest and their affiliations shall be listed on the call for entry. No juror or employee of the organization holding the contest shall be eligible to enter the contest.
3. Criteria for judging the entries and specifications

for the artwork to be submitted in all rounds shall be clearly defined in the call for entry as a guide to both entrants and jurors.

4. Deadlines and process for notification of acceptance or rejection of all entries shall be listed in the call for entry.

5. Any and all uses for any and all entries shall be clearly listed in the call for entries, with terms for any rights to be transferred.

6. For the first round, tear sheets, slides, photographs, or other reproductions of existing work shall be requested in order to judge the appropriateness of style, technique, and proficiency of the entrants. This round shall result in the choice of finalists. If samples from this round will not be returned to the entrants, that fact shall be clearly listed in the call for entries.

7. The number of finalists chosen after the first round should be small. The finalists shall then be required to submit sketches or comprehensive drawings for final judging.

8. Agreements shall be made with each finalist prior to the beginning of the final stage of the work (Graphic Artists Guild contracts or the equivalent can be used). The agreements shall include the nature of the artwork required, deadlines, credit line and copyright ownership for the artist, and the amount of the award.

9. Any work of finalists not received by the required deadline or not in the form required and agreed upon shall be disqualified. All rights to the artwork that has been disqualified shall remain with the artist.

10. The winners shall produce camera-ready or finished art according to the specifications listed in the call for entry. Artwork submitted shall not be altered in any way without the express permission of the artist.

11. The value of any award to the winners shall be at least commensurate with fair market value of the rights transferred. The first-place winner shall receive an award that is significantly greater than that of other winners.

12. The contest holder shall insure original artwork in its possession against loss or damage until it is returned to the artist.

CONTESTS FOR NONPROFIT PURPOSES

1. The call for entry shall clearly define all rules governing contest entries, specifications for work entered, any and all fees for entry, and any and all rights to be transferred by any entrants to the contest holder.

2. Jurors for the contest and their affiliations shall be listed on the call for entry. No juror or employee of the organization holding the contest shall be eligible to enter the contest.

3. Criteria for judging the entries and specifications for the artwork to be submitted in all rounds shall be clearly defined in the call as a guide to both entrants and jurors.

4. Deadlines and process for notification of acceptance or rejection of all entries shall be listed in the call for entry.

5. Any and all uses for any and all entries shall be clearly listed in the call for entries, with terms for any rights to be transferred.

6. For the first round, tear sheets, slides, photographs, or other reproductions of existing work shall be requested in order to judge the appropriateness of style, technique, and proficiency of the entrants. This round shall result in the choice of finalists. If samples from this round will not be returned to the entrants, that fact shall be clearly listed in the call for entries.

7. The number of finalists chosen after the first round should be small. The finalists shall then be required to submit sketches or comprehensive drawings for final judging.

8. Agreements shall be made with each finalist prior to the beginning of the final stage of the work (Graphic Artists Guild contracts or the equivalent can be used). The agreements shall include the nature of the artwork required, deadlines, credit line and copyright ownership for the artist, and the amount of the award.

9. Any work of finalists not received by the required deadline or not in the form required and agreed upon shall be disqualified. All rights to the artwork that has been disqualified shall remain with the artist.

10. The winners shall produce camera-ready or finished art according to the specifications listed in the call for entry. Artwork submitted shall not be altered in any way without the express permission of the artist.

11. The value of the award should, if possible, be commensurate with the fair market price for the job, though exceptions may be made depending on the budget and use of the artwork for the contest.

12. The contest holder shall insure original artwork in its possession against loss or damage until it is returned to the artist.

Over the intervening years since the above guidelines were developed, graphic artists have raised other concerns: Who is judging the work? Is the work or the artist being judged? Are competitors who are unknown and unconnected treated as fairly as those whose work is familiar to judges?

In an effort to keep informed about the latest practices and to address the above concerns, the Guild did a follow-up survey, which was sent to 40 associations, publications, sourcebooks, and paper companies that sponsor competitions and contests. The survey asked a number of questions, including: Are entrance fees reasonable? Is speculative work required? What rights are entrants asked to give up? How are submissions handled and returned? What are the odds of winning? Twenty-one competition holders responded.

The results of the survey were both reassuring and troubling. On the one hand, the study indicated that most sponsors of annual competitions are reputable organizations making good faith efforts to design fair and ethical contests and competitions. They are not guilty of the kinds of questionable practices engaged in by one-shot contest holders, such as the manufacturer who requests original artwork created on speculation, to which the artist must sign over all rights. On the other hand, the study revealed that some contests are still conducted in ways that are ethically ambiguous.

The most troubling area involves judging. When entries are identified by artist, the likelihood increases that judges will vote for friends and colleagues or for names they recognize. Of course, there is no way to prevent judges from recognizing an entrant's work, even without an attached name. And in certain cases, like book competitions, it is impossible to remove the name of the illustrator. But more could be done to create a firewall between judges and judged. A numerical coding system would ensure both anonymity and proper identification of entries. Entrants could be asked to mask their signatures and credit lines from flat art and discs.

Being a competition judge can add a prestigious feather to an artist's or designer's cap, but it also seems to improve the chances of winning. Temptations are inevitable when judges are permitted to enter their own work, no matter what safeguards exist. Though the competition holders surveyed insisted that their rules prevent bias and promote impartiality, the Guild's analysis of the judging raised some questions about the appearance of bias.

Some artists refuse to enter certain competitions because they believe the judges will not choose their work. Though that may seem unlikely to some, it is not, if competition and contest holders draw continually from the same pool of judges. Competition and contest holders could eliminate bias and promote impartiality by both excluding judges from entering competitions and looking for ways to expand the pool of judges, so competitions and contests do not appear to be closed enterprises. These measures would open up the process and create conditions that would allow new, unfamiliar talent to emerge.

Before entering a contest, artists should ask themselves, "What is the real value of contests and competitions to the award winners, and how does that compare with the value derived by the sponsors?" It is difficult to measure the benefits to winners because they involve intangibles like exposure and prestige. But trade publications, for example, have much to gain. Not only are competitions and contests a source of considerable revenue from entrance fees ($35 and higher per image), magazines fill their award issues with work they do not have to commission. A search of art contests and competitions for all types of visual media found entry fees as high as $200 per work. Competitions involving digital media and media with motion tend to have much higher entry fees than those for print media.

Nor should the artist assume that contests with no entry fees are in their best interest. The sponsors of these contests are often businesses looking for art, designs, illustrations, logos, etc., that they can use on their products or marketing materials—in other words, free art and design services.

Contests and competitions may be part of every graphic artist's marketing plan, but entering them requires time, energy, thought, and money. Artists and designers need to analyze competitions and contests with care, weigh the value of the awards offered, estimate the chances of winning, and evaluate whether safeguards create an open, even-handed contest or competition.

Health & Safety Issues

Graphic artists encounter several health and safety issues in their occupations. Some hazards are due to the materials and equipment they use. Graphic artists who also create fine art have an even greater exposure to potentially dangerous substances. Other health and safety concerns are caused by the physical and mental aspects of the job.

Most employers are required by the U.S. Department of Labor's Occupational Safety and Health Administration (OSHA) to provide a safe and healthful environment for their employees. OSHA sets and enforces standards to accomplish this goal, as well as provides training, outreach, education, and assistance. Most companies that meet three basic conditions are required to adhere to OSHA regulations: employers who control the actions of their employees, exercise command and power over their employees, and have the authority to fire employees. Even those companies that use independent contractors, who are not legally employees of the business, are typically covered by OSHA if the employers maintain control over workers' actions. Small businesses with 10 or fewer employees are exempt from some OSHA injury-reporting requirements.

While most employees and independent contractors are protected under OSHA standards, there are no such protections for the self-employed. It is up to freelancers to self-monitor their workplaces and studios and to educate themselves about hazardous substances and equipment they may be using.

Hazardous Substances

Common hazardous substances used by graphic artists and fine artists include heavy metals, chemicals, solvents, and volatile organic compounds. They can enter the body via skin contact or by breathing gaseous fumes and dusts. Some can even enter by accidental ingestion. It should be noted that even odorless substances can be harmful. Hazardous substances typically found in the artist's workplace include

* Acids (printing)
* Arsenic (paints and dyes)
* Cadmium (paints)
* Fiberglass (sculptures)
* Formaldehyde (paints and varnishes)
* Lead (paint, printing inks, glazes, other art supplies)
* Polyester Resin (sculptures, molds, coating/sealing artwork)
* Silica dust (ceramic clays)
* Solvents: hexane, benzene, toluene (graphic arts materials)
* Toxic metals (glazes)
* Volatile organic compounds: lacquers, thinners, aerosol sprays, and inks

Everyone is familiar with arsenic being used as a means of poisoning a person to death throughout history and in literature. Although it's a natural chemical element found in our food and water, high-level exposure and repeated exposure over time can cause skin and lung cancer,

breathing problems, decreased intelligence, and peripheral nervous system problems. Lead is another heavy metal that is a natural chemical element. The ill-effects of lead poisoning are well documented. They include kidney damage, arthritis, memory and learning difficulties, reduced IQ, behavioral problems, miscarriage, reduced sperm count, and even high blood pressure and anemia.

Another carcinogen is the rare metal cadmium, which gives artists' paints their brilliant colors and lightfastness. It's also responsible for several kidney and liver ailments. Inhaling it can cause a host of respiratory problems and flu-like symptoms.

Polyester resin is highly toxic, causing burns, allergic reactions, and serious irritation of the eyes and skin, even with brief contact. The higher the exposure, the greater the possibility of developing cancer. Like polyester resin, contact with fiberglass can cause irritation and burns. Inhalation can cause serious breathing problems. Repeated exposure can cause cancer. Formaldehyde, which has a wide range of uses in the creation of art, can cause leukemia and brain cancer with prolonged exposure.

There are several dangerous substances that can be inhaled while mixing clay, one being silica dust. Chronic inhalation of silica dust can cause silicosis, with symptoms including shortness of breath, dry cough, emphysema, and a high susceptibility to lung infections, such as tuberculosis. The disease may take years to develop.

Visual artists use many products in spray form, including fixatives, retouching sprays, paint sprays, varnishes, and adhesive sprays. Sprays are especially hazardous because dangerous pigments and solvents are more easily inhaled than when applied by brush. Aerosol sprays also contain propellants, which are highly flammable. The fine mist produced by airbrushing is also a serious inhalant hazard, especially solvents containing paint, because of artists working so closely to their art.

There are many other hazards associated with art materials and processes that are too numerous to mention here. The website of the Princeton University Office of Health and Safety is an excellent resource for artists to easily find out which substances they use are hazardous. They are organized by discipline (painting and drawing, ceramics, lithography and relief printing, photography, and sculpture). Specific hazardous substances are described in detail with their health risks and precautions for working with them. There is also a section on waste disposal for the visual arts. The site can be accessed at https://ehs.princeton.edu/health-safety-the-campus-community/art-theater-safety/art-safety.

Some general safety precautions to take in your studio to cut down on health risks associated with hazardous substances:

READ WARNINGS LABELS & SAFETY DATA SHEETS

Always read Directions for Use labels on art supplies, as well as any warnings. The American Society of Testing (ASTM) wrote the health labeling standard adopted into Federal Law. Look for health warnings on art supply labels that say, "Health Label conforms to ASTM D-4236."

If you use chemicals in your work, manufacturers and importers are required by OSHA to include container labels and Safety Data Sheets (SDSs) for any chemicals that are hazardous. Look for these and read them carefully. SDSs use a standardized format, which include such information as **Identification** (product identifier, manufacturer, recommended use and restrictions, emergency phone number, etc.), **Hazard(s) identification, First Aid measures, Handling and storage, Exposure controls/personal protection, Toxicological information** (routes of exposure, related symptoms, acute and chronic effects, etc.), and other pertinent information.

MINIMIZE EXPOSURE

Whenever possible, look for safer substitutes for substances that you know are hazardous. For example, manufacturers have now developed lines of oil, acrylic, and watercolor paints that are cadmium-free.

You can minimize your exposure to hazardous and toxic substances by adhering to recommended safety precautions, which may include wearing protective gear, such as gloves, safety goggles, and respirator masks.

Do not eat, drink, or smoke in your studio if you use hazardous materials. Doing so can lead to accidental ingestion of harmful substances (plus smoking around chemicals poses other dangers). Move these activities outside your studio and be sure to wash your hands thoroughly first. Likewise, keep pets and young children out of your studio. Pets can accidentally inhale or ingest a harmful substance by sniffing or licking, and young children are notorious for putting their fingers in their mouth. Exposure to lead, in particular, is most harmful to the developing brain.

IMPROVE VENTILATION

Proper ventilation is one of the most important ways to minimize hazardous exposure in the artist's work space, and one of the most overlooked. Without proper ventilation, chemical fumes can rise and pool at the ceiling, even when there is no detectable smell. This lingering cloud of chemicals can not only cause health risks with chronic exposure, but potentially start a fire in your studio.

Artists who use oil-based paints are one of the most at-risk groups if their studios are improperly ventilated because of the use of solvents in their work. Environmental hygienists recommend that air in an art studio should be exchanged ideally 10 times an hour, with 6 to 10 times being acceptable. The use of an open window or door, ceiling fans, and air conditioners do not adequately exchange air. While air purifiers can help significantly reduce the amount of harmful materials in the air, they cannot completely eliminate the hazardous elements.

Two types of ventilation that can be used to improve your studio's ventilation are *dilution ventilation* and *local exhaust ventilation.*

Dilution ventilation attempts to lower the concentration of harmful elements and vapors by bringing in fresh air to dilute the contaminated air. The easiest and least costly way to do this is through cross-ventilation by putting a fan in one window that blows in fresh air and a fan in another window that blows contaminated air outward. The windows cannot be on the same side of the room; ideally, they should be on opposite sides of the room. Artists should position themselves so that the fresh air being blown in is behind them, blowing fumes away from their face out the other window. The fans provide the power to exchange air much more effectively than just two open windows. Industrial strength fans for windows can be purchased at big box stores. Fan sizes are measured by how much air they can move in a minute, or cubic feet per minute (CFM). Purchase fans to match the size of your room.

Dilution ventilation is adequate for situations where fumes are of low toxicity or there are very small amounts of moderately toxic vapors, such as

* Painting
* Black & white photo developing
* Small amounts of adhesive, ink, or shellac

Local exhaust ventilation attempts to trap the fumes and airborne elements at their source, before they can enter the air, and then vent them outside and away from the studio. This method is most commonly accomplished with hoods placed over or very near the source of pollution. The contaminated air is then pulled away through ducts. Often the ducts will connect to an air cleaner that will filter the air before it is pumped outside. There are different hood designs and ventilation systems, some more efficient than others, for specific situations. Research ventilation systems and hoods for the type of work you most commonly do.

Local exhaust ventilation should be used for controlling dust and moderately toxic and highly toxic fumes and for removing large amounts of particles and vapors, such as

* High dust processes (woodworking, grinding, plaster mixing and carving, sculpting, using pastels)
* Spray painting and spraying substances in aerosol cans
* Silkscreen printing
* Acid etching
* Welding

Musculoskeletal Disorders

The digital age has brought about increased health concerns. For graphic artists and other professionals, there is a high risk of becoming seriously injured from working at computers for extended periods of time.

Musculoskeletal disorders (MSDs) are injuries or pain in the human musculoskeletal system, including the joints, ligaments, muscles, nerves, tendons, and structures that support the limbs, neck, and back. MSDs can arise from a sudden exertion (e.g., lifting a heavy object), or they can arise from making the same motions repeatedly, repetitive strain, or from repeated exposure to force, vibration, or awkward posture. An example of a repetitive motion disorder is carpal tunnel syndrome. Past studies by the National Academy of Sciences (NAS), the Institute of Medicine, and the Occupational Safety and Health Administration (OSHA) have concluded there is strong scientific evidence that exposure to ergonomic hazards in the workplace causes musculoskeletal disorders.

Graphic artists and others who work on a computer all day frequently suffer from the MSDs caused by repetitive motion (typing and clicking a computer mouse) and strain, and repeated exposure to awkward posture. Most workplace MSD episodes involve multiple parts of the body. For graphic artists, injuries can occur to the hands, arms, wrists, shoulders, and back. MSDs are a national problem as well as a global one. MSDs are the most frequent health complaint by European, United States, and Asian Pacific workers, and the third leading reason for disability and early retirement in the United States. MSDs cost the economy billions of dollars annually in compensation costs, lost wages, and lost productivity. According to the United States Department of Labor, Bureau of Labor Statistics, the number of reported musculoskeletal injuries and illnesses causing days away from work in 2015 was 356,910. The number of cases involving 31 or more days away from work was 115,680, with 12 being the median number of days away from work.

Blue Light Exposure

Of most recent concern is the health risk caused by exposure to blue light emitted by modern electronics, especially screen devices. Blue light is another name for high-energy visible (HEV) light in the blue and violet part of the light spectrum. The evolution in digital screen technology has advanced dramatically over the years, and many of today's electronic devices use LED backlight technology to help enhance screen brightness and clarity. These LEDs emit very strong blue light waves. Cell phones, computers, tablets and flat-screen televisions are just a few of the devices that use this technology.

Eye care professionals actually have a diagnostic term for the computer-related eye strain caused by blue light—*digital eyestrain syndrome*. Its symptoms include dry, irritated eyes, blurred vision, headaches, and neck and back pain. A serious medical condition that affects learning and work productivity, digital eyestrain has overtaken carpal tunnel syndrome as the number one computer-related health complaint.

While digital eye strain condition affects the general population, it is especially damaging to professionals who spend extended periods of time in front of a computer screen. Medical research is showing that blue light exposure causes even more dangerous long-term health risks than digital eye strain. A Harvard medical study stated that "High Energy Visible (HEV) blue light has been identified for years as the most dangerous light for the retina. After chronic exposure, one can expect to see long-range growth in the number of macular degenerations, glaucomas, and retinal degenerative diseases."

Other studies have shown that exposure to blue light seems to accelerate age-related macular degeneration (AMD) more than any other rays in the spectrum and that increased exposure to blue light by individuals in their teens, twenties, and thirties, increases the onset of AMD by 10 years, effectively doubling their chance of going blind in their lifetime. Harvard researchers also have linked working the night shift and exposure to blue light at night to several types of cancer (breast, prostate), diabetes, heart disease, obesity, and an increased risk for depression.

Other Health Risks

Graphic artists also suffer from tension headaches, stress disorders, chronic fatigue, and obesity. All of these conditions are related, having similar causes. For example, tension headaches are caused by sitting in the same position all day doing the same thing (e.g., working on a computer). They can also be caused by stress, eye strain, fatigue, physical inactivity, and anxiety.

Stress disorders can be caused by a high-stress job and working long and irregular hours. They can trigger stress-induced insomnia. Staying awake all night can lead to fatigue.

Fatigue is feeling weary and tired, which can last from a day to several months. When it becomes chronic, getting rest does not relieve it.

Lastly, the sedentary nature of the job can lead to obesity. The health risks of obesity are well documented.

Workplace Safeguards

While employers are responsible for creating a safe work environment, self-employed creators should make a safe setup a priority to avoid future disability. A number of preventive measures can reduce the risk of injury. The design of a workstation, including desk height, chair posture, and placement of keyboard, printer stand, and monitor, are important.

Overhead lighting should be indirect and glare-reduced. Correct posture at the computer and taking frequent breaks are good ways to reduce stress and hand, wrist, arm, back, and shoulder strain. A 15-minute break for each two hours of work is recommended by the Communications Workers of America; hourly breaks are ideal. Doing simple hand stretches during a break is recommended. A physician or clinic specializing in occupational health may be able to provide proper diagnosis and correct treatment.

The following recommendations for protecting eyes from the dangers of blue light (as well as more detailed information about digital eyestrain syndrome) can be found on the University of Montreal, School of Optometry website, bluelightexposed.com, as well as on allaboutvision.com:

* Remind yourself to blink more often. Staring at a digtal screen can affect the number of times you blink, causing eyes to dry.
* Take frequent breaks, move away from the screen, and wear computer glasses while on a device for two or more hours.
* Change the background color of digital devices from bright white to cool gray to help reduce digital eyestrain.
* Clean your screen. A dust-free, smudge-free screen helps reduce glare.
* If you wear corrective lenses, ask your eye doctor about the type of vision correction and lens features that will best suit your needs for viewing your computer and other digital devices and protecting your eyes from blue light. A number of lens manufacturers have introduced special glare-reducing anti-reflective coatings that also block blue light from both natural sunlight and digital devices.
* If you don't wear corrective lenses, special purpose computer glasses are available without an eyeglass prescription.
* Use physical blue light filters on your devices. They are available for smartphones, tablets, and computer screens and prevent significant amounts of blue light emitted from these devices from reaching your eyes without affecting the visibility of the display. Some are made with thin tempered glass that also protects your device's screen from scratches.

There are also blue light filter apps available for screen devices, such as Night Shift, Night Mode, Twilight, f.lux, and Iris. Most smartphones and computers come with a basic app built in for filtering light. They work by masking or "filtering" blue light on the screen to a warmer part of the spectrum. While they do reduce some of the light that is emitted by the display, they are not totally effective. They provide better protection when used with light filtering glasses. Another downside of both screen filters and filter apps can be increased eye strain because they reduce contrast. In addition, the distortion of true colors on the screen display can make it difficult to focus the eyes. Of the three solutions, blue light filtering glasses provide the best protection against digital eye strain and for preventing eye damage.

Other ideas for maintaining your physical and mental health can be found previously in this chapter in the section, Self-Employment Issues.

An excellent resource book for artists and art educators with more in-depth information is *The Artist's Complete Health and Safety Guide, Fourth Edition* (2019) by Monona Rossol. For a list of organizations and websites that provide publications and/or information on artists' health and safety issues, see Part 5, Resources & References.

Final Note

There are advantages and disadvantages of both staff-employment and self-employment situations. Only an individual artist can decide which option is best for his/her economic situation, lifestyle, personality, and temperament. Likewise, each artist should decide individually whether to enter art contests or design competitions, provide free services, work on speculation or on a contingent basis, and decide what to charge for his/her work.

The Graphic Artists Guild's purpose in publishing this book is to inform the artist fully so that he/she can make educated decisions about pricing work and negotiating fair agreements.

The information provided in the first three chapters of this book will give you business confidence and help you avoid costly mistakes that can undermine your professional success. The next chapter, Maximizing Income, will provide you with additional ideas and strategies to ensure that you make a sustainable living.

{ 4 }

Maximizing Income

This chapter begins with the self-promotion and marketing strategies that self-employed artists must practice on an ongoing basis to attract prospective clients and to ensure that their business is growing, with new jobs continuously coming in. It then explores the many and diverse ways that artists can maximize their income for a more sustainable livelihood, from selling additional rights to their artwork to sharing their knowledge to using their passion projects to promote themselves and attract new clients.

MAXIMIZING *the income potential of artwork both enables artists to sustain and improve their business and provides art buyers with options for solving their needs. While reuse—the sale of additional rights to existing artwork—has long been standard practice, this market has exploded in recent years, while licensing and merchandising markets for new artwork have also grown.*

The Internet and digital media have provided graphic artists with many additional options for maximizing their income. Social media has opened up many new and less expensive avenues for artists to promote themselves and their art. Likewise, online platforms provide new opportunities for marketing art and reaching thousands of new customers looking for unique images and patterns for decorating their homes and clothing, accessorizing, and gift-giving. Many graphic artists have long supplemented their creative income with jobs in the education sector, as teachers and adjunct professors in schools and colleges. Social media, the Internet, and digital technology also have broadened educational opportunities for increasing an artist's income.

The most powerful aspect of the Internet as a tool for maximizing income is its capability to cross-promote all of an artist's marketing initiatives with very little additional time and effort.

Self-Promotion & Marketing

One of the most vital, but frequently neglected, aspects of being a graphic artist—which applies to all artists in all disciplines who function as independent contractors—is self-promotion. Every graphic artist should see promotion as a top priority in maintaining a consistent, steady flow of work. It is best to avoid the obvious dilemma: when it is busy, there's no time for it; when it is not, it is too late.

Graphic artists need to show potential clients their work and position themselves advantageously to develop ongoing client relationships or to get more work or a better type of work. Promotion also enhances the studio's image or identity. It shows a creator's thinking: his/her ability to innovate, attract attention, and articulate a unique style or approach.

Keys to successful marketing include establishing a clear identity for a studio or firm, targeting desirable clients, and routinely reminding prospective clients of available services through ongoing promotion.

Establishing an Identity

Pinpointing the kind of work you want to do, what interests you most, and what you do best helps define a clear identity for your studio or firm. If you have trouble doing that, it may be useful to hire a management consultant to help you devise a marketing plan.

Targeting Clientele

Defining the ideal client and then creating a market strategy to target those potential clients is critical. If you want to develop new business in a particular industry, such as banking or health care, research departments in those organizations that use graphic art services. Then follow up with direct mailings.

Maintaining a Contact List

An essential aspect of good marketing is compiling and maintaining a list of contacts and updating it at least once a year to keep it fresh and relevant. Lists targeted to specific industries can be purchased, or you can ask for referrals from current clients, business acquaintances, suppliers, or even generous colleagues. Another resource is a marketing consultant who can help you develop lists and devise mailings based on what has worked for other clients in the past.

Besides current and former clients, your contact list should include prospective clients and other professional that you've met in person, had correspondence with, or interacted with on social media—anyone who has shown an interest in your work or ideas. Prospective clients should be defined as the ideal clients you would like to work with, not people in general.

Scheduling Promotions

To be effective, graphic artists need to schedule promotions at key intervals throughout the year. Sending out an attractive and creative periodic marketing piece that also contains useful information will be appreciated by the client. The information might be something that is helpful to the artist-client relationship of the targeted clientele, or it might be tips on a more general subject that most people would find interesting or useful.

At the very least, try to make a memorable statement at least once a year. Sending out an e-mail with a recent illustration or a press release about your latest professional award acts as a timely reminder; including a link to your website makes the piece doubly effective.

Ongoing Promotion

Staying on the radar screen of existing and prospective clients is vital for the continued growth of your business. You want them to be repeat customers. Not all clients, though, will be regular clients. Some do not have a need for graphic arts services every year or two, but when they do have a need—even if it's five years from now—you want them to remember you and have your current contact info.

The best marketing plans integrate a combination of strategies that utilize print, digital and social media, and face-to-face communication and that cross-promote among all of them. For example, an artist can generate interest in an upcoming exhibit of his/her art by blogging about the process of creating a work for it, sending out a postcard announcement, and tweeting a countdown to the date on Twitter. The exhibit itself not only showcases the artist's creativity but also provides opportunity for the artist to meet and engage with prospective clients, discuss business services, and have business cards and brochures on hand for attendees to take with them. Photos or video from the event can be posted on the artist's website, Instagram, or Facebook to continue generating interest in the artist's work.

Marketing plans should be continually adjusted, based on which strategies prove to be the most and least successful for your situation. Colleagues, vendors, and friends should also be targeted in promotional efforts because they can be a source of referral to new clients or they might become future clients themselves.

TRADITIONAL STRATEGIES

Though most people do not like sending out mass mailings or making cold calls, they are among the many traditional ways of attracting new business. Often, the traditional methods of self-promotion require printing and mailing costs. You should use them only if you enjoy doing them and you get results; otherwise, they may be a waste of time and money. If you are on a tight budget, you will see in the Online Strategies section below that there are online equivalents for many of the traditional methods of self-promotion that are more affordable.

HANDWRITTEN NOTES

It may seem old school, but Maria Brophy, business consultant to creatives, highly recommends that artists use the handwritten note as part of their ongoing marketing strategy. A handwritten note will make you stand out in a digital world where no one sends anything handwritten anymore. It shows that you care enough about your clients to take the time to personally write them a note. She suggests you send clients a thank-you note every time they buy a piece of your art or purchase your services. It should be sent shortly after delivery of the art or project. You can also set up a system where you send out a handwritten note to a few past clients and customers each week, letting them know that you are thinking of them.

You might consider having a number of note cards printed up with a copy of one of your recent designs or illustrations on the front. Your customers will not only receive your personal note but a memento of your art as well—a visual reminder of your talent. The point is to make it look personal, not like an ad.

HOLIDAY CARDS & CAMPAIGNS

Some graphic artists send out a self-designed or illustrated holiday card or e-card to clients and colleagues. A holiday card accomplishes both social and business purposes: it lets clients know they are thought of and appreciated; it keeps the artist in clients' minds; and it showcases the artist's creativity (especially talents that the client might not normally see). Clients are known to keep memorable holiday cards on display in their offices. To be more noticeable, you might send out a unique greeting for a holiday other than the December holidays or for a holiday that ties in with the image that you want to project. For example, if your firm wants to promote green design, you might send out a card on Earth Day.

For major and repeat clients, some artists expand the holiday card concept to a gift that showcases their talent. The most common are useful items that keep the artist in the client's mind all year, such as a calendar. Other artists hold annual events to thank clients and supporters, such as a studio open house with artwork offered at discounted prices.

You can get very creative with a holiday-themed campaign, in the form of note cards, e-cards, e-mails, blog posts, or Instagram posts. Throughout the year there are lesser known holidays and observances, in the form of "national" months, weeks, and days being celebrated. Some are serious, practical, or tied to organizations and occupations, while others are humorous or whimsical, for example, American Diabetes Alert Day, Stress Awareness Month, Take a Chance Day, Optimism Month, Children's Authors and Illustrators Week, No Brainer Day, Near Miss Day, National Smile Week, and Backward Day. Your campaign could be a weekly holiday post, showing your illustration skills and sense of humor or tying the holidays into your prospective clients' interests or business or your own services.

POSTCARD MAILERS

An example of a postcard promotional campaign might be a series of postcards with a common theme but with changing copy sent out periodically. It is recommended that you send one out consistently every 1–2 months for at least a year to make an impact. The front of the card should feature one strong image. On the back, include a call to action with your contact information.

CONNECT IN PERSON

As your business grows, you should try to connect personally with former and newly interested clients and customers periodically. The purpose is not to sell but to nourish and maintain your relationship. For local clients, ask them out for coffee or lunch. You might invite them to an event that would be of interest to both of you, either personally or professionally.

As part of your marketing plan, call a specified number of clients or customers each day. Perhaps it's only two to five but make it a habit. Asking them how they are doing and if there is anything you can help them with lets them know you are interested in their lives and reminds them that you are available. Keep notes on clients' interests so that you can notify them of events, etc., that they might be interested in attending. You can supplement personal contact with e-mails containing links to articles, events, business tips, etc., that you know would interest specific clients.

ONLINE STRATEGIES

The Internet, combined with social media, offers artists limitless ways to promote and cross-promote themselves, their skills, and their work. Not only does social media reach thousands of people, but most platforms are also free or very inexpensive. Following are some of the online tools graphic artists are using for marketing and promotion:

HTML E-NEWSLETTERS

Sending a newsletter by e-mail is an inexpensive and powerful way to connect with your network. HTML e-newsletters are formatted e-mails, with color, font styles, and images, so they are more attractive and professional-looking than an everyday e-mail. Create a consistent format so that your newsletter is easily recognizable to recipients as your brand and less likely to be deleted as spam. Also be consistent about when you send it out—the same time every week or month.

The information included in an e-newsletter can be purely business, such as updating existing and potential clients about new art or projects you are working on or new services you are offering. It might also include a recent job you've completed with a description of an obstacle you overcame or a new skill you utilized in the process. These experiences become part of your story. An e-newsletter might also be a combination of business and general interest information.

If you think sending an e-newsletter is too much work, keep it short and simple. Use one image, a short description, and add a call for action with contact information, and a live link to your website or online store. Recipients are more likely to view something short, and sending short newsletters frequently is more effective than sending long ones infrequently.

Newsletters can also be targeted to specific clients or businesses. Regardless of the kind of information included, e-newsletters should provide something that the recipient will find useful, interesting, or entertaining, either in the text and images or through live links to other useful resources. Remember, the purpose is for you to stand out in the receiver's mind.

There are a number of HTML e-mail providers that artists can use to ensure that they are in compliance with the United States CAN-SPAM Act of 2003. The penalties for noncompliance can be extremely costly. The Federal Trade Commission also provides a Compliance Guide for Business on its website at https://www.ftc.gov/tips-advice/business-center/guidance/can-spam-act-compliance-guide-business.

The Canadian Anti-Spam Law (CASL), which went into effect in 2016, governs all messages sent into and out of Canada, but does not include messages simply routed through Canada. Information and regulations can be found on the Canadian Radio-television and Telecommunications Commission website, with answers to frequently asked questions at https://crtc.gc.ca/eng/com500/faq500.htm.

As of May 25, 2018, messages sent to or received from the European Union are covered by the General Data Protection Regulation (GDPR) law. You can read more about GDPR at EUGDPR.org. For a comparison of the features of CAN-SPAM, CASL, and GDPR in chart form, visit https://www.relationshipone.com/blog/guide-can-spam-casl-gdpr/.

PERSONAL WEBSITES

For visual creators, a personal website is a necessity for creating a business identity, describing and promoting services, and displaying examples of work. Keep it fresh by updating info and changing images frequently. Promote your website by including the URL in any print materials you send out.

To drive business to your site, include a live link to your site from wherever you can—e-mail, social media, and other digital media. Make sure you are linking from sites with which you want to be associated. Many professional organizations offer their members a link from their website to those of their members.

PORTFOLIO WEBSITES & PAGES

Portfolio websites are sites specifically designed for creative professionals to display their work—for a monthly or annual fee. Some allow artists to sell work from the site. The amount of text allowed varies but usually includes at least the artist's contact information and an artist's statement. These sites often provide layout and design options for displaying work. They can be a relatively inexpensive alternative for artists who don't have their own website. Before posting work on one of these sites, read its terms and conditions section to make sure you are not relinquishing any copyrights by posting your work.

Some professional organization websites offer their members a portfolio "page" to display work. The cost of displaying work is either nominal or offered free as a benefit of membership. An example is the Member Portfolios section of the Graphic Artists Guild website (www.graphicartistsguild.org/guild-member-portfolios/).

ONLINE DIRECTORIES

These are online versions of established advertising directories (see the Sources of Illustration and Design Talent section in Chapter 2). For an annual fee, artists can display their work, list their disciplines and artistic styles, and provide their contact information. Many include a live link to the artist's personal website.

Social media is a powerful way for graphic artists to promote and market their art and services and connect with potential clients, as well as with professionals working in the same or related fields. A social media presence increases your visibility on the Internet, especially if you post images and/or video, because search engines favor them.

Social media professionals give the following advice when considering using social media to promote your brand:

* **First, explore various social media platforms to understand how they work, the features they offer, the audience, any costs involved, ease of use, etc.** You can research the sites themselves to learn much of this information, but also do an online search with your questions to find out other creatives' experiences with specific platforms. You will also find articles that list the pros and cons of each platform, geared to artists.
* **Don't try to build all platforms at once.** Initially, pick one platform and stick with it. Use its insights and analytics features to find out what works and what doesn't and adjust your efforts accordingly. You can branch out to other platforms once you are more experienced with using social media.
* **Choose a platform that plays to your strengths and your situation.** If you are an enthusiastic, extroverted type of person who is passionate talking about your art or discipline and likes being in front of the camera, YouTube would be a good platform for you. If you are an introvert who doesn't like calling attention to yourself, you might feel more comfortable trying to establish a presence on Twitter or LinkedIn, where you can comment on the posts of others in your field or join discussions. Also consider the audience you want to reach.
* **Limit involvement to no more than three platforms.** Otherwise you are taking too much time away from your creative process.

Once you are involved in social media, use the following strategies to increase your presence and followers:

* **Educate.** Share what you know and what you are learning in the areas in which you want to become known as an expert. Don't be a generalist.
* **Network in your niche.** Add value to other experts and network with their communities by sharing on online groups and blogs.
* **Be proactive.** Promote yourself by offering to share content with other creatives just starting out and by collaborating with other professionals in a joint cause or effort.
* **Be consistent.** Blog, post, or interact frequently on a regular basis—for most platforms, at least once a day and for Twitter, multiple times per day. If you are making videos, create a content calendar and pick a certain day of the week or month when you will publish your video and promote it on your social platforms, so your audience knows exactly what to expect from you and when to expect it.

Blogs. The best feature of blogs is their interactive capability, which enables bloggers to share information and solutions to problems with other people in their field as well as with prospective clients. Artists can create their own blog on, or linked to, their website, or they can increase their visibility by contributing to other professionals' art, business, communication, or technology-related blogs on a regular basis. Many professional organizations have blogs on their websites where members can share information with each other.

Blogs are an excellent way to demonstrate your expertise on a particular subject that ties in with the services you provide, without doing a hard sell. They also reveal something about your personality in a way that traditional self-promotion does not. Lauren Hom discusses the power of her blog, Daily Dishonesty, and how it jumpstarted her career in Part 4. If you decide to create your own blog, be aware of the time it takes to post messages frequently in order to keep it fresh and make it a resource that people will want to keep coming back to.

Following are some specific social media platforms for artists to consider for promotion and marketing purposes:

Instagram, a social networking app for sharing photos and videos from a smartphone, provides a very visual, casual engagement with fans and clients. For artists, it's a good place to show off their work and build an audience. You can share a variety of content—works-in-progress, time lapses, videos, and finished work. It's also an excellent place to network with magazines and arts organizations, many of whom love to repost and help artistic content go viral. It is also known to be used by collectors to find artwork.

Hashtags are the key to others finding your content because they are powerful search tools. It's recommended that you use at least seven hashtags in your posts. If you have a personal account, convert it to a business account, which will allow you to advertise and will give you access to analytics that will show you the peak times for your posts.

By studying this data, you will see when your followers are most engaged. Then plan to post at those times. A business account also lets you add links to your stories once you have 10,000+ followers.

Make sure you engage with your audience daily to help gain more followers. You can engage in two ways. "Like" your followers' posts; they will notice and do the same for you. Also, leave comments that show you are interested in the content of the person posting. However, be sincere and make your comments genuine.

Facebook, the largest social networking site, has universal reach with an average of 1.59 billion users logging on daily. It's a good place to network both professionally and personally and to build microcommunities and niche interest groups.

As an art marketing tool, Facebook enables you to share all kinds of posts, including photos, videos, links to websites, podcasts, and blogs, and you can easily link to other social media channels and share posts from Twitter, Instagram, and Pinterest.

To keep your personal and professional lives separate, sign up for a free Business Page. A business account allows you to set up a Facebook Shop for selling your art. It also provides you with free insights on your fans, and you can follow how well your posts are doing. A drawback of the Facebook business account is that the algorithms are becoming more focused on paying for your posts to be seen in the news feed

Twitter is easy to use and an excellent medium for searching and interjecting yourself into a conversation. You also can pin your latest work on your profile so when people look you up, it's the first thing they see. Your images will stand out amidst all the text on Twitter. To promote an image, you can pair a thumbnail of it with a link to your website. Consider using Twitter as a quick promo. Because Twitter moves so quickly with all the news, you will need to post at regular intervals for maximum exposure.

Pinterest, a visual search engine and web-based bulletin board, is the perfect social platform for visual artists and artisans to show off and market their work, as well as get inspiration and business tips. Pinterest users love to see and buy products, so there is a built-in audience of potential customers, especially those who enjoy decorating and crafting. Consumers are not the only ones looking for creative work on Pinterest. Graphic artists are being contacted for commissions by art directors who saw their work on Pinterest.

Pinterest is also an excellent option for long-term exposure. When you "pin" an image on Pinterest, it cre-ates a clickable link to the website where the image is located. So, if someone pins an image from your blog or website, every time another Pinterest user clicks it, you get free traffic. By getting people to pin or re-pin images from your website on Pinterest on a regular basis, you are guaranteeing a steady stream of traffic for months, or even years. Pinterest gives higher priority to pins saved by the content creator, so a good strategy is to save your pins to multiple relevant boards.

Unlike other social media, you don't need a lot of followers to see results. Your pins will be seen by Pinterest users who don't even follow you. Another advantage over some other platforms is Pinterest's business accounts are not given lower priority in users' news feeds. A free business account gives you access to analytics and insights and enables you to advertise with "promoted" pins and sell art directly with "buyable" pins.

Tumblr, a huge microblogging and social network, is user-friendly and frequented by thousands of creative individuals, making it a prime environment for sharing work. It is home to 475 million blogs and has over a half-billion visitors every month.

A Tumblr page can function as a complete website, adding to its power for discoverability and exposure. Templates and the custom HTML/CSS feature allow users to do what they want with their own Tumblog. With the queue feature, you can program posts of your work weeks in advance and at intervals that you set yourself.

YouTube, a video sharing website owned by Google, provides plenty of opportunities, through the use of videos, to promote and market yourself, your art, and your services. If you can video your art process, it will involve people in your creative world—an excellent way to connect with potential customers and clients and develop a following. It's also an excellent platform to monetize, sponsor, partner, and create additional revenue channels. Your content can be embedded on almost all platforms which allows you to share your video all over the web.

Behance is mainly a portfolio site owned by Adobe, and it's somewhat more professionally oriented than the other platforms mentioned. It's free to sign up and present your work. It gives you statistics and metrics for views and comments about your work. It's a good choice to show off both personal and professional projects in a way that's easy for potential clients to discover. As an online community, it provides plenty of opportunities to interact and network within your field, as well as others. There's also a chance to be featured in curated galleries and networks.

Dribble is a community of designers who share screen shots of work in progress, making it a good place to get feedback on a project. It's by invitation only, which makes it difficult to get on. The plus side is that the work is of higher quality than most portfolio sites. It also has a job board where major companies post jobs and users can search for work.

LinkedIn is the world's largest professional network and platform for business, so a well-thought-out LinkedIn profile is a good idea, especially for artists trying to attract corporate clients. It also allows former co-workers and clients to leave recommendations, acting as an online résumé that potential clients will look for. It's a good idea to vet recommendations for validity, to make sure they are from people you know and for skills you actually have or want to promote.

For professional tips and up-to-date information on marketing with social media platforms, visit Louise Myers Visual Social Media blog (https://louisem.com/).

ONLINE CAMPAIGN SERIES

You can use social media, your blog, and e-mail to generate interest in and greater exposure for your work by creating and posting an online campaign series, for example, One Month of Painting Waterfalls in New York State Parks, 30 Days of Political Cartoons, Two Weeks of Street Photos in Cuba; Illustrating the 12 Days of Christmas, 14 Days of Hand-Lettered Valentines, etc.). An online campaign costs very little and will attract new and existing customers. Some new customers may be attracted by the subject matter itself and discover you in the process.

There are many ways to do this, but the first step is to choose the topic and the number of days you will commit to the campaign, and then announce it on all the social media you are on with a link to where the campaign will be posted. Continue to announce it daily for the duration of the campaign. For works such as paintings that take more time to complete, post daily photos of the work with a description. You can show works in progress or sketches. For additional interest, tell a story about each work and include photos of you working on it. You can even generate sales by mentioning that the finished work is for sale and giving contact info on how to purchase it.

For photographers and artists whose work takes less time to complete, instead of posting work-in-progress photos, post one image a day and sell limited-edition prints of it.

At first there will be a slow response, but as each day goes on, the campaign will gain momentum as viewers get involved and want to see what your next post or image will be.

A different version of the live campaign is to post stages of a work or project in progress, such as a painting, a mural, or a linoleum block print, on your blog, Facebook, Instagram, etc. With each post, you can describe aspects of your technique and/or difficulties you may encounter. This strategy builds interest in your work and an appreciation of your skills and creates a personal connection between you and your audience. If you plan to sell the work, it can also help increase sales.

VIDEOS

Video has become a powerful component of social marketing and marketing in general. It offers even small businesses massive opportunities for promotion and marketing. Why should you consider video in your marketing plan? As of 2019, video accounted for 80% of all online traffic. According to *Forbes,* 90% of consumers indicate product videos directly inform their purchase decisions. Businesses that utilize video content experience a 41% increase in traffic through web searches as compared to those that don't use video in their content strategies. More than half of marketing experts also agree that video gives the best return on investment. Over 76 percent of marketers and small business owners that have used video marketing said that it had a direct impact on their business. Furthermore, businesses using video grow company revenue 49 percent faster year-over-year than those who don't use it.

Gone are the days when video production required a budget of thousands of dollars and expensive equipment. For online use, you can use your smart phone to produce videos with very little additional equipment. More information on creating online videos can be found in the section, Instructional/Tutorial Videos & Courses, later in this chapter.

There are several ways to use video for self-promotion and marketing. Include video in your social media presence. According to results of a survey by Animoto, consumers rank video as their number one favorite type of content to see from brands on social media, and 93% of marketers using video on social media say it has landed them a new customer. According to *Small Business Trends*, video generates 12 times the shares that text and images combined do on social media.

As the second largest search engine, YouTube offers you opportunities to get in front of potential customers and clients searching for how-to videos related to your industry, products, or services.

You can also incorporate video on your website. The average customer spends 88% more time on a website if it has video. Some ways you can increase visitor engagement are by including an introductory video on your landing page, videos promoting your products or services, a demonstration of your artistic technique or process, a how-to video, a blog teaser, and a video ad. An About Us video works especially well for small and growing businesses. It lets you show off the people and story behind your business—enabling visitors to connect with you on a more personal level. Likewise, so does a product video when your product or service has an interesting backstory. These videos can be repurposed for sharing on social media and YouTube.

Video can also be added to your e-mail promotions for an increase in open and click-through rates. A video does not have to play in your e-mail for results—mention video in the subject line and link out to it. Campaign Monitor offers a guide on how to use video in e-mail marketing at https://www.campaignmonitor.com/resources/guides/video-in-email/.

Videos do not have to be limited to online use. You can also use them at events and trade shows.

For tips and tricks on using video for marketing, see Animoto's *Small Business Marketing with Video* at https://sproutsocial.com/insights/guides/small-business-marketing-101/#small-business-marketing-with-video.

Additional Self-Promotion & Marketing Resources

As a self-employed graphic artist, it may help to think of your career as a long-term promotion or identity campaign. It is actually a building process that lets clients know you have longevity and staying power. If you persist, promotion should pay off, but you have to be willing to invest both time and money to make it work. Whatever you do, make sure you get noticed. The first rule of promotion is to get the client's attention. Whether you use traditional or online promotional methods or a combination of both, remember that self-promotion takes time, consistency, and persistence to pay off.

There are numerous resources available for artists and freelancers to learn about self-promotion and marketing: books, magazines, websites and blogs, online videos, your local Chamber of Commerce, courses, workshops, and presentations at conferences and trade shows. For a list of books and other media on self-promotion and marketing, see Part 5 Resources & References.

Creating Multiple Revenue Streams

As discussed in Chapter 3, the life of a self-employed graphic artist can be quite unpredictable financially, especially when just starting your career. There will be no income while you look for your next project or commission. Even if you are busy with client work, you may not have income for several months until you finish a project. Once you finish and bill a job, payment may be delayed.

Successful graphic artists have found ways to supplement the unpredictable income with other sources of revenue to make their financial situation more stable. Creating additional sources of income does not mean having to take a part-time job as a ride-share driver or some other job totally unrelated to your art. You can use your creative skills and your existing art to create multiple streams of revenue. The ideal revenue stream is *passive income*—money that is coming in with very little additional work on your part once you set it up.

The following sections describe several ways self-employed graphic artists can create multiple revenue streams to make their livelihood more sustainable. Some involve taking part-time jobs in their profession, others involve developing other markets for their art and skills, and some are sources of passive income.

Sell Reuse Rights

Reuse is an opportunity for all artists and an important area of income for many. The artist, authorized agent, or copyright holder sells the right to reproduce artwork originally commissioned for one specified use, for new or additional uses. Because the work has already been created, reuse is a form of passive revenue

Reuse has many different names. By trade custom, the term *stock art* in general illustration markets means copyrighted artwork for which the user negotiates a pay-per-use license or usage fee. Stock art also includes typographic alphabets (usually prepared in digital form and licensed to buyers by type houses), social media icons, and dingbats—non-typographic decorative elements in font format.

Reuse may also be called *secondary rights* (though it may actually be the third, fourth, or one-hundredth time the rights have been sold). In publishing they are called *subsidiary rights* and are grants of usage in addition to what the project was originally commissioned for, such as when a chapter from a book is sold to a magazine before the book is published. In merchandising, where existing art may sell for many different uses to many different clients, grants of usage rights are called *licensing*.

Selling reuse rights represents a logical step in extending the value of artwork through the length of the copyright. Over the artist's lifetime plus 70 years, judicious control of a work's copyright and uses can generate much more income for an illustrator than the original rights grant. The Internet and the more prevalent use of mobile devices have increased the demand for images.

The growing market for reuse fuels the debate about whether stock illustration sales reduce new commissions or harm artists by overexposing or under-controlling the appearance of an illustration. The continuous improvements and growth in technology heighten the debate. Methods of cataloging and presenting stock art have improved dramatically, thanks to advances in computers, digital storage, and the Internet. Digital technology has increased compact storage, as well as enabled quicker searches, retrievals, and presentations; reduced the risk of artwork being swiped or copied; and accelerated transmission and digital delivery to platemaking or electronic end products. And technology also enables graphic artists to customize existing images to meet the needs of a new client and charge fees that reflect the customized image.

Reuse may be sought by the original client, who wishes to expand the original project or use it in a new campaign. Or a prospective buyer may want to use art seen in an online directory, stock catalog, or other promotional material. Some buyers may even plan a proposed project around a particular image; if the desired image is not available, they will have to be flexible about using other work that is available or commission original work. Sometimes artists envision and market a reuse; for example, an artist may propose using an existing image for a greeting card, calendar, or editorial insert.

The aesthetic is different when using existing artwork rather than commissioned illustration; the art buyer knows exactly what he/she is getting. The client's risk of being unfavorably surprised is avoided. On the other hand, an element of creativity is eliminated, as is the traditional excitement of collaboration between art director and illustrator and the thrill of creating/receiving a unique new illustration.

The economic climate and the growth in the use of stock illustration are creating new niches for existing artwork. It is up to each artist to seek them out in order to better fulfill the artwork's potential value. Artists interested in reselling rights must make individual marketing decisions about the best avenues for reuse sales for their inventory of images.

Any discussion of reuse is based on an artist's control and ownership of rights. Artists who relinquish control by accepting work made for hire and all-rights conditions are forever locked out of reuse markets and other sources of potential income.

Who Should Handle Reuse Sales?

Artists, artists' representatives, and stock agencies may each claim they know the reuse market best and can negotiate the most appropriate reuse fees.

ARTISTS

Many artists like to handle their own reuse sales, but there are advantages and disadvantages to that arrangement. On the one hand, artists have to handle all the usual record keeping connected with an illustration assignment without the excitement of creating a new image. On the other hand, a little paperwork can produce welcome additional income from an inventory of existing images.

Handling reuse sales themselves allows artists to determine the client's needs firsthand and to custom tailor the agreement, fee, and quality of the artwork's reproduction. Knowing their own body of work, artists may come up with more options or an image better suited to the client's needs, while at the same time establishing a relationship that might result in future assignments. If a potential client contacts an artist with a possible commission but an insufficient budget, the artist can suggest reusing an existing image that conveys a similar message. At least one artist offering stock images recognized this client need and now provides a service in which he customizes his stock images to meet clients' exact needs. Artists may feel they are best qualified to set reuse fees because of their knowledge of their own work relative to the field, their reputation, and their comfort with negotiating.

To handle sales of reuse rights, artists must be willing to practice good rights management—maintaining accurate records of usage rights agreements for all illustrations (see the section on Keeping Track, in Chapter 1); monitoring sales to prevent conflicts and unauthorized usage; and handling contracts, invoices, and shipping. This is in addition to managing all the other usual overhead tasks of the illustration business. Artists who maintain careful records can sell reuse rights to images that could not be handled through a stock agency (agencies often require images with completely or widely available rights). If necessary, artists may be able to negotiate the reversion of desired reuse rights from a client.

Reuse pricing is as complex as pricing for original commissioned art, and no percentage of an original commissioned fee has been set that is common to all markets. Reuse rights are usually sold at less than the rate of commissioned work, though not if the artist controls the sale and determines that the new use warrants a higher rate. The primary criterion for setting pricing should be how the client chooses to use the work. If the client will derive great value from its reuse of the work, then the artist should feel free to set a fee, commensurate with the new use, that is higher than that for the original use. Artists should also take the usual factors—size, geographic region, exclusivity of market, time frame, and media—into consideration when setting reuse prices. Generally, it is wise not to commit to a reuse fee in your original contract for commissioned work. Just stipulate that there will be a reuse fee to be negotiated later. When the request is made, base the fee on the factors outlined above.

To maximize stock illustration sales, some artists feature images available for reuse in targeted promotions or on their websites. If you feature art on a website, it needs to be displayed in a format that is protected against unauthorized use (see the section on Unauthorized Reuse & Alterations later in this chapter).

ARTISTS' REPRESENTATIVES

Artists' representatives may sell reuse rights on behalf of artists as part of the normal artist-agent agreement. Reps are in a good position to negotiate reuse fees, custom-tailor reuse agreements to the clients' needs, and monitor compliance with purchase agreements. Often these agreements are handled just like newly commissioned work: the artist usually receives 70–75% of the fee, with 30–25% going to the rep. Artists usually retain the right to refuse a sale; they also receive tear sheets of the final printed piece.

Though this type of contract has been standard for commissioned artwork, reps may choose to handle reuse differently from commissioned art. For example, while the usual artist-agent split of 75/25% is a clear advantage to the artist over the 50/50% split of usual stock agency agreements (see below), reps may change the percentage split to match those in stock agreements if they want their businesses to more closely resemble stock agency marketing. Artists are always free to negotiate more favorable terms.

Many reps prefer to handle reuse sales of images originally commissioned through their efforts, or appearing on promotional materials carrying their name, rather than have the artist or a stock house manage them. Having negotiated one-time or limited rights in the initial agreement, reps often feel they deserve the opportunity to market the rights that were reserved to the artist through their efforts. Artist-agent contracts should specify whether the rep will handle such sales and, if so, whether that is an exclusive arrangement. Artists and reps whose relationships predate the rise of the reuse market can attach a letter of agreement to their contract, detailing the new arrangements.

Artists' reps who have long-standing relationships with their artists and handled the initial agreement with the client are well positioned to market reuses that both protect the artist's reputation and avoid stepping on the original client's toes. Some reps also handle reuses of images that did not originate with them. Among the marketing techniques employed by some reps are establishing a special stock division on terms similar to those at stock agencies and developing special promotions of images judged to be particularly marketable. It may take a different kind of marketing to achieve successful, sustained reuse sales; the clients are not necessarily the same as those for commissioned work. Only the artist's rep can decide whether it is in his/her interest and ability to pursue stock illustration sales.

STOCK AGENCIES

Stock illustration was introduced by stock agencies or houses that were already established as sources of stock photography; several illustration-only agencies, including international ones, have since been founded to handle stock art. A leading global market research company, Technavio, headquartered in London, has taken a look at the global still image market and concluded that it will exceed $4 billion by 2020, growing at a compound annual growth rate of over 7% from 2016–2020. Of primary concern to illustrators is that stock illustration sales may, as with stock photography, reduce the demand for originally commissioned work.

Though stock illustration evolved from stock photography, the significant differences in how artwork and photography are created affect each genre's opportunities in the stock image market. Photographers create many images in the course of doing business; illustrators create fewer images over their lifetime. This means that illustrators have fewer potentially income-producing copyrights. But the growth of the stock illustration business argues that a market exists. As demand grows, illustrators hope the market will provide them with additional, and more lucrative, sources of income.

HOW AGENCIES SELL STOCK ILLUSTRATION

Today, stock images are bought and sold via online stock sites. Digital directories allow buyers to research numerous images themselves. Once purchased, the images are downloaded to the buyer. Some online services are set up to enable the buyer to search for and locate an image by describing it in simple language or in keywords. This service is usually free until an image is chosen, but online registration may be required prior to being permitted to search the images.

There are two major licensing arrangements for stock: *rights-managed (RM)* and *royalty-free (RF)*.

Rights-managed stock refers to a copyright license which, if purchased by a user, allows the one-time use of the image as specified by the license. If the user wants to use the image for other uses, an additional license needs to be purchased. RM licenses can be granted on a nonexclusive or exclusive basis.

Royalty-free stock is often confused with being free or copyright-free. This is not the case at all. There is a fee for using the image, and the artist still owns the copyright. The term is meant to distinguish it from rights-managed stock licensing arrangements, in which the user often must pay a royalty to the artist, agency, or both every time the image is used. Generally, in RF licensing, the user is granted a determined set of rights to use the image in a variety of ways, for a one-time, flat fee.

The major stock agencies generally sell both rights-managed and royalty-free stock. A *microstock* agency deals in royalty-free licenses, which include subscription-based licenses.

The stock agency and the illustrator usually split the proceeds of whatever rights the agency sells, The artist-agency split varies widely. In general, most major illustration stock agencies pay the artist 50% and keep 50%. Higher royalties may be paid to exclusive contributors. Also, royalties often are paid on a tiered system, based on such factors as the number of years the artist has been with the agency, the number of downloads the artist's images receive, and whether the art is a single-image download or part of a subscription. In general, the greater the number of downloads an artist's work receives, the greater the amount of the royalty, and single-image downloads pay more than downloads that are part of a subscription. Sometimes there also is a point system involved in how much an artist receives. Many of the newer royalty-free stock houses give artists a flat fee for each use, which is the least profitable option.

Increasingly, there is no difference between domestic and foreign rights. However, if a foreign agency is involved, you still earn the same percentage that is stated in your contract but on the amount minus what is withheld by the foreign agency. For example, if your contract with the stock agency says you are to receive 50% of rights sold, but the U.S. agency negotiates a 50/50 split with the foreign agency, you will receive 50% of 50%, or what is left after the foreign agency takes its 50%. Fifty percent of 50% is only 25% of the total.

The royalty-free agencies are changing the face of stock photography and illustration, making them increasingly competitive and less profitable. Stock agencies usually quote reuse prices, though still negotiable, by referring to in-house charts that rely upon such factors as market, reproduction size, print run, and number of pho-tos to be used as benchmarks. For instance, a large sale of many images may result in a low price per image, with the profit to the agency derived from search fees charged to the client for each hour the agency's staff searches their libraries.

Artists may find that fees negotiated by stock agencies are significantly lower than they would negotiate for themselves. Agencies send out periodic checks with sales reports, usually quarterly or monthly, that list the sale, the client's name, and sometimes the media in which it appeared, but not the terms of the reuse. Many artists feel the last information is vital in order to accurately calculate the income generated from each reuse. Although some agencies might request tear sheets, they do not guarantee that they will send samples to the artists.

Artists under contract to a stock agency do not have the right to refuse a sale, except by indicating in the contract any off-limit markets such as pornography or cigarette and liquor advertising. Some agencies do contact artists at their discretion to discuss a proposed sale.

Some stock agencies grant clients the right to alter, tint, crop, or otherwise manipulate images; others do not. This right is usually listed in the agency's delivery memo, which states standard terms governing the client's purchase of rights, but it is usually not addressed in the artist-agency contract. Very few agencies discuss intended alterations with the artist or arrange to have the client contact the artist to discuss changes.

NEW COMMISSIONS

When a client commissions new work from an artist through a stock agency and the agency acts as agent and negotiates the fee with the client, the agency usually takes a 25–30% commission—depending on the stock house—and in this economic climate, fees are up for grabs. Increasingly, anything goes. When new work is commissioned through a stock agency for an illustrator who has a representative, the agency allows the rep to negotiate the price and takes a smaller finder's fee (usually 10%), or the agency has the buyer contact the rep directly.

Some illustrators without reps do not wish to have a stock agency represent them for commissioned work. Illustrators have negotiated artist-agency contracts in which the artist handles the fee and contract negotiations directly with the client and pays the agency a 10% finder's fee for attracting new work rather than an agency's full commission. Some agencies do not request a finder's fee for commission referrals. However, beware of the terms of the contract—most demand payment for the life of your work with the client. And many will charge fees well in excess of the 10% suggested here unless you negotiate otherwise.

4–1 Should Clients Use Stock Agencies to Purchase Artwork?

PROS

✳ Agencies provide complete, available images that can be delivered immediately with ensured results.
✳ An art director saves time negotiating directly with the agency, rather than with the artist, client, and/or the designer.
✳ Stock may serve as an introduction to an artist's work that leads to commissioned assignments for future needs.

CONS

✳ Clients miss the chance to discover the artist's skills as a problem-solver and creative collaborator.
✳ Searching through large numbers of files is time-consuming, and the cost of the designer's time plus the use fee may exceed the price of custom art.

4–2 Should Artists Use a Stock Agency to Market Their Artwork?

PROS

✳ Agencies offer the chance of generating high-volume reuse sales for little additional work on the artist's part.
✳ Artists have more time to create while the agency does the selling.
✳ Artists can pick specific images to be licensed to an agency while retaining others to market personally.
✳ Stock agency sales may help introduce an artist's work to new clients or new markets.
✳ The burden of keeping up with new technology and markets is left to the agency.
✳ Some agencies are expert at getting their images before buyers.

In short, the stock agency offers artists the possibility of additional sales for less work on their part.

CONS

✳ The artist cannot determine or negotiate the fee for a sale.
✳ The artist pays a high commission (50% or more) for each sale.
✳ The artist yields control over the integrity of the art and where it appears.
✳ Many stock houses are large, impersonal corporations that seek control and rights to art that may not be in the artist's best interests.
✳ Increased use of stock may negatively affect the market for originally commissioned works.

PROS & CONS OF WORKING WITH STOCK AGENCIES

There is no question that artists want to maximize the income potential from a lifetime of work, leaving all such revenues to their heirs. There is, however, considerable controversy in the industry about how best to do that. See Figures 4–1 and 4–2 for the pros and cons of clients using stock houses to purchase art, and artists using stock agencies to market their work.

Trade Practices & Contracts for Reuse Sales

The artist, artist's rep, or stock agency must be clear about which reproduction rights were transferred to the previous buyer and which the artist retained. It is, of course, illegal to sell a usage that breaches an existing contract on exclusivity of market, time frame, geographic region, and so on. It is accepted practice that an artist or agent will not sell a use that competes with another use, though the definition of competing uses may be hard to articulate. In general, a reuse should not be in the same market and time frame, nor for a competing client or product.

Paperwork relating to the sale of an image should always be reviewed carefully if there is any doubt about rights previously sold. Contracts for reuse rights, whether drawn up by artists, their reps, or stock agencies, should state clearly what usage is being granted and the intended market, the size of the reproduction, the print run, the length of the agreement, and so on. Other negotiating points might include reasonable payment schedules, alteration policies, access to accounting records, receipt of copies of delivery memos, and tear sheets. (For more information on artist-agent agreements, see Chapter 2, Professional Relationships.)

Artists who wish to have their stock illustration sales conducted by artists' representatives or agencies should discuss all reuse agreements and contracts carefully, so all terms are fully understood and agreed upon by both parties. Artists considering prewritten contracts should remember that many points are negotiable; they may wish to consult a lawyer and/or other artists before signing a contract.

Artists considering signing with a stock illustration agency or artists' rep should ask to review a copy of the firm's standard delivery memo or invoice, which states the standard terms by which a client buys rights. Information such as whether tear sheets will be provided, or alterations permitted, is usually located in this agreement rather than in the contract the artist signs.

Likewise, errors by agencies reporting fees received would be minimized if artists received copies of the delivery memo or invoice with regularly reported sales and income, allowing them to verify prices and terms of sales. Ensuring that artists see the terms of sale and a sample of the published result would also aid in monitoring the client's compliance with the delivery memo. Some artist-agency agreements include the right to audit the agency's books by a certified public accountant

CLIP ART & RIGHTS-FREE ART

Grants of reuse rights for art sold as stock are not the same as clip art. Clip art consists of images that, once acquired, come with a grant of license for any use (though specific terms depend on the license agreement). Clip art can be any artwork that is in the public domain or camera- or computer-ready art to which all rights have been sold by the artist, with the understanding that such art may be altered, cropped, retouched, and used as often as desired. Clip art is available to the public in books, on CDs, and as digital downloads. When an artist's inventory is sold as a collection, some clip art distributors pay the artist a royalty on sales and give them name credit.

Clip art competes with both commissioned art and stock illustration. With digital imaging capability, designers can create new artwork solely by combining and altering clip art, although that may not be cost-effective when one considers the designer's investment of time and effort against the cost of a commissioned illustration.

One controversial way to market an artist's entire inventory as clip art is on rights-free CDs. Companies usually offer artists royalties on sales of the original discs but not on any additional uses, since all rights are sold outright. The purchasers may then use the work in any way they choose, including manipulating, combining, or otherwise changing the original for placement on products, in ads, or as characters in feature films.

Selling artwork on rights-free CDs gives the artist the opportunity to sell a large number of images at one time for an up-front fee, and to receive royalties on sales of the CDs, but not on the images.

The availability of downloadable rights-free art has also created new options for graphic designers, who have the increased technological means of manipulating them. However, the tradeoff is that designers lose the experience of working with a knowledgeable and creative illustrator who can create new artwork custom-made to specifically meet their needs. Users of clipart also need to read the specific terms of each licensing agreement very carefully because they are not all the same.

ROYALTY-FREE STOCK

Graphic artists who use royalty-free stock images (also known as microstock) in their work need to carefully read the terms of use. Contributing artists retain the copyright to their work, even when their artwork is sold as "royalty-free," and the terms of use prohibit purchasers from using images for logos or artwork on which they will claim copyright.

UNAUTHORIZED REUSE & ALTERATIONS

Reproduction of an image without the artist's or copyright holder's permission constitutes unauthorized reuse. It involves copyright infringement, and the infringer may be liable for attorney's fees and statutory damages if pursued in court. The same may be true of unauthorized alteration of an artist's image. For more information, see Chapter 11, Legal Rights & Issues.

An art user who wishes to "pick up" an image from an already published source should first contact the artist to arrange for permission and payment of an appropriate usage fee. Failure to reach the artist is not sufficient excuse for unauthorized use of an image; legal due diligence (an earnest, concerted effort to obtain the necessary information) must be demonstrated.

Stories abound of artists' portfolio work being used without permission for client presentations. Digital images have made it even easier for those who engage in questionable business practices to produce "ripamatics" and include them in presentations—and artists are rarely, if ever, consulted, much less compensated. However, some stock photo houses permit limited comping use of their images, so it's important to check for this when reviewing their client agreement.

Artists who display their work via digital catalogs can use electronic watermarks, digital time stamping, and registries to protect their copyrights. Such methods clearly indicate ownership for protected art, as opposed to rights-free clip art, and are available as software. All such efforts have some merit, but the only sure way to completely protect one's electronic property is by registering the work with the U.S. Copyright Office (see the Copyright section of Chapter 11, Legal Rights & Issues).

An artist, artists' rep, or stock agency who notices an unauthorized reuse will usually contact the infringer and request an appropriate fee. Other remedies include legal action, which may involve receiving damages and court fees from the user. Both artists and buyers should clearly specify in writing the particular rights bought or sold, including whether the client has permission to scan or alter the art electronically. While vigilance and follow-through are important, a well-written agreement is currently the best overall protection for all parties' rights.

License Your Art

Licensing is big business, presenting tremendous opportunities for graphic artists of all disciplines to generate revenue in new markets. According to *The Licensing Letter's Annual Licensing Business Survey*, retail sales of licensed products in the United States and Canada in 2018 totaled $110.49 billion.

In 2018, the top six licensing property types in retail sales in the United States and Canada were trademarks/brands (26.8% of market); fashion (19.9%); sports (14.5%); entertainment/character (11.7%); celebrities (5.5%); and art and artists (5.3%).

The amount of revenue you can expect to make on licensing as an artist depends on how well your art applies to commercial products, how popular your images are, and how much time you are willing to put into licensing efforts.

Art Licensing

To get an idea of what products offer the most opportunity for artists licensing their work, product categories are listed below by their share of total retail sales for the art-licensing market in 2018.

24.5%-Stationery/Paper	4.0%-Apparel
17.9%-Gifts & Novelties	1.5%-Other
15.9%-Publishing	
10.4%-Housewares	
7.7%-Infant Products	
7.6%-Domestics	
5.7%-Accessories	
4.7%-Furniture/Home Furnishings	

4–3 Art Licensing Categories

Some of the many categories in which artists can license their designs and illustrations include—

* Accessories (jewelry, buttons, headbands, etc.)
* Apparel (T-shirts, hats, other clothing items)
* Crafts (stickers, scrapbooking items, rubber stamps, craft kits, etc.)
* Domestics (bedding, rugs, and throws)
* Electronics (cell phone cases, screen savers, electronic games)
* Games/toys (everything from puzzles to plush)
* Garden (flags, banners, birdhouses, gardening products)
* Gift and collectibles (candles, picture frames, boxes, figurines)
* Gift packaging (gift wrap, tissue, bags, cards)
* Home décor (wallpaper, wall décor, etc.)
* Housewares (tabletop, kitchen, etc.)
* Home furnishings (lamps, tables, chairs, etc.)
* Infant products (bibs, baby bedding, baby clothing, diapers)
* Kitchenware (cutting boards, coasters, towels, trivets, etc.)
* Novelty (magnets, key chains, pencil toppers, etc.)
* Party (paper goods, balloons, decorations)
* Personal care (soap, fragrances, etc.)
* Pet products (food bowls, treats, clothes, etc.)
* Publishing (books, calendars, bank checks)
* Stationery & paper goods (greeting cards, stationery, notepads, etc.)
* Tabletop (melamine, ceramic, china, glassware

See Figure 4-3 for examples of products that are especially suitable for artists who want to license their designs.

Artists interested in licensing their art can keep up with current trends online. There are several blogs devoted to art licensing that cover the annual art licensing trade shows and report on types of art and subject matter that are trending.

ART LICENSING BASICS

Two terms are of particular importance in licensing: *licensor* and *licensee*. The artist or owner/creator of the design or property is called the licensor. The entity that acquires the rights to use the design or property is referred to as the licensee. In art licensing, artists license the right to reproduce their work on a specific product (e.g., a photo album), in a certain territory (e.g., North

America, Australia, worldwide, etc.), for a specified period of time (which is usually two to three years), and sometimes for a particular distribution channel (e.g., mass market, specialty, home shopping, etc.). The artist/licensor maintains the right to license the same design in North America for a different product—perhaps a magnet or a mug—or to license the rights for the same product to a manufacturer who will only sell the product in Asia, South America, or somewhere else in the world not specified in the first licensing agreement.

The artist should avoid entering "all rights" licensing agreements because a single licensee does not produce product in every category. The ability to license the same design in different product categories and territories allows artists to maximize the earning potential of a particular image. It is extremely important to keep a rights database to track which rights have been licensed for each design.

PAYMENT METHODS: FLAT FEE VS. ROYALTY

Unlike other categories of licensing, art licensing does not necessarily involve royalties. Artists can license their work based on either a **flat-fee payment** or on a **royalty basis**.

The advantage to a flat-fee license is that the artist receives money up front, and therefore will not be dependent on the design selling successfully to get further income from it. Also, manufacturers tend to pay a higher flat fee than an advance against royalties. For example, a flat fee for a greeting card design generally ranges between $250 and $900, while an advance—if one is offered—against the average 5–6% royalty tends be between $100 and $400. Because the gift and stationery industries are facing economic challenges, many manufacturers have stopped offering advances. They feel that they are spending tens of thousands of dollars to bring a product to market and that the artists should share in the risk.

According to *The Licensing Letter*'s Annual Licensing Business Survey, the average royalty rate in 2018 in the United States and Canada for licensed merchandise was 8.81%. However, royalty rates vary depending on the industry and are broken down by property type and product category: for example, the average rate based on books was 7.95% (with a range of 6–14%), while art and artists properties paid an average of 6.11% (4–12%). Gift and novelties products paid average royalties of 8.71% (4–16%) versus only 6.34% (3–14%) for housewares products.

Rates also vary by distribution channel. For example, if a product is sold in the mass market (i.e., a major retailer, such as Walmart or Target), the artist may only get a 3–4% royalty, while the same product could receive an 8% royalty if sold in the specialty market (retail gift stores). However, the higher royalty may not generate the largest income. Artists must also take into consideration the potential volume of sales. Artists who have a product at Walmart will invariably make more money, even at a 3% royalty rate, than they would if the product were sold in a gift store at a 9% royalty.

Royalty rates are also negotiable. If no advance is offered, an artist may ask for a higher royalty.

When working on a royalty basis, there is a difference between licensing an existing illustration and asking an artist to spend time creating something new. If a company commissions a design on a royalty basis, it is appropriate to pay the artist an advance in order to cover the time the artist must spend creating the artwork. If the company just wants to license an artist's existing work, an advance is not as critical, as the artist has not had to spend additional time and will start receiving royalty income sooner than if an advance had to be paid off. In other words, no advance means that the artist receives the royalty income sooner.

Some companies, especially start-up concerns, may not have an effective distribution system in place, and if they can't get the product into stores, there will be no sales, so they won't be paying any royalties on it. Artists are advised not to work on a royalty arrangement with start-up companies.

To determine if a royalty arrangement is appropriate, an artist should first ask how many pieces the client plans to produce for its initial and subsequent manufacturing runs. Then the artist can evaluate the options and strike the best deal.

The licensing revenue statistics used in the above three sections were provided by and used with permission of The Licensing Letter, ©2019, www.thelicensingletter.com, info@thelicensingletter.com.

CREATING LICENSABLE ARTWORK

It is important for an artist who is thinking of entering the licensing market to understand why companies manufacture product and what types of designs they are looking for before creating designs specifically for licensing. Many of the companies that license art manufacture gift items. Art appropriate for Christmas and other seasonal needs, as well as life events (birth, birthday, wedding, etc.) is always sought after by licensees.

In the competitive licensing world, it is advisable for artists to provide their artwork in a format that is easy for their licensees to apply to product templates. The best way to do that is to create a "themed collection"—a group of coordinated images that an art director can mix and match to create a saleable product line. This includes a central illustration (or a pair of illustrations) with coordinating frames, borders, background patterns, and icons. It is important to provide these digitally, in layered Photoshop files.

DEVELOPING A MARKETING PLAN

One step in developing a marketing plan is to become familiar with the different categories in which artists can license their designs. See Figure 4-3 for a sample of licensing categories.

Artists should select and prioritize the categories in which they wish to find a licensee, and then research each one to identify those licensees that have a good reputation. Resources and methods for researching categories include trade shows, trade magazines, websites and blogs, books, licensing consultants, networking with other artists who license.

There are tradeshows geared to each of the marketing categories. Attending them can help artists identify companies they would like to approach. If attending a tradeshow isn't feasible, it is possible to gain a lot of information about a company by surfing the Internet and reading trade magazines and books on art licensing. *Licensing Art 101*, *3rd Edition* by Michael Woodward is very informative. A licensing consultant can also help artists identify companies to approach, and networking with other artists who are licensing their work already is an effective way to get information about which manufacturers are easy and desirable to work with. There is an e-mail licensing group on Yahoo, which many designers find helpful (http://groups.yahoo.com/group/TheArtofLicensing/) and an Art of Licensing Group on LinkedIn (https://www.linkedin.com/groups/149470/).

LICENSING AGENTS

Some agents specialize in licensing, but many artists' reps also handle licensing. The advantage of working with a licensing agent or a rep is that agents have contacts with creative directors at a number of companies and can get their client's work seen by the right people. Agents usually handle all the marketing, contract negotiation, billing, and paperwork, so artists are able to concentrate on what they do best—create art. Often agents also provide valuable advice on trends, colors, and themes.

The main disadvantage of working with agents is that they generally take a 40–50% commission, and sometimes require a monthly retainer until a licensee is secured. However, some artists' reps charge the same commission for licensing as they do for other work. Another disadvan-

tage of agents is that because they represent more than one artist, they cannot focus exclusively on the needs of an individual artist. (For more about working with agents, see Chapter 2, Professional Relationships.)

An artist-agent relationship is similar to a marriage—a good one takes work. Licensing agents often specialize in specific product categories or property types, so it makes sense for graphic artists to contact agents in their specialty. Once such an agent is found, the Graphic Artists Guild recommends interviewing the artists the agent already represents to get an idea of what can be expected from the relationship. Some artists hire a licensing consultant (who charges hourly for advice) to help determine if having an agent is in their best interest. Before signing with an agent, be sure you are comfortable with the agent's contract, especially the termination clause.

NONTRADITIONAL LICENSING

All the information discussed above refers to traditional licensing, in which you license your art to manufacturers, who place it on products and sell it in the mass market or to mainstream retailers. Art consultant for creatives Maria Brophy recommends licensing your art to nontraditional markets because you can make more money than in the traditional markets.

Some nontraditional markets she suggests exploring are advertising campaigns, company brands, point-of-purchase displays, online web banners, boutique retailers, niche markets, and any other usage that doesn't fall under traditional licensing.

There are no set royalty rates or dollar amounts for licensing deals in nontraditional markets because fewer artists are doing them, so you can negotiate your own deal. If you are creating new art instead of existing art for a licensee, then make sure you ask for a large enough advance to cover your time.

PROTECTING IDEAS

Whether dealing with potential licensees or with a licensing agent, graphic artists should be careful to protect their ideas by copyrighting their work and by using a nondisclosure agreement, which protects ideas that are not yet fixed in a tangible, copyrightable form. (A model Nondisclosure Agreement for Submitting Ideas is found in the Appendix.)

LICENSING RESOURCES

Three good sources for licensors, licensees, and licensing agents are the *North American Licensing Industry Buyers Guide*, *The Licensing Letter*, and the International

Licensing Industry Merchandiser's Association (LIMA). Another excellent book on licensing is *Licensing Art & Design* by Caryn Leland. Model licensing agreements, reprinted with permission from the book, appear in the Appendix: Contracts & Forms. (For contact information and additional resources, see Part 5, Resources & References.)

Market Your Art

Limited-Edition Prints

While original artwork may sell for thousands of dollars, lithography and serigraphy (silkscreen printing), and most recently, *giclée* printing have made the collection of limited-edition prints, numbered and signed by the graphic artist, within reach of the average collector.

Giclée prints are created using a high-resolution digital scanner. The scan is then printed with an 8–12-color inkjet printer using archival-quality pigment-based inks. The giclée printing process results in greater color accuracy than any other reproduction method used today—so good that giclées have been passed off by unscrupulous art dealers as original works of art.

Artists who want to make their work available to a larger audience can produce prints of their original art (paintings, drawings, photographs, etc.) with a quality that rivals that of traditional silver-halide and gelatin printing processes. Another advantage of giclée printing is prints can be printed on demand, one at a time, avoiding the cost of a large-quantity print run as in offset lithography. As with other limited editions, the file used to create the prints is destroyed at the end of the run to ensure that the work will remain valuable. Signed, numbered, limited edition giclée prints often enable artists to make a sustainable living from their work.

The giclée print is attractive to collectors because they can own a reproduction of a piece of art that rivals museum-quality at a fraction of the cost of an original. Also, giclées can be custom sized to fit the collector's space. There is no difference in resolution between a small print and a large one.

Giclées are more expensive to reproduce than bulk prints made using traditional lithography, and they are priced accordingly.

Art for limited-edition prints may be created independently by graphic artists or under contract with a gallery. Every gallery is different, but generally they pay artists 50–65% of the sale price for limited-edition prints.

In many cases, the prints are submitted to a gallery on spec. The gallery receives a similar commission, although it is more likely to be on the lower end if it's placed on spec. If the gallery is responsible for all production costs, advertising, and promotion, graphic artists traditionally receive less.

A typical edition ranges from 100–250 prints. Each print is usually numbered and signed by the graphic artist. The agreement normally guarantees the artist a certain number of proofs to use in any way he or she wishes. Artists should be aware that limited editions numbering 200 or fewer are granted special moral rights protections under the Visual Artists Rights Act (VARA). These protections include

* The right to claim authorship
* The right to prevent the use of one's name on any work the author did not create
* The right to prevent use of one's name on any work that has been distorted, mutilated, or modified in a way that would be prejudicial to the author's honor or reputation
* The right to prevent distortion, mutilation, or modification that would prejudice the author's honor or reputation

Additionally, authors of works of "recognized stature" may prohibit intentional or grossly negligent destruction of a work.

Marketing can make or break a limited-edition venture. Market research should be conducted prior to entering into a binding agreement, making significant outlays of money, or investing time in creating the art. The market for limited-edition prints is regulated by law in a number of states, including Arkansas, California, Georgia, Hawaii, Illinois, Maryland, Michigan, Minnesota, New York, North Carolina, Oregon, and South Carolina. Extensive disclosures or disclaimers may have to accompany limited-edition prints sold in these states.

Trade practices for graphic artists creating limited-edition prints are the same as those for greeting card, novelty, and retail goods illustration (see Chapter 7, Illustration).

Original Art & Sketches

Graphic artists in certain disciplines supplement their income from commercial work by selling original art and sketches created during the assignment. Original art done by comic book artists is returned to the artists (usually divided between the penciler and the inker). There is a large market for cartoon art composed of fans and collectors. Artists often sell it directly to collectors on their websites or through an agent.

Selling Art Online

The Internet provides artists with several avenues for selling art online.

FROM YOUR OWN WEBSITE

Some artists sell their art from their own websites. They have complete control over the entire process, including pricing, but setting up and managing your own shopping cart can be expensive and quite time-consuming. In order to sell enough to make it worthwhile, you must drive a high volume of traffic to your site, which requires a huge investment in time constantly promoting the site through numerous channels.

You will also need to fulfill all orders yourself, which includes invoicing, packing, shipping, collecting sales tax, and keeping records of sales. Storage space is also a consideration for keeping an inventory of art, products created from your art, and shipping supplies. Consider carefully the cost of materials plus your time to create and promote your art as well as to fulfill orders to see if it makes sense financially to sell from your own website. If you will be making only a few cents on an item, you might consider selling from third-party sites instead.

FROM THIRD-PARTY SITES

There are variations on how these sites work. Two common online models are third-party marketplaces where you set up a "shop" on their platform to sell your original art, crafts, and products and print-on-demand (POD) selling platforms, where you can upload images of your art and have them reproduced on a variety of products, including wall art, clothing and accessories, and decorative household and personal items—everything from pillows to cell phone cases.

THIRD-PARTY MARKETPLACES

One of the more popular third-party marketplaces is Etsy. The main advantage of this type of site is you don't have the expense of setting up and running a shopping cart on your own site. The third-party site may also handle and collect payments for you for a fee and provide a sales tax calculator. However, you are responsible for fulfillment services for any sales made through the site. Fees charged by sites may include listing fees, transaction fees, and processing fees.

PRINT-ON-DEMAND SELLING PLATFORMS

POD sites take most of the work out of selling. They handle both sales and fulfillment and pay you monthly. The other plus is your work is seen by thousands of new site visitors every month—far more traffic than you could drive to your own website.

However, the tradeoff is you make only a fraction of the listing price for each item. Royalties vary from site to site, but they may be as low as 10% of sales. The potential of a high volume of sales may make up for the low royalties. Also, some sites pay higher royalties than you would receive if you licensed your art.

You should research each site you are considering and read its terms of agreement very carefully before you decide to use it to sell your work. Make sure that you retain the copyright to your work. Look at the caliber of art on the site. What is the royalty rate and how do you get paid? You can also ask other artists who use the sites about how financially rewarding they are or do an online search for reviews of the site. It is recommended that for maximum exposure and increased sales you put your art on multiple sites, so make sure a site allows nonexclusivity.

Creating a Niche Market

Artists who want to stand out from the crowd should explore developing a niche market for their art. Instead of trying to sell your art or services to everyone who could use them, focus on one group or demographic of potential customers who could benefit most from your offering. A niche market could stand apart from others because of geographic area; a demographic feature, such as age or gender; profession; lifestyle, activity, or habits; behavior; culture; style; occasion; purpose; or need.

Some examples of artists who create for a niche market are a painter whose specialty is pet portraits, an illustrator who hand-letters and illustrates *ketubot* (Jewish wedding contracts), and a graphic artist who has combined his illustration skills with his love of baseball to paint one-of-a-kind custom baseball gloves. In the latter example, Sean Kane's customers are fans and baseball professionals who commission his gloves as collectibles and as unique, memorable gifts. Read how Sean developed his niche market in Part 4.

To help determine your niche, start by considering the activities or hobbies you love doing the most, what you are most passionate about, the one thing that sets your work apart, a past project you really enjoyed and why it was easy for you, and what you want to focus your time and effort on. You can even develop a niche by using your art to raise awareness of a cause or need.

Develop your reputation in your niche by focusing on

one style, theme, or product until you get really good at it. Eventually, you will become known as the expert in that niche and you will get known for your work.

Target your marketing efforts directly to likely buyers, not people in general. The most likely buyer is someone who loves or appreciates your work, someone who can connect with your work or sees the value in it, and someone who shares your personal values or lifestyle. Plus, a characteristic often overlooked by artists—someone who is capable of paying your price. To connect more personally with your targeted customers, whenever possible, include stories about your art and your life in your promotional efforts.

Create & Sell at Live Events

If you are comfortable creating art and talking about it in front of strangers, live events can be a source of not only revenue but also a way to promote your work.

Creating Art at Events

Cartoonists and caricature artists often are hired to sketch guests at corporate events and private occasions, for both children and adults. Guests get to keep caricatures of themselves as a memento of the event or as a party favor. This type of activity can be done by all kinds of artists who can work quickly and who are creative in matching their art or subject matter to the theme of the event.

CORPORATE ANNUAL MEETINGS

Large companies and corporations book their annual meetings at luxurious venues and hire event planners to make the event memorable for guests. Planners often hire artists as part of the entertainment. Artists are paid from several hundred dollars to in excess of $5,000 for a three-to-four-hour event. How much you can expect to be paid is determined by several factors: the geographic area, your reputation, the size of the event planning company, etc.

To tap into this market, do an online search for event planners in your area and then contact their account manager by e-mail. Introduce yourself and briefly describe your skill, talent, medium, and what you are willing to do live. Include a link to a website, a digital brochure, or photos that showcases your work. Describe what makes you unique or why you would be interesting to guests. Perhaps you can create caricatures of guests as sports figures or action heroes; you are known for your illustrations/paintings of vintage cars, historical subjects, horses, botani-

cals, or food; and so on. Include your contact information and a price list on a separate sheet.

If you don't hear back within a week, follow up with a phone call. When you talk with the accounts manager, ask lots of questions—the kind of clients they do work for, the most popular event themes, what are they looking for artists to do, and most importantly, how can you make their job easier. Event planners look for reliability. With all the arrangements they have to make and the details they have to attend to, especially the day of the event, they want someone who shows up for the job and who needs very little attention. So ask ahead of time about exactly where you will set up and request any special equipment or furniture you might need. It's a good idea to physically check out the venue and space ahead of time so you know where to go and if the accommodations will be adequate for what you are doing. Once you know the theme of the event, you can arrange to bring props that will liven up your space to fit in with the theme but coordinate with the events planner in advance to make sure your props are acceptable. Be sure to bring business cards and a bio about you and your work that you can put on display in your workspace.

Event planners also like being able to purchase small related items from an artist that can be used as giveaways to guests, such as small framed prints, objects with the artists art on them, or objects related to the art or theme. They also like artists who are personable and can interact with guests about their art.

You should make sure to get a signed agreement in advance for the services you will be providing. The agreement should include your pricing for your time (including set up and tear down), and any ancillary items the event planner will be purchasing from you. It should also specify a nonrefundable 50% deposit to paid upon signing, with the stipulation that you will be paid the remaining 50% at the event. For full-day events, charge a day rate plus any expenses (meals, hotel, travel, etc.).

Make sure in any agreement that you have a clause that states that you retain the copyright to your art. This is especially important if you are creating one large piece for the event. You might offer to sell it to the client.

CHARITY EVENTS

Charity events can be both a source of income and an opportunity to promote yourself. Charities hold galas and black-tie events, often as fundraisers with auctions. If you are asked to do live art at one of these events, make sure you are getting paid for your time by treating them like corporate events with a signed contract.

If you are pressed to donate something, you could

consider donating a piece of your art for their auction, making sure your name is promoted along with the piece and your copyright is retained. Another option, if you are just producing one piece of art at the event, is to offer to donate that for their auction. A third option that guests can bid on is to donate two to three hours of your time for live sketching at a private party. This option can serve to get your name out there among people who do a lot of entertaining. If you give art lessons and workshops, you might consider donating a free lesson or free space in one of your workshops.

FASHION EVENTS

Fashion and lifestyle illustrators are often hired to do live sketching at fashion-related events. These events may take place at private parties, runway shows, exhibits, fashion boutiques, and department stores. For example, a store may hold a special event introducing the season's latest line by a specific fashion designer for its big-spending customers. The illustrator is hired to do portraits of guests. Sometimes illustrators are hired by magazines to cover the event, and other times they are hired by the fashion houses themselves. Illustrators who do this type of work report being paid $1,000–$2,000 per event, usually for a two-hour minimum. Supplies and transportation are negotiated separately. In Part 4, illustrator Bil Donovan describes how live sketching at a fashion event resulted in a lucrative contract with a major fashion house.

Selling Art at Live Events

Selling your art at live events gets you out in front of people, where you can get immediate feedback from potential customers.

ART FAIRS & FESTIVALS

Art fairs and festivals are one of the most common ways to sell art live. However, before you commit time and energy to these ventures, you need to consider the costs carefully to see if the financial investment can be offset by potential sales or promotional benefits. Entry fees can be costly, and there is an initial outlay of money for the booth setup and display materials. Most likely you will incur travel-related expenses.

You also need to consider what type of vendors will be exhibiting. Art fairs and festivals run the gamut from people reselling mass-produced merchandise to art produced from craft kits to high-end, unique arts and crafts. Look for fairs and festivals that are juried and require that all merchandise displayed has been hand-produced

by the artist. If you consider yourself a fine artist or highly skilled craftsperson, you don't want your work displayed between vendors selling tchotchkes and kitsch. Nor will you find your perfect customer at these types of shows. They are more likely to attract people who are looking for a day's outing or inexpensive things to buy. The entry qualifications don't tell the whole story. Visit a fair or festival you are considering selling at and talk to other exhibitors, especially ones who have done it for a few years. They can tell you if the investment is worth it or not, and they might also be able to recommend other shows. Also check out different types of booth setups to get ideas for your own booth and how to display your art.

When you prepare your work for an art fair, consider having merchandise at different levels of pricing to accommodate the wallets of different types of attendees. For example, if you mainly sell large original paintings, you might also offer smaller high-quality prints of the paintings or your art reproduced on note cards and select household items.

For resources listing juried fine art fairs, see Part 5: Resources & References.

TRADE SHOWS

Professional trade shows also have hefty booth fees plus setup and travel costs. However, the expense could be viewed as a long-term investment if the show will put your work in front of potential wholesale buyers who can get your art in retail outlets or licensing agents who can get your work on merchandise.

See Part 5, for a list of Conferences, Trade Shows, & Merchandise Markets where you can promote and sell your art.

PRIVATE HOME SHOWS

Some artists turn their home into a gallery for a weekend every year to sell their work. If you do not have an appropriate space, consider asking a friend who does, in exchange for a piece of your art. You also can rent a public space, sharing the cost with a few other hand-selected artists. Having more than one artist may increase attendance. If you do this every year on the same weekend, it will become an annual event that the locals look forward to. For a larger turnout and better publicity, schedule it the same weekend as an annual tourist event in your area.

TOURIST AREAS

For artists who specialize in local scenery, architecture, or landmarks, tourist areas can be a source of increased sales. Tourists love to shop for unique souvenirs as mementos of the places they visit. If you do not have a shop, consider partnering with a restaurant, landmark, or venue frequented by tourists so that you can do live sketching or painting on site. This will attract potential customers, and you can have a supply of finished pieces with you ready to sell.

Self-Publish

Advancements in technology have made it much simpler and less expensive for artists to self-publish books of their art, their art techniques and processes, their knowledge on a certain topic, or a narrative they have illustrated. Many graphic artists already have the software programs needed to self-publish a book in their professional toolbox. A self-published book can promote your art and make you discoverable as an artist, expand your audience to people who admire your work and want to support it but cannot afford original art, and most importantly, provide a passive stream of revenue while you work on other creative projects.

A self-published book does not have to be a four-color, large format, professionally printed coffee-table book, although it can be. Artists also are publishing smaller and less expensive formats. Examples include how-to PDF files, downloadable from an artist's website; pocket-sized promo books of their art to hand out to prospective clients; their art converted to line drawings and marketed as coloring books for adults and children; and how-to workbooks teaching art techniques.

Some artists and photographers who have previously published books of their work through traditional publishing houses have turned to self-publishing because of the control they have over the process and quality. There are several online resources you can access to learn about the ins and outs of self-publishing, some geared specifically to artists. A few of the things you should consider: the format—e-book or a printed book; color or black and white; whether to lay out the book yourself or hire a designer; whether to print on demand or print a run of books; which printer to work with; how to sell the book; and how to promote it.

The format of the book will depend partially on its purpose. If you want it to be a small pocket-sized book as a promotional piece to give to clients, then it would work best printed. If your book will be mostly text and you want to sell it online, you might consider an e-book. If you have design experience, especially with publications, and layout software, you might want to design it yourself. However, if it will be an e-book, you need to learn the lay-

out and file specifications required by the various e-book formats and publishers or hire someone experienced in designing e-books. If the book includes text, it also pays to hire a copy editor to check for grammar, spelling, and usage mistakes. Printing on demand requires less initial outlay of money, but you make less per copy sold, while having a run printed requires a larger investment up front, but you will earn much more per copy, assuming the book sells.

If the book will be printed, there are numerous choices and types of printers. Artists who have researched and used more than one type of printer report that while foreign printers may be less expensive, there can be problems with delays and miscommunication due to language barriers. You can have more control and success with local printers. One self-publishing artist found that the printer she was most happy with on quality, service, and price was her local FedEx store. The quality of the end product is the most important factor as it reflects on your reputation as a professional.

There are numerous self-publishing companies and platforms that can help you get your book published and out to your audience. You can sell from some of these platforms, but they will charge a fee for the service on each book sold, which will reduce your profit. You can also create a shopping cart on your website and sell directly from it. Another option, if it's a print book, is to shop it around to local independent bookstores that sell self-published books.

Promote your book as you would promote your art. Show it prominently on your website's landing page. Start a Facebook page devoted to it. Tweet, post, and blog about it on all your social media. Include a photo of the cover, a description, relevant hashtags, calls to action, and a link to where people can buy it.

Share Your Knowledge

There are many ways that artists can share knowledge about their art to earn extra income.

Educator

Artists have often used a career in education to subsidize their art. Some work full-time as art professors or teachers and create their art on the side. Besides the obvious financial benefits of a full-time, salaried job, there are other benefits as well. As art educators, they have to keep up to date regarding the trends, techniques, equipment, and software for their disciplines. Through their colleagues and the institutions they work for, they have access to networks of other art professionals both locally and nationally. They also may have access to facilities and equipment they could not afford on their own. They also receive inspiration daily from their colleagues and students.

Other artists supplement their income with part-time educational jobs, such as adjunct professors, only teaching one or two courses, so they have more time to spend on their own art.

Workshop Creator

Freelance artists can create other educational opportunities to support their art. For example, if you are a painter, illustrator, cartoonist, web designer, lettering artist, you could create a workshop that teaches your skill to children or other adults. If your first workshop proves successful, you could expand your offering by teaching other techniques or more advanced courses.

There are artists who teach courses in their homes or studios, but if that's not a possibility, there are other ways of doing it. You might teach a workshop or course through a local arts organization, community center, your school district's adult education program, a private studio that offers art courses, or a summer camp. You might partner with a local restaurant, winery, or inn to offer a painting or sketching class or workshop. For the course fee, you offer the lesson and the restaurant provides wine and appetizers, and then you share the profits. In mild weather, you can offer outdoor painting and sketching in public places, but be sure to have a backup plan for inclement weather.

Presenter or Speaker at Professional Conferences

If you are quite experienced and known in your discipline or have expertise in a specific software, business practices for artists, marketing, utilizing social media, interactive design, etc., professional conferences are another possibility for giving a workshop. If you have a talent for public speaking and can motivate others, you might consider speaking at a professional conference on a topic relevant to other artists. Workshops can be geared to a more specific audience, whereas a speech or talk needs to reach a wider group of people. Having an interesting story to tell or experience to share will be more inspiring.

For some conferences, a call for submission goes out for workshop presenters and speakers. For others, presenters are invited to speak.

For a list of professional conferences of interest to graphic artists, refer to Part 5: Resources & References.

Instructional/Tutorial Videos & Online Courses

Creating and selling instructional or tutorial videos is another way that freelancers can diversify their revenue and make their monthly income more stable. Once a video or online course is produced and the cost of production is recovered by initial sales, most of the work is done and the income becomes passive. You will have to continue to market your videos or courses. Social media provides many opportunities for marketing them.

The most-watched YouTube videos are tutorials, according to social media strategist and consultant Sunny Lenarduzzi. A how-to video or course lets you showcase your expertise. You might be asking yourself why anyone would pay to watch your video when there are so many free videos on YouTube. Some of the reasons people pay for content is that paid content is usually more accessible and in one place, saving time searching around the Internet for what you want; it is easier to vet an original creator than someone whose content that has been reposted numerous times; the content is more comprehensive than "freebies"; people value things more when they have a price tag; and many people will also pay for content as a way to support their favorite artists or contribute to a community or movement.

To generate interest in the videos you are selling, do some mini ones first that you share for free on social media (teasers for the paid content)—an effective strategy for not only promoting your videos but also for creating followers and getting yourself and your work known. A good way to get noticed is to create a video that answers a question that no one else is answering. It might be a question you hear often from your clients or a question that you've seen frequently in the comments or Q&A sections on blogs or social media. Since you are the one answering the question, you will appear to be an expert. You can also use video to share a tip based on your industry expertise.

You do not need expensive equipment to produce online videos. Decent videos can be produced using your smartphone with a minimum of additional equipment. Do an online search for how to produce YouTube and Instagram videos. There are several excellent tutorials on YouTube explaining the technical aspects of recording using a smartphone. Once you understand what to do technically, there are other tutorials that explain how to produce effective video content that attracts viewers and keeps them watching.

You can sell your videos from your own website or online store, or you can use a third-party video hosting service, where you can sell your videos on a subscription basis or a one-time purchase basis.

If you want to create and sell courses online, there are several different platforms for doing so, with varying features. An excellent resource that describes the various platforms, how they differ from each other, and their pricing structures is *15+ Platforms to Create and Sell Online Courses (and counting)* by Jeff Cobb of Learning Revolution. His website includes other informative articles about creating and launching online courses (https://www.learningrevolution.net/sell-online-courses/).

School Visits

Schools, especially elementary schools, often have funds for arts education through grants or their parent-teacher associations to bring in visual and performing artists for presentations, workshops, and performances. Children's book illustrators have found that this can be a source of additional income and promotion for the books they illustrate and/or author. Educators like author/illustrator visits because they generate an interest in reading. Ideas for author/illustrator visits might originate with an individual teacher whose class is reading one of your books, the librarian, the art teacher, or an arts education committee.

If you are interested in doing these types of visits, contact schools in your area to find out who is in charge of bringing in outside artists. Then send that person a brochure or links to your website about your work and the school services you offer. Some states that have funding for arts education programs may also maintain lists of presenters; they can be helpful in making contact with schools.

School visits can take several different formats, so have ideas and content in mind with pricing before you contact schools. To generate more interest among students, suggest that the classes you will be visiting read your book(s) prior to your visit. If your books are mainly for younger children, you might do a reading to several small groups, talk about how you create your illustrations, and do some quick sketches of your main characters, which you can donate to the school at the end of the visit. You might also set aside time to sign copies of your books that the children bring. This is a great way to promote your most recently published title.

Similar activities can be done with older elementary and middle-school students, but with more focus on literary techniques (if you are also the author), artistic style and technique, and illustration as an occupation. For high-school art classes, your visit could take the form of a workshop for students in one of your artistic mediums.

Two things are key to successful school visits. First, you have to really like talking to kids. You need to know what is appropriate for different age groups to engage them and keep their interest. You also need to understand something about classroom management and setting expectations, with follow-through. Otherwise, a presentation can quickly turn to chaos, especially in a large room, such as a gym or cafeteria. Visual aids are extremely important, since just talking or holding up a book doesn't hold kids' interest for very long.

The second key to success is to treat a school visit as seriously as the rest of your craft. You need to plan ahead. Approach the presentation like a lesson plan: what are you going to share, how will the audience participate, and what will be the outcomes at the end? Your plan will need to change from book to book and will be different for each grade level. Ideally, you should know something about the standards and curriculum for each grade level, so your content is appropriate for students and useful for teachers. Talking with teachers ahead of time will be beneficial to both of you for planning your visit.

Illustrators who do school visits on a regular basis have discovered that they can also be a lot of fun. Some schools go all out to welcome the illustrators and authors. Students might dress in costumes depicting the artist's characters, decorate the school with murals of their own drawings of the characters, and so on. Children's imaginations are boundless when they are inspired.

Prior to the visit, get a signed agreement, including contact information (both yours and the school's), dates, times, an outline of your services, and your fees (which should include travel expenses if you are going outside your vicinity) and payment method. Due to the possibility that schools may be closed unexpectedly for weather, etc., you should consider including a nonrefundable down payment and a cancellation clause.

Follow up a visit by posting photos or videos from it on your website with a thank you and brief description of how much you enjoyed the visit. Showing your connection with the students and your enthusiasm will go a long way toward getting more school jobs.

An alternative to the in-person school visit for schools outside your travel range is the Skype visit. It is generally priced lower than an on-site visit, but you still need to plan ahead, as well as test the technology.

Follow Your Passion

You may have started a passion project on the side as a creative outlet that you were not getting from your job or your client work. The intrinsic beauty of passion projects are they help keep you motivated and inspired. Creating something you really love has value in itself. It's fun and it's rewarding. A side project can also give you the opportunity to try something new and steer your portfolio in a new direction.

If you are just starting your career, passion projects give you unique pieces for your portfolio and a point of view that is distinctively yours. In a job interview, they can help you stand out from the competition by showing your creativity, work ethic, and personality. Graphic designer Louise Fili is a proponent of passion projects: "I feel very strongly that every designer has to have his /her own personal projects because it's the only way that you really grow and find your design voice."

In more practical terms, passion projects, combined with the promotional power of the Internet, can also lead to additional income. Hand-letterer and designer Lauren Hom blogs about how passion projects are her secret weapon. Read how Lauren used side projects to kick-start her creative career at a relatively young age in Part 4.

Generate interest and exposure for your passion projects by posting about them often on all the social media platforms you are on, starting with your own blog if you have one. Include photos or videos of not just finished projects, but also of you working on them throughout the process—a strategy to create followers and keep them interested enough to keep coming back to view your work.

Learn More

For more in-depth information on maximizing income from your art, an excellent resource from art business consultant Maria Brophy is *Art, Money & Success.* Find more information and resources on her blog (https:// mariabrophy.com/).

An excellent resource for how to utilize social media, especially YouTube, to promote and monetize your art is social media consultant and brand strategist Sunny Lenarduzzi (https://sunnylenarduzzi.com/). She offers many free videos and podcasts on business tips for entrepreneurs, including such topics as finding a niche that pays.

Grow Professionally

As you grow your career, you will need to grow as a professional. There are many resources available to help you increase your knowledge of your field as well as other disciplines in the graphic arts (see Part 5, Resources & References). It will also be helpful to learn about the industries and markets for which you do work, such as corporate culture, education, advertising, entertainment, publishing, and technology.

Start by joining a professional organization in your discipline. The membership fee is money well spent for the benefits you receive in return. Generally, you will have access to other members you can consult for advice, as well as continuing education opportunities. Professional organizations maintain websites that include industry news and issues. Some even offer portfolio pages for members; others post employment opportunities. Many websites include blogs that give you an opportunity to participate in discussions pertinent to your discipline. Professional organizations with local chapters may offer local or regional events, such as mixers, exhibits, workshops, and seminars on topics of interest to graphic artists.

Try to attend a national or regional conference or tradeshow every couple of years. Trade shows provide excellent opportunities to learn about the latest developments and trends in your field, as well as to communicate and share with other professionals. Most offer numerous seminars and workshops for increasing your knowledge and updating your skills. Sometimes you can even be inspired by one of the featured speakers, who represent the top in their field.

Read, watch, learn. You can get all sorts of information and free advice from books, industry magazines, and online resources such as websites, blogs, and discussion groups on social networking sites. The Internet also offers numerous videos geared to the creative professional and tutorials on using social media and various software programs.

Part 1 has introduced you to the essential business practices you need to start on the road to becoming an organized and well-informed professional graphic artist capable of making a sustainable living from your talents. In Part 2, you will gain more specific knowledge about the trade customs, salaries, and pricing for the major graphic arts disciplines as well as many specialties within those disciplines.

Salaries, Pricing Guidelines, & Trade Practices

{ 5 }

Graphic Design

This chapter describes several specialties within graphic design and the many different business environments in which graphic designers apply their talent and skill. Their clients include corporations, advertising agencies, small businesses, manufacturers, non-profit organizations, publishers, retailers, entrepreneurs, and educational institutions, encompassing all facets of commercial, social, and cultural life.

GRAPHIC DESIGNERS *use design elements —color, typography, illustration, photography, animation, and printing or programming techniques—to organize ideas visually in order to convey a desired impact and message. In addition to exercising aesthetic judgment and project management skills, the professional graphic designer draws on experience in evaluating and developing effective communication concepts and strategies that enhance a client's image, service, or product. For a general discussion of the scope of what designers do, review the Graphic Designer Professional Relationships section in Chapter 2.*

Graphic design is applied in a wide variety of visual communications, including, but not limited to, printed materials such as periodicals, books, and advertisements; packaging and products; and identity systems and promotional campaigns for business and industry through logos and collateral promotion. Graphic design talent is also crucial to digital communications, advertising, and social media on the Internet; interactive media; and to the broadcasting and film industries. (For more information on Web design and design for other digital platforms, see Chapter 6, Web/Interactive Design.)

According to the results of the 2019 Design Census, created by Google and AIGA, 70% of graphic designers who responded work as full-time salaried employees at a company, design firm, or other entity, where they may be principals or staff designers. Another 18% work as freelancers or self-employed/small business owners, and 4% work as educators. Graphic designers generally work with or hire other graphic designers, illustrators, production artists, and photographers. Almost all graphic designers buy and sell art.

The Design Census also found that almost 50% of designers work in either very small companies of 1–10 employees (25%) or very large companies of 1,000+ employees (22%). Because the level of experience of a design practice, the scope of project services provided, and the overhead expenses may vary considerably, graphic design is one of the most difficult areas for which to identify pricing practices. Most design firms negotiate a project fee, while a freelancer's base fee is often billed at an hourly rate. Regardless of whether or not a freelancer starts with a base hourly rate for time, each project is unique and needs to be priced according to the variables and components of the project as well as the end usage.

Graphic Design Salaries
Overview

The salary figures provided in this chapter reflect the current market for professional graphic designers holding full-time staff positions in the United States. The salaries listed for each position reflect starting pay only, meaning the salary an employee would receive when first starting at a company, but not necessarily an entry-level salary, because employees start at companies with various levels of experience.

The salary figures do not include benefits and perks, such as health insurance, paid time off, retirement savings plans, maternity/paternity leave, workplace wellness programs, free food, flexible work arrangements, etc.—since these can vary widely among employers. In general, many employers do offer a benefits package to full-time employees that includes vacation, holiday, and sick pay. For health insurance, employees are frequently required to contribute part of their premiums and to use health maintenance organizations (HMOs). Bonuses, stock options, and retirement plans may be available, but these benefits usually depend upon company policy regarding salaried personnel. Job seekers should evaluate the entire package when weighing offers.

Salary Ranges

In most corporate settings each job title has a salary range, and new employees are often hired at the low end of the range to provide room for future raises. The following U.S. design salary ranges are taken from *The Creative Group 2021 Salary Guide*. They are based on job searches, negotiations, and placements managed by The Creative Group's staffing and recruiting professionals.

The ranges represent national averages, with the lower figure representing the 25th percentile and the higher figure representing the 75th percentile. The Creative Group defines figures at the 25th percentile as salaries of employees who may be new to the position or still developing relevant skills, or in a low-demand role. Figures at the 75th percentile represent salaries of employees who have more experience than is typical or most or all relevant skills, or in a high-demand role. The *Salary Guide* also provides salary figures at the 50th and 95th percentiles.

Salary ranges can be further adjusted for specific U.S. and Canadian cities by using the variance numbers on pages 17–19 and page 30 of the *Salary Guide*. *The Creative Group 2021 Salary Guide*, as well as a salary calculator for customizing pay ranges for more than 550 cities, can

be accessed at http://creativegroup.com/salary-center.

* **Creative Director** $93,000–140,250[1]
* **Art Director** $68,750–103,000[1]
* **Project Manager** $57,250–82,750[1]
* **Studio Manager** $54,500–77,500[1]
* **Graphic Designer** $43,250–68,000[1]
* **Production Artist** $43,000–60,250[1]
* **Environmental Designer** $55,500–81,250[1]
* **Package Designer** $48,500–71,000[1]

Below are annual salary ranges, as of September 2020, for additional job titles from ZipRecruiter, an online employment marketplace. The ranges represent U.S. salaries from the 25th to the 75th percentile; ZipRecruiter considers figures below the 25th percentile and above the 75th percentile as outlier figures.

* **Book Designer** $33,000–62,500[2]
* **Broadcast Designer** $60,000–94,000[2]
* **Exhibit Designer** $41,500–60,500[2]
* **Photo Retoucher** $21,000–54,000[2]
* **Publication Designer** $40,000–80,000[2]

Freelance Graphic Design
Economic Outlook

The economic outlook for freelance graphic designers has changed considerably during the last two decades. Freelancing itself has become a force to be reckoned with in the labor market.

In a study published in 2016 by Paychex, who analyzed 400,000 freelancers' resumes posted on the job site, Indeed.com, they found that the freelance economy took off during the new millennium. Between 2000 and 2014, freelance jobs listed on the resumes they examined increased by over 500%.

Several factors contributed to this dramatic increase in the gig economy. While some graphic designers may have started freelancing during the recession of 2008 when staff opportunities dried up, many of today's workers prefer the flexibility of the freelance lifestyle, which accommodates family time, travel, and hobbies. Businesses are also more interested in hiring freelancers. For many companies, the need to cut payroll and insurance

---

1. Salaries reprinted with permission from *The Creative Group 2021 Salary Guide,* ©2020 Robert Half International.
2. Source of salary ranges: ZipRecruiter (www.ziprecruiter.com), as of September 29, 2020.

expenditures has led to an increase in outsourcing. For graphic designers, this has been a double-edged sword. While it has increased freelancing opportunities, it has also caused layoffs in the profession.

Technology has also played a role in the increase in freelancing. In the past, companies may have been reluctant to hire remote workers, but today's technology enables freelancers to stay seamlessly connected with their clients. At no time in recent history has the ability of employees to work remotely been more valuable for businesses than in the coronavirus pandemic of 2020.

Technology also empowers freelancers to conquer what is arguably their biggest challenge: finding work. The spike in freelancing coincides with the launch of numerous online marketplaces in the late 1990s and the 2000s, dedicated to connecting independent contractors with potential clients. These platforms completely revolutionized the playing field for freelancers.

According to the Paychex study, graphic designers dominate the world of freelancing in 34 states. The most freelancing opportunities exist, not surprisingly, in large cities, such as Los Angeles and New York, and around tech centers, such as Seattle and Denver. Graphic designer's gigs are more varied than ever.

The growth of freelancing is not slowing down. In 2019, freelancers earned an estimated $1 trillion, or almost 5% of the Gross Domestic Product, contributing a significant share to the U.S. economy—more than industries such as construction and transportation.

"Freelancing in America: 2019," an annual study commissioned by the Freelancers Union and Upwork, the world's leading freelancing website, found that from 2014 to 2019, the number of full-time freelancers increased from 17% to 28%, and freelancing is becoming more of a long-term career choice. For the first time, as many freelancers said they view this way of working as a long-term career choice as they do a temporary way to make money. The study also found that freelancing provides opportunities and flexibility for those who otherwise might not be able to work for a traditional employer due to personal circumstances. These trends are expected to continue into the future. Although all generations surveyed had more than 25% of its workers freelancing, 40% of millennials (ages 23–38) and a majority (53%) of Gen Z workers (ages 18–22) freelanced. While freelancing has become a long-term career choice for an increasingly diverse group, they continue to face significant challenges, such as access to affordable healthcare and protections so they can get paid fairly and on time for the work they do.

Historically, a major problem for graphic designers and other freelancers has been collecting the money owed them by clients. More than 70% of gig workers in New York City report having been cheated out of payments, paid many months late, or paid less than they were owed. The Freelancers Union launched a campaign to support and publicize a bill introduced by Councilman Brad Lander to address this problem. As a result of this campaign, the Freelance Isn't Free Law was signed into law in New York City on November 16, 2016. (For a detailed explanation of this law, see the section on The Importance of Contracts for Freelancers in Chapter 12.)

These challenges and others facing freelancers are discussed thoroughly in Chapter 3, Professional Issues.

Trade Practices

WRITTEN AGREEMENTS

Since designers work with a variety of graphic resources, it is important that all conditions and expectations be spelled out in writing in a contract, letter of agreement, or purchase order before the work begins. (See Chapter 12, Standard Contracts & Business Tools for more detailed information about these documents, and the Appendix: Contracts & Forms for samples of each type.)

The information to include in a written agreement is also discussed in Chapter 1 under the section, Keeping Track. Some considerations specific to graphic design agreements are discussed below:

Payment: Larger projects are often broken down into smaller payments made at more frequent intervals, rather than the total fee being paid at the completion of the project. For example, a third of the payment might be made upon signing the agreement, a third upon approval of design comps, and the final third within 30 days of delivery of digital files for production. Payment for other large projects might be broken down by quarters or by significant junctures in the project. Very lengthy projects might be negotiated to be paid on a monthly retainer basis.

Rights: Most contracts include a section specifying how, when, where, and the duration for which the design will be used. The extent of use determines which copyrights the client needs and will be a factor in establishing appropriate fees. Graphic designers are often entitled to credit and copyright, unless another arrangement is negotiated.

Subcontractors: Designers often contract with freelance illustrators, other designers, and photographers for work on a limited-use basis for specific projects. Unless specified otherwise in writing, it is assumed that the creator owns the copyrights to the work, not the client or the designer. It is fairly common, therefore, for copyrights to be held by several different contributors to a project, who may all deserve the same acknowledgment and rights on the piece or group of pieces. (For a more in-depth discussion of these and related issues, see Chapter 11, Legal Rights & Issues.)

Payment is due in a timely manner to sub-contractors hired by the designer, regardless of when the designer receives payment from the client.

All terms and conditions of working with independent artists should be clearly outlined in writing (in a contract, letter of agreement, or estimate and confirmation form) and reviewed prior to the commission. (See Chapter 12, Standard Contracts & Business Tools.)

Reimbursable Expenses: In addition to the designer's fee, expenses reimbursed by the client typically include sub-contractors' fees, digital output and file storage, supplies, travel, and overnight shipping services. Data indicate that the markup for these services, when charged, usually ranges from 10 to 30%, but it can go as high as 50%, depending on the discipline. The markup reimburses the designer for supervisory and handling time and helps ensure that all work is done to the designer's specifications and standards of quality. Reimbursable expenses can be billed monthly, upon completion of project phases, or upon completion of the project.

Responsibilities of the client: The client is usually responsible for copywriting, providing copy in an electronic form, proofreading, and sometimes press approval.

Consultation fees: When a graphic designer is called in by a client to advise on a project or design decision, consultation fees are often based on an hourly rate.

GENERAL TRADE PRACTICES

The following trade practices have been used historically for graphic design and thus are accepted as standard:

1. The intended use of the design, the price, and the terms of sale must be stated clearly in the contract, letter of agreement, or purchase order.
2. The usage of a design influences the price. If the design will be featured over an extensive geographical area or is an all-rights sale, fees are significantly higher than when used locally, within a selected area, or for limited usage.
3. Depending on the discipline, many designers charge higher fees for rush work, either as an additional percentage of the original fee or as an additional flat fee. A job may be considered a rush if the designer

is requested to do the work on a greatly abbreviated schedule.

4. If a client wants to use a design for something other than the original purpose negotiated in the agreement, the designer should negotiate reuse arrangements with the original commissioning party with speed, efficiency, and respect for the client's needs. It is recommended that the designer add the terms of reuse in the initial contract (for example, "Reuse will be granted for two years at 50% of the original fee per instance"). Note that the secondary use of a design may be of greater value than the primary use. Although there is no set formula for reuse fees, surveys indicate that designers in certain disciplines add a reuse fee as a percentage of the fee that would have been charged had the work been originally commissioned for the anticipated use.

5. Return of original artwork, computer discs, or digital files to the designer should be automatic and should be done in a timely manner, unless otherwise negotiated. Note: This may affect sales tax requirements in some states.

6. If a job is canceled through the fault of someone other than the designer, a cancellation fee, or "kill fee," is charged. Depending upon the stage at which the job is terminated, the fee paid should reflect all work completed or hours spent, and any out-of-pocket expenses.

7. A rejection fee is usually agreed upon if the assignment is terminated because the client finds the preliminary or finished work to be less than satisfactory. Depending on the reason for the rejection, the rejection fee for finished work is often equivalent to the charge for the number of hours spent on the job. (See the Cancellation and Rejection Fees section under Pricing Your Services in Chapter 1.)

8. No new or additional designer or firm should be hired to work on a project after a commission begins, without the original designer's knowledge and consent. The original designer may then choose, without prejudice or loss of fees owed for work completed, to resign from the account or to agree to collaborate with the new design firm.

9. Major revisions or alterations initiated by the client (*author alterations*, or *AAs*) are usually billed at the designer's hourly rate. In such cases, the designer will apprise the client of anticipated billing and obtain authorization prior to executing the additional work.

10. Designers are entitled to a minimum of five samples of the final piece.

The Graphic Artists Guild strongly opposes the following practices and recommends avoiding them:

1. **Working on speculation:** Designers considering this work arrangement assume all risks and should take them into consideration when offered such arrangements. (Read more about Speculation under Entrepreneurial Issues in Chapter 3.)

2. **Work-made-for-hire contracts:** In these types of contracts, authorship and all rights that go with it are transferred to the commissioning party, and the independent designer is treated as an employee for copyright purposes only. The independent designer receives no employee benefits and loses the right to claim authorship or to profit from future use of the work forever. *Work made for hire* is a narrow exception to copyright law, and it only applies to certain situations. For example, corporate logo designs are ineligible to be done under work-made-for-hire contracts because they do not fit its legal definition. (In-depth information on work-made-for-hire contracts can be found in Chapter 11, Legal Rights & Issues.)

However, *all-rights transfers* of such work to clients are common. Graphic artists often ask what the difference is between work-made-for-hire contracts and all-rights transfers. Work-made-for-hire contracts strip away not only the graphic artist's rights, but his/her authorship as well. All-rights transfers are preferable because the artist retains authorship and statutory termination rights.

Using the Pricing Charts

When using the pricing charts in this chapter to figure out how to price a design job, consider them as only a starting point. There is no one set price—each project has its own specifications, design considerations, and level of complexity. These prices, which reflect the responses of established design professionals, are meant as a point of reference only. They do not necessarily reflect such important factors as geographical differences in cost of living; deadlines; job complexity; reputation and experience of a particular designer; research; technique or unique quality of expression; number of deliverables; and extraordinary or extensive use of the finished design, or the usage rights being transferred. Flat fee pricing in this book is often given in ranges, based on the lowest and highest figures that design professionals have reported for that type of job. Those professionals at the top of their field, with a

5–1 Median Hourly Rates Paid to Graphic Design Freelancers*

Creative Director	$ 125
Art Director	$ 125
Senior Designer	$ 100
Designer	$ 80
Print Production Manager	$ 75
Print Production Artist	$ 65

The median hourly rates in this chart were compiled from the results of a national survey of graphic artists conducted by the Graphic Artists Guild in 2020. Responses reflect hourly rates paid to freelance designers by other graphic artists during 2018 and 2019.

*Note: A median is the middle number between the highest and lowest values in a set of sorted data. Therefore, the hourly rates reported on the survey may be significantly higher or lower than the median, depending on the industry, geographic area, size of market, type of media, and a designer's skill level and years of experience.

national or even international reputation, may be able to charge fees even higher than those listed in the charts.

View the prices in the charts as guidelines only. More importantly, you will need to estimate how long you think a particular project will take and multiply the hours by your hourly rate to get a sense of what a realistic base price might be. Then add on the estimated cost of materials, outside services that you are responsible for, the usage rights you are granting, etc., to arrive at a project price. Even if you present a flat project fee to the client, you need to figure out in advance how much time it will take you to do the job. Doing so will also help you schedule the project realistically.

A formula for determining your hourly rate is provided in Chapter 1, Essential Business Practices. Sample Median Hourly Rates for different types of freelance design responsibilities are provided in Figure 5–1 to use as a guide.

Corporate Graphic Design

Corporate graphic designers specialize in business communications, identity programs, brand standards, signage, internal and promotional publications, and annual reports for companies and institutions such as hospitals, universities, and museums. A team specializing in this area of design may include a principal of the firm, an art director, designer(s), production manager, copywriter, and project manager. Or a graphic design department can consist of one person, who handles multiple functions.

Since graphic design projects often involve long-term strategic research and development, corporate designers are frequently brought in at the earliest planning stages. Some corporate designers work on retainer and also act as design consultants in peripheral areas in addition to their main projects. They may be involved in the creation of brand standards or a brand's graphic standards.

Phases of a Project

A corporate design project begins once a client accepts the design proposal outlining the scope of the project, its budget, schedule, and the terms under which it will be executed.

A project might be broken down into three or five phases, depending on the amount and complexity of the work being done or on how much detail the client wants to see. Below is an expanded five-phase project. Often, in a three-phase project, Phases 2 and 3 (Concept Development and Design Refinement) are combined as are Phases 4 and 5 (Design Implementation and Production). An example of a three-phase project is given under the Corporate Identity section.

Phase 1. Research & Planning: This phase is concerned with gathering information and establishing design criteria. It often requires spending a great deal of time with the client to define the needs, objectives, and problems to be solved, as well as identify the primary audience, the primary message, and the client's main competitors.

Phase 2. Concept development: After the designer and client have reached an agreement concerning the basic project, visual solutions are pursued that meet the stated objectives. This phase results in a presentation showing only the ideas that the design team feels are viable, appropriate, and meet the prescribed criteria.

Phase 3. Design refinement: At this stage, the design team refines the accepted design, which may include general format, typography, color, other elements, and the assignment of illustration and/or photography. A final presentation may be made to the client explaining the refined applications. Any changes in budget and/or schedule are agreed upon at this point.

Phase 4. Design implementation: Decisions on all related art direction, including commissioned illustrations and photography, typography, copywriting, layouts or digital files, and all other elements, are final at this point. Designer errors or printer errors (PEs) are not billable after this point, but all AAs are. The client may make changes in files or on press only through the designer. Conversely, the designer may execute design alterations, either in files or on press, only with the client's final approval.

Phase 5. Production: This phase only applies to design projects that have specific deliverables. It may be a matter of going on press, supervising the fabrication or manufacturing of products, or launching a website. Supervision is the key to this phase, since achieving the designer's vision depends on the precision and quality attained in this final step. After the end product is approved, the project is considered billable.

Corporate Identity

The objective of a properly executed corporate identity program is the accurate visual presentation of an organization's unique personality. The client's initial focus may be on the development of a new "mark" or logo, but a complex procedure involving several phases and a wide range of expertise is required to furnish a full-fledged, professionally executed corporate identity program.

A typical three-phase corporate identity program includes the following:

Phase 1. Research & Planning: This phase of the program focuses on gathering information and establishing design image criteria. A creative brief is developed by the designer after interviewing the client.

If applicable, an audit of all existing branded materials is conducted to weigh any existing brand equity. Identities of competitors are collected to ensure differentiation. Main criteria are brand recognition and brand awareness.

A significant sampling of visual materials is collected and evaluated, and interviews are conducted with various relevant audiences. Communication objectives, a plan of action, and a nomenclature (hierarchy and system of language to be used within the identity system) are established.

A large potential part of identity projects is naming/renaming. If naming is needed, exploration of a name is started with brainstorming, considering mouth-feel and possible confusion with other words. Then a trademark search and available URL search is conducted once choices are narrowed.

Phase 2. Design development: In this creative phase, design ideas for the mark, logo, or other primary identification device are developed. Applications to stationery, signage, and digital media must also be presented to demonstrate the versatility of each design, as well as legibility in one color versus full color. Recommendations are also made regarding color schemes and secondary typography. The design selection process should be made according to the approved image criteria, not based on individual taste or subjective preference.

Phase 3. Implementation: This phase of the program is where the brand is expanded beyond the logo concept. Sufficient application formats must be developed to visually demonstrate the nature of the corporate identification system. Guidelines (usually in the form of a brand standards manual or a brand's graphics standards manual) establish the management-endorsed design policy and implementation procedures. Rules governing proper usage of the program's design elements, formats, templates, typography/font application, and nomenclature are presented, including reproduction materials for graphics and color guidelines.

Finally, organizations that want to make the most effective use of a visual corporate identity program either contract for a long-term consulting agreement with the design firm or establish a properly administered in-house communications department. A third option is to utilize a combination of both.

A corporate identity project often involves the creation of or redesign of an organization's website. Website Design and pricing is covered in Chapter 6

Logo Design

Logos are the most recognizable representation of a company or an organization. Although they are relatively small images, they contain a lot of meaning about the company. Good logos convey the core principles of an organization and what that organization does. And, in an age of visual overload, logos need to communicate quickly and effectively for their brand.

Although the design of a logo may be the first component to be developed in a comprehensive corporate identity program (see above), a designer may be contacted initially to design only a logo. This is often the case with clients who are starting small businesses. Or, in other cases, a company already has an established identity program but wants to redesign an existing logo.

The best logo designs have the following attributes and answer the following questions:

1. **Simplicity:** Is the design simple, yet distinctive enough, to be easily recognizable? Not too busy, distracting, or confusing. Often, a black and white version of the logo will be needed. The logo should be able to be reduced to only one color and still maintain a great presence.
2. **Memorability:** Can it be recognized quickly? Is it unique? Will people be able to get it in only a second or two?
3. **Timelessness:** Will it still be a great logo, years or even decades from now? A timeless logo may be contemporary, but it is not trendy.
4. **Versatility:** Can it be scaled to different sizes without losing quality or clarity? Will it work across all media and applications, from a business card to a phone screen to the side of a truck?
5. **Relevance:** Does it resonate with the targeted audience and is it appropriate for the industry of the business? Does it reflect the services it offers or tie to the organization's vision?

These attributes of effective logo design cannot be found by simply using templates, pieced-together clip art, and recycled stock images because they have not been created with the client's specific company, industry, and targeted audience in mind. The best logos are created by professional designers who do extensive research to understand the client's company, its customers, and the uniqueness of the products or services it offers and then custom design a distinctive logo to reflect those factors.

The process used for designing a logo is similar to other corporate identity projects (see previous section). It includes the following steps: researching the client and the industry, brainstorming and sketching, executing the design, presenting it to the client in applications relevant to the client's needs, revising and getting approval, and delivering it to the client in various file formats for numerous applications: viewing, print, and web. Black and white monotone versions are also supplied. The logo is created in a vector format so that it can be scaled to a wide variety of sizes without loss of quality or sharpness.

Branding Design

While corporate identity is about the look and feel of the business, branding relates to the emotional relationship between a customer and a business and its products. Often, a sense of differentiation or exoticism is evoked by a brand campaign to captivate the consumer. Branding is also a response to the proliferation of information anywhere, anytime, in any form. A unique and identifiable

5–2 Comparative Fees for Corporate Graphic Design

The pricing ranges in this chart do not constitute specific prices for particular jobs. The buyer and seller are free to negotiate, with each designer independently deciding how to price the work, after taking all factors into account. Reading the more detailed information, Pricing Your Services, provided in Chapter 1, will help in pricing projects for your specific situation.

Hourly Rates

Designer	PRINCIPAL OF FIRM	CONSULTANT
$65–175	$120–200	$100–250

Flat Project Fees (Initial Deposit: 25–50% of estimated fees & expenses)

	GLOBAL/NATIONAL CLIENT	REGIONAL/LOCAL CLIENT
Comprehensive Branding/ID	$7,500–50,000	$1,500–20,000
Comprehensive Logo Design	$4,375–30,000	$1,250–15,000
Limited Logo Design	$1,500–17,500	$1,000–7,500
Stationery System	$1,000–15,000	$750–8,000
Comprehensive Website Design–Static	$3,000–30,000	$2,000–10,000
Comprehensive Website Design–Dynamic	$6,500–50,000	$3,000–40,000
Annual Report (print)	$7,500–15,000	$1,500–7,000
Annual Report (downloadable PDF)	————————	$1,500–7,000

Additional Fees

MARKUPS (% above cost)

Out-of-pocket expenses	10–30%
Outside services	10–50%

EXTRA ROUND OF REVISIONS   100–150%
(Not included in original agreement; % of original fee)

USAGE (% of original fee)

Total copyright transfer	125–300%
Sale of original artwork	80–200%

CANCELLATION & REJECTION FEES (% of original project fee)

Prior to completion of concept phase	25–50%
After completion of preliminary work	50–75%
After completion of finished work	70–100%

Designers who charge by the hour bill for the number of hours worked up to the date of cancellation or rejection, plus any expenses incurred.

RUSH WORK (% added onto normal fee)

24-hour turnaround	25–100%
48-hour turnaround	20–100%
Holidays & weekends	25–100%

The above rates and fees were compiled from the results of a national survey of graphic artists conducted by the Graphic Artists Guild in 2020. Responses were based on rates charged in 2018 and 2019.

look associated with a certain product makes its design—including advertising, packaging, and direct mail promotion—more important than ever.

Designers use the usual tools of form, color, texture, graphics, typestyle, and other imagery to evoke emotions connecting a consumer to a brand so the consumer will continue to buy it. Designers who specialize as brand identity consultants need to have a special understanding of the universal emotional, psychological, and visceral meanings of color, shape, and form. They usually also take into account the brand essence, brand loyalty, marketing considerations (such as demographics and psychographics), and other factors when working on a branding design. Armed with that knowledge, brand designers show that well-defined, well-designed brand imagery applied consistently can produce big dividends for many commodities.

Annual Reports

It should be noted that quality print versions of annual reports, a former mainstay of corporate graphic design, are rare. Companies have replaced printed reports with online versions that are designed and produced in-house, with the work being done by their website designer. Midsize companies put their annual reports online, too, for economic reasons, but as 8½" x 11" PDF files. Not-for-profits thank donors online and through their newsletters.

Pricing

Corporate design projects are often quoted and billed by phase, with an initial fee representing 25 to 50% of total estimated fees and reimbursable expenses to ensure that the designer will be paid if the project is canceled in mid-schedule.

Billing is handled in a number of ways. During the first phase, the designer will arrange to bill on either an hourly or project basis. If clients prefer to be billed on a project basis, they usually establish an acceptable limit ("cap") on the total amount, but the designer needs to clearly spell out at the onset of a project that the client cannot request unlimited revisions without additional compensation. For large or lengthy projects, bills may be sent out periodically (usually monthly) or at the completion of each phase of the project.

Bills for expenses and outside services usually include a markup (except for costs incurred for client-approved travel). Sales tax is rarely included in expense estimates and is usually billed periodically or at the end of the project along with AAs, which are billed at a predetermined hourly rate. Some vendors (such as printers) in some states may require proof of resale (such as a resale permit issued by the county or state) prior to billing; otherwise, sales tax may be added to the invoice.

Costs related to production or printing are the responsibility of the client and may be billed by the studio or directly to the client, depending on a particular designer's practice. The printer and all other professionals working with the designer are accountable to the designer and are ethically bound to follow the designer's directions while working on the project, regardless of who pays the printer. This becomes a matter of practicality as well, since the designer orchestrates many elements and must control them to ensure consistency.

See Figure 5-2 for sample Corporate Graphic Design fees.

Advertising & Promotion Design

Advertising designers must have a sophisticated knowledge of marketing, sales, and advertising print production in addition to design skills. Because they are experts in a variety of disciplines, they can successfully coordinate a company's visual identity with its marketing. Consequently, more and more of these designers are being asked by clients to replace advertising agencies. In these cases, designers often apply for agency status to be eligible for the "agency discount" when placing advertising with magazines and newspapers.

Specific Trade Customs

It is common practice for several agencies to pitch the client (known as the "account") on speculation, presenting ideas for upcoming advertising campaigns. The investment and risks involved are usually accepted by advertising agencies because of the tremendous ongoing rewards that may be gained from media placement, should the agency win the account. Graphic designers, who do not enjoy the media placement commissions, must assess these speculative risks much more critically. Since ideas are a designer's stock in trade, it is the industry's standard not to do work on speculation.

The designer's role is to work as part of a creative team composed of a copywriter, an account executive, and/or a public relations professional. When the designer works as part of a team, the proposal presented to the client usually includes a strategy as well as a design solution.

Since the Internet, tablets, and mobile devices are a major presence and revenue source for most newspapers and magazines, designers have to be able to create artwork for both print and digital. It is best to ask ahead of time if both digital and print media will be used, because each requires a different preparation of artwork. When designing for dual formats, the artwork needs to be created first in RGB at a high resolution (at least 300 ppi) and then optimized to somewhat lower resolutions for the Internet and digital devices. Then the RGB artwork is converted to CMYK with the resolution of 300 ppi maintained as a minimum for print production.

When images are converted from RGB to CMYK, they can suffer a loss in quality, since RGB has a larger color spectrum than CMYK has. This drastic "dulling" effect needs to be compensated for by adjusting hue and saturation. To be on the safe side, many designers will design to accommodate possible additional future use. A designer can always downsample artwork from 300 ppi to a lower resolution but cannot upsample from a lower resolution to 300 ppi.

Pricing

The designer agrees to work with an advertising agency for at least the length of the entire advertising campaign, a long-term rather than project-based relationship. Traditionally, most graphic design firm fees have been based on hourly or per-project estimates, and designers have not enjoyed a percentage of the ongoing revenue generated from a successful campaign, although many alternative arrangements are possible.

In a survey of U.S. graphic designers conducted by the Graphic Artists Guild in 2020, respondents working freelance in advertising and promotion design reported that they charge either an hourly rate based upon a total estimated number of hours, or a flat fee based on the scope of the project. A designer may also negotiate a retainer. Some designers are able to negotiate a percentage of the total project fee to be paid up front upon signing a retainer agreement. When working on retainer, some designers discount their rates.

If the designer is hired to create a single ad, a price based on the type of placement is negotiated. Ad placement on the inside front cover, for example, is more expensive than the back of the book. Circulation figures of a publication also affect the price of an ad. A full-color, full-page advertisement in *Rolling Stone* magazine usually commands a higher fee than a small black-and-white ad in a limited-run trade publication. (For more information on how advertising factors affect pricing, see Chapter 1, Essential Business Practices.)

Graphic designers who specialize in advertising and promotion design often handle posters, press kits, outdoor advertising and promotion, as well as graphics for Internet, mobile, and tablet advertising and e-mail promotions, so consistent application of graphic design is essential across all channels of advertising.

Since designers working in this field hire other graphic artists on a freelance basis and purchase art and photography on behalf of their clients, they must have a good working knowledge of advertising illustration and photography, including trade customs that govern both fields.

The price ranges in Figure 5-3 assume limited use of advertising design with up to five insertions within a specified media for one year. Unlimited usage increases fees and is charged as a percentage of the original price.

5–3 Comparative Fees for Advertising & Promotion Design

The pricing ranges in this chart do not constitute specific prices for particular jobs. The buyer and seller are free to negotiate, with each designer independently deciding how to price the work, after taking all factors into account. Reading the more detailed information, Pricing Your Services, provided in Chapter 1, will help in pricing projects for your specific situation.

Hourly Rates

DESIGNER	PRINCIPAL OF FIRM	CONSULTANT
$30–125	$75–125	$50–150

Flat Project Fees

MAGAZINE ADS (PRINT)	COVER	SPREAD	FULL-PAGE	½-PAGE	¼-PAGE
Consumer Magazines	$500–5,000+	$500–2,500+	$300–900+	$150–600+	$125–400+
Business Magazines	$750–5,000	$700–1,800+	$350–1,000+	$350–750+	$150–500+

Flat Project Fees

MAGAZINE ADS (DIGITAL)	STATIC	ANIMATED	INTERACTIVE
Consumer–Online	$125–1,200	————	$250–1,500
Web Banner Ad	$120–800+	$200–1,000	$250–800+
Tablet/Mobile	$150–600+	$250–750	$250–800+
Business–Online	$125–800	————	$150–800+
Web Banner Ad	$150–800	$350–800	$200–500+
Tablet/Mobile	$350–800	$750–1,200	$350–1,000

NEWSPAPER ADS (PRINT)	FULL-PAGE	½-PAGE
Daily	$100–4,500	$75–1,500
Weekly	$100–1,000	$75–500

NEWSPAPER ADS (DIGITAL)	STATIC	ANIMATED	INTERACTIVE
Web Banner Ad	$75–500	$100–800	$100–800

BILLBOARDS

Print	$200–4,000
Digital	$100–3,000

Additional Fees

MARKUPS (% above designer's cost)

Out-of-pocket expenses	5–50%
Outside services	5–65%

EXTRA ROUND OF REVISIONS 110–150%
(Not included in original agreement; % of original fee)

USAGE (% of original fee)

Reuse in original market	100–120%
Unlimited in any media, incl. digital for 1 yr.	100–200%
Total copyright transfer	125–300%
Sale of original art	100–300%
Stock sale or existing art	100–125%

CANCELLATION & REJECTION FEES (% of original project fee)

Prior to completion of concept phase	25–50%
After completion of preliminary work	50–100%
After completion of finished work	50–100%

Designers who charge by the hour bill for the number of hours worked up to the date of cancellation or rejection, plus any expenses incurred.

RUSH WORK (% added on to normal fee)

24-hour turnaround	25–100%
48-hour turnaround	10–100%
Holidays & weekends	20–100%

The above rates and fees were compiled from the results of a national survey of graphic artists conducted by the Graphic Artists Guild in 2020. Responses were based on rates charged in 2018 and 2019.

The percentage increases as the number of media and length of time increases. Likewise, a complete transfer of copyrights increases fees by a high percentage of the original price. All reimbursable out-of-pocket expenses incurred, including digital file preparation, are billed separately.

Collateral Design

Graphic designers who specialize in collateral material create brochures, catalogs, press kits, and direct mail packages. While clients generally retain advertising agencies to handle major campaigns for products and/or services, they often commission or retain a design firm to furnish these pieces.

Like advertising designers whose work is intended to elicit a specific response, collateral designers must have a sophisticated awareness of advertising, marketing, and sales. They often receive art and photography from the client or need to research stock images, so it is important to know how the rights to those visuals are transferred. If additional rights are needed, their transfer should be negotiated before the design or production stages. Graphic designers traditionally sell specific uses to the client—for example, first-time print runs. See Figure 5-4 for Collateral Design fees.

Package Design

Visually pleasing package design creates an emotional connection between a brand and consumers, influencing their decision to choose a particular product from the vast number of other brands on the shelf. With a strong understanding of the link between marketing strategy and design, package designers use color, form, graphics, typography, size, and materials to enhance the consumer's experience with the product, which will ultimately help build brand awareness.

A Multifaceted Discipline

In addition to design principles, package designers have in-depth knowledge of branding strategies, trends, and concept development. They also understand the relationship of design objectives to technological and marketing requirements, materials and their limitations, government regulations affecting the package, and printing and reproduction processes.

Packaging, which by its nature ends up as three-dimensional forms, requires the ability to design in three dimensions and foresee that result while working with two-dimensional layouts. Technical aspects include being able to render the designs to clients so that they can visualize their products in three dimensions either through use of 3-D modeling or through creating physical mockups. Skill and experience with bookbinding are helpful if not essential.

Some categories of packaging involve actual development of new packaging forms (custom bottle shapes, new bindery designs, use of new substrate materials). This requires being able to work with manufacturers that not only print the pieces but develop the initial dieline from the designer's concept so that they can cost-effectively manufacture a piece at scale and within a budget dictated by the price point of the product.

Package design is a demanding discipline, combining advertising, form, function, and style with an understanding of people, culture, and the consumer mindset. Therefore, it can involve months of market research, development, and test marketing.

MATERIALS & CONSTRUCTION FACTORS

The designer considers appropriate materials for two types of packaging: the primary packaging (such as glass, aluminum, plastic, or paperboard), which encases an individual product and protects it, as well as secondary packaging that holds several individual products for shipment and displays (such as a corrugated box or a pallet wrap). Packaging materials may be used in combination, such as the waxed paper or plastic bag inside a cereal box.

When choosing packaging materials, the designer also considers which fits best with the company's brand aesthetic and environmental commitments. Aesthetics also matter to buyers, the ones who determine whether a product makes it to the shelf or not. Some buyers, especially for large accounts, can be pickier than the consumer. For instance, they might reject carrying a good product if the packaging looks cheap. To appeal to cost-conscious consumers, the challenge is to create packaging that is both attractive and affordable

Today, environmental issues also play a role in package design, with more eco-friendly packaging materials being developed—sustainable alternatives to environmentally unfriendly materials. Designers are designing for recycling and reuse, replacing plastics with bioplastics or paper, and increasing recycled content. To address the mounting concerns over plastic waste, 25 of the biggest brands have partnered to create a subscription deliv-

5–4 Comparative Fees for Collateral Design

The pricing ranges in this chart do not constitute specific prices for particular jobs. The buyer and seller are free to negotiate, with each designer independently deciding how to price the work, after taking all factors into account. Reading the more detailed information, Pricing Your Services, provided in Chapter 1, will help in pricing projects for your specific situation.

Hourly Rates

DESIGNER	PRINCIPAL OF FIRM	CONSULTANT
$35–150+	$75–150	$75–150

Flat Project Fees

	GLOBAL/NATIONAL	REGIONAL/LOCAL
Direct Mail Package		
Simple	$800–5,000	$500-3,000
Complex	$2,000-7,000	$1,000–5,000
Press/Media Kit		
Simple	$800–3,000	$500–2,000
Complex	$1,000–4,500	$750–3,000
Product/Service Catalog		
Simple	$500–10,000	$500-5,000
Complex	$1,000–15,000	$1,000–7,500
Brochure (6-panel, 4x9")		
Simple	$300–5,000	$125–2,500
Complex	$500–7,500	$400–3,500
Brochure (8.5x11", self-cover)		
Simple (8 pgs.)	$200–5,400	$200–3,500
Complex (8 pgs,)	$600–6,500	$250–5,000
Simple (16 pgs.)	$600–8,400	$480–5,400
Complex (16 pgs.)	$1,000–9,400	$480–7,400

Additional Fees

MARKUPS (% above cost)	
Out-of-pocket expenses	10–50%
Outside services	10–50%

EXTRA ROUND OF REVISIONS	100–150%

(Not included in original agreement; % of original fee)

USAGE (% of original fee)	
Reuse in original market	100–150%
Total copyright transfer	120–300%

CANCELLATION & REJECTION FEES

(% of original project fee)

Prior to completion of concept phase	25–50%
After completion of preliminary work	50–75%
After completion of finished work	100%

Designers who charge by the hour bill for the number of hours worked up to the date of cancellation or rejection, plus any expenses incurred.

RUSH WORK (% added on to normal fee)	
24- to 48-hour turnaround	20–100%
Holidays & weekends	25–100%

The above rates and fees were compiled from the results of a national survey of graphic artists conducted by the Graphic Artists Guild in 2020. Responses were based on rates charged in 2018 and 2019.

ery service that will offer products in durable, refillable packaging. Initially tested in limited markets in 2019, Loop (www.loopstore.com) is based on the milkman home delivery model. UPS drivers will drop off a reusable tote of products. Once they are used, consumers can schedule the used containers to be picked up and filled containers to be dropped off. Loop will handle the cleaning and reuse aspects of the packaging. Each company designed its own packaging, so its brand image has been retained. Initial testing was positive enough that Loop is being expanded to retail stores.

The choice of package construction is also affected by how the product is meant to be displayed. Will it stand freely, lay down, be hung, or stacked? The size of the package is important to ensure that it fits in standard shelving and display configurations and apparatus.

And finally, the designer needs to consider materials and construction from the perspective of consumer use and accessibility. In general, packaging should not be unwieldy or hard to pick up, and it should be easy to open quickly without creating a mess or having openers break off. Package design should be inclusive—designed to be used by as many people as possible, regardless of disability, age, gender, or other demographics. Key accessibility guidelines include designing packaging that is easy to open and use for those with limited functional abilities and labelling that is highly legible. If packaging is accessible to the elderly (with eyesight and weakness issues) and people with physical disabilities and health conditions, it benefits all consumers.

MANUFACTURING CONSIDERATIONS

Being knowledgeable about the manufacturing of packaging makes a big difference as it does with any class of product—understanding the different media involved in the processes, from flexography to specialty offset, digital printing, the use of spot varnishes, foil-stamping, embossing, metalized papers, and coated versus uncoated stock, and being able to get the most out of them for the best graphic impact. Being on a first-name basis with the art department of the printers and manufacturers and earning their trust and confidence is part of the work.

BUDGETARY ISSUES

It is recommended to ask for the client's budget. They always have a budget in mind, and it will not have much wiggle room. You are either going to accept the work at the budgeted price or not. If you cannot make enough money on it to pay your overhead, do not take the project.

To work within a client's budget without sacrificing fees, designers may need to downscale the project. There are several ways to downscale projects for clients with smaller budgets by reducing the number of components, choosing a less expensive material, using fewer colors, etc.

Designers should make sure to keep track of the revision hours and whether the work has veered off the initial scope of the project. It is helpful to remind clients when they stray beyond their own budget in time and scope due to excessive revisions.

Pricing Factors

The scope of a package design project can range from a single component, such as a simple hang tag or a label, to numerous components, including shipping containers. Not only does the number of components affect pricing, but so do the hours spent with the client in discovery and consultation, the amount of market research, number of designs and revisions, accessibility requirements, and turnaround time. Expanded services might include sourcing and manufacturing, printing, creation of a prototype, photography, and illustration.

Other factors that can affect pricing are the size of the business, the scale of the distribution range of the product, and usage rights. Due to the many aspects and variables involved in the package design process, it is generally priced at a flat fee.

Specific Markets

Many branding and graphic design firms create packaging as part of a client's total project, but some design firms specialize only in packaging design. There are also package designers who specialize in a specific market. In addition to the general practices already described for packaging design, each specific market has its own requirements. Four of these markets are described in the following sections.

Food & Beverage Packaging

Packaging design for food and beverages has special consideration that packaging design for other retail products does not.

PACKAGING CONSIDERATIONS

Brand identity is only one of four primary functions of the package for this industry. The designer balances shelf appeal with product protection, safety, and freshness. The designer needs to be mindful of these functions when selecting materials and types of containers. These functions also affect labeling components.

The main goal of product protection is to keep food and beverages safe during transportation, handling, and distribution. Protecting perishable products throughout the supply chain requires consideration of the primary packaging that will encase individual products from a perspective of food safety and shelf life.

A secondary concern of product protection is to avoid the loss of profit from returned or rejected product, due to damage and breakage. While the consumer is the end buyer, there are other buyers along the supply chain, such as distributors and retailers, who will reject product with damaged packaging, for both aesthetic and safety reasons.

PRODUCT SAFETY
The correct packaging material helps to ensure product safety, thereby eliminating or reducing food recalls and hazards. While using food-grade materials in packaging is mandatory, there are other hazards that can occur at the packaging stage. For example, designers need to consider the safety of inks and coatings used on the packaging because they can migrate into food and beverages. Contamination can occur at any point in the supply chain, and a product recall can potentially destroy a brand's credibility, reduce sales, and possibly result in a lawsuit. The cost of destroying and replacing product alone can be prohibitive.

Designers need to be aware of labeling laws and Food and Drug Administration (FDA) regulations that require certain information to be included on food and beverage packaging for the consumer's protection. Labeling requirements include, among other items, an ingredient list, nutritional facts label, the possible effects of consumption or use, and the batch ID and manufacturing date so the product can be traced in the event of a recall or discarded on the expiration date. The FDA also has very specific rules of how, what, and where label text needs to be positioned. Even the size of the text and label matters to the FDA. Most consumers think of contaminated product as being the reason for a recall, but products are also recalled for improper packaging and labeling.

PRODUCT FRESHNESS & QUALITY
Proper packaging materials and sealing methods can increase a product's freshness and maintain its appearance, taste, shelf life, and quality. A great packaging design may initially attract consumers, but if the product does not taste fresh, a potentially loyal customer is lost. Designers need to keep up to date with new packaging technology advancements that help manufacturers extend a product's shelf life and better control product freshness. They also need to understand the barrier properties of materials that affect air and moisture getting into the product, as well as flavor. They need to know which products need wraps with air barriers and which ones need to breathe.

The construction of the package and the rigidity or flexibility of the material also affect how to best support the physical quality of the product from the factory to the retail shelf. Consumers will not be happy if they open a bag of chips or crackers and find they have been broken into little pieces during transit.

Beer, Wine, & Spirits Packaging

As a subset of food packaging, the design of bottle labels, cans, and the carriers and cartons that go with beer, wine, and spirits do not have quite the same degree of focus on food safety, aside from protecting the glass from breakage and the cans from becoming dented. There is not as much bindery design or choice of materials involved as the structures for labels and cans and their carriers and cartons are fairly well established, aside from design for spirits which is more likely to include custom bottle design.

Branding is a far more important concern. The graphics for beer and wine are in a highly competitive market. Breweries and wineries depend on shelf appeal and brand recognition as a primary incentive for making a sale, so a designer needs to have or develop a savvy and a passion for creating brands that have appeal and can lead to loyalties and cult status among customers, who have an increasingly sophisticated taste for graphics. Not only does the packaging need to stand out on the shelf in a crowd of other products, it needs to help tell the story of the beer, wine, brewery, winery and be part of developing a following. With the high price of luxury wine and the competition for craft beer, the value that designers can impart to this process is significant. This applies to all kinds of packaging, but especially the premium and craft alcohol market.

With the laws governing the sale of alcohol, designers also need to have a clear grasp of the elements of required information, including size and wording of aspects like alcohol content, container size, and what can and cannot be said about the product in the description for the labels

Cosmetics Packaging

The aesthetic aspects of package design are extremely important in the cosmetics industry, in which products are often touted as making customers more beautiful, attractive, youthful, or sexy. The packaging is expected to be an extension of those claims, especially high-end beauty products that are tied to a celebrity brand. Other brands that want to appeal to customers who are more concerned with a natural or healthy look or with environmentally friendly materials need to reflect those concerns in their packaging design.

TARGET MARKET

Understanding the target market is also a major factor in designing packaging for the cosmetics industry. What will appeal to a teenager will not be the same as what will appeal to a busy mom or a mature woman. Ethnicity might also be a consideration, for example, a line of cosmetics that has been developed to match the skin tones of women of color. Gender is also a factor—men might want to have softer skin or to smell good, but the packaging still needs to have masculine appeal.

LAYERS OF PACKAGING

Cosmetic packaging may involve designing up to three layers of primary packaging. The outermost layer is what consumers will open to find inner packaging. This bag or box is what customers see when they purchase cosmetics at a large retailer or online store. Inner packaging houses the product. It may be a presentation box, a sleeve, wrapping, or a just a thin piece of plastic. The third layer is the actual container that houses the product that the customer will use; for example, it may be a skin cream jar, a lipstick or mascara tube, a perfume bottle, or a plastic case of eye shadow.

Generally, the more expensive the brand, the more layers of packaging it will have. In some cases, more than one layer of packaging is used due to the fragility of the product container, such as a glass bottle. For other products, the primary container may be sealed in a plastic layer to keep the product from being contaminated or to preserve its freshness.

LABELING

Cosmetics are often referred to as "personal care prod-ucts" or located in the "health and beauty" sections of drug and department stores. However, the FDA does not define personal care products by law, but it does define what products are *cosmetics* and what are *drugs*. Some personal care products are classified as both cosmetics and drugs. The package designer needs to know which category a product falls under because it makes a difference in the information required on package labels. There are specific FDA labeling requirements for each category of products, as well as for both outer and inner packaging. Requirements common to both are a list of ingredients and warning and caution statements.

Consumers check ingredients because they may be afraid of chemicals or they have experienced allergic reactions to certain ingredients. They also check warning labels and expiration dates for safety reasons, especially on products with a short shelf life.

Today, consumers are interested in products and design that are organic, natural, and sustainable. In addition to labeling components required by law, information should be visible that speaks to the targeted market of a product so that it is differentiated from similar products on the shelf, for example, "non-allergenic," "clinically-tested," "fragrance-free," "for aging and mature skin," "with sunscreen," "100% natural and vegan," and "cruelty-free."

Entertainment Packaging

Entertainment Packaging is a separate entity unto itself. Unlike package design for products, it is package design for the artist/musician or a film/filmmaker. Both are very different art forms with different approaches.

MUSIC

Despite the increasing popularity and convenience of listening to music via digital downloads and streaming services, there is still a market for physical CDs and vinyl. In fact, vinyl is making a huge comeback in Jazz, Blues, and Rock, fueled by its unique sound and nostalgic appeal.

There is still a viable amount of work for package designers in the music industry. Besides packaging for CDs and vinyl, box sets are currently hot. The profession is even recognized at the Grammys, with awards given for Best Album Package and Best Box Set.

Music packaging is about showing visual concepts of the music on the album. An "album," whether on CD or vinyl, is a collection of songs. In creating the booklet, the art director and designer try to create a visual experience for the band's audience to coincide with the music. The main purpose of the booklet's interior is to deliver liner notes, a more in-depth glimpse of the musician or band, their philosophy, and their music at this moment in time. Each album concept changes with the latest music. Some artists require lyrics in all of their booklets; some are more interested in the photographs, the production credits, and the visuals that move their message.

Most Pop artists prefer photography on the covers of their albums, while Jazz, New Age, Rock, or Alternative music may prefer an illustration, painting, or a conceptual photograph on their covers, with the band or artist's image on the back cover. It is the responsibility of the project's art director to fit the right photography or illustration and design with the music. Package designers working with a record label may also get to organize and produce the photo shoot. While photography is the mainstay of most music projects, having a good retouch artist on hand is an essential part of creating the finished booklet.

In addition to album packaging and booklets, the music industry is a source of many ways for graphic designers to make money, such as designing single covers, social media banners, 8–10-page websites, banner ads on music-related sites, posters, postcards, printed invitations to listening parties, bio flyers (digital or printed), ads in magazines such as *Billboard*, and e-mail blast ads. Music festivals provide additional income opportunities in poster and merchandise design.

FORMAT & DESIGN

CD, vinyl, and digital releases are totally different formats with different industry packaging requirements, so they require separate design considerations. A package designer may get a project that requires designing for multiple formats, which also impacts the design process. Depending on a client's needs, a project may include such items as 30 x 30" or larger posters and huge fabric banners. Package designers try to anticipate at the start of the project the largest item the client may need, and size the art accordingly. To make sure color matches, work is started with RGB images and converted to CMYK, where color is adjusted, and then converted back to RGB for finished digital covers.

Album covers are designed at the highest resolution possible because they may also be used as a magazine ad or a poster. Vinyl covers are 12 x 12" at 300 dpi in a CMYK format.

Album covers for iTunes distribution now have to be 8 x 8" at 300 dpi in an RGB JPEG format.

There are no industry restrictions as to what wording can be put on a physical CD cover, aside from considerations of avoiding censorship due to nudity or profanity.

It can also include a sticker with additional information, and sticker placement can be incorporated in the cover design. This is not the case with the digital cover of a CD distributed by iTunes. They are more specific and have strict guidelines as to what can be put on a cover. Also, there are no stickers allowed on digital albums. If a designer is doing a vinyl cover as well, it would be considered a third design because of the larger size. Stickers on a vinyl cover are also larger than those on a CD and will need a redesign from CD packaging.

Physical CD booklets are 4.75 x 4.75" (300 dpi, CMYK). A standard booklet is 4, 8, or 12 pages; a roll fold booklet can be 6, 8, or 10 pages. The standard components of physical CD packaging for music include a CD booklet, tray card, and a CD label.

Booklets for digital downloads are totally different from physical CD booklets in size and design. A digital booklet is 11" wide x 8.264" high at 72 dpi, RGB, with a minimum of 4 pages, and the entire document cannot exceed 8–10 MB. It may contain lyrics, production notes, and photos of the artist or band. Because of the file size restrictions for download, the number of photographs used may need to be reduced. Sometimes the digital booklet is done by an in-house designer at a record

Due to the differences in sizes, a designer who is doing booklets for both a CD and a digital download cannot just save the CD booklet as a PDF and download it to iTunes. The digital booklet is a total redesign project, so the designer should charge for two layouts.

PRICING & PAYMENT

Pricing for music package design is affected by how big the recording artist's name is in music sales. Genre is also tied to music sales, so it too impacts package pricing. In recent years, Pop, or Popular music, has been the top category, while during the 1970s–90s, Rock dominated. Because Pop's artists cross all genres, making the most money and selling the most albums, they have the highest design budgets. The status of the other genres changes frequently, with R&B/Hip Hop/Urban and Country also in the top four. Experienced music design professionals indicate that at this writing, pricing for typical music package design projects, by genre, is as follows:

* Popular: $5,000–10,000+
* Country: $3,000–8,000
* R&B/Hip Hop/Urban: $3,000–8,000
* Rock: $3,000–5,000
* Alternative & Dance/Electronic: $2,500–4,000
* Jazz/Blues/Traditional Pop: $2,500–4,000

* Americana & Roots & Gospel: $2,500–3,000
* Classical/Opera/Soundtracks for Visual Media: $2,000–3,000
* Independent Artists: $500–2,500

Jazz, Blues, and Traditional Pop rely on boxed sets to sell older artists, and they have shown an increase in vinyl sales. Projects for Independent Artists can vary budget-wise: some artists are just starting their careers and have no money and no record deal, others are very loyal and pay very well, and many are moderately successful and want a quality job to go with their music.

Because CD, vinyl, and digital releases are totally different formats requiring different design considerations, designers working on a project with multiple formats need separate or additional fee structures for the various formats.

Few clients, except big name Pop artists, like Taylor Swift, have the budgets for a full-blown project with all the collateral pieces. Each artist has different priorities. There are several options for downscaling projects for clients with smaller budgets. Since a photographer's budget is usually 2–3 times the designer's budget, the length of on-location photo shoots can be reduced and moved to the studio. Buying stock photos is not a good option because recording artists are selling a product and want a unique look. If a designer decides to go that route anyway, it is recommended that he/she negotiate with a legitimate stock rep for only the usage needed. Also, buying usage for multiple images at one time can be a cost savings. Another option for designers with good photo skills is to take the photos themselves.

Another area that can be downscaled is the type of booklet and the number of formats and pages. Instead of putting lyrics in the CD booklet, which takes up a lot of pages, lyrics can be put on the artist's website, saving paper and printing costs.

The larger the client, the longer it may take to get paid, but you will get paid. The smaller or the independent client may pay sooner, but they can also be less dependable in their payments, so you have to protect yourself and your work. Always ask for a 50% deposit before starting a project.

FILM

Today, if film is packaged, the packaging is for DVD/Blu-ray discs. DVD/Blu-ray packaging is driven by the movie studio's marketing machine and must convey a two-hour film with a powerful image and some great marketing copy. All the art created for films is called key art. Whether the designer is creating the original one-sheet movie art or the DVD package, both are referred to as key art. Key art involves creating a logo/title treatment and a really powerful image to capture the main theme of the film.

Movie key art is designed to be seen on a large one-sheet poster at the movie theaters, while DVDs are designed to pop out at a much smaller size from video store shelves that display multiple titles. Rarely is the key art from the movie one-sheet used for the DVD packaging. The logos and the images are usually changed to reflect the smaller size and the newest marketing tactics, such as "Academy Award Winner," etc. The new key art is created from scratch, including the film's title treatment. In this process, several key art comps are created. Most studios require more than 2-3. Depending on the size of the budget, up to 10 comps are required.

The design of the DVD package includes a disc label and a wrapper that slides into a plastic case. A secondary package uses a Digi-Pak format, where the key art is printed on cardboard boxes. The wrapper includes a front cover, spine, back cover with scenes from the movie, a synopsis, a specific billing block for the credits in the movie, and a barcode. It is customary for one design studio to work on all the assets for the film. It is very common to do the DVD plus the Blu-ray packaging and disc labels, as well as a screener package for the retail buyer ("not for sale"), a place card for rentals, a trade ad, a sell sheet, etc.

While key art for films involves photography, the end-product is more like photo illustration. Art directors rarely have the luxury to reshoot the actors in a studio setting, due to the fact they are off on other movies. The original costumes and hair styles are long gone by the time the DVD/Blu-ray art is being created. Unlike other kinds of packaging design, having a great photo imaging person/illustration artist/Photoshop artist in the design studio is essential to working on key art packaging.

PRICING

Like music packaging, film packaging pricing is similarly affected: the bigger the actors and the greater the film's success at the box office, the larger the marketing

5–5 Comparative Fees for Package Design

Hourly Rates
$50–170

The above rates were compiled from the results of a national survey of graphic artists conducted by the Graphic Artists Guild in 2020. Responses were based on rates charged in 2018 and 2019.

budget for the film's release at the DVD level. Since less prominent or newer artists and smaller films have fewer sales, their budgets are smaller. Budgets can range from $10,000 a campaign at an independent studio to $20,000–$30,000 for a mid-size campaign at a larger movie studio. Hollywood takes all rights to package design so designers must be compensated well for design work because there will be no further compensation. Usage rights for U.S. distribution are built into a designer's fees. However, usage rights for merchandising (i.e., putting the package design on a T-shirt or a poster) can, and should, be negotiated separately.

See Figure 5-5 for hourly rates for Package Design.

Publication Design

Publication designers create the format and look of printed, digital, and online magazines, tabloids, and newspapers, or white papers (usually PDFs). These have an editorial point of view and often contain advertising.

Magazines

Contrary to early dire predictions, magazines are not dead. According to the 2019 whitepaper, *The Future of Media*, released by the network for global media, FIPP, in collaboration with UPM Communication Papers, "despite the emergence of digital channels, print continues to thrive." Specifically referring to magazines, the report cites, "The top 25 print magazines reach more adults and teens than the top 25 prime time shows. And, despite generational differences, magazine consumption is strong."

While some magazines are dropping their print editions and moving to a digital-only platform, the white paper credits print's resilience to "being driven by its ability to fit in with and alongside a universe that combines all platforms. Successful magazines have reinvented themselves as brands that serve their audience via a range of channels, of which print is just one." Some of the more successful magazine publishers have realized that it is not a question of print versus digital, but what should the mix of print and digital be?

A current trend is using multichannel publishing to differentiate content in order to allow each channel (print, web, mobile), to play to its specific strengths. Industry experts say the key is understanding how customers want to engage with the publication and then making it as simple as possible to do so. This philosophy is evident in not only how content is delivered but in subscription choices as well.

Major magazines that are successfully publishing both print and digital versions are *Vogue, National Geographic, Rolling Stone, The Atlantic. Harvard Business Review,* and *Forbes.* They also have apps for accessing content on mobile devices. The best example of a long-time traditional print magazine that is successfully using all channels, including social media, is *National Geographic.* Its editor-in-chief, Susan Goldberg, explained in an interview, "We try to use all those contents as much as we can across all platforms that can make the most sense from the content and economic perspective. The two are very interconnected—almost nothing we do is purely print or just digital." As a result, *National Geographic* was ranked the number one brand on social media in 2017 with over 350 million followers globally across all platforms, and it was the first brand to top 100 million Instagram followers.

Digital media is creating opportunities for publication designers with interactive skills who can translate static print layouts into tighter, interactive digital designs. In addition to the solid background in graphic design, typography, and software (InDesign, Illustrator, Photoshop) that print publication designers need, those designing for interactive media need such skills as a working knowledge of HTML and Digital Publishing Suite; experience with motion graphics, content management systems, and designing user interface (UI) elements; and an understanding of web and smartphone/tablet usability principles.

Newspapers

Newspapers have not fared as well as magazines in the transition from print to digital. While digital advertising is increasing, the market is dominated by only a handful of giant social network services and search engines that create little original content of their own. With the exception of a few large-sized newspapers (the *New York Times,* the *Washington Post,* and the *Wall Street Journal*), the newspaper industry is failing to keep up with the transition from print to digital modes of consumption. For the small- to medium-sized newspapers that represent the bulk of the industry, there has been an overall drop in revenues led by diminishing revenues from print products. Along with declining revenues, an increasing number of newspapers are closing their doors, and the number of employees in the print news sector fell 45% between 2008 and 2017.

Other reasons for the demise of the print newspaper are a fragmented readership, misinformation and disinformation, and increased competition from corporate media. Today's readers are not loyal to a single publication. Instead, they peruse news articles online via shared links on mega-platforms and curation sites like Facebook and Google. The deregulation of media consolidation in 1996 has led to numerous corporate mergers, resulting in a decline in the number of media corporations from about 50 in the 1980s to six today, which own over 90% of the entire U.S. media industry.

As a result of the current state of the print newspaper, much of the work graphic designers did for this industry has dried up. However, there is still work available for in-house corporate and institutional publications.

Specific Trade Customs

Today, many publishers complement their design staff with freelance or independent designers. Non-staff designers may be hired to design the format for a new magazine or tabloid; redesign an existing magazine or a special issue, section, or feature within a magazine; or develop a magazine prototype used by an editorial team to pitch a new magazine, either in-house or to a publishing company. Frequently, freelance designers continue on after a job is finished as consultants for periodic oversight, either on retainer or for a fee based on an estimated number of hours per issue. The freelancer may work with one or more staff associate art directors, assistant art directors, and/or designers and production artists. This is common in large publishing companies that have numerous publications (such as trade/technical journals or how-to magazines).

At the planning stage for each issue of the publication, the key editorial staff (most often the editor-in-chief, section editors, and key writers for the issue) meet with the art director and appropriate staff to hold a story and cover conference. During this session, the strategy for several issues is mapped out, with a major focus on the current issue. A direction is established, and concepts may be determined at this time. Then the art director commissions art for the issue within yearly budget constraints. That may involve locating new creative talent (illustrators and photographers) whose styles are appropriate for the new design. Since editors assume authority for the publication, they have approval over dummies and storyboards. The publisher most often has final approval over the entire package, and revisions are frequently required.

Freelance designers who are commissioned to work on publications are often expected to sign all-rights or work-made-for-hire contracts. Due to the nature of publication design, the publisher owns the rights to what is produced. Designers should weigh all their options before accepting assignments under these conditions. (For more informa-

tion, see the Work-Made-for-Hire section in Chapter 11, Legal Rights & Issues.)

Pricing

Because nameplates (logos) are the anchors of most magazines, they are the anchors of most magazine design work. Consequently, fees for magazine design are front-loaded toward logo design since its development takes place at the beginning of the project. If logo design is not required (an existing magazine wishes a new design without changing its nameplate), the design fee will be weighted more toward cover design.

Standard procedure is to bill the design and development fee in segments, no matter what the size or cost of the job. For larger projects, a third of the payment is usually made upon signing the agreement, a third upon approval of design comprehensives, and the final third within 30 days of delivery of electronic files or printed pieces. For smaller projects, half is customary at the outset, with the balance due upon submission of final layouts.

Fees for publication design vary as widely as the magazines themselves. The complexity of the work involved and the scope of the project are always considerations. Some other factors affecting price are the magazine's audience (consumer, trade, or corporate/in-house), the number of pages, production, whether the publisher is an individual or small or large corporation, the size and stature of the designer or design firm, and the urgency of the schedule. The lower end of the fee range is appropriate for a redesign that only requires the designer to create one or two cover designs and a few inside spreads. If the client requires a full-blown dummy issue to demonstrate every possible variation that might occur in the magazine, a proportionately higher fee is customarily charged. Another factor that affects fees is whether the freelance design team has to provide written guidelines and digital templates for the in-house art department to use.

The majority of publication designers price jobs either at an hourly rate or as a flat fee based on the job specifications, depending on the specific project. A small number charge a page rate or a per-issue rate.

See Figure 5-6 for Publication Design hourly rates and fees.

Book Jacket or Cover Design

Book jacket designers create the look of the jacket or cover of a book, or of a series of books, using the graphic ele-

5–6 Comparative Fees for Publication Design

The pricing in this chart does not constitute specific prices for particular jobs. The buyer and seller are free to negotiate, with each designer independently deciding how to price the work, after taking all factors into account. Reading the more detailed information, Pricing Your Services, provided in Chapter 1, will help in pricing projects for your specific situation.

Hourly Rates

DESIGNER	PRINCIPAL OF FIRM	CONSULTANT
$50–120+	$120–170	$120–150

Additional Fees

MARKUPS (% above designer's cost)

Out-of-pocket expenses	5–30%
Outside services	5–50%

CANCELLATION & REJECTION FEES (% of original project fee)

Prior to completion of concept phase	20–50%
After completion of preliminary work	50–75%
After completion of finished work	100%

Designers who charge by the hour bill for the number of hours worked up to the date of cancellation or rejection, plus any expenses incurred.

RUSH WORK (% added on to normal fee)

24-hour turnaround	25–100%
48-hour turnaround	20–50%
Holidays & weekends	40–100%

The above rates and fees were compiled from the results of a national survey of graphic artists conducted by the Graphic Artists Guild in 2020. Responses were based on rates charged in 2018 and 2019.

ments of typography, illustration, photography, and/or specially designed letterforms.

The publishing industry has two major categories: Trade and Education. What defines the titles within those categories is how much money the book can potentially make in the marketplace and how large of a budget is assigned to the title. For trade books, the categories of mass, major, and young adult determine how much money will be spent on a particular title.

Within the publishing organization, a book may be identified as an A-, B-, or C-level book, based on market research and potential sales. Once a trade book reaches the store shelf, publishers often depend on the consumer "judging the book by its cover" as a way of guiding their purchasing behavior.

For textbooks, the categories are college, and el-hi (elementary/high school). Unlike the purchasing scenario of a trade book, where people are generally purchasing the book for themselves, in the education market, someone other than the end user is making the purchasing decision. Therefore, the cover image and overall design is meant to appeal to the purchaser, rather than the end user.

Relationships between Cover Design & Book Categories

Online retailers have greatly expanded the outlets for selling books, and e-readers and other mobile devices with their wireless delivery systems have changed how book content is packaged and how consumers access and read it. The following book categories originated when only printed books existed.

TRADE

Trade books are designed for a specific target audience in either specialized or general consumer markets and traditionally were sold primarily through bookstores. Today, they also are available through online booksellers.

HARDCOVERS

Trade books are traditionally hardcover. For most major trade books, the cover image is a key factor in driving the sales of the book.

TRADE PAPERBACKS

A trade paperback is a soft cover edition of a trade hardback, often published a year after the first printing. In certain cases, the soft cover edition of an existing hardcover title might receive a new cover design if it is targeted to be repurposed for a particular market segment or to fit a specific genre or category.

MASS-MARKET PAPERBACK

Mass-market books are designed to appeal to a broader market and are sold predominantly through mass channels that extend beyond traditional trade outlets. Mass-market sources may include newsstands, drug stores, and chain and department stores, in addition to bookstores, libraries, and the Internet. For the client, a mass-market book is often produced in a standard size and format and has lower production costs. The cover design of a mass-market title is critical to its sales.

Textbooks are designed for classroom use rather than general consumption. There are several ancillary components to textbook design. The cover is designed to appeal to specific grades, subject matters, and sometimes, specific geographic locations.

Specific Trade Customs

After accepting the job, the designer is given a brief synopsis of the book and a marketing and sales strategy. The purchase order (PO) or contract usually reflects terms and fees that are agreed upon in writing by the publisher's art director and the designer.

COPYRIGHT & CREDIT

Copyright and credit for the designer should be agreed upon before work begins. When credit is given, it usually appears on the back flap or on the back of the cover, though it occasionally appears on the copyright page. If other commissioned elements such as illustration, calligraphy, or custom fonts appear on the cover, they should be credited as well.

USAGE RIGHTS

Usage rights should also be agreed upon and stated clearly in the contract or written agreement. Generally, publishers have a standard contract they use. However, not all publishers' contracts are the same, so it is important to read each contract and try to negotiate additional edition fees.

Reputable publishers pay for additional paperback and electronic rights. Designers should clarify these provisions in a written agreement with the publisher, as well as specify any additional payments expected for use of the art by another domestic publisher, by book clubs, foreign publishers, or by film, television, or other media. Many, but not all, publishers pay the designer an agreed upon fee for one edition, such as hardcover, and if the cover design is used for paperback at any point (often a year later), generally a 50% of the original design fee is paid. Likewise, designers should be paid extra for physical audio book covers, although generally they earn a smaller fee. Foreign editions are sometimes published, too. Because book cover fees in general are low, these usage fees

for additional editions are extremely beneficial to the designer.

To further protect themselves, book jacket designers should specify on their invoices that the artwork is prepared only for the named edition and title and provide the International Standard Book Number (ISBN) (if available). Since each edition (hardcover, paperback, foreign language, e-book, etc.) requires a different ISBN, including it on a contract or invoice helps protect the designer in the event a publisher tries to use a cover design or art for future editions beyond the original usage without compensating the designer. It should be noted that an enhanced e-book requires a different ISBN than the non-enhanced version of the same e-book; therefore, it is considered a separate edition.

Pricing

Many designers sell one-time reproduction rights; however, current practice varies. In some cases, artists have found their work appearing on the paperback edition or in electronic form as an e-book, without permission or additional payment from the publisher, years after a hardcover jacket was issued. To catch unauthorized usage, it is a good practice to periodically do an online search of the book to see what formats it is being sold as.

The designer may prepare from two to four sketches or comps for presentation, which are supplied to the client most commonly in digital form (as PDF or JPEG files) or alternatively as color prints if the client prefers. Another one or two variations may be requested. If more than three comps are required, industry sources indicate that it is customary for an additional fee to be paid.

Generally, the comp should be as close as possible in appearance to the finished piece. Such tight comps can entail expenses, and traditionally all out-of-pocket expenses in the sketch stage are billable to the client. For instance, high-quality color prints that may be used in comps are billable directly to the client. However, many clients approve JPEG or PDF proofs on screen, and there is no printed comp.

The nature of publishing leads to a high rate of rejection of comp presentations. Current industry practices indicate that this risk is accepted by designers and publishers, who agree to a rejection fee, reflecting the amount of work completed at the time of the project's termination. Recent data indicate that the usual rejection fee is 50% of the agreed-upon design fee for an accepted job. Any incurred expenses also are paid.

Once the comp is approved, the designer purchases the high-resolution stock art or executes or commissions the illustration, lettering, or other graphic elements used in the finished art. Production costs for necessities such as, but not necessarily limited to, photographic processing, type, and digital output are generally billed by the designer in addition to the design fee. Such costs are directly assumed by the client. Markups and handling fees for outside services are charged to cover expenses incurred when the publisher does not pick them up directly.

E-Book Cover Design

PRINT VERSUS E-BOOK MARKETS

Despite early signs a decade ago that print books were going to be overtaken by e-books, print books have proven to have staying power. In fact, the 2019 annual report of the Association of American Publishers states that in 2018, revenue from print books totaled $22.6 billion, while revenue from e-books totaled $2.04 billion. These figures included trade and educational books as well as fiction. Surprisingly, the percentage of millennials that read print in 2017 (75%) was higher than the national average of all ages (67%).

Why do print books continue to be popular? According to Meryl Halls, managing director of the Booksellers' Association in the U.K., "I think the physical object is very appealing. Publishers are producing incredibly gorgeous books, so the cover designs are often gorgeous, they're beautiful objects. In an interview with CNBC, she added, "People love to display what they've read. The book lover loves to have a record of what they've read…. It's about decorating your home, it's about collecting." This is all good news for book cover designers.

Others cite the physicality of print books beyond their aesthetics for their enduring popularity—they like the feel and smell of books. Print books also make more meaningful and beautiful gifts than a digital file.

According to Nielsen Book International, genres that do well in print include nature, cookery, and children's books, while people prefer to read crime, romantic novels and thrillers—genres composed mostly of text—via e-readers. E-books are also more useful for readers with certain physical handicaps and for those with poor eyesight, as they can turn the pages easier and adjust the size of the font to make the print legible. Print publishers and designers have not been responsive to a growing elderly population with vision problems; instead, fonts used in print periodicals and books have been getting smaller in size and lighter in weight over the past few decades. E-books have also proven to be a more lucrative source of revenue than print books for self-published authors.

The takeaways for designers are books are not dead and both print and digital books exist side by side, each with their own strengths. Designers who understand and can work in both markets will be more successful.

DESIGN DIFFERENCES

Traditional (print) book covers have three basic purposes: to identify the book's title and author, to protect the interior pages, and to sell books. As a sales tool, the cover is a finely tuned representation of the book's genre and the message it wants to send. Since an e-book does not exist in any physical reality other than as a digital file, it doesn't need a protective cover.

Although there is no need for a physical cover, e-book "covers" continue to exist as a form of advertising. A well-designed e-book cover is what makes readers initially select a book they know nothing about from the hundreds of other cover images online. And, even though there is no need for the e-book cover to be any particular physical shape, since the text will reflow into the form and shape of the e-reader into which it is loaded, some retailers insist on the "covers" being the conventional vertical rectangle, regardless of the shape of the original print version or the fact that many books exist only as e-books.

E-book covers present unique design challenges for the creator. Potential buyers are not browsing through bookstores picking up physical books and leafing through them; instead they are searching online through long lists of thumbnail-size images of the covers that serve as product icons. The cover designer has a split second to grab readers' attention so hopefully they will click on the image and read the summary or sample pages. Covers must create immediate visual interest and titles must be legible.

When creating such a small-sized cover, the design needs to be simple. If there is an existing cover for a print edition, it cannot just be sized down for the e-book version. Any elements that won't be legible or readable at thumbnail size must be taken out. It is best to keep only the title, author, and one primary graphic that instantly communicates something about the tone and genre of the book. Subtle colors and thin or script typefaces should be avoided. Likewise, special type effects such as outlines, drop shadows, bevel/emboss, and textures need to be used judiciously and cautiously. They might look great on a computer monitor, but on a smaller e-reader, tablet, or smartphone screen, they may be lost entirely, or worse, make the type illegible. Illustrations must be chosen with great care for tone, emotion, and contrast.

Although e-book covers are used at different sizes by online retailers, they are best designed for the smallest size at which they will be used, which is the thumbnail size

5–7 Comparative Fees for Book Jacket or Cover Design

The price ranges in this chart do not constitute specific prices for particular jobs. The buyer and seller are free to negotiate, with each designer independently deciding how to price the work, after taking all factors into account, including any online editions, such as e-books and downloadable electronic formats. Reading the more detailed information, Pricing Your Services, provided in Chapter 1, will help in pricing projects for your specific situation.

Hourly Rates $45–100+

Flat Project Fees

	ONE INITIAL CONCEPT	ONE ADDIT. CONCEPT (PER SKETCH)
HARDCOVER		
Mass Market	$500–2,500	$200–500+
Trade	$400–2,000+	$200–500+
Textbook	$350–1,500+	$100–500+
Young Adult	$350–1,000+	$200–500+
Self-Published	$300–2,000	$100–600+
Voluntary Termination Fee (% of original fee) 50–60+%		
PAPERBACK		
Mass Market	$500–1,250+	$200–500+
Trade	$400–1,500+	$100–500+
Textbook	$350–1,500+	$100–500+
Young Adult	$350–1,500+	$200–500+
Self-Published	$100–1,500	$100–600
Voluntary Termination Fee (% of original fee) 20–60+% (self-published)		50–60+% (all others)

E-BOOKS	COMPLEX	SIMPLE
Original Design	$600–1,500+	$150–1,000+
Based on Existing Print Cover	$250–1,000+	$75–500+

Additional Fees (% of original fee)

EXTRA ROUND OF REVISIONS (Not included in original agreement)	100–150%	
REUSE IN ORIGINAL MARKET	120–190%	

CANCELLATION & REJECTION FEES

Prior to completion of concept phase	20–50%
After completion of preliminary work	30–75%
After completion of finished work	50–100%

Designers who charge by the hour bill for the number of hours worked up to the date of cancellation or rejection, plus any expenses incurred.

RUSH WORK (% added on to normal fee)   10–100%

The above rates and fees were compiled from the results of a national survey of graphic artists conducted by the Graphic Artists Guild in 2020. Responses were based on rates charged in 2018 and 2019.

used on search pages. If potential customers cannot read the title or cannot tell what the cover image is, they will skim right over the cover to the next title. If the design passes the thumbnail test, then it also will look good at larger sizes.

As with other digital media, image resolution is also a consideration when designing e-book covers. Each of the major e-book publishing services has its own minimum and ideal resolution requirements in pixels for e-book covers. These specifications can change, so designers should research the latest requirements.

Branding is also a challenge for e-book designers. Many e-book authors have had success writing a series of books. An important part of the branding for both the series and the author is for the reader to be able to immediately recognize a title as part of a series. In print book design, the combination of the graphic elements on a cover with the typography of the title is considered as making up the basic brand of the book. The same holds true for e-book design, but because covers have to be simplified for the small size of online display, cover designers have to create branding for a series more efficiently. Simple branding techniques for an e-book series might be color-coordinated covers, common design elements, or a simple logo.

See Figure 5-7 for Book Jacket and Cover Design fees.

Interior Book Design

Book designers develop the style and visual flow of a book's interior by combining the graphic elements of typography, illustration, and photography. The job description for book designers ranges from highly creative to somewhat mechanical.

Book Design Categories

There are four basic book design categories for print books: mass market, trade, college textbook, and elementary through high school-level textbook (el-hi). Some unusual projects or books for small presses may not fit into those categories. In such cases, designers traditionally use their hourly rates as the basis for a fee. If the design is to be used for a series of books, a reuse fee should be negotiated.

MASS MARKET

Mass-market book interior designs, when called for, are usually simple and low-budget. These books can be a page-per-page reduction of the trade version or printed on low-quality paper with a type of press that cannot reproduce fine detail. Most indie authors settle for this level, or an even less polished level, of interior design. Unfortunately, it keeps them from setting themselves apart from the crowd.

TRADE

The complexity of design for trade books is determined by the genre and specific format of the book:

Simple: A straightforward book such as a novel or short book of poetry. Design includes a layout showing a title page, a chapter opening, a text spread, and front matter spreads. Simple books are generally done in-house but may be given to a freelance designer if the publisher is small and does not have an in-house design department.

Average: General nonfiction, poetry, anthologies, or illustrated books designed on a grid system. Design may include front matter (half title, title, copyright, dedication, acknowledgments, preface, contents, list of illustrations, introduction, ad card), part opening, chapter opening, text with three to six levels of heads, tabular matter, illustrations and/or photographs, extracts, footnotes, and simple back matter such as bibliography and index. The design, excluding the front matter, is set in sample pages for the publisher and approved before the complete manuscript is formatted.

A freelance designer might also offer an independent author or small business client sample pages for a simple novel. Self-publishing authors who are looking for professional design are doing so because they want a specific look that they know they cannot achieve themselves.

Complex: Books that require special treatment of each page or more complex printing techniques, such as four-color books, cookbooks, workbooks, catalogs, and elaborate art or picture books.

COLLEGE-LEVEL TEXTBOOK

The design of college-level textbooks involves three phases: presentation of concept, full design of all elements, and final design with style sheets for the compositor.

Simple: These are mostly straight text with up to three levels of heads, simple tables, and/or art.

Average: These have up to six levels of heads, tables and/

or charts, extracts, footnotes, and illustrations, diagrams, and/or photographs laid out on a grid system.

Complex: These are usually foreign language texts, or two-, three-, or four-color texts, complicated workbooks, catalogs, or illustrated books that require special treatment of each page.

ELEMENTARY THROUGH HIGH SCHOOL-LEVEL (EL-HI) TEXTBOOK

El-hi textbooks tend to be more visually oriented than college-level texts and therefore more design intensive.

The Design Transmittal

Before the designer can begin, the manuscript must be reviewed to ascertain how many elements will need to be designed and how the hierarchy of the various heads should be organized. This is done in the form of a design transmittal, which lists all elements in the manuscript along with the page number of the first instance. Design transmittals are sometimes prepared by the publisher's editorial department and will accompany the design packet supplied to the designer. However, more often designers are handed a manuscript and have to go through it themselves to find the elements. This is also common practice in self-publishing projects because authors may not know the parts of a book and how significant they are for the design. Designers may elect to create a questionnaire for authors that helps elicit this information.

The design transmittal includes a copy of the manuscript or a selection of representative copy for sample pages, a summary of all typographic elements, and a description of the book's production specifications (trim size, desired number of pages, number of ink colors, and so on). The publisher should also reiterate the design directives discussed during the consultation. It is really important at this stage for the designer to get a clear idea of what the client wants, in order to avoid time-consuming revisions. A designer may ask clients for examples of interiors they like if they have a hard time describing what they want visually. If a cover image or cover rough exists, the designer should ask to see it to make sure the interior will match the cover in style and genre. To prevent problems later on, some designers show clients a designed preliminary page or two, to make sure they are going in the right direction.

The design fee is based on the complexity of the manuscript as demonstrated primarily by the number of elements listed on the design transmittal. If the designer finds additional elements during the design process or if the transmittal otherwise misrepresents the complexity level of the manuscript, the design fee may be increased accordingly to compensate for the additional work necessary. The publisher should also indicate whether any particular visual style is desired. The designer's pricing is based on the publisher's preparation of the design transmittal. When the designer's assignment includes this responsibility, it should be reflected in a higher fee.

Design Process

After the fee is agreed upon, the designer prepares layouts. These typically include the title page, a sample of front-matter heads such as "Introduction," a sample chapter opener, a sample part title (if applicable), and double-page spreads showing the text setting along with most or all text elements. These may include extracts, poetry, sidebars, and so forth. These examples are needed for the publisher to evaluate and approve the design and are used as a guide during production.

Today, the trend is away from writing formal type specs for the typesetter and more toward setting up digital files in page layout software such as Adobe InDesign, which includes style sheets, master pages, and sample pages that hopefully cover all contingencies.

Publishers may use an in-house or a compositor's production facility to take the book from layout to page makeup. In those cases, the designer will be required to check the first set of page proofs to make sure the compositor has followed all design specifications. Other publishers may give designers digital files of type and art and have them make up the pages electronically. The designer charges an additional per-page rate for type composition or page layout if that is part of the job.

DUMMY/PAGE MAKEUP

After the book design is approved, the design is applied via style sheets to the text manuscript—either by the copy editor, compositor, or production person. Next, the dummy or first-pass pages will be created by either the compositor or designer. Some publishing projects require special coding, such as XML and ETM, and this work may be done by software specialists. However, many books are still produced by typesetting houses, production artists, or freelancers. Most interior book designers who serve the indie community will do both the design and the typesetting.

Dummy/page makeup is charged on a per-page rate, which includes one round of minor corrections. See Figure 5-9 for typical page rates. Author's alterations (AAs) and editor's alterations (EAs) after page makeup are usually charged at an hourly rate in addition to the page rate. However, some publishers require that all revision cycles be included in the page price. Final pages are created after first-pass pages are proofread and reviewed by the publisher.

Trade Practices & Pricing

MASS MARKET, TRADE, & COLLEGE TEXTBOOK

The design fee reflects design complexity. A basic fee for mass market, trade, or college textbooks includes the following services:

* Initial consultation with the publisher, packager, or other contractor to discuss the project. This consultation can be accomplished in person or by phone or e-mail.
* Analysis of the manuscript to confirm that the scope of work complies with the publisher's design transmittal.
* Castoff of the manuscript. Casting-off is estimating the number of pages in the final book by performing an in-depth character count of the manuscript. This may be done during the initial consultation, but sometimes the cast-off has to wait until the final manuscript is ready and all or most of the graphics are acquired. Sometimes the design has to be adjusted at this stage in order to make the page count correct. The designer may adjust the final invoice to account for variations in page count from the estimate.
* Sample layouts showing principal elements.
* Speccing /markup of the manuscript.
* Preparation of templates for the approved layouts. Digital files with style sheets may be provided by the designer for use by the compositor, or a comp order may be supplied, which contains all specs necessary for the compositor to create his/her own style sheets.
* Follow-through, including a check of first-pass pages.

If a publisher requests minor changes in the design, revisions are included in the basic design fee. If major changes are requested, the design fee may have to be renegotiated, or changes may be billed at the designer's hourly rate. The prices in Figure 5-8 are based on the preparation of as many layouts as the designer feels are necessary to show major design elements. When the client wishes to see highly detailed layouts, a higher fee is usually charged.

5–8 Comparative Fees for Interior Book Design

The price ranges in this chart do not constitute specific prices for particular jobs. The buyer and seller are free to negotiate, with each designer independently deciding how to price the work, after taking all factors into account, including any online editions, such as e-books and downloadable electronic formats. Reading the more detailed information, Pricing Your Services, provided in Chapter 1, will help in pricing projects for your specific situation

Hourly rates

Design	$50–100+
AAs or EAs (after page makeup)	$40–105+

Dummy Page Markup (per page)

Trade Book	$2–25
Self-Published	$2–25+

Flat Project Fees

EL-HI Textbook	$350–2,000
College Textbook	$350–2,000+
Mass Market	$350–5,000
Trade	$450–8,200
Self-Published	$300–3,000+

The above rates and fees were compiled from the results of a national survey of graphic artists conducted by the Graphic Artists Guild in 2020. Responses were based on rates charged in 2018 and 2019.

EL-HI TEXTBOOK

El-hi textbook design and production are structured a bit differently. Four-color basal math, reading, science, social studies, etc., generally follow this course:

* Meeting of designers, editors, and photo researchers: with sample manuscript in hand, they sketch out what the pages should look like prior to delivery of the full manuscript.
* Concept sketches: usually thumbnail size, 30 to 50% of the actual page size.
* Design prototypes: the specs are sometimes included, but if they are extremely complicated, there could be an additional fee for the specs/design brief.
* Page production: includes 3 rounds of proofing and

all associated proofreading fees. Additional steps (charged separately) may include:

+ Art or photo research or acquisition.
+ Art or photo database management/trafficking.
+ Photo shoot set-up, including props, styling, and so on.

ADDITIONAL CHARGES

Project management; supervision or art direction of an art program, including hiring and coordinating illustrators or photographers; extra conference time; trips to the publisher; page makeup or dummying; and time spent doing other production work are billed in addition to the design fee. The cost of specially commissioned work and other supplies is traditionally a billable expense.

E-Book Design & Conversion

E-books are most often published as digital editions of existing print books, converted to be read on e-readers, tablet computers, and some mobile phones. However, e-books can also originate in digital form with no pre-existing print version. Original e-books are often self-published.

Although e-books were slow to catch on at first with the reading public, they have become widely popular in the past decade. By the second quarter of 2012, U.S. publishers for the first time netted more sales revenue from e-books than from hardcovers. Currently, sales in the e-book market have flattened out, with a renewed interest in print books, as discussed in the previous section, Book Jacket or Cover Design.

Many textbooks are now available as e-books. Recent surveys have found that despite the advantages of using e-books over print books, a high percentage (72–92%) of college students prefer print textbooks, citing the distractions, eye strain, and headaches associated with reading on a screen. There also is a move in some elementary and secondary school districts to use e-books and tablets, rather than physical textbooks, mainly for the savings in cost and storage. The move from print to digital textbooks in K-12 classrooms currently remains a controversial issue with numerous pros and cons for both sides, including academic, economic, technological, environmental, and health-related issues.

E-book design and conversion are specialties requiring the graphic designer to be familiar with the various file formats used by the numerous e-book readers, as well as their limitations, and the specifications of the particular devices, in order to format, adapt, and tweak print content to function seamlessly electronically. There is no magic wand or click of the mouse to convert a print book to an e-book. Authors and publishers are often overwhelmed by the sheer number of e-book formats and publishing options available, opening the door to opportunities for graphic designers who have the skill set to do e-book formatting and conversion. InDesign has made the conversion process easier for designers with the ability to export to the EPUB format in both reflowable and fixed layout options.

E-BOOK TYPES

There are basically two types of e-books—*reflowable e-books* and *fixed-layout e-books*. An e-book might also be referred to as an "enhanced e-book." This is not really a type, but refers to enhancements, or extra features, that make an e-book more interesting or interactive. Enhancements can also add content and functionality that is not possible in a print book.

REFLOWABLE E-BOOKS

In e-books, like those read on the monochrome Kindle, NOOK, or Kobo e-readers, the text file is reflowable, meaning that the text adapts to the screen size of the device it is being read on. The user can also change the font and type size, completely overriding the designer's choice. While this is a very useful feature for readers with poor eyesight, it creates challenges for the designer, since the page layouts and design of the print version cannot be retained. To compound the problem, the size of the screen varies by the type of device and by manufacturer. Each dedicated device needs its own formatting. The reflowable e-book is best for books such as novels that are comprised mainly of text. Non-standard paragraphs, such as lists, outlines, and poetry, require special design treatment. Tables and charts can be problematic and must be inserted as images.

FIXED-LAYOUT E-BOOKS

Fixed-layout e-books are e-books that replicate the look of print books, with color screens, two-page spreads and text over graphics. It is a popular format for children's books, graphic novels, cookbooks, technical manuals, and textbooks—books that are heavily designed or illustrated. Unlike reflowable e-books, fixed-layout e-books can preserve the same layout and design as their print counterparts. Text and images are "fixed" to the same point on a page.

The most common fixed-layout e-book formats are:

∗ KF8 and Kindle Textbook Creator for Amazon Kindle Devices

- ePUB3 for Apple, Google, and Kobo
- PagePerfect and NOOK Kids for Barnes & Noble.

Of the fixed formats, Apple's EPUB format offers the most enhancements. Most fixed-layout books are children's books because the Barnes & Noble and the Amazon formats do not support non-fiction that well. Apple's platform also supports narration integration, as well as some animation and interactivity, options that are not currently available in the other fixed layout formats. In addition to the EPUB3 fixed layout format, Apple's iBooks platform also supports another format called iBooks Author, a tool for creating non-fiction fixed-layout e-books, especially textbooks (discussed in the next section).

With the introduction of e-book/tablets, the e-book reading experience has evolved from just words to a rich multimedia experience. Monochrome e-readers with their E-ink displays that don't fade in bright sunlight still excel at plain text. However, Apple's improved iPad—with four times the number of pixels as the original, and its 9.7-inch color display—was the first e-reader device that rivaled both the crisp text and brilliant images of ink on paper. These improvements in the technology are being explored by publishers, who are publishing e-book versions of hardcover titles (including novels) at half the price, with enhancements not found in the print edition, such as video interviews with authors, pop-up galleries of illustrations of characters and objects mentioned in the text, zoomable maps, interactive infographics, puzzles, etc.

E-BOOK FORMATS

There have been numerous e-book formats. As technology has advanced, some have become stronger with support and development and others have disappeared. The following are the most commonly recognized formats today:

- **EPUB2** is the most widely supported vendor-independent XML-based (as opposed to PDF) e-book format. It is supported by the largest number of e-readers. The EPUB format, developed as an industry-wide standard for e-books, is maintained by the World Wide Web Consortium (W3C), an international community of member organizations and the public working together to develop Web standards. EPUB is based on a variety of other technologies and standards, like Open e-book and XHTML 1.1. By combining these standards, it has the advantage of being able to format almost every shape and size of e-book. EPUB books can be read on Windows and Apple computers with Adobe Digital Editions; on the Barnes & Noble NOOK and

NOOK Color; on the iPad, iPhone, iPod Touch, and the Android system, using a variety of apps; on Linux computers and other handheld devices using special software; and online in Bookworm and in Ibis Reader, a web-based reading system that can be accessed by mobile phones and computers.

- **EPUB3**, the latest version of the EPUB format, was released in 2011. It is now officially supported on all reading systems. EPUB3 was updated to include better support for foreign languages, embedded media, and other core features and enhancements. It also has a fixed layout formatting option that is beginning to be adopted for children's e-books and even for non-fiction titles.

- **iBooks Author** is a proprietary e-book format created by Apple and intended for complex non-fiction e-books, such as textbooks, cookbooks, etc. The iBooks Author format is only able to be read in the iBooks environment, and it can only be created in the iBooks Author program on a Macintosh computer. iBooks Author files are fixed layout—the design is static and does not allow the reader to change the font size or other visual settings. However, iBooks Author also has an option for creating a reflowable version of the content that can be accessed by changing the orientation of the device. iBooks Author format is not recommended for children's e-books because it does not have support for a read aloud function that is available in standard children's fixed layout e-books for Apple. iBooks Author files are similar to EPUB files in structure, but they are not the same format and are not interchangeable with EPUB files.

- **Kindle Format 8 (KF8)** is Amazon's successor to the old Mobipocket format, and has been updated to include a variety of new features and functionality. KF8 has support for HTML5 and CSS3, and it also has a built-in fixed-layout format that is especially well-suited for children's e-books. KF8 e-books can be read on any of the Kindle devices, as well as in any of the Kindle Apps for PC, Mac, iOS, Android, etc.

PUBLISHING AGGREGATORS

Digital self-publishers looking for a wider distribution beyond Amazon for their e-books should consider a *publishing aggregator,* a self-publishing service that lets them upload a manuscript to one place and then distributes their book to multiple channels, including various retailers, libraries, and stores around the world. Working with an aggregator bypasses many of the formatting complexities self-publishers would have to deal with if they attempted to upload their book to each individual retailer. Three of the larger aggregators today are Smashwords (www.smashwords.com), Draft2Digital (www.draft2digital.com), and the newer PublishDrive (www.publishdrive.com).

In addition to making formatting easier, these platforms take care of the administrative aspects and distribution, as well as make royalty calculations easier because all sales are consolidated into one central location. They do charge 10–15% of sales for their services, but that cost should be balanced against the time it would take indie authors and small publishers to commit to customizing their book's content, formatting, and other aspects of publishing to meet the specific requirements of each different retail site.

All three services have their pros and cons, as well as unique features, so they should be researched thoroughly before choosing one.

PRICING

Interior e-book design pricing differs by the type and complexity of service. Services may be offered individually or as package deals with the price of the package increasing with the number of manuscript pages and the number or complexity of the services included.

An example of a relatively inexpensive individual service is the preparation of a fiction file by a designer to meet specifications for conversion (flat fee). Most design and formatting services for fiction are charged as flat rates according to a tiered system based on either the number of words or number of pages. Non-fiction, such as children's books or other heavily formatted or illustrated books, may be priced by a variety of methods, such as by the page, by the hour, or by complexity and number of chapters. The most time-consuming and labor-intensive formatting, and therefore the most expensive, is for fixed-layout books. Requiring the highest level of design, they are usually custom priced.

Designers determine the complexity of a basic e-book project based on the time it will take to develop the e-book files. Affecting the length of time are many factors, such as the source file type, the number of internal and external hyperlink features, and whether there are images, charts, or tables; back matter (indexes and glossaries); extra page features (footnotes, lists, sidebars, pull quotes); special formatting (scripts, screenplays, poetry, etc.); foreign languages; mathematical and other special symbols; complex page design. Enhancements such as narration, animation, video, interactivity, etc., may be outsourced services and billed additionally. Time should also be built into the budget for previewing the book on various devices.

See Figure 5-8 for pricing for Interior Book Design.

Book Packaging & Consulting

Book packaging and book consulting services are other possible sources of work for self-employed book designers.

Book Packaging

Occasionally, an organization (for profit or nonprofit), an independent writer, and/or a book designer collaborate to create a "package" that is then sold (or gifted) directly to its member organization or to a traditional publisher for public distribution to create book sales and revenue. Such a package includes completely finished digital files, relieving the publisher or funding organization of any production responsibilities. Generally, this way of working is most common when the idea for the book originates with the organization, writer, or designer who wishes to maintain control over the manuscript copy content, design, illustrations, or photographic images used to create the book. This also would include the physical attributes of the book, including trim size, decoration, reproduction processes that best present the book in the marketplace (i.e., offset printing, letterpress, or silk-screen printing vs digital printing and/or e-book platforms).

With the emergence of self-publishing companies on the Internet, there is an increased demand for book packaging. Online companies that specialize in print on demand (POD) publishing (printing one copy at a time) make it easier and more affordable for an author to self-publish. However, to achieve a professional look, authors still need the services of a professional designer or other traditional publishing services, including distribution guidance.

The goals for book packaging for the self-publishing market are the same as for traditionally published authors: represent the book inside with a presentation that will pique the interest of its intended audience and make the reading process familiar, clear, and visually appealing to help keep reader's attention. In terms of design, there should be no difference between a self-published and a traditionally published book. The packaging designer considers the genre and intended audience, and digital on-demand printing limitations. among other factors, when making packaging decisions. It is a service that is especially needed for first-time authors.

The charge for this service may be included in a designer's fees for book design.

Book Consulting

BOOK SHEPHERDING

An all-inclusive consulting service geared to self-publishers is book shepherding. A book shepherd guides self-publishers through complicated book projects and the confusing maze of the rapidly changing publishing industry, advising them on all aspects of the publishing process, from developing the manuscript through marketing and distribution. A professional book shepherd, like a packager, often has in-depth prior experience in the field of publishing or authoring as well as valuable connections to industry experts, which can help authors avoid the pitfalls of self-publishing and save them from costly mistakes. Book shepherds put together creative teams for any skills they don't have themselves, so for independent book designers, aligning themselves with a book shepherd can be another potential source of income.

HYBRID PUBLISHERS

There is a new breed of fee-based professional book publishing services emerging called the "hybrid publisher," which is a cross between the self-publisher and the traditional publisher. While book shepherding describes the process of herding creative individuals through a project to create a unique book with impact in the marketplace, the hybrid publisher brings more book publishing expertise to the table and an additional entrepreneurial "partnership" approach. Hybrid publishers are willing to share in the marketplace risk with the author. They do this by offering reasonable or discounted fees upfront and sharing in the marketplace profitability by paying the author a higher royalty of the net profits than is offered by traditional book publishers.

Typography, Lettering, & Calligraphy

Graphic design utilizes both typography and lettering, and sometimes calligraphy. All three share certain visual concepts, but they are quite different disciplines.

Typography

Typography refers to a repeatable system of letters, as well as the art and technique of arranging type in a way that makes it legible, clear, and visually appealing to the reader. When choosing type for a project, graphic designers consider letter style, appearance, and structure and how well they work within a layout, color scheme, etc. The choice of a typeface can make the difference between good and bad design. However, the art of typography is much more than that. When selecting type, graphic designers consider the relationship between the look of the text and what the text says, in order to bring the words to life. The choice of type has the power to express different emotions, moods, and atmospheres, as well as convey specific messages.

In digital media, typography is a vital component of user interface design. Just as with printed materials, good typography establishes a strong visual hierarchy and provides a graphic balance to web pages. It guides and informs users, optimizes readability and accessibility, and ensures an excellent user experience.

Typography is used for both text and headlines in print, digital, and interactive media in all areas of the communications and entertainment industries, in advertising and promotion, corporate identity, packaging, and publishing. The typographic choices made by graphic designers are evident in all aspects of our everyday life—from the magazines we read, the products we buy, to the movies we watch, the social media we engage in, the websites we visit, and the apps we download on our phones.

Lettering

Although typography is a core component of graphic design, some graphic artists also specialize in the discipline of lettering. *Lettering* is the art of drawing single letterforms individually and in a customized way, for a specific use through a process of sketching, refining, and final execution. This differentiates lettering from type design (see the Type Design section below), which is creating a system of letters (typefaces) that always look the same in any combination. Unlike type, lettering is generally not used for text; it is mainly used for purposes where display type would be used.

Graphic artists who specialize in lettering find work in advertising, editorial, and packaging design, creating various unique headlines and titles that support a brand, or in corporate design, creating custom logotypes (see more about logo design under the Corporate Design section). The work of the lettering artist also can be found on stationery, greeting cards, wall art, and all types of decorative household goods.

TYPES OF LETTERING

Within the discipline of lettering, there are various sub-specialties.

HAND LETTERING

Originally, as its name suggests, *hand lettering* was done manually. The digital age has had a major impact on lettering, since graphic artists can now manipulate and customize fonts on a computer. There are even typefaces that mimic the look of hand lettering.

Today, some artists still render lettering and lettering animation completely by hand, but others do the entire process digitally, and still others use a combination of methods. Increasingly lettering artists draw sketches manually and then complete the work digitally. However, there are many variations in the workflow: letters may be drawn first and then refined; they may be outlined and then filled in; they may begin with an already drawn form or typeface and then altered, either manually on paper or digitally after the work is scanned into a computer; or they may be started in a computer program, such as Adobe Illustrator, and then customized.

Typically, lettering artists use a variety of pencils, pens, brushes, brush pens, and felt markers to create their work. However, any method of creating handmade letters is considered hand lettering, including needle and thread. Engraving and similar arts are related to lettering.

TACTILE LETTERING

Tactile lettering is a specialty within lettering, in which letters are created by hand, out of paper or other physical objects. The lettering may be designed first on a computer, then the objects are painstakingly positioned on a sketch of the design and photographed. The choice of objects used to create the lettering are limitless—candy, food, coins, nature (leaves, flowers, seeds, stones, feathers, etc.), and manufactured items, adding visual and symbolic meaning to the words, titles, and slogans created. Tactile lettering also can be animated by moving the objects and using stop-motion videotaping techniques.

TYPOGRAPHIC ILLUSTRATION

Some lettering projects involve merging the art of typography (arranging letters) with illustration, commonly referred to as *typographic illustration*. In these assignments, lettering is not simply a headline but might be a full page or an image made up of hand-lettered words or a combination of lettering integrated with smaller illustrations or icons. It can also take the form of concepts illustrated with various words in the shape of a person or object. Not all typographic illustration uses hand-lettered words; sometimes pre-fabricated typefaces are used with modifications, or they are arranged in a unique way to express an idea. Typographic illustration is a way to convey a message or emotion through lettering. Examples of typographic illustration can be found in a variety of media, such as a magazine or book cover, a feature article, or an advertisement.

HANDWRITING & CALLIGRAPHY

Related to hand lettering are handwriting and calligraphy, but there is a fundamental difference. While hand lettering involves drawing individual letter forms, the movement of *handwriting* is done in one gesture and focuses on the flow of writing letterforms. Handwriting is characterized by using a casual-looking script style of lettering. Handwriting campaigns are often used in advertising and packaging design. Sometimes the product name is handwritten (e.g., Gardenburger®); in other instances, handwriting is reserved for sub-branding (e.g., light carb, vanilla, etc.).

Calligraphy is a form of handwriting, and although it can look lightweight and effortless, its execution is usually very planned and deliberate. It is marked by a variation in width for the upstrokes and downstrokes of each letter. Traditionally, calligraphy involves writing with ink and pens with nibs or brushes. It is important for calligraphers to master the rhythm of their hand and tools as part of their skill and technique. Unlike hand lettering, calligraphy has been used historically for long passages of text, including entire books, prior to the advent of the printing press. The most famous modern example of a book handwritten with calligraphy is *The St. John's Bible,* commissioned in 1998.

Specific Trade Customs

The work of lettering artists is similar to that of illustrators. Upon agreement of the terms, usage rights, and fee for the project, a letterer prepares a sketch or sketches of possible solutions to a specific problem. Sketch fees alone usually do not include usage rights that must be transferred in writing. Upon acceptance of the sketches or comp, the lettering artist prepares finished art for reproduction.

Graphic artists who want to modify a font to create a logo need to refer to the font's End User License Agreement (EULA) to confirm that modifying the font is allowed. Not all font publishers allow modification of existing typefaces, so the issue needs to be researched on a case-by-case basis.

Pricing

Many factors affect the pricing of lettering. A primary factor is usage, which may be further broken down by geographic area, time period, market, and type of media (print, digital, or both).

In logo design work, usage terms include an all-rights transfer, as the company or organization will need rights to use the work indefinitely and exclusively.

In the publishing field, pricing is affected by whether the lettering is being done for a new release or the re-release of an old book, and whether it's a hardcover or a paperback book, with romance being its own category. Hardcovers pay more than paperbacks. The fame of the author and the use of the cover are other pricing considerations. A new title for a well-known, best-selling author commands a higher fee than for an unknown author. The highest prices are paid when the cover becomes a product—the style of the lettering becomes the author's brand or franchise. Likewise, the lettering of a TV show or movie title may also become a brand or franchise.

When pricing headlines created for advertising, the lettering artist may take into account the size of the ad and the relative size of the headline, and refer to advertising illustration fees based on ad size (1/4-page, 1/2-page, etc.). Fees for lettering done as design for social media use can depend on the size of the brand and whether the design will be used elsewhere for print. See Figure 7-1 for Comparative Fees for Advertising Illustration.

Artists usually receive half of the total fee upon delivery of sketches. (Increasingly, more time is spent on sketches and less on completing the digital finish.) Some lettering artists and calligraphers include in their contracts a nonrefundable deposit of 50% of the project.

Fees for lettering done as part of a package design, depend on, among other factors, whether the client hired the artist directly, which is unusual, or a design firm or advertising agency hired the artist, which is more common. In the latter case, the fee is usually significantly less, reflecting in-house input into the design and the agency's

reluctance to part with any more of the client's fee for services than is necessary.

For all tactile lettering, rates can depend on the amount of copy, the intricacy of letterforms, the complexity of the animation, the ease or difficulty in working with a particular product or material, as well as the size of the brand/company for which the work is being done.

A project requiring typographic illustration may be priced more like illustration, but it may depend on how complex the lettering portion is.

Type Design

Type design is the art and process of creating systems of alphanumeric characters and symbols, called *typefaces* that always look the same in any combination and that are output as *fonts*, the software installed on a computer. Type design work is performed by a type designer who blends elements of art and math, along with optical corrections to accommodate for the peculiarities of human perception.

Digital typefaces are the foundation for today's print, branding, interactive, and app design. Perhaps because of their constant use and exposure, they tend to be taken for granted by most of the viewing public. Many thousands of typefaces exist today, giving graphic designers the ability to depict the feeling, mood, tone, and very essence of a message through type.

The terms *typeface* and *font* are often used interchangeably, but technically there is a difference. Typeface refers to the appearance and design of a collection of related characters as a whole. In both traditional typesetting and modern usage, font refers to the delivery mechanism of the typeface design. In traditional (manual) typesetting, the font is made from metal or wood. Today, the font is primarily a digital file, although traditional typesetting is still practiced as an artisan pursuit and a niche market.

OpenType is currently the standard file format for typeface design. OpenType fonts are nearly operating system platform neutral, allowing the typeface designer to build fonts that can tackle complex typography, including glyph variants like small caps and different numeral styles, and that support significantly more languages and scripts than its predecessor technologies. OpenType also allows for contextual substitution, in which fonts respond to what is typed by the type user. This lets script typefaces become more like hand lettering, and other possibilities.

With OpenType, users have come to expect typefaces that can cover a much broader set of languages than in the PostScript/TrueType font days. Today, extended language support is the main driver of growth in the font industry.

Variable fonts, a new font format, was added to the OpenType standard in 2016. With variable fonts, a single font file has the capability to seamlessly transition between multiple weights and styles of a typeface design. For example, instead of a font having discrete weights, the user can use a slider or some other means to specify any of at least a hundred weights, from the lightest to the boldest. The variable capability was added with the World Wide Web in mind, since a single variable font file (about the size of two static fonts) can take the place of any number of discrete font files, thereby reducing the amount of data needed to be downloaded to display a web page.

Variable fonts need a decent amount of technical knowledge to produce, but the tools are improving. Nevertheless, type designers are coming up with very creative uses for this new capability beyond web-page efficiency.

Specific Trade Customs

Each year, hundreds of new fonts are created, ranging from simple display fonts to trendy fonts to complex, sophisticated font families. The designers who create these fonts are often self-employed, running their own small type foundry, or they may be staff designers working at the larger type foundries or at companies, such as Adobe. Typeface design work can be either commissioned or noncommissioned (produced independently, on speculation). Sometimes, a font that was originally commissioned might be licensed retail if the exclusivity has lapsed or never existed. As software, fonts are licensed while the designer, in most cases, retains ownership.

USAGE ISSUES

The distinction between a typeface and a font matters in terms of intellectual property law. In the United States, copyright protection does not extend to type design, as it does in some other Western countries, including the United Kingdom and Germany. However, novel and non-obvious typeface designs are subject to protection by *design patents*, a form of legal protection granted to the ornamental design of a functional item. Also, a distinctive new name of a typeface can be trademarked.

Because the actual shapes of letters are not copyrightable under U.S. copyright law, the U.S. Copyright Office will not register digital vector fonts or any digital data that merely represents the electronic depiction of type designs. However, the Copyright Office may register a computer program that creates or uses certain type designs, but the registration covers only the source code that generates these designs, not the typeface, typefont, lettering, or calligraphy itself. Also, some pictorial elements that are incorporated into letter forms may be registrable, but only if they are conceptually separable from the letter shape. Examples include representation of an oak tree in the shape of a letter T, or flourishes, such as swirls, vector ornaments, scrollwork, borders and frames, added to the letter forms. (For further clarification of these issues, see Sections 723 and 906.4 of *The Compendium of U.S. Copyright Office Practices.*)

The standard for the use of a font is that a license is required for each individual font used on a computer. Under the license, fonts can be licensed by computer, CPU, or user (where a user is permitted a number of installations). In the case of a business, it is possible to license all users of an entity or to license as described above. These End User License Agreements (EULAs) generally state that fonts may only be used on machines that have a valid license. The licenses are nontransferable, meaning the fonts cannot be shared by multiple computers or given to others. Such licenses typically only apply to the font file itself (which is a computer program), and not to the shape of the typeface, as long as it is manipulated outside the software (e.g., in graphic design software).

Designers are sometimes asked to modify existing fonts. Before doing this, one must always check the End User License Agreement (EULA) that governs the use of the font software to see if such modifications are permitted under the terms of the license. Most often, this kind of work is not allowed by font licensors, except by the original designer. If this work is allowed by the EULA, it is generally priced at an hourly fee based on the type of modifications needed. Persons hiring type designers to perform this type of work are required to present the type designer with valid authorizations to do the work, and ethical typeface designers will check with the original foundry to see if such modification is permissible.

Pricing

NONCOMMISSIONED WORK

Many fonts are developed without commissions and offered to the design public for licensing. Many type designers choose to contract with resellers and sometimes larger type foundries to sell their fonts, rather than sell the licenses themselves. Royalty rates paid to the typeface designer for these arrangements range from 15 to 75%. The higher figure comes from smaller distributors, often after showing good sales. Resellers might use a license they issue, but most often they provide a license issued by the font designer (so that even though the purchase is made through the reseller, the licensor is the foundry that designed the type). Additionally, many font foundries make their fonts available via Adobe Creative Cloud and are paid a negotiated guaranteed minimum monthly royalty (with quarterly overage reporting) based on use of the fonts by Adobe CC customers who pay no fee in addition to the Adobe CC subscription. Interfacing with other type designers through professional conferences is the best way to find out what is going on in the field and who the most favorable distributors are.

Not all font licenses grant permission for the same uses. Because font designers have very limited ability to control the use of their fonts on computers (Digital Rights Management), it is important to read and understand a font license as you make use of the font. You cannot assume the font will be able to push an alert if you are doing something that is not covered by your license. It is standard that a basic level license grants permission to install the fonts software on machines for direct use to create images. In most cases, distribution of static rasterized images is permitted (e.g., printing in a magazine). However, many licenses treat some forms of static rasterized distribution as different and require additional licensing (e.g., product packaging, products, broadcast, logos, large volume).

Not all basic level licenses permit commercial use, so that any commercial use at all might require additional licensing. Almost no basic licenses permit application embedding or self-hosted web embedding (where the fonts are contained inside other software and rendered live by that software). All font licenses granted through Adobe Creative Cloud (a popular distributor of high-quality independent fonts) permit all possible static image use (commercial, product, broadcast, etc.). Usage rights not permitted under a given license are almost always available as "add-on" licensing through the foundry or reseller.

COMMISSIONED WORK

Pricing for commissioned typeface design is based on the following components that make up a commission:

Glyphs are the individual characters that make up the font's character set. A glyph can be drawn, for instance an "n" or it can be a composite, when two or more drawn forms are combined, like the "n" and tilde for "ñ". The designer works with the client to determine what languages the work needs to support and what other glyphs (numerals, punctuation, ligatures, symbols, etc.) are needed.

Fonts include the complete set of glyphs in a single style: letters, numbers, punctuation marks, ligatures, alternate glyphs (like special initial caps and swashes), foreign or mathematical symbols, and accent marks. Spacing and *kerning* (spacing exceptions for specific letter combinations) are integral to the overall quality of the font.

Families are clusters of related fonts that bear the names of their parent typefaces. The fonts in a family can vary in slope (roman or italic), weight (bold, regular, light, etc.), or width (condensed or expanded). Sometimes they include serif, semi-serif, semi-sans, and sans serif variations. Display faces often have families comprised of fonts that do not differ in slope or weight, but in decoration or another element of the design.

With the new technology supporting variable fonts, every aspect of the font can vary, creating an enormous range of style for every typeface design, basically making the simple structure of light, roman, and bold, for example, obsolete. There will be every weight possible between thin and extra bold.

Master Font Families are made by creating "master" styles which can be interpolated to create the in-between weights. Most 8-weight families have 6 masters (3 for the upright and 3 for the italic). Most of the labor in making a font family is in the mastering so that a commission of three styles where they all come from the same master is less labor-intensive than a commission where they are all separate masters (e.g., light, regular, bold).

Text faces are designed to be easily read in long blocks of copy, and they perform best between 6-point and 14-point.

Display faces differ from text faces in that they are designed to stand out and are suitable only for headlines or call-outs rather than large passages of text. Display faces are usually set in 14-point or larger. They sometimes have a smaller character set than a text face, but in the case of a display face that has a lot of alternate glyphs, this may be the opposite.

Typeface design involves creating the upper and lowercase letters, numbers, ligatures, and punctuation, as well as alternate and special characters. Creating complete font families requires multiple rounds of finished drawings or printouts, with minute adjustments between rounds. Setting text in a range of sizes and outputting to a variety of devices to ensure legibility takes time and patience.

The fee for a typeface commission should reflect the required number and variation of styles, weights, and alternate sets (small caps, lining figures, symbols). The more fully drawn glyphs a font needs, the higher the price will be. Composite (component) glyphs, although made of reused parts, still cost for the time to assemble and test the glyphs. Multiple weight/style type families will generally be priced at a lower per-font price, depending on how many weights and styles are ultimately created. Creating scripts for a design for non-alphabetic languages such as Mandarin Chinese and Japanese, and for non-Latin alphabetic languages, such as Arabic, Cyrillic, Greek, Hebrew, Indic, or Thai, is a highly specialized skill. All work is priced on a project-by-project basis.

The usage and market will also largely determine the overall price (i.e., the cost to license the fonts in addition to having them made). Does the client need just print fonts, or do they need fonts for the Web and apps, a simplified set for office users? On how many devices will the client want to install the font? Likewise, does the client need the rights to distribute the font to third parties (e.g., a company wanting to give it to its advertising partners, etc.)? For example, a single font for editorial use does not command the same price as a single font for a multinational corporation who wants to distribute it to third parties.

The exclusivity period for a typeface also affects pricing, as the retail licensing value of a font may be higher after a period of exposure as a corporate exclusive. Generally, corporate clients want a minimum of three to five years of exclusivity. In some cases, longer exclusivity periods demand a higher price, and a design with no exclusivity would be priced lower.

Many large corporations pay a large sum to own a font (meaning the designer transfers the rights rather than licenses the font) in order to avoid millions in licensing fees. An all-rights contract, where the designer transfers all rights to the client, would increase the price dramatically.

Type designers may also offer clients additional services, such as modification of spacing metrics, creation of custom kerning, expansion of existing character sets to include special characters, and coding for specialized language uses. The pricing for these services varies widely. They may be priced according to the client's intended use or they may be priced as labor with the licensing separate and dependent on use. In some special cases, a client may need fonts to work in their own proprietary software, which requires special mastering.

Since variable fonts are relatively new, pricing standards have yet to be established, either for commissioned or noncommissioned variable fonts.

The process of producing a viable Open-Type font with OpenType "features" is a highly technical discipline requiring a knowledge not only of type design, but also of programming and code. The production of a typeface involves additional work separate from the original design and font making. Some of this work may be contracted out to professionals who specialize in font engineering. Their services include *mastering*, the process of preparing final font files by making sure all glyphs have the correct Unicode values, that the styles are linked correctly, that all styles show up in font menus, and that the vertical metrics are set so that accents do not get cut off and web fonts perform correctly.

Other services include OpenType programming, the creation of variable and/or web fonts and *hinting* (or *instructing*), an essential process which involves modifying fonts with mathematical instructions to function optimally at small sizes and in low-resolution environments. Now that many computers and devices have higher resolutions, hinting is less of an issue than it once was, except in developing countries and with older computers. Once done manually, most hinting today is done with automated tools. Manual hinting specialists command a high free for the service, due to its painstaking and time-consuming nature.

Digital Imaging & Photo Retouching & Restoration

Today's technology enables graphic artists to become experts at manipulating and altering photographs and other images to better meet a client's needs. Photo manipulation includes such skills as color correcting, distorting, or enhancing an image; replacing backgrounds; and creating complex composites.

Digital Imaging

A digital imaging specialist is primarily responsible for creating quality digital images from photos, film, or digital media files provided by clients. If files are provided in hard-copy format, the specialist scans and converts the images into an electronic format. Once the image is digitized, it can be enhanced or manipulated as needed for a particular project.

Since the advent of digital photography, the role of a digital imaging specialist is to handle everything that needs to be done post-capture: image evaluation, image processing, image enhancement, and image manipulation. Image enhancement includes adjusting the color, tone, brightness, contrast, lighting, etc. Image manipulation involves the edits necessary for the photo to work within the design or page layout—cropping, resizing, rotating, etc. Digital imaging specialists are also responsible for color management, color correction, and prepress.

Imaging specialists may also be skilled in retouching—the art of cleaning up undesirable elements in a photograph (see below).

The work of an imaging specialist is done with photo-editing software, such as Adobe Photoshop, Affinity Photo, or Corel PaintShop Pro, as well as Adobe Illustrator and Adobe InDesign.

Photo Retouching & Restoration

Photo retouchers, also called *image editors*, are graphic artists who alter and enhance an existing photograph. The retouching work requested by the client often includes the same type of image manipulation that Digital Imaging Specialists handle—adjusting tone, color, contrast, lighting, sharpening, noise reduction—along with portrait retouching, image compositing, selective color changes, and adding, removing, or transforming individual elements within the photograph.

Originally, retouching was done manually, by applying bleach, dyes, gouache, or transparent watercolor to the photograph or transparency/chrome with a paintbrush or airbrush. Today, it is done digitally, using software programs such as Adobe Photoshop and Affinity Photo. The resulting image usually appears untouched. This "invisible art" requires a highly skilled hand and eye to be successful. Therefore, the retoucher most often specializes in one area of retouching and concentrates on the skills and technical knowledge of that area.

Photo retouchers perform their magic for many industries—advertising, publishing, and fashion/beauty, among others—as well as for fine art photographers and portrait studios.

Photo restorers use digital tools to add or subtract areas of a damaged or faded photograph in order to return the image to its original condition. The artist may have to remove scratches, stains, or tears; adjust the color bal-

5–9 Comparative Fees for Digital Imaging & Photo Retouching & Restoration

The pricing in this chart does not constitute specific prices for particular jobs. The buyer and seller are free to negotiate, with each designer independently deciding how to price the work, after taking all factors into account. Reading the more detailed information, Pricing Your Services, provided in Chapter 1, will help in pricing projects for your specific situation

Hourly Rates

Digital Imaging	$40–100+
Photo Retouching	$40–125+
Photo Restoration	$55–100+

Additional Fees

CANCELLATION & REJECTION FEES

(% of original project fee)	
Prior to completion of concept phase	25–50%
After completion of preliminary work	25–75%
After completion of finished work	75–100%

Designers who charge by the hour bill for the number of hours worked up to the date of cancellation or rejection, plus any expenses incurred.

RUSH WORK (% added on to normal fee)

24-hour turnaround	20–100%
48-hour turnaround	20–100%
Holidays & weekends	20–100%

The above rates and fees were compiled from the results of a national survey of graphic artists conducted by the Graphic Artists Guild in 2020. Responses were based on rates charged in 2018 and 2019.

ance and contrast; and even recreate missing sections of the image. Like photo retouching, photo restoration was historically done manually. Today, most restoration work is done digitally by scanning the photograph into an image editing program and modifying the scanned image file, then outputting that digital file to photo paper on a high-quality printer.

Old photographs are irreplaceable, having both historical and sentimental value. Photo restorers work for customers who want to preserve family photos and records, as well as for historical societies, museums, and art galleries.

When pricing a photo retouching or restoration project, the artist must take several factors into account:

Complexity: The work required can run the gamut in changes to the photo from simply removing dust spots and blemishes to actually creating realistic hand-wrought backgrounds, shapes, or figures or compositing two or more photos together to create a montage. The complexity of the work results in a wide range of hourly rates for these services. Lower fees are charged for simple retouching, such as removing telephone lines from the sky behind a building or removing blemishes and acne from a face. Fees at the higher end of the range would be charged for such jobs as restoring an old photo that has missing areas or has been ripped or stained across the eyes, mouth, or other areas of a person's face. Also commanding a higher fee would be a job combining two photos into one, for example a group shot in which one or more persons are added or subtracted, requiring that the body parts of others are moved around.

Rush Work: Retouching and restoration, by their nature, should not be rushed. It is important to know how much retouchers and restorers charge for accelerated schedules. Normal turnaround time for an average project is three days, and "rush" rates usually go into effect for projects with less than three days' turn-around.

Rights: Unlike other graphic artists, photo retouchers and restorers always work with an existing piece of art and are not usually entitled to copyright or reuse fees. The fee that they charge, usually based on an hourly rate, represents the total income from that project—unlike other artists who may benefit from future uses of a work. See Figure 5–9 for Digital Imaging & Photo Retouching & Restoration Fees.

Experiential/Environmental Graphic Design

Experiential graphic design (or XGD), also called *environmental graphic design*, involves the orchestration of typography, color, imagery, form, technology and, especially, content to create environments that communicate. Experiential graphic designers plan, design, and specify communications in the built and natural environment. Because of the term "environmental" in the former name, the discipline is often mistakenly thought of as "green" design (the use of recycled paper, soy inks, etc.) or design focusing on sustainability or improving the environment.

Experiential graphic design merges the communication skills of a graphic designer with the architect's understanding of space and structure. It encompasses distinct but overlapping areas: wayfinding systems, architectural graphics, signage and sign programs, exhibit design, retail design, and themed or branded spaces. The field embraces a wide range of disciplines including graphic design, architectural, interior, landscape, digital, and industrial design.

Design solutions are most often three-dimensional and expressed visually. Increasingly, XGD involves the use of digital technologies and systems that present dynamic content through motion graphics, making possible rich interactions between a user in a place and the information being provided. This vital field offers a rich diversity of projects in many environments from offices, campuses, hospitals, airports, cities, parks, transportation and sports facilities, to hotels, museums, zoos, retail stores, theme parks, and cruise ships, to name a few.

Signage and wayfinding programs provide site and navigational information to visitors, travelers, patients, or customers, among others. *Wayfinding* is an industry term referring to the design and implementation of directional systems that guide people through complex spaces. Signage helps to identify and brand a specific place, and when used as part of a larger wayfinding program, they help people determine orientation and they assist with navigation.

Wayfinding can be broken down into two areas: direction and orientation, and identification and regulation. Design elements as sculptural or architectural features and such aids as color-coding and graphic symbols may be used to increase ease in navigation. The practitioners of the discipline of experiential graphic design in recent years have set the standards for wayfinding in transportation centers (airports, railway and subway stations), hospitals, museums, and on city streets and highways.

According to the article, "What Is Experiential Design," by Peter Dixon (https://segd.org/what-we-do), "Learning and immersive environments such as museum exhibitions, and public, civic and landscape place-making programs have benefited from the multi-disciplinary talents of designers to shape experiences that orient, inform, educate and delight users and visitors.

"Retail stores, entertainment and hospitality destinations—theme parks, hotels, casinos, sports venues, shopping malls—and other 'branded environments' are using the tools and story-telling approaches of XGD to create more engaging and meaningful interactions with their customers."

Environmental graphic designers come predominantly from the fields of graphic, industrial, architectural, interior, and landscape design. They work closely with architects, engineers, city planners, fabricators, and construction firms.

Education & Skills Required

Projects vary widely in scale and size; consequently, environmental graphic designers need extensive knowledge of building design, project management, codes and regulations, fabrication shop practices, and construction. Also, knowledge of design possibilities and limitations, such as how materials react to weather or how distance, lighting, and speed affect the legibility of type, is crucial.

Designers seeking employment in environmental graphic design should try to apprentice either with someone already working in the field or in the graphics department of an architectural firm. They must be able to read working drawings and understand architectural scale. Useful study also includes architectural drafting, 2-D and 3-D design software, digital interactive skills, motion graphics, corporate identity and information systems design, packaging, psychology, fine art, literature, and cultural anthropology.

Specific Trade Customs

An environmental graphic design team is multidisciplinary and often includes a principal of the firm, a senior project designer, assistant designers, and additional artists and consultants who are often hired freelance for specific skills when needed.

Since these projects frequently involve long-term research and development, environmental graphic designers are often brought in at the earliest stages. In addition, many environmental graphic design offices work on retainer and act as design consultants in peripheral areas in addition to their main projects.

In the specific design of signage, often professional and governmental codes regulate and guide the design and where the signage must be located. Consequently, environmental graphic designers are required to know and follow standards established by the Society for Environmental Graphic Design (SEGD), the American Institute of Architects (AIA), and the Construction Specifications Institute (CSI), as well as local zoning laws, municipal sign ordinances, state and local building codes, fire codes, and other government regulations. A significant example of such regulations is the Americans with Disabilities Act (ADA), which affects the interior and exterior signs of all public facilities in the United States. The ADA calls for the removal of all architectural and communications barriers to those with special needs. The original ADA regulations, revised in 2010 and referred to as "the 2010 ADA Standards for Accessible Design," became enforceable on March 15, 2012. Compliance with the 2010 Standards is required for new construction and alterations under Titles II and III, as well as for program accessibility and barrier removal.

ADA Accessibility Guidelines are available from the United States Department of Justice at 800-514-0301 (voice); 800-514-0383 (TTY); and www.ada.gov/2010ADAstandards_index.htm. SEGD educates and helps define the practice of environ-mental graphic design. It also monitors and provides members with updates on related ADA regulations.

The Graphic Artists Guild Foundation and the National Endowment for the Arts published the "Disability Access Symbols Project." The project collected and standardized a graphic vocabulary of 12 symbols indicating accessibility, such as wheelchair access for mobility-challenged people, audio description services for visually challenged people, and listening devices for the hard of hearing. The symbols may be used in signage, floor plans, and other materials promoting the accessibility of places, events, or programs. SEGD also offers tested symbol sets such as healthcare and safety symbols. Download the Disability Access Symbols at https://graphicartistsguild.org/downloadable-disability-access-symbols/.

PROJECT PROPOSALS

The project begins once a client accepts a design proposal, which outlines the scope of the project, the services to be provided, consultant/client responsibilities, project fees, schedule, and terms and conditions under which it will be executed, including ownership, usage, and liability. Most environmental graphic design projects are quoted and billed by phase, with an initial fee representing 10 to 30% of total fees and reimbursable expenses.

Phase 1. Programming: Concerned with gathering information and establishing design criteria, this phase often requires spending a great deal of time with the client or on-site to define the needs and problems to be solved.

Phase 2. Schematic design: After the designer and client have reached an agreement concerning the basic program, design solutions are pursued that solve the stated problems. Much of this phase involves concept development and investigation of the functional aspects with consulting fabricators. This process results in a presentation showing only those ideas that the design team feels are viable and appropriate and meet the pre-scribed criteria. Preliminary expectations for factors such as electrical, lighting, and structural details are coordinated with the other consultants.

Phase 3. Design development: At this stage, the design team refines the accepted design, and a final presentation is made, explaining the applications. Once the client and designer have chosen a definite direction, specific information is sought from the fabricator, including preliminary cost and schedule estimates.

Phase 4. Contract documentation: The project is fully documented for implementation, which includes preparing working drawings, specifications, and reproducible artwork, where appropriate. Decisions are final at this point. Any changes made by the client after this point are billable as additional work, although designer errors are not.

Phase 5. Contract administration (including pre-bid qualification and bid assistance): This phase involves quality checking and coordinating product manufacturing. Oversight is key to this phase, since so much depends on the precision and quality achieved in this final step. Fabrication is usually billed on approved phased performance benchmarks. After the end product is approved, the project is paid in full. The designer normally retains the right to execute any design intent corrections in the fabrication process.

Pricing & Billing

Experiential design jobs are custom projects with numerous components and many variables, so it is next-to-impossible to give accurate pricing guidelines for freelancers. Even two seemingly identical projects can end up with significantly different final costs, depending on the type of materials used. There is some comparative pricing for Exhibit & Display Design provided in Figure 5–10.

Billing expenses and fees may be handled in a number of ways. Early in the project, the designer should arrange to bill as a lump sum or on an hourly, progressive, or project basis. If clients prefer to be billed on a project basis, the client usually establishes an acceptable cap on the total amount billed, although the designer must make it clear that the client is not entitled to unlimited revisions.

Expenses for work done directly with clients are usually billed with markups, including costs incurred for client-approved travel. Client alterations are usually billed at the firm's predetermined hourly rates.

The fabricator is accountable to the designer and is ethically bound to follow the designer's intent and direction while working on the project. This, of course, becomes a matter of practicality, since the designer orchestrates many elements and must oversee them all to ensure consistency. However, final fabrication and installation of the project is normally handled in a separate contract for direct billing between the client and the fabricator.

Visit the Society for Experiential/Environmental Graphic Design's website (www.segd.org) for more information.

Exhibit & Display Design

Exhibit and interior display design are growing specialties within Experiential Design. The field includes permanent installation work in natural history and art museums, science and technology education centers, and travel and tourism information centers, as well as temporary exhibits and promotional venues such as trade shows, conventions, conferences, other special events, and window and interior displays in retail stores and boutiques. Many companies are solely devoted to the unique design, production, and logistical problems related to these assignments.

Corporate Exhibits & Displays

Exhibit and display design in the corporate setting includes on-site signage for conferences and events and displays of corporate initiatives or sponsored projects. Corporate displays can be found in-house or at a traveling venue.

Educational Exhibits

Developing permanent installations whose main purpose is to educate rather than promote or sell is one example of this type of interpretive design. Exhibit designers work closely with an architect or planning firm to customize the space to meet the project's particular communications needs. Exhibit designers may have other specialists on staff or consult with graphic designers, signage experts, lighting designers, photography and film output vendors, and illustrators. These jobs are generally estimated on a project basis by the design firm. The permanence of the display is often a factor in negotiating prices.

It is critical for the exhibit designer to establish the scope of the work before negotiating a contract. The scope of work should identify the approximate size (square footage) of the exhibit; all likely elements such as cases/objects, graphics, vignettes, audiovisual, or computer

5–10 Comparative Fees for Exhibit & Display Design

The pricing in this chart does not constitute specific prices for particular jobs. The buyer and seller are free to negotiate, with each designer independently deciding how to price the work, after taking all factors into account.

Hourly Rates $75–150

Additional Fees

MARKUPS (% above designer's cost)

Out-of-pocket expenses	10–25%
Outside services	10–50%

EXTRA ROUND OF REVISIONS   110–145%
(Not included in original agreement; % of original fee)

CANCELLATION & REJECTION FEES
(% of original project fee)

Prior to completion of concept phase	20–50%
After completion of preliminary work	50–100%
After completion of finished work	100%

Designers who charge by the hour bill for the number of hours worked up to the date of cancellation or rejection, plus any expenses incurred.

RUSH WORK (% added on to normal fee)

24-hour turnaround	10–100%
48-hour turnaround	10–120%
Holidays & weekends	10–150%

The above rates and fees were compiled from the results of a national survey of graphic artists conducted by the Graphic Artists Guild in 2020. Responses were based on rates charged in 2018 and 2019.

components; and the persons who will be responsible for various input, including research, curating, scriptwriting, architectural and engineering services, new illustration or photography, photo research, obtaining objects and negotiating loans, and construction supervision. If the client is an established museum, it will likely provide the majority of these functions, while organizations new to doing exhibitions may want the designer to assemble a team to perform all such functions.

As organizations weigh the actual costs of realizing their needs, they may also hire exhibit designers to do feasibility studies to determine the scope of work for a prospective project. A feasibility study includes doing a site survey of existing conditions, developing a narrative or story line, locating sources of images and information, and assembling a firm description of, and bid on, the project so the prospective client may seriously consider what they can afford to spend. The only caution for the exhibit designer is to conduct the study under a separate contract and not as part of the potential project, in case the client decides to cancel it as a result of the study.

Trade Show Exhibits

In trade show exhibit design, a client usually has a group of specialists (an "exhibits group") design the traveling exhibition, taking into consideration the detailed and specific needs of the design message, the need to customize the exhibit from venue to venue, and the unique traveling and setup/breakdown requirements. Freelance artists are often hired to fulfill particular graphic design needs, such as typography, photography, motion graphics, illustration, and overall creative direction. Printed collateral materials are often needed at the show sites and are prepared in parallel with the overall exhibition design.

SPECIFIC TRADE CUSTOMS & PRICING

Project proposals follow the phases previously outlined for environmental graphic design. Fees for exhibit projects are usually negotiated with a "not to exceed" figure. As with other types of design involving construction, change orders are customary as the scope of work evolves. Expenses are generally added to the negotiated fees. Specific contract terms may depend on the client, so determining the client's needs and establishing a collegial working relationship are important from the start.

When pricing trade show exhibits, the artist-designer should consider not only the specific nature of the usage but also that such shows have a limited calendar life of a year or two. Advertising and institutional pricing guidelines should be the starting points for negotiating prices, with the understanding that exhibit usages are not as extensive as those for advertising and broadcast.

For traveling exhibits—which can include many other kinds of exhibits beside trade show exhibits— additional factors affect pricing. If an exhibition is to travel, then it must be designed with that in mind; materials, durability, shipping weight, and ease of assembly and disassembly need to be considered. Generally, designing an exhibit to travel involves additional work and thus a higher fee. Venues often need aspects of the traveling exhibit to be tailored to their particular spaces, so space planning and trimming to fit are also involved. If future venues are scheduled and the designer knows about them at the start of the project, then some of the cost may be included in the initial fee. If venues are added later, an additional fee is charged by the designer. See Figure 5-10 for selected Exhibit & Display Design fees.

Retail Displays

For window and interior displays in retail stores and boutiques that change on a monthly or more frequent schedule, designers usually work on a per-project basis, though many have contracts for a specified period of time or number of projects.

SPECIFIC TRADE CUSTOMS & PRICING

While there are no industry standards for this specialty, certain conditions generally prevail. Designers customarily present sketches or drawings on spec for a proposed project. The price of the sketches may be figured into the overall budget, which includes the cost of materials (asking for a deposit up front for materials is standard practice).

Display designers are responsible for providing all materials, props, and backgrounds to be used in displays (except permanent fixtures such as mannequins). Unless otherwise specified, these become their property (except permanent fixtures), even if they were built or purchased for a specific project. Designers may subsequently rent or sell these materials, though not to a competing retail outlet unless they are significantly altered first. Designers are responsible for the durability of all displays; any repairs due to weak or faulty construction are assumed to be the designer's responsibility.

Broadcast Design

The work of a broadcast designer involves all aspects of traditional graphic design plus the added dimensions of motion and sound. Broadcast designers work primarily in the media and entertainment industries, either in staff positions or as freelancers hired temporarily for a specific project. They develop and maintain a visual corporate image for an electronic media company, such as a television station, advertising agency, film production facility, or a broadcasting corporation.

Broadcast design jobs are advertised most frequently as Motion Graphic Designer or Motion Graphic Artist because they generally require work with animation and 3-D design elements. They might also be adver-tised as Broadcast Designer or Graphic Artist/Broadcast Designer jobs. A job title might reflect the major responsibilities of the position, but in general, a broadcast designer is expected to conceptualize and design for broadcast, print, web, and mobile apps, being conscious of color, space, composition, typography, and audio. For many positions, especially Motion Design, there is also an emphasis on animation and visual storytelling.

The work of designers in this field is visible in all sports, news, music, and network programming. Broadcast design includes creating the look for an entire show, channel, or network, with opening graphics and bumpers (shorter clips of an opening animation that identifies a broadcast). Some examples include the on-air look and sound of any television station or network as well as the logo, ID, lead-ins for movies, and graphics that promote shows. Most television programs begin with a title sequence designed by a broadcast designer. News and sports programs are packed with the work of broadcast designers. Almost every commercial includes some work by a broadcast designer; sometimes, entire commercials are created by broadcast designers.

Skills Required

Designers in this field, especially those working on live programming, must have the ability and temperament for working in an extremely fast-paced, deadline-driven environment with short timelines. They also must be flexible—being able to work as a team player as well as independently and being able to juggle multiple projects simultaneously.

Broadcast designers might work alongside reporters to develop story graphics and with producers and directors to create the look and feel for various program. They also direct production staff and even assist clients in creating commercials.

For on-air functions, broadcast designers are required to be illustrators, animators, and type designers. They must be knowledgeable about animation techniques, and, on occasion, must prepare and shoot animation.

Broadcast designers, even in jobs advertised as Motion Designers or Motion Artists, also may be responsible for devising off-air collateral—everything from small-space program-listing ads to full-page newspaper ads for print media, as well as trade publication ads, booklets, brochures, invitations, posters, and other material. In that capacity, they double as corporate designers, coordinating everything from the on-air look to the application of identity logos/marks from stationery, memo pads, and sales promotion materials to new vehicle or even helicopter markings. They must also be adept at designing for websites and digital and social media, with an interest in pop culture.

Scenic design may be another area of responsibility. It requires understanding construction techniques, materials, and paints, and an awareness of staging, furnishing, lighting, spatial relationships, and camera angles.

Art directors in this field must be skilled managers, proficient in organization, budgeting, purchasing, directing staff, and working with upper management. The most effective broadcast designers are those who combine great creative talent with numerous specific skills. There is a strong benefit to having an affinity for technological creative tools and techniques. Important skills beyond those of traditional graphic design include the ability to direct a live-action shoot; a working knowledge of a variety of animation techniques; video compositing and editing; and straight computer graphics.

Broadcast designers must stay abreast of technological advances in both hardware and software. The software programs most commonly used in broadcast design are Adobe Photoshop, Illustrator, After Effects, and Premiere Pro; Apple's Final Cut Pro; Maxon Cinema 4D, and Avid Maestro.

Pricing

Freelance Broadcast Designers are paid rates similar to freelance graphic design in general, with more experienced designers and those having specialized skills, such as animation, being able to command higher compensation. The size of the hiring company and the broadcast market also affect compensation.

Greeting Card & Novelty Design

Greeting card and novelty design is often done by graphic designers, surface designers, and illustrators, although some artists specialize in this field. Opportunities abound to have art or design published on greeting cards as well as on holiday decorations, posters, magnets, mugs, T-shirts, stationery, and gift or boutique-type products.

Naturally, not all designs can make the transition from card to mug to paper plate, but many of them do, making them profitable ventures for their creators. Some leading art licensors in the stationery and gift industry develop their own brands and license their designs to a broad range of product manufacturers to maximize their income potential. There is a good market for artists who can sketch product concepts quickly for giftware and other product companies. Also, there are a lot of opportunities if you like to work on licensed properties and can follow a style guide.

Some top leading licensors command good advances, royalty percentages, and project art fees. Commissioned licensed work is also done as well. Since manufacturing materials, resources, and requirements for production of various items often limit their display and design, research into those factors is extremely important for artists who are considering a career designing for this industry or for those who are interested in it as another outlet for licensing their art. While this section will focus on greeting card design, the general information is applicable to novelties as well. (For more information on licensing, see Chapter 1, Essential Business Practices.)

Greeting Card Design

Greeting cards touch the lives of millions of people each day. They comfort, inspire, celebrate, and communicate a range of emotions. Greeting cards are one of our culture's foremost tools of communication, and the greeting card industry has a constant, continual need for art. While there are staff designers at the large greeting card companies, most greeting card designers are self-employed, either as small or niche business owners or as freelancers.

A great greeting card is a marriage of art and verse—a card's message is communicated through both the design and the verse. The design makes a customer pick up a card, but the verse will make her either purchase the card or return it to the rack and search for one that better expresses what she wants to say. Thus, the designer needs to create an illustration eye-catching enough to capture the customer's attention, and the art needs to reflect the card's message. Greeting cards, like other products that feature copy and are designed to touch someone's heart, are part of the industry's "social expressions" category.

INDUSTRY OVERVIEW

Before embarking on a freelance career as a greeting card designer, it is important to understand certain facts about the industry. Most of the past decade has seen the greeting card market shrink, so designers should consider creating designs that can be licensed for other products as well as cards.

According to the Greeting Card Association, the greeting card industry today generates $6.5 billion in retail sales from consumer purchases of more than 7–8 billion cards. Of the total greeting cards purchased annually, roughly half are seasonal, and the remaining half are for everyday card-sending occasions. Christmas is the most popular seasonal card-sending holiday, followed by Valentine's Day, Mother's Day, Father's Day, Graduation, and Easter cards. Birthday cards account for most of the sales volume for everyday card sales, followed by a number of secondary occasions that include sympathy, thank you, wedding, thinking of you, get well, new baby, and congratulations. Nine out of ten American households purchase an average of 30 greeting cards each year. with women purchase more than 80% of all greeting cards.

According to Dun & Bradstreet First Research, there are 100 print greeting card publishers in the United States, with nearly 100% of revenue concentrated in the top 50 companies. However, small companies compete effectively by offering unique or specialized products. Many publishers license designs from freelance artists. Competitors to the print market include online companies and photo services that publish digital greeting cards, photos, and videos, as well as social media outlets such as Facebook and Instagram.

The two largest print publishers are Hallmark Cards and American Greetings Corp, LLC (AGC), a vertically integrated company whose brands include Carlton Cards, Gibson, and Papyrus, among others. Both companies have an online presence, selling their print cards as well as personalized and electronic greeting cards (e-cards). The online market is not as concentrated as the print market. Although Hallmark and ACG are the largest players, according to IBIS*World,* their market share decreased during 2014–19, due to intense competition from smaller brands.

Despite the competition from e-mail, text, and social media companies that make it easier to send instant greetings, more people, especially young people, are sending greeting cards. While the industry has been struggling for the past decade, younger people and millennials, in particular, are credited with keeping the industry afloat. In 2018, the industry showed 3% growth. Not only are millennials buying physical cards, but they are buying fancier specialty cards with a higher price tag. Millennials have shown a preference for retro technologies like paper books and vinyl records. Research has shown that nostalgia works by evoking sensory input through tangible objects that trigger memories, such as people who are no longer in our lives or a longing for past events because they seem to be better in some way than the present. The ability for paper cards to engage multiple senses—touch, smell, and sight, and now hearing with audio cards—makes them powerful as memory aids and emotional triggers.

Millennials are embracing all greeting card formats and outlets, such as digital apps that allow them to send personalized cards with a click of a button and to upload a picture from their phone and write a personalized message in their own handwriting, which the company then mails to the recipient. They also shop for greeting cards from some of the big photo-printing companies, such as Shutterfly and Vistaprint, where they can upload personal pictures to customize stationery and greeting cards.

Millennials are also starting their own greeting card companies or lines to create a more personalized experience and to make cards more relatable to younger consumers. Their offerings feature pop-up 3-D images, hand-painted artwork, LED lights, sounds, and even animated cartoons that can be accessed with a mobile phone. One of the most successful small greeting card start-ups is Lovepop, which has sold more than 5 million of its handmade pop-up cards featuring laser-cut pieces of kirigami art since it launched in 2014. It sells 90% of its cards directly to consumers online.

GETTING STARTED

When creating designs to license in the greeting card industry, it is advisable to stick with the more popular and saleable categories, such as birthday and Christmas. The chances of getting a design published increase substantially when artists concentrate their designs efforts on high-volume cards. The Greeting Card Association's website, www.greetingcard.org, has a wealth of helpful information for designers trying to break into the industry, including tips for artists and writers, current industry statistics and trends, paper and envelope sizes, and an updated list of its member organizations (with contact information) who are accepting submissions.

TIPS OF THE TRADE

Many card stores still use racks that obscure the bottom half of the card, so it is important to get the message—"Happy Birthday," "Merry Christmas," or other text—into the top third of the card. If the design does not have words, try to place the strongest design element where it will be seen. Also, be aware that most racks do not accommodate horizontal cards, so artists who are designing on spec are advised to use a vertical 5 x 7-inch format. When creating work on spec, it is not necessary to design the inside of the card. The cover illustration is enough for art directors to decide if the look and feel are appropriate for their company.

Marketing Designs for Cards & Novelties

Some artists use a licensing agent to market their work, while others prefer to represent themselves. (For more information on licensing agents, see Chapter 4, Maximizing Income.) Artists who represent themselves need to decide which companies to approach. Research is extremely important to learn how their work can translate best to potential clients' product ranges. Shopping the market to see what products are available and how the art is applied to the product formats can put an artist way ahead of the equally talented competition.

One way to select a company is to view their complete product line, which can be done by attending one of the national or regional stationery and gift shows, such as the National Stationery Show, which is held in New York City every May, or the Atlanta Gift Show, which is held in January and July. SURTEX, held in May in New York City, is an international show that focuses on selling and licensing art and design for numerous industries, including greeting cards, gift wrap, and other paper products. (A more comprehensive list of shows can be found in Part 5, Resources & References. Given the COVID-19 pandemic, check the shows' websites for updates as to whether they will be held in 2021.)

Reading industry publications, such as GREETINGS etc., the official publication of the Greeting Card Association, is a great way to research different card companies—and to stay on top of industry trends. You can also explore individual card company websites to research their offerings to see if your art is a good match for their line. For example, one card company specializes in Christian and spirituality-themed cards. Another company wants photos of animals, but only in their natural habitats—no photos taken in zoos or with humans. Familiarizing yourself with a company's offerings and philosophy before you submit your art will save you unnecessary rejection.

Before making a submission, contact the company and request their artist/photographer guidelines (Hallmark and American Greetings do not accept unsolicited freelance submissions.) Many companies post submission guidelines on their website. The guidelines will say what to send, to whom to send it, when to send it, and how to send it. For example, most companies prefer to look at digital submissions (with specific file-size limits), but occasionally a company will request color photocopies. Some companies will review any work at any time; others have a specific submissions schedule (e.g., they look for Christmas submissions in September and do not want to see Valentine or birthday ideas at that time). Artists who submit their work according to the company guidelines have a better chance of getting their submissions reviewed.

Each submission should include the artist's name and contact information, along with a design number and the copyright symbol. Artists should keep a record of all designs they have submitted.

Pricing

Determining which rights are being acquired is critical when pricing a design. Most greeting card designers license their work either on a *flat fee* basis or for an *advance against royalties*. Licensing gives a company the right to reproduce a design for a certain product (e.g., greeting cards or mugs), a specified time period (generally three to five years), and a specific territory (e.g., North America or worldwide). (A more detailed discussion of licensing can be found in the Art Licensing section of Chapter 4, Maximizing Income.) Some companies attempt to use a "work-made-for-hire" agreement because they want to own all the rights to the finished design. The Graphic Artists Guild does not recommend creating work under a work-made-for-hire arrangement because the artist loses all rights to the art and, therefore, all potential future revenue.

The advantage to a flat-fee license is that the artist receives money in advance and therefore will not be dependent on the design selling successfully to generate income from it. Also, manufacturers tend to pay a higher flat fee than an advance against royalties. For example, a flat fee for a greeting card design generally ranges between $275 and $500, while an advance—if one is offered—against what is typically a 4-to-6% royalty tends to be between $150 and $300. However, it is possible to negotiate both a higher royalty percentage and a higher advance, especially if a licensee asks for exclusivity in a certain territory or product type.

The ranges in pricing reflect differences in the complexity of the design, whether multiple pages (cover and inside) of design are used, and the quantity printed. It's important for artists to know that if the advance against royalty is the amount equivalent to what they would earn if the initial print run sells or if the amount of the flat fee buyout is equivalent to the advance, they are not taking any undue risks to ask for royalties. In fact, it can be a win-win situation: the artist is rewarded for designing great-selling art with money on the back half (when the royalties surpass the advance), and the client then has artists devoted to making work that helps their product perform well in the marketplace. This is a team partnership where licensing benefits both parties.

5–11 Comparative Fees for Greeting Card Design

The pricing ranges in this chart do not constitute specific prices for particular jobs. The buyer and seller are free to negotiate, with each designer independently deciding how to price the work, after taking all factors into account. Reading the more detailed information, Pricing Your Services, provided in Chapter 1, will help in pricing projects for your specific situation.

Flat Fees: Print Greeting Cards

COVER	$75–2,000
COVER & INSIDE	$100–2,500

Fees vary widely by the specific publisher and the reputation of the designer.

Additional Fees (% of original project fee)

EXTRA ROUND OF REVISIONS	115–150%

(Not included in original agreement)

CANCELLATION & REJECTION FEES

Prior to completion of concept phase	10–50%
After completion of preliminary work	50–80%
After completion of finished work	80–100%

Designers who charge by the hour bill for the number of hours worked up to the date of cancellation or rejection, plus any expenses incurred.

RUSH WORK (% added on to normal fee)

24-hour turnaround	30–100%
48-hour turnaround	20–50%
Holidays & weekends	20–100%

The above rates and fees were compiled from the results of a national survey of graphic artists conducted by the Graphic Artists Guild in 2020. Responses were based on rates charged in 2018 and 2019.

Royalties are paid on the wholesale price of the card. Related products, such as gift wrap and boxed stationery sets, which are more complicated to execute, may command higher prices. To determine if a royalty fee will be profitable, it is best to ask how many pieces the client plans to produce for their initial and ensuing press runs. Then evaluate the options and strike the best deal. Generally, while mass market retailers offer lower royalty percentages, the sheer number of potential sales can make a royalty arrangement attractive in these situations.

The price should also reflect how complicated a design is and how much time will be required to produce it. Other factors can affect the price, including samples and the artist's credit. Most card companies provide six to twelve free samples of the finished product, but it is possible to negotiate for a larger number. A proper copyright notice should accompany the artwork. Designers should specify in the licensing agreement that name and copyright credit be given to them on both products and packaging. A credit line on all products develops the recognition of the artists and their brands and is essential to building their future as art licensors. Artists just starting out are sometimes willing to accept a smaller fee in return for their credit and extra samples.

The artist should receive a cancellation fee if a project is canceled, either because the artist did not execute the assignment in a satisfactory fashion or because the client changed its mind about the project. If the artist completes the requested assignment but the project does not move forward, a general kill fee is half the flat fee arrangement or all of a royalty advance (since there will be no royalties). If the artist completes the assignment but the design was found lacking, one quarter to one third of the agreed-upon price may be more appropriate. (For more discussion of cancellation fees, see the Cancellation & Rejection Fees section of Chapter 1, Essential Business Practices.)

See Figure 5–11 for fees for Greeting Card Design.

Commissioning Procedures

For situations in which a designer is commissioned to create new art for a product according to a client's specifications (as opposed to licensing existing work), most companies will send the artist a commissioning form that spells out all the details of what they want. Many companies also include a contract with the commissioning form, so there is no misunderstanding about what licensing rights they wish to acquire. However, in any client dealings, it is best for artists to have their own standard contracts that they offer to the client first. By offering their own contract first, artists establish their professionalism in the field and let the client know they value their work.

The commissioning form should include the due date for the sketches, color comps, and finished art. Many companies include prices for the sketches separately from the finished art. Then, if the project is terminated after the sketch stage, the artist knows how much he or she will be paid. If a company communicates clearly what is expected and the sketches do not reflect those requirements, the firm expects the artist to try again at no additional charge. If, however, the company changes its mind about what is wanted, then it should expect to pay for the artist to rework the sketch.

Contracts

It is essential that artists have a contract, signed by both parties, before beginning work on a project. At the least, artists should have a signed letter of agreement that defines the terms until the exact contract can be signed. If the client insists on using its own contract, artists can still send the client their own contract and suggest that they negotiate a compromise that is mutually fair and beneficial to both parties. Many artists feel that they have no right to ask for changes when they are offered only the client's contract. This is not true—negotiation is key, and artists often cross out wording and terms that they feel are unfair, unacceptable, or unnecessary. Any changes in the contract should be initialed by both parties. If the client does not accept reasonable changes requested by the artist, the artist should consider walking away from the deal. Ultimately, the artist must decide if the deal is worth it and whether or not they can live with the terms of the deal.

Some of the variables in a contract include the following:

Property: Design(s).

Products: What the company plans to produce or manufacture using the designs.

Territory: Where the company can sell the products. Many companies sell worldwide and therefore need to obtain worldwide rights to the design.

Term: Length of time the company is allowed to manufacture products with this particular design. The average greeting card has a shelf life of three years, but companies usually ask for a five-year term and often an extension term (an additional time period of one to three years).

Renewal fee: Percentage of the original compensation to be paid to the artist if the company wishes to continue to use the design for an additional period. In a flat-fee contract, the artist needs an additional incentive to allow the company to continue to produce the design; otherwise, the artist could license that design elsewhere. In a royalty contract, a renewal fee clause is optional since the artist is compensated by additional royalties. Designers should ask for a renewal fee of 100% of the original agreed-upon flat-fee price. A second advance is not always paid for a renewal, but the royalty is the same.

Automatic renewal clause: It may not be advantageous to the artist to have an automatic renewal clause in the contract because many things can change during the life of a contract, which may not be in an artist's best interest. For example, the client may sell the artist's work to a company that the artist does not want to be associated with, or the client did not produce good sales figures. The artist needs the right to end with that company and enter into an agreement with a company that will be more lucrative.

Out clause: the main reason to have a provision to get out of the contract is if the client does not put the artist's work into commercially feasible quantities within six to eight months of signing the deal. The client should not tie up the rights to the artist's work for three years if it is not going to actually put the art into production. Other reasons for including an out clause are if the client does not pay on time, goes bankrupt, etc.

Two other items are important to include in the contract:

Samples: Companies customarily give artists a number of samples in the quantity in which their product is sold. For example, greeting cards are usually sold by the half-dozen or dozen, so the artist ordinarily receives 6 or 12 samples. Mugs and other gift products are sold individually or in lots of two or three, so the artist may receive fewer samples. If more samples are needed as useful giveaways, the artist can request more at the manufacturer's cost price. A clause should be added that if the product is liquidated, the artist should be offered the product first at the liquidation price. In any selloff period, artists should still receive their royalty percentage on the selloff, too.

Artist's Credit: Artists should always specify that their name and copyright credit appear on both products and packaging.

Additional Resources

Licensing Art 101, 3rd Ed. by Michael Woodward. A well-written, comprehensive handbook on licensing designs, which includes a chapter devoted to greeting cards. Available through Amazon.com.

Artist & Graphic Designer's Market. Published annually by Writer's Digest Books, it features a section devoted to greeting cards.

Infographic Design

Infographics, the contracted term for information graphics, give life to information, data, and knowledge through signs, charts, graphs, diagrams, maps, and other visual elements. This visual illustration of information gives meaning to otherwise complex ideas and presents information in a manner that is easily understood, memorable, and enjoyable.

Designing infographics involves presenting complex information so that it can be easily understood at a glance, as in the age-old adage, "a picture is worth a thousand words." Infographics serve as visual shorthand for everyday concepts, and they also illustrate information that would be cumbersome as text alone. In some cases, infographics have a secondary use. They may be used to save space, for example when cooking directions are printed on a product package in pictures and numbers, with very few words. Pictorial directions for using or assembling a product to be marketed globally also save on translating the directions into multiple languages.

Infographics predate writing as a means of communication. Cave drawings are probably the earliest known example. People were also creating and using maps before the advent of written language. Although the art form of infographics has its roots in print, they are now widely used in all types of digital media. Their use has increased with the growth of the Internet, where social media has made them wildly popular. They are particularly suited to our short attention spans in an age of information overload.

Today, the work of infographic designers—ranging from the simple to the highly technical—can be seen everywhere and in all types of media. One of the more common usages of infographics is traffic signs and other public signs with their stylized human figures, icons, and emblems to represent concepts such as stop, go, yield, caution, and the direction of traffic. Public places such as airports, train stations, parks, and museums usually have some sort of integrated signage system with standardized icons and stylized maps. Modern maps, especially route maps for transit systems, use infographic techniques to integrate a variety of information, such as the conceptual layout of the transit network, transfer points, and local landmarks.

Print, online, and broadcast media use infographics in the creation of weather maps and graphs illustrating statistical data. Infographics, frequently used in children's books as well as most textbooks in the form of maps and all types of charts and graphs, can be powerful learning tools. They are especially common in scientific literature, where technical illustrators use them to illustrate physical systems, especially ones that cannot be photographed, such as cutaway diagrams, astronomical diagrams, and images of microscopic or sub-microscopic systems. (See the Technical Illustration section in Chapter 7.)

Mathematicians, statisticians, and computer scientists develop and communicate concepts using infographics. All types of manuals employ infographics, ranging from a consumer manual showing how to put a piece of furniture together to technical manuals that make extensive use of diagrams and common icons to highlight warnings, dangers, and standards certifications.

Infographics are also used extensively in the business world to provide snapshots of fiscal data, such as sales revenue, profit and loss over time, a comparison breakdown of types of expenditures, etc. Annual reports often use an abundance of infographics to make fiscal data easy for shareholders to digest. They are also used for project and organizational planning, to describe processes and procedures, and to make sales pitches.

Infographics & Data Visualization

A term that is often used interchangeably by the general public with infographics is *data visualization*. While some experts and practitioners of information design try to make fine distinctions between the two terms, the distinctions are not always that clear.

In simplest terms, a data visualization is a graphical representation of quantifiable data, usually by means of a chart, graph, or map. Although it can be created by hand, it can always be (and usually is) generated by applying automated methods on top of the data.

An infographic is a combination of design elements, text, and data visualization with an editorial objective—to point out relationships, show a process, tell a story, or sell a product—that cannot be automatically discerned from the data alone. An infographic requires the application of a creative process with some understanding of the underlying data and its context. However, neither a visualization nor an infographic is objective, and both require hand-tuning and understanding of the data.

The distinction lies in the process by which the final product is created. The data visualization process is generative—taking raw numbers and creating a visual representation through some formula or algorithm. There may be hidden patterns or trends in the numbers that the designer uncovers while working with the data set. In the creation of an infographic, the designer uses data that has already been processed—the outcome is already known—and then manually creates a visual representation of these numbers.

Both can be static, animated, or interactive. Despite the perceived distinctions between the two, users will probably not recognize the difference or care about the creative process. They are looking at a data visualization or an infographic as a way to gain information about a topic. For them, the value is in the end-product.

5–12 Comparative Fees for Infographic & Icon Design

The pricing ranges in this chart do not constitute specific prices for particular jobs. The buyer and seller are free to negotiate, with each designer independently deciding how to price the work, after taking all factors into account. Reading the more detailed information, Pricing Your Services, provided in Chapter 1, will help in pricing projects for your specific situation.

Hourly Rates

Infographic Design	$50–150+
Icon Design	$50–150+

Additional Fees (% of original project fee)

EXTRA ROUND OF REVISIONS   110–150%
(Not included in original agreement)

CANCELLATION & REJECTION FEES

Prior to completion of concept phase	25–50%
After completion of preliminary work	50–75%
After completion of finished work	75–100%

Designers who charge by the hour bill for the number of hours worked up to the date of cancellation or rejection, plus any expenses incurred.

RUSH WORK (% added on to normal fee)

24-hour turnaround	20–100%
48-hour turnaround	10–50%
Holidays & weekends	10–100%

The above rates and fees were compiled from the results of a national survey of graphic artists conducted by the Graphic Artists Guild in 2020. Responses were based on rates charged in 2018 and 2019.

Design Considerations

As in other types of graphic design, infographic designers follow the principles of effective design and aesthetics, but information and data are their first and most important concerns. If data is the foundation of an infographic assignment, a designer needs to take the time to learn what each specific dataset is about, where it's from, the methodology used, and what makes it interesting and unique. A good designer will represent data accurately and clearly, letting the data speak and not decorate it with extraneous visual elements that obscure what's important. One of the infographic designer's challenges is to find creative ways to visually compare extremely large numbers so that the user comprehends their relationship. Selecting the appropriate type of digital visualization for the subject matter and for displaying the data—map, chart, timeline, diagram, etc.—is especially important, as each type has its specific functions, and within each general type, there are numerous sub-types. Part of the infographic should include the source of the data to make the information credible.

Not all infographics are data-based. Since the whole point of an infographic is making complex information user-friendly, the designer's goal is to create the infographic so it can be read and understood at a glance. One way that designers do this is by telling a visual story without relying too heavily on text. They also make boring and complex information more engaging by presenting it in the context of a visual metaphor—one that is understood by everyone. When trying to communicate information about a product or process, designers might take great effort with the visual aspects to draw viewers into the infographic and compel them to stay by making it very detailed, fun, or engaging.

Pricing & Specific Trade Practices

Infographic designers commonly price their work at either an hourly rate or a flat project fee estimated beforehand. The majority charge an extra fee for rush work.

Hourly rates for infographic design can be found in Figure 5–12, and examples of flat-fee pricing for infographics can be found in Figure 7–10, Comparative Fees for Technical Illustration in Chapter 7.

Icon Design

Icon design is the process of creating a graphic symbol that represents a real, fantasy, or abstract thing, concept, motive, or action. Unlike a logo, an icon relies solely on an image—not letters or words—for its meaning. An icon is a way of creating an immediate, visual understanding between what the creator means and what the viewer sees. Icons, in the form of pictograms and ideograms, were used over 5,000 years ago by the ancient Chinese, Egyptians, and Sumerians, who eventually developed them into logographic writing systems. In more modern times, icons have been used in all types of print media. Icon design is an aspect of almost every graphic art sub-discipline featured in this book, especially corporate, advertising, and package design and illustration; collateral, environmental, exhibit, and display design; and book, technical, medical, and scientific illustration.

Icons for digital media were first developed in the 1970s by Xerox as a means of making computers easier for novices to use. The first large-scale commercial application of icons was on the Macintosh personal computer, introduced in 1984. Today, every major operating system employs an icon-based graphical user interface (GUI). Icons are created to represent programs, files, directories or folders, devices, and selections on the toolbar. They are used on the desktop as well as within application programs. Icons play a crucial role in the navigational systems and user interfaces of interactive media. The demand for icon design rose dramatically with the widespread use of interactive media—computer programs, websites, blogs, and video games, and most recently with the proliferation of touch screen displays and mobile media. Every app on a smart phone or tablet screen has its own icon.

While the name icon design implies that it is a graphic design discipline, the work involved can be more illustrative—the marriage of spot illustration with information graphics. Graphic artists who specialize in icon design often create infographics as well. The pricing of icon design is also more similar to illustration than it is to graphic design.

Design Considerations

Icons are designed within a designated shape and must stay within the confines of that shape, while a logo, for example, has no shape boundaries. Icons are designed, and often priced, as sets, ranging from a small set of five or six icons to larger sets of 50+ icons. Designing in sets creates certain challenges for the designer. Designing icons for interactive versus print media has its own challenges, due to the fact that icons for the screen usually need to be smaller. This is especially true for mobile devices.

Whether they are created for print, websites, or mobile applications, icons are part of a graphic system and must work harmoniously with the other graphic elements in that system. Each icon must also work aesthetically with the other icons within the set. At the same time, each icon must differ enough to be distinguishable from the other icons in the set and still work together as a whole. Successful icon designers recommend conceptualizing the images for the entire set and planning how they will work together before beginning actual illustration activities. Thinking through the entire set will save valuable redesign time.

For an icon set to work aesthetically within a website, for example, the style chosen for the set needs to be similar to or complement the style of the site. Icons within a set should be of the same artistic style, drawn from the same perspective, have a single light source (from the same angle), and cast consistent reflections and shadows.

The most successful icons are simplistic and iconic, with as few elements as possible. A maximum of three is recommended. This is especially true of icons designed for small screens. They must be recognizable at very small sizes. The software available today allows icon artists to add a high degree of realism and illustrative detail to icons; however, details can be lost or even create visual confusion at very small sizes. Handheld devices are often used in less than optimal situations—low light, distracting glare and reflections, etc.—so a simple and bold design helps to increase usability. The decision to use a more graphic, symbolic style versus a more illustrative, realistic style also depends on what the icon is portraying. Realism is more appropriate for concepts that can be represented by a physical object, rather than with abstract concepts.

Icons are best designed at the size at which they will be used. For example, a vector-based icon design should not just be scaled to any size. An icon that looks good at 256 x 256 pixels will be a blurry mess if scaled down to 16 x 16 pixels. For this reason, it is best not to use words in icons, especially if designing for small screens. The words will be unreadable. If a designer is commissioned to create an icon set for use at various sizes, extra time needs to be built into the project. A base design can be used as a starting point, but then each output size needs its own optimized design.

Icon designers also consider the audience or user. If the product or app will be used or sold internationally, special consideration is given to national and cultural differences. A symbol used for one culture might have no meaning, a different meaning, or even an offensive meaning in another culture. Therefore, it's necessary to use universal imagery that is easily recognizable by most everyone. Think of the icons used on the dashboard controls for your car's various systems or the international traffic signage used on roadways.

Pricing & Specific Trade Practices

Icon design is charged either by the hour or as a flat rate per set. The price of an icon set is determined by the number of icons, the complexity and originality of the design, and the type of usage. Designers charge more for complex or realistic-looking designs with more illustrative detail than for simple graphic designs. The base price for a set is for non-exclusive use. The media and duration of use vary by project, so designers need to specify those terms of usage in their contracts. For example, if an icon set is designed for a website or a phone app, it would involve an online usage agreement. If the client decides at a later date to use the set for print, an additional fee for that usage would need to be negotiated. Although the designer may try at the onset of the project to get the client to anticipate future usage of the icons, clients often decide to purchase an all-rights transfer to avoid any messy negotiations later on.

If a client wants exclusive usage, then the designer charges considerably more. Knowing this, savvy clients will try to buy an all-rights transfer, so the designer cannot sell rights to anyone else. It is in the artist's best interest (and will save the client unnecessary expense) to determine the client's exact needs and sell the client only those rights and retain the remaining rights. The majority of icon designers charge extra for rush work.

It is not unheard of for icon designers to repurpose unused icons and icons of very general concepts (e-mail, print, save, etc.) into another client's set. An unused concept also may spur development of a more complete set for sale as stock. Some designers develop nothing but stock sets. It is a more acceptable practice in the industry for designers to sell stock sets off their own websites than on traditional stock sites.

Icon sets sold on stock websites may cost considerably less than the cost of a custom-designed set. While some clients may be attracted to the seemingly lower cost of stock icons, astute designers can promote the advantages of having a custom set designed. The icon designer creates a set based on the client's specific needs, coordinates it with the style of the environment in which it will be used, and sizes it accordingly. No matter how large a stock set is, it seldom contains every icon that is needed for the client's project. It would be very time-consuming and costly for a designer to try to create additional icons to match the stock set. Hiring an artist to design a custom set also allows the client the flexibility of having more icons of the same style added to the set in the future, if the need arises.

Hourly rates for icon design are given in Figure 5–12. Also refer to the pricing charts in Chapter 7, Illustration, especially the prices for spot illustration, to get an idea of what to charge for icon design.

Production Art

Production art is most commonly the responsibility of production artists, whose combination of creative and technical skills make them an indispensable part of the creative design team. The production artist provides the link between the conceptual design and the tangible result. The lines between the roles of the production artist and the graphic designer may be blurred because in some smaller organizations, the graphic designer might be responsible for both roles.

Production artists originally performed paste-up duties for the advertising industry, but the position has evolved to include prepress work for both print and digital projects in various industries, including design, advertising, marketing, motion pictures, and computer systems design. Today's production artists assist design teams primarily in producing print, packaging, advertising, point-of-purchase, and digital graphics. They are the final checkpoint in the creative design process and ensure that all deliverables are produced on time. Production artists might also be responsible for archiving and updating graphic files.

They review final copy, layouts, and content in print or digital form. Using specialized software, they make sure that projects and products accurately meet all of a client's requirements and that images are of the highest possible quality. Their digital imaging skills include scaling, cropping, retouching, repositioning, and other manipulation skills. In finalizing products, artists may suggest improvements and modify formats to increase the quality of production and ensure that standards are met.

Production artists also make sure the design concept works for the various formats and platforms it will be displayed on, such as brochures, billboards, web banner ads, social media posts, mobile apps, etc. One of the most common duties for production artists is preflight formatting, as well as collecting, processing, checking, and uploading files.

Skills

In addition to their unique combination of design and technical skills, successful production artists are organized, accurate, and able to work quickly but remain extremely detail oriented, as they often complete the last step in a rushed process. They often work on several projects simultaneously. They also are good communicators and team players who can work collaboratively with art directors, designers, developers, and outside vendors. They should be able to troubleshoot problems as they arise with both the creative team and the printer.

The scope of knowledge a production artist needs includes a strong foundation in graphic design, including typography and layout skills, a solid understanding of conventional and digital printing processes and guidelines, and experience with digital content, such as websites, social media, online advertising, and media campaigns.

The software that is commonly part of a production artist's skill set includes Adobe InDesign, Illustrator,

5–13 Comparative Fees for Production Art

The pricing in this chart does not constitute specific prices for particular jobs. The buyer and seller are free to negotiate, with each designer independently deciding how to price the work, after taking all factors into account. Reading the more detailed information, Pricing Your Services, provided in Chapter 1, will help in pricing projects for your specific situation.

Hourly Rates $20–125

Additional Fees

RUSH WORK (% added onto normal fee)

24-hour turnaround   40–100%

48-hour turnaround   20–100%

Holidays & Weekends 75–100%

The above rates and fees were compiled from the results of a national survey of graphic artists conducted by the Graphic Artists Guild in 2020. Responses were based on rates charged in 2018 and 2019.

Photoshop, Dreamweaver, and Acrobat; Quark Xpress; Markzware FlightCheck; Macromedia Flash; Interwoven TeamSite; and Microsoft Project. Increasingly, production artists need some experience using CSS, HTML, and JavaScript to change how a web page or application looks and behaves for the end user.

Pricing

The complexity of the job determines the production artist's pricing. Another factor that affects pricing is the skill required for the job. Production artists who have multiple and specialized skill sets and are equally adept in both the print and digital worlds can command higher compensation.

See Figure 5–1 for Median Hourly Rates Paid to Freelance Production Artists and Figure 5–13 for ranges of hourly rates and rush fees for Production Art. Salary ranges for Production Artist are provided under the Graphic Design Salaries section at the beginning of this chapter.

{ 6 }

Web/
Interactive
Design

This chapter focuses on the continually evolving area of web-based design and technologies: creating and enhancing an ever-expanding array of digital interactive media and the support marketing required to promote these media. The interactive design field includes website design and development; rich Internet applications (RIAs); online advertising and e-mail marketing; social media; software applications for tablet and mobile devices, computer games, e-commerce, and kiosks; and other standalone software applications.

With the burgeoning growth of the Internet and digital media, products, and services, especially in regard to the mobile space, comes a ballooning need for fresh content to keep people clicking and touching away—apps, videos, photos, illustrations, and animations. Web and interactive designers and developers lead this field by creating content for these markets. These creators work for a range of industries, including commerce, marketing, publishing, entertainment, and education.

The technological means of protecting copyright and reuse do not always keep up with the rapid growth and newest forms of digital media, and trade practices for traditional media may not always apply to digital. Therefore, it is important for graphic artists working in the ever-evolving digital field to research and stay current about the latest laws, practices, and mechanisms that can be used to protect their intellectual property.

The Digital Marketplace

The digital marketplace has exploded in the past 15 years, due to advances in mobile technology and the increased use of social media. Today, almost every business and institution, from large corporations and national retailers to small, local service providers have some type of web presence. All types and sizes of businesses and media outlets—as well as millions of individuals—have embraced social media as well.

E-commerce also has continued to grow steadily. According to digitalcommerce360.com, e-commerce had $601.75 billion in sales in 2019, representing a 16% share of total U.S. retail sales. This growth in penetration represented the largest percentage from year to year, since the U.S, Department of Commerce first started tracking annual e-commerce in 2000.

With the proliferation of mobile devices, we have become not only a digital society but a mobile, interactive one. E-commerce has evolved to include enhancements to, and applications beyond, desktop websites. Both advertising and the shopping experience have become more sophisticated. Advertisers have embraced digital technology, not only with banner and display ads in all types of digital media, but with mobile apps that allow QR codes in both print and digital ads to be read by a smartphone, giving consumers information about a product or the capability to purchase it.

Major print magazines and newspapers have online editions, with additional components such as video clips and interactive features, which we can access from just about anywhere using tablets or smartphones. We can choose from a takeout menu using our smartphone or tablet en route to the restaurant where our order will be ready for pickup. If we are not sure how to get there, we can use an app that enables our smartphone with GPS. Through the Web of Things (WoT), the world around us is becoming smarter and more responsive, from smart homes, offices, and devices to cars that drive themselves.

Open Source Code has also contributed to the rise of the digital marketplace by creating new models of ownership and licenses, which allow software to be freely used, modified, and shared. They enable expensive CMS systems and themes to be sold at low cost and even given away for free. This has speeded up the development process by years, compared to the Closed Source model.

These newer technologies and devices have changed the very fabric of our society because people are connected globally, and we receive information instantly. We no longer receive news passively in a top-down structure. News gathering has become much more of a participatory process and collective voice as news outlets receive, and even encourage, eyewitness accounts by citizens of news events sent via their mobile phones. Citizen-recorded eyewitness images of police brutality were a major force in public support of the Black Lives Matter movement that started in the United States and grew worldwide. Presidential election campaigns, mass demonstrations, and even insurgent uprisings against repressive governments throughout the world have been organized and orchestrated through the use of social media and digital technology.

There is a demand for graphic artists who can design and develop content and structure for websites and other online media, as well as for new products and applications (apps) for smartphones, tablet computers, and wearable devices. Graphic artists with diverse skill sets and experience in both print and interactive media have a competitive edge in attracting potential clients.

Salaries

Overview

The salary figures provided in this chapter reflect the current market for selected professional web and interactive designers and developers holding full-time staff positions in the United States.

The salary figures do not include benefits and perks, such as health insurance, paid time off, retirement savings plans, maternity/paternity leave, workplace wellness programs, free food, flexible work arrangements, etc.— since these can vary widely among employers. In general, many employers do offer a benefits package to full-time employees that includes vacation, holiday, and sick pay. For health insurance, employees are frequently required to contribute part of their premiums and to use health maintenance organizations (HMOs). Bonuses, stock options, and retirement plans may be available, but these benefits usually depend upon company policy regarding salaried personnel. Job seekers should evaluate the entire package when weighing offers.

Digital Design & Production

In most corporate settings, each job title has a salary range, and new employees are often hired at the low end of the range to provide room for future raises. The following U.S. digital design and production salary ranges are taken from *The Creative Group 2021 Salary Guide*. They are based on job searches, negotiations and placements managed by The Creative Group's staffing and recruiting professionals.

The ranges represent national averages, with the lower figure representing the 25th percentile and the higher figure representing the 75th percentile. The Creative Group defines figures at the 25th percentile as salaries of employees who may be new to the position or still developing relevant skills, or in a low-demand role. Figures at the 75th percentile represent salaries of employees who have more experience than is typical or most or all relevant skills, or in a high-demand role. The *Salary Guide* also provides salary figures at the 50th and 95th percentiles.

Salary ranges can be further adjusted for specific U.S. and Canadian cities by using the variance numbers on pages 17–19 and page 30 of the *Salary Guide*. *The Creative Group 2021 Salary Guide*, as well as a salary calculator for customizing pay ranges for more than 550 cities, can be accessed at http://creativegroup.com/salary-center.

The salaries listed for each of the following positions reflect starting pay only, meaning the salary an employee would receive when first starting at a company, but not necessarily an entry-level salary, because employees start at companies with various levels of experience:

* **User Experience (UX) Director** $111,250–153,750[1]
* **User Experience (UX) Designer** $75,750–118,500[1]
* **Interactive Art Director** $77,500–105,000[1]
* **Interaction Designer** $66,500–89,250[1]
* **Information Architect** $81,000–117,750[1]
* **Web Designer** $58,750–86,500[1]
* **Web Production Artist** $45,250–63,500[1]
* **Mobile Designer** $67,000–101,500[1]
* **Visual Designer** $65,250–101,750[1]
* **Multimedia Designer** $55,500–84,000[1]

Web & Mobile Development

The following are average annual salaries in the United States for select web and mobile job titles, updated by Indeed.com in September 2020. They are base salaries; however, many web and mobile development professionals also earn cash bonuses of approximately $2,000–4,000 annually.

* **Front-End Developer** $109,391[2]
* **Back-End Developer** $127,913[2]

* **Full-Stack Developer** $112,710[2]
* **Mobile Developer** $123,589[2]

Designing for Interactive Media
Job Roles & Skills

The digital workspace that evolved in graphic design, using layout programs such as QuarkXPress and Adobe InDesign, came directly from traditional typesetting and film applications and shares much of the vocabulary, measuring systems, and printing terms. Designing for the Web, mobile, and applications requires a different toolset and vocabulary. The need for entirely new disciplines has emerged. Computer languages are not fixed—they are continually evolving with new functions and versions. The same is true of hardware, devices, and their features, such as mobile phones, wearables, and screen sizes. Practitioners in technology must be agile, experienced, and confident in how to handle the constant changes in an industry that reinvents itself almost daily.

Some graphic artists have evolved their skill sets into hybrid roles that combine the experience of designers with developers. Traditionally, designers create the visual experience but usually do not write the code for it, as compared with web developers who translate the visual experience into a tangible one by coding it and often simultaneously redesigning it to work in a real world scenario. A good web developer is often expected to also be a web designer because of the nature of responsive design. This has created new hybrid roles, such as "web fixers" and "full stack developers," which were born of the demand to meet the needs of the industry and client expectations. These roles continually evolve at the pace of technology.

WEB DESIGNERS

Web designers determine the look and feel of a website, while also making sure the site is easy to interact with. Their work is critical in making sure visitors engage and spend more time on a site. Designers also focus on branding elements for a site and may be involved with creating all branding materials for a client in addition to the website.

Web professionals who work on the design side need to have a good understanding of visual design—the elements and basic principles of design, typography, layout principles, color theory, etc.—as well as the skills of a graphic designer. They also need to understand how people will interact with a design. They analyze the latest trends in web design. Designers use Photoshop, Sketch,

---

1. Salary ranges are reprinted with permission from *The Creative Group 2021 Salary Guide 2021* ©2020 Robert Half International.

2. Salary estimates are based on salaries submitted anonymously to Indeed by employees and users and collected from past and present job posts on Indeed in the previous 36 months.

or Illustrator to deliver appropriate design files to the development team.

Web designers' tools also include wireframes and prototypes. A wireframe is a visual map that lays out the skeleton of the site. By creating wireframes, using software such as Adobe XD, Figma, Balsamiq, etc., web designers can visualize and plan out the way a site will be arranged. A wireframe also allows designers to share their site plans and progress with developer teams, clients, test users, and other stakeholders. A prototype is a more developed website model than a wireframe and can be used for site testing before a site's final release. Depending on where a site is in its development cycle, a prototype can consist of anything from a paper mockup sketch to a fully functioning digital model.

Designers also need to be concerned with accessibility (a11y), a measure of how accessible a computer system is to all people (for a more in-depth discussion of accessibility as it applies to websites and web apps, refer to Best Practices under the Freelancing section later in this chapter).

Since web design covers a lot of responsibilities, some designers may specialize in certain aspects of the design.

UX DESIGNERS

User experience (UX) designers make sure the site keeps visitors engaged. They analyze data before putting things into practice. The also run complex tests and restructure the site when needed to keep the user experience optimal. UX designer is a very fluid term in the industry, with the breakdown of roles on a particular project determined by the individual UX designer's strengths and skills: some UX designers have skill sets that are more IA and visual design oriented, while others are very proficient programmers, who utilize those skills in their work.

INFORMATION ARCHITECTS (IA)

Information architects (IA) are designers who create a visual representation of a website or an app's infrastructure, features, and hierarchy. The level of detail is up to the designer, so it may also include navigation, application functions and behaviors, content, and flows.

UI DESIGNERS

User interface (UI) designers handle how well users can interact with the elements on the site. The user interface is everything a visitor sees when accessing a website, and it needs to be well-crafted to fit the way users expect to navigate through the site.

VISUAL DESIGNERS

The responsibilities of both a UX designer and a UI designer can be merged into one job—the visual designer. Visual designers create interfaces that are both visually pleasing and convenient to use. The skills of a visual designer include both creativity and programming. They are responsible for crafting a unified image of a brand across all digital communication platforms, which may include Internet and intranet sites, games, movies, kiosks, and wearables. They ensure that the voice, look, and feel of the brand remains consistent.

ACCESSIBILITY SPECIALIST

Accessibility specialists focus on creating interfaces and user experiences that work towards making products accessible to everyone, including those with disabilities. They evaluate accessibility compliance; work with UX, UI, and product designers; and research and test products and services for accessibility. They have experience with assistive technology (screen readers, screen magnifiers, etc.), human/computer interaction, prototyping, wireframing, and data analysis.

WEB DEVELOPERS

Web developers handle the implementation stage of building a website. After the designers figure out the structure and goals of the site, developers step in to make them become a reality—to make them live, functioning sites. Web developers can specialize in different parts of the process.

FRONT-END DEVELOPERS

Front-end development, also known as client-side development, involves programming all the public-facing visuals and elements of a site's design. Front-end developers often collaborate with web designers. Front-end developers should have strong programming skills, but as opposed to back-end developers, they only work with elements that are visible to the user.

Front-end developers use hypertext markup language (HTML), a coding language, to define the parts of an individual web page (which part of the page is a header, a footer, where paragraphs belong, and where images, graphics, and videos are placed), giving the page structure. They also use Cascading Style Sheets (CSS), the code that handles the visual appearance of websites—a page's fonts, background colors, paragraph formatting, etc. Together HTML and CSS are the combination that builds the structure and style basis for any web page. Front-end developers also should have a basic understanding of JavaScript, the programming language that interacts with HTML and CSS to create the three layers of web design: structures, styles, and behaviors.

In addition to building websites from scratch with HTML, CSS, and JavaScript, web developers can build them with software programs called *content management systems* (CMS), such as WordPress, Joomla, and Drupal, which do not require knowing how to code. The industry standard CMS is WordPress, which can be downloaded free from WordPress.org. CMS sites are a popular alternative for clients who do not need a site built from the ground up or who want to be able to update content on their own later on. Content management systems (CMS) also streamline the process of changing web content that needs to be updated regularly, such as blog posts or events.

BACK-END DEVELOPERS

The back end refers to what the user cannot see on a site. It has to do with the core structure of a website—the processes that make it function. Back-end developers do not have anything to do with the aesthetics of the site. They build servers and databases.

Back-end developers are logical thinkers with heavy technical knowledge and strong programming skills. They are proficient in JavaScript, which adds interactivity to static elements. It works with XML files and communicates asynchronously with a web server through an approach called AJAX, which enables websites to load faster and various embedded objects to update without requiring a complete page reload.

JavaScript is a versatile programming language. For one, it is a full-stack language that can be used to build both the front and back ends. JavaScript libraries, such as jQuery, are collections of pre-written JavaScript code that can be plugged into web projects, saving developers time on recreating basic JavaScript functions like interactive forms and image galleries. Another feature is JavaScript frameworks, such as React.js, which are collections of JS libraries that can be used as larger scale templates for web projects. Frameworks not only provide pre-written code, but they also provide a structure for where JavaScript code should be placed, helping projects become more efficiently and uniformly arranged.

Developers also learn back-end programming languages, such as PHP, Java, Perl, C++, etc. There are pros and cons to different languages, and some are more appropriate for certain applications (mobile, gaming, etc.) than others. PHP is popular because it is an open-source language that is supported by a strong community. Web developers also use Structured Query Language (SQL), a scripting tool that interfaces with databases. For designers, a basic understanding of it will help inform design choices that reduce rework for developers.

Web professionals need to be able to design responsive websites that look great at various sizes to support the wide range of user devices and screen sizes being used. There is also a need for web developers who can develop mobile applications, especially those that interface with websites.

FULL-STACK DEVELOPERS

Full-stack developers have the skills to work on all the layers (or stacks) of a website, including elements from both back- and front-end development. They can use several types of programming languages and are both technical and creative. Full-stack developers are proficient at working across multiple stacks. Many projects require at least a web stack and a mobile stack; others evolve to need a native application stack, complete with databases, servers, and systems engineering.

The average stack of a full-stack developer might be HTML, CSS, JavaScript, a server-side language (PHP, .NET, etc.), and database code (SQL or MySQL), which are all used together to create AJAX and responsive design.

A Team Approach

Many clients casually interchange the concepts and challenges of design between print and interactive media. And even though both processes begin with concept and content, the functional and production methods of the two are profoundly different. While graphic design is the largest part of a print project, it is just one of several considerations in an interactive design project.

Because technology changes so rapidly and clients change their mind so often, the need for a more flexible web development model arose to solve the problems with traditional development in designing for interactive media. Also, the Web is not linear—it is a complex web. Therefore, the production process should not be linear either. The web of design and development can be carefully woven by teams (or sometimes an individual), but in either case, they need to adapt to change quickly and easily.

An interactive design project is made up of a team of several individuals with specific skills, but there are at least two different core approaches to the process: the *Traditional* approach and the *Agile* approach.

The Traditional approach is predictive in nature, seeking to plan out all aspects of the project. It is based on the idea that the client or the team will be able to predict and anticipate all problems and needs related to the project. This approach demands extensive planning and paperwork.

The Agile approach, which was originally created for software development, responds to real world scenarios as they happen or change, based on the idea that team members cannot possibly predict nor anticipate all problems and needs related to the project. In this way, the team is assumed to know best how to solve problems and is allowed to execute the project with far more speed and agility.

THE TRADITIONAL APPROACH

The team for an interactive project, using the Traditional approach, consists of two major teams: Design and Development, each of which can be further divided into specific roles. Generally, the larger the project, the more team members there will be and the more specific their roles will be.

For example, in very small projects, one designer may do everything on the design side, while in larger projects, there may be more than one type of designer. There will be a graphic designer, also referred to as the visual designer, and there may be functional designers, such as an information architect (IA), a user experience (UX) designer, and a user interface (UI) designer. UX design not only involves UI design but some interactive design and IA as well.

The various designer roles may be filled by different individuals (or companies), but they frequently overlap somewhat, even on a moderate-sized web project. For small projects, the interactive designer may wear multiple hats, but in most cases will team with a programmer for the more technical aspects of the job. Full-stack developers and web fixers have the skills to do both the design and development aspects of a project and can replace the need for a team.

THE AGILE APPROACH

There are several types of Agile project management methodologies. One of these is *Scrum*. The Scrum model is designed for teams of three to nine members, who break their work into actions, called *sprints,* that can be completed within a defined and fixed period of time—usually a specific number of weeks.

The Scrum model works well for the team approach because it recognizes *requirements volatility*—frequent changes to the requirements of a project from the design phase to implementation. For example, clients, target audiences, and consumers will change their minds about what they want or need, constantly causing unpredictable challenges. Likewise, technology changes often enough to present even more complicated problems, such as responsive design for mobile devices, browser variations, and new hardware features, such as tablet or monitor screen sizes and resolutions. Therefore, the Traditional approach is not very well-suited for many modern web development projects because of the rapid rate of change in the industry.

In the Scrum model, the teams are structured as follows:

The product owner, representing the product's stakeholders and the voice of the customer, is responsible for the backlog (an ordered list of everything that is known to be needed in the product) and is accountable for maximizing the value that the team delivers.

The development team is responsible for delivering product increments every sprint (the sprint goal). The team members carry out all tasks required to build the product increments (analysis, design, development, testing, technical writing, etc.).

The Scrum Master, who facilitates the project, is accountable for removing impediments to the ability of the team to deliver the product goals and deliverables.

All three—the product owner, the development team, and the scrum master—work together to determine the sprint goals for the project.

The Interactive Production Process

To give an idea of what an interactive production process might look like, described below are the players and work flow involved in a sample interactive project—the design or redesign of a commercial website with a budget of $50,000 to $1,000,000, which covers a broad range of commercial sites.

THE PLAYERS

CLIENT-SIDE RELATIONSHIP OWNER

Depending on the size of the project and the company involved, this role might be filled by a company executive, a manager of a specific department within the company, or a project or product manager for the specific initiative being built.

Whenever possible, try to have a single primary point of contact for the client and make sure that person has the appropriate authority within his/her organization to grant approvals. The project will go more smoothly if the client contact is an executive or has executive support— someone who can sign off on projects, approve them, and cut through the red tape because one thing is certain: the project will change.

PROJECT-SIDE RELATIONSHIP OWNER

Project teams are assembled in at least 20 different ways, known as *methodologies and frameworks*. A client may choose every part of their project team and maintain contracts and relationships with strategists, UX designers, visual designers, developers, and copywriters separately; development firms and agencies may bid on projects to be carried out by internal staff or a network of contractors; and lastly, one firm or agency may submit and win the project proposal and then sub-contract sections of the project to another firm or individual.

In the Traditional development model, it is critical to understand the relationships involved and have project proposals, statements of work, contracts, and agreements in place with the appropriate parties before beginning. This is a very different approach from the Agile model and also needs to be clarified at the start. The question that needs to be asked is "If this becomes an Agile project, are we prepared to transition out of the Traditional model and original plan?"

In the Agile model, the work is expected to change constantly. Therefore, the price changes as well, so monthly retainers are favored, since everyone on board already knows the project cannot possibly be fully planned out. The Traditional model would quickly fail in an Agile development project because endless paperwork would constantly disable progress, and the amount of time required to document and sign off on such changes is too high and vastly efficient.

STRATEGIST/PROJECT MANAGER

This role may be filled by the project-side relationship owner in the case of a project manager at an agency. In some cases, this might be a separate contractor or employee engaged to gather requirements; write creative briefs, functional briefs, and technical specifications; develop and maintain project plans and schedules; and coordinate the project team.

The project team is composed of four parallel branches that play different but equally important roles in the design of the site: design, development, content, and operations. Key players working in the first three areas include the following:

INFORMATION ARCHITECT (IA) & USER EXPERIENCE DESIGNER (UX)

These roles may in some cases be filled by the same person as the strategist or project manager, but they are almost always different from the visual designer. The IA is engaged with understanding the situation and developing personas, user stories, and building out page-level wireframes and interaction models. While a UX designer can do that too, he/she generally also works out designs in Photoshop and/or Illustrator, knowing how things need to be delivered for execution. UX designers might not be the best at being an IA or a visual designer, but in many cases, they are the glue between the creative team and integrators and developers.

This step ensures that requirements are being met in a way that wraps the flow of the design around the user and the goals of the design before the project proceeds to the visual design process. This is often a key learning phase in the project. This is one of the areas that expands or contracts greatly with overall project cost, as very large websites often invest several months in this process. This roadmap may also be used to allow the development team to begin programming tasks before the visual design is complete.

VISUAL DESIGNER

Once UX design for at least the homepage and overall sitemap is complete (and for larger sites, a detailed creative brief written), sites proceed to visual design. This often commences with an initial creative explorations phase done on one site template (often the homepage, although for complex dynamic sites, it is often helpful to include the lowest-level detail page as well, such as a product detail page for an e-commerce website) where 3-5 completely different style variations are developed, in many cases, by different designers (all of whom are paid for their work for this phase of the process). Freelance designers working on simpler websites might only develop one or two style variations. The variations are refined and narrowed down until one design is chosen. It should be noted that since UX designers possess both visual design and IA skills, a UX designer may be hired to work out the design details involved in this phase, instead of a designer whose skills are limited to visual design only.

Making site maps, flow charts, and simple storyboards can help the designer assess the scope of an interactive design project and serve as an early catalog of the level of graphics required. Web designers often determine file names and sizes on these charts before beginning design concepts. Occasionally, a designer may negotiate payment for a sample to determine the time and therefore the scope of the project. Creating a development (Beta) site based on the mandatory design specifications for any smooth-running web project, with a basic skeleton and outline, is another possibility. Such a site allows the client to review and make changes while the content is easy to manipulate.

When beginning a project using the Traditional model that includes creative exploration, expectations should be clear about the number of variations and revisions allowed for this phase. However, in Agile web development, it is understood that the number of total revisions is unknowable. Once a style decision has been made, if necessary, contracts proceed with the appropriate designer.

The chosen style is then iterated out to page templates as defined in the UX/Wireframes phase. It is also critical to specify a number of revisions in this phase, as each template may go through several rounds of changes. With the Agile approach, using the Scrum model, these revision phases could be viewed as sprints; they are actually continual and expected revision phases. It is generally known, understood, and accepted in Agile development that base designs will likely change anywhere from 5-30% in post-production in order to produce working real-world results, to achieve better SEO scores, and to follow web standards.

DEVELOPMENT TEAM

Once a sufficient backlog of requirements is approved (including enough functional or visual direction to begin programming), the development team begins their work, starting with the front-end developer who takes the designer's comps and builds them into actual pages, using HTML/CSS and following web standards. (On some projects, an UX designer or other designer may be expected to do HTML/CSS as a requirement of the delivery of assets to developers.)

Developers are also responsible for adding logic of any kind and wiring things all together, especially at the back end, and for data access and other dynamic elements of a given website or application. The development process varies significantly among different types of websites.

Developers often have an additional set of responsibilities and expectations placed on them:

* Preserve web standards to ensure the success of the final product.
* Perceive, predict, and inform the client of potential problems.
* Educate, train, and collaborate with the team about best practices.
* Fill various technology gaps, such as server management, security, and even IT support.

In some situations, the design team may not consider web standards or break from them in such a way to cause various levels of product failure. The developers have a duty to educate the other teams and members before coding the final application. Coding a final system that lacks web standards may cause it to have to be redone, rebuilt, or completely scrapped—a colossal waste of time and resources. Similar responsibilities are placed on the SEO team (see following section on SEO/SEM/SMM Strategists).

CONTENT STRATEGIST/COPYWRITER

While not strictly necessary, this is an extremely helpful role to have involved in a project. Clients tend to underestimate the need for new, quality content (or overestimate their ability to produce it in a timely manner). Many sites have been delayed once it became clear that the "lorem ipsum" text needed to be replaced and there was nothing to put in its place. Even when the copy is supplied by the client, it may need to be re-worked to be more web optimized—to create a better overall user flow and message hierarchy and to avoid redundancy. If at all possible, the content strategist/copywriter should be involved in the UX and visual design process so there is a clear idea from the beginning where each bit of content is created, who is responsible for creating it, and how it is created/edited.

This role is especially important for content management system (CMS)-driven sites. Making sure that the design accurately takes into account all possible inputs (and/or that inputs are restricted appropriately) is one of the biggest factors that can make a development process run smoothly and ensure a finished, dynamic website that looks as good as the design comps.

OPERATIONS TEAM

Web operations teams are tasked with a variety of responsibilities, including, but not limited to, the deployment and instrumentation of web applications; the monitoring, error isolation, escalation, and repair of problems; conducting performance management, availability reporting, and other administration; and measuring the impact of changes to content, applications, networks, and infrastructure. Once a website has launched, it requires maintenance in order to be refreshed, updated, and corrected on a regular basis. In the pricing and planning of a website, it is important to take long-term maintenance responsibilities and pricing into account, especially for CMS-driven websites that will periodically need to be updated with security patches and updates to external application programming interfaces (APIs)—such as Facebook, Twitter, and Salesforce.

SEO/SEM/SMM STRATEGISTS

Each of these roles can easily expand into entire teams or can be handled by an individual with the right experience, such as a seasoned web fixer or full-stack developer. They are all inextricably bound to web standards throughout every area of online marketing, operations, client needs, and end user interactions.

SEO (search engine optimization) includes responsibilities such as modifying and rebuilding websites, adding Schema.org specifications, speed tuning, mobile testing, and responsive design, as well as writing, revising and generating new content; keyword strategies; and inbound and internal linking campaigns.

SEM (search engine marketing) includes pay-per-click campaigns; building, fine tuning, monitoring, and adjusting landing pages, as well as building and maintaining the campaigns that link to them.

SMM (social media management) includes, among other responsibilities, creating thoughtful social media experiences, integrating those experience into a website or online media, monitoring the official channels and social media pages of the client, and ensuring that every single page on a website is sharable, optimized, and ready for consumption on social media.

Some methods demand that strategy for SEO/SEM/SMM is done prior to any design work, including the logo. Other methods consider these roles to be optional, ancillary, or arbitrary to the core build.

Website Design/Development

Web designers and developers have many different options to choose from when building a client's site, depending on its intended purpose or function.

Types of Websites

Although there are various general types of websites, each individual site is unique and may actually be a combination of types. For example, many corporate sites include a blog, a news section, and a gallery component. Many social network sites have review sections, event listings, blogs, and galleries, etc. Considerations about the type of website also include mobile versus other screen and form factors (see the Mobile Design/Development section later in this chapter). In addition, a website can be built so that the information is either static or dynamic.

STATIC SITES

Static websites deliver information to the user that does not change over time and remains in the same form as sent by the web server. All the pages exist as physical (HTML) files on the server, whether visitors to the site load them on their web browsers or not. Static sites are coded in HTML, CSS, JavaScript, and jQuery, and they display the same information to everyone.

The advantages of a static site: they are relatively easy to build; they can be developed relatively quickly; they require little code maintenance; and they are indexed easily by search engines.

The disadvantages: they cannot do the complex tasks required by many online services; updating the entire site can be time-consuming and cumbersome; and there is no isolation of content and design.

In the days of the early Web, when simple HTML websites that did not need to be changed often were common, static sites were more cost effective than a CMS system or a dynamic website. This is no longer completely true—the industry has changed drastically because of the Open Source Community. Today, with fast-paced social media and rapidly changing technology, static sites are nearing extinction, simply because social media and CMS templates and page builders are readily available, much cheaper (sometimes free), and offer the ability for anyone to access technology that can create, edit, and update dynamic content via a CMS system, for less than the cost of building and maintaining a static site a decade ago.

DYNAMIC SITES

Most sites on the Web today are dynamic. Dynamic websites generally consist of code, a database containing content, and a system of templates. This architecture separates the content from the design—often called the presentation layer—which means that these database-driven sites can be updated by external content feeds, website content editors, or even end users, and can display appropriate content for a variety of factors, such as user details, screen size, and numerous activity-triggered indicators.

Database-driven websites use back-end programming languages such as PHP, ASP.NET, Java, and Ruby to generate HTML pages and use front-end languages, such as CSS and JavaScript, as well as images, to style and position content on pages. These sites may utilize an existing content management system (CMS), such as WordPress, Joomla, or Drupal, or be custom created using frameworks such as Angular, Ruby, Laravel, and Django.

When designing for dynamic websites, it is critical to keep in mind the difference between designs and templates. Since these sites build pages according to sets of rules, style guidelines, and content pulled from the database, the exact layout as presented in the designs will likely never occur. Designers should keep this in mind to create a design system that can accommodate different types of images, lengths of headlines and body text, and other ways in which the site's actual content may stray from the test content used in the design process. Flexibility and forward-thinking are key to successful design.

E-commerce sites contain many additional dynamic features making the individual user's viewing and ordering experiences unique. The availability of an item may change based on the user's size or color preference. "You may also like" suggestions are shown to the viewer, based on his/her browsing choices or even on past purchases. Sites containing large amounts of information such as an encyclopedia site, news sites, and real-time sites such as an e-ticketing site are also dynamic.

The advantages of a dynamic site: they can do more complex tasks and the isolation of data and design allows programmers and content writers to work independently. They are faster and easier to update because only the database needs changing; CSS can be updated, and graphics, new templates, widgets, plug-ins, etc. can be added.

The disadvantages of a dynamic site: they can take longer and be more difficult to build; they require code maintenance and security updates; and since content is dynamic, there is less-than-complete control over how a page design will display as content changes over time. They may also be more vulnerable to hackers and spambots, so additional measures, monitoring, and maintenance may be required.

Technically, a dynamic website is never finished. Instead, it reaches version states that developers refer to as *alpha* (prerelease) or *beta* (stable), similar to operating systems and software. These release states often use version and subversion numbering (1.0, 1.5, 2.0, 3.5.7, etc.) which can refer to a theme, a CMS system, a plug-in, or even the website itself.

Designing for Multiple Devices

In the past, website designers only had to be concerned with designing for desktop or laptop computers, both relatively large screens. On these large-screen devices, there was plenty of room to offer the user several ways to navigate around the site. However, on the increasingly shrinking screens of tablets and mobile devices, there is not enough space to offer multiple navigation options, much less cram all the same features on the screen.

Moreover, there are numerous devices now, all with different form factors that can access a website (see the Web of Things section later in this chapter). This means that designers have to start thinking more flexibly about how to build websites.

How do designers address these issues? In the past, they might have had to design separate versions of a site for different platforms and various screen sizes. Now it is important to build websites that can adapt to any device. The current standard for accomplishing this is Responsive Web Design.

RESPONSIVE WEB DESIGN

Responsive Web Design refers to a fluidly constructed web page layout that scales from handheld device displays to large, high-resolution computer displays using flexible typography, flexible images, fluid grids, and CSS3 media queries.

Responsive Web Design allows sites to be designed for multiple viewing situations, whether on a 24-inch monitor or on a mobile device. The design adjusts to the size of the web browser or the device viewport to maintain the hierarchy of the information on the site without losing the impact of the design. Because all web-based systems can be designed to fit multiple screen sizes, the need for several variations of an entire website or system may arise. Commonly there will be three: desktop, tablet, and mobile. They may all look completely different or only have minor variations. These designs can actually be programmed by the development team to change for every single type of device so that a single website can be built that gracefully adapts to each device's constraints and capabilities.

Knowledge of this process has changed the requirements designers need to be familiar with because liquid layouts and re-flowing design mist be integrated into the development arena, once again blurring the lines between these disciplines and growing into a vast system of hybrid roles and types of professionals. Developers have had to evolve to understand design and vice versa. The design team needs to discuss Responsive Design with the programming and development team members simply because the possibilities are limitless.

Building the Site

Because the Web is liquid, nearly all websites will drastically change in production, during development, and after launch, by responding to client requests, customer needs, and changes in technology, such as new devices or integrations. There are several approaches to building websites available today for designers and developers, requiring various levels of skills. More importantly, each site will be different, so the needs and goals of a particular site need to be determined first, in order to choose the most efficient and powerful tools to accomplish those needs and goals. For some sites, it makes sense to code the site from scratch, while others benefit from a content management system (CMS). Some of the most-used approaches to building websites are discussed below.

CMS PLATFORM-BASED

Websites built with content management system (CMS) software provide website authoring, collaboration, and administration tools designed to allow users with little knowledge of web programming languages or markup languages to create and manage website content with relative ease. This can be an advantage for both designers and their clients.

The CMS of choice for many web designers and bloggers is WordPress, an open-source project with an enormous user base and a large Open Source developer community. It is a powerful and versatile platform, and relatively easy to use, even for web designers who do not know how to code. Those who do know how to code can access its full potential. There is a massive selection of site templates (or "themes") available, many of them free, as well as many plug-ins to expand its capabilities.

Other CMS platform-based tools include Magento, Drupal, Expression Engine, Joomla, and Shopify. All support e-commerce sites.

Designing for CMS-driven websites can pose some fundamental challenges for designers coming from the print world. Understanding the need to approach a page design as a template or style guide instead of a static layout is critical in making sure a design moves smoothly from concept to execution. This often requires some technical understanding of how the page will be constructed from the back end so that the designer can accurately gauge overflow of content elements and recommend text length limits or other restrictions where necessary.

NON-CMS HTML

Non-CMS HTML websites are built by developers with the mark-up language HTML, cascading style sheets (CSS), and JavaScript. The pages are static (with no database), and while there is little or no maintenance required, changes in the site are difficult to make without a knowledge of HTML/CSS. For this reason their popularity has declined along with the concept of the static website.

WEB-BUILDER TOOLS

Online web-builder tools allow designers to create websites without manual code editing, though most include CSS coding modules for advanced customizations. The software (or platform) is easy to use and can be used to build full-featured, mobile-friendly sites on a budget. Some of the better web-builder tools are Squarespace, Weebly, WIX, Duda, SiteBuilder, Shopify, and WordPress. These systems have evolved to meet a very specific need, one that is in high demand: getting a website up and running immediately.

Hosting companies offer rental versions of these web-builder tools for a monthly fee. This rental concept or *software as a service* (SaSS) has filled the large price gap that existed between the static website versus the dynamic website and offers a temporary alternative to a full custom build. These SaSS visual builders (VB) are technically CMS systems because they allow users to manage, change, and interact with the content. However, they are not usually fully customizable, and you do not own the final product and cannot take it with you if you leave the platform. This is the defining difference between Content Management and SaSS or VB systems. The CMS, complete with its files, database, content and design, belongs to the customer and it can be moved to other hosting accounts and usually does not have any monthly fee (other than hosting) associated with it, while the SaSS or VB systems are owned by the company that made them.

CUSTOM WEB DEVELOPMENT

There are limitless possibilities when building websites from scratch. Custom web development incorporates programming and responsive web design. Non-CMS HTML sites can be built using Dreamweaver or other WYSIWYG editors (Notepad++, KomodoEdit, Brackets, etc.). Other sites might be CMS platform-based, for example, when developers design and build their own themes for WordPress sites.

An *integrated development environment (IDE)* is a system that facilitates application development and builds and edits websites or any aspect of a web-based application/platform. Using an IDE allows developers to encompass all programming tasks within a single application. IDEs eliminate the need for developers to write code in a text editor, then run the compiler or upload the files via FTP and look for error messages—all with different tools. By providing a suite of combined tools in one environment, the IDE solves the problem of constantly switching tools, making the process much faster.

Some designers create dynamic sites with non-CMS HTML, a database, and custom programming, using a combination of HTML, CSS, JavaScript, jQuery, and PHP (or another programming language, such as Ruby, etc.).

Some projects require a lot of flexibility and intensive use of advanced web technologies. If this is the case, a truly customized solution that fits the project's needs will have to be developed. Open-source CMS platforms that provide solutions for complex projects are Drupal, WordPress, Joomla, Magento (specifically for e-commerce), and Dolphin (social media).

Establishing Roles & Responsibilities

Concept and content and how they function determine the success or failure of an increasing number of complex websites. Visual and behavioral aspects of interface architecture, programming, and code play vital roles. If the web designer only has responsibility for creating the visual interface, not the programming, it is essential that the designer have a clearly structured relationship with a trusted programmer or be familiar with the many existing web-building applications. The designer is expected to provide the programmer with all the objectives and details for interactivity.

The programmer, in turn, is responsible for producing alpha and beta site testing versions and may also be responsible for providing the documentation necessary to implement the work (a change log). Thorough advance planning is necessary because once programming begins, any changes to the program or to the artistic elements will incur high charges in Traditional development projects. If the project is understood to be an Agile web development project, revision phases are far more cost-effective because Agile development tactics are rapid and do not require the same amount of planning and paperwork.

Clients should review all materials received at agreed-upon intervals from the project team and give a detailed list of comments and suggestions for revision at specific deadlines. Changes are easiest to implement if they are made before production of the finished work. Designers report treating postproduction changes as author's alterations and charging fees accordingly.

The Proposal or Statement of Work

A proposal or statement of work, including estimated fees and anticipated expenses for each item, is usually presented to the client before work begins (many clients like to work with a bottom-line number). The statement of work is a general agreement that details many of the following factors:

* Project objectives and requirements.
* Project team members with clearly delineated responsibilities.
* Type of project and method (traditional, agile, scrum, etc.)

* Project timeline or Gantt chart.
* A visual representation of proposed site architecture (site map).
* Intended use of the work.
* Technical constraints and exclusions.
* Number of devices covered in responsive design; number of browsers covered during cross-browser compliance checking.
* Art phases and nature of all deliverables.
* Warranty and limitation of liability.
* Disclosures, such as PCI compliance or EU laws on cookies, privacy, and data collection.
* Licenses and third-party cost disclosures for hosting, registration costs, or dependent systems (e.g., payment gateway fees, SaSS fees, etc.).
* Collateral and extra costs (e.g., fees and penalties associated with various laws, such as CAN-SPAM Act or ADA requirements).
* Terms of payment (including budget limit, line of credit for labor, revisions, enhancements, overtime, etc.).

In addition, designers frequently describe relationships with subcontractors (such as illustrators, animators, or programmers), design specifications (requirements and deliverables for both the client and the designer, milestones for review, and accountability factors), billing procedures, and contract terms. See the following section for more detailed information about contract terms.

Also outlined in the statement of work is the number or complexity of the templates, the maximum number of revisions, the way in which comps of project phases will be presented and approved, and the format in which they are needed. More about Developing a Design Proposal can be found in Chapter 1, Essential Business Practices. Web Designer & Developer Professional Relationships are discussed in Chapter 2, Professional Relationships.

It is customary for proposals to be submitted to clients as a complimentary service, although fees and expenses accrued thereafter on a client's behalf and with the client's consent are billable. If the client accepts the proposal, the written terms and conditions are confirmed with the signatures of the client, programmer, and designer. Frequently, a deposit is also requested before work begins. Once a client accepts the design proposal and any appropriate deposits have been received, actual work begins.

CONTRACT TERMS

Examples of many contract terms specific to digital media can be found in the model contracts for digital media and website design in the Appendix: Contracts &

Forms. Components of contracts for design and illustration also may apply to digital media (see the Trade Practices sections in Chapter 5, Graphic Design and Chapter 7, Illustration).

DELIVERABLES

Deliverables are all the items that a designer agrees to deliver to the client, including digital files and images. It is important to delineate all the deliverable parts so that both the designer and the client understand the full scope of the project. Depending on the complexity of the project, the designer may divide it into several different phases with corresponding deliverables that will eventually be incorporated in the website. Things such as content development (copy and graphics), interface design, back-end coding, graphics optimization, search engine optimization, positioning statements, and concepts must be considered separate project modules and priced as different line items.

Many contracts fail to describe deliverables in sufficient detail, leaving both designer and client vulnerable to miscommunication and dissatisfaction during the contract phase and, even worse, with the results. Creating an in-depth specification sheet and flowchart will help the designer avoid major headaches and keep the project on track.

A full, clear description includes the size and scope of the work, using appropriate measurements (such as time, file size, number of screens or pages, complexity of linking and navigational elements, segment of programming source code, and site assets); intermediate review timetables and the deliverables required at those stages; the technical needs of the product such as medium, electronic file format, and style guides; copyright ownership of the deliverables; modules that conform to the function specifications; the kinds and types of revisions included in the fee; and the terms of acceptance.

EXPENSES

It is a widespread industry practice for the client to reimburse direct and indirect expenses, as specified in the contract. If precise amounts are not known at the time of signing, they are estimated, and the client should be given the option to approve any costs in excess of those projected in the original agreement. Direct costs include fonts, plug-ins, and software subscriptions, as well as commissioning new or licensing existing images, animation, and sound; hiring voice talent; and signing run-time licenses. Note that use of graphics on printed pieces, such as photos, illustrations, and logos, must be quoted separately. Other expenses include travel, research materials, and media costs (such as DVDs). For designers who bill

hourly, remember to consider capital investment when establishing fees. (See the Hourly Rate Formula section in Chapter 1, Essential Business Practices.)

PAY RATE

Rates depend upon project scope and complexity. Even if the client wants a bottom-line rate, an estimate must start with the expected time it will take to complete the project. Most projects are bid in two parts. The first part includes the design, architecture, and user interface. The second part includes additional back-end programming.

PAYMENT TERMS

Depending on the length of the project, fees may be paid in a lump sum within a set period (30 days) after completion, or at periodic intervals when the timeline is longer. Fees are often tied to acceptance of deliverables, but if there is only one review, payment may also be divided into three increments: a third on signing the contract, a third upon review of deliverables, and the last portion upon completion. Some design firms request up to 50% of the payment upon proposal acceptance, to cover hiring freelance programmers and coders. (See more about pricing in the section on Freelancing later in this chapter.)

Agile web development projects and long-term maintenance contracts also offer clients the following payment options:

* **Monthly installment payments** to finance a website (with or without a finance fee). For example: 20 monthly payments of $500 per month to pay off a $10,000 website.
* **Tabs or labor credit lines** extended to the client, allowing for new work requests to be placed on the fly and paid later. For example, a $1,000 line of labor credit is extended to handle maintenance and post-launch procedures such as minor revisions.
* **Monthly retainers** for which on-call support may be covered/provided. The type and limitations of the support need to be defined. For example, a monthly retainer of $1,000, which includes 24 x 7 on-call webmaster SEO services; limited to a maximum of 15 phone calls not exceeding 15 hours per month.

These types of payment options are typical and expected in situations where Agile web development assumes the client relationship will not have any clearly defined end but has many goals which require a wide variety of skills and means to work toward. These options are not usually applicable nor expected for Traditional models, which assume that the client relationship ends after clearly defined goals are accomplished.

Traditional web development projects often start using clearly defined goals and later evolve into Agile web development projects, which is natural and common. Recognition and anticipation of client needs as either Traditional or Agile is an essential and intuitive skill, which a seasoned developer should be able to identify before drafting elaborate documentation that might never be met or have any clearly defined end.

CANCELLATION FEES

A negotiated cancellation fee may range from a portion of the cost to the entire cost of work, depending on the project status at the time of cancellation and the terms of the contract. Terms should stipulate that upon cancellation, all rights—publication and other—revert to the designer; the client shall assume responsibility for all collection and legal fees necessitated by default in payment; and a nondisclosure clause limits the review of the project to the client and specifically prohibits the client from showing the project to other designers. (An example of a Nondisclosure Agreement for Submitting Ideas can be found in the Appendix.)

SCHEDULE

While the timing of deliverables is an important contractual commitment, all digital media projects require specific time frames, including those with intangible deliverables, for example, provision of services. Contracts that include schedules should include contingency provisions to be met in the event deadlines are missed by either designer or client.

COPYRIGHT

One critical copyright concern related to digital media is ownership of the rights to deliverables. Obviously, the creator should ensure that the necessary rights to all work used to create the final product are properly licensed or purchased for use or confirmed to be in the public domain. Digital media creators often negotiate for the copyright to the final deliverable; if this proves difficult, creators then attempt to retain rights to intermediate deliverables. Signing a work-made-for-hire agreement transfers ownership of all materials and concepts to the client and should be avoided in all circumstances. For a full discussion of copyright issues, see Chapter 11, Legal Rights & Issues.

NONCOMPETE CLAUSES

Noncompete clauses restrict an artist from creating work perceived to be in competition with a client. Noncompete clauses are therefore troublesome for creators, as they limit their potential client base. Clients, however, are legitimately concerned that work resembling theirs will appear in the same market at an overlapping time. A compromise may be a stipulation that the graphic artist will not create work that is in conflict with the client's. If it appears difficult to eliminate a non-compete clause, traditional limitations appropriate to the project may be negotiated, such as time limits, geography, or usage. Occasionally, designers may propose clauses that offer the client the right to refuse new product ideas before they are offered to other clients. For an example of a Non-Compete Clause, refer to the Appendix: Contracts & Forms.

CREDIT

Appropriate attribution and publicizing of credit can enhance a designer's reputation and ability to get work and are therefore important points of negotiation. Production studios, for instance, have initiated negotiations with clients about credits. As in film, video, and television, there are often many creators in website design, and credit may be difficult to negotiate, at least initially. Credit options may include the creation of a colophon/credit page, a link to the designer's site or e-mail address, or an embedded comment in the HTML code, such as "Another cool site by The Designer."

DEMONSTRATION RIGHTS

Demonstration rights are essential for self-promotion. They refer to the designer's right to show a client's work as a part of the designer's portfolio. Since the designer is the creator, the designer owns the copyright of the visuals, unless stipulated otherwise in the statement of work. However, clients may raise understandable concerns about preempting launch publicity or revealing work to possible competitors. Compromises may have to be negotiated, such as permitting only portions of the work to be shown or delaying unlimited rights until after the product is released.

LIABILITY

Liability raises a range of concerns. The client is usually responsible for obtaining permissions for any materials, including code and software, submit-ted to the designer. Similarly, the designer is usually responsible for obtaining necessary clearances for all subcontracted work (illustration, photography, animation, or any programming—both front-end and back-end), unless the client assumes that responsibility. The designer should also define to what extent the website will be compatible with existing technologies, software, and platforms and to what extent each party is responsible for the smooth operation of the website. For instance, subcontracted programmers are responsible for the functionality and legality of their code (they must define all copyright terms relating to their code with the client) and any bugs or incompatibilities. It should be clearly spelled out that any lack of projected hits (number of visits to a site), sales, or awards are not the designer's responsibility. The designer should retain the right to reuse code at a later date. Reuse of photography, motion graphics, and copywriting must also be negotiated.

The Information Gathering Phase

CLIENT GOALS

* Will the website be a new site or the redesign of an existing site?
* What are the client's business goals, and how will a website or redesigned site advance them? What does the client envision? What message should the website convey?
* Are there any compliance requirements (such as accessibility) that need to be reflected in the web design?
* What are the demographics of the primary audience for the website? Age, gender, professions, disciplines, interests? (Designers should warn clients that if the target is a broad-based, international audience, with potentially slow connections, old browsers, or expensive service, design options may be limited.)
* What are the secondary goals of the website? Is this an informational site or an avenue for Internet-based marketing or revenue?
* What subjects, in order of priority, does the client want to cover on the website? Have the client define the separate areas of subject matter and describe in detail the unique qualities of the business.
* Is the web copy written? What content needs to be created?
* Does the client have any existing design elements (logos, treatments) or design guidelines (brand style guide) that the designer should follow? Does the client have existing photography or video content they would like to incorporate?
* Does the client require original illustration, photography, video, or animation on the site? If so, is the animation going to be entirely original, or will the client be providing imagery (screen shots, product shots, etc.) that needs to be animated?
* Does the client need a new logo or new collateral marketing materials and media, for consistency with the new website? If so, these design services should be quoted in addition to the website proposal, as a separate contract.

* Does the client want to incorporate additional publicity for the website utilizing social media such as Facebook, Twitter, or an online blog?

CLIENT EDUCATION

To get a true picture of what the client needs, it is helpful to know how much the client understands about the Internet and what maintaining the website will involve in the long term:

* **Prior experience:** Has the client been part of a web development project before? If yes, have them describe their experience: what went right, what went wrong, how they would improve the experience this time around. Be sure that clients accurately describe what they want.
* **Current Internet capabilities:** With what service does the client have Internet access and what kind of connection? Does the client have a domain name registered and with which registrar? Does the client have a web hosting account and with which host?
* **Adequate resources:** Does the client have the staff to respond to an anticipated upsurge in e-mail? If not, the project manager should explain that the client may develop a negative online reputation if people do not receive immediate responses. Does the client have the resources to maintain a presence on social networking sites or to keep a blog current, if this is part of the overall website strategy?
* **Maintenance:** If the client plans to institute in-house site maintenance, is there someone on staff with the capability and time to do it? Or does the client want the designer to do it? Designers considering site maintenance arrangements should look carefully at the ability of their own organization to do it at least biweekly or monthly changes.

Depending on the answers to these and similar questions, it may be helpful to devote some time to providing basic education about the Internet.

Start-up businesses that want a website but do not yet have a logo or a comprehensive brand identity may need to be educated about the importance, value, and reusability of a well-planned identity, discrete and separate from the website application. Some web designers recommend that clients without a logo or identity engage with them on an identity design project first, before the creation of a web presence. This practice ensures that the designer is not giving the client a "free" brand identity, and that the client is not using a website project as a back door to create an integrated identity. Keeping the identity design and web design projects separate avoids potential misunderstandings and dissatisfaction between the client and the designer.

PLANNING

* **Final project approval:** If someone other than the client's team has that authority, then the designer needs to make sure that person has a basic understanding of web technologies.
* **Registering a domain name:** If the client has not already registered a domain name or wants a new one, what top-level domain name would the client like, and do they want a generic extension or one of the restricted extensions? What are two or three alternative domain names in case the first choice is already taken?
* **Expected site traffic and content access:** What is the expected site traffic and what content will the site be accessing at once? Sites with higher web traffic and content such as multiple streaming videos may require different server needs.
* **Client's source materials:** Are they in a usable electronic form? If not, the designer may need to educate the client about how to submit materials in formats as consistent and compatible as possible. The designer should always request high-resolution versions of files so compression levels can be controlled for final graphics and PDF files. If necessary, the designer should provide the client with a variety of options and be prepared to do conversions.
* **Advanced functionality:** Does the site require advanced functionality, such as database functionality? Does the site need to be coded in a special language? Is the site going to be updated automatically through a server-side database and the implementation of a Common Gateway Interface (CGI) script, or does the site need a content management system (CMS)?
* **Cross-browser compatibility:** What devices does the client expect the site to be able to be viewed on? The designer needs to understand the complexities of cross-browser compatibility and the elements that will be supported so that the site is functional on all browsers and devices. An excellent reference to help keep current on compatibility issues is http://caniuse.com/, which provides tables outlining the support of individual elements from HTML5, CSS3, SVG, JP ASI, etc., in various desktop and mobile browsers.

* **Social media integration:** Does the client have any social media accounts? If not, do they want to add any? If one exists or they want to add more, would they like social-share and/or social-follow links on their site? Blogs would do well by adding social share links, while static sites may not want them unless they have a section that offers general info that could boost Internet visibility if shared. The designer can advise about where on the site these links should be placed, as well as how they should look.
* **E-commerce requirements:** Does the site require the ability to securely process credit card transactions; need the development of shopping cart strategies, survey forms, advanced configurator sales selectors, online games and interactive demonstrations, or online chat, message boards, user forums, and blogs?
* **Web hosting:** Will the site be hosted on the client's server or with another provider? If in-house, the client's information technologies department should be included in the planning meetings.
* **Marketing & advertising:** Once the website is launched, what are the client's marketing plans? What will they be creating and how will the marketing affect the website and vice versa? What is the timeline for the marketing efforts? Who are the individuals and/or agencies that will be coordinating the marketing/advertising? Meeting with these people during the planning phase of the project will help to understand the overall picture of where this website fits in the overall marketing plan.

PREPARING TO DESIGN

* If the project is the redesign of an existing site, does the client want any additions or deletions?
* What look and feel would the client like for the site? Does the client have a specific genre, culture, or style in mind and why? However, the client's personal aesthetic preferences should not dictate what is in the best interest of the business goals.
* The designer should ask for any existing materials with which the web design needs to be consistent in branding: corporate identity programs, collateral marketing materials, product packaging, preproduction sketches, or media (DVDs, video games, etc.).
* Does the client desire graphics interactivity and/ or multimedia (also involving content development and site mapping)? These typically include JavaScript effects, animated GIFs, videos or podcasts, sound files, PDF downloads, animation, and interactivity. Be sure to advise the client that

these features will be estimated/charged in addition to, and not as part of, the basic design proposal.

Creative Brief

Once the proposal is accepted and all questions satisfactorily answered, the designer should write an internal brief for the creative team, summarizing the client's vision for website design. This overview of the work should reflect the information obtained from the above questions. Since its purpose is to inform team members about the job, each member should receive a copy and become familiar with it. The project manager also uses it to organize the workflow. Figure 6-1 illustrates a sample Creative Brief Outline

---

6–1 Sample Creative Brief Outline for Web Design

1. Assess Current Situation
* Is there an existing brand online/offline?
* Are there existing brand guidelines: logos, color palettes, etc.?
* Define any existing products/offerings. Is it a relatively competitive/saturated market?
* What is the value proposition for the target demographic?

2. Business Requirements & Objectives
* Define target goal and list adjectives describing it.
* What is the scope of the project?
* Why does the business want to do this? Is this the right choice?
* What features will need to be included in the website architecture and design to achieve this goal?
* Tone and manner (descriptive adjectives) for the site?
* What legal requirements might there be?

3. Demographics & Target Audience(s)
* Describe the model personas or users and their behavioral patterns
* Know the target demographics' web comfort level, probable hardware, spending patterns, software, and browser usage.
* What is their comfort level with interactive online features, etc.?
* Interview members of the target demographic; what do they think?

4. Barriers & Assumptions
* Define barriers and client assumptions that could hinder achieving the objectives of the website (e.g., competition, inadequate web technologies, etc.).
* Educate client about technologies and solutions which can be utilized to mitigate or overcome barriers (e.g., search engine optimization to counter lack of awareness of client's website, utilizing a blog to drive traffic to the site, etc.).

* Who is the main client contact person for achieving resolutions?

5. Strategies
* Outline how the website will be designed and mplemented, including coordination with back-end designers.
* Outline how site will be launched, including steps to publicize the launch.
* Outline how site will be maintained on an ongoing basis.
* Is there a content strategy?
* What is the SEO strategy?
* What are the accessibility and usability strategies and issues for the site?

6. Define Functionality with User Stories/Scenarios
* Create user "stories" that concisely capture what each persona or user does or needs to do with website or digital experience.
* Write stories from the point of view of the personas in non-technical language client and users will understand.
* Key story components: user, outcome when interacting with site, and value of interaction. (*As a* <user role>, *I want* <goal/desire> *so that* <benefit>.)

7. Project Mood Board
* Add logos and other branding-related images.
* Collect images that evoke the feeling of the desired vision of the site, after working out the above.

8. The Creative Vision
* What are the vision and story for the site?
* What do we want the interaction models and IA/ Wireframes to lead us to?
* What does the mood board tell us? Color, vision, palette, emotional feel: how do these change the brand or affect brand perception, design guidelines, and new vision?
* What do our user stories look like?
* Digital designs and design process?

---

that can be easily adapted to suit the needs of a particular project.

Copyright Protection Concerns

From the moment a website is launched, the information or graphics can be downloaded freely by anyone who wants them. It is all too easy for it to fall prey to illegal copying or element downloading. Even graphics that appear as very-low-resolution images can readily be reused. Using techniques such as JavaScript to disable the right-click feature on the mouse makes it more difficult for images to be copied, but there are ways around that.

Software technology enables designers to embed invisible comments (digital watermarks) and numeric signatures in the file's binary data. While this offers minimal protection, it does not prevent copying or swiping. The best way to legally protect graphics on the Web is to clearly spell out any permitted uses of the images and the text on the site. (For more about copyright in the digital environment, see the Digital Millennium Copyright Act section in Chapter 11, Legal Rights & Issues.)

United States copyright and libel law is applied to Internet content, but enforcement in the global Internet environment is extremely difficult. If a designer sees one of his or her graphics on someone else's page (the most frequent offense), common practice is to send an e-mail and ask the person to take it down, as web etiquette requires. Most frequently, the offender does not realize it is illegal to use other people's graphics. However, if the user has copied the graphic artist's work without permission and refuses to remove it, this illegal act is grounds for legal action.

Beware of worms, spiders, or search robots. Bitmap worms are programs that scan the Web for graphics, collecting them into icon and so-called clip art collections and then presenting them on a different site as so-called public domain art. The graphic artist can check hit reports to see who is spending time at the site. A single visitor downloading several megabytes of images is a warning that something illegal has been going on.

Protecting and enforcing one's legal rights in the digital world is easier said than done. Designers and artists are encouraged to register the site's content and images with the U.S. Copyright Office (for information on registration procedures, see Chapter 11, Legal Rights & Issues).

The Web of Things

The need for interactive design is not limited to websites, apps, and mobile devices. There is a whole world of nonstandard computing devices that connect to Wi-Fi and can transmit data, known as the *Internet of Things (IoT)*. Common examples from everyday life are video doorbells, security systems, electronic appliances, smart speakers (e.g., Alexa and Google Home), cars, baby monitors, smart watches, and wearable health monitors. The IoT also includes military systems and industrial applications as well, for example, laser cutters and automated machines using CnC (computer numerical control).

The *Web of Things (WoT)* refers to the approaches, software architectural styles, and programming patterns that allow many of these real-world objects to be part of the World Wide Web. They may be created in the realm of industrial design, but they need apps, application programming interfaces, and web-based graphic user interfaces to control and translate them into useful human tools, using the language of design and object-oriented programming. Designing for the WoT is now an important part of web standards. It is increasingly common for web designers, full stack developers, and web fixers to be employed to assist industrial designers in the hardware design and development process.

Mobile Design/Development

Mobile sites and apps are currently a huge growth area in technology. There is a proliferation of choices and platforms available for advertising campaigns and programs with a mobile component. Graphic artists are needed to design and illustrate content that will be effective on miniature screens held at arm's length as well as on the vast screens of electronic billboards seen from moving cars, and every size in between. Mobile apps are represented onscreen by icons, which have created a demand for icon design beyond those used for websites. Designers and programmers are also needed for navigational and Global Positioning Systems (GPS), such as an auto GPS or a GPS application on smart phones, as well as a plethora of other sensors and features.

Mobile Websites

According to Fueled.com, the mobile market has grown substantially over the years, and industry experts predict continued growth. In 2018, mobile traffic accounted for 52.2% of toral website traffic in the United States, and 3.6 hours that adults spend consuming digital media occurred on smartphones, ahead of desktops, laptops, and other connected devices.

These statistics have very positive implications for advertisers who are considering mobile advertising—and

6–2 Best Practices for Mobile Sites

1. Prioritize the Content

Many people use their mobile device on the go—in a hurried, rushed state. Combined with small touch screens, it doesn't make for easy search or navigation. When designing for a mobile experience, minimalism rules. Each page, including the homepage, should have just one central focus.

Keep clutter to a minimum. Prioritize and hide some of the content where prudent. Reposition the things most important to mobile users to the top. Content can also be hidden behind tappable and swipeable areas. For example, instead of showing an entire section with its body text, show just the title, with a little supporting graphic that can be made interactive/clickable. When clicked, the full body text can appear. This can help shorten what would otherwise be an intensely long page.

2. Keep It Simple

Keep navigation menus simple and accessible. When designing a mobile navigation menu, consider the limitations of small screens and try to make the most with little available space. The traditional desktop website menu bar at the top of the page eats up precious screen space on a mobile site. Instead, make the menu a drop-down accordion or icon on the top left or right of the mobile screen. Avoid multi-level menus as much as possible.

3. Make It Quick

The mobile web is all about quick actions and results. Browsing a mobile website in search of something is more tiresome than on a PC, but it can be made easier by adding a search bar, allowing site visitors to quickly type in what they're looking for. The search bar saves time and reduces the number of steps visitors need to take before finding what they need.

4. Easy Does It

Engagements on mobile sites should be designed to make them easy for users. Typing on a mobile touchpad is awkward and tedious. Keep that in mind when adding features that require users' input. If forms are used, try to minimize the required entry fields. When possible, pre-fill fields with defaults. Use auto-fill for commonly used fields. When asking for opinions, give a choice of icons or emojis that can be clicked instead of requiring typed responses.

If there are any atypical gestures, like a swipe to move to the next page or a horizontal scroll, don't assume users will pick up on these. Tell them how to use these features with a small arrow or a hovering message—whatever it takes to make it easy for them to find what they're looking for.

5. Design for Readability

Legibility is especially important on a mobile site. Make sure content is easy to read and truly optimized for the device size. Choose font sizes and weights than can be easily read at small sizes. Balance the headings and body font sizes for the size of the device. A good rule of thumb on mobile is to strive for around 60–75 characters per line of body copy for optimal legibility. Other important factors affecting readability are color contrast between type and backgrounds and ample spacing.

6. Make It Flexible & Fluid

Mobile devices come in many different dimensions, with various viewport widths between 320 and 1280 pixels and lengths between 568 and 1366 pixels. Don't just design for a 320-pixel screen width. Keeping the layout flexible and fluid ensures it displays properly on different portrait and landscape screen sizes.

7. Create Responsive Imagery

A desktop page may need an image at 1200 pixels wide for full resolution, while the mobile version of that page may only need that image at 400 pixels wide. For an optimal responsive experience, it's best to use two different versions of the same image for mobile and desktop. What's more, in addition to typical mobile devices with standard resolution screens, there are also high-resolution devices which require graphics with density scale factors of @2x and @3x.

Scalable Vector Graphics (SVGs) are a must-have for any responsive design that is utilizing illustrations like icons. Unlike image files (JPEG/PNG/GIF), SVGs are infinitely scalable—any icon or graphic will remain ultra-sharp across all experiences without having to worry about resolution. Also, SVGs are often a far smaller file size than image files, so they can save on the site's load time, which on a mobile experience can mean the difference between someone sticking around or leaving

8. Design for Touch

On mobile, buttons and links will be tapped by a human finger, not by a precise mouse click, so they need to have larger interactive areas to accommodate this difference. On average, it's recommended that any clickable on a mobile device be at least 45 pixels in height. This will help ensure that there are fewer errors in navigation and minimize potential frustration. Also, don't just rely on touch inputs. There are many mobile devices that use styluses, and some older ones that still use directional key pads.

9. Take Advantage of Device Features

Mobile devices have many features like GPS, gyroscopes, and other sensors that are not available on desktop devices, such as "slide to unlock" or the ability to make phone calls. Figure out how to use these features to make the mobile experience for websites even better. Simple features can be added like "Tap to Call" the phone number on the contact page, easier sharing across social media platforms, or GPS to offer location-specific information and services.

10. Be Reachable

Mobile internet users expect quick and simple access to the most important information that a site offers, and that includes contact info. If visitors need to get in touch and are unable to easily find what they need, they might lose patience and decide to move on.

---

for web designers and graphic artists who have the skills to create mobile websites and content.

Although web designers have the skills to create mobile sites, mobile site design should not be approached as simply making a small-screen version of a website. The designer and the advertiser need to take into consideration users' mobile experiences and how they interact with their mobile devices. Best practices for designing mobile sites can be found in Figure 6–2.

Mobile Apps

The increasing number of smartphone users in the global market has led to a tremendous increase in the number of apps that consumers use on their phones. The Apple App Store offers 1.85 million of these apps, while Google Play has over 2.6 million apps. These numbers are expected to increase in the future. According to eMarketer, in 2019, the average person spent 90% of their mobile time in apps versus the mobile web. Statista reported that the global mobile app revenue was about $461.7 billion in 2019, over double of what it was in 2016. This growth in mobile phone app usage has created a demand and opportunities for graphic artists to design, develop, and illustrate content for these devices. Apps are not limited to personal use and entertainment. Mobile components are also integral parts of advertising campaigns and programs.

SKILLS NEEDED

Many of the skills that web designers and developers already have are transferable to mobile app design, according to experts working in the field.

TECHNICAL

Mobile apps are compact application software programs that perform specific tasks for the mobile user. They frequently serve to provide users with similar services to those they access on their desktop computers; however, apps are generally small, individual software units with limited function. They are a move away from the integrated software systems generally found on desktops or laptops. Instead, each app provides limited and isolated functionality, such as a game, a calculator, mobile web browsing, etc. Their specificity has become part of their desirability because they allow users to hand pick what their devices are able to do. There are three types of mobile apps:

* **Native apps** are installed on a device, either pre-installed or downloaded for free or for a small fee from websites (app stores). They are developed specifically for a particular operating system (OS) platform, using the associated software development kit (SDK) and integrated development environment (IDE), in order to take more advantage of the device's functions. The advantage is they are fast, reliable, and powerful. The disadvantage is that they have to be written in different code for each mobile OS (such as Swift or Objective-C for iOS devices and Java or Kotlin for Android). Also, of the different types of apps, native apps are the costliest to develop.

* **Mobile web apps** are server-side apps, accessed from the Internet. The software is written as web pages in HTML and CSS with the interactive parts in HTML5 or server-side technology like Python, Ruby, PHP, or ASP.NET, etc. This means that the same app can be used by most devices that can surf the Web, regardless of brand. A mobile web app performs specified tasks for the mobile user, usually by downloading part of the application to the device for local processing each time it is used. Web apps are less costly to develop than native apps, but their weakness is that they cannot access all of a device's capabilities.

✳ **Hybrid apps** combine the common web-based development environments with the power of native applications. Like native apps, hybrid apps run on the device, but like mobile web apps, they are written with web technologies (HTML, CSS, and JavaScript) but use a native host like Apache Cordova. A web-to-native abstraction layer enables access to device capabilities that are not accessible in mobile web applications, such as the accelerator, camera, and local storage.

Web professionals who have proficiency in the latest versions of HTML and CSS standards and are fluent with JavaScript can start off by designing and developing web apps and hybrid apps. Help with the hybrid process is available through books and online resources. Experimenting with HTML, CSS, and JavaScript to design apps can be a great way to get acquainted with the platform.

Those who want to build native apps need more of a programming background than a web development one, and the learning curve can be steep. Fortunately, for the vast majority of apps, it is possible to do remarkable things using web technologies to achieve similar results to writing native code. However, building apps with eye-popping graphics, animations, native widgets, and full access to the entire device, requires software built with the device's native language. Time-critical functions, such as the high frame-rate requirements of fast action games, also require using the native language of a device or operating system. Those who are just starting to design native apps might want to partner with a more experienced coder.

DESIGN

While many web design concepts still apply, designing for mobile experiences differs in important ways from designing for the desktop (see the Mobile Websites section above). It is recommended that one way to start learning app design is by researching the market: look at and compare existing apps and study their functionality and the elements they are using that are already part of the device's offerings. How could they be improved to be easier to use? Study very successful mobile apps to see why they are effective. It may be helpful to start by choosing one platform and learning it very well, rather than trying to learn everything all at once.

During the app design process, the mobile designer needs to consider the following:

The User & the User Experience: Mobile users interact differently with mobile devices compared to the way they interact with a non-mobile device, such as a desktop computer. It is important to understand the difference. Users can use their mobile devices wherever they are; on the go, in any manner of motion; and at a moment's notice. However, there is no single type of mobile user. Yes, there is the stereotypical on-the-go, distracted user, but there are also mobile users who use their apps in more prolonged, relaxing situations or while waiting for long periods of time (at the doctor's office, for a delayed flight, on a long trip, etc.). In these situations, users can give a lot of attention and time to exploring the app.

The difference in user experiences is also affected by the device itself. There is a functional difference between designing apps for tablets and for other mobile devices. The difference between the two often revolves around the expected use. Where the desktop or laptop computer experience for a given service can be seen as the main hub, mobile applications have a focus on doing things quickly, on-the-go, with more limited interaction, whereas tablet experiences often focus on a more cinematic "browse" entertainment experience or an interactive learning experience. While this is often more of a user experience and information architecture challenge than a visual design challenge, designers should be aware of the root differences between different screen experiences and be aware of technology limitations, navigation gestures, and page-size concerns.

Studying these patterns of use and designing apps to fit different lifestyles is similar to designing a website. Regardless of the medium, it needs to be designed around a target audience.

Device Capabilities & Limitations: Mobile designers need to consider the capabilities and limitations of the specific devices themselves as well as the requirements of the different platforms the app will be used on. Mobile devices (smartphones, mobile phones, tablets, e-readers, etc.) differ greatly in form and capabilities. Just because mobile devices are smaller, they should not be thought of as simplified versions of desktops. Many mobile devices have built-in features that make them more powerful than desktops, such as touch, microphone, camera, accelerometer, compass, gyroscope, GPS, etc., and research shows that users expect to be able to do more from their mobile devices, not less. The device's features shape how the target audience uses it and how they will expect to use an app.

The smaller screen size does present challenges for the mobile designer. Economy of design is important—what is left out is as important as what is left in. Every feature or element needs to be considered carefully—is including it worth the tradeoffs of added complexity and the need for more user time and attention? Menus need to be simpler with not too many choices. Finding ways to separate elements spatially is also a design consideration. Due to the smaller screen space, padding between elements needs to be considerably fewer pixels than on a desktop, so the designer might use other visual devices to suggest separation, such as rounded corners around perimeters and different color backgrounds.

Another consideration is thinking of ways an app can work in both screen orientations—landscape and vertical.

Ergonomic & Visibility Issues: For touchscreen devices, the designer needs to consider ergonomic issues, since navigating with fingers and thumbs can create comfort and visibility issues with the interface. Where does the thumb naturally come to rest on the screen? Where should controls be placed so they can be accessed easily (even one-handed) without obscuring content? Navigation and controls in apps for certain mobile devices may be better suited placed at the bottom of the screen—just the opposite of programs designed for desktops and laptops.

Stability: A good app also needs to be stable—well-tested and crash-free.

THE APP DESIGN PROCESS

DETERMINE THE APP'S PRIMARY TASK
Once an idea for an app has been conceived, the application functionality needs to be narrowed down to the core of what the app will do. The most successful apps focus on one primary task. To determine what the primary task will be, you need to write a concise explanation, called the *Product Definition Statement*, describing the app's main purpose and intended audience. The statement should include three parts:

* **The differentiator:** what differentiates this app from existing ones doing the same or similar things? (easy to use, simpler, faster, time-saver, convenient, expanded capability, etc.)
* **The solution:** what problem does it solve or need does it meet? This is the main purpose for designing the app.
* **The intended audience:** who will benefit most from this app? Who will most likely use it (18–24-year-old male gamers, senior citizens with poor eyesight, traveling business professionals, etc.)?

A Product Definition Statement for a particular educational app, for example, might be: *The "Look at My Face"*
app teaches young children with autism [intended audience] *how to recognize social cues in facial expressions* [solution] *using an entertaining, interactive game format that can be navigated by the student, independently of the teacher* [differentiator].

RESEARCH THE MARKET
The research phase starts by looking for existing solutions to see what is already available. A search should not be limited to other mobile apps. You may find products similar to your proposed app outside the mobile marketplace as desktop applications, web apps, and even offline products. An online search can include the iTunes App Store and the Google Play Store.

Once you discover what is available, a deeper look will uncover potential technical limitations. For example, you might be envisioning an app for a certain device, only to find out its software development kit doesn't support the functionality you want the app to have. Also, you need to think about how many hits the app might get because some search engines start charging a fee once a certain daily volume of search requests in an app is exceeded.

However, what is a technical limitation today may not be in the future, so you can still plan for future functionality in the design.

KNOW THE TARGET AUDIENCE
Knowing your specific target audience is very important in defining a design style, typography, and layout. Will your app appeal to 18–22-year-old female college students or mid-level corporate executives? Try developing "personas" to understand what your targeted demographic wants to see, and the context in which they will use the app. Once you define personas, place them in real-life mobile circumstances. Where are they and what is their form of mobility— jogging in a city park, riding to work on a city bus, being chauffeured across town to a business meeting, sleeping on a trans-Atlantic flight, etc.?

DESIGN THE SITEMAP
Sitemaps for mobile apps are critical to designing an intuitive flow and simple and usable controls. Unlike website sitemaps, mobile apps should not present the user with multiple ways to get to one place. Due to the smaller screen space and the on-the-go mobile experience, there should be only one way to get there.

CREATE THE WIREFRAME & PAPER PROTOTYPING
Data collected from the use case scenarios will define the content and controls that need to be present on the screens defined in the sitemap. From there you have to

design a preliminary layout that will account for each of these design elements. Define a grid and establish the importance of information using the color, shape, and size of design elements.

Since users hold touchscreen mobile devices in a way that the thumb position is typically pointed towards the middle of the screen, to help them navigate around the app quickly, give them controls that allow them to move around holding the device with just one hand. Also think about how you can minimize users' input, so they do not waste time entering a lot of text. Provide them with choices from a menu instead.

Paper prototyping will save a lot of time when designing mobile apps. Much like any design or illustration process, having iterations of your design allows you to explore a wider variety of design options. Using sticky notes or index cards is useful for re-ordering, adding, or deleting screens until the flow is right.

CREATE FINAL FILES

Once you have fine-tuned your paper prototypes, your sketches can be brought to life in Photoshop or Sketch. Templates for different devices, as well as specifications on how to set up your files at the proper size and resolution, can be found on the Internet at http://mobile.tutsplus.com.

Tablet Apps

Despite the overwhelming popularity and convenience of smartphones, tablets still have a place in the market, due to their larger screen size and longer battery life. Both advantages make them better for entertainment use, such as movie watching, game playing, and book reading. They are also often preferred for mobile business use due to the screen size, which provides larger displays in which users can view multiple sets of data or information at once.

Tablet app design is similar to, but functionally different from, mobile app design. The difference between the two often revolves around the expected use. Where the desktop or laptop computer experience for a given service can be seen as the main hub, mobile applications have a focus on doing things quickly, on-the-go, with limited interaction, whereas tablet experiences often focus on a more cinematic "browse" entertainment experience.

The popularity of tablets, both at home and in schools, also has created a demand for educational apps, starting at the preschool level. Educational apps present concepts in an entertaining, game-like way with enhancements such as voice and sound effects. Again, unlike mobile apps, the experience is a more prolonged, engaged one.

Tablet usage is also an important factor in e-commerce. According to statistics researched by aioma.com, it is predicted that m-commerce, which includes all mobile devices, will account for over half of e-commerce sales by 2021. Online shopping is one of the top activities for 43% of smartphone users and 17% of tablet users. However, while smartphone users are the most enthusiastic shoppers, the average purchase by tablet users has a value $10 higher than that of phone users. Tablet shoppers also have a higher conversion rate (percentage of visitors to an e-commerce site or app who actually make a purchase) than smartphone shoppers (5.2% vs. under 3%).

While the difference between mobile and tablet apps is often more of a user experience/information architecture challenge than a visual design challenge, designers should be aware of the root differences between different screen experiences and be aware of technology limitations, navigation gestures, and page-size concerns from extraneous graphics.

Other Digital Media

While work in certain print media may be drying up, the need for illustration and design skills is being transferred to the digital arena. In the past, other than website design, work for digital media was often viewed (and priced) as add-ons to or as additional usages of larger print projects. Today, designers and illustrators are increasingly being asked to produce work directly for digital platforms as standalone projects, not tied to print. Advances in technology also have opened up opportunities for artists in digital media that did not even exist 15 years ago. Described below are some of the areas in digital media not already discussed, which need the skills of designers, illustrators, and animators.

Events, Presentations, Displays

Graphic artists are creating ambient graphics (still or motion), video, and animation for all types of events and displays. These uses may be commercial—to advertise, promote, demonstrate, and launch products and books—or they may be simply to enhance the experience at events such as art openings. Artists and programmers are needed for touch screen displays, kiosk systems at shopping malls and tradeshows, and large-scale permanent installations that can be found in museums.

Computer Software Applications

As more and more service businesses and government agencies, such as banking, medicine, the Department of Motor Vehicles, and the Internal Revenue Service, switch from print to electronic records and services, there will be a greater need for computer software applications that are designed and programmed to make the experience easy and user-friendly for the consumer. There will also be a greater need for information worker software for the employees who are creating, processing, and managing all this electronic data, as well as software to train them. Software applications include Customer Resource Managers (CRM), used internally to track sales and customer information in a database, and content management systems (CMS), which may be internal intranet and extranet based.

The proliferation of digital entertainment also requires software for those who create it, as well as for the user to access and consume it. Entertainment software includes gaming engines and video games. Software Development Kits (SDK) allow software to be developed within a kit environment for an already existing system, such as the Sony PSP and even the iPhone.

E-Marketing

One form of e-mail & viral marketing is the *personalized URL (PURL)*. A PURL is a web page or microsite that is tailored to an individual visitor through the use of variable fields and pages that are linked to a database that contains information about each potential visitor. For each recipient on the database's list, the web address is unique, as is the content of the web page. For example, a college could send out an HTML e-mail inviting potential students to visit its website. After clicking on the link to the site, a student who has an interest in science would see lots of photos of labs, etc.; another student interested in theatre would see the same website, but the photos and text would talk about the theatre department. Both web pages would have a personal greeting such as, "Welcome to XXX U., John Doe" (or whatever the name is), and the URLs would also be personalized with the recipient's name, such as "www.xxxuniversity.edu/johndoe." The high degree of personalization involved in creating PURLs requires additional web design and a great quantity and variety of visual content.

Blogs & Social Networking Sites

More and more businesses and organizations have realized the value of hosting blogs and joining social networking sites to promote their products and services or to advance their causes. Graphic artists are being requested to design and illustrate pages and custom graphics for these sites, such as covers and profile graphics for Facebook and Twitter. WordPress is the most popular blogging software utilized by designers.

Other forms of digital media are discussed in Chapters 5, 7, 8, and 9.

Freelancing
Trade Practices

The following trade practices are meant to protect both the freelancer and the client and prevent misunderstandings:

WRITTEN AGREEMENTS

Whether hired by the client as a freelancer, by the designer or developer as a sub-contractor, or by someone else, all individuals hired to work on a web/interactive project should have a written agreement or contract, signed by both parties, in hand before starting work. Written agreements are recommended for all freelancers and sub-contractors, but especially in a team environment and for projects with many phases, components, and/or deliverables. Your responsibilities should be clearly spelled out in the agreement, including your relationship(s) with the rest of the team. For a detailed list of various items that should be included in the written contract, see the Contract Terms under The Proposal or Statement of Work section, earlier in this chapter. The Digital Media Invoice and the Website Design & Maintenance Order Form, found in the Appendix, can be used as guides for writing agreements.

When pitching to design a website, a freelance web designer may need to hire consultants or sub-contractors on creative deliverables such as wireframes, animation, photography, illustration, videography, and programming. If web designers hire a programmer, they should define the ownership rights of the program code (some are in the public domain and/or Open Source licensed; others are proprietary, protected, patented, or Closed Source licensed) in all contractual arrangements with the programmer, who creates it from a variety of computer languages.

Most programmers hired to write code for a proprietary website are asked to sign a work-for-hire agreement. A programmer rarely maintains ownership of the code for a finished website, although for some highly complex websites, code is sometimes licensed to the customer, with limited-usage rights.

Accessibility (a11y) is a measure of how accessible a computer system is to all people, including those with disabilities or impairments (e.g., hearing loss, visual impairment, limited dexterity, etc.). A11y concerns both software and hardware and how they are configured in order to enable a disabled or impaired person to use a computer system successfully. A website developed with accessibility in mind might have text-to-speech capabilities or output for special Braille hardware.

In today's Internet-driven world, inclusive technology is an important issue to ensure that access is equitable for everyone. Websites and web apps can (and should) be designed to be understood by the widest possible audience, which includes making accommodations for not only disabilities and impairments, but for conditions like colorblindness, dyslexia and dyscalculia, seizure and migraine triggers, as well as reading comprehension level and cognitive load.

Accessibility is not just a social issue. Some client organizations are required by law or other legal mandates that their websites be accessible. These include certain governmental, educational, and non-governmental/industry entities. Other organizations and corporations, while not mandated by law, have their own accessibility policies. Accessibility also makes good business sense, so designers should explore the issue with clients as a possible goal for their website, even if the client is not bound by requirements.

So, it is important for designers to find out at the very beginning of a project if the client is governed by any accessibility laws, mandates, or policies so that these requirements can be built into the design or redesign. It is almost always easier, more effective, and less expensive to incorporate accessibility early in the process, rather than later.

Developers need to evaluate accessibility throughout the development process to identify accessibility problems early, when it is easier to address them. Simple steps, such as changing settings in a browser, can help evaluate some aspects of accessibility. Comprehensive evaluation to determine if a website meets all accessibility guidelines takes more effort. There are evaluation tools available; however, no tool alone can determine if a site meets guidelines. Knowledgeable human evaluation is required to determine if a site is accessible.

To create websites and apps that are compliant with the Americans with Disabilities Act (ADA), the recom-

mended guidelines to follow are the *Web Content Accessibility Guidelines* (WCAG) found on the W3C website (https://www.w3.org/WAI/standards-guidelines/wcag/). The website is an excellent source of information regarding all aspects of accessibility as they apply to the Web.

There are no counterparts in the world of the Web comparable to consumer protection laws, other than optional web standards. Consequently, many unscrupulous practices have evolved. These include selling cheap $35 themes to clients as "full websites" and charging the same fee one would expect for a full website. Other practices involve deliberately hiding the fact that a ready-made theme from a template site is being used, by obscuring the credit line on the theme or by obscuring or removing the CMS system that is being used and presenting the website as a full custom build. In many cases, these practices can technically be "100% legal" if the Open Source License is left intact; however, they are frowned on because they allow agencies and freelancers to overcharge for their work, which has an overall negative effect on the integrity of the entire industry.

The generally accepted ethical way to handle Open Source CMS systems, themes, and ready-made mass-produced templates is to expressly notify the client, in writing, of the following:

* Other companies or websites may be using the exact same theme.
* The Open Source theme or plug-ins used cannot be copyrighted or patented.

When estimating and billing,

* Make clients aware that they will have to buy licenses for any fonts used or transferred to their systems, as well as any site enhancements and functionality, such as plug-ins, themes, and interactive features.
* Licenses, assets, domain names, and hosting should be purchased in the client's name and not inappropriately.

The true cost of the project should reflect the actual labor used and should not mislead the client with padded fees that reflect the going rate of legitimate custom builds.

Pricing Interactive Media

There is no typical interactive multimedia project. The size of a client and its needs vary greatly, as do the methods and vehicles used to best meet its online business and branding needs. All these variables greatly affect the size, complexity, and price of a project.

The cost of designing and developing interactive media can range dramatically, due to the numerous factors and variables involved in pricing a project. For example, the cost of a website can range from a limited makeover, for a few thousand dollars at the low end, to the major launch of an e-commerce site for several million dollars at the high end. The cost of building an iPad app (design, coding, testing, infrastructure, validation, and project management) can range from $35,000 for a simple app to at least $200,000 for a high-end one.

FACTORS AFFECTING PRICING

Traditional print pricing criteria of size, placement, or number of insertions do not apply to artwork used in digital media, where the end user often determines the sequence, timing, and repetitions of the work. The global nature of the Internet eliminates locale as a factor in website design. Geographic distribution remains relevant for some digital media markets such as games, kiosks, point-of-purchase displays, and training programs.

COST PER USER

One rule of thumb that can be used when pricing a project is that the number of people a web-based system will serve over one year is equivalent to the cost of a website. Each end user has a cost and a value—what it costs to both reach that user and support the website. So, for example, if it is determined that the per-user cost is $0.05, then 1 million users might require a website in the $50,000 range, but if the per-user cost is $1.00, then 1 million users might require a website in the $1,000,000 range. Knowing the cost per user is important. A key practice in discovering if a website and a company are capable of supporting its users is to calculate an estimated cost per user.

For example, on a social media website for a large corporation, where each user might upload 10 gigs of data per year, the server and hosting costs could be very high. On the opposite end of the scale, a simple informational website for a small business may have no user storage requirements, and the only cost consideration would be how many people can visit the site at the same time without crashing it. The small busines owner would be able to use low-cost shared hosting, and the large corporation might need an entire cloud. It is important to understand that the end user is often who the website is really for and understanding the cost of that user on the system is a key part in consulting a business on the cost of production.

DESIGNER/DEVELOPER'S SKILLS

Designers and developers' fees for interactive work also range widely, depending upon their skills, portfolio, and the complexity of the project. Professionals working in the interactive industry also stress that the skills needed on the team to accomplish the specifications of the job can also affect pricing. For example, a highly skilled animator's hourly rate can be much higher than the hourly rates of the rest of the team. It is also wise to figure in adequate time for proper testing of a website or an app and budget funds to hire a few outsiders to test it.

OTHER FACTORS AFFECTING THE PRICE

In a 2020 survey conducted by the Graphic Artists Guild, developers and programmers were asked to check all the factors that affect the price of an original website. The factors that were chosen by over 50% of the respondents are

* Number of site features (100%)
* Type and number of deliverables; number of pages (88%)
* Number of original graphic elements to be built (75%)
* Complexity of navigation; unique functionality; time constraints imposed by client; client size (63%)

While 63% developers and programmers responded that client size impacted their pricing, approximately 50% of website designers reported that their pricing was affected by client size.

METHODS OF PRICING

VALUE-BASED

The principle of value-based pricing (keying prices to the work's role in the client's business) is as valid in the digital world as in other media. Generally, the wider and greater the benefit of a website, digital ad, or some other media, the higher the value to the client. This may be gauged in relation to projected sales, increased customers, or to the client's track record on previous or similar projects. (More about value-based pricing can be found in Chapter 1, Essential Business Practices and Dan Mall's interview in Part 4).

HOURLY & FLAT FEES

Self-employed professionals working in interactive media generally charge either by the hour for their services or charge a flat project fee, depending on the circumstances and scope of the project. An hourly rate is also charged when the client cannot give a clear scope of the work.

Occasionally a client prefers to set a fixed price for a project. In such instances, an accepted industry practice is for designers to increase fees to accommodate unexpected changes, rush work, and overages that can occur during the course of a job. Alterations and changes should also be tracked, charged, and billed separately.

Normally, for projects using the Traditional approach, firm bids are given, and the designer does not adjust the final price unless the client changes the scope of the work, regardless of whether or not the designer goes under or over the quoted amount of time. If the client increases the scope of the work, the changes should be put in a written agreement signed by both parties, with corresponding additional fees for the extra services or deliverables.

PRICING PRACTICES TO AVOID

Designers should know that although web server software collects data on the number of visits to a site, that number can easily be manipulated and should never be used to establish pricing. The project should be completed and fully paid for by the time a site is launched.

Also beware of the company that promises a percentage of future revenue in lieu of payment for services rendered; that amounts to working on speculation, which is cautioned against in Chapter 3, Professional Issues. Either an hourly or flat-fee pay rate should be addressed and take precedence over royalties or promised stock options.

A range of hourly rates for several different types of freelance interactive jobs are given in Figure 6–3. Ranges of flat project fees for non-e-commerce website design can be found in Figure 6–4.

USAGE RIGHTS

It is recommended that designers transfer rights only for known media delivery, which should be specifically listed in the contract. Some usage payments are made as flat fees; others may be treated as an advance against a royalty, based on total distribution. In rare instances, companies have even allocated royalties to the freelancers they have hired for particular jobs.

ADDITIONAL FEES

Additional fees may be charged by freelancers working in web/interactive design, for stock photo usage, font usage, and software licensing, but there is no industry standard. Some include font usage in their base price, while others charge an additional fee at cost. Likewise, some designers charge stock photo and software licensing at cost. Other website designers also charge a mark-up for stock images, font usage rights, and software licensing (see Figure 6-4 for percentages of markups).

For some web design projects in which analytics and SEO/SEM are required, they are included in the base price; for others, they are considered an additional charge. The design of fan/business social media pages (Facebook, Yelp, etc.) is always billed as an additional charge.

CLIENT TRAINING

Client training is charged in several different ways; there does not seem to be an industry standard. Some designers

6–3 Comparative Fees for Web/Interactive

The pricing ranges in this chart do not constitute specific prices for particular jobs. The buyer and seller are free to negotiate, with each designer independently deciding how to price the work, after taking all factors into account.

Hourly Freelance Rates

User Experience Design (UX)	$85–130+
Informational Architect (IA)	$60–130+
User Interface Development (UI)	$60–130+
Web Designer	$60–130+
Web/Interactive Visual Designer	$85–150+
Web/Interactive Project Management	$85–130+
Web Content Strategist	$60–130+
Interactive Strategy	$85–130+
Web Front-End Developer	$60–130+
Web Programmer	$60–150+
Mobile Interface Design	$60–130+

Additional Fees

CANCELLATION & REJECTION FEES

(% of original project fee)

Prior to completion of concept phase	25–50%
After completion of preliminary work	50–75%
After completion of finished work	70–100%

RUSH FEES

25–100% (% added on to regular rate)

The fees provided in this chart were compiled from the results of a national survey of graphic artists conducted by the Graphic Artists Guild in 2020. Responses reflect fees charged in 2018 and 2019.

6–4 Comparative Fees for Website Design

The pricing ranges in this chart do not constitute specific prices for particular jobs. The buyer and seller are free to negotiate, with each designer independently deciding how to price the work, after taking all factors into account.

Flat Fees

Usual and customary fees for research and design of all visual aspects and elements of website look and feel; organization and architecture of website, including site map, and informational hierarchy and relationships; supervision of illustration, photography, and animation; testing on browsers and mobile devices for responsive design.

Non-E-Commerce Sites

	SMALL CLIENT	MEDIUM CLIENT	LARGE CLIENT
CMS Platform-based	$500–10,000+	$1,000–26,000	$1,000–30,000
	1-10 PAGES	11-30 PAGES	31+ PAGES
Non-CMS HTML	$250–8,000+	$750–14,000+	$2,000–30,000+
Web Builder Tools	$200–10,000	$400–13,000	$600–15,000

Additional Fees

MARKUPS (% added on to the cost of an item or service by the designer)

Stock Imagery, Video, Audio	10–50%
Software Licenses	10–50%
Outsourced Services	10–50%
Social Media Page Graphics	10–30%
Design of HTML E-mail/Newsletter	10–30%
SEO/SEM	10–50%
Analytics	10–25%
Arranging Web Hosting	10–50%

(Some Web Designers do not price the above as additional fees. Instead, they list them as line items in the project price. Others charge the client at cost for these items and do not add markups.)

RUSH FEES

15–100% (% added on to original fee)

Client Training

Hourly $60–130

(Some web professionals figure client training into their base project fee.)

Website Maintenance

Hourly $60–125+

Monthly Retainer $50–500+

(Cost of monthly retainers will vary greatly, depending on the maximum amount of time and/or specific   services listed in the retainer agreement.)

The fees provided in this chart were compiled from the results of a national survey of graphic artists conducted by the Graphic Artists Guild in 2020. Responses reflect fees charged in 2018 and 2019.

and developers build it into the base price of the project, while others show it as an additional charge. For those who consider it an extra fee, some charge a flat fee for a specified number of hours and/or calls, some charge by the hour, and others charge a monthly or annual retainer with a specified number of maximum calls or hours. (See examples of these arrangements in the previous section on Payment Terms under Contract Terms.)

MAINTENANCE AGREEMENTS

If web pages are going to need to be regularly updated, it is common to have the client sign an MSA (Master Service Agreement), separate from the web design, for ongoing maintenance beyond the scope of work. Without an MSA, clients will tend to ask a lot of questions and ask designers/developers to make basic updates to the site well after the launch. Often, clients could answer the questions they ask on their own with a little bit of research, and if they know they will be paying for a web professional's time, they will be more likely to do that little bit of research themselves. The person who will be responsible for updating—whether the designer or developer, an individual on the client's staff, or a third party—should be described in the contract, along with all corresponding data.

Maintenance agreements can be charged at an hourly rate, as a monthly/quarterly retainer, or annual contract. For retainers and contracts, the type and frequency of maintenance should be specified.

CANCELLATION/REJECTION/RUSH FEES

Cancellation, rejection, and rush fees are common in interactive design. If work is rejected or cancelled, a percentage of the total project, based on work completed at time of cancellation/rejection, is charged. All survey respondents reported charging full price for necessary expenses incurred up to the time of rejection or cancellation.

Rush fees are charged by designers and developers whenever they are not following the specific time frames defined in their process for that type of job. For example, if a client wants a website completed in six weeks, and the designer would typically require 8 weeks for the specific scope of work the client wants, then the job would require a rush fee.

{7}

Illustration

This chapter details the different markets where illustrators, mainly independent contractors, sell their creative product and reproduction rights to their artwork. The accepted trade practices that govern the buying and selling of artwork are provided for each market.

ILLUSTRATORS *are graphic artists who create artwork for any number of different markets. Most illustrators are freelancers (independent contractors) who maintain their own studios and work for a variety of clients, rather than salaried staff artists working for one employer. Some fields in which illustrators work on staff include animation studios and comic book and greeting card companies. While some freelance illustrators hire representatives or agents to promote their work to art buyers, many do their own promotion and marketing. (For a thorough discussion of artist's representatives, see Chapter 2, Professional Relationships.)*

Illustrators use a variety of traditional and new techniques and tools, including pen and ink, airbrush, acrylic and oil painting, watercolor, collage, multidimensional structures, and computer software and hardware. Most have a signature style, while some are sought for their versatility. Illustrators are responsible for proper file preparation, maintaining a color-calibrated monitor, and understanding how their work will be reproduced to maintain the quality of the final printed piece.

Original or specially commissioned illustration is sold primarily on the basis of usage and reproduction rights, but other factors are important as well. Original artwork, unless sold separately, usually remains the property of the illustrator.

Usage rights are generally sold according to the client's needs. Other uses for a work may be sold to other clients, as long as they are non-competitive or do not compromise the commissioning client's market. Clients that manage their businesses well only buy rights particular to the project, since it is not economical to pay for additional rights that are not needed and that will not be used.

Trends in Illustration

While there will always be trends in illustration style—looks and techniques that come and go and return again, there are also trends that affect markets for illustrators. Going into the second decade of the new millennium, these are some of the areas in which illustration is growing and changing:

A Merging of Illustration and Animation. Social media has been an important new market for illustrators during the last decade, but with increased competition for viewers' attention, there will be an increased demand for illustration work to become interactive. The use of the animated GIF has already blurred the lines between moving images and illustration. Another trend is the animation of select details in static illustrations, instead of everything moving. Animated details add dimension to illustrations by drawing viewer's attention to specific details or something significant.

A Resurgence of Physical and Traditional Techniques. As a reaction to the impersonal look of digital illustrations, recently there has been a renewed interest and demand for traditional illustration techniques, such as linocut, silkscreen, and letter press.

Hand-Lettering Is Thriving. Despite the multitude of typefaces available, all types of hand-lettering are currently popular in advertising, packaging, editorial, book covers, greeting cards, and publishing.

Illustration Has Overtaken Photography in Branding. One of the biggest trends currently affecting illustration is the desire for a more artful aesthetic in branding. The movement was originally led by boutique independent brands, such as craft beers, who wanted to distinguish themselves from large corporations. It has now caught on with the big brands, who want to be more appealing and stay relevant to their consumers—to the point that illustration is playing a much bigger role than photography in branding.

Illustration Salaries

Salaries for full-time illustrators vary by the type of illustration and the industry. Job descriptions for illustrators are often actually a combination of graphic design and illustration. Below are salary ranges for select types of illustration jobs. The ranges represent national averages in the United States, with the lower figure representing the 25th percentile and the higher figure representing the 75th percentile. The salary figures do not include benefits and perks, such as health insurance, paid time off, retirement savings plans, maternity/paternity leave, workplace wellness programs, free food, flexible work arrangements, etc., since these can vary widely among employers.

THE CREATIVE GROUP[1]
* **Illustrator/Infographics Designer** $45,500–64,250

ZIP RECRUITER[2]
* **Advertising Illustrator** $32.500–47,500
* **Architectural Illustrator** $42,500–59,000
* **Book Illustrator** $31,500–73,000
* **Concept Artist** $45,000–69,500
* **Graphic Recorder** $31,000–50,000
* **Science Illustrator** $36,000–93,500*
* **Storyboard Artist** $41,500–97,000
* **Technical Illustrator** $42.500–60,000

Freelance Illustration
A Note about Pricing

Pricing illustration work is complex. From the results of past pricing surveys conducted by the Graphic Artists Guild, it is evident that pricing methods can vary by the discipline, by industry or market, by complexity or amount of detail required by the client, and by the individual illustrator, as well as the illustrator's reputation. Some illustrators use multiple methods of pricing, depending on the industry or market. Usage, re-use, royalties, licensing arrangements, etc., also can vary widely.

The bottom line is if you are a self-employed illustrator, you need to figure out how to price your work in order to make a living wage and also realize that all contracts offered by a client are negotiable. More in-depth information about pricing and negotiating the terms of an offer can be found in Chapter 1, Essential Business Practices.

CHARGE YOUR TRUE WORTH

The information in this book is intended to encourage illustrators to evaluate the true worth of their work and seek it aggressively.

---

*Category includes natural science as well as other sciences.
1. Salary range reprinted with permission from *The Creative Group 2021 Salary Guide*, ©2020 Robert Half International.
2. Source of salary ranges: ZipRecruiter (www.ziprecruiter.com), as of September 28, 2020.

THE VALUE OF INTELLECTUAL PROPERTY

The value of intellectual property (IP) has ballooned as markets have become global. The U.S. Department of Commerce recognized the value of IP in its report, *Intellectual Properties and the U.S. Economy: 2016 Update*:

Innovation and creative endeavors are indispensable elements that drive economic growth and sustain the competitive edge of the U.S. economy. The last century recorded unprecedented improvements in the health, economic well-being, and overall quality of life for the entire U.S. population. As the world leader in innovation, U.S. companies have relied on intellectual property (IP) as one of the leading tools with which such advances were promoted and realized. Patents, trademarks, and copyrights are the principal means for establishing ownership rights to the creations, inventions, and brands that can be used to generate tangible economic benefits to their owner.

When pricing their work, illustrators need to keep in mind that as part of an IP-intensive industry, they are professionals who provide a valuable service that helps clients succeed in business. The value of their service is much more than the time it takes to do a job. The value includes their unique skills, expertise, and experience. Their work is their livelihood, so they should factor these things into their fees, as well as the cost of doing business (expenses and overhead) and their cost of living.

NEGOTIATE FAVORABLE TERMS

The need for illustrators to negotiate contracts with favorable terms, such as higher royalty rates, increased usage fees, more visible credit, and promotional opportunities for themselves, is even more important when faced with clients who offer lower fees. The onus of a client's shrinking budget should not be placed on the illustrator. Nor should a client's business structure affect how an illustrator prices a job. For example, a business's not-for-profit status does not mean the business has no funds or budgets to pay for services. Savvy illustrators will suggest less expensive solutions for a client with a smaller budget, rather than lower their fees.

VALUE YOUR WORTH & YOUR PROFESSION

While some illustrators may feel pressured to lower fees to keep work coming in during slow economic periods, it is not recommended. Once fees are reduced, it is difficult to justify raising them again when the economy rebounds and fees stabilize. Plus, illustrators who do this are not only devaluing their own worth, but the worth of the entire graphic arts profession. Likewise, when the cost of living is steadily climbing, it is financial suicide to start charging less for services.

Also beware of giving a new client a large break on pricing just to get the work. If the client becomes a steady customer, it may be awkward to start charging your normal fees. If you do offer a discount to a new client, it should be reasonable, and you should make the client aware that it is a one-time deal and state your normal fees.

EMBRACE CHANGE

It is inevitable that many types of print media will be replaced eventually by digital media. Opportunities for illustration work are already shifting from print to digital formats. Illustrators are encouraged to seek out and take advantage of new opportunities in digital media (refer to Chapter 6, Web/Interactive Design and Chapter 9, Animation & Motion) as well as explore new markets for the re-use of their art, such as selling stock and licensing their images for use on products (see Chapter 4, Maximizing Income).

EDUCATE CLIENTS

Make persistent, concerted efforts to educate clients about the true value of what you do. It is in clients' best interest to see artists as partners in creating their message, and in everyone's best interest when artists are treated with respect and rewarded with the compensation their work deserves.

THE PRICING CHARTS

When using the pricing charts in this chapter to figure out how to price an illustration job, consider them as only a starting point. There is no one set price—each project has its own specifications, artistic considerations, and level of complexity. These figures, reflecting the responses of established professionals, are meant as a point of reference only, and do not necessarily reflect such important factors as geographical differences in cost of living; deadlines; job complexity; reputation and experience of a particular illustrator; research; technique or unique quality of expression; and extraordinary or extensive use of the finished illustration, reflected in the usage rights being transferred. Flat fee pricing in this book is often given in ranges, based on the lowest and highest figures that professional artists have reported for that type of job. Those professionals at the top of their field, with a national or even international reputation, may be able to charge fees even higher than those listed in the charts.

View the prices in the charts as guidelines only. More importantly, you will need to estimate how long you think a particular project will take and multiply the hours by your hourly rate to get a sense of what a realistic base price might be. Then add on the estimated cost of materials, the usage rights you are granting, etc., to arrive at a project price. Even if you present a flat project fee to the client, you need to figure out how much time it will take you to do the job. Doing so will also help you schedule the project realistically. A formula for determining your hourly rate is provided in Chapter 1, Essential Business Practices.

General Trade Practices for Illustration

The following general trade practices have been used traditionally and thus have become accepted as standard. Please see individual market sections for additional trade practices specific to those markets.

1. The intended use of the art, the price, and terms of sale must be clearly stated in a contract, purchase order, or letter of agreement.

2. The artwork cannot be altered in any way, except for what occurs during the normal printing process, without the written consent of the artist. Since it is easy to alter art electronically, clients should inform the artist if they wish to alter the artwork and then do so only with the permission and supervision of the illustrator. Anything less is a violation of professional good faith and ethical practice.

3. Return of artwork to the artist, whether physical original artwork or on a digital file, should be automatic, with art "unaltered and undamaged except for normal use and wear," unless otherwise negotiated or noted in the individual market sections in this chapter.

4. If artwork will be used for something other than its original purpose, such as for an electronic database or a website, that fee is usually negotiated as early as possible. Note that secondary use of an illustration may be of greater value than the primary use. Reuse fees vary according to the individual market. (See individual market sections.)

5. Illustrators should negotiate reuse arrangements with the original commissioning party with speed, efficiency, and respect for the client's position.

6. Artists generally charge higher fees for rush work, which vary according to the individual market. (See individual market sections.)

7. If the illustrator satisfies the client's requirements but the finished work is not used, full compensation should be made. If a job is canceled after the work has begun, through no fault of the artist, a cancellation or kill fee is often provided. Depending upon the stage at which the job is terminated, this fee must cover all work done, including research time, sketches, billable expenses, and compensation for lost opportunities resulting from the artist's refusing other offers in order to make time available for the commission. In addition, clients who put commissions on hold or withhold approval for commissions for longer than 30 days should secure the assignment by paying a deposit up front. Cancellation fee terms should be included in the illustrator's written agreement or contract.

8. A rejection fee is agreed upon if the assignment is terminated because the preliminary or finished work is found to be unsatisfactory and steps to correct the problem have been exhausted. The rejection fee for finished work often has been 100% of the full price, depending upon the reason for rejection and the complexity of the job. When the job is rejected at the sketch stage, surveys indicate that the customary fee is 25 to 50% of the original price. This fee may be less for quick, rough sketches and up to 100% for highly rendered, time-consuming work. Rejection fee terms should also be spelled out in the illustrator's contract.

9. Artists considering working on speculation assume all risks and should evaluate the risks carefully when offered such arrangements. For a thorough discussion of the risks, see the Entrepreneurial Issues section in Chapter 3, Professional Issues.

10. The Graphic Artists Guild is opposed to the use of work-made-for-hire contracts, in which authorship and all rights that go with it are transferred to the commissioning party and the independent artist is treated as an employee for copyright purposes only. The independent artist receives no employee benefits and loses the right to claim authorship or to profit from future use of the work forever. For example, in the Guild's view, advertising is not eligible as work made for hire, as it does not fall under any of the nine eligible categories defined under U.S. Copyright Law. Additional information on work made for hire can be found in Chapter 11, Legal Rights & Issues.

11. Customary and usual out-of-pocket expenses such as props, costumes, model fees, travel costs, production costs, shipping, picture reference, and consultation time are billed to the client separately. An expense estimate is usually included in the original written agreement or as an amendment to the agreement.

All prices for freelance illustration in this book are based on surveys of artists in the United States. See related material in other sections of this book, especially in Chapter 1, Essential Business Practices, and Chapter 12, Standard Contracts & Business Tools.

Advertising Illustration

Illustrators are hired to provide visuals for products or services for specific advertising needs. The illustrator's first contact in this market is usually an art buyer, who solicits and receives portfolios and often, especially in the larger agencies, remains the primary conduit for the flow of work. For creative guidance, however, illustrators usually work with art directors, account executives, copywriters, and heads of the agency's creative group. The terms and fees for art are normally negotiated with the agency's art buyer or art director by the illustrator or the artist's representative. (For a description of these roles, see Chapter 2, Professional Relationships.)

Traditionally, premium prices for illustration have been paid in the advertising field, where the highest degree of professionalism and performance is expected from artists working within unusually strict time demands. Illustrators must meet their deadlines or risk damaging their reputation or that of their rep. It is important that illustrators communicate with the agency if the deadline is too short. Agencies are very team based and communicate well. The illustrator becomes part of the advertising team while on the project.

However, illustrators report that advertising seems especially affected during slow economic periods, with budgets tightening and fees decreasing. Generally, advertising illustration prices are negotiated strictly on a use basis, with extra pay added for the sale of residual or all rights, complexity of style, or extra-tight deadlines. Most magazines have set prices in their budgets, with children's magazines paying at the low end and business magazines somewhat higher.

Advertisements are usually thought of in terms of the number of times they run. Therefore, sale of usage rights may refer to limited or unlimited use in a specific media and geographic area within a specified time period; for example, they may be "limited to one to five insertions in consumer magazines in the United States for one year." The media, distribution area, and time period for which advertising rights are sold should be clearly defined and the price agreed upon before the project starts.

Agencies expect illustrators to work in a specific style represented in their portfolios and to follow a sketch supplied by the agency and approved by the client. Changes and last-minute alterations are common, since many advertisements are created by committee and illustrators may need to please several people of varying opinions. Many illustrators set fees that include a finite number and type of alterations, such as "one reasonable revision." Additional changes, especially significant ones, necessitate additional charges, and artists tend to be flexible, giving valued and responsible clients some leeway.

Some illustrators have learned to anticipate several different uses. For example, art commissioned for a magazine ad may end up having corresponding billboard and web uses. They prepare the art layered and ready for unanticipated usage requests. Clients appreciate the illustrator's forethought.

Specific Trade Practices

In addition to the general trade practices listed in the beginning of this chapter, the following trade practices for advertising illustration have been used traditionally and thus are accepted as standard:

1. Illustrators working in advertising normally sell rights to one to five insertions of their artwork, within a given medium and a given market, for one year from date of first use, unless otherwise stated.
2. Reuse fees: from 100 to 150% of the fee that would have been charged had the illustration been commissioned for the new use.
3. Charge for rush work: an additional 15 to 100%, depending on how tight the rushed deadline is.

See Figure 7–1 for Comparative Fees for Advertising and Collateral Illustration.

Preproduction Illustration

Artists who specialize in preproduction art service the advertising, television, and motion picture industries and usually are called upon to produce high-caliber professional work within extremely tight deadlines that necessitate both freelancers and full-time staff to frequently work weekends. It is a discipline with a lot of work-life balance disruption.

Types

Although some artists specialize, nearly all are engaged in three areas of preproduction art: comps (common abbreviation for "comprehensives"), storyboards, and animatics.

7–1 Comparative Fees for Advertising & Collateral Illustration

The fees in this chart do not reflect any specific trade practices and do not constitute specific prices for particular jobs. The buyer and seller are free to negotiate, with each artist independently deciding how to price the work, after taking all factors into account. Reading the more detailed information, Pricing Your Services, provided in Chapter 1, will help in pricing projects for your specific situation.

Hourly Rates

Advertising	$30–150
Exhibits/Displays	$20–105
(trade shows & retail displays)	

Per-Illustration Fees

Complex	$375–12,000
Simple	$150–3,000

Additional Fees

EXTRA ROUND OF REVISIONS	100–150%
(Not covered in original agreement; % of original fee)	

USAGE (% of original project fee)	
Reuse in original market	100–150%
Unlimited use, print only	100–200%
(no geographic or time limits)	
Unlimited use in all media for one year	125–200%
Total copyright transfer	100–300%
Sale of original art	110–200%

CANCELLATION & REJECTION	
(% of original project fee)	
Prior to completion of sketches	25–50%
After completion of sketches	45–75%
After completion of finished art	50–100%

Illustrators who charge by the hour bill for the number of hours worked up to the date of cancellation or rejection, plus any expenses incurred.

RUSH FEES (% added onto normal fee)	
24-hour turnaround	20–100%
48-hour turnaround	15–100%
Holidays & weekends	20–100%

The above rates and fees were compiled from the results of a national survey of graphic artists conducted by the Graphic Artists Guild in 2020. Responses were based on rates charged in 2018 and 2019.

COMPS

A *comp* is a mock-up of a proposed advertisement and other printed promotional material, usually consisting of a "visual" (a rendering of the illustration or photo to be used in the finished piece), headlines, and body text. The comp shows the relative size and position of images and text A preproduction illustrator creates the visual and the ad agency does the headlines, copy, and logos.

STORYBOARDS

A storyboard is a visual presentation of a proposed television commercial, program, or feature film, using sequential frames. Most storyboards are created digitally, using a graphic pad/device, such as a Wacom Cintiq, Cintiq Companion, or Wacom Mobile Studio Pro. Many artists use Adobe Photoshop to draw their boards. Some use Sketchbook Pro, which is the industry standard, especially for animation productions.

Storyboard frames vary by screen ratio, for example, frames for HDTV boards are 16:9, while frames for widescreen movies are 2.35:1. Board formats also vary by frames per page and orientation. Live-action boards are usually stacked three frames high on a portrait page. Animation boards are three frames arranged horizontally on a landscape page. Some agencies prefer six frames per page, but television series and films never do. Artists are usually asked to provide files of individual storyboard panels on delivery as well as pages or PDF files of the complete project.

In advertising, storyboards are generally used within an agency to present the concept of the proposed commercial to the client. An important component of preproduction artwork in advertising is the "key" frame, a large single frame used with other frames to establish the overall mood or to portray the highlight or key moment of the commercial. The key frame must be given extra attention—and compensation—since it carries most of the narrative burden.

For feature films or television, especially those that are animated, storyboard renderings are used by producers to envision creative concepts and to evaluate a concept's visual qualities and continuity. Used most often as a reference to an accompanying script, the storyboards and text are videotaped as an *animatic* a critical element in determining a property's value as entertainment and as a visual production (see below). Storyboards are the visual blueprint producers rely upon to budget and help avoid cost overruns. Most animated TV show production is now paperless, and all art is drawn on digital interactive tablets, which makes editing and correcting easier. (More specific information about animation can be found in Chapter 9.)

Storyboards for motion picture and television features are generally black-and-white and emphasize camera angles and moves. Because a larger number of frames are generally produced for feature-length storyboards, the rendering style that is the most in demand is quick, clean, and realistic. Artists who create storyboards for motion picture and television features must work more closely with other members of the creative team than is customary in advertising preproduction. And artists often scout locations or work on location.

ANIMATICS

An *animatic* is a limited-animation video using camera movements, a select number of drawings, some animation, and a soundtrack. Video storyboards use only storyboard art (no moving parts), and movement is achieved with simple camera moves. Most animated projects, TV shows, and movies create animatics of the entire production. They are played in production meetings to help the crew see the director's vision.

Animatics are also used in TV commercial production. A director might use an animatic to perfect the shots or to get approval from the client, as it is easier to understand the action in an animatic than by looking at printed boards.

Artists must know in advance whether film or video will be used, since each has its own special requirements. A good grasp of current TV commercial, film, and music-video styles is crucial to success in this field. Most art is now created digitally. Some older artists still work in pencil and ink and scan their work digitally.

Fees & Pricing Factors

Usually, preproduction artists charge fees based on their time or they charge a bulk fee. For high-end color animatics, the fee might depend upon factors such as the number of subjects in a given frame, type of background required, and the tightness of the deadline. In pricing high-end animatics, one background illustration and one to one-and-a-half cut-out figures comprise one frame. Two figures and their moving parts can constitute one frame when backgrounds are used for several scenes.

Artist fees for television or feature-film storyboards have traditionally been based on the value of the production—its budget and its intended distribution. Fees for high-budget productions generally are higher than fees for low-budget productions. Fees for this discipline are seldom based on complexity as deadlines are so tight, there is little time to do more detailed work. Even on the biggest movies, storyboards are barely more than thumbnail drawings.

Some agencies, production companies, producers, and individuals may request that artists sign nondisclosure or noncompete agreements to protect trade secrets and creative properties for specified periods. These conditions may restrict an artist's opportunities for future work; this is a factor that should be seriously considered when negotiating fees. Some agencies also request that artists work in-house, and this should be taken into account when establishing a fee.

Hourly rates are rarely used, but they may be appropriate for consultation time if the artist participates in the design of the scene or sequences.

In some cases, a per-diem rate is paid when the artist works on-site for extended periods. Be aware that requiring an illustrator to work on site may open an artist to reclassification as an employee rather than as an independent contractor; that may put the client and the artist at risk, depending on how the client treats the artist. If an artist does not work for other clients, on-site work may also endanger an artist's home office deduction. (See the Employment Issues section in Chapter 3, Professional Issues.)

A growing trend in large city markets is for advertising agencies to have exclusive contracts with artist's representatives and preproduction art studios in exchange for lower fees but more-or-less steady work. Artists who are not represented by a designated studio cannot work with a particular ad agency, regardless of past affiliations with art directors. Exclusive ad agency/studio contracts therefore force artists to work with a particular representative, thereby forfeiting a percentage of their income and jeopardizing the artist's status as an independent contractor. The consequent reduction in competition among studios and artists raises concerns about restraint-of-trade issues.

Another factor affecting ad agency practices is cost consultants. Many ad agency clients retain the services

7–2 Comparative Fees for Preproduction Illustration

The fees in this chart do not reflect any specific trade practices and do not constitute specific prices for particular jobs. The buyer and seller are free to negotiate, with each artist independently deciding how to price the work, after taking all factors into account. Reading the more detailed information, Pricing Your Services, provided in Chapter 1, will help in pricing projects for your specific situation.

Per Diem Rates
$125–900

Rush Fees (% added onto normal fee)

24-hour turnaround	35–100%
48-hour turnaround	25–75%
Holidays/Weekends	50–100%

Rush Fees are dependent on industry. They apply mostly to advertising. Not applicable to film and television.

The above rates and fees were compiled from the results of a national survey of graphic artists conducted by the Graphic Artists Guild in 2020. Responses were based on rates charged in 2018 and 2019.

of consultants who control agency expenditures and seek to define suppliers' fees. Artist suppliers are rarely able to negotiate directly with these cost consultants but must work through the agencies. This situation makes it important for artists to marshal a firm negotiating stance with agencies in order to maintain industry standards.

If a project is for a Hollywood studio, an artist is required to join the union in order to work. Therefore, artists need to subtract union dues when figuring the actual total compensation for a job.

Specific Trade Practices

In addition to the general trade practices listed in the beginning of this chapter, the following trade practices for preproduction illustration have been used traditionally and thus are accepted as standard:

1. Return of original artwork to the artist is not automatic unless otherwise negotiated. Artists who work for a Hollywood studio may have to sign over all rights to art, since the property belongs to the studio.

2. Preproduction artists usually grant all rights for preproduction work. Since this work is very product-specific (campaigns are often confidential, and the media used—for example, markers—are impermanent), frames are almost never reusable. Higher fees for this work have compensated for the loss of rights, though many art directors will return artwork for an artist's self-promotional use.

3. Rush fees are specific to the type of project. Usually they are only charged for commercial work. They are not charged in TV and film work. When time is an issue, instead of a rush fee, an illustrator may negotiate the level of finished work, suggesting black and white rather than color, pencil rather than ink, or less detail. The reality is that no matter how much financial compensation is offered, there is only so much volume and so much "finished" work an illustrator can do under a tight deadline.

See Figure 7–2 for Comparative Fees for Preproduction Illustration.

Corporate, Organizational, & Institutional Illustration

An illustrator creating corporate or institutional illustrations works with graphic designers, art directors, or in-house personnel such as writers, advertising/marketing managers, or communication directors to create visuals for annual reports, in-house publications, and other material targeted to internal or non-advertising outside specific audiences. The assignment is made by the public relations department of the corporation or an outside agency or design firm, and the illustrator is often called upon to determine the concept and design of the art. Particularly in annual reports, illustrations are "think pieces" that contribute substantially to enhancing the corporation or institution's public image.

Illustrators who do corporate work report that more and more emphasis is being directed to Web-only projects, such as PDF "booklets" and PDF "brochures," that function much like print pieces but are strictly digital. Some companies have replaced their printed annual reports with online versions. Since these digital pieces are not add-ons to a print project, pricing should be at least equal to print for these jobs. If clients resist paying print prices and want to pay less, it can be argued that there is no difference on the illustration side as to how this work is completed—the process is the same. Furthermore, the Web has more distribution potential than print, and in many cases, these online PDFs are available for download and can be printed an unlimited amount of times by any-one who has access—potentially globally.

Clients include Fortune 500 companies, smaller companies, and public relations firms, as well as educational institutions, government agencies, and not-for-profit groups and associations. An organization with a "not-for-profit" designation does not operate at a deficit; some, in fact, such as AARP, with approximately 38 million members, have enormous resources. Other examples of not-for-profits include trade associations and business leagues, hospitals and health-service organizations, professional membership societies, trade unions, philanthropies, museums and other arts groups, and charitable and educational organizations. Whether a client is for-profit or not-for-profit, pricing varies according to its size, resources, and profitability.

Annual Reports

An annual report—the yearly fiscal report by a corporation to its stockholders and the financial community—is an important means for a company to promote itself. Designers of annual reports often seek thoughtful, provocative illustrations to offset the written and financial material while projecting the company's public image powerfully and effectively.

Illustration fees are usually based on the corporation's size and the nature of the annual report and are usually negotiated on a one-time-use basis only. When dealing with large assignments in this area, artists should be prepared to set a fee for selling original art, since annual report clients frequently make such requests.

In-House Newsletters

Corporate in-house newsletters are distributed at no charge to company employees, retirees, and supporters. Traditionally printed, newsletters today may be print, a downloadable PDF, or both. Illustrators may be hired to illustrate a feature article or story, if not handled by an agency using royalty-free material. Usually the work involves spot illustration which is charged as a flat fee.

Corporate Magazines

Corporate magazines, including university and prep school alumni publications, are distributed to alumni, shareholders, policy-makers, industry members, customers, and students at no charge. They may be available as a printed publication, an online downloadable PDF, or in both formats.

Corporate magazine illustration pays similar to edi-torial magazine prices (see Figure 7–7). Fees include one-time rights. Corporate magazines also buy more stock illustration than mainstream editorial magazines.

Corporate Calendars

Illustration prices for company calendars can vary greatly and usually depend upon the size of the company, the complexity of the subject, and the intended use. Calendars designed for internal use only generally pay less than calendars distributed to consumers for promotion or sale.

Corporate Portraits

Corporations and organizations will reach out to illustrators to do portraits, since traditional portrait painters are frequently outside the price range of many corporate buyers. Portraits are commissioned for a variety of reasons: to honor retiring leaders, commemorate anniversaries within organizations, or to honor historically important people posthumously. They are also commissioned for places of honor within company spaces, to honor philanthropy, for commemorative collateral publication and web promotion, and for company literature of the traditional nature. Another market for these assignments is state legislatures, which commission a lot of portraiture of long-term legislators. These portraits are usually larger in size and have decent budgets.

PRICING

Generally, portrait assignments start with a commission for display usage first, and then any other uses descend from that. Size is a consideration in pricing. If the portrait will be hanging in a large public place, it needs to be at least 20 x 24 inches, plus matting and framing, to create presence on the wall. Because the client will be buying the original artwork, pricing is determined by the artist's requirements for selling originals, as well as size, since it affects time spent and materials. Therefore, a client would expect to pay more for larger works.

Pricing for smaller works that include sale of original art to client start at about $2,000. Commissions for larger works can easily jump up to the $8,000–10,000 range and above for sizes over 30 inches for any one dimension. Larger sizes usually involve traditional oil or acrylic painting on canvas.

If the portrait were only going to be used in reproduction usage and not for display, the illustrator would need to price the piece like any other illustration assignment.

7–3 Comparative Fees for Corporate, Organizational, & Institutional Illustration

The fees in this chart do not reflect any specific trade practices and do not constitute specific prices for particular jobs. The buyer and seller are free to negotiate, with each artist independently deciding how to price the work, after taking all factors into account. Reading the more detailed information, Pricing Your Services, provided in Chapter 1, will help in pricing projects for your specific situation.

Hourly Rates

Publications	$60–150
(annual reports, in-house newsletters, business>consumer magazines)	
Special event invitations	$40–150
Native digital illustrations	$40–120+

Per-Illustration Fees

Corporate Logo

Major Corporation	$1,000–8,000
Minor Corporation	$300–4,000
Very Small Business	$200–3,000
(e.g., law firms, wineries, "mom & pop" retail, etc.)	

Special Event Invitation

Complex	$150–1,500
Simple	$75–500

Additional Fees (% of original fee)

EXTRA ROUND OF REVISIONS	110–130%
(Not covered in original agreement)	

USAGE

Reuse in original market	125–150%
Unlimited use, print only	100–150%
(no geographic or time limits)	
Unlimited use in all media for one year	150–200%
Total copyright transfer	100–300%
Sale of original art	100–200%

CANCELLATION & REJECTION

Prior to completion of sketches	25–50%
After completion of sketches	50–75%
After completion of finished art	80–100%

Illustrators who charge by the hour bill for the number of hours worked up to the date of cancellation or rejection, plus any expenses incurred.

RUSH FEES (% added onto normal fee)

24-hour turnaround	20–100%
48-hour turnaround	20–50%
Holidays & weekends	20–100%

The above rates and fees were compiled from the results of a national survey of graphic artists conducted by the Graphic Artists Guild in 2020. Responses were based on rates charged in 2018 and 2019.

USAGE

Illustrators retain copyright in portraiture work, even if the original art is sold. Any additional usage beyond display, as well as the terms of usage, needs to be stipulated in the agreement in detail, so the illustrator is pricing the job accurately. Portrait illustrators should always be able to use or re-market non-conflicting usage of the piece outside of a certain timeframe (e.g., one to two years after the assignment is finished). In terms of fair use, they should be able to use the piece for personal promotion immediately after the job is completed.

Non-Advertising Website Illustration

Corporate illustration work for non-advertising purposes on a website includes presenting information that is pri-

marily aimed to educate the consumer and promote the company's products, services, and reputation. This type of illustration pays similar to or slightly lower than online editorial magazines.

Graphic Recording & Facilitation

An illustration specialty that has gained popularity in the past decade is *graphic recording*, also referred to as *visual note taking* or *scribing*. Graphic recording involves translating verbal ideas into visual maps during events. Graphic recorders are hired by corporations and organizations to draw live during meetings, focus groups, speaking events, workshops, and conferences to create a visual capture of what speakers discuss or present during the event. They need to work quickly, using both imagery and words, to capture the essence of what is being said.

Graphic recorders can work either at in-person or virtual events. When working with live audiences, they generally use a very large drawing surface, markers, and pastels. They may start with a blank canvas or with a customized template designed to support and guide the conversation in a particular direction, which is determined by working with the client ahead of time. The finished piece might be one continuous drawing or several panels. Graphic recorders can also work digitally on a tablet, with their drawing projected in real time on a digital projector screen or patched into high-definition monitors.

Artists also may be hired to do digital-virtual graphic recording for situations in which the client cannot get their team or audience together in one physical location or for reasons of social distancing as in the COVID-19 pandemic. Digital-virtual recording works well for video meetings, classes, webinars, and international conferences.

In both situations, audiences see the drawing unfold live while the event happens. This entertaining aspect supports greater participant engagement and focus. The visuals help participants better understand complex content and see "the big picture." Digital-virtual recording supports content-sharing among teams or participants both during and after the event.

Similar to graphic recording is *Graphic Facilitation.* While the graphic recorder is a silent observer—listening, synthesizing, and summarizing information visually, the graphic facilitator is both leading the discussion and drawing. The facilitator's role includes planning the agenda and guiding the group through the meeting. Due to the added responsibility of leading the meeting, the facilitator's imagery will be less embellished than that of the graphic recorder.

CUSTOMARY PRACTICES

As part of their graphic recording services, illustrators also take digital photos of the finished posters, clean them up digitally if needed, and provide the client with the files. These digital copies of the illustrations are very useful to the client. The files can be sent to event attendees as a follow-up for future review or they can be posted on social media. Clients can have smaller versions of the event poster printed on collateral, such as notebooks and calendar covers, or they can have it printed as large-scale signage.

Graphic recorders may be asked by corporate or government clients to sign nondisclosure agreements, due to the confidential nature of the information being presented.

Illustrators should make sure they have a written, signed agreement or contract with the client, in advance of the event. The exact dates of the event and the services being provided should be outlined with their corresponding fees, as well as extra expenses such as travel. Any equipment or physical space the illustrator will need during the event should also be specified; illustrators report that clients do not necessarily think of these things.

The illustrator should also include a booking policy and a cancellation policy and any related charges. A specific cancellation policy can help protect both the illustrator and the client in the case of unforeseen circumstances, such as illness, bad weather, natural disasters, and travel delays. Veterans in the industry also prepare as much as possible for unforeseen problems, for example, scheduling the travel day prior to the day of the event in case of delayed or cancelled flights and having a substitute graphic recorder available in case of illness.

PRICING

Due to the time needed to set up and tear down materials and equipment, most graphic recorders charge a day rate for their services. The day rate includes pre-event coordination with the client, a specified number of hours of sketching, and post-meeting digital photographing of the finished illustration(s), photo retouching, and delivery of the digital files. Some illustrators include materials in their day rate; others charge extra for materials. Some charge a deposit, up to 50% of the cost, for booking the event, but they may also offer a discount for clients who book several months in advance. Travel expenses are not included in the day rate.

Some graphic recorders also offer a flat or package rate for the entire job, which is more inclusive than the day rate. It can include domestic airline fees, meals, and ground transportation, as well as a specific number of hours of drawing per day.

Rush fees may be charged for bookings with a week or less notice. Overtime may be charged for drawing that goes beyond the artist's normal work hours.

Specific Trade Practices

In addition to the general trade practices listed in the beginning of this chapter, the following trade practices have been used traditionally in much of Corporate, Organizational, and Institutional Illustration, and thus are accepted as standard (Customary Practices for Graphic Recording & Facilitation, can be found in a previous section):

1. Artists working in these fields normally sell only first reproduction rights unless otherwise stated.
2. Reuse fee: from 125 to 150% of the fee that would have been charged had the illustration been commissioned for the new use.
3. Charge for rush work: an additional 20 to 100%.

See Figure 7–3 for Corporate, Organizational, & Institutional Fees.

Book Illustration

The publishing business has undergone tremendous growth and change in the last 20 years. Most well-known publishing houses have been acquired by multinational conglomerates here and abroad, and many smaller houses have been either eliminated or incorporated as imprints. Worldwide paper prices continue to increase the pressure on publishers' bottom lines. The sale of books online first surpassed the sale of books in brick-and-mortar stores back in 2013, and today, the e-retailer Amazon dominates both online print and e-book sales. All these factors have contributed to the demise of independent bookstores.

Book Jackets & Covers

Book jacket and cover illustration or design is the second most important ingredient in the promotion and sale of a book, superseded only by the fame and success of the author. Pricing illustration in the book publishing market is complex, so all the factors involved need serious attention. Romance, science fiction, and other genre paperback covers can command higher fees than some hardcover jackets, especially when the projected audience is very large. Artists who design and illustrate jackets may approach their work differently from other graphic artists. (Also see the Book Jacket Design section in Chapter 5, Graphic Design.)

Factors that prompt additional fees and that are negotiated before the assignment is confirmed include changes in approach and direction after sketches are completed, requiring new sketches; additional promotional uses above and beyond what is common trade practice (using the art separately from the cover without the title or author's name); and extremely tight color comps done for sales meetings and catalogs.

MASS MARKET & TRADE BOOKS

Mass-market books have large print runs and appeal to a wide audience. They include best sellers, mysteries, thrillers, gothic novels, fantasy, science fiction, historical novels, and modern romance novels. Trade books include poetry, serious fiction, biography, how-to books, and more scholarly works that appeal to a special audience. When pricing work in these areas, the size of the print run is traditionally taken into account.

Because of their larger print runs and higher gross sales, mass-market books very often generate higher fees for illustrators. A hardcover assignment might also include paperback rights, for which an additional 50% of the original fee is customarily charged. Occasionally, the fee for a book with a very large paperback print run may amount to an additional 75% of the original fee, or possibly more.

Currently, publishers like Knopf Doubleday/Random House rarely do wraparound covers. The backs are usually reserved for quotes from book reviews. Advertising rights for the book are included with no extra payment, as long as the image is used in context of the book. Otherwise, an extra payment can be negotiated with credit given to the illustrator. See Figure 7–4 for Comparative Fees for Book Jacket/Cover Illustration .

SECONDARY RIGHTS USE

Another way illustrators earn additional fees is to license a cover illustration for use on foreign editions of a book. This type of secondary (or subsidiary) rights usage is growing; however, fees vary widely from country to country and use to use, with few standards. Most artists or their representatives usually negotiate fees for such rights and do not simply accept what is offered. Breaking down the fee for each use (both hardback and paperback, for example) and stipulating a particular length of time for the sale, with an option to renew, are ways to boost and maximize fees. By also specifying "up to x number of copies" in their contracts, illustrators can bill extra if the book becomes a much bigger seller than originally anticipated.

Domestic book club rights are usually included in the original hardcover fee; however, in some instances a book club edition might be huge and make the book into a bestseller—for example, books chosen for Oprah's Book Club. Audio book covers are negotiated as separate subsidiary rights. All other residual rights, especially movie and television rights, are reserved by the artist and transfer of those and all other rights is negotiated by the artist and the client. By reserving non-book and merchandise rights for themselves, illustrators can generate additional income from the illustration by selling prints, calendars, mugs, etc.

To ensure that illustrators are compensated for any

7–4 Comparative Fees for Book Jacket/Cover Illustration

The fees in this chart do not reflect any specific trade practices and do not constitute specific prices for particular jobs. The buyer and seller are free to negotiate, with each artist independently deciding how to price the work, after taking all factors into account. Reading the more detailed information, Pricing Your Services, provided in Chapter 1, will help in pricing projects for your specific situation.

Hourly Rates

$50–150

Flat Fees

	FRONT COVER	WRAPAROUND JACKET
HARD COVER		
Major Trade	$1,000–3,000	$1,500–4,500
Small Print Run	$500–1,500	$800–2,000
Small Press	$500–1,000	——
Young Adult/Chapter	$1,000–2,000	$1,500–2,500
Textbook	$1,200–2,000 -	——
PAPERBACK		
Mass Market (major distribution, 4 x 7")	$400–2,000	$800–4,500
Major Trade (5.5 x 8.5")	$1,000–3,500	$1,000–5,000
Average Trade	$350–2,000	$800–2,500
Self-Published POD	$250–1,500	$500–2,000
Young Adult/Chapter	$350–1,500	$600–2,500
Comic Book (major publisher)	$750–3,500	$800–5,000
Textbook	$650–3,500	——

Additional Fees (% of original fee)

EXTRA ROUND OF REVISIONS	105–150%
(Not covered in original agreement)	

USAGE	
Reuse in original market	120–175%
Unlimited use in all media for one year	100–200%
Total copyright transfer	100–250%
Sale of original art	100–200%

RUSH FEES (% added onto normal fee)	
24-hour turnaround	50–100%
48-hour turnaround	20–100%
Holidays & weekends	25–200%

The above rates and fees were compiled from the results of a national survey of graphic artists conducted by the Graphic Artists Guild in 2020. Responses were based on rates charged in 2018 and 2019.

additional editions and secondary rights beyond those included in the original fee, it is advisable to specify the International Standard Book Number (ISBN) in the terms of the contract. Since each edition has a different ISBN, the publisher cannot assume additional usage of artwork in subsequent editions if the contract is clearly limited to a specific edition.

Illustrators should be wary of contracts that use the term "work for hire." If you agree to work for hire, the client will own all rights to reuse your work without additional compensation. If these terms are not agreeable to you, renegotiate the contract or do not accept the job. In general, work-for-hire terms apply to work done by staff employees of a company. For very specific and limited situations in which work for hire applies to independent contractors, refer to the section, Work-Made-for-Hire Criteria, in Chapter 11, Legal Rights & Issues.

Book Interiors

Illustrations have long been recognized as an important ingredient in the editorial and marketing value of a book. Book illustrators work with editors, art directors, book designers, or book packagers to create anything from simple instructional line drawings to full-color-spread illustrations for textbooks, picture books, children's and young adult books, novelty books, and special reprints of classics, among other trade genres. The importance of illustration to a specific book may be significant or limited, depending on needs determined by the publisher.

PRICING

Pricing for book illustration is figured as either a flat fee, a per-page rate, a per-illustration rate, or as a royalty arrangement. Outside of children's books, it is rare for royalties to be paid for book illustration. If such an opportunity arises, check Figure 7–6, Comparative Fees for Children's Picture Book Illustration, for details on an appropriate royalty. (See Figure 7–5 for other pricing options for interior illustration.)

PACKAGERS VS. PUBLISHERS

Book packagers are independent suppliers that take over for publishers some or all of the functions of preparing a book. Often, they initiate a project, find writers and illustrators, arrange for whatever extras may be involved, and strike a deal with a publisher, usually supplying a set number of bound books at a set price. When a book is conceived by the packager rather than the publisher, the artist will be asked to sign a contract with the packager rather than the publisher, even before the packager has contracted for the project with a publisher. (Additional information about packagers can be found in the Book Packaging & Consulting section in Chapter 5, Graphic Design.)

Book packagers often offer illustrators either a flat fee or a 10% royalty. This royalty is not figured on the book's list price, as with some publishers' contracts, but on what the packager will receive from the publisher for the finished books ("base selling price"). Since publishers generally set a book's retail price at four to five times the cost of its production, illustrators should be aware that 10% of the base selling price amounts to a 2 to 2.5% royalty of the list price.

Publishers generally allot 10% (or 5%, in the case of mass-market material) of list price for the author's and illustrator's royalties. When a publisher uses a packager to produce a book, that 10% may be absorbed by the publisher or may be paid to the packager in addition to the base selling price. Sometimes that share is paid to a licenser in exchange for the right to publish a book about a popular property (cartoon characters, for instance), and a packager is hired to create the book. In some cases, particularly where the project originates with the author-artist, all or some of those list-price royalties may be paid to the artist. It is the publisher's choice to do so; the packager is not likely to promise an artist any of the publisher's royalties.

Thus, the compensation offered to artists who work through packagers is generally at a lower rate than work that comes directly from publishers, although two factors may somewhat mitigate this difference. Because a packager's contract with a publisher is indexed to the sale of a predetermined number of books, paid up-front, the packager will pay the artist's royalty on the full print run before publication. If a second printing is ordered, royalties on that print run will again be paid in full, rather than if and when the books are sold. This arrangement brings payment to the artist somewhat sooner than the standard publisher's contract. Rights to reuse the artwork (in other editions or promotions, for example) are often considered when negotiating the advance or the fee.

OTHER FACTORS AFFECTING PRICING

Other factors affecting advances and fees in this complex area include the type of book and the importance of the author, the artist's reputation and record of commercial success, the size of the print order, and the length of time estimated for the total project.

PAYMENT TERMS

Traditionally, illustrators receive partial payment for long projects: by quarters, thirds, or halves. There are several variations of each of these arrangements. An

7–5 Comparative Fees for Book Interior Illustration

The fees in this chart do not reflect any specific trade practices and do not constitute specific prices for particular jobs. The buyer and seller are free to negotiate, with each artist independently deciding how to price the work, after taking all factors into account. Reading the more detailed information, Pricing Your Services, provided in Chapter 1, will help in pricing projects for your specific situation.

Per-Page Rate
$110–400

Flat Fees

	SPREAD	FULL-PAGE	½-PAGE	¼-PAGE/SPOT
HARD COVER				
Adult & Young Adult	$300–2,500	$300–1,500	$300–800	$100–400
Textbook	$500–1,500	$350–2,000	$250–1,000	$100–500
Self-published POD	$400–1,000	$200–800	$350–500	$75–350
SOFTCOVER				
Juvenile workbook	$500–1,500	$400–1,000	$200–500	$75–300

Additional Fees (% of original fee)

EXTRA ROUND OF REVISIONS (Not covered in original agreement)	100–185%
USAGE	
Reuse in original market	125–175%
Unlimited use in any media for 1 year	100–200%
Domestic reprint, paperback, book club, digest, anthology, or serial	100–175%
Total copyright transfer	100–300%
Sale of original art	100–200%
RUSH FEES (% added onto normal fee)	
24-hour turnaround	50–100%
48-hour turnaround	20–100%
Holidays & weekends	20–50%

The above rates and fees were compiled from the results of a national survey of graphic artists conducted by the Graphic Artists Guild in 2020. Responses were based on rates charged in 2018 and 2019.

---

example of an arrangement paid in halves might be half upon signing, and half within 30 days of delivery of finished art. An example of a contract paid in thirds might be a third of the total fee paid upon approval of sketches, a third upon delivery of half of the finished art, and the remainder within 30 days of delivery of the finished art. Another type of arrangement for long projects is to be paid on a monthly retainer. The illustrator's fee for the total project is divided by the number of months in the project to arrive at a monthly payment.

Regardless of the partial payment arrangement, the deposit should be worded in the contract to constitute the kill fee. That way, if the client kills the project, the illustrator does not have to return the deposit.

For more details about payment structures, see the Payment Terms section under Children's Books.

7–6 Comparative Fees for Children's Picture Book Illustration

The fees in this chart do not reflect any specific trade practices and do not constitute specific prices for particular jobs. The buyer and seller are free to negotiate, with each artist independently deciding how to price the work, after taking all factors into account. Reading the more detailed information, Pricing Your Services, provided in Chapter 1, will help in pricing projects for your specific situation.

Page Rates
$60–200

Flat Fees
Hardcover

(cover plus 30-48 interior pages)	$3,500–25,000

Board Book

(cover plus 32 pages or less)	$1,500–15,000

(Most board books have an average of 16-24 pages.)

Royalty Rates*
Author & Illustrator

Children's Picture Book	7–12%

Illustrator only

Children's Picture Book	3.5–6%
Board Book	2.5%

*Royalty rates are from industry sources. Advances vary widely, depending on the publisher and the reputation/experience of the author and/or illustrator. First-time book authors and illustrators can expect to receive smaller advances. If an advance is given, the amount of the advance must be earned back from the sale of books before royalties will be paid.

Additional Compensation

Number of free copies to illustrator	10–19
Illustrator's discount off list price	20–50%

The above rates and fees (unless otherwise noted) were compiled from the results of a national survey of graphic artists conducted by the Graphic Artists Guild in 2020. Responses were based on rates charged in 2018 and 2019.

Children's Books

The illustrator's contribution to a children's book can range widely, from the entire contents of a wordless picture book to a jacket illustration for a young adult novel. Another market in children's books for illustrators who can work with style guides is illustrating licensed-property picture books, such as Star Wars, Marvel, or Mickey Mouse.

Pricing usually falls into two categories: a flat fee, for books in which the illustrator's contribution is usually substantially less than the author's, or a royalty contract, in which the contributions of author and illustrator are comparable or in which the illustrator is also the author. Publishers will pay more plus royalties to successful writer/illustrator teams.

Packagers often pay a flat fee, but most publishers will negotiate a royalty reflecting the percentage of art versus text. The artist's share can range from 3.5 to 6%, depending upon the reputation of the artist versus the author.

FLAT-FEE CONTRACTS

Publishers' flat-fee contracts tend to stipulate all possible rights to the art in return for a one-time fee. Illustrators should negotiate to retain rights not needed by the client or negotiate additional payment for additional uses, such as the sale of paperback rights. Holding non-book or merchandising rights is particularly vital; otherwise, illustrators lose the opportunity for additional income and will not be able to retain the rights to a copyrighted character.

CHAPTER & YOUNG ADULT BOOKS

Chapter books for ages 8 to 12 and young adult books for children over 12 may be illustrated for a flat fee. A typical flat-fee book contract commissions a full-color wraparound jacket. From 1 to 14 black-and-white interior illustrations of various sizes may be included in a chapter book. Interior illustrations for young adult books are also paid per illustration or per page. (See Figures 7–5 and 7–6 for flat fees paid for children's book illustration.)

JUVENILE WORKBOOKS

One category of children's books—the juvenile workbook—is handled quite differently from others. Workbooks are assigned through brokers or publishers' agents, representing many illustrators working in varied styles, who have traditionally established pricing for each book with the publisher. Budgets for workbooks vary considerably, depending on the size of the publisher, the location, publication schedules, and the artist's experience. Illustrator fees for these projects may also vary considerably, and it is always preferable to work directly with the publisher.

Workbooks are usually priced per page, per half page, or per spot. Although fees are traditionally quite low, an entire workbook can add up to a considerable amount of work. Artists who are able to produce this kind of artwork quickly may find this field quite lucrative and feel secure knowing that months of work lie ahead. Artists should note that in order to meet increasingly rushed publishing deadlines, a book with a considerable amount of illustration may be divided among several illustrators.

ROYALTY CONTRACTS

An *advance against royalties* is paid for most children's picture books, storybooks, and middle-grade readers. However, overseas publishers tend to pay a flat rate, usually in three installments.

The *advance* is an amount of money the publisher pays the illustrator prior to publication. The *royalty* is the percentage of the list price that the illustrator will receive for each book sold, but the payment of royalties does not start until the royalties earned exceed the amount of the advance. If the author and the artist are separate individuals, a full royalty on the book's list price is commonly split 50–50 between the two creators. The royalty and the size of the advance are based on the illustrator's reputation, experience, and the publisher's budget.

To have a better understanding of royalty contracts, book illustrators should familiarize themselves with the terminology they may find in a publisher's royalty contract. To protect themselves and the use of their work, they may want to make sure that many of these terms are included in the contracts they sign.

ROYALTY CONTRACT TERMS

Grant of rights: The illustrator grants to the publisher the right to use the art as specified within the contract.

Alterations: The art cannot be altered in any way by the publisher, except as part of the normal printing process, without the written consent of the artist. (It is all too easy to alter art electronically, but this should not be allowed.)

Delivery: Sets deadlines for finished art and sometimes for rough sketches. Often this clause has also specified what payments are due the artist if the project is canceled or rejected (see the Cancellation & Rejection Fees section in Chapter 3, Professional Issues).

Warranty: This states that the illustrator has not infringed the copyrights of others or broken any other laws in granting rights to the publisher.

Indemnity: The illustrator shares the cost of defending any lawsuit brought over the art. An artist who is found to have broken the terms of the warranty bears the entire cost of the lawsuit and any damages that may result. The indemnity provision might present more risk than the illustrator is willing to accept. Without an attorney, it may be difficult to counter this provision effectively, but it is possible. An illustrator should request to be indemnified by the publisher for any suits arising from a request on the publisher's part, such as making a character look like a famous person.

Copyright: The publisher agrees to register the copyright to the work in the artist's name.

Agreement to publish: The book will be published within a specific period of time, usually 18 months from receipt of finished art. If the publisher fails to do so, the rights should revert back to the artist (reversion rights).

Paperback advance: If an advance against royalties is to be paid for the original publisher's paperback edition, that is usually negotiated at the time of the original contract. The royalty rate is usually less than for the hardcover edition.

Escalation: For trade books, royalties of 10% (for author and illustrator combined) are often raised to 12.5% or higher after sales reach 20,000 copies. Though mass-market books usually have lower royalty rates, these also can be raised based on sales.

De-escalation: Some publisher's contracts stipulate that royalty rates may decrease dramatically under two conditions: when high discounts are given to distributors or other buyers, or when book sales from a low-quantity reprint are slow. Not all publishers include these clauses in their contracts; it is in the artist's interest to strike them or at least to try to negotiate better terms.

There can be some justification for the illustrator to accept a lower royalty rate for a book whose sales are vastly increased by a high discount negotiated between the publisher and booksellers. It is also common practice for the royalty to decline incrementally once discounts exceed 50%. It is less favorable for the artist to accept the terms offered by some publishers whereby any discount above 50%, for example, produces royalties based on the "amount received" (the wholesale price) rather than the book's list price. This arrangement immediately reduces the royalty rate by at least half.

Illustrators have found it desirable to ensure that this deep discount is given only for "special sales" and is not part of the publisher's normal trade practice. The latter could mean that the publisher uses these discounts to gain sales at the expense of the artist and/or author. Deep discounts are also customary in book-fair sales and publishers' own book clubs. The artist should try to limit or eliminate all special sales. The artist's royalty payments will decline when books are discounted and the backlist is diminished.

By accepting a royalty decrease for a slow-selling reprint, the illustrator may give the publisher incentive to keep the book in print, but the terms of the decrease should have limitations. For instance, the book should have been in print at least two years, be in a reprint edition of 2,500 or fewer copies, and have sales of fewer than 500 copies in one royalty period. Under these conditions, the royalty might drop to 75% or even 50% of the original rate.

A foreign-language edition to be sold domestically may also be published with a lower royalty rate, as it is costlier to produce than a simple reprint and may have limited sales potential. Terms may be set, however, to escalate to a normal royalty rate if sales exceed low expectations.

Subsidiary sales: Income derived from the publisher selling any rights to a third party is divided between publisher and artist and/or author, depending on whether the rights involve art, text, or both. The percentage earned by the illustrator for each type of use is variable and is determined by negotiation. The possible use of a character in a greeting card or poster, for example, can be a valuable source of additional income for the artist. The area of electronic rights, either as a subsidiary right or as income derived from the publisher's own electronic products, is still ambiguous and changes constantly. Some publishing contracts leave the category unresolved, stating specifically that terms for electronic rights will be agreed upon mutually when and if the need arises. If that is not possible, the artist should limit those rights to three to five years, with an automatic reversion to the artist whether or not they are used by that time.

Author's copies: Publishers' contracts usually provide 6 free copies to the author, but additional copies often can be negotiated. Most publishers offer the artist a 20-to-50% discount off the list price on purchases of their book. Some publishers will pay royalties on these sales; others do not.

Schedule of statements and payments: This defines when and how accounting will be made. Normally, a royalty period is six months, with the appropriate royalty payment made four months and one day after the period closes. A useful clause found in many contracts allows access by the artist or a designated accountant to examine the publisher's books and records. If, in a given royalty period, errors of 5% or more are found in the publisher's favor, the publisher will correct the underpayment and pay the cost of the examination up to the amount of the error. If an audit costs more than the error, the artist must pay the difference.

Pass-through clause: This takes effect when the illustrator's share of a subsidiary sale exceeds $1,000. The publisher will then send payment within 30 days of receipt rather than holding it until the semiannual royalty reporting date.

Remaindering: If the book is to be remaindered (sold at a huge discount, often at the end of a print run), the publisher should notify the illustrator and allow him or her to buy any number of copies at the remaindered price.

Return of artwork: Most art is delivered digitally, and publishers no longer want original art. However, if original art is sent, the art remains the property of the artist, and it should be returned "unaltered and undamaged except for normal use and wear" after publication, if not sooner. Since publishers are responsible for the art while it is in their possession, a value should be placed on the cover and inside illustrations in the event of possible loss, damage, or negligence by the publisher.

Termination of agreement: This states that if a work is not, or will not be, available in any edition in the United States, it is out of print. At that time, the illustrator may request in writing that all rights return to the artist. The publisher usually has six months to declare an intent to reprint and a reasonable amount of time in which to issue a new edition. Failing this, the agreement is terminated, and all rights return to the artist.

In some boilerplate contracts, "out-of-print" is defined too narrowly, or the time allowed the publisher is unreasonably long. Some contracts also grant the illustrator the right to purchase any existing film, plates, or die stamps within 30 days after termination.

Quality control: Occasionally a provision is added to contracts that allows the illustrator to consult on the design of the book and to view bluelines, color separations, and proofs while corrections can still be made. A good working relationship and an informal agreement with the art director are probably as good as a guarantee of this actually occurring.

Revisions without the artist's consent: A clause prohibiting this from occurring is good insurance for protecting the integrity of the work.

Many of these contractual points may not add up to

much money for any one book, or even a lifetime of books. However, illustrators can effectively manage their careers only if they retain control over their work. Therefore, it makes sense to negotiate the best possible contract, not merely the best possible advance.

In order for the illustrator (especially a first-time illustrator new to the picture book genre) to properly evaluate an advance fee offer from a publisher, it is essential the illustrator fully comprehends how much time it will take to complete a picture book project, which is typically a huge amount of work. To determine the total time involved, illustrators needs to estimate the time it will take to initially read and comprehend the text, organize their visual plan for the illustrations, gather reference material, create the storyboard/rough sketches, followed by final sketches which are presented to the editor and art director. Once they have reviewed the final sketches, usually additional time is required to make any necessary modifications to the sketches in order to obtain full approval to proceed to the final art stage.

The most common number of pages in children's printed picture books are multiples of eight (24, 32, 40, 48), although page count can vary with print-on-demand books. Generally, the final art required for a 32–page picture book is 13-14 spreads of illustrations (integrated with the text) plus cover art, jacket flap art, title page art, and dedication/copyright page art. The art for these peripheral pages is sometimes created by culling details or vignettes from the completed interior illustrations. Some picture books will also require endpaper art. Once the illustrator provides all the final illustrations for review, some modifications may be required. Overall time involved for the illustrator to complete all sketches and final art can vary significantly, depending on the artist's personal style/complexity and execution process. Generally, it falls within a range of 5–10 months, with most illustrators taking 6 or 7 months.

The advance is designed to reflect the anticipated earnings of the book and will rarely exceed the royalty due on the sales of the book's entire first printing. So, realistically, an advance fee offered by a publisher rarely fully compensates the illustrator's initial efforts and time to create the illustrations. The financial lure is that the illustrator will receive a back-end royalty (usually 5%) of sales once the earned royalties accumulate above the amount of the advance that has already been paid to the illustrator. At that point, the illustrator will receive a royalty payment every 6 months.

It is to the illustrator's advantage to negotiate as large an advance as possible, since it may not be earned back by sales, or it may take considerable time before any royalties are actually paid. Not every picture book sells well enough to generate significant royalties at all. Only about 15% generate royalties which will accumulate enough to compensate for the lack in the illustrator's advance fee. The publisher is taking an educated risk that a picture book will be successful, so illustrators are essentially taking a risk along with the publisher, evidenced by not being fully compensated up front for their time and efforts creating the illustrations. If over time, an illustrator develops a track record of being associated with many successful picture books that sell very well, then the illustrator can demand higher and higher advance fees. Until then, the illustrator should be prepared to accept most picture book projects as a labor of love. A royalty arrangement is not recommended for small press and self-published books.

It is important when negotiating the contract with the publisher that the advance is paid in a timely manner. Most publishers offer one of two time frames for paying the advance: 1) 50% of the advance paid upon signing the contract with the remaining 50% paid on delivery of the final art; or 2) 33.3% paid on signing the contract, 33.3% upon delivery of all sketches, with the remaining 33.3% upon delivery of all final art. However, some publishers will offer a third option, which entails paying the final portion of the advance *upon publication of the book*. This means that the illustrator would not receive the final payment portion of the advance until nearly a year after they have turned in final art. Consider this third option unacceptable and demand either option (1) or (2). Payment of the advance should always be paid in full upon delivery of the final art, never upon publication of the book. In addition to the advance, all the artist's out-of-pocket expenses should be paid.

An appropriate advance will be earned back within two (and up to ten) years after publication. If the advance is earned back after only three months of release, either the advance was too low or the book was an unanticipated good seller. If an advance is earned back within the first six-month royalty period, it is a sign that a higher advance would have been more appropriate, a point to consider when negotiating future contracts.

It is also to the illustrator's advantage to secure only nonrefundable advances to be paid against royalties. Artists should scrutinize contracts to confirm that the advance does not have to be refunded if a sufficient number of books are not sold. A nonrefundable advance also constitutes a kill fee if the project is cancelled or never comes to completion, so the illustrator should be satisfied with the advance in case the project is never printed. The publisher's right to reject the art should be clearly defined and limited in the contract, and any changes requested by the publisher should be defined as "reasonable." If the artist has submitted pencil drawings that were approved and has not deviated from them in creating the finished art, the artist should be paid the complete advance for the time spent—even if the art is rejected.

Illustrators may also want to stipulate in the contract that the usage returns to them after a certain period of time. That way, the art does not end up in limbo if the publisher fails to publish, and the artist can then publish or resell it.

Royalty contracts are complicated and vary from publisher to publisher. "Boilerplate" authors' contracts rarely are written with artists in mind, and they can be difficult to comprehend. The Graphic Artists Guild strongly recommends that an attorney or agent with a track record in publishing children's books review any contract if it contains terms about which the illustrator is uncertain, especially if it is the artist's first book contract. Even publishers' boilerplate contracts can be amended if the changes are agreeable to both parties. Among sections of a royalty contract that are often negotiated are the lists of the royalty percentages for the publisher's uses of the work ("publisher's direct") and for the sale of subsidiary rights.

Specific Trade Practices

In addition to the general trade practices listed in the beginning of this chapter, the following trade practices have been used traditionally for book illustration and thus are accepted as standard:

1. Book illustrators normally license only first reproduction rights for one edition unless otherwise stated.
2. Reuse fees: from 125 to 175% of the fee that would have been charged had the illustration been commissioned for the new use.
3. Charge for rush work: usually an additional 20 to 100%, depending on how tight the deadline is.
4. When satisfactory art has been produced but the publisher, for whatever reason, decides not to use it, the full payment customarily goes to the artist, and rights to the unused work are not transferred to the publisher.

Editorial Illustration

Editorial illustrators are commissioned by designers or by art directors of consumer and trade magazines, newspapers, and online outlets to illustrate specific stories, covers, columns, blogs, or other editorial material in print or digital media. Increasingly, editorial illustrators are being asked by publications to create animated GIFs for online use, either as the main illustration or as an animated version of the still illustration, used to accompany it or lead into it.

Usually the art director has first discussed with the editor the slant and intended literary and graphic impact of a piece and then communicates it to the illustrator before the artist prepares sketches. Often illustrators prepare several sketches that explore a range of approaches to the problem. Editorial art is often commissioned under tight deadlines, especially for news publications and weekly magazines and newspapers. Monthly magazines generally offer longer deadlines.

Some editorial illustrators have encountered a problem with ethics now that all work is handled digitally. Some uninformed art directors and editors have digitally altered the illustrator's work without permission. Be sure to stipulate in any written agreement that artwork may not be cropped or altered in any way without first obtaining the artist's permission.

The Internet has created additional factors that illustrators need to consider when pricing a job. It is up to the individual illustrator to determine if posting illustration on the Web, only within the context of the original use, is included or not in the fee charged for a print project. Art directors are trying to negotiate print as secondary usage for Internet-driven assignments in which the primary market is online because they think it will be cheaper. Some illustrators argue that web usage should never be priced less than print usage because the art still takes the same amount of time to execute, plus art created for the Web reaches a larger audience, so in theory it should be worth more.

Publications today do not exist solely in print, so work must be posted in their online counterparts. One solution to the print versus digital usage problem is illustrators including *first-time North American print and web rights* in their standard fee, rather than asking for additional usage compensation. However, if you feel the compensation is not sufficient for the additional usage you are providing, you should increase your fees to reflect it.

Magazines

Fees for editorial assignments have traditionally been tied to the magazine's circulation and geographic distribution, which in turn determine its advertising rates and therefore its income. A magazine's prestige, as well as its circulation and ad revenue, can affect illustration rates.

7–7 Comparative Fees for Editorial Illustration

The fees in this chart do not reflect any specific trade practices and do not constitute specific prices for particular jobs. The buyer and seller are free to negotiate, with each artist independently deciding how to price the work, after taking all factors into account. Reading the more detailed information, Pricing Your Services, provided in Chapter 1, will help in pricing projects for your specific situation.

Hourly Rates
$60–200

Per-Illustration Fees

	COMPLEX	SIMPLE
Magazines	$300–2,000	$100–1,000
Newspapers	$500–1,500	$100–800

	STATIC
Non-commercial website/blog	$50–500

Flat Fees

EDITORIAL (PRINT)	COVER[1]	SPREAD	FULL-PAGE	½-PAGE	¼-PAGE/SPOT
Magazines					
High/above average[2]	$1,200–3,000	$800–2,000	$750–1,500	$450–750	$250–500
Average[3]	$1,100–1,500	$600–2,000	$600–1,000	$400–600	$200–500
Lower than average[4]	$400–1,500	$800–1,500	$300–1,250	$300–750	$150–500
Newspapers					
Nat'l/major & mid metro	$600–2,500	$800–2,500	$500–1,200	$450–650	$150–500
Small metro/local weekly	$300–1,500	——	$100–750	——	$50–300

1. Cover for newspapers refers to section cover.

2. Reader's Digest, Time, Bloomberg, Sports Illustrated, Business Week, Playboy, The New Yorker, GC.

3. Family Circle, Atlantic Monthly, New Republic, Mother Jones, MORE, Women's Health.

4. Single interest, trade, institutional, or professional. (ex., Field & Stream, Institutional Hospitals, Architectural Record).

Additional Fees

EXTRA ROUND OF REVISIONS		CANCELLATION & REJECTION
(Not covered in original agreement; % of original fee)	110–140%	(% of original project fee)
		Prior to completion of sketches 20–50%
USAGE (% of original project fee)		After completion of sketches 50–75%
Reuse in original market	100–150%	After completion of finished art 50–100%
Unlimited use, print only (no geographic or time limits)	100–200%	
Unlimited use in all media for one year	100–250%	Illustrators who charge by the hour bill for the num-
Total copyright transfer	100–300%	ber of hours worked up to the date of cancellation or
Sale of original art	100–200%	rejection, plus any expenses incurred.

The above rates and fees were compiled from the results of a national survey of graphic artists conducted by the Graphic Artists Guild in 2020. Responses were based on rates charged in 2018 and 2019.

For example, *Time*, *Reader's Digest*, and *Bloomberg Business Week*, pay some of the industry's highest rates for illustration, while *Family Circle* only pays average rates, yet all four magazines have national circulation. Circulation and distribution information is usually available from advertising and subscription departments of magazines.

Editorial magazine illustration is also priced by what fraction of a magazine's page it occupies. Spread illustrations occupy two facing pages. If a spread illustration occupies only half of each page, one historical basis for fee negotiation has been to add the partial page rate. Keep in mind that if only the title or very little text is used on the spread, it could be interpreted as a full-spread illustration. In these cases, discretion should be used.

Spot illustrations were once considered to be small in size—one column wide and less than a quarter page. Although quarter-page illustrations are not spots, some magazines (particularly those with lower budgets) make no distinction between the two. In recent years art directors have tended to call any illustration that is less than half a page a spot illustration. This practice fails to accurately describe the commissioned illustration and undermines established trade practices to the artist's detriment.

Newspapers

For pricing purposes, some newspapers, such as *The New York Times*, *The Washington Post,* and *The Wall Street Journal* are considered large-circulation national publications. They carry national and international news and are distributed both nationally and internationally. Medium-circulation newspapers are generally regional in nature, sell outside the city where they are published, often carry national news, and publish four-color supplements and weekend magazines. Local newspapers, naturally, have the lowest circulation, and their size of readership varies widely and is usually taken into account when determining fees. It is worth noting that this is one of the lowest-paying fields of illustration and is valued, especially for new and emerging talent, as a trade-off for providing exposure and published portfolio pieces.

Specific Trade Practices

In addition to the general trade practices listed in the beginning of this chapter, the following trade practices have been used traditionally for editorial illustration and thus are accepted as standard:

1. Editorial illustrators normally sell only first-time reproduction rights, unless otherwise stated.

2. Reuse fee: from 100 to 150% of the fee that would have been charged had the illustration been commissioned for the new use.
3. An additional charge for rush work, although reviewers are reporting rush fees are more difficult to get because art directors are tied to predetermined budgets.

See Figure 7–7 for Comparative Fees for Editorial Illustration.

Reportage Illustration

Reportage illustrators record real situations and live events on site by sketching, drawing, and painting. Like documentary photographers, these visual reporters cover a wide variety of subjects in locations at home and abroad, from public events to exotic travel destinations to war zones.

This type of illustrator is hired for a variety of reasons. On-site illustration has more of a sense of place and spontaneity than work done in the studio. If the reportage drawing is of an event, then it also becomes a documentation of what happened, in real time without editing. This becomes useful in journalistic assignments, where the illustrator also acts as a witness.

Reportage illustrators also can capture the essence of a situation, whether it's an emotion or a particular dynamic or tension. By selectively emphasizing certain aspects of a scene, they can draw the viewers' attention to what they want them to focus on. For these reasons, reportage illustrators are often commissioned for editorial assignments.

In other situations, a client might want an overview of a place or event. A reportage illustration can cover more in one image than a camera can. It can also be more opinionated or inventive in its presentation. Montage is a useful form of reportage illustration for this kind of purpose.

Sometimes, a client wants a 'reportage style' illustration of a place that no longer exists, an episode in history, or an imaginary place. An experienced reportage illustrator can create these images from a mixture of reference and on-site work.

Specific Trade Practices

Most reportage work is done directly on location, but each illustrator's workflow varies somewhat. For example, corrections might be done in the studio. Sometimes color is done separately in the studio to avoid issues with color changes the client might request. Because the illustration is created live, on location, clients do not always require preliminary sketches. However, it is good practice when working in the field to back up your illustration with a photo reference in case the client asks for something after the fact that you may not have drawn. Good communication with the client ahead of time—including some rough thumbnails—will help alleviate these types of problems.

When clients send an illustrator on location, they should cover the cost of travel (including car rental) and lodging as well as provide a stipend for meals. If the client does not have this type of budget, it's up to illustrators to decide if the fee being paid warrants the expenses they will have to cover themselves. If the travel is local or regional, you may decide the compensation is worth taking the assignment anyway.

Pricing

In general, most reportage illustration is priced by usage, as are most other kinds of illustration. Fees reflect the type of use and the media and market in which it will be used. For example, if it will be used for a print advertisement, then it would most likely be priced higher than if it were to be used for a spot editorial.

Sometimes reportage illustrators are asked to draw at an event. Most often, this kind of work is drawing portraits at department stores or at social events. In these cases, a day rate is charged that includes giving the finished drawings to the attendees.

Courtroom Sketch Art

The talents of reportage illustrators are also needed in restrictive environments where cameras are not allowed. The most familiar type of reportage illustration is the work of the courtroom sketch artist. Generally, cameras are banned in federal courts, and their use in state courts varies by state. Cameras also can be at the judge's discretion. In high-profile and newsworthy cases where cameras are not allowed, news outlets and publications hire courtroom artists to document the proceedings.

Speed is essential in this discipline, as well as being able to find just the right scene to recap an entire day or trial. The artist is not just sketching people but capturing a moment in time. Because they must work very quickly, most courtroom artists use a sketch pad and graphite or colored pencils, pastels, or chalk.

Deadlines can also be very tight for this type of work. There is a lot of pressure to turn the art around quickly in time for newscasts. A typical court day starts around 9 a.m. for high-profile cases, and news outlets want first sketches by the first recess, which is approximately 10:30 a.m., in time for the 11:00 a.m. or noon newscast, and then during every recess after that—so, the pace is grueling.

SPECIFIC TRADE PRACTICES

Courtroom sketch artists also supplement their income by selling original art and prints of their work. Judges, winning attorneys, witnesses, and police officers in high-profile cases often will ask to buy a sketch. Some sketch artists also do commissions of attorneys in court, a request often made by those who have just graduated from law school. Another source of income is drawing meetings at judge and lawyer conventions with the same look and feel as courtroom sketching.

Courtroom art is done by freelance illustrators. To break into the field and get assignments, it is recommended that an illustrator be seen in the courtroom sketching the proceedings as that is where reporters and field producers are looking for drawings—on location. This can be done at trials not requiring a press pass. You should dress professionally as if you belong there, and during recesses, discreetly but noticeably display your drawing somewhere outside the courtroom.

PRICING

Courtroom sketch artists generally price their work by the day. The news network, or affiliate channel, wants to make sure they have an artist there for them on a particular day (or series of days), for the extent of the day court is in session. A day rate is necessary due to the uncertainty of when key witnesses will testify. While a good reporter, working with the illustrator, will most often have insight and inside information as to what specific days key figures will take the stand, they may not know what time of day they will be examined or cross-examined. Paying a day rate reinforces that plans are made by the day and reassures that the hired artist is covering the day.

In the case of high-profile prominent ongoing trials, the artist might offer a weekly rate, which can be more appealing to the networks for scheduling and security of confirmation as well as for budgetary considerations. A weekly rate also allows for better planning and focus by the illustrator.

USAGE
Usage fees are worked out in advance with the client, and the artist maintains ownership of the art. Usually, usage is non-exclusive, but if the client wants exclusive usage, the artist charges a higher fee. It is to the artist's advantage—and uniquely essential for courtroom illustration—to grant non-exclusive rights. It is a work environment

where the competing clients are all present and aware of the artist's work. Therefore, it is possible and likely that other media representatives will approach an ambitious illustrator, offering on the spot to purchase secondary rights to the work for their own broadcast or publication. For heated, ongoing trials, illustrators have been known to work several channels per day.

However, on some occasions for very large trials, one company is designated to hire the artist at a low rate and distribute the art as they see fit. This is a far less lucrative situation for the artist.

OTHER FEES

Generally, media outlets are more likely to hire local sketch artists. However, if an artist has to travel long distances, any travel-related expenses are factored into the day rate. During an intense trial day, there is little time to go out to eat, so courtroom illustrator cuisine might be a power bar while working through lunch.

Rush fees are not charged in this discipline, as illustrators already know to expect very tight deadlines. Nor is overtime charged, as the normal court day is scheduled for set hours. The aspects of the work are taken into account and worked out in advance when negotiating the day rate.

Photo Illustration

Photo illustrators specialize in creating works of art by altering photographs or creating composite images— compilations of multiple images. They may use some of the same artistic treatments employed by retouchers and restorers (see the section on Digital Imaging & Photo Retouching & Restoration in Chapter 5). Most of photo illustration is done digitally, but it may also be done by hand or by using a combination of both.

The subject matter of a photo illustration is often conceptual, and can be thought-provoking or humorous, which makes it a good choice for editorial illustration and political satire. Photo illustration is also used in advertising. There is much controversy, however, about using photo illustration in news. Photo illustration is a powerful tool that can have dramatic consequences, and if a photo is altered, it can distort the accuracy of historical events and the objectivity of news reporting; for example, evidence that published photographs of a 2006 bombing in Lebanon had been digitally manipulated to make the damage seem more severe caused outrage in the U. S. press. While there have been examples of controversial manipulation of "documentary" photos since the early days of the medium, digital photography and Photoshop have made the process easier and less detectable to the untrained eye.

Photo illustrators are creators who, like other artists, control all the rights to their creations. Photo illustration is priced similarly to other forms of illustration. See Advertising Illustration and Editorial Illustration sections.

Package Illustration

Package illustrators create art for the packaging used for all types of retail products, some of which include apparel, electronics, food and beverages, health and beauty aids, toys and games, and music and film recordings. The illustrator's contribution to packaging consists of components of the final package, such as a label, that can be revised many times by both the designer and client due to the complexity of the end product packaging. Because it is often a single component of the package design, it would appear as an intact element on other uses (Web, print, broadcast, etc.). Some package illustrations become part of the product's branding.

Music Recordings

In the past, the demand for engaging, forceful, highly creative packaging for vinyl record albums attracted the best of talented editorial and advertising illustrators, who in turn created a new art form. Many record album covers have become collector's items. Several books have been published on record album cover art, and an ongoing market is active in collecting and selling.

Since 1988, the sale of vinyl recordings declined, as they were replaced by CD and DVD formats, which had much smaller and simpler covers. Digital downloads and streaming services also became popular ways to deliver music, cutting into the need for physical album covers. Since 2015, however, there has been a resurgence of music recorded as vinyl albums. Regardless of the physical format of the recording, cover images are needed for advertising purposes. Commissions for vinyl and CD/DVD cover illustration can be lucrative. Based on current data, fees vary widely, depending on the recording artist or group, the genre of music, the particular label and recording company, and the desirability and fame of the illustrator. For a detailed description of music packaging and pricing factors, refer to the Package Design section in Chapter 5.

With the growth of independent record companies specializing in specific genres and the opportunities of working directly with the recording artists themselves and their management through exposure and notice via social media, there are many total-package assignments (including illustration, type treatment, and overall design) for diligent creators willing to search for them. Fees for complex recording packages have gone to higher than $10,000. This kind of assignment, however, requires many meetings, sketches, and changes.

Tie-ins of the music packaging art with posters and other printed usage on everything from bottle openers to hoodies to belt buckles should be considered at the very first discussions of the project when pricing. This is directly associated with the growth of the merchandising culture of music and touring and the need of the music artists to make up income with the industry drop-off in music sales royalties.

Most recording companies have subsidiary labels, featuring various recording artists and types of music. The minor labels of major recording companies are usually reserved for less-commercial works and re-releases of previous recordings. In all cases, only recording company publication rights are transferred, and the original art is returned to the artist. Tie-in poster rights are sometimes included.

It is common in the music packaging market for the musicians, their management, or the project's producers to purchase the original art. The artist should be prepared with a dollar amount in case this happens. Possible tie-ins with DVD marketing should also be kept in mind when considering an appropriate fee for the image.

One illustrator who has worked extensively with major recording companies advises artists working in the field to employ a lawyer experienced in the entertainment industry to negotiate contracts for them. Otherwise, the artist may be unknowingly exploited because of lack of experience. The contract should contain a clause clearly spelling out that additions and alterations will lead to extra charges.

Other Products

While packaging for the Entertainment industry is somewhat standard, packaging for other industries varies widely in size, shape, and the materials used. (See the Package Design section in Chapter 5 for a detailed look at what is involved in packaging for the Food and Beverage; the Beer, Wine, and Spirits; and the Cosmetics industries.)

SPECIAL CONSIDERATIONS

To deliver the best product possible, it is important for package illustrators to understand the reproduction limitations of certain substrates, such as aluminum, recycled cardboard, etc., on which the illustration will be reproduced. Some substrates only allow for a limited level of detail. The illustrator may have to follow very strict guidelines when developing the art so that it will print properly. Some special techniques, such as foil or embossing, also have limitations and may necessitate working together with the printer during the illustration process to ensure that it will reproduce well.

For these reasons, the illustrator should ask the client during the initial stages of a project—where will the illustration be used, will it be printed, are any special printing techniques being used, is there a budget for special techniques, and are there packaging limitations? This discussion should also include the standard discussion of style and execution. If the illustrator also will be responsible for logo design or the entire package design, the future of the brand must be considered. Will there be product or flavor profile offshoots that might need to be illustrated in the future?

PRICING

Pricing is determined by the complexity of the illustration, the size and prominence of the printed illustration on the package, the size and importance of the client, and the number of usage rights needed.

Package illustration assignments for Food and Beverage clients range in scope from illustrating only the flavor elements, such as lime rinds, or standalone fruits in various executions to illustrating the full package design background. Sometimes illustrators are hired to design the layout or even the typography in addition to illustrating the package. These additional services will increase pricing and may be billed as separate line items.

An illustrator might also be hired for a package design for comp, and if the package is chosen, the artist will receive 150–250% of the comp rate for finalization and usage rights.

Illustrators also may license their existing work for use on packaging. It simply has to be changed to fit the correct dimensions of the package or to adhere to printing limitations.

Clients from the Food and Beverage and the Health and Beauty industries almost always request a full buyout of rights. Instead, it is in the best interest of both parties for the illustrator to specify exactly the rights that the client needs so that the illustrator retains unused rights and markets for possible future revenue, and the client is not wasting money on rights it doesn't need. For example, acceptable rights might include "unlimited, exclusive packaging rights in the United States for the specified product only. Original artwork belongs to the artist."

7–8 Comparative Fees for Package Illustration

The fees in this chart do not reflect any specific trade practices and do not constitute specific prices for particular jobs. The buyer and seller are free to negotiate, with each artist independently deciding how to price the work, after taking all factors into account. Reading the more detailed information, Pricing Your Services, provided in Chapter 1, will help in pricing projects for your specific situation.

Hourly Rates
$40–75

Per-Illustration Fees
$500–5,000
(High end of range represents more complex illustrations)

Additional Fees (% of original fee)

ADDITIONAL ROUND OF REVISIONS (Not covered in original agreement)	110–150%

CANCELLATION & REJECTION	
Prior to completion of sketches	25–50%
After completion of sketches	50%
After completion of finished art	50–100%

Illustrators who charge by the hour bill for the number of hours worked up to the date of cancellation or rejection, plus any expenses incurred.

RUSH FEES (% added onto normal fee)	20–50%

The above rates and fees were compiled from the results of a national survey of graphic artists conducted by the Graphic Artists Guild in 2020. Responses were based on rates charged in 2018 and 2019.

Specific Trade Practices

In addition to the general trade practices listed in the beginning of this chapter, the following trade practices have been used traditionally for package illustration and thus are accepted as standard:

1. Package illustrators normally sell only first reproduction rights unless otherwise stated.

2. Charge for rush work: an additional 20 to 50%. However, rush fees have been more difficult to get in recent years.

See Figure 7–8 for Fees for Package Illustration.

Fashion & Lifestyle Illustration

Fashion illustrators specialize in drawing clothed figures and accessories in a specific style or "look" for use by brands, retailers, advertising agencies, graphic design studios, corporations/manufacturers, and in editorials for magazines and newspapers. Sometimes fashion illustrators are required to create an illustration with only a photo or *croquis* (working sketch) of the garment for reference; the illustrator must invent the drape of the garment on a model, the light source, or even the garment itself.

The application of the techniques and styles exclusive to fashion illustration have also been used to create lifestyle illustration. These illustrations may be general in appearance but have a stylization that reflects a background in fashion illustration. Due to the nature of lifestyle illustration, artists will need to research, find, and/or create reference to suit the needs of a particular assignment. Lifestyle illustration is priced the same as fashion.

Although the advertising market for apparel and accessory illustration has declined in recent years, illustrations are still commissioned for work with a fashion theme in the growing beauty and cosmetic areas, as well as in the development of crossover markets that are well suited to an illustrative style. Such illustration is generally used as comp or finished art for magazine or newspaper editorial, print advertising, storyboards, television/video, packaging, display, collateral material, and product development or test presentations. Internet displays and sales venues are relatively new markets. There is also work available for illustrators working in this genre to create spot illustrations or figures for personal blogs and fashion websites, as well as illustrations for Twitter avatars and Facebook pages. While these clients do not generally have large budgets, illustrators are able to charge $250 to $500 for a very quick illustration. Done in bulk, this type of work can be a lucrative source of income.

In addition to creating work for publishing, fashion illustrators also are commissioned by retailers and fashion designers to appear at various fashion-related events to create fashion drawings and portraits of customers on the spot. These assignments usually involve fashion illustrators drawing for two to three hours, but the timeframe may be longer, depending on the client and the event.

Illustrators should be wary of projects that require far more technical details and revisions than normal for fashion illustration. There are clients who pose as designers, but actually use the illustrator to design their lines for them. These types of projects, which might include shoes, handbags, hats, gloves, and other accessories, border on product development and should be priced accordingly.

Pricing

Current data indicate that the two most important factors determining fees are the type and extent of usage and the complexity of the job. Other factors that affect pricing are market (such as corporate, advertising, or editorial), size and prestige of the account, volume of work, the illustrator's experience and desirability, and deadlines.

Most apparel illustration is paid on a per-figure basis, with an additional charge for backgrounds. When more than three figures are shown (four to ten), a group rate can be charged at a lower rate, usually 80 to 90% of an artist's single-figure rate. In volume work (considered any amount over ten figures), such as catalog, brochure, or instructional use, the per-figure price is negotiated at a volume rate, usually 75% of an artist's single-figure rate. Mailers and catalogs also have been a part of a larger package where if the client is cosmetics, then the use of the illustration will be negotiated for a usage fee for display/in-store signage, advertising, and mailers. Accessory illustration is generally paid on a per-item basis. With the exception of specialized work, accessory illustration rates are generally 40 to 75% of an artist's per-figure prices. When more than three items are shown, additional items can be charged at a lower unit price.

Fashion illustrators are also hired to create covers and fully illustrated books. These projects are usually negotiated with a flat fee and royalty for the use of the illustrator's work.

For live sketching at fashion events, illustrators may charge a flat rate for their participation in the event or an hourly rate for their time.

When doing work for fashion designers, illustrators may have to educate them on copyright, usage, and pricing practices. For example, if an illustrator is hired by a designer to draw figures for a sales meeting, and then later the designer decides to use the finished art for a lookbook for New York Fashion Week, it is a separate use and therefore an additional fee. Usage and how it is priced can be explained to the designer upfront when estimating an initial job by asking the designer if he/she foresees wanting to use the illustrations for any other purpose in the future. It is generally more economical for the designer to have any additional usage built into the initial project, rather than negotiating a second contract for an additional use.

Specific Trade Practices

In addition to the general trade practices listed in the beginning of this chapter, the following trade practices have been used traditionally for fashion and lifestyle Illustration and thus are accepted as standard:

1. Fashion/lifestyle illustrators normally sell first reproduction rights unless otherwise stated.
2. All corrections/revisions should be made in the preliminary sketch stage. All client changes, particularly in finished art, traditionally require an additional charge; the amount depends on the number and complexity of the changes.

Pricing much of fashion and lifestyle illustration depends on the media and end use. Refer to the sections Advertising Illustration, Editorial Illustration, and Book Illustration for guidance.

Greeting Card & Retail Product Illustration

The greeting card and paper novelty fields continue to be highly competitive cost-driven markets. New greeting card companies and fresh card lines constantly enter—and exit—the industry. While the largest card publishers continue to hold the lion's share of the market, they have been facing fierce competition from smaller brands in the last few years. Since success or failure in this business is based largely on the public's buying habits, greeting card designs lend themselves particularly well to royalty or licensing arrangements.

Artwork for retail products such as novelty merchandise, apparel, china, giftware, toys, and other manufactured items is traditionally purchased through licensing agreements. Calendars and posters for retail sale may also use licensing or royalty agreements. For more information about uses of this type of illustration, refer to the Greeting Card & Novelty Design section in Chapter 5, Graphic Design; the License Your Art section in Chapter 4, Maximizing Income; and the Book Illustration section earlier in this chapter.

Greeting Cards

Greeting card sales in such mass-market outlets as supermarkets and big box retailers helped fuel sales growth over the past decade. The benefits of royalty agreements cannot be overstated, although the major card companies (Hallmark and American Greetings) are resistant to outsourcing creative work, keeping it in-house or with "first look" independent contractors who work at high volume. Cards for new niche markets, such as people of color, multicultural families, single-parent households, and same-sex couples, have been introduced, with anticipated sales growth during the next decade.

Although the major companies generally publish cards developed by staff artists, they do commission or buy some outside work. The rest of the industry, however, depends heavily on freelance illustration and design. Freelancers may earn income both from creating an inventory of their own illustrations and designs, which they license to producers/manufacturers and by selling commissioned works. They usually develop different styles for different clients in order to minimize competition.

Designs, usually created in full color, generally fit into everyday or seasonal lines. Everyday cards include birthday, anniversary, get well, friendship, juvenile, religious/inspirational, congratulations, sympathy, and other occasions. Christmas cards comprise the vast majority of seasonal greetings, making up more than a third of all cards sold and as much as 50 to 100% of some card companies' offerings. Other seasonal cards include Valentine's Day, Easter, Mother's and Father's Days, Hanukkah, and other holidays. Current survey data indicate that cards with special effects, such as embossing, die-cuts, or pop-ups, command larger fees.

Artists whose cards sell well may propose that the company commission them to develop an entire line of cards, which involves from 20 to 36 stylistically similar cards with a variety of greetings. In cases where an artist's cards become top sellers and the style is strongly identified with the company, the value of the artist's work to the company is recognized with equity and other compensation. Exclusive arrangements providing royalties are negotiated on occasion; artists are advised, however, to develop a solid relationship with the client before considering such an agreement.

Greeting card designs are licensed either on an advance-against-royalty basis or for a flat fee. The royalty is usually a percentage of the wholesale price, unless the company sells retail or online retail as well, in which case the royalty can be a combination of wholesale and retail. In most cases, a nonrefundable advance is paid in anticipation of royalties. This reflects the fact that production and distribution schedules require a year to 18 months before a design reaches the marketplace. Royalties and licensing are discussed further in Chapter 4, Maximizing Income.

Companies that offer a flat fee often offer a portion (25–50%) of the payment upon completion of concept sketches, and the remaining once the final art is delivered. Sometimes these companies will end up executing the sketch concepts in-house, so there may not be a "final art" stage for the illustrator.

Many greeting card companies purchase rights in the greeting card product category only, for a specified period of time (usually three to five years), in a specific market (e.g., North America or worldwide), with the artists retaining rights in all the other product categories (e.g., apparel, home furnishings, etc.). Unlike smaller companies that only seek rights to a design for one or two product categories, larger greeting card companies like Hallmark and American Greetings tend to look for buying a design outright. It is not in the best interest of illustrators to give up all rights to their work because it prevents them from being able to license their art on other products, providing a revenue stream for years to come. If such a contract is agreed to, the illustrator's usage fee should be much higher than a limited-use contract.

Artists should not do revisions on a proposed design before a contract, describing payment and terms, is signed by both client and artist. Nor should artists accept contract terms that they are uncomfortable with or that are not in their best economic interest. All contracts are open to changes and negotiation. Savvy artists can negotiate for themselves to use their own contract, or they can make changes in the company's contract. However, artists who find contracts confusing or overwhelming should consult a lawyer or a consultant who reviews contracts before signing.

Retail Products

A wide array of designs and illustrations are in demand for T-shirts, towels, mugs, tote bags, and other novelty items. Whether a design or illustration is specifically developed by the artist for marketing as a product or sold as a spin-off of a nationally known character, it is usually done under a licensing agreement.

In such agreements, an artist, designer, or owner of artwork rights permits ("licenses") another party to use the art for a limited specific purpose, for a specified time, in a specified territory, in return for a fee or royalty. For a detailed discussion of licensing, see Chapter 4, Maximizing Income. An excellent book on the subject is *Licensing*

7–9 Comparative Fees for Greeting Card & Retail Product Illustration

The fees in this chart do not reflect any specific trade practices and do not constitute specific prices for particular jobs. The buyer and seller are free to negotiate, with each artist independently deciding how to price the work, after taking all factors into account. Reading the more detailed information, Pricing Your Services, provided in Chapter 1, will help in pricing projects for your specific situation.

Hourly Rates
$70–260
Rates will vary widely by the reputation of the artist and type of product.

Royalty Rates
Original Print Greeting Card	3–10%

Flat Fee Pricing
Original Print Greeting Card	$100–2,000
Poster	$200–1,000+

Additional Fees (% of original fee)

EXTRA ROUND OF REVISIONS	25–100%
(Not covered in original agreement)	

USAGE	
Reuse in original market	20–100%
Sale of original art	50–125%

CANCELLATION & REJECTION	
(% of original project fee)	
Prior to completion of sketches	25–50%
After completion of sketches	25–75%
After completion of finished art	50–100%

Illustrators who charge by the hour bill for the number of hours worked up to the date of cancellation or rejection, plus any expenses incurred.

RUSH FEES (% added onto normal fee)	25–100%

The above rates and fees were compiled from the results of a national survey of graphic artists conducted by the Graphic Artists Guild in 2020. Responses were based on rates charged in 2018 and 2019.

Art and Design, by Caryn Leland, published by Allworth Press (see Part 5, Resources & References). Model licensing agreements, reprinted with permission of the author, appear in the Appendix: Contracts & Forms.

Specific Trade Practices

In addition to the general trade practices listed in the beginning of this chapter, the following trade practices have been used traditionally for greeting card and retail product illustration and thus are accepted as standard:

1. Artists illustrating greeting cards and retail products normally sell only first reproduction rights, unless otherwise stated.
2. Reuse Fees: Although there is no set formula, current surveys indicate up to 100% of the fee that would have been charged had the illustration been commissioned for the new use.
3. Charge for rush work: an additional 25 to 100%.

See Figure 7–9 for Comparative Fees for Greeting Card & Retail Product Illustration.

Medical Illustration

Medical illustrators train extensively to work in a surprisingly broad range of fields, including medicine, surgical training, forensics, research, art, design, web development, visual technology, media, communication, education, management, and even game development. Their job is to translate complex technical information into easily understood and efficient images to clearly convey how bodies work, how medicines interact, what happens under stress or trauma, or any of a nearly endless range of conditions that may need to be expressed.

The market for accurate and well-rendered medical depictions is strong. Medical illustrators may be employed by medical, dental, and veterinary schools, as well as teaching and research medical centers. Animation studios and multimedia production houses also hire medical illustrators on a freelance or full-time basis, as do medical publishers, pharmaceutical houses, advertising agencies, and attorneys. Most medical artists create 2-D illustrations in Photoshop, Illustrator, or Painter and 3-D models and animation using Maya, Cinema 4D, Autodesk 3ds Max, and LightWave 3D.

Training & Certification

Not surprisingly, anatomical accuracy is critical to success. To achieve this degree of verisimilitude, many medical artists earn a Master's Degree from an accredited graduate program. There are currently three very competitive programs in the United States and one in Canada that are accredited by the Commission on Accreditation of Allied Health Education Programs (CAAHEP), regarded as the premier sanctioning body. Course work includes human gross anatomy (with detailed dissection); histology; physiology; embryology; neuroanatomy and neurobiology; pathology; illustration techniques; anatomical and surgical illustration; modeling; prosthetics; graphic and exhibit design and construction; medical photography; television and multimedia production; computer graphics, specifically 3D/CGI; business management; instructional design; and production technology.

Some medical illustrators demonstrate competency by becoming board certified. A Certified Medical Illustrator (CMI) is tested on subjects covering business practices, ethics, biomedical science, and drawing, and undergoes a rigorous portfolio review. To maintain certification, they must continue their education and must have their certification renewed every five years. The National Commission for Certifying Agencies (NCCA) establishes the standards by which all medical illustrators are evaluated.

Specific Trade Practices

In addition to the general trade practices listed in the beginning of this chapter, the following trade practices have been used traditionally for medical illustration and are accepted as standard:

1. Illustrators normally sell only first reproduction rights unless otherwise stated. Additional rights are traditionally licensed on a one-time basis, with separate payment for each and every use. Artists retain copyright to all 3-D models and scenes.
2. Fees for licensed medical animation are based on final rendered frames.
3. Due to the proprietary nature of much of the work associated with medical illustration, artists frequently sign nondisclosure agreements prohibiting discussion of work-in-progress and prohibiting exhibit or display of art until a specified date.

Professionals in the field report that there is a current trend for clients to want to own everything, including 3-D models, so it is extremely important that usage rights and ownership of work is spelled out in contracts.

Being forced into work-for-hire arrangements is also a constant battle. Work for hire generally does not apply to self-employed illustrators—only to staff illustrators doing work for their employer. However, under U.S. copyright law, there are nine narrow exceptions to self-employed artists retaining copyright to their work, including contributions to a collective work or an instructional text. Illustrators should familiarize themselves with all nine exceptions, which are outlined in Chapter 11, Legal Rights & Issues. If an illustrator's work for a client does not fall under one of the exceptions *and* if both the client and illustrator do not agree in writing to a work-for-hire arrangement, then the work does not qualify as work for hire. Clients may not understand that allowable work for hire is on a project-by-project basis, dependent on end use of the illustration.

For the most up-to-date information about the profession and salaries, visit the website of the Association of Medical Illustrators at www.ami.org.

Natural Science Illustration

Natural science illustrators create accurate and detailed images of scientific subjects, including anthropology, astronomy, botany, cartography, geology, paleontology, and zoology, often working directly with scientists and designers to illustrate books and journals or to create exhibits and educational materials for universities, research centers, state and federal government departments, museums, zoos, botanical gardens, and aquaria. Natural science illustration is expanding into all areas of graphic communications and commercial applications, such as special interest magazines, environmental design, merchandise and package illustration, advertising, computer graphics, audio-visuals, and model-making and murals for museums and zoos.

Education & Skills

Scientific illustrators must be versatile in more than one technique or medium, using everything from traditional pencils and paints to digital media; often they must be skilled in using optical equipment and precision measuring devices. A thorough understanding of the subject matter is essential. Many scientific illustrators have advanced degrees or strong backgrounds in science as well as art. However, the lack of a science degree is not necessarily a hindrance to success in this field. Several schools of higher education offer certificate programs in natural science illustration.

The illustrator often must pictorially reconstruct an entire object from incomplete specimens and poor-quality photographs or conceptualize an informed interpretation. Specimens must be correctly delineated to show proportion, coloration, anatomical structures, and other diagnostic features. The illustrator may clarify complex three-dimensional structures, emphasize important details, and idealize an individual specimen in ways not possible by photography. Scientific illustrations are judged for their accuracy, readability, and beauty.

Pricing Factors

Scientific illustrators who create works for books and journals report that work-made-for-hire contracts are unfortunately all too common in the field, especially in the textbook industry. Textbooks are often compilations of the work of many different contributors. Both textbooks and compilations are two allowable work-for-hire exceptions under U.S. Copyright Law. Illustrators should familiarize themselves with all nine allowable exceptions because not all natural science assignments qualify as work for hire (see the complete list in Chapter 11, Legal Rights & Issues).

Opportunities and payment for natural science illustrators in the K-12 textbook market have been especially hard hit by the outsourcing of work overseas. As more and more printing was sent out of the country, composition houses in India began opening art studios and doing illustration work very cheaply. Some major U.S. educational publishers are now offering illustrators pricing structures based on these foreign economies. These prices are 1/6 to 1/4 of what is customary and do not support an artist's livelihood in the U.S. economy. However, some illustrators report still being able to negotiate fees that are customary.

Another problem facing natural science illustration is that more and more works are computer generated; therefore, the function of illustrators is frequently viewed as mere data entry, and although their work is integral to the scientific data provided, illustrators are often not even credited. To protect illustrators' rights in this field, and because it may take years for the work to be accepted for publication, practitioners recommend pricing work appropriately for first (and probably only) use, requesting final payment upon submission of the work, and providing scanned images rather than original artwork.

In addition to intended usage and rights transferred, the factors that affect pricing in this field include research and consultation time, travel, reference materials, and the complexity of the project, which sometimes require extra stages of concept development and approvals. Scientific illustrations may contain extremely fine details and communicate complex ideas and therefore may command higher prices than less "information dense" work of the same printed size.

One source of work that has increased for scientific illustrators is scientific/academic journal cover art, due to competition among researchers. However, illustrators should beware of some of the problems working in this area. First, the journals require that the researchers pay for the artwork, with no guarantee that the art will be chosen. The journals also require all commercial rights, if not all rights, to the art, and again the burden of payment falls to the researcher for all-rights licensing. The researcher often does not understand this, so the illustrator needs to clarify and explain how usage and licensing work. Otherwise, the scientist gets the art from the illustrator and unthinkingly signs away the illustrator's rights to the art without the illustrator realizing it. So, the illustrator needs to be very clear upfront—and in writing—that the scientist owes payment for the work regardless if the art is used. In these situations, the illustrator should structure fees so that he/she receives a flat fee for creation and submission, and then charge a separate fee for usage if the art is chosen to be published.

Specific Trade Practices

In addition to the general trade practices listed in the beginning of this chapter, the following trade practices have been used traditionally for natural science illustration and thus are accepted as standard:

1. Natural science illustrators normally sell only first reproduction rights, unless otherwise stated.
2. Rush work is charged as an additional percentage of the normal fee.

Technical Illustration

Technical illustrators create images that convey or explain complex information visually. Subjects include highly accurate renderings of machinery, instruments, scientific subjects (such as geological formations and chemical reactions), space technology, or virtually any subject that requires precise interpretation in illustration. Technical illustrators often work directly with a scientist, engineer, technician, product manager, or communications specialist to achieve the most explicit and accurate visualization of the subject and/or information. Being trained in mechanical drafting, computer-aided design (CAD) and/or 3-D software, mathematics, diagrams, blueprints, and production gives technical illustrators specific and required skills.

Technical illustration is used in all areas of graphics communication in this age of sophisticated technology. Some of the areas that most commonly require this specialized art are industrial publications, technical manuals, instructions for use (required by the FDA), training materials, annual reports, special or single-interest magazines, packaging, advertising and sales materials, corporate, editorial, web graphics, trade show graphics, and audiovisuals. These artists most often create their work digitally.

Information graphics or infographics are often employed by technical illustrators. These visual representations of information, data, and knowledge are used where complex information must be explained quickly and clearly. They include maps, charts, diagrams, and graphs. Infographics can be found everywhere and in all types of media. They have both everyday and scientific uses. While they often serve as visual shorthand in everyday life (traffic signs), in science and technical literature they are used to illustrate physical systems, especially ones that cannot be photographed, such as cutaways, astronomical diagrams, and images of microscopic systems. (See more about infographics in Chapter 5, Graphic Design).

Pricing Factors

Whenever possible, technical illustrators should retain control of their copyrights. However, technical illustration is often covered by a nondisclosure agreement, involves trade secrets or proprietary information, is for an internal/private audience, or is very specific, so it may lack broad appeal. For these reasons, opportunities for reuse is often limited in this field. Nonetheless, it can be valuable for illustrators to build a library of their work that can later be reused with alterations in new work. Given the complexities of some assignments, this practice can help illustrators complete jobs faster.

In addition to intended usage and rights transferred, the factors that affect pricing in this field include research and consultation time, travel, reference materials, and project complexity. The quality and number of available assets, such as CAD models provided by the client or those in the illustrator's personal library, also affect pricing as they may save the illustrator considerable time.

7–10 Comparative Fees for Technical Illustration

The fees in this chart do not reflect any specific trade practices and do not constitute specific prices for particular jobs. The buyer and seller are free to negotiate, with each artist independently deciding how to price the work, after taking all factors into account. Reading the more detailed information, Pricing Your Services, provided in Chapter 1, will help in pricing projects for your specific situation.

Hourly Rates
$70–100

Flat Fees
Cutaway (industrial subject)	$750–3,000+
Infographic (print)	$150–3,000
Editorial (magazine)	
Spread	$1,000–2,200
¼ page/spot	$200–800

Additional Fees (% of original fee)
EXTRA ROUND OF REVISIONS	110–150%
(Not covered in original agreement)	
USAGE	
Unlimited use, print only	100–175%
(no geographic or time limits)	
Unlimited use in all media for one year	130–150%
Total copyright transfer	100–250%
CANCELLATION & REJECTION	
Prior to completion of sketches	20–50%
After completion of sketches	40–75%
After completion of finished art	80–100%

Illustrators who charge by the hour bill for the number of hours worked up to the date of cancellation or rejection, plus any expenses incurred.

RUSH FEES (% added onto normal fee)	
24-hour turnaround	25–100%
48-hour turnaround	20–30%
Holidays & weekends	25–100%

The above rates and fees were compiled from the results of a national survey of graphic artists conducted by the Graphic Artists Guild in 2020. Responses were based on rates charged in 2018 and 2019.

The fees and completion time for technical illustration vary considerably according to the complexity of the assignment and quality of the reference materials. A single complex illustration, such as a cutaway of a ship, can sometimes take six weeks to three months to complete, while simpler cutaways of common household items, such as the interior of a mattress, are done in hours. Many illustrators prefer to shoot their own photographs for reference but often work from reference materials supplied by the client.

Specific Trade Practices

In addition to the general trade practices listed in the beginning of this chapter, the following specific trade practices have been used traditionally for technical illustration and thus are accepted as standard:

1. Technical illustrators normally sell only first reproduction rights unless otherwise stated. Some clients, especially corporate clients (engineers and manufacturers), often come to a project expecting full rights or unlimited use, so they may need to be educated upfront about copyright and usage-right pricing.
2. Charge for rush work: often an additional 20 to 100%.

See Figure 7–10 for Comparative Fees for Technical Illustration.

Architectural Illustration/ Visualization

Architectural illustrators/visualization artists (also known as renderers) are hired by an architect, designer, or real estate developer to create accurate representations (computer generated [CG] rendering and animation, sketches, drawings, or paintings) of exterior or interior design projects. They also are frequently commissioned to create conceptual, evocative imagery that relies more on impressionism than accuracy or realism. In the past, architectural illustration was done by hand, but today most of it is done digitally.

When this discipline was delivered exclusively via non-digital means, the field was primarily a commodity-driven market—the client requested an illustration and a fee was paid to the artist. While the delivery of images and animations still exists (mostly on the digital side), many mature and more established companies have eventually diversified their firms to become real estate marketing studios. Architectural illustration/visualization remain a staple of these companies, but their services now have expanded to include architectural design, branding, marketing strategy and collateral, sales center design, architectural and live-action films, virtual and augmented (VR/AR) experiences, websites, mobile app development, etc. This diversification of services came about because of the difficulty of visualization companies to grow and be successful while trying to survive the inevitable swings of the real-estate market.

Types of Work & Usage

Architectural illustrators work in a variety of media. The finished art is in the form of one or a combination of several media: CG image, animation, watercolor, colored pencil, marker, gouache, pen and ink, airbrush, and/or pastel. Many illustrators take advantage of 3-D modeling, 3-D rendering, and CAD (Computer Aided Design) applications with capabilities that range from producing preliminary layouts to complete final renderings. Not only are they extremely useful for their speed and accuracy, but they also allow the artist to quickly choose views, materials, and lighting that serve the client's needs.

Illustrators may be commissioned by real estate developers and/or their advertising agencies to create art for promotional purposes. In most of these situations, the illustrator retains the copyright but allows clients to use the image or film without limitations.

When the artist is asked to provide renderings to be used by the client in a design competition, the artist may be asked to provide them at a lower fee or to participate on an unpaid basis. In this speculative arrangement, the artist usually negotiates additional compensation or a bonus if the client wins the competition. The amount of the bonus depends on the size of the original discount and the value of the contract the client will secure from winning the competition. It is customary that the illustrator will recoup his/her invested time through future work on the project if the team wins.

Illustrators working non-digitally often sell the original illustration for design presentation purposes, but the copyright and the reproduction rights are usually retained by the artist. Some artists provide their drawings to clients on a temporary "use basis," with eventual return of the original.

Pricing Factors

Architectural illustrators/visualization artists are hired for their unique illustrative styles and their accuracy in depicting the building, space, color, and/or materials.

7–11 Comparative Fees for Architectural Illustration & Visualization

The fees in this chart do not reflect any specific trade practices and do not constitute specific prices for particular jobs. The buyer and seller are free to negotiate, with each artist independently deciding how to price the work, after taking all factors into account. Reading the more detailed information, Pricing Your Services, provided in Chapter 1, will help in pricing projects for your specific situation.

Hourly Rates
$75–125 (rendering)

Additional Fees

EXTRA ROUND OF REVISIONS	110–150%
(Not covered in original agreement; % of original fee)	
RUSH FEES (% added onto normal fee)	25–100%

The above rates and fees were compiled from the results of a national survey of graphic artists conducted by the Graphic Artists Guild in 2020. Responses were based on rates charged in 2018 and 2019.

They usually have a background in architectural, interior, or industrial design and have chosen this specialized field after part-time or freelance experience in the business. As a result of these unique qualifications, they are often hired to work on a rendering project while the design is in progress. In this situation, it is customary for the renderer to bill hourly plus expenses. Hourly rates are based on the artist's skill set and the complexity of the work. Illustrators often work from a variety of reference materials, depending on the end use and the level of detail required by the client, ranging from rough schematic design sketches with verbal descriptions to photorealistic computer-generated 3-D imagery.

Factors involved in pricing include the complexity of the design project (which depends upon the views and amount of detail required), the number of images, the length of the 3-D animation (sometimes billed by the second), the media to be used, and the amount of time required for travel and consultation for the project. The size of the finished hand-rendered piece was once a main consideration when pricing but is not as important today as most work is scanned to create various sizes. For digital work, the resolution of the imagery—for example, a low-res image versus an 8K image—affects pricing.

Other expenses that might make up the budget for a project, especially for live-action photography and film, include photography, camera/film crews, actors, and the rental of green-screen studio time, helicopters, etc.

Specific Trade Practices

In addition to the general trade practices listed in the beginning of this chapter, the following specific practices have been used traditionally for architectural illustration/visualization and thus are accepted as standard:

1. Charge for rush work: often an additional 25 to 100%.
2. A client may request that the illustrator enter into a nondisclosure agreement that would prevent the artist from showing or publishing (for self-promotion) the artwork for a specific period of time. Any conditions limiting an artist's ability to exploit artwork have been factors in negotiating fees. Nondisclosure agreements customarily have a provision allowing use with written permission from the client.
3. As digital media is easily transferable and distributable, reuse fees and restrictions on specific use are difficult to implement. However, proper image credits should be contractually enforced when images are published.
4. While copyrights and ownership of digital images should, in theory, be treated the same as traditional hand renderings, many clients (usually larger corporate clients) may insist that the results of the creation process are "works made for hire" and demand ownership. It is sound practice to ensure that the contract stipulates that ownership remains with the artist. In the event that the client is adamant, a higher fee for transfer should be negotiated.
5. Distribution of the final digital art is accomplished via e-mail or a file sharing service.

See Figure 7–11 for Comparative Fees for Architectural & Visualization Illustration.

Dimensional (3-D) Illustration

Dimensional illustration includes, but is not limited to, paper, soft, or relief sculpture; paper/photo collage; assemblage; plastic, wood, and/or metal fabrications; clay imagery; food sculpture; fabric/stitchery; and other types of mixed media. Dimensional illustrators create original 3-D artwork, varying from low-relief collage to sculptural assemblage that is usually shown from one vantage point. This genre includes traditional illustrators, model makers, paper sculptors, and fabric artists whose work is created for a wide range of uses in the same markets as that of other illustrators, predominantly in advertising and editorial. Some dimensional illustrators also seek work in related markets creating architectural models; window displays; museum exhibits; convention display booths; prototypes for toys and giftware; sculpture for building interiors; food styling; animation; and sets, props, costumes, and puppets for TV commercials and performances.

Any 3-D illustration to be used in print must have two images: the original dimensional artwork and a photograph (transparency or slide) or digital image to be submitted for reproduction. Typically, the client buys one-time usage rights.

Photographing the Artwork

Because many dimensional illustrators like to maintain control over the entire process, they choose to photograph their own work. In addition to making the final image, they may take preliminary photos, often digital, to establish camera angles or to submit as sketches or comps. Another advantage of photographing the artwork is that it may be constructed without regard to permanence or the need for transportation or reassembly. Dimensional illustrators thereby eliminate the expense of hiring a photographer, scheduling such services under deadline pressure, and any possible confusion over copyright. The 3-D illustrator who chooses to do his/her own photography is obligated to make a considerable investment in equipment and supplies and in mastering the techniques needed to produce suitable high-quality reproductions.

Dimensional illustrators who opt to use the services of a professional photographer must consider copyright issues carefully. As the creator of the original work, 3-D illustrators implicitly grant authorization to create a 2-D derivative of their work. Frequently, however, once artwork is photographed for use, it is difficult for 3-D illustrators to control uses and distributions or even obtain copies of their work. This situation can occur under the most ordinary arrangements: when the client hires both the artist and the photographer, when the photographer hires the artist, and even when the artist hires the photographer.

Fortunately, most art directors and photographers function under the assumption that the final photographic image does not belong to either the dimensional illustrator or the photographer, but to both. The reasons for this are logical: the photo could not have been created without the dimensional illustration and is therefore a derived image. So, photographers should not assume ownership and full rights to an image when that image is derived fully from a dimensional illustrator's work. In most relationships involving model makers, a photographer or client who wants to assume all rights to the work and the derivative photograph will offer to buy out the artist for a fee significantly higher than that offered for first rights.

It is sound practice, as always, to ascertain in advance the client's and the photographer's rights. The best protection dimensional illustrators have is a written agreement; a simple letter to the other party is needed to confirm basic terms.

3-D ILLUSTRATOR & PHOTOGRAPHER HIRED BY CLIENT

Dimensional illustrators should consider the following in situations where the client hires both the illustrator and the photographer:

License: Specify the precise scope of the license granted to the client for use of the illustration and its photographic reproductions.

Assignments: Limit the client's agreements with all third parties (including the photographer) for use of any reproductions of the illustration, photographic and otherwise.

Rights reserved: Obtain permission to make unfettered use of the photograph (a transparency is preferable so additional reproductions can be made).

Credit: Require the client and the photographer to provide a specific credit to the artist whenever the photograph is used (i.e., Photography © 2000 John Photographer, Artwork © 2000 Jane Artist).

PHOTOGRAPHER HIRED BY 3-D ILLUSTRATOR

In cases where a dimensional illustrator hires the photographer, the illustrator should specify the following:

Grant of rights: The rights granted the photographer and the limits of the photographer's exercise of copyright in the photograph.

Permission: The anticipated use of the photograph.

Credit: The credit to be used at all times with the photograph.

Access: If the illustrator is free to reproduce the photograph without using the photographer's services. If so, a negative or a transparency that can be duplicated should be obtained.

3-D ILLUSTRATOR HIRED BY PHOTOGRAPHER

In situations where a dimensional illustrator is retained by the photographer, the illustrator should consider the following:

License: Specify the rights granted to the photographer and the photographer's permitted uses of the photograph depicting the illustrator's work.

Authorship: Retain the copyright of the illustration and, if possible, share joint copyright of the photograph.

Rights reserved: Specify that the illustrator may use his/her illustration freely and without restriction (including having it re-photographed by another photographer).

Credit: Specify the credit that the photograph must carry.

Access: Obtain rights to use the photograph and to obtain a transparency or copy of the negative.

Pricing

Pricing ultimately depends on the client's intended use. Typically, as with 2-D illustration, clients buy one-time publication rights. Artwork created for permanent exhibit or for broadcast media is priced relative to those markets.

There are several factors that specifically affect pricing for 3-D illustration and should be considered when negotiating with a client. In today's cost-cutting environment, 3-D illustrators are often asked to price their work on a scale similar to that for 2-D art (work painted, drawn, or bitmapped on a flat surface). Because of the complexity of 3-D versus 2-D art, the materials and techniques needed to create a 3-D piece may require considerable investment on the artist's part, because photographing the artwork requires an extra process and expense, and because the 3-D illustrator offers the client greater potential for use (since the lighting and perspective can be varied when photographing it), the comparison of 3-D to 2-D art is not realistic.

Often 3-D pieces are used to promote the client's product in a public place: a shop window or a counter display. Generally, a 3-D display is more valuable to a client than a flat picture because of the number of opportunities to exploit the work.

MATERIALS, EQUIPMENT, & SUPPORT SERVICES

The materials used to build a 3-D project can be much more expensive than art supplies used in 2-D illustration. Model-making materials used in miniature sets or architectural models, real objects used in assemblages, rare fabrics used in fabric collages, and casting resins for molded sculpture can add significantly to the cost of a job. It is up to the individual artist to determine if expenses for materials will be included in the original creator's fee or billed separately. If included, the artist should consider unforeseen circumstances that might lead to additional expenses and include an allowance for changes.

Model makers must maintain large facilities and extensive equipment to produce their work—often not just a single piece of sculpture, but also a complete setting. And they may need to hire extra help for especially detailed or large projects. If the deadline is short, the model maker may not only have to hire help but may also have to refuse other valuable work in order to meet the client's needs. The client should be aware that giving the artist sufficient time to complete the project is an important factor in controlling costs. Because the model maker's overhead is higher than that for the typical 2-D illustrator, these added expenses are generally reflected in a model maker's fees. A client who requests a piece of sculpture that has been cast from a living model, molded on a vacuum-forming unit, and "gold" plated should expect to pay a considerably higher price than for digitally produced flat art. If cost is a primary concern to the client, dimensional illustrators frequently offer options, such as simplifying the artwork or, if possible, creating a smaller original.

PHOTOGRAPHY COSTS

In order to photograph 3-D pieces, the dimensional illustrator also must invest in photography and lighting equipment or pay for the services of a photographer. Another pricing consideration is the number of different photographic images that may be needed for a variety of uses.

Billing

Few clients like surprises, so it is advisable to estimate costs as closely as possible at the time of the agreement. Clients should be informed of the potential for additional expenditures for supplies and be alerted in advance when photographic expenses and materials will be billed separately. It is good practice, when billing separately, to submit receipts and/or an itemized list with the invoice. Expenses for projects that require support services (mold making, vacuum forming, plating, engraving, or foundry casting) can increase significantly. The client should be fully informed of any such anticipated expenses, which, again, can either be billed separately or reflected in the artist's creative fee.

Specific Trade Practices

In addition to the general trade practices listed in the beginning of this chapter, the following trade practices have been used traditionally for Dimensional Illustration and thus are accepted as standard:

1. If the client wishes to display the artwork, dimensional illustrators have reportedly charged a fee in addition to the base one-time use price. The display usage fee should be agreed upon in the initial purchase order.
2. The payment terms should be negotiated prior to the sale, and these terms should be stated on the invoice, including provisions for late payment. As they largely reflect the graphic artist's labor, invoices should be made payable upon receipt.
3. An advance payment, termed a "material advance," may be requested for large projects.
4. Additional payment is routinely paid to an artist when (a) the client requests artwork changes that were not part of the original agreement, and (b) sales taxes must be collected on all artwork, except when original work is returned to the dimensional illustrator.
5. Terms of joint authorship and ownership of the photographic image should be accepted by all parties (the dimensional illustrator, the photographer, and, where applicable, the client) and stated in the agreement. Data indicates that a dimensional illustrator who allows the copyright to become the property of the photographer receives substantially higher compensation than for work with shared copyright.
6. If a job is cancelled, ownership of all artwork and copyright is retained by the artist. If a job based on

"documentary" work or other original art belonging to a client is canceled, payment of a time and/or labor charge is common.

7. Customary and usual expenses, such as travel costs, consultation time, shipping and mailing charges, and other out-of-pocket expenses for materials (film, model-making supplies, casting resins, and fabric), as well as fees for production services not performed by the dimensional illustrator (such as vacuum forming), outside services such as photography and processing, model fees, and additional production staff are usually billed to the client separately as they occur. An expense estimate, which states that the estimate is subject to amendment, can be included in the original written agreement with the client.

Fantastic Art

Although all illustration is imaginative, much of it, inspired by everyday experience and culture, reflects the real world. Illustrators who specialize in fantastic art help us view the world in an extraordinarily different way—they create the unimaginable, the unknown, and the futuristic. Creators of fantasy, science fiction, space fantasy, horror, the grotesque, and the surreal produce images that amaze, delight, enchant, enthrall, and sometimes scare us.

Traditionally, fantastic art has been largely confined to illustration and painting. Today, it is commonly found in films, TV programs, comic books and graphic novels, children's literature, video games, and collectible card games, but it may also be used for editorial and advertising purposes for a variety of media and products. The genre includes elements of magic, mysticism, the occult, and supernatural forces. Stories are often set in exotic and alien fantasy worlds or based on tales from mythology and folklore.

Fantastic art is generally priced according to the market for which it is commissioned, such as children's book illustration, comic book art, video game art, etc. Some illustrators working in this genre also sell their originals as fine art and limited edition prints of the originals to collectors. They promote and market their art online via personal websites and blogs and social networking sites, as well as at comic and science fiction conventions. An annual juried art contest devoted to fantastic art is sponsored by and published as *Spectrum: The Best in Contemporary Fantastic Art*. Entry forms are available at www.spectrumfantasticart.com.

Concept Art

A popular discipline within the fantasy art genre is concept art. A concept artist is in charge of the creation of new ideas and concepts that develop the look and feel of video games, animations, movies, short films, comic books, and advertising. The concept artist is a visual problem solver who helps game developers, movie directors, and other creatives give life to their vision. Artists visualize and create art for characters, clothing, creatures, worlds, architecture, technology, and vehicles that do not yet exist.

While the concept artist role is not new, having been used by animation studios for at least a century, the demand for concept artists is at an all-time high due to the explosive growth of the visual and multimedia entertainment sector.

Concept art is a form of illustration that involves the presentation of ideas that grow over many iterations. The concept artist starts by working from a brief, supplied by the art or creative director, that lays out design factors such as color schemes, rough design concepts, environmental background, real world examples, and any other factors that the lead creators are looking for in the final product. The artist takes the brief and sketches many rough thumbnails, leading to a design prototype. Lead designers, creatives, and other developers will then add their ideas and critiques to the design for the concept artist to incorporate into his/her next draft. The process continues back and forth until everyone is satisfied. Visual effects teams and animators execute these ideas and use them for production. In the motion picture and digital media industry, concept artists also help design storyboards, which detail camera moves.

Concept art is not only used to develop a work but also to show the project's progress to directors, clients, and investors. Once the development of the work is complete, concept art may be reworked and used for advertising and promotion of the end product.

SKILLS NEEDED

While concept art can be created in any medium, the field has truly launched itself forward and embraced modern technology. The majority of concept artists today work in their preferred digital format, from 2-D painting programs to 3-D rendering software to a combination of both. Most work on tablets or desktop computers. In addition to mastering technology, concept artists need to know how to paint quickly and be proficient in their understanding of anatomy, color theory, lighting, and perspective. They must also be able to "see" in three dimensions. Drawings are presented in front, back, and profile views. Some concept artists specialize in world building, architecture, or character/creature design.

WORK ENVIRONMENT & PRICING

Many concept artists work in a highly collaborative team environment in a studio, although some are hired as freelancers or do a combination of studio and remote work. Due to the short deadlines, concept artists have to create new ideas and convey elaborate concepts frequently and very quickly, so it is advantageous for them to build a strong visual library of ideas, shapes, fabrics, textures, and other similar concepts.

Concept artists can be found in several different disciplines, so pricing for freelance work would be similar to other forms of illustration in those disciplines.

{ 8 }

Cartooning
& Comics

This chapter discusses the markets available for both staff and freelance cartoonists and comic artists. While staff positions for editorial cartooning are shrinking, and the market is highly competitive, especially for newspaper syndication, there are increasing opportunities in digital media, alternative comic books, and graphic novels.

CARTOONIST *is commonly used to mean both a cartoonist and a comic artist, but there are differences in the media that these illustrators create.*

A cartoonist *is a creator of ideas, who makes political points or tells jokes using only one compelling picture. A cartoonist may specialize in types of cartoons that range from a gag (a visual joke with the punch line in the caption) to more detailed cartoons that include editorial, political, or adult subject matter, among other topics. Cartoons appear to be easy to create because they are relatively simple in style, but in fact, creating cartoons is a highly demanding specialization, usually requiring a long apprenticeship—years of practice developing a style and sense of humor.*

By contrast, comic artists *are visual storytellers who use sequential images to develop characters, various points of view, and plots through comic strips, comic books, or book-length graphic novels. Developing comics can be incredibly complex, detailed, and time-consuming.*

Most cartoonists and comic artists are freelancers, though some work on staff at newspapers and other publications, including magazines and digital formats. In addition, cartoons and comics are used by publishing houses; advertising agencies; greeting card publishers; and television, animation, motion picture, and commercial art studios. Cartoons and comics are also sought by editors and art directors to enhance textbooks, training materials, in-house publications, novelty items, and posters. Although the field has traditionally been dominated by men, the number of published works by women is on the rise.

Magazine Cartooning

The magazine cartoon is probably the most popular of the graphic arts; media surveys invariably place cartoons among readers' first preferences. Magazine or gag cartoons are created by freelance cartoonists who usually conceive the idea, draw the cartoon, and then offer it for sale to appropriate magazines. Magazine cartoonists bring a unique blend of writing and drawing skills to every piece. A magazine cartoon must be staged as graphic theater that instantly communicates a situation and characters. A good gag cartoon says it faster and with more impact than a paragraph of descriptive words and, most importantly, makes you laugh.

Pricing

The pricing of freestanding magazine cartoons is different from that of other forms of illustration. Cartoons are purchased as a complete editorial element, similar to a freelance feature article, at fixed rates determined by each publication. It should also be noted that it is often an editor, rather than an art director, who is responsible for selecting or assigning cartoons. A handful of magazines (such as *The New Yorker*) give additional compensation to those cartoonist contributors who are closely identified with that particular magazine. In those instances, the cartoonist may have a contract providing an annual signature fee, bonuses, and, in a few cases, fringe benefits in return for first look at the cartoons. When a cartoonist works with a writer, often called a "gagman," the writer gets 25% of the fee paid by the publication. Future payments for re-use of cartoons are usually worked out between the writer and artist, especially if they work together regularly.

Among the factors affecting prices for magazine cartoons are whether the cartoon is black and white or color; the size of reproduction; the magazine's geographical distribution, circulation, impact, and influence; the importance of cartoons as a regular editorial element; the extent of the rights being purchased; and the national reputation of the cartoonist. Since the list is composed of objective and subjective factors and the mix in each case is different, rates vary considerably from magazine to magazine. Magazines do not usually publicize what they pay for cartoons, so cartoonists should contact the publications that they want to submit work to about rates.

See Figure 8-1 for a few sample rates paid by magazines for cartoons. Because many cartoonists and humorous illustrators work in overlapping markets, readers should also refer to Chapter 7, Illustration, for related topics.

Submitting Art

Unless a cartoonist is under contract to a magazine, art submission is normally done on a speculative basis, which means the artist assumes all risks with no promise of payment unless the work is bought. It is important to have an organized plan. Artists should review cartoons found in their targeted publications and submit work that reflects that style. It is helpful to check first with a magazine to find out if it is still looking at unsolicited material.

To a beginning cartoonist, patience and persistence are a must. Presuming they are appropriate, not only will continued submittals provide practice, but they will familiarize an editor with your style and capabilities, setting the stage for eventual successes. In addition to submitting cartoons, another way to get noticed by magazine editors and publishers is to have a strong online presence of your work, either on your own website or on a third-party portfolio site.

Submission guidelines for most magazines are available online on the publication's website. Check each specific magazine's submission policy—some prefer digital submissions, sent as PDF attachments to e-mails; others require submissions uploaded to a specific site; and a few still accept hard copies sent by U.S. mail. Below are some very general guidelines:

* Send between 10 and 20 single- or multi-panel cartoons to a magazine at one time. Each cartoon should fill the center of an 8 1/2 x 11-inch sheet.
* If submitting hard copies, do not send originals!
* Never send the same cartoon to more than one U.S. publisher at a time. Multiple submissions, however, are acceptable to many European and other overseas publishers.
* Label each cartoon with your name, address, phone number/fax, and e-mail address. For personal inventory control, discreetly number each piece.
* To have mailed cartoons returned, include a self-addressed stamped envelope.
* Keep good records about what was sent to whom, and when. See the Appendix for a sample Artwork Inventory Form.

Trade Practices

In the ideal relationship between cartoon buyer and seller, the following trade practices would be accepted as standard. In reality, many transactions do not go smoothly, and the artist must be prepared to adapt when problems arise. It is up to artists to behave in their best self-interest

8–1 Sample Fees for Magazine & Custom Cartooning

Magazine Cartoons

(Fees paid to individual cartoonists per cartoon; original cartoons, unless noted otherwise)

PRINT

Reader's Digest	$150
The Funny Times	$30–60 (reprint)
The New Yorker	$200
Woman's World	$150

DIGITAL

AC Business Media	$190 (website cartoons)
The New Yorker	$200 (web exclusive)
The Weekly Humorist:	$20

PRINT & DIGITAL

Playboy	$80

Custom Cartooning

(Fees paid to individual cartoonists per cartoon)

Corporate internal use	$700
Personal blogs	$200–300

Additional Fees (% of original fee)

USAGE

Reuse in original market	115–170%
Sale of original art	100–500%

CANCELLATION & REJECTION

(% of original project fee)

Prior to completion of sketches	0–50%
After completion of sketches	25–50%
After completion of finished art	40–100%

Illustrators who charge by the hour bill for the number of hours worked up to the date of cancellation or rejection, plus any expenses incurred.

RUSH FEES (% added onto normal fee)

24-hour turnaround	50–75%
48-hour turnaround	25–50%
Holidays & weekends	10–50%

The above rates and fees were compiled from the results of a national survey of graphic artists conducted by the Graphic Artists Guild in 2020. Responses were based on rates charged in 2018 and 2019.

and even be prepared to lose a sale if conditions do not meet their expectations.

1. Payment is due upon acceptance of the work, net 30 days, never on publication.
2. Artists normally sell only first reproduction rights unless otherwise stated.
3. Under copyright law, cartoonists retain copyright ownership of all work they create. Copyright can be transferred only in writing.
4. Purchasers should make selections promptly (within two to four weeks) and promptly return cartoons not purchased.
5. Return of original artwork to the artist is expected unless otherwise negotiated.
6. The Graphic Artists Guild is opposed to the use of work-made-for-hire contracts, in which authorship and all rights that go with it are transferred to the commissioning party and the independent artist is treated as an employee for copyright purposes only. The independent artist receives no employee benefits and loses the right to claim authorship or to profit from future use of the work forever. In any situation, cartoons created by the initiative of the artist are ineligible to be works-made-for-hire.
7. The terms of sale should be specified in writing in a contract or on the invoice.

Editorial Cartooning

Editorial or political cartoons have had a long history in America, going back to the colonies and Benjamin Franklin's 1753 cartoon, "Join or Die," which illustrated how a complex political issue could be distilled into a single, powerful image. The art form came of age in the United States during the Civil War, when cartoonist Thomas Nash created some of the most recognizable images in U.S. politics that are still used today, including Uncle Sam, the Democratic donkey, and the Republican elephant. To this day, editorial cartoons have been a popular contribution to political dissent, epitomizing freedom of expression in America.

Staff Cartoonists

A few fortunate editorial cartoonists still work on staff at newspapers, but these positions are rare. Their salaries vary greatly with the circulation and status of the paper and the reputation and experience of the cartoonist. Although editorial cartoonists are generally paid less than illustrators in other markets, the job provides both fringe benefits and more stability than freelancing. Some editorial cartoonists can compensate for the disparity in income by selling reprints.

Other advantages afforded staff cartoonists are they often have significant exposure and name recognition by being published in a widely circulated newspaper. Some are syndicated nationally while on staff with a base paper. As with comic strip artists, their earnings received from syndication depend on the terms of their specific contracts and the number and size of the newspapers buying their work (see the Newspaper Syndication section later in this chapter).

At the turn of the last century, there were about 2,000 editorial cartoonists employed on staff at daily newspapers in the United States. Despite editorial cartoons often going viral on social media, the number of full-time staff cartoonists is rapidly shrinking, from approximately 100 ten years ago to only about 30 today, after heavy journalism lay-offs in the media industry in 2019. Their demise mirrors the state of newspapers themselves: the number of publications, especially major dailies, is shrinking, creating ever-increasing budget constraints at the remaining papers. As budgets tightened, the relative creative freedom editorial cartoonists once enjoyed, came under tighter scrutiny by editors.

Ironically, social media (fueled by the current divisiveness reflected in U.S. society) has also contributed to the demise of the staff editorial cartoonist. The outraged moralistic mobs on social media ranting against political cartoons with either a far-left or far-right slant have caused newspapers—afraid of losing even more revenue and subscribers—to buckle under the backlash. For example, *The New York Times* first terminated syndicated cartoons in 2019 over the furor of a cartoon printed in its international edition, and then a few months later, ended its in-house political cartoons as well. Even several newspapers that still have cartoonists on staff furloughed them during the COVID-19 pandemic.

The position of staff editorial cartoonists may be diminished, but their visual commentary remains as popular and as relevant as ever, especially in the current political climate. As former *International New York Times* editorial cartoonist Patrick Chappatte wrote, "Political cartoons were born with democracy. And they are challenged when freedom is."

Two digital start-up endeavors, The Nib and Counterpoint, begun by editorial cartoonists, are aiming to show how the popularity of cartoons can be harnessed into a successful online business model or stable new revenue stream for editorial cartoonists.

Freelance Cartoonists

Sometimes freelance editorial cartoonists sell their work to major, daily newspaper op-ed pages or to weekly news magazines. Rates vary, but they are generally based on the placement of the work, such as the leisure or advertising section, the column width of the piece, whether the drawing is an original or a reprint, and the reputation of the artist. Well-known artists generally are sought for large commissions such as covers. Freelance editorial cartoonists without national recognition are rarely considered. Artists should check with individual papers regarding their interest in freelance contributions before sending work.

Comics Journalism

Comics journalism, also referred to as *graphic journalism*, is a form of visual storytelling that covers news or nonfiction events using the framework of comics—a combination of words and drawn images. Instead of the one or two panels depictive of editorial cartoons, comics journalists might use the comic strip or the longer graphic novel format to cover real-life events and issues for news organizations, publications, or publishers. Historically, prior to photography, pictorial representation—usually engravings—of news events were used in publications, but today graphic journalism is at an all-time peak.

Most recently, writers, journalists, and illustrators have used graphic journalism to cover foreign and domestic affairs. Word balloons are actual quotes and sources are actual people featured in each story. There is no strict format: there may be narrative and explanatory text as well as word bubbles and other types of illustration may be included, such as infographics. Examples of topics covered by comics journalists include corporate crime, the history and plight of the Palestinian people, a series on Cuban culture and politics, a look inside death row, and a series chronicling a Syrian refugee family resettling in the United States, among others.

Comics journalism is published in many different formats as well, such as standalone comic books and graphic novels, serialization in the Sunday edition of a newspaper over several months, multiple-part series, and as collaborations with established publications and small presses. The genre also appears online on comics websites, such as Drawing the Times, Cartoon Movement, Graphic Journalism, and The Nib.

Syndication

Many freelance cartoonists develop comic strips, panels, or editorial cartoons for major national and international syndicates that edit, print, package, market, and distribute them to newspapers and magazines throughout the world. Since the number of newspapers using syndicated material is limited, the field is highly competitive. Few new strips are introduced in any given year by the major syndicates (perhaps only one or two per syndicate), and sales of these new features are usually limited to the somewhat rare instance of an existing feature being dropped. The more numerous smaller syndicates typically offer better contract terms but provide fewer services and much less sales support. The last alternative, self-syndication, allows cartoonists to retain all rights to their work and to keep all profits. The trade-off is that cartoonists must be their own salespersons. Self-syndication also can be difficult because newspapers prefer to buy comics from dependable syndicates that screen and manage the artists. Secondary markets such as weekly newspapers and alterative newspapers are less dependent on the major syndicates and more agreeable to working with self-syndicated cartoonists.

Submissions

Most syndicates have specific guidelines for submissions, which vary by syndicate. For example, some accept submissions only via U.S. mail, others accept only by e-mail, and some will accept either method. Syndicate submission guidelines usually are available on the company's website. The following are generally accepted guidelines for syndicate submissions, but artists should check the individual syndicate's requirements before submitting:

* Submissions usually include a presentation kit comprised of a "character sheet" (drawings of all characters, their names, and perhaps a descriptive paragraph) and a minimum of 24 daily strips and two Sunday strips.
* It is customary practice to send the same strip submission package to all syndicates simultaneously. Acceptance by more than one may add to the artist's negotiation leverage.

Trade Practices

When a cartoonist is selling a strip, it is tempting to sign the first contract offered. No matter how tempting it is, cartoonists owe it to themselves to prepare to negotiate contracts as well as they can and to understand all terms thoroughly. There is no substitute for knowledgeable legal counsel in contract negotiations. A syndication attorney with expertise in cartooning, visual arts, copyright, and/or literary property contracts is recommended.

When establishing a relationship with a reputable attorney, it is important to be explicit and upfront about both the work to be done and the cost. Transparency will pay dividends in efficiency and money.

Foremost among the terms that are changing in the field are the monetary split between the syndicate and the artist, ownership of the feature, and the length of the contract. The split for newly syndicated cartoonists is still fixed at the customary 50/50, but it is more common for artists renewing their contracts to achieve a better split, such as 60/40 or even higher. A few artists are winning a percentage of gross rather than net receipts.

Syndicates in the past have demanded copyright ownership of the feature, and a few still begin negotiations by requesting it. Artists benefit so much more economically and artistically from retaining ownership that over the last decade it has become standard for artists to win this point in negotiations. Artists must be alert to the many contract terms syndicates promote to undercut the value of the artists' copyright. For example, most syndicates demand a right of first refusal for renewals, and some major syndicates even require that they be paid their income split for some period of time after termination of the contract.

Contracts for newly syndicated artists that formerly ran for 20-year terms are being negotiated with much shorter renewal dates that are based on the syndicate achieving satisfactory sales of the feature. The flexibility created by ownership of the feature and periodic renegotiations benefit the cartoonist, whose bargaining leverage may increase considerably over the contract period if the work is successful, and who may therefore be able to negotiate better terms upon renewal. Depending on the other contract terms and the attitude of the syndicate (which varies considerably), the initial contract term, plus a fairly easy-to-achieve renewal, can be expected to last for a combined 10 to 15 years (3,650 to 5,475 cartoons). Under these circumstances, artists should not sign syndicate contracts unless the terms are acceptable for the long-term.

A number of well-known cartoonists have negotiated or renegotiated contracts with major syndicates on terms more favorable to the artist, such as shorter contracts, better income splits, guaranteed minimums, signing bonuses, and the right of the cartoonist to own and manage their potentially lucrative licensing rights. Cartoonists who are offered a syndicate contract should keep these terms in mind.

Syndicated cartoonists' earnings are based on the number of newspapers that carry their strips or panels and the circulation levels of these papers. Syndicates charge more money to sell content to large publications with higher circulation numbers. For example, small newspapers may pay less than $5 per week for a comic while large papers pay higher fees of $10, $20, $50, or more for a week's worth of cartoons. Comic strips also earn a higher price according to their popularity within a given market. Publications measure popularity not only by reader feedback but with page clicks of comics that appear online.

Progressive changes in syndicated contract terms reflect the decision of individual cartoonists to fight for more control over their creations and the increasing importance of character licensing in today's markets. In their contracts, savvy artists stipulate that the syndicate has the right to sell the strip only to newspapers and periodicals, with the artist retaining all other rights, including book rights. Cartoonists who negotiate effectively can benefit from their cartoon's success in the marketplace and can establish the potential for an ongoing stream of revenue in the future.

Following is a list of the largest syndicates. For the most current information, visit the websites of the individual syndicates.

NORTH AMERICAN COMIC SYNDICATES

Creators Syndicate, Inc.
310-337-7003
www.creators.com/submissions
Submissions: digital only
Home to *Heathcliff, Liberty Meadows*, and *Speed Bump*

King Features Syndicate, Inc. & ComicsKingdom.com
(Member of Hearst Entertainment & Syndication
   Group)
Submissions Editor—Comics
628 Virginia Drive, Orlando, FL 32803
212-969-7550
www.kingfeatures.com/contact-us/submission-
   guidelines
E-mail: submissions@comicskingdom.com
Submissions: mail or e-mail
Home to *The Amazing Spider-Man, Bizarro,* and *Zits*

Tribune Content Agency
www.tribunecontentagency.com/submissions
Submissions: electronic only
Home to *9 to 5, Dick Tracy,* and *Pluggers*

Universal Uclick (and GoComics)
(a subsidiary of Andrews McMeel Syndication)
E-mail: submissions@amuniversal.com
Submissions: e-mail only (files must be under 8 MB)
Home to *Calvin and Hobbes, Doonesbury, Garfield*, and
   Peanuts

Washington Post News Service & Syndicate
E-mail: cartoonsubmission@washpost.com
Submissions: e-mail (only as a multi-page PDF)
Home to *Candorville, Pickles*, and *Rudy Park*

Online Cartoon Sales

Online syndication of print cartoons, as well as syndication of cartoons that appear exclusively online, is a rapidly expanding market for cartoon material. Cartoons are now often offered as content on advertising-supported websites, or as opt-in syndicated content from search engines and content portals. Innovations such as animated and interactive editorial cartoons have also been introduced. While the market develops, there is real income potential here, and one encouraging trend is the development of online sites, such as goats (www.goats.com), Universal Uclick (www.syndication.andrewsmcmeel.com), and Cartoon Resource (www.cartoonresource.com), to name a few, that sell to a variety of markets and/or hire cartoonists.

Many online purchasers of cartoon rights offer very different business terms in their contracts than traditional print syndicates do. Artists should consider very carefully the specific rights they grant and how those rights are likely to be used in the electronic world. Like many publishers today, syndicates are attempting to retain exclusive electronic publication rights, and artists should consider this carefully when granting rights and negotiating fees. For more information on copyright and the Internet, see Chapter 11, Legal Rights & Issues.

Self-Syndicated Webcomics

Self-syndication online is fast becoming a legitimate way to market a comic strip or graphic feature. Several comic strips have created financially sustainable websites by utilizing a free content model, which is then subsidized through the selling of advertising, books, the original comic art, and other art-based merchandising.

Webcomic artists report that another source of subsidization for their comics is Patreon (www.patreon.com), an online membership platform for fans and a way for artists to achieve sustainable income to keep on creating. Fans pledge a monthly fee on a tiered subscription system in return for such things as sneak peeks, behind-the-scenes access, bonus materials, and online classes—the larger the pledge, the more perks the fan receives. Depending on the subscription tier, Patreon takes a 5–12% monthly commission from pledges, and the artist receives the remainder. In addition, whereas mainstream print syndication has editorial control of content, the Web allows for unlimited creative freedom and the ability to easily reach both broad and niche audiences.

Successful webcomics include *Penny Arcade* (www.penny-arcade.com), *Schlock Mercenary* (www.schlock-mercenary.com), *PvP* (www.pvponline.com), and *Saturday Morning Breakfast Cereal* (www.smbc-comics.com).

Comic Books

According to Comichron, sales of comic books for the Direct Market during 2019 ended on a note of growth as comics shops bought $528.1 million in comic books, graphic novels, and magazines from Diamond Comic Distributors, an increase of 2.23% or $11.5 million over 2018's total of $516.6 million. The beginning of the new decade promised another good year. January 2020 experienced something that never had happened before in the history of comics—an issue of *Wonder Woman* outsold all other comics that month, and the next month was the strongest February in three years. But, then COVID-19 hit in March and disrupted the industry: by mid-month, spring conventions had been cancelled and many businesses were required to close or cut hours to slow the spread. Supply-chain disruptions caused cash flow problems across the industry, forcing Diamond to announce it could no longer pay publishers. The full impact of the pandemic on this industry has yet to be seen.

Licensing prospects in TV, movies, video games, toys, and consumer products have emerged as the driving factors in determining if a comic book series will be continued. Sales rates that would have seemed low or of marginal profitability in the past are accepted today because of fear that discontinuation would affect licensing possibilities. For further information, see the Licensing and Merchandising section later in this chapter and Chapter 4, Maximizing Income.

Comic books, which are cinematic in style, lend themselves to film adaptation and have become a popular source of movie concepts. Writers conceive a story and develop a script or plot, often indicating specific views of the action to be portrayed. Some companies use a style in which scene descriptions and full dialogue are given just like in a screenplay. Others do not indicate panel breaks or even specify the number of panels and may or may not indicate page breaks, giving the artist much more freedom in which to make a graphic statement.

Each monthly comic book (averaging 22 pages of story, with another ten pages of ads and letters) is produced in 28 days to meet distribution deadlines. (Some contracts used in the industry may contain a clause that penalizes the artist if deadlines are missed.) Such high-pressure working conditions mean that comic books are mass-produced in assembly-line fashion. Publishers divide production among people with special skills who complete a specific component in the process and then pass the work on to the next stage of production.

Artistic Specialties & Job Roles

Specialists in comic books generally include writers, pencil artists (pencilers), lettering artists (letterers), ink artists (inkers), and coloring artists (colorists). The editor generally assumes a tracking role, guiding the work along the path from freelancer to freelancer, to meet the company's deadlines and, on rare occasions, also serving as art director. The trend in at least the last decade shows an increasing number of comic book artists who write, draw, and ink their own stories, but even for such specialists, the rigors of the four-week deadline require severe discipline.

When comic books are created traditionally, pencilers lay out the action from the typewritten script and finish the art on Bristol board. The penciled board is passed on to the letterer, who letters the balloon text in ink and inks the balloon and panel borders. Next, the board goes to the inker, who inks the figures and backgrounds on each panel. (Background artists, if used, are usually subcontractors, assistants, or interns.) After the boards are reduced to 6 x 9-inch or 8.5 x 11-inch Strathmore paper, they are passed on to the colorist, who hand-colors and color-codes the photocopies of all 22 pages of the book. The boards and coded reductions are then sent to the separator, and finally the colored photocopies are sent to the printer for manufacture.

Digital technology has changed much of this process. Today, lettering is done exclusively on the computer, using font programs capable of approximating a letterer's handwriting. Both Marvel and DC Comics now have in-house lettering departments. A fairly recent trade practice, which is becoming more widespread, is inking pages on a blueline print. The pencilers scan their pencil drawings and transmit them digitally to the inker who then prints them out onto a sheet of Bristol board to ink. Once the inking is done, the inker scans the finished page and transmits them digitally to the publisher, whether the inks are on blueline printout or over the original pencils. Like lettering, coloring is also done exclusively on the computer. Color artists are still needed to do the computer coloring, but due to the necessary learning curve and the cost of the equipment, a more sizable initial investment is needed to become a colorist than in the past. Colorists submit their work on disk, which is then "edited" at the publishing company before being sent to a separator for creation of the final film.

Pricing

Freelance artists working in this industry are expected to meet minimum production quotas. They report being paid a page rate set by the publisher for each page completed. Page rates vary according to specialization, but overall, they have barely increased in decades.

Since comic books are paid on the piecework system, the faster an artist works, the more he or she will earn, although, in order to meet production deadlines, artists are expected to complete a minimum number of pages in each production cycle. Letterers, for example, are expected to complete at least 66 pages over three weeks but strive to complete ten pages per day, five days a week. Many artists must work ten hours a day, six days a week, to make a living wage. In a survey done in 2015 by comics artist David Harper of www.sktchd.com, almost 60% of the 186 comic book artists who responded reported they cannot make a living from comic book art alone. Page rates at independent publishers are even lower than mainstream comic publishers. Comic book publishers generally pay artists a lower page rate for reprinting an original publication.

As in other genres, the more popular an artist or writer, the higher the company's projected sales. Therefore, all aspects of compensation, including royalties, are open to negotiation.

If a comic book's net domestic sales exceed 75,000 copies, a royalty on the excess is usually paid to the writer, penciler (or other layout artist), and inker. However, few titles actually earn royalties. In the last decade, it's been a general practice to give royalties only to the top ten selling comic books. If royalties are paid, they are usually graduated according to the degree of creative input and the number of units sold, but generally range from 2% to 5% of the cover price. Artists who perform more than one function receive a higher royalty; if several creators are involved in a project, they all share the royalties.

Freelance agreements with the major comic book publishers provide for the return of original art. The

8–2 Page Rates Paid by Comic Book Publishers

Scripts	$25–125
Inks	$20–160
Line Art	$20–225
Colors	$18–135
Letters	$5–45
Cover	$150–800
Script & Art	$31–250
All Art	$70–300

The above page rate ranges were compiled from the results of a survey of comics professionals, conducted by Creator Resource in 2017. There were 142 respondents who anonymously reported page rates they had been paid by comic book publishers. Creator Resource also broke the data down by publisher. To see which publishers were represented and how rates differ by publisher, go to http://www.creatorresource.com/page-rates-2017/.

artist(s) may assign, sell, or transfer ownership only of the physical original. Since several artists work on a given piece, ownership of the original art must be negotiated; normally only the penciler and inker receive original artwork, though a hand-painted piece is given to the colorist. In the traditional process, the penciler receives two-thirds of the originals, and the inker receives one-third. When the pages have been inked on blueline, the penciler retains the pencil drawings, and the inker keeps the inked pages. The artists, however, do not retain any of the copyrights to the work, as the contracts usually contain a work-made-for-hire clause, which transfers legal authorship and all rights to the publisher. For more detailed information about work made for hire, see Chapter 11, Legal Rights & Issues.

Figure 8–2 lists representative page rates for comic book art by type of skill. The data was collected anonymously from a sample of 142 comics professionals in a survey conducted by Creator Resource. The price ranges in the chart do not reflect any of the above considerations and do not constitute specific prices for particular jobs. The buyer and seller are free to negotiate, with each artist independently deciding how to price the work, after taking all factors into account.

Alternative Comic Books

Alternative comics, while not new, became very popular in the late 1990s and have led to a burgeoning interest in longer comic stories, including book-length graphic novels (see later in this chapter). Alternative comics promote the comic-book medium as an art form for creative expression rather than as an assembly-line business. The result has been a form of comic books more highly regarded as an adult form of literature. With editors and art directors counted as fans, small-press or self-published creators of comic books have found inroads into commercial and editorial illustration.

Unlike other cartooning markets, the alternative comic book market is not dominated by work-made-for-hire contracts. Usually the artist also writes the stories and frequently acts as the publisher and distributor. Or, creator-owned art may be done speculatively and submitted to publishers on a freelance basis similar to the way gag cartoons are. Often, these stories are bought by small presses at a low page rate, such as $50 a page. In some cases, they may be contributed to smaller presses that cannot afford to pay but give artists the opportunity to have their work in print and circulation. For artists who feel strongly about their work, the major advantage of working this way is the ability to maintain full control of the content and the copyrights.

Trade Practices

The following trade practices for comic book art have been used traditionally, and thus are accepted as standard:

1. The intended use of the art must be stated clearly in a contract, purchase order, or letter of agreement stating the price and terms of sale.

2. In non-work-for-hire contracts, artists normally sell first North American reproduction rights only, unless otherwise stated. Ancillary rights (TV, movie, European distribution, paper or hardback printing, or character licensing) are negotiable and are often shared by the publisher and the artist for a fixed period of up to five years, at which time full rights revert to the artist. (It is wise for creators of alternative comics to retain ancillary rights, especially for TV and movies, since there is a growing interest in these rights.)

3. If the artwork is to be used for other than its original purpose, the price for that usage should be negotiated as soon as possible. The secondary use of the art may be of greater value than the primary use. Artists should negotiate reuse arrangements with the original commissioning party with speed, efficiency, and respect for the client's position.

4. Deadlines for delivery of finished art and rough sketches should be outlined in the contract. The clause should also specify what payments are due to the artist in the event the project is canceled or rejected. For negotiable fee suggestions, see the sections describing cancellation ("kill") and rejections fees in Chapter 3, Professional Issues.

5. The artist guarantees that the art is original and does not infringe on the copyrights of others and that the artist has the authority to grant rights to the publisher.

6. An artist can request to be indemnified by the publisher for any suits arising from the use of the art by the publisher that might infringe on the rights of others, and also against any suits arising from a request on the publisher's part, such as making a character look like a famous person or an existing image.

7. In the case of creator-owned art (versus work-made-for-hire art), the publisher agrees to copyright the work in the artist's name.

8. For non-work-made-for-hire contracts, revisions without the artist's consent are unacceptable; artists should be consulted to protect the integrity of their work.

9. Fees should be established to be paid to the artist in the event artwork is lost or damaged due to the publisher's negligence.

10. The publisher agrees to publish the book within a specific period of time, and upon failure to do so, the rights revert back to the artist (sometimes called reversion rights).

11. Royalties, if paid, are graduated according to the degree of creative input and the units sold, but they are figured as a percentage of the cover price. Royalties are paid either quarterly or semi-annually, at which time the artist receives a statement of sales.

12. Return of original artwork to the artist is automatic unless otherwise negotiated. The artwork is often divided between the artists working on the project (primarily the penciler and inker). Most artists view original artwork as a subsidiary income, selling it either directly to collectors or through an agent.

13. Publishers usually provide the artist with up to 10 free copies of the book, but additional copies are often negotiated. Most publishers offer the artist a discount off the list price on purchases of the book.

14. Artists considering working on speculation often assume all risks and should take these into consideration when offered such arrangements; for details, see the Speculation section in Chapter 3, Professional Issues.

Although work-made-for-hire contracts dominate most areas of this field (except for alternative comics), the Graphic Artists Guild is opposed to their use because authorship and all rights that go with it are transferred to the commissioning party and the independent artist is treated as an employee for copyright purposes only. The independent artist receives no employee benefits and loses the right to claim authorship or to profit from future use of the work forever. Additional information on works made for hire can be found in Chapter 11, Legal Rights & Issues.

Book-Length Formats

Several different types of comic-strip products in book-length form are found on the market.

Cartoon & Comic Collections

The traditional book format for cartoons or comic strips is the collection or anthology, in which cartoons that were originally published in newspapers or magazines are collected into a single volume.

Similarly, comic books are often reprinted as a collection of stories in book format. In the comics industry, they are referred to as trade paperbacks, but they may have either a soft or hard cover. Trade paperbacks feature either one story arc from a single title or a common theme or story arc connecting stories from several titles. The collection often includes additional art, such as alternate cover art, that did not appear in the original serialized comic books.

For reprints in book format, major comic book publishers pay artists a rate equal to either one half of the original page rate or a royalty based on the type of original work performed. The royalty is divided among the contributing artists and pro-rated by the portion of original art an artist did. For example, if the book has 100 pages and the royalty rate is 1%, an artist who created 10 of those 100 pages will receive a royalty of one-tenth of 1% or .10%.

Graphic Novels

A graphic novel (GN) is a lengthy narrative in comic strip form, published as a book. GNs are published as trade paperbacks or hard covers by either comic book publishers or by mainstream literary publishing houses. There are publishers and imprints that specialize in graphic novels, such as First Second, Graphix, and Papercutz. In 2019, Random House launched Random House Graphic, an imprint dedicated to graphic novels for the children's market.

The term "graphic novel" is evolving and generally refers to either a collection of stories initially published serially in comic books or an original, long-form narrative. The term has frequently been used to differentiate works from comic books designed for children or juveniles and to imply that the work is of a more serious, literary nature. However, the growth of the graphic novel genre for children and teens has exploded during the past decade—in both fiction and non-fiction (see following section).

In the publishing trade, the term graphic novel is sometimes extended to material that would not be considered a novel if produced in another medium. Collections of comic strips that do not form a continuous story, anthologies, collections of loosely related pieces, and even non-fiction comics are categorized by libraries and bookstores as "graphic novels" (similar to the manner in which dramatic stories are included in "comic" books). A comic created and published as a single narrative without prior appearance in a magazine, comic book, or newspaper is sometimes identified as an original graphic novel (OGN).

Overall sales of graphic novels in the United States and Canada in 2018 totaled $635 million, according to a joint estimate by ICv2 (www.ICv2.com) and Comichron (www.comichron.com). The popularity of the genre in the United States can be partly attributed to the graphic novel's Japanese cousin, *manga*. Outside of Japan, manga refers to comics originally published in Japan or works derivative of their artistic style. Literally translated as "whimsical pictures," manga has a long tradition dating back to the late 1800s and today represents a multi-billion-dollar global market. Wildly popular in Japan, manga encompasses a very diverse range of subjects and themes for readers of all ages and interests. Popular manga, aimed at mainstream readers, frequently involves science fiction, action, fantasy, and comedy. According to Time.com, manga is credited with expanding the traditionally male-dominated American comics market. This trend has caused major publishing houses to eagerly embrace the graphic novel genre. Today, there is an increasing interest by females in all comics: it is estimated that about 50% of adult comic book and graphic novel readers combined are female. The trend also is partially attributed to Marvel and DC featuring more female characters.

France and Belgium also have a long tradition in comics and comic books. Known by the French term, *bande dessinée* (literally "drawn strip"), Franco-Belgian comics are often viewed in the United States as equivalent to graphic novels, due to their more serious subject matter, but they may be long or short; bound or in magazine format.

GRAPHIC NOVELS FOR THE EDUCATION MARKET

The popularity of graphic novels over the past decade has extended to the elementary-school market. School librarians recognized early on that students were attracted to the genre and the demand was so high, they could barely keep titles on the shelf. Always looking for a way to get reluctant readers interested in reading, they began ordering whatever graphic novels were available. As publishers took notice and more titles were published for this market, librarians were able to make more educated choices about what they purchased.

Teachers, always exploring new ways to engage their students who have varied learning styles, also embraced the genre as a way of reaching visual learners. Struggling and reluctant readers are often put off when faced with a large block of text, but graphic novels are far less intimidating with their often fun and playful visuals. Graphic novels have proven to help students build literacy skills as well as gain reading motivation. The genre's emphasis on dialogue has also been a big help to learners of English as a new language.

According to Comichron, the biggest factor in increased sales for 2018 in the book channel for the comic book and graphic novel market (which includes chain bookstores, mass merchants, major online retailers, and Scholastic Book Fairs) was the sale of kid's graphic novels. The genre has grown beyond stories about superheroes. Teachers are using graphic memoirs and personal narratives in numerous ways for teaching literary elements and writing. Classic literature titles are also being published in a graphic novel format—not abridged or condensed versions, but faithful adaptations.

The genre has expanded to include non-fiction titles in science and social studies to augment the curriculum. These might be short graphic novels, such as a series about people of historical significance, or a standalone science topic. While there are strong publishing programs in non-fiction for young students and adults, there's not as much for middle and high school students—a market that publishers are looking to reach next.

Education is a growing market as well for comic artists seeking work. Comics and graphic novels now receive prominent attention at professional and educational conferences. In 2015, Comic-Con International added a special three-day line up of educational panels.

Pricing & Trade Practices

In the case of cartoon collections and graphic novels, book contracts vary widely—by publisher, genre, success of the author, and individual book—so it is advisable to consult a qualified literary agent who has connections in the comics publishing industry or a lawyer, especially one with experience in negotiating comics contracts. One place to look for an appropriate lawyer is at comics conventions; they often are presenters or serve on panels.

PUBLISHING OPTIONS

TRADITIONAL LITERARY BOOK PUBLISHERS

Contracts for graphic novels published by major book publishers are structured like other book deals: the contract specifies an advance and a royalty percentage. Once the royalties have paid back the advance, then the artist starts receiving the royalties. Advances vary greatly; royalties generally range from 2% to 10%, sometimes with escalators (increased royalties) once a sales point of 15,000 copies is reached. An illustrator who is also the author receives a higher royalty than an artist who does only the illustration. Higher royalties are given for hardcover books than for paperbacks. First-time comic authors cannot expect a very high advance and should know that an advance is not meant to support them while they work on the book. Very successful graphic novelists with a successful publishing record are able to negotiate higher rates.

Book publishers will want exclusive rights to publish and distribute the story and artwork. For that exclusive license, the publisher will pay an advance plus royalties. The copyright can be jointly held by the author and the illustrator if they are separate individuals working collaboratively. Sometimes, the author gets a publishing deal, and the artist is hired to do the illustrations. There are several different arrangements for how the writer and the artist are hired and by whom, and these arrangements affect how the advance and royalties are split. Both the working arrangement and the money split as well as all the related details should be spelled out in the contract(s).

Traditional book publishers often use the same boilerplate contracts for graphic novels that they use for prose books, with similar terms: grant of rights, territories, advances, royalties, delivery deadlines, editorial control, etc. In some cases, publishers are not familiar with the process of creating a graphic novel and how it differs from prose. Graphic novelists should review contracts carefully for terms and conditions that do not align well with the comics profession or work process and revise the contract accordingly.

Lawyer and contract expert, Katie Lane, recommends that graphic novelists first reach out to a lawyer when they are presented with a Deal Memo from the publisher. It is easier to negotiate changes and improve terms at that point in the process, since the Deal Memo will dictate what terms will show up in the contract.

Negotiating a book publishing contract can be a long process, taking place over several phone calls. Ms. Lane advises graphic novelists to be persistent and consistent in their message regarding terms, etc., even if it seems as if they have to repeat their concerns over and over again. In a traditional publishing house, many people work on a book project, so it is important that everyone you talk to hears your concerns. Preliminary talks may be with an editor, so it is good to get sticking points hashed out in advance because final contract negotiations may be with a contract negotiator, not the editor.

COMIC BOOK COMPANIES

Rates for graphic novels published by comic book companies are determined by either the page or the book (with covers sometimes negotiated separately). Arrangements vary by publisher, and royalties vary by book contract, even within the same publisher. Mainstream comic book publishers tend to pay by the page, while independent and small press publishers tend to pay 8–10% of the cover price for each book sold. Generally, any royalties tend to be lower than those paid by traditional book publishers.

Independent publishers often work on a model in which one artist is responsible for the complete work, from writing to finished art. Graphic novelists who work with independent publishers often retain the copyright to their work and are able to negotiate a percentage of profits from licensing everything from merchandise to movie and broadcast rights.

Comic book companies do not use Deal Memos as often as traditional book publishers do. However, graphic novelists still need to thoroughly understand all aspects and terms of the deal that is being offered. How does it fit into your life and career goals, will you still be able and have the time to work on other projects, etc.?

If you are not doing both the writing and drawing yourself and have been hired to work with a writer, the publishing company might try to present you both with a single contract. It is preferable for each of you to have your own contract with the publisher. Your agents or lawyers can communicate with each other to make sure there are common terms in each of your contracts. With separate contracts, you are less likely to be affected negatively if the other person breaks his/her contract.

SELF-PUBLICATION

The third publishing option for graphic novelists is to self-publish their book. Unlike working with a publisher, they will need to contract with printers and distributors themselves to manufacture and distribute it. To make it financially viable, they attempt to print it for 20% or less of the cover price. The books are then sold to comic distributors, such as Diamond, who resell them to comic shops and bookstores. The self-publisher receives 40% of the cover price from Diamond. Some graphic novelists have been able to make self-publishing a profitable venture.

ADDITIONAL CONTRACT CONSIDERATIONS

When presented with a contract, graphic novelists should not just accept unfavorable or unreasonable terms or ones that they are not comfortable with. Contracts between graphic novelists and publishers or distributors are negotiable. It is important for the artist to establish expectations up front on such matters as page length, whether sub-contractor(s) will need to be hired, the party responsible for production (scanning, book design, etc.), and the form in which the finished book will be delivered (original art or on disk). More and more publishers look for all aspects of production to be done by the artist. While this arrangement allows the artist to control the end-product, it is a huge additional workload, which should be factored into the artist's overall fee.

When reviewing a publisher's contract, make sure definitions for terminology are used consistently throughout the contract. Be aware of option clauses, such as ones in which you agree that the publisher will have first dibs on the next book you publish. Timelines can change and delays can happen. You may have other publishing projects you are already working on that end up being ready to be published first or for which you can get a better publishing deal. While some option clauses are fair, others have the effect of holding the author hostage. Also find out what terms are discretionary in a contract. What is the publisher's policy for enforcing terms, such as delays?

If you find as the project progresses that you cannot meet a deadline, you need to let your agent and the publisher know immediately. There are many people at a publishing company—not just an editor—working on your graphic novel to bring it to market. If you cannot meet a deadline, it impacts a lot of people and can even negatively affect the relationship your agent has built with the publisher. Schedules can be adjusted if you let the publisher know in advance, but if you just sit on it and miss the deadline, you will annoy a lot of people and possibly jeopardize your chances for a future publishing deal.

Although not recommended, if you are asked to sign

a work-for-hire contract, which gives the publisher or client the copyright to your work, make sure you review and understand the nine exceptions under U.S. Copyright Law in which work-for-hire contracts are permissible (listed in Chapter 11, Legal Rights & Issues). To compensate you for all the rights you are relinquishing, a work-for-hire contract should pay you more than other types of contracts in which you retain your copyright.

Graphic novelists need to follow through on all aspects of publication, such as getting the publisher to show them proofs, and be involved at all levels of promotion to ensure that the book is accurately described. Authors can expect that much of the promotion will fall on them, for example, book parties and promotion after publication. Taking on this responsibility can make a big difference in book sales; however, this expense also should be factored into the artist's advance or overall fee. It is in the creator's best interest to find out who follows foreign and domestic sales and to establish relationships with those departments to ensure these aspects of promotion are addressed.

To help maximize sales, it is also worth getting the publisher to assign a specific category to a book-length comic—memoir, politics, fiction, adaptation, etc.—in addition to the general genre of graphic novel. For example, a comic categorized as "autobiography" is more likely to be placed in multiple sections of a bookstore, which is more desirable than simply being relegated to a mixed-together graphic novel/manga section.

For further information, refer to the definitions of royalty contract terms found in the Children's Book Illustration section in Chapter 7, Illustration. Negotiating is covered under Chapter 1, Essential Business Practices, and contracts are discussed in depth in Chapter 12, Standard Contracts & Business Tools.

Reuse

Even during periods of growth, magazines have not proportionately increased payments to cartoonists and other artists. To make a viable income, cartoonists try to sell drawings repeatedly to secondary markets for use either in merchandising (T-shirts, coffee mugs, etc.) or in books as part of an anthology, textbook, or collection, which in turn will usually generate more reprints. Another option is selling cartoons as stock on websites that specialize in illustration and/or cartoons. Before entering into an agreement with a stock site, artists need to read its terms very carefully regarding exclusivity, payment amounts and arrangements, and to make sure they are retaining copyrights to their work. Reuse sales can be made in the United States and worldwide.

Trade Practices

Each publication has its own criteria for establishing a fee for reprints. Obviously, some drawings will generate additional fees, and others will not. Rarely, one will turn out to be immensely popular and more than cover the meager earnings from the others.

Artists should be sure to specify the terms of the sale in a contract or on the invoice. For example, if the work is to appear in traditional print media, such as a textbook, the following should be included:

For one-time, nonexclusive, English language, North American print rights only, in one hardcover edition, to be published by [name of publisher], entitled [title of publication]. All additional requests for usage by your organization or any other publication, except as specified above, are to be referred to [name of artist] to determine the appropriate reprint fee.

Trade practices allow for additional printings of the same edition without additional fees, but any change in the content of a book or in the arrangements of its elements would constitute a new edition that would be considered an additional use.

If the publisher wishes to purchase electronic publishing rights, the cartoonist should limit the license for use of the work to a specific period of time, such as a year, after which any additional or continued rights would be renegotiated. Language should also be included that prohibits changes to the work without the artist's approval and supervision.

For additional information on reuse, see Chapter 4, Maximizing Income.

Licensing & Merchandising

According to Licensing International's *Global Licensing Survey,* in 2018, the United States and Canada combined was the largest market for global licensed merchandise and services, accounting for 58% of the world's $280.3 billion in retail sales. The largest property type in licensed retail sales consistently has been entertainment and characters. When characters, such as Disney's Star Wars and Universal's Minions are licensed for a range of products, from toys and apparel to designer sheets and stationery, their creators can earn considerable additional income if they retain all or a significant percentage of the subsidiary rights to the property.

It is sometimes assumed that only nationally known syndicated characters are sought by licensing agents or manufacturers. With the tremendous growth in this area, however, there are now possibilities for cartoonists to develop characters specifically for product use. Cartoonists interested in pursuing this potentially lucrative application of their work should consult an attorney specializing in this field to ensure adequate copyright protection before presenting work to licensers or manufacturers.

Trade shows for character licensing and merchandising are held several times a year around the country. They provide a place for creators, licensors, syndicates, and manufacturers to explore business opportunities. To obtain a list of shows, see Part 5, Resources & References or contact the International Licensing Industry Merchandisers Association at www.licensing.org. For an extensive discussion of these opportunities, consult Chapter 4, Maximizing Income.

{ 9 }

Animation
& Motion

This chapter discusses the growing number of jobs involving animation and motion graphic design and illustration. Character animation and animated special effects are used in a wide range of applications—everything from feature films, TV commercials, and video games to biomedical research and simulator rides in theme parks. Likewise, motion graphics, which give the illusion of movement or transformation, are utilized in all screen-based media, especially entertainment and advertising.

CHARACTER ANIMATION—*such as flip books—started long before motion picture film was produced in the late 19th century. Film animation was introduced in 1900 and was effectively adapted for industrial uses in 1917 and for commercial uses in 1921. It has since been adapted for educational uses as well. In recent years, computers have enabled animation artists, who are skilled at creating the illusion of movement, to create images never before seen outside the imagination.*

*Today there is a huge demand for computer animation and effects, especially for animated entertainment content, partly driven by the expanding new medium of streaming services' constant need for product. Applications for animation are not limited to entertainment—they span varied fields and interests, such as biomedical research; scientific and educational films; litigation arts (forensic animation); television commercials, titles, and station IDs; feature films; visual effects in motion pictures, interactive games, and mobile devices; virtual-reality software and simulator rides for theme parks; spot sequences created for broadband Internet; and much more. Animated films (*Avatar *(2009),* The Lion King *(1994),* 101 Dalmatians *(1961), and* Snow White and the Seven Dwarfs *(1937)) figure prominently in the lists of the top 20 box-office-earning films of all time in the United States (adjusted for inflation).*

Animation is also in demand as an art form. Independent animated films, in a broad spectrum of styles and with their own markets and distribution channels, are usually shown at film festivals or competitions that showcase the artist's work. Independent filmmakers often create production companies to solicit development funds. Balancing art and commerce, they also bring their style to TV commercials and other commissioned projects.

The need to communicate a message that is compelling and stands out in the massive amount of screen content that society consumes daily has led to many opportunities for motion graphic designers. There is also an increasing demand for illustrators who can add motion to their work.

Animation

Traditional animators once worked with line drawings that were inked and then painted onto *cels* (celluloids, or cellulose acetate sheets) with watercolor or gouache. The process was difficult, time-consuming, and expensive. Often several animators were assigned to specific characters, backgrounds, or other segments of a project. The end result was almost always a team effort by a number of artists, each with his or her own area of expertise.

Computer animation has increased the level of sophistication, as in such mass-market movie successes as Disney's *Frozen* and *Zootopia*, Pixar/Disney's *Coco*, DreamWorks' *Shrek* films, and Twentieth Century Fox/Blue Sky Studio's *Ice Age* series. However, traditional hand-drawn 2-D animation endures and continues to delight viewers as evidenced in both films—Cartoon Saloon's *The Breadwinner* and Disney Animation's *The Princess and the Frog*—and TV shows—Disney's *Gravity* and Cartoon Network's *Steven Universe*. The 2016 Disney release, *Moana*, while largely produced in 3-D computer animation, creatively combined hand-drawn 2-D animation in the creation of Maui's conscience, the character Mini-Maui, who is embedded in Maui's intricate tattoos.

To be successful in today's market, an animator must be able to tell a story, have an in-depth understanding of creating lifelike movement, be proficient in traditional and computer animation techniques, and understand filming techniques, including timing, staging, lighting, squashing and stretching, and easing in and out. Animation artists may also work as illustrators, cartoonists, and designers for film.

Types of Animation

2-D ANIMATION

2-D animation created for TV, film, etc., can be hand-drawn in the traditional style, using pen and ink, or created with computer-generated imagery (CGI)—images produced digitally using a software program. However today, even drawings done by hand, as well as the backgrounds, are drawn directly into computer programs, using Cintiqs or Wacom tablets. Characters are created and/or edited using either 2-D bitmap or 2-D vector graphics. 2-D computer animation is used for cartoons and some special effects. 2-D morphing tools allow for the integration of dissimilar imagery into cohesive visuals. Software commonly used for 2-D animation includes Toon Boom Harmony, TV Paint Animation, Adobe Animate, After Effects with DUIK plugin, and Adobe Photoshop. Nuke is used for compositing CG animation.

Rendering, used in both 2-D and 3-D computer animation, is the process of getting the final assembled animation scenes or pieces out of the computer in the format of a sequence of individual frames. The aim of rendering is to generate a series of individual pixel-based frames or a video clip.

Artists who create storyboards (visual presentations using sequential frames) for commercials and movie effects sequences can enhance the impact of their storyboards with programs such as Toon Boon Storyboard Pro, which allows them to create simple movement and effects with still images. A moving storyboard, called an *animatic,* is a video using camera movements, a select number of drawings, a limited amount of 2-D animation, and a sound track (for a detailed explanation of storyboards and animatics, see the Preproduction Illustration section in Chapter 7, Illustration). After Effects is used heavily to create TV commercials in the motion graphics industry and for corporate sales presentations, as well as for some web animations and feature films.

3-D OR COMPUTER ANIMATION

3-D animation uses modeling and/or digitizing to create objects that not only have shape and dimension but also can be viewed from any angle. Computer-generated imagery (CGI) is commonly used in 3-D computer animation when doing special effects. With the help of a complex rendering program, the artist can project the object onto a screen or into a virtual environment. Then 2-D texture maps (a surface pattern like wallpaper) are often applied to the 3-D image to give it a realistic surface.

THE 3-D PROCESS

The process of creating a 3-D animation is complex, involving many tasks and numerous people with different skill sets. The structure and framework used to push such a complicated process forward efficiently and affordably is the *3-D animation pipeline*, a system of people, hardware, and software aligned to work in a specific sequential order. The production pipeline has three main stages: pre-production, production, and post-production. Each segment of the 3-D industry may use the stages somewhat differently, but the main structure stays intact. Likewise, the specifics of a pipeline may differ by project, but the three stages remain the same.

Pre-production is the researching, designing, and planning phase of the entire project, which is split between two teams: the design team and the management team. The design team creates the idea, story, and designs, while the management team prepares the production plan, which includes the budget, teams, and timeframes. This phase includes the following steps: idea generation, story creation, scriptwriting, storyboarding, and animatics (animating the storyboard), and design (concept, character, costumes, props, environment). The overall mood is also established in this phase.

Production is where all the pre-production efforts transform into action. Visual elements will be handed out to the designated teams and artists. Team leaders make sure quality and time frames match those of the pre-determined plan and that all goes smoothly. The steps in this phase are 3-D layout, modeling, texturing, rigging, and animation; VFX; lighting; and rendering.

Post-production is where final touches are added to make the animation look more polished and professional. The possible steps in post-production include compositing, 2-D VFX, color correction, and final output. The most common output format is digital video which is compatible with most digital devices and can be played on the Internet.

THE 3-D INDUSTRY

Motion picture computer animation is the highest echelon of the field. Perhaps the most well known of all animation houses today are Pixar/Disney, Walt Disney Animation Studios, DreamWorks Animation, and Industrial Light & Magic (acquired by The Walt Disney Company in 2012). These studios write a great deal of their own software because so much of what they produce is unprecedented in the industry.

Many animated features are sold internationally and dubbed in any number of foreign languages. Mainstream family animated features based on action, movement, and physical humor work well in many different cultures and can be easily dubbed when necessary. Sometimes scenes may need to be edited out if they do not translate well or might be offensive to another culture.

Computer animation is also used in the video game industry. 3-D animators primarily give life to game characters and creatures, but sometimes animation is also applied to objects, scenery, and environmental effects. See the following section on Video Game Art.

Architectural animation, called Architectural Previsualization or Previz, allows artists to create realistic simulations of environments, which clients can "walk through" even though they have not yet been built. An efficient design tool, it helps the architect avoid expensive construction mistakes by making alterations before work begins.

Previz is also a process in the pre-production of a movie, commercial, or music video, which involves mapping out scenes before the principal photography takes place. It can utilize a combination of photography, storyboards, and animatics. The renderings can range from simple stick figures and modest drawings to detailed, artistic illustrations that border on fine art.

High-quality computer animation formerly required access to sophisticated and expensive equipment, but with technological advances, broadcast-quality output (used primarily for TV commercials and video games) is readily available, though by no means inexpensive. Full-feature quality is equally attainable, but it takes more time to render. Graphics software now available off the shelf is designed to run on different platforms, including Windows, MAC-OS, and Linux (most commonly used by the larger studios).

Most large motion picture studios use proprietary software or commercial software with lots of custom code. Maya from Autodesk is the modeling tool of choice, but other software, such as 3D Max, LightWave, Modo, and Zbrush, have been used as well for this purpose. Mid-size studios and visual effects (VFX) shops use commercial software like Maya, Houdini, 3DS Max (Autodesk), and After Effects, along with custom software and code. Nuke is used mostly as a final compositing tool in visual effects. 3DSds Max is a very popular 3-D application also used in the creation of video games. Cinema 4D is a 3-D modeling, animation, and rendering application often used by small shops and freelance animators, game designers, and architects, most frequently for motion graphics. There are also open source applications available that have been used to create high-quality films, most prominently the 3-D content creation suite, Blender (www.blender.org).

STOP-MOTION ANIMATION

Stop-motion animation is a filmaking technique in which objects are physically manipulated in small increments between individually photographed frames so that they will appear to exhibit independent motion or change when the series of frames is played back. Traditionally, stop-motion uses hand-made puppets, clay figures (*claymation*), or any other three-dimensional objects to narrate a story. Puppet animation often requires the artist to create movie sets to scale that depict the story line and can be filmed from many angles. Aardmann Animation (creators of *Wallace & Gromit*) in Bristol, UK, and Laika (*Kubo and the Two Strings*), in Portland, OR, are the better-known practitioners of stop-motion animation techniques. Dragonframe is the industry standard stop-motion animation software.

While stop-motion is still done traditionally,

contemporary top motion studios have taken advantage of 3-D printing and digital fabrication techniques to augment their work. Moving an object frame by frame to create the illusion of animation is a painstaking process. Instead of manipulating clay in between shots, an array of detailed parts, created with a 3-D printer, can be interchanged accordingly, in a much more efficient workflow. Laika Studios used 3-D printing in *Kubo and the Two Strings* to create thousands of different facial expressions for the characters. For Kubo alone, they created 11,007 unique mouth positions and 4,429 brow motions that when combined resulted in over 48 million different possible expressions. In addition to interchangeable parts, 3-D printing has been used to fabricate entire puppets, set pieces, and scenery. Its use is not limited to films. It also used in stop-motion ads and videos.

MOTION CAPTURE ANIMATION

Motion capture (also known as *motion tracking* and *mocap*) is the process of recording movement and translating that movement onto a digital model. It is used in military, entertainment (movies and video games), sports, and medical applications. In filmmaking, it refers to recording actions of human actors and using that information to animate digital character models in 2-D or 3-D computer animation. The process involves sampling movements of one or more actors many times per second. Then this animation data is mapped to a 3-D model and manipulated and modified by CG animators, so the model performs the same actions as the actor. This is comparable to the older technique of rotoscope. When motion capture involves faces or fingers or captures facial expressions, it is often called *performance capture*.

James Cameron's *Avatar* used motion capture to create the Na'vi that inhabit Pandora, and *The Adventures of Tintin*, directed by Steven Spielberg, is a 3-D motion-capture computer-animated film.

Careers in Animation

Animation companies are growing, and movie studios and game companies are adding computer animation divisions. As more and more interactive services are put online, there will be an even greater demand for designers, animators, directors, and programmers. Mobile devices, as well as the Internet, have spawned numerous opportunities for 2-D projects. Opportunities in animation are not limited to the entertainment industry. Artists with animation skills are hired by design firms, advertising agencies, publishers, software companies, and educational institutions, such as teaching hospitals.

Education and training for a career in animation can be found at universities and colleges, as well as at professional schools. The level of education offered ranges from certificate programs and associate degrees to Bachelor of Arts and Master of Fine Arts degrees in animation. It also is possible to earn a degree in animation online. Educational preparation includes a combination of academic and hands-on learning experiences in animation drawing and practices, 3-D programming, computer graphics, video effects, and graphic design, as well as courses geared to specific positions on the animation team and to specific industries.

Having a solid background and foundation in all types of animation techniques only enhances an artist's chances for employment. Many animation studios prefer to hire artists who have traditional animation and fine artistry skills and the ability to tell a story, in addition to computer training and experience, since the technology changes so quickly. Programmers and technical directors are responsible for the technological aspects. Today's cutting-edge techniques can be outdated almost before a project is completed, so it may sometimes feel that a significant part of a computer animator's job is keeping current with the evolution of animation technology.

Many animation artists who work for studios in the entertainment industry are represented by the Motion Picture Screen Cartoonists (MPSC) of the International Alliance of Theatrical Stage Employees (IATSE). Its members also include freelancers. Various locals of the union are located in different cities; for instance, Los Angeles is home to Local 839, also known as The Animation Guild (www.animationguild.org). There are also nonunion animation artists, but most artists, writers, and technicians employed by animation studios are covered by the collective bargaining agreements negotiated by MPSC. Some of the big-name studios with which Local 839 currently has negotiated contracts include Cartoon Network Studios, DreamWorks Animation, Marvel Animation Studio, Universal Animation Studios, Walt Disney Television Animation, and Warner Bros. Animation.

THE ANIMATION TEAM

Almost all animation is created by a team in a studio. The players on the team will vary, depending on the size/complexity of the project, the type of animation, and the size of the studio. On smaller productions and in smaller studios, some of the roles will be combined. Below is a partial list of some of those roles:

Producer: Hires the team, organizes the schedule, locates investors, manages expenses, handles distribution, and is responsible for the budget and the overall development of the project. The Producer has the huge task of ensuring the right crew is doing the right thing, for the right amount of time, at the right time. On larger productions, a Producer would need more production support, which is provided by the Supervisory Team.

Production Assistant: Responsible for assisting in the smooth running of the production. This position can be found in most all departments of an animation studio.

Writer: Identifies the subject of the film, defines the characters, and develops the story line and dialogue.

Character Designer: Creates the look and feel of animated characters. Blends skills from illustration, concept art, and animation to bring characters to life and flesh out their look. May be hired at any stage of the process—to provide simple character sketches at the beginning, more technical drawings or a finished painting of a character during production, turnarounds and expression sheets for the modelling department, or all of these things.

Concept Artist: Works closely with a Director at the very beginning of a project to dream up the intended look and feel of the characters and environments in a film. Once the concept art is approved, modelling can begin. Needs to be an excellent illustrator as well as proficient in software such as Zbrush.

Visual Development Artist: Like the concept artist, the vis-dev artist provides early inspirational work to help define the look and style of the film. However, the role is more concerned with creating the background, environments, colors, and lighting that accompany characters, as well as visualizing more complex shots. The artist must be facile in both traditional skills and current software such as Photoshop, as well as Zbrush to create 3-D sculpts and sketches. Some larger motion picture studios may hire a sculptor to create clay maquettes of characters for visual reference for traditional animators and for digitizing purposes.

Director: Responsible for carrying out the vision of a project and for the supervision and coordination of everything, making sure all elements work together, including layouts, storyboards, the actions of the characters, voice talent, and timing.

Art Director: Oversees creation of the project's visual style, supervises visual development artists in the preproduction phase, and in consultation with the director oversees functions from the color-modeling process to color timing the film prints. Some projects hire a separate production design supervisor so the art director can focus on color and lighting.

Storyboard Artist: The Storyboard Artist creates storyboards representing the scope of the film's action, breaking the story down into specific scenes and showing the film's sequential development in proper scale. The visuals for each major scene include character poses, facial expressions, and backgrounds, as well as animation directions, such as a character lifting its arm or exiting the scene. In some productions (especially in TV animation), the storyboard artist might also be responsible for writing the script.

Previs Artist: Storyboards may not be done for VFX projects. Instead, a Previs Artist creates rough, usually greyscale 3-D models and environments, to place in a scene for mapping out the general camera angles, layout, and animation for a scene. On larger, more complex productions, previs is a key step in order to get a proof of concept of the planned CG, approved by the Director/Vendor.

2-D Layout Artist: In traditional 2-D hand-drawn animation, layout artists define the perspective of the animation frames by drawing the environment or background layout of exterior and interior spaces in which the animated characters will function. The relative size of the objects in the background, as compared to the action in the foreground, influences how viewers perceive the scene. Artists base what will appear in the image on the storyboard, but they more clearly define what appears in an animation frame.

Background Artist/Matte Painter: Paints/color-styles the background layout. This job is now done both with traditional tools and digitally.

Color Stylist: Chooses colors for the characters and props; works in conjunction with the art director and background artist.

Modeler: Builds 3-D characters and environments based on the concept art.

Texture artist: Brings flat color and texture to a prop, character, or environment. Some artists specialize in character work and others in texturing the hard surface models. Artists need to understand how a model has been made in order to plan for how best to achieve the look they want. An understanding of lighting fundamentals also is useful.

Rigger: Creates the bone structure of a 3-D character model. This bone structure is used to manipulate the 3-D model like a puppet for animation. Needs to have an understanding of performance and anatomy, as well as a firm grasp of coding languages.

Animator: Working from storyboards and animatics, animators breathe life and personality into a modeled character by making it move, talk, and express emotions. Animators study movement, timing, staging, and gestures—the nuances that make a performance believable. In this way, their role is closer to that of an actor than of a technician. Creates "roughs," thumbnail sketches, and models of the characters depicting their range of movement, key poses, expressions, and emotions.

Assistant Animator (Inbetweener): Prepares drawings to fill the intervals between key poses or frames. Inbetweeners also refine the sketches, clean up and tighten lines, and darken shadows.

Junior Animator: The entry-level job in 3-D computer animation (the role of Assistant Animator rarely exists in CGI).

Lighting Artist/Lighting TD: Gives the 3-D models and animations their lifelike look and enhances the atmosphere, tone, depth, and mood of a scene with strategically placed and angled lighting. Needs to have an eye for color, tone, atmosphere, and composition—understanding how light reflecting on objects in nature and the real world determines how the eye perceives them.

Director of Photography (DoP): Directs the filming and lighting of stop motion animation. For a feature animation, this may involve supervising multiple shooting units all operating simultaneously. On smaller budget productions, the roles of DoP and Cinematographer are combined.

3-D Layout Artist: In 3-D animation, a layout artist is the director of photography (DoP). Like the DoP of a live-action movie, the layout artist makes decisions about lenses and camera angles and movements but with a virtual camera within 3-D animation software. 3-D layout artists work from storyboards and tidy up the animatics, and they work out the timing and the placement of the characters at key points within each shot. They also do a rough version of the lighting and produce the shots.

Cinematographer/Scene Planner: Films the movie. Cinematographers are commonly used in 3-D and stop motion productions today. In motion picture production a Scene Planner, formerly a traditional camera operator, digitally refines the more sophisticated camera movements to accent the action.

Editor: Cuts together rendered footage, matching the images to the soundtrack. Prepares footage for duplication and printing.

Renderer: A position in 3-D animation, involving the process of converting computer data and out-putting it as a sequence of viewable images.

Render wrangler: A quality-control position in the computer graphics field, this person makes sure the animation is rendered correctly. The wrangler is the last person to view the animation before its final output to film or video.

Compositor: Working at the end of the production process, compositors creatively combine material from various sources, such as rendered CG animation, special effects, graphics, 2-D animation, live action, static background plates, etc., into the final image. They ensure that the established style is respected and continuity is maintained. Uses tools such as, Adobe After Effects, Black Magic Fusion, The Foundry's Nuke, and some proprietary compositing software in major studios.

Puppet Builder/Fabricator: In stop-motion animation, puppet building involves many skills, such as sculpting, mold making, armature (skeleton) building, casting of all the separate puppet pieces, painting, hair styling, and costume fabrication. In a stop-motion major feature film, puppet building involves a team of many skilled artists and craftspeople, each assigned to a specific skill.

Costume Designer: In stop-motion animation, the costume designer creates outfits and accessories that express elements of each character's personality. The challenge is to create realistic-looking outfits for "actors" (puppets) the size of a doll, working with thin, lightweight fabrics that allow these tiny characters to move, walk, run, or dance like real people.

Video Game Art

Video game artists bring to the player the vision set out by the designers, art directors, and producers. Whether the virtual worlds inhabited by the characters and objects are highly realistic, futuristic, fantastic, minimalistic, or mythical, they need the imagination and artistic and technological skills of 2-D and 3-D artists and animators to bring them to life. From the concept artist, who works with the art director to establish the game's style, to the 3-D modeler who brings those concepts into existence, artists play a crucial role in the creation of a game. There are many other positions in the video game industry; however, this section is only concerned with those that require the skills of artists and animators. It should be noted that a game designer is not a graphic designer; a game designer typically determines the overall vision of the game—its storylines and plots, user interfaces, in-game objectives, map, scenarios, the degree of difficulty, and character development. The game designer is also responsible for writing the game design document.

The video game industry is a huge market, fueled by its customers' craving for new entertainment and fascination with technology. It is also an evolving and quickly changing industry. There are games that can be played remotely by multiple players scattered all over the world, who can talk to each other while playing. There are the wireless motion sensing controller games that simulate the swing and the sound of a tennis racket, golf club, or other sports equipment. Another genre is the episodic game, which is produced and sold in small units that build into a recognizable series. Play is no longer limited to a video console or a handheld device designed solely for gaming—games are played on computers, online, on social networking sites, and on smart phones. Now there is a hybrid console that transforms from a home console to a portable system, enabling play anywhere with the same device. The ever-increasing types of games and platforms on which to play them have expanded the demographics of those who play as well as created numerous opportunities for artists.

Careers in Video Game Art

Artists work on video games as 3-D Environment Artists, Animators, Character Animators, Special Effects Animators, Modelers, Character Modelers, Character Riggers, Concept Artists, Storyboard Artists, Level Designers, Motion Capture Artists, and Texture Map Artists, as well as Art Directors.

JOB DESCRIPTIONS

Art Director improves the process, quality, and productivity of art development while promoting artistic and job harmony.

Concept / Layout / Storyboard Artist creates original envi-

ronments, objects, and storyboards under the guidance of the visual effects art director.

2-D Artist works primarily on 2-D games; for 3-D games, works on textures for 3-D models, as well as 2-D User Interface elements in the game. Concept art for 3-D games is often first visualized and drawn in 2-D.

3-D Environment Artist designs and constructs 3D environments for game landscapes including the terrain, buildings, vegetation, and vehicles.

Texture Map Artist creates 2-D graphic art used to define the surface qualities of a 3-D computer model.

Animator creates movement for characters, objects, and natural phenomenon.

Character Animator specializes in the creation of realistic character movement.

Character Modeler utilizes concept art to create and build 3-D computer-modeled characters.

In the past few years, artists working in the video game industry have had to deal with diminished opportunities due to outsourcing. Art can easily be created and refined outside the main studio, so it's easy for companies to send art-based work overseas, where labor is cheaper. There are still many opportunities for artists in the United States, but the desired skill set for full-time, in-house artists is changing. Art managers, who can speak the language of artists and who have an artistically trained eye, are needed to supervise the flow of outsourced work in and out of the studio. Concept artists, technical artists, riggers, and animators are among the other art jobs that need to stay in house.

SKILLS NEEDED

Artists who have some technical knowledge, especially a scripting language or a general knowledge of programming, are more desirable job candidates than artists who have none. Artistic talent alone is not enough to stay in demand in the game industry. To become invaluable to the team and company they work for, artists must be able to creatively collaborate with others, as well as be talented. The spectacular visuals of a game require technical wizardry, artistic persistence, and clever design—all working together. To deal with the endless number of problems inherent in the process of making a game and to keep the game going forward in a creative, productive way, artists must also be creative problem solvers. Other important skills required of artists in this field are a consistent, solid work ethic and the ability to deliver clean, organized work.

For artists working in this ever-evolving field, it is extremely important to develop and hone their traditional artistic skills and at the same time keep ahead of technology. They need to know the media they are creating art for by having a deep understanding of the hardware, tools, and engines they use to produce it.

Game artists and animators should be familiar with at least one 3-D software application, such as Autodesk's 3DS Max, Maya, and Softimage XSI; Zbrush; and Blender, as well as 2-D graphics tools, especially Photoshop. They should have a foundational knowledge of fine arts first, upon which they can build additional digital skills. Some game artists have additional experience in web design, others have studied hand-drawn animation, and some are former sculptors and painters. Becoming more common in art departments as technology becomes more advanced are technical artists—artists who specialize in the software and hardware side of things. They are typically mid- to senior-level positions. Smaller game studios may prefer generalists who can work in different roles when necessary.

Motion Graphic Design

When you watch the opening titles of a movie or a TV show, you are seeing the work of Motion Graphic Designers. Motion Graphic Design (or simply Motion Graphics or *Mograph*) is graphic design for media that has motion. Motion graphic artists create imagery for television, video, film, computers, websites, and mobile devices—any media that has a screen. Motion graphics use video and/or animation technology to create the illusion of motion or a transforming appearance.

According to Steve Curran, the author of *Motion Graphics: Graphic Design for Broadcast and Film*, "The art of motion graphics combines the arts of design, filmmaking, sound, music design, and animation in solutions that solve communication problems, educate an audience, add to the entertainment experience, or extend the value of a brand." Computer animation may focus on using animated characters to tell a story, while motion graphics utilize type, photography, video, 2-D elements, and 3-D objects to communicate messages. Motion graphics are best for outlining or emphasizing facts, illustrating a point, breaking down complex concepts, and presenting services or products in a memorable way.

Motion graphics is not the same as animation, but it shares many of the same principles, such as timing, staging, etc., and much of the software used for animation is also used to create motion graphics that add animation, video, and interactivity to web pages. Some of the software most commonly used in motion graphic design today are Adobe After Effects, Nuke, Blackmagic Fusion 9, Maxon's Cinema 4D, and Autodesk's 3D Max and Maya. Maya has been the dominant 3-D motion graphics software for many years, but now has real competition from Cinema 4D. A good knowledge of Photoshop is very helpful for creating textures, modifying images, and creating designs, among other things. It is also a good prerequisite for learning and using the previously mentioned software. Adobe Illustrator is also becoming an important tool in the motion graphics industry. There is also a wide range of software and libraries/frameworks that help in the creation of motion graphics for web applications, such as Velocity.js, Popmotion.js., and GreenSock Animation Platform (GSAP-JS).

Motion Graphics done specifically for television is called Broadcast Design. However, Broadcast Design includes the design of all the print collateral used by a TV station as well as motion graphics. For a more detailed description of Broadcast Design, see Chapter 5, Graphic Design.

Motion Illustration

Motion illustration or *motion-based illustration* is a relatively young art form. It is at the intersection of illustration, motion design, and animation, and the process requires skills from all three disciplines. The types of work that illustrators are creating that involve motion have some shared characteristics. Like static illustration, a motion illustration project completes a typical illustration task, such as advertising or editorial, and the idea behind the illustration can be understood immediately. The motion is used in a supporting role to the pictorial design—to help advance the visual concept.

In a digital landscape visually cluttered with competing brands and services, one of the best ways to get consumers' attention is through moving images. This has led to a demand for illustration for motion graphics, animated GIFs, and short animations by the producers of online ads, TV commercials, mobile apps, and websites, as well as independent filmmakers. Motion illustration is also used for editorial applications. For example, a newspaper or magazine might commission both static and animated versions of the same image to support print and electronic versions of the publication. Children's books and comics also use motion illustration technology.

There is no single technique for adding motion to illustration. Illustrators are using a variety of tools, software, and processes, resulting in unique effects and styles. Illustrators who can add motion graphics and animation skills to their toolbox will be in a strong position to win more work and boost their careers. Illustrators who are already doing this kind of work have clients of varying sizes, from various industries with a variety of needs.

Animated GIFs

The GIF (Graphic Interchange Format) was invented in 1987 as a way to animate images in the smallest file size. A series of images or soundless videos, a GIF will loop continuously without anyone needing to click play. GIFs have been used to bring life to static web pages, but in recent years they have made a huge comeback and are wildly popular, filling the demand for low cost, fun, and highly visual motion graphics. GIFs also have the capability to add more context or emotion in a much shorter message. These fast-paced (2–5 seconds), eye-catching, and easily shareable animations makes them perfect for all types of advertising and social media applications, but their uses are endless. They have been used to build brand awareness and create a brand personality. Because they are dynamic, they can show off details and highlight key functions of a product that static images cannot. Their looping feature makes them the perfect medium for how-to presentations, step-by-step tutorials, and recipes. They also work well for animating data and building excitement for a product or a release by providing a sneak peek.

All of these applications have created opportunities for illustrators to add GIFs to the services they offer clients. Animated GIFs can be created in Photoshop, either from videos or illustrations and vector artwork. There also are several online tools available for creating GIFs. The process takes a little longer in Photoshop than with the dedicated GIF-builder apps, but it gives the most freedom to create exactly what you want.

Whiteboard Animation

Another popular form of motion that requires the skills of an illustrator is *whiteboard animation,* also referred to by many other names: *whiteboard video, RSA-style animation, video scribing, fast draw,* and *sketchboard animation.* Whiteboard animation is a specific type of video that uses the process of creating a series of drawn pictures on a whiteboard that are recorded in sequence and played back to create an animated presentation. Time-lapsed techniques and stop-motion animation are often used to liven the hand-drawn illustrations; for example, making it appear as if the illustrator is drawing very quickly.

There are several techniques used to arrive at the end result, such as filming the illustrator making the drawings then speeding up the camera. Another method is having the artist sketch out all the drawings first, then filming the hand erasing the lines with an empty marker, and then running the film in reverse to create the drawing effect. A third way is to create the sketches digitally on a tablet; then a green-screened hand is added by compositing it over the drawing. This last method creates more polished and professional illustrations and makes it easier to implement client revisions and add animations. Sound is also added during the process—usually a voice-over and when appropriate, sound effects and music.

Watching a hand draw an illustration so that the art is revealed as it is created is mesmerizing, making whiteboard animation a perfect vehicle for making complicated concepts easy to understand. Commonly used for explainer videos and for educational and business purposes, whiteboard animation is also an effective and exciting way to advertise and market services and products. The technique can be seen in several national TV commercials from major advertisers.

Studios who do whiteboard animation look for illustrators who not only have excellent drawing skills but who are also adept at translating complicated concepts to the visual dimension.

Job Markets & Salaries
Animation & Motion

The job market for animation and motion design is varied, highly competitive, and expected to grow 4% between 2018 and 2028, at about the same rate of growth as the average for all occupations. According to the U.S. Bureau of Labor Statistics (BLS), which includes both animators and motion designers in the category Special Effects Artists and Animators, there were 71,600 animators and special effects artists working in the field in 2019. The majority (59%) were self-employed. The Bureau projects that the need for animators will grow, "due to increased demand for animation and visual effects in video games, movies, and television." An exploding desire for animated entertainment content, due in part to the expanding medium of streaming services and its constant need for product, is increasing opportunities for animation artists as well. Multimedia artists also will be needed to create applications for mobile devices. Job growth may be slowed, however, by companies hiring animators and artists who work overseas. Despite positive job growth, there will be competition for job openings because many recent graduates are interested in entering the occupation.

Most multi-media and animator jobs are in the motion picture and video industries. Many large production houses have entry-level positions for production assistants and junior animators, and many of these people later become animators and, eventually, directors.

Artists working in this area are always thinking about where to line up their next job because they are often hired as contractors. Summer is usually a dead time for features. For this work, animators usually have one-year contracts, while some VFX jobs have six-month contracts. Television series projects can take from several months to three years to produce, with the biggest push during March and April to get pilots out after development. If hired for a TV series, there is a hiatus of a month to a year waiting for production on the next season to start up. TV commercial work usually lasts a few weeks to a few months, with the busiest time being November to April.

Other industries in which animators can find work are computer systems design and related services; software publishers; advertising, public relations, and related services; other information services; manufacturing; and the medical, technical, and aerospace industries.

In May 2019, the BLS reported that the five industries that pay the highest annual mean salaries for animation and special effects are found in the Motion Picture and Video industry ($100,910), Professional and Commercial Equipment and Supplies Merchant Wholesalers ($92,530), Aerospace Product and Parts Manufacturing ($92,440), Employment Services ($91,430), and Other Information Services ($90,710).

The School of Motion also conducted their own survey, specifically of the motion design field, *Motion Design Industry Survey: 2019 Insights* (https://www.schoolofmotion.com/blog/2019-motion-design-survey). According to the results, the average annual income for Motion Designers in the United States is $87,900, based on 30+ hours per week.

In showing work, portfolios of storyboards, backgrounds, model sheets, and similar items are useful. Artists seeking entry-level positions should include samples of their basic artistic skills, especially life drawing. Almost every employer has a printed summary of portfolio requirements. It pays for artists to do some research into the kind of images a company has used in the past and then make sure their portfolios reflect both their strengths and the company's focus.

To show the true nature of their ability to animate movement, animation and motion artists submit a "demo reel" of their work as a link to their personal website or to YouTube or a password-protected Vimeo site. When pre-

paring a demo reel, read the job description very carefully to ensure you have a reel that demonstrates the skills the employer is looking for and that represents the type of work the studio does. Likewise, your demo reel should reflect the kind of work you want to do. If you want to do photorealistic styled VFX creature animation, then do not include cartoony, cute, childlike work on your reel.

Computer animation companies look for three types of employees: artists to do animation, visual development, storyboards, design, and the more technical artistic skills, such as modeling and lighting; technical directors/technicians who support the artists by writing code and adjusting CG tools to find technical solutions for what they are trying to achieve; and engineers for technical support and maintenance.

Trained computer animators will find positions with film and video production studios, special effects production houses, television stations, and video game producers. Stop-motion and special effects studios also seek artists with experience in ball-and-socket puppets, set and model building (creating highly realistic miniatures used in special effects), armatures, mold making, and costume design for puppets.

Artists should include a clause in their contracts that gives them the right to use their work for self-promotion. It is time consuming for an artist to create a demo reel of his or her most current techniques and accomplishments, so retaining the right to show already-produced work can be a tremendous advantage. In feature films, because competition is very high, some studios will refuse to look at reels that include scenes from non-released productions. Artists who post a studio's proprietary work on their websites without prior agreement are asking for trouble. To alleviate clients' fears that a feature or an ad will be shown before its release, set a timeline in your contract for when it can be used in your portfolio "in a professionally aesthetic manner."

In the CGI industry, it is common for artists to do additional work on their own time to create demo reels for applying to studios. Websites, such as The 11 Second Club (www.11secondclub.com), provide a free platform to test and train skills for animation. Similar websites are devoted to specific skills, such as lighting and rigging.

According to the MPSC, going rates for animation artists have increased dramatically in the past decade. The weekly salary levels in Figure 9-1 were supplied by The Animation Guild, Local 839, IATSE, and represent the anonymous poll of its members taken in 2018. You also can review The Animation Guild website (www.animationguild.org) for the latest contract provisions and wage scales. Sample animation job titles with current journey wage scales are given in Figure 9–2.

9–1 Weekly Salaries for Animation Artists

Select Job Titles from the IATSE Member Survey 2018

CLASSIFICATION	JOURNEY MINIMUM[1]	MINIMUM REPORTED[2]	MEDIAN AVERAGE[3]	MAXIMUM REPORTED
Directors[4]	$2,304.60	$938	$2,375	$9,014
Story Artist/Writer[4]	$2,004.00	$1,438	$2,237	$7,480
Production Board[4]	$2,304.40	$1,000	$2,200	$3,200
Character Layout[4]	$2,004.00	$1,347	$2,023	$2,884
Background Painter[4]	$2,004.00	$1,000	$1,950	$2,500
Art Directors[4]	$2,304.60	$1,313	$2,200	$5,044
Visual Development[4]	$2,004.00	$1,097	$2,011	$3,500
Model Designers[4]	$2,004.00	$1,300	$2,000	$2,947
Color Key/Color Stylist[4]	$1,714.80	$1,176	$1,700	$2,400
Technical Directors[4] (lev 1/cat 1)	$2,004.00	$926	$1,916	$3,116
Lighters (lev 1/cat 1)[4]	$2,004.00	$1,094	$1,955	$3,368
Surface/Texture Artist (lev I, cat 1)[4]	$2,004.00	$1,100	$2,000	$2,500
3-D Compositor (lev 1/cat 1)[4]	$1,793.20	$1,320	$1,813	$3,548
2-D Compositor[4]	$1,424.80	$1,550	$2,100	$2,500
3-D Animators (lev 1/cat 1)[4]	$2,.004.00	$920	$2,000	$6,316
3-D Modelers (lev 1/cat 1)[4]	$2,004.00	$1,400	$2,165	$2,526
2-D Animators (lev 1/cat 1)[4]	$2,004.00	$1,333	$1,800	$2,947
Effects Animators (lev 1/cat 1)[4]	$2,004.00	$1,142	$1,924	$3,000
Animation Checking[4]	$1,714.80	$1,600	$1,750	$2,000

1. Rates shown are from the second period of the 2018–2021 CBA.

2. Many of the minimums are for persons working at non-union shops, or at less than journey level.

3. The median average represents the middle rate when the results were listed in order from lowest to highest. The numbers should be viewed in the context of the minimums and maximums reported.

4. Not all persons working in this category are under the Animation Guild's jurisdiction.

Reprinted with permission from the Animation Guild, Local 839, IATSE, Member Salary Survey, 2018. All salaries are computed on a 40-hour week. The salary figures, which represent what members reported they were paid in the previous 12 months working at both union and non-union shops, and reflect the "going rate," as opposed to the CBA (Collective Bargaining Agreement) minimums. The listing of "Journey Minimum" shows the union minimums for the various job categories. Reported salaries have been rounded to the nearest dollar.

INDUSTRY RESOURCES

More industry-related information, such as salaries, career prospects, animation companies, workshops/classes, events, and even job listings can be found in *Animation Magazine* (www.animationmagazine.net), on Animation World Network (www. awn.com), at Creative Talent Network (CTN) (www.creativetalentnetwork.com), and Animation Industry Database (www. aidb.com). ACM SIGGRAPH (https://dl.acm.org/sig/siggraph), a special interest group for computer graphics, sponsors the annual SIGGRAPH conference. For a comprehensive list of annual international animation festivals, visit www.animation-festivals.com.

9–2 Hourly & Weekly Salary Rates
Animation Unit Journey Minimums

Select Animation Titles

(For period 8/2/20–7/31/21)

TITLE	HOURLY*	WEEKLY
Production Board	$59.34	$2,373.60
Animator, Background, Layout, Model Designer**	$51.60	$2,064.00
Assistant Animator, Storyboard Revisionist, Assistant Background, Assistant Layout, Assistant Model Designer	$44.16	$1,766.40
Breakdown	$38.78	$1,551.20
Inbetweener	$37.35	$1,494.00
Story Sketch	$46.36	$1,854.40
Inker	$36.94	$1,477.60
Special Effects	$38.21	$1,528.40

Minimum scale for daily employees shall be 117.719% (which rate is inclusive of vacation and holiday pay) of the minimum basic hourly rate provided herein for such employee's classification.

**An Animator, Background, or Layout person designated by the Producer to be responsible for and supervise the work of others in his classification shall be paid the key rate of 15% above the minimum Journey rate for his classification during such an assignment.*

Reprinted with permission from The Animation Guild and Affiliated Optical Electronic and Graphic Arts, Local 839, IATSE Contract, Effective July 29, 2018 through July 31, 2021. (For additional job titles, rates for other time periods, rates for specific studios, and other information about the above rates, see CBA Wage Minimums 2018–2021 at http://animationguild.org/contracts-wages/.)

Video Game Art

Today the video game industry is huge and employs many thousands of people globally. With 59% of Americans playing video games, there is an enormous market for games to be created and sold each year. Total consumer spending on video games is over $70 billion annually.

In the early days of the industry, the games were quite simple with primitive art that could be done by one artist. As the gaming systems became more powerful—evolving from two-dimensions to three-dimensions in full-color, the art became more important and more sophisticated. As a result, the art that was once done by a single artist has split into many different art specialties, each with its own tools and techniques.

WORKING CONDITIONS

Generally, there are three types of workers in the video game industry: full-time employees on staff at the game companies and studios, contract workers who are hired by staffing (temp) agencies, and freelancers. Contract workers often have some benefits enjoyed by employees, such as health insurance, and they are eligible for unemployment benefits between contract periods. Contract workers are governed by state laws that define how long they can work for a company before a mandatory waiting period sets in. Overtime work and the overtime pay rate vary by state laws and individual staffing firms' policies. Freelancers are self-employed, securing and paying their own benefits, and they are not eligible for unemployment insurance. Staff employees are often bound by non-compete clauses and are sometimes prevented from freelancing for direct competitors or from freelancing at all. Contractors and freelancers are not bound by these restrictions.

FREQUENT LAYOFFS

Despite the popularity of games, the video game industry goes through frequent ups and downs, even in a single year. Unfortunately, it is often the art jobs that are hit the hardest during the down cycles. Fortunately, games cannot be made without art, and despite the fluctuations, there has been a steady increase in the demand for artists over time. Many companies are willing to hire artists on a contract basis until the up cycle starts again.

CRUNCH TIME

The gaming industry is also noted for "crunch," the time period just before a launch, when employees are expected to put in 100-hour weeks with no extra pay. In past decades that crunch period was limited to the weeks just before a game's release date because there would not be any changes or updates, unless there was a sequel. However, with games now being connected to the Internet, crunch has gotten worse. Today, game studios are constantly updating and refreshing their existing games, partly through downloadable content, such as new weapons or levels that players can purchase. The demand by gamers for this content is very profitable for the studios, resulting in yet more pressure on workers for months and sometimes years after a game's release date.

SALARIES

Like most jobs, game artist salaries are based on years of experience and areas of expertise. "Lead" and "senior" positions have more responsibility and require more experience, so there is higher compensation.

According to the *Game Industry Career Guide*'s Video Game Artist Salary for 2020, artists' salaries start around $35,000 for entry-level positions and can grow to $90,000 or higher for senior or lead positions. The average annual salary ranges for video game artists are as follows:

* **Game Artist (generalist)** $45,000–95,000
* **Concept Artist** $45,000–100,000
* **Character Artist** $45,000–70,000
* **Environment Artist** $55,000–120,000
* **Technical Artist** $40,000–105,000 (min. 3 years prior experience)
* **Character Animator** $40,00–100,000
* **2D Artist** $60,000–75,000
* **Lead Artist** $73,000–105,00 (min. 3 years prior experience)
* **Art Director** $110,000 (min. 6 years prior experience)

There are other factors besides experience that can affect salaries, including the size of the company. According to the *Career Guide*, larger companies, generally have larger project budgets than smaller companies, so they can pay game artists higher salaries, in some cases, significantly higher than the above-average salaries. Stylistic fit is another factor. Artists who can get into a studio that has a style that matches a style they excel at, and which they can do easily and quickly, will have greater earning potential. Both the abilities to specialize and to generalize can be assets, depending on the team. Smaller teams place value on an artist who can work in many different styles or roles, while larger teams tend to value artists who are highly specialized in one area and who can consistently produce high-quality, expert-level work in that area.

The salary survey and in-depth information about careers in the video game industry can be found at www.gameindustrycareerguide.com.

BREAKING INTO THE INDUSTRY

Many of the things you need to do before actually starting a job search are similar to what animators and motion artists would do in other industries. You definitely need an online portfolio of work that is focused on the type of work you want to do, as well as what game studios are looking for. If you want an animation position, you need a demo reel as well.

If you did not go to college or went to a traditional art college and not a school specific to the video game industry, there are lots of online tutorials and courses where you can learn more about creating video game art (e,g,, YouTube, Gnomon, 3dtotal, Udemy, and Lynda). Depending on the type of art or animation position you are most interested in, you should familiarize yourself with the software used in the industry, such as Photoshop, Maya, and Zbrush. Blender is a free program to learn 3-D Modeling.

Some of the better websites to look for jobs in the gaming industry are Indeed Jobs (www.indeed.com), Game Job Hunter (www.gamejobhunter.com), and Zip Recruiter (www.ziprecruiter.com). Looking on Indeed is a big time-saver because it is a job aggregator, meaning it combines job openings from several different job sites in one place. Game Job Hunter has fewer jobs listed, but they tend to be high-quality and up to date, and it is a good place to find jobs in video game art. Zip Recruiter has the ability to send your resume to hundreds of employers a day.

Other strategies for finding employment and getting noticed are posting your work on discussion boards, blog applying for an internship at a gaming studio, participating in game jams, and continually honing your skills and applying for jobs even after rejection.

To get their foot in the door of a studio, sometimes artists take a different position other than exactly what they want (e.g., 2-D artist instead of 3-D artist). This strategy has its advantages. Instead of waiting months and years for the right job, you will be learning the industry, building a network, and getting entrance into a studio you want to work at. Studios prefer to hire people they know and trust from inside the company, and you will be hearing about internal job openings before they are made public.

Freelance Animation & Motion
Finding Work

Before you can start pitching a job, you need to do your homework: know where to look for freelance animation and motion design jobs and research what potential employers are looking for in your area of interest.

SOURCES OF FREELANCE OPPORTUNITIES

There are opportunities for animators and motion designers in numerous industries in a variety of companies, so do not limit yourself to looking only for studio work or only in the entertainment industry. You can gain experience and build your skills in other areas that will help you get studio work if that is your goal. Below are some of the places to find job listings and/or post your work:

Websites of studios that interest you: some studios post jobs on their own websites, so start there.

Industry-specific websites: Some of these sites feature job listings as well as industry news, etc., for example, Animation World Network (www.awn.com), Motionographer (www.motionographer.com), and Gamasutra (www.gamasutra.com).

Employment websites and job boards that specialize in creative jobs: Most feature freelance opportunities, as well as part-time and full-time employment (for a list of creative staffing agencies and job boards, see Part 5, Resources & References).

Professional organizations: Joining industry organizations often gives you access to job listings on their websites, as well as many other benefits.

Forums and animation Facebook groups: A lot of animators hire others to help them out when a big project comes in, and they will often turn to a forum or Facebook group they are a part of to find freelancers.

Social media and art websites: In addition to Facebook, create an account on these sites and keep them updated.

Portfolio sites and platforms that feature creative work: Make sure you have an account on sites such as Behance, ArtStation, Deviant Art, Draw Crowd, and Pinterest.

NETWORKING

In the School of Motion's *Motion Design Industry Survey,* freelancers reported that word of mouth is overwhelmingly the most common way they find work—over five times as many responses as the next most popular sources of work, which were Instagram and Facebook. This result indicates the importance of networking, maintaining contacts, and establishing good relationships within the industry.

CREATE A PROFESSIONAL PRESENCE

You will want to present yourself not just as talented or having a particular skillset, but also as a professional. Some advice from industry insiders that tell prospective clients that you mean business include the following:

* Get a website with an e-mail feature instead of just using a g-mail account.
* Include an About page with a decent bio and a quality photo of you.
* Have a portfolio site with some work on it (if you do not have your own website, use a third-party portfolio site and list the link in all your correspondence).
* Create a Demo Reel focused on the type of work you want to do (e.g., animation, modeling, VFX, etc.) and make it accessible from your website.
* Open a LinkedIn account and fill out your profile.
* Do a social media scrub to eliminate anything that a client might consider unprofessional, inappropriate, or insensitive or that you might consider embarrassing. Social media posts and photographs stay on the Internet forever. Jason W. Bay, author of the *Game Industry Career Guide,* gives step-by-step directions on how to do a social media scrub in one of his blog posts (www.gameindustrycareerguide.com/scrub-social-media-before-job-search/#more-4836).
* Prepare your own written Agreement form that can be filled in with the particulars of a job. It should outline your studio policy regarding such things as your work hours (per day, per week), compensation for overtime, cancelled bookings, cancellation and rejection terms, rush work, usage terms (for projects that are not work-for-hire), attribution, etc. By presenting clients with your Agreement

first, instead of waiting for clients to give you their Agreement, you are making it clear what your policy is regarding working conditions, plus you are presenting yourself as a prepared and informed professional.

Pitching is basically contacting prospective clients and telling them why you are the best person for the job. You can use the following tips for writing an e-mail to reply to actual advertised freelance jobs or to introduce yourself to a company or studio from which you would like to get work. You want your first impression to be favorable and you want them to read it, so include the pertinent information without overwhelming them:

* Introduce yourself and tell what you do (e.g., "freelance animator specializing in stop motion animation," "freelance 3-D modeling expert," "freelance concept artist specializing in video games," etc.).
* Explain where you saw their call for work and convey excitement about a specific part of the job (if not an actual job, something about their company) that interests you.
* Include links to your website with your demo reel and one other piece of work that is relevant to the job.
* Request a follow-up e-mail, letting them know you are looking forward to speaking with them and that you are available for alternative means of contact (telephone, Skype, etc.).

Trade Practices

ANIMATION & MOTION DESIGN

Both animation and motion design are often done as part of a larger, collaborative work, such as a motion picture or another type of audiovisual media. In these situations, it falls under acceptable criteria for work made for hire, meaning that the client owns all rights to the work. Full copyright to the finished work is transferred to the client once full payment is received. Animators and motion designers generally retain the right to use the work for self-promotion. Some animators also successfully negotiate for the ownership of the rights to original audio and the illustrations, when applicable. In corporate and broadcast work, the animator commonly retains ownership of the elements he/she created (scenes, models, textures, etc.) to produce the final product. Some designers

are able to negotiate terms so that their work files remain their property. They may also stipulate that the client is not allowed to modify the finished work and that attribution be made to the designer as the creator.

Freelancers who do work that is not part of a work-made-for-hire agreement may include specific usage rights in their base project price, but the specific rights will vary by project. The transfer to the client of all rights to the final artwork is charged at a higher than the base project price.

ART TESTS

Expect to do an art test regardless of your skill when you apply to a studio, especially when just starting your career. This is most common for game studios, but not uncommon in motion graphics, series, and features. If you are unable to do the test for whatever reason, bring this up to the studio to see if there are other options available.

THE HOLD SYSTEM

Freelancers should be aware of the "hold system," a practice used in some localities. A *hold* is a voluntary courtesy offered by a freelancer to a studio to help in the early days of staffing a potential job. If a studio is interested in working with you on a future project, it will ask you for your day rate. The studio can either accept your rate or negotiate you down. Once both parties agree to the rate, the studio could book you on the spot (guaranteeing you work for certain dates), but what happens more often is it will put you on a hold. When agreeing to a hold, you are saying that you will not take any other work or make other plans that could interfere with a potential booking for an agreed upon set of days. In other words, the studio has first dibs on you for your services for a certain time period. You have not been booked for the job and you are not getting paid.

In the meantime, if a second studio is interested in hiring you, you would need to check back with the first studio to see if it wants to materialize its hold (actually book you) or release you from the hold. It is customary to give the first studio 24 hours to reply to a challenge for your time. Sometimes the second studio is not ready to book you yet either, so you are put on a *second hold*. This scenario can repeat itself until you have multiple holds. When a studio is finally ready to book you, you will need to check back with your holds according to the hold order, giving each studio the opportunity to either book you or release its hold. If you are offered a hold, you want to ask for specific dates, and if you get booked, to ask how long you are actually booked for.

Some freelancers make it a policy not to do holds and only accept official bookings. The hold system is more common with production studios than smaller companies. In some situations, freelancers work on a project basis, rather than a day rate, and charge a flat fee. It is also recommended to include cancellation clauses in contracts, making the client liable for your time in the event that a project is cancelled after you are booked for studio time.

TIME ABUSE

Time abuse can be a problem in the motion industry. Freelancers are usually contracted to work 8- to 10-hour days but end up working much longer (up to 16 hours), often without additional compensation. To counteract this practice, freelancers need to put clauses in their contracts that they will receive additional compensation for work done beyond the contracted number of hours per day. It was reported by motion graphic artists that these written agreements are usually honored by the client.

ESTABLISH A STUDIO POLICY

Many of these issues can be dealt with upfront if freelancers have their own written agreement prepared in advance that provides their studio policy (see the previous section, Creating a Professional Presence). You can even excerpt your studio policy from your written agreement to create a separate document that is linked to your booking e-mails so that a client knows upfront what your requirements are. Freelancers can create better working conditions for themselves by being proactive, rather than viewing themselves as passive victims.

VIDEO GAME ART

If you are thinking about freelancing, industry professionals recommend trying to get a full-time staff job at a game company first. Working on a game team will provide experience and help you grow and master your skill set, as well as build your portfolio of shipped titles. It will be next to impossible to get hired for freelance jobs if you do not have a track record of shipped games. Working in a game studio will help you build a professional network. If you develop positive relationships with the people you meet and work with on the job, they can play a key role in helping you get gigs when you become a freelancer in the future.

Like their counterparts in motion graphics, freelancers who do work in the video game industry report that most of their work comes from word of mouth, past clients, and social media, so building a professional network of connections first through a staff job is a valuable asset when striking out on your own.

Freelancers can find opportunities on the same job sites as artists looking for full-time employment (see

previous section on Job Markets & Salaries). It is recommended to avoid third-party sites like Fiverr that underpay and devalue skills.

MOTION ILLUSTRATION

Artists who create illustrations for motion do not necessarily need to know how to animate themselves, but they need to understand the animation process and prepare their illustrations accordingly. Other than for whiteboard animation, the process of creating the art is different from creating a still image. It needs to be prepared in layers so that it can be animated. It also needs to be created in pieces so it can be put in motion. Therefore, the workflow is different, as well as timelines.

Illustrators who have additional animation-related skills, such as storyboarding, may find even more opportunities in this field.

Pricing

ANIMATION

Like all self-employed graphic artists, animators need to set pricing for a project in a signed written agreement or contract with the client before work is begun. Methods of pricing, as well as the level of compensation for animation, vary by industry and media.

In some industries, animation is priced by the completed second or minute. Some freelance animators also price by the project or by the hour, and in some cases, by the day.

In addition to the length of the finished animated sequence, there are many other factors that animators consider when determining the price of a job:

* Scope of the project
* Existing/available assets provided by client
* Client's budget, schedule, and deadlines
* Whether work is on-site or off-site
* Animation type/technique (2-D, 3-D, stop-motion, mixed media, etc.)
* Style of animation (photo realistic vs. stylized realism vs cartoon, etc.)
* Estimation of time needed for execution
* Number of characters and amount and intricacy of movement.
* Complexity or intensity of rendering
* Number of iterations allowed
* Amount of preproduction planning/research needed
* Estimate of post-production time
* Necessity to do script, storyboards, or audio

9–3 Additional Freelance Fees for Animation & Motion Graphics

The fees in this chart do not reflect any specific trade practices and do not constitute specific prices for particular jobs. The buyer and seller are free to negotiate, with each artist independently deciding how to price the work, after taking all factors into account. Reading the more detailed information, Pricing Your Services, provided in Chapter 1, will help in pricing projects for your specific situation.

Additional Fees

EXTRA ROUND OF REVISIONS　100–130%
(Not covered in original agreement; % of original fee)

CANCELLATION & REJECTION
(% of original project fee)

Prior to completion of concept or sketch phase	25–30%
After completion of concept or sketch phase	40–70%
After completion of finished work	100%

Illustrators who charge by the hour bill for the number of hours worked up to the date of cancellation or rejection, plus any expenses incurred.

MARKUPS (% added onto cost of outside services, such as voice-overs, custom music, etc.)

Animation	10–100%
Motion Graphics	10–50%

RUSH FEES (% added onto normal fee)

24-hour turnaround	50–100%
48-hour turnaround	20–50%
Holidays & weekends	25–100%

The above fees were compiled from the results of a national survey of graphic artists conducted by the Graphic Artists Guild in 2020. Responses were based on fees charged in 2018 and 2019.

* Scale of the team required to assemble; need for any other third-party services and additional equipment
* Delivery formats and versions of work (e.g., varying commercial lengths and foreign versions)
* Size and type of client
* Repeat vs. new client
* Usage factors
* Original work vs. existing piece
* Possibility of more work (as in a long-term series)

Obviously, not every factor will be considered for every job. It depends on the particular project and the animator's schedule.

A good starting point for determining freelance fees for animation is to look at the union wage scale for the same type of work. The Animation Guild Local 839, IATSE website (www.animationguild.org) includes detailed information on its latest collective bargaining agreement, including wage scales, hours of employment, working conditions, and general employment practices found in the industry. The contract provides for several levels of experience. Experienced artists, referred to as journey artists, enjoy a higher wage scale than artists who have been in the business for less than a year or two. See Figure 9-2 for examples of minimum hourly and weekly salary rates for selected unit journey titles.

Wage scales are not the only factor freelance animators and motion designers should look at when establishing basic fees. They should take into consideration benefits that are often covered at least partially by employers, such as health, disability, and life insurance; paid holidays and vacation days; 401(k) plans; retirement benefits; etc. Freelancers must pay for these expenses themselves, so they should be factored into their rates. There are other non-billable business costs that take up a lot of a freelancer's time, which should be considered when setting fees, such as preparing proposals and contracts, promotion, invoicing, registering copyrights, etc. If an animator has a non-home studio, overhead also has to be considered. Freelancers also need to adjust their rates for taxes—automatically deducted from a staff animator's salary—that they will have to pay at the end of the year or quarterly.

The bottom line is you need to establish pricing that will provide you with a sustainable livelihood. To help you determine how much income you need to make a bare minimum living wage, MIT has developed the *Living Wage Calculator* (www.livingwage.mit.edu) for states and various cities in the United States. It is further divided by the number of children you are supporting and whether you have a non-employed spouse.

MOTION DESIGN

Freelance motion graphic design work is priced several different ways. According to the results of the *Motion Design Industry Survey*, 55.4% of freelance motion designers reported they charge clients a project fee, 28% a day rate, and 16.6% charge by the hour. It can also be priced by the finished onscreen second or minute. The method of pricing may be determined by the size of the project, the industry, or the client's preference. Larger projects often come with a fixed budget.

Although the *Motion Design Industry Survey* was international, it did publish some freelance pricing results that were more "U.S. Centric." On average, freelancers earned $47,390 annually in the previous year, with a range of $10,000–300,000; however, not all worked freelance for 40 hours per week. The average number of hours per week respondents reported working freelance was 23. However, when the survey results compared full-time freelancers to full-time salaried employees, freelancers earned an average of $90,800 per year versus $70,700 for employees, with freelancers working an average of 41.9 hours per week compared to 40.8 for employees.

The average hourly rate that freelancers charged was $67, with a range of $20–300 per hour. The average day rate was $498, with a range of $200–1,000.

When estimating a job, determining factors include the scope and complexity of the work, the estimated amount of time it will take, and other factors that animators consider (see the previous Animation section). When presented with a fixed budget, the graphic artist will adjust the amount of work to fit within the budget. Even projects priced by a flat fee or by the finished second/minute may have an hourly rate clause for rush work and additional modifications.

It is customary to charge the client additional fees for extra rounds of revisions not in the original contract and for such expenses as stock footage, font licenses, props, equipment rental (cameras, lighting, etc.), rendering services, professional custom artwork, sound design, music composition and licenses, voice-overs, recording mixes, and any other third-party services. Of those who charge additional fees for services, approximately half mark up the cost of services, such as voice-overs and custom music, and the rest charge for these services at cost.

Sample additional fees charged by Animators and Motion Designers are found in Figure 9-3. For more detailed information about pricing your services, refer to Chapter 1, Essential Business Practices. Additional information about self-employment issues can be found in Chapter 3, Professional Issues.

VIDEO GAME ART

According to Zip Recruiter, as of July 2020, freelance video game artists earn an average of $68,832 per year. The range from the 25th to 75th percentile is $37,500–84,500. The average hourly rate is $33, with a range of $18.03–40.62 from the 25th to the 75th percentiles. These figures represent all video game art titles combined.

MOTION ILLUSTRATION

Some illustrators doing work for motion report being paid per project or per scene, although other pricing arrangements are possible and vary by industry. A scene may be composed of multiple illustrations. As in other types of illustration, the end use is also a consideration when pricing. For example, will the animation or animated GIFs be used in advertising, for editorial purposes, or in the entertainment industry?

Other factors to consider when pricing include the size of the client and the budget, usage (where motion illustration will be viewed and for how long), and how complex the motion is, which determines how complicated each illustration will be to create. Requests for additional services besides creating the actual illustrations, such as storyboarding, should be charged extra.

Pricing for the various illustration disciplines can be found in Chapter 7, Illustration.

{ 10 }

Surface Pattern Design

This chapter focuses on decorative patterns created primarily for printed products that are mass manufactured. Once exclusively rendered by hand, designs in some segments of the industry are now fully computer-generated. Although computer use has been integrated into the entire process—from design concept to retail sale—there remains a demand for the creative skills or "hand" of the traditional designer.

SURFACE PATTERN DESIGNERS *create repetitive and engineered decorative patterns used to adorn products for the apparel, home fashions, paper product, giftware, and craft industries. Surface pattern designers create stand-alone designs referred to as* leads, *or a design group consisting of a lead and coordinating designs, which are purchased, commissioned, and sometimes licensed by a company. This work is further developed for specific or cross-product end-uses in the preproduction phase, forming the foundation used by manufacturers to mass produce decorative retail products with consumer appeal.*

Definitions of Surface Pattern, Surface, & Textile Design

This chapter focuses primarily on the Surface Pattern Design profession, but there are other terms used to describe the design treatment of knitted and woven textile products. Sometimes these terms are used interchangeably, but there are significant differences among them.

Surface Pattern Designers create 2-D designs that are mass manufactured onto surfaces via printing or for decorative knitted and woven textile products. Due to the variety of designs created, each segment of the industry has creative parameters dictated by consumer appeal and technical specifications required for mass production.

Surface Designers, by contrast, create a single decorative treatment through surface manipulation, such as dyeing, painting, embroidery, etc., to a product blank, such as a scarf, pillow, etc. These items are not intended for mass production but for direct sale at craft fairs, boutiques, and specialty stores. A surface technique, however, could be developed on a fabric swatch or other substrate, scanned, and developed digitally into repeat to be part of a printed line; many special looks, textures, etc., can be derived from surface treatments. Surface designers enjoy the freedom of creative expression and are not restricted by mass production considerations.

Textile Designers are often considered to be technical designers, creating 3-D structures via a draw-in (weft) and peg plan (warp) to create a woven structure. A knit structure involves rows, stitches, and other technical parameters such as gauge. Even with modern technology, professional textile designers require a unique skill set and special knowledge. The term is sometimes used erroneously as an umbrella term including Surface Pattern Design.

The Role of Surface Pattern Designers

Surface pattern designers work either as independent freelancers, freelancers in service studios, or as full-time employees in the studios of design companies, converters, and manufacturers. Service studio staff include art directors, full-time in-house creative staff, CAD designers, and depending on size, a sales staff. Converters and manufacturers have creative, production, and sales staffs. Design companies have the largest number of employees depending on their product line(s) and size. Employees can range from entry-level colorists/CAD assistants to stylists, senior stylists up to vice-presidents of design, prop stylists, and sales teams.

Freelance designers, regardless of the industry, must be cognizant of trends at all times. For trends and inspiration, they may research online; subscribe to trade publications or design magazines; join professional organizations or groups via the Internet; and visit trade shows, museums, libraries, fabric stores, bookstores, or retail shops.

Trends & Color Forecasting

Design trends and color palettes are of the utmost importance to entice consumer attraction to decorative designs. Prior to the influx of technology, the American garment industry drew from the European market, with American designers studying the European trade shows to identify trends and, where possible, purchase designs for the upcoming apparel seasons. After being applied to apparel products, these "looks" would then emerge in home fashions and other industry segments. Technology has changed this, effectively dissolving creative borders. Whereas Europe once set and led design trends, in today's global marketplace American design plays an important role in driving trends. Companies that are able to respond quickly to "what will sell" has changed the "Europe-first" design aesthetic of the industry. European studios have sold work in America for years; today the competition with American studios has paralleled.

Being aware of future trends and the consumers' color "tastes" is a vital part of creating successful decorative designs. Trend and color forecasts are often compiled from research conducted by professional organizations, individual design consultants, or a company's in-house stylist/senior stylist. Trend forecasts mainly contain imagery but can also include color palettes, both resulting from analyzing consumer preferences and other factors influencing changes in taste. Political and social climates, major art exhibits, movies, music, trade journals, magazines, and research done at national and international trade shows can all have a bearing on what kind of "imagery" or "theme" will be the next hot trend. Color forecasts usually do not include imagery; the palettes are derived from trend projections that define the palettes of colors that can be expected to rise, fall, or maintain popularity in coming seasons.

These projections are condensed by design firms visually, in the form of story, presentation, or as they are referred to in fashion, mood boards. The boards serve as communication tools to "tell the story" of the upcoming design group, line, or collection. Generally, trends and color palettes change more rapidly for apparel than for home products, as these changes involve a greater financial commitment for the consumer. A freelance designer may be privy to some of this information when commissioned by a company to develop designs with a particular look and palette. Professional decorative pattern designers who are accustomed to following trends and color fluctuations, are often able to predict with amazing accuracy when the consumer will tire of a particular motif, look, or color palette.

The Design Process

Surface pattern designers stay cognizant of future trends and the consumer's emerging color tastes as the first step in the creative process. Surface pattern designers create speculative work—original designs sold at trade shows, by an agent, or directly to studios or design firms. When commissioned, they are hired to work as problem solvers to create designs steered by the client's needs.

Designs can be executed by hand using traditional media in a variety of techniques, usually on paper, or digitally via graphic software, or both. They are accompanied by computer printouts, external digital storage, or both. They can range from a one-color small-scale pattern, to a larger-scale, highly illustrative design, or a collection with a lead design and several coordinating designs. Designs created for traditional print production and digital pre-production samples are often presented with color *gams*, or color chips, which consist of each color in the design. The gams or color chips are created as solids, regardless of the media used.

Designs for multi-colored wovens may be presented with a yarn chart showing the colors that result from the interlaced yarns. Knitted textiles are created by the interlooping of yarns and may be accompanied by yarn samples called *poms* for color matching. Designs for printed, woven, and knitted products go through similar preproduction, production, and post-production processes—regardless of end use.

Designs for printed textiles used for apparel are created in the form of a *croquis*, a full-color design concept or sketch. The croquis is purchased by an apparel company and then developed into a repeat to meet the technical specifications of the manufacturer.

Home fashion products are vast and commonly designed as repetitive designs with respect to production methods relative to the end-use or as an engineered design, a full-color design created to fit a specific product's dimensions. In the home fashion industry, hard goods, such as kitchen and bathroom accessories, may begin as a black and white sketch that is developed with color and mechanicals to show several 3-D views of the product.

Paper products, crafts, and giftware may begin with a pencil sketch, an engineered design, or a repeated design; depending on the product, they may also require mechanicals.

Computer-Aided Design

Computer-aided design (CAD) has had a profound effect on the surface pattern design process for printed, woven, and knitted products as it has on many other creative fields. The Internet now makes it possible for an individual or corporation to work worldwide in a matter of seconds, and computer-aided manufacturing (CAM) is becoming a global standard. Many time-consuming tasks, such as layout revisions, creating colorways (new color combinations), and developing coordinate designs by hand, have been essentially eliminated, speeding up the process from design creation to retail sale.

Formerly, during the pre-production phase, a stylist in the home fashions industry would provide the designer with visual references, color direction, relevant technical design information, and written specs for the lead design. Many hours or days were spent creating the lead design, based on the stylist's instructions. After the initial lead design layout, color palette, and technique sample were reviewed, revisions were completed, if needed. Upon approval of the lead design, coordinate designs and colorways were developed in the company's studio. Finally, the lead and coordinate engraving areas were rendered in preparation for production. The pre-production process could demand a long timeline if the designs required large repeats, had extensive color palettes, and/or had a unique rendering technique.

The production process was often time-consuming as well. The approved design(s) had to be color separated, screens engraved, colorants mixed, and printing machinery prepared. The stylist would then have to approve the strike-offs (printed samples) for accuracy; again, revisions would be made and the production process would halt until the revisions were complete.

Today, digital methods have eliminated many laborious procedures. Many design studios have digitized their design archives. A stylist can now provide freelance designers with visual references and technical information via e-mail, or the in-house CAD designer can research independently and create original designs. Revisions are done quickly.

Although there are many fully digital designs, hand-rendered designs are still in demand. However, even a hand-rendered design is converted to digital for production. Hand-painted coordinates and colorways have become obsolete and are now done in-house by the studio's CAD staff. Once a lead design has been approved, everything moves to a digital format. Traditional printing requires the design(s) to be scanned, color reduced, cleaned, and then repeated. Coordinates and colorways are then developed to work with the lead. All the design components are then color separated; the type of separation depends on the production method. The digitally separated files are then used for engraving.

Many studios use the Pantone Textile color system, now digital, to ensure continuity of color in a product line. All of the design's preproduction and postproduction information is entered into a database, to be accessed easily for future reference and/or for revisions to color palettes or coordinate designs. Color printouts on paper are used to check color balance, layout, motif scale, etc. Digitally printed fabric samples are available immediately, eliminating regular mill visits by the stylist. The time-consuming, costly mill runs, which now necessitate trips overseas, are monitored via e-mail to ensure production specifications are met.

Digitally printed fabric samples are also used for product prototypes and go directly to the showroom. Designs are also digitally mapped onto a product to display on a website or for presentation to buyers. Orders, including different sizes and colors, require a much shorter sales cycle, resulting in easier and quicker customization of a design in a relatively short turnaround time.

Numerous graphic software programs that drive CAD—freeware, one-time purchase, subscription-based, industry-level, and proprietary (software developed for a specific company)—are becoming more complex and sophisticated. Designers who know how to use such CAD packages appropriately are increasingly sought out in the pattern design marketplace. Industry-level and proprietary software are often too expensive for a freelancer to afford. Therefore, it is important for any freelance designer wishing to enter the field today to be creatively and technically proficient with the most widely used software such as Adobe Creative Cloud's Illustrator and Photoshop for design development and pre-production prep and InDesign for design presentation. Even though Adobe Illustrator now has a patternmaker function that can be used to develop repetitive designs, if a designer is not fully versed in color theory, industry repeats, and layouts, computer usage only serves to quickly create a lot of unmarketable digital designs.

Jobs available for someone with professional surface pattern design CAD experience are varied and include both in-house and freelance positions. For example, during a rush, a freelancer might be hired by a studio to paint a rough design, scan it, and refine it digitally. Although CAD designers are generally pushing salaries higher, salaries or rates can vary widely from industry to industry (see Surface Pattern Design Salaries at the end of this chapter).

Product Categories

Printed Designs

Printed decorative textiles are one of the products produced for the largest segments of industry that utilizes the skills of the surface pattern designer. The apparel market uses the largest quantity of decorative textile prints for end-uses ranging from yard goods and garments to accessories for personal, corporate, and athletic use. Printed decorative home fashion fabrics are produced for both indoor and outdoor use for the residential segment (home/personal) as well as for the commercial segments (hospitality, institutional, corporate, educational, and transportation).

Digital design techniques are used more frequently for designs simulating textural or faux looks that originally could only be done by hand-rendering techniques. Even so, as each design is unique, often the initial rendering is still done by hand using assorted media: gouache, dye, watercolor, collage, etc., on paper, scanned, and developed as an engineered or repetitive design. Apparel design studios that create textile prints for the fashion market create four or more seasonal collections a year, often devising as many as 250 designs or color variations a month to sell to textile or garment manufacturers. Design studios that create textile prints for home fashions do not usually follow a seasonal schedule, as each market area is different, depending on the end-use. For example, collections in the tabletop market for novelty table linen end-uses could include fall/winter, spring/summer, and holiday/seasonal, whereas collections for the bedding, carpeting, or upholstery markets would not.

DOMESTICS

Printed textiles for domestics include those for bedding, bath, kitchen, and tabletop products. The designs used for soft goods, such as a bath or kitchen towel design, are translated and developed mostly by CAD for use on hard goods (bath and kitchen accessories). These products are considered 3-D and are executed in much the same way as products for giftware.

TABLETOP

Tabletop includes domestic soft goods—table linens such as tablecloths, napkins, placemats, etc.—and hard goods—tableware such as dinnerware and serviceware. Table linens may be cut and sewn from a textile with a repeated design fabric or engineered. Dinnerware designs are applied to fine china, stoneware, melamine, etc.

WALLCOVERING

Wallcoverings are decorative soft goods, predominantly printed on a paper substrate for residential use, but there also are fabric- and vinyl-based wallcoverings for both residential and commercial use. The popularity of wallcovering fluctuates frequently, and developments in printing and technology have impacted the design options for residential and commercial wallcoverings. LED, glass fibers, glass beads, etc., have contributed to the use of wallcovering as an accent in commercial venues.

Wall murals, wallies (removable wall stickers), removable wallcovering, sculpted designs, etc., have increased use in the residential segment. Though many American textile printing facilities have closed as production increasingly moved abroad, wallcovering production has not followed and remains steadfast throughout the United States. The most common decorative wallcovering hard goods are ceramic tiles, which come in a variety of sizes, colors and patterns.

FLOORCOVERING

Floorcoverings do not traditionally include bathmats/rugs. Decorative soft, hard, and resilient floorcoverings are used in both residential and commercial settings. Soft floor coverings are considered textile products and include wall-to-wall carpeting, area rugs, and runners, which often coordinate and come in specific industry sizes. There are also customized floorcovering packages created and sold exclusively to individual clients. Wall-to-wall carpeting comes in either continuous rolls to cover floors from wall to wall, or in "modules" called carpet tiles or squares. Residential and commercial carpeting patterns can vary from subtle textures, to bold colorful graphics, to flecks of color against neutral grounds to minimize soil and vacuum marks, and to hide traffic patterns.

Hard floorcoverings include wood, stone, and ceramic products. Ceramic products are commonly more decorative than wood and stone. Resilient floorcoverings include rubber, vinyl, and cork. Vinyl is usually the most decorative and is often used to simulate stone and wood looks.

PAPER PRODUCTS

Paper Products are largely driven by holidays, special events, and celebrations. With the global marketplace being a norm, the industry has responded to this. Larger companies have specialized teams/departments that tailor products to various ethnic and religious events, holidays, and celebrations. Designs can be spilt into specific categories. Gift-giving products could include gift wrap, gift bags, and tags. Party goods/celebration could include paper plates, napkins, tableware, decorations, invitations, and thank-you cards.

Other areas, sometimes referred to as "personal expression" or "memory keeping," could include album covers, picture frames, note cards, scrapbooking papers, etc. There are also novelty products such as magnets, mouse pads, bookmarks, recipe boxes, notepads, etc. Extensive knowledge of graphic software is a necessity for freelancing in this industry.

CRAFT

Craft includes products such as quilting fabrics, which have imagery that ranges from simple geometrics to extremely detailed, intricate holiday prints. All quilting fabrics are printed and are often sold in packs with a central theme. The craft industry uses much the same range of imagery as paper products and more. Recently, quilting has become quite popular with consumers, and there are companies who only produce fabrics for this purpose.

Hobby-based crafts include needlepoint, embroidery, and latch hook kits. The role of the designer here is to create designs that are printed on a base fabric or mesh that is then completed with the needlework technique designated. These images can be simple or complex and are usually multi-colored. Both of these areas utilize computer-generated work depending on the company's needs.

GIFTWARE

Giftware is probably the one area where the skills of the surface pattern designer are used solely for 3-D products, such as ornaments, figurines, decorative boxes, etc. There is a unique skill set required to design for this area; since many products are three–dimensional, the designer must be able to visually represent to the client different views or mechanicals of the design placement on the product. The ability to use 3-D rendering software used to be a plus, but with 3-D rendering becoming a function of graphic software, such as Adobe Photoshop and Illustrator, this requirement is slowly becoming. a necessity. The freelance designer who possesses knowledge of how to use this function correctly and effectively has an advantage.

Woven Designs

TEXTILES

Decorative woven textiles are created by interlacing two sets of yarns—a warp and a weft—on a loom. The patterns created can be very simple or extremely complex, requiring expert knowledge of woven structures. Color, texture, density, and number of yarns used are also necessary design decisions. The woven design industry has become highly computerized (the first computer was the jacquard loom with punch cards), and it is essential for anyone in the field to be computer literate. Woven designs can be visualized on a computer screen or by weaving an actual sample on a handloom (though that term is deceptive because most handlooms are now computerized). Today, software packages simulate yarn type and weave textures so finely that they look real.

Most CAD software packages for woven designs are proprietary and used by companies to turn a design sketch or squiggle into a woven fabric. Hand-rendered designs are often used for producing decorative woven jacquard fabrics. The rendered design, depending on complexity, may be rendered in highly contrasting colors to easily identify the placement of different weaves. The design is then scanned, color-reduced, and a weave is specified (plotted) for each color (yarn) throughout the design; for example, the red in a design could be a twill, the blue a satin, etc. The digital file is then downloaded to the loom and woven.

Most studios specializing in woven fabrics have a creative staff. If the studio has its own loom, a sample weaver, also known as a hand weaver, will execute the designer or stylist's weave specifications. Between the designer/stylist and the sample weaver, there may be other levels and titles, depending on the responsibilities, ability, and experience of the weaver. In a small studio, the designer and the weaver may be the same person. Some studios may not have their own looms and may distribute the work to independent contractors. Despite the predominance of CAD in production, CAD designers have not replaced hand-weavers for sampling. Woven textiles are used for heavier apparel garments and residential and commercial upholstery.

DOMESTICS

Decorative woven textiles are used for bath, kitchen, and top-of-bed products. Some woven bedding and bath products are embellished with embroidery, fringe, appliqué, etc. Due to the global marketplace, the bedding industry has seen a surge in embellishments for top-of-bed products.

TABLETOP

Decorative wovens used for table linens may also be further embellished with embroidery, beading, etc.

Decorative floorcovering products that are woven are either produced manually or by machine. They are more widely used in residential than commercial settings due to the higher production cost. Products include wall-to-wall carpeting, area rugs, carpet tiles, and runners with a plethora of designs ranging from abstract to traditional.

Knitted Designs

Knitting yarn or thread into fabric on a machine is based on the same principle as knitting by hand—yarns are interlooped horizontally and vertically to create a continuous textile. Different combinations of loops create different knit structures. Before computers existed, a knit pattern was programmed on punch cards, which directed a knitting machine to reproduce it. Today, just like woven textiles, knits are increasingly produced by CAD programs, and hand-rendered designs created by surface pattern designers are widely used for developing knitted textiles.

Knits are used predominantly in the apparel industry. Knit designers develop stitch structures and color combinations for four seasons. They either work as staff designers for knitwear companies, which have their own showrooms, or work as independent contractors through studios that act as brokers and take swatches on consignment. Buyers purchase knit designs from the studios and produce their own original knitted garments. The design process is increasingly computerized, speeding up the entire cycle, and large companies tend to dominate the production end of the business.

Embroidery, the most popular of current embellishment techniques, is often used on knits. Just think of the many different logos embroidered on knitted designer golf shirts. The introduction of high-speed, multi-head, computerized embroidery machines in the late 1970s opened up the industry just when hand-embroidered jeans became popular. Knit designers have taken advantage of the new opportunities to include embroidery in their designs. Knit designers may find it helpful to have a basic understanding of embroidery stitches or to consult a specialist, in order to successfully incorporate the needlework in their designs. With the bulk of manufacturing handled abroad, most studios rely on design work created here; therefore, since enough handwork is still required, CAD does not dominate the design phase of the business. That leaves the field, driven by the American market, wide open for independent knit designers who choose to pursue their own artistic vision.

Licensing & Royalties
Licensing Agreements

When a designer who owns the copyright and reproduction rights to a design or designs, permits another party—usually a company—to use the work for a specific purpose(s), the designer spells out the terms of usage in a licensing agreement between the two parties. The terms specified in the licensing agreement include the use, the length of time, the market, and the geographic area. In return for permitting the use, the designer receives a flat fee or an advance against royalties, plus a percentage of sales (see Royalty Arrangements below), with those terms also spelled out in the licensing agreement. Usage can be exclusive to a particular market or geographic area, or non-exclusive. A design can be licensed at the same time for multiple products (usually in different markets); for example, a design may be licensed to one party for paper products and another for dinnerware. The designer retains the right to use the design during the licensing period for any other purpose not specified in the licensing agreement(s). Upon expiration of an exclusive license, the right to use the design reverts to the designer of origin unless another contract is negotiated.

There is no standard license. Licenses vary by the needs of the client and by what is most economically advantageous for the designer who owns the copyright and reproduction rights to a design. The designer may grant the client one-time usage rights of a design for a specified product, a specified length of time (which could be based on a set number of production runs, rather than calendar time), and within a specific geographic area in return for a larger flat fee and no royalties. This sort of arrangement is good for the designer who feels the design being licensed will not actually sell very well. The gamble with this type of negotiation is if the design becomes a best seller, the designer cannot collect any additional revenue from the client but can still market to other product areas.

In the surface pattern design industries, licensing agreements are normally negotiated for an entire line, collection, or group of products for a particular market. For example, a licensing agreement for bedding could include designs for a number of entire "beds" (top-of-bed comforter, duvet covers, and shams, as well as inner bed sheets and pillowcases, and so on). A license for bath products could include a shower curtain, rugs/bathmats, towel sets, and accessories. Licenses are not usually granted for a single product, such as a shower curtain or beach towel. The home fashions industry tends to license with a brand to produce products under their label as consumer awareness directly impacts revenue.

Although any design can be licensed, in the apparel market it is rare because designs have such a short life.

Licensing today is becoming more difficult, even with the use of CAD. It is imperative for the freelance surface pattern designer to possess a specific skill set: the ability to conduct relevant research and to spot trends; to possess an extensive knowledge of color theory, repeats, and layouts; to understand the differences and similarities between lead designs and coordinates, in addition to being familiar with creative limitations dictated by production and end-use.

More thorough discussions of licensing can be found in Chapter 1, Essential Business Practices and Chapter 11, Legal Rights & Issues. Model licensing agreements appear in the Appendix: Contracts & Forms. *Licensing Art & Design* by Caryn R. Leland is listed in Part 5, Resources & References.

Royalty Arrangements

Designers work directly with clients or via a licensing agent to determine whether a royalty arrangement is in the best interests of both parties in relation to design usage. Arrangements may include a non-refundable advance payment to the designer called an "advance against royalties," paid before the product is sold. At minimum, many designers negotiate advances to cover their expenses. Often advances are equal to the price of the work if it were sold outright. Royalties are a percentage of total sales paid to the designer, based on the product's wholesale price. The advance is deducted from sales; once the entire advance has been realized by the licensor, then the designer will begin to receive royalties. Royalty percentages and advances vary from industry to industry; high-volume items may be as low as a fraction of a percent. Percentages are negotiated individually and will vary with the designer or brand's reputation or significance to the consumer. They can range from 1 to 5% of the wholesale price and can differ from product to product. See Figure 10-1 for Sample Advances & Royalties by product type.

Working with Representatives

Surface pattern designers frequently work with representatives or agents who have the legal right to act on behalf of the designers they represent only in the manner agreed to by both parties. A model Surface Pattern Designer-Agent Agreement can be found in the Appendix: Contracts & Forms. A complete discussion of the artist/representative relationship is found in Chapter 2, Professional Relationships.

Trade Practices

The following trade practices have guided the industry and are particularly relevant to freelance surface pattern designers. The Graphic Artists Guild strongly recommends confirming all agreements in writing. Designers should read any agreement carefully and should consider the benefits of restricting the sale of rights to specific markets. (For detailed information on negotiating and model contract provisions, see Chapter 1, Essential Business Practices; Chapter 3, Professional Issues; and the Surface Pattern Design business and legal forms in the Appendix: Contracts & Forms.)

Speculation: Speculative ventures, whether in financial markets or in the creative industries, are fraught with risk. Individuals who choose this course risk loss of capital and all expenses. Designers who create speculative work with the hope of selling at a trade show or who accept speculative assignments (whether directly from a client or by entering a contest or competition), risk the loss of fees, expenses, and the potential opportunity to pursue other compensated assignments. In most circumstances, all the risks are placed on the designer, with the client or contest holder assuming none. For example, some buyers will decide whether or not to purchase a design only upon approval of finished work. Each designer should make an independent decision about acceptance of speculative assignments based upon a careful evaluation of the risks and benefits of accepting them and of the designer's particular circumstances.

Many surface pattern designers, choosing to act as entrepreneurs, create original design collections or groups and try to market them in a variety of ways. For example, if a designer develops a collection for the domestic market and enters into a licensing agreement with a manufacturer who agrees to pay an advance against royalty sales, the designer and the manufacturer share the risk in the mutual investment. The compensation to both parties is speculative, meaning both are dependent on the sale of the product. Designers who create works on assignment or commission always receive payment for their work. (To help ensure payment, see the Surface Pattern Designer Estimate and Confirmation Form in the Appendix: Contracts & Forms.)

Billing for a Sale: When a sale is made, a receipt or invoice is presented by the designer that states the terms of the sale and is signed by the client. The terms of payment should be negotiated prior to the sale, and these terms should be stated on the invoice. Because invoices largely reflect the designer's labor, they should be made payable upon receipt. Companies often take 30 days to pay invoices. If payment is legitimately delayed, the designer may wish to accommodate the buyer and grant a reasonable extension, but the new deadline should be presented in writing. Any transfer of copyright or usage rights should be contingent upon full payment of the designer's invoice.

Granting extensions should be viewed as a professional courtesy on the part of the designer, not the buyer's right. Some designers may demand a late fee—usually a percentage of the outstanding balance—as compensation for a delay in payment. Designers who employ this practice usually notify their clients of the policy in writing before any work is accepted. This practice should be used particularly when longer extensions are granted.

Cancellation (kill) Fees: Clients usually pay the designer a cancellation fee if the assignment is cancelled for reasons beyond the designer's control. The amount of the fee varies considerably, ranging from 30% to 100%, depending upon the percentage of work completed. Some professional designers prefer to receive 50% of the agreed-upon fee up front for commissioned work, which transfers to a kill fee if the job is terminated. (See Chapter 3, Professional Issues, for a detailed discussion of kill fees.)

Unless otherwise agreed to, the client usually obtains all the originally agreed-upon rights to the use of the design(s) upon payment of the cancellation fee. Under a royalty arrangement, all rights to the artwork, as well as possession of the original art, generally revert to the designer upon cancellation.

If a job based on documentary/vintage or original work belonging to a client is canceled, payment of a time and/or labor charge is a widely accepted industry custom.

Client Responsibilities: It is common practice for a client to approve a layout with a technique sample, a portion of the design rendered on paper with the intended medium and technique, using the full color palette proposed for the finished design. Designers may request additional payment when the client requires major changes and/or additions to the design that were not part of the original approved design. Designers should be flexible enough to accept the working procedures with clients from different markets, as the design needs, timelines, etc., vary within the industry. A design for apparel, for example, requires a different procedure and creative needs than that for a wallcovering. Sales taxes, if due in accordance with state laws, must be collected on all designs.

Credit to Designer: In the past, in acknowledgement of the creative work designers provided, many received credit and their copyright notice printed on the selvage of the textile or somewhere else on the product if other than a textile. Today this practice is nonexistent and only occurs when negotiated as part of a licensing agreement.

Expenses: Additional expenses outside of the agreed-upon design fee, such as travel, accommodations, consultation time, shipping and mailing charges, and other out-of-pocket expenses, if applicable, could be billed to the client, separately or included in the original work agreement. Regardless, clients should be made fully aware of these possible charges, and they should be included in the original agreement to be billed separately, as they occur, or as part of the "design project." Designers should always save receipts whenever possible and submit copies with their invoice to avoid any disputes.

Holding Work: In the past, the practice of holding work was pertinent only to speculative work. Although previous experience with a client who wished to hold work prior to purchase was generally the guide for allowing this practice, designers today usually do not consent to any holding period. In addition to risking that the work may be damaged or lost, with today's technology, designers run the risk of their design being digitally appropriated, for want of a better term. Most stylist and design directors have the authority to purchase designs on the spot, and they normally do so. When that is impossible, having a signed holding form with a disclosure agreement is recommended. The length of the holding period of three days is permitted by some designers, but most limit this time to several hours or one day.

Quantity Sales: Each design is unique, and the creation can vary in labor intensity. A factor that many designers feel should not warrant a discount is when a number of designs are purchased at the same time. The exception to this may occur if a designer has created a design collection with a lead, and several coordinates; the designer could sell them individually, only if they are designed to work with or without the rest of the collection, but would have better luck selling them as a group with a break in price. Nevertheless, designers should decide independently how to price their work.

Return of Original Work: Commissioned designs and speculative designs sold without a licensing agreement are very rarely returned, as the production process often mutilates the work to the point that it is useless. Surface pattern designers should negotiate to obtain samples of their printed designs or finished products for display and portfolio use.

Rush Work: Expedited or rush work will usually increase the original fee, and as with all charges, the parties to the transaction must agree upon a fair rush fee.

Uses and Limitations: The intended use of commissioned or licensed work is generally stated clearly in a contract, purchase order, invoice, or letter of agreement that states the price and terms of sale. If a company commissions a design, it usually holds the copyright and can use the design as it wishes.

If a client decides to use a previously or currently commissioned design for products other than originally stated in the contract, the designer of origin is customarily offered the opportunity to create the redesign to fit the new format. An example of this would be reformatting a wall covering design for a matching printed fabric. Common practice is for the designer to receive additional compensation for such extended uses. If no specific limits on usage were stated in the original contract and changes do not have to be made to the design to render it usable for a new product, the designer usually will not be offered additional payment for the new use of the design.

If the original was a speculative design purchased outright, the company can use the design for whatever products it wishes. If a designer enters into a licensing agreement to use a design specifically for bedding, the designer should always ensure in the agreement with the client that the same design can be licensed in another uncompetitive market, such as paper products, dinnerware, etc.

Reuse Fees: Specific uses, and terms for uses other than those initially specified, should be negotiated in advance whenever possible. Secondary use of a design can sometimes be of greater value than its primary use. Therefore, there is no set formula for reuse fees.

Surface Pattern Design Salaries

Depending on the industry segment, there are varying job titles as well as responsibilities. Most employment opportunities, when searched, are found under the heading of Textile Design and sometimes Graphic Design, although Surface Pattern Design encompasses much more than either of these terms suggests. Within these titles, positions for non-textile products, i.e., paper products, may

also be located. Today's marketplace is competitive and almost no one, designer or not, does just one thing anymore. Nearly all design/product development positions not only require creative skills and production knowledge, but often require the designer to gain an understanding of the business/retail side as well.

The content provided is an overall view of common titles, responsibilities, and average salary ranges across the United States. Salaries are also affected by the applicant's extent of education/degree, prior industry experience, the size of the company, geographic location, bonuses, stock options, and other incentives.

Assistant CAD/Textile/Graphic Designers are entry-level designers, one to two years out of college, with less than 5 years of experience. These creatives are guided by the Associate CAD Designer. They usually have to be trained on the correct software procedures to prepare original, purchased designs, or company archives for the CAD Designer (or a higher position) to start refining the designs. Responsibilities may include scanning and cleaning artwork, color reducing, putting into repeat and possibly developing some colorways. They may also create simple prints and some slight design changes to the composition. They should be capable of working on multiple projects simultaneously with various deadlines. In addition, participation in meetings for product development is expected to gain an understanding of the business, trends, and a basic knowledge of manufacturing principles and production requirements. **$40,000–50,000 +/-**

Associate CAD/Textile/Graphic Designers have, in addition to a degree, up to 5 years' experience. They possess the skills of the Assistant CAD Designer and are guided by the Senior CAD Designer to assist in creating new designs for products that reflect current market trends. Responsibilities may include collecting market data on future trends, including fabrication, material, color, and design; translating trends into concepts that reflect the company's business needs and goals; creating and editing design collections; development of multiple colorways from seasonal color palettes; and producing trend and color-boards and storyboards for presentation to customers and sales teams. They also manage multiple projects simultaneously with various deadlines, and collaborate with product development and design teams to ensure designs manufacturability; and they correspond regularly with factories to articulate printing needs, track and maintain design samples, design development, and approval. **$51,000–60,000+/-**

CAD/Textile/Graphic Designers have a lot more responsibility than Assistant Designers. They are expected to multitask as directed by the Senior CAD Designer and/or Design Director to establish the overall seasonal print direction. The skill set demands creative talent, speed, and proficiency using CAD for design development and management as they oversee and provide requirements to the Assistant and/or Associate CAD designers on design projects. Responsibilities may include presenting product and concept ideas to design, merchandising, and sourcing teams; collaborating daily with cross-functional teams such as product design, product development, pattern design, and vendors; creating original designs from scratch, expanding the work prepared by the Assistant and/or Associate CAD Designers to make aesthetic changes and ensure all technical requirements are met. At this level, many designers begin changing jobs, and are able to negotiate raises (usually 15%). **$52,000–75,000 +/-**

Senior CAD/Textile/Graphic Designers provide on-trend creative/design direction, workload management, and training and coaching in specialized CAD software to the creative team (including the Associate CAD and CAD Designers). Other responsibilities may include researching pattern and color trends worldwide; initiating special CAD projects assigned by senior management to implement design concepts consistent with brand strategies; developing and presenting CAD concepts to director and design development teams; approving design layouts and repeats, original color palette, and new colorways preproduction. They also manage communication with international and domestic vendors on product production for the approval of designs for sampling, and mass production with factories to the specifications of the Director of Design. **$72,000–85,000 +/-**

CAD/Textile/Graphic Design Managers have very similar roles and responsibilities at a lot of companies, and report to the Director of Design. They have the most creative license and are responsible for creatively leading the CAD team. Responsibilities may include overseeing all product categories; leading, managing, and training the design team; creating the main/key designs for collections; overseeing all aspects of development for collections; approving all final designs; presenting to senior management; and working with vendors. Senior Designers and above (manager, director) are expected to own a creative cyclical aesthetic, have budget responsibilities, and manage and hire employees. In addition, they travel to keep abreast of current trends and to stay well informed of changes in the marketplace, ensuring

that the right creative path is determined months in advance to meet a client's brand/item and price point. A Senior Designer at one company may have just as much ownership or seniority as a Design Manager at another company. When there are open positions in industry for managers and directors, Senior Designers and above are considered for them because the responsibilities are so fluid. At this level, the salary is dependent on experience. **$100,000–160,000 +/-**

Creative Directors oversee all activities of the CAD team (sometimes multiple departments for Art/Design Directors) and report to the Vice President of Design and above. Responsibilities may include leading product design strategy and development processes within the defined market sector and/or cross-product categories; building and maintaining market segment products, design, styling, and color needs; encompassing styling duties, particularly to be a trend leader, and set design direction; overseeing the senior design team; managing budgets; attending applicable meetings; and international travel. Many Directors have held multiple positions at different companies. Depending on the size of the company, they may also be responsible for overseeing advertising, packaging, and showrooms. The salary range at this level is also dependent upon experience. **$175,000–250,000+/-**

Vice Presidents/Senior Vice Presidents/Executive Vice Presidents of Design lead the entire design team (Design, CAD, Trend/Concept, sometimes Technical Design) and are responsible for ensuring that work of the entire design department is produced on time and on budget. They work with merchandising and sales to set the direction and fulfill the sales goals for the company. They may also be responsible for overseeing licensing activities. Depending on the size of the company and amount of creative responsibility, the vice presidents also may be responsible for over-seeing advertising, packaging, showrooms, etc. Salary ranges vary based on company structure and experience level Note: Many companies have eliminated or are considering eliminating Design Directors or Vice Presidents of Design, to eliminate hefty salaries. Pertinent feedback is provided from the sales team and the Vice President of Marketing, and the design team (Manager and below) is entrusted with rolling out the creative initiatives. As some Design Directors or Vice Presidents of Design are not familiar with the graphic software used—Adobe Photoshop and Illustrator, industry software such as NedGraphics, and PDM (product data management) and PLM (product lifecycle management) software—companies prefer having design leadership (usually manager level) that can create designs and/or contribute more than just managerial skills. The salary range at this level is also dependent upon experience. **$275,000–350,000**

Pricing Freelance Design

A freelance designer's fee can be determined by several factors, including a track record of success, associated research, complexity of the rendering technique, number of colors, size of croquis for apparel, whether the design is engineered or in repeat, design revisions, turnaround time, and transfer of copyright and usage rights. In certain circumstances, freelance designers may charge by the hour or by the day, instead of a flat fee. (See Figure 10-2 for Hourly and Day Rates.)

The Comparative Flat Fees for Surface Pattern Design provided in Figures 10-3 through 10-10 reflect input from established professionals in the United States and are meant as a point of reference only. All flat fees reflect a +/- range for each purchased speculative design and/or commissioned design. Final fees can be based on design complexity, number of colors, quantity of speculative designs purchased, or services commissioned at one time. Company size and level of distribution can also be contributing factors.

Typically, fee ranges do not consider the designer's geographic location, differences in cost of living, or intended end-use of speculative design(s) purchased. The buyer and seller are free to negotiate independently to decide how to price purchased or commissioned work(s) after taking all factors into account.

10–1 Surface Pattern Design ✳ Licensing[1]—Sample Advances & Royalty

QUILTING FABRIC	Advance Against Royalties[2]	Royalty Percent[3]
By the Yard: printed	$0.00–500± per pattern $0.10–0.25 per yard printed	2%± Big Box/Mass Market[4] 2–8%± Independent Retailers[5]
Collections: 3 to 8 patterns	$0.00–500± collection	2–8%± Big Box/Mass Market 5%± per Collection

DOMESTICS	Advance Against Royalties[2]	Royalty Percent[3]
BATH PRODUCTS		
Soft Goods (3-pc. towel ensemble: wash cloth; hand, guest/face towels)	$0.00–10,000±	3–6%± Big Box/Mass Market 5%± Independent Retailers
Hard Goods (Accessories: toothbrush holder, lotion dispenser, soap dish, tumbler, tissue cover, and wastebasket)	Not Common	3–6%± Big Box/Mass Market 5%± Independent Retailers
BEDDING PRODUCTS		
Top of Bed (throws, blankets, quilts, coverlets, bedspreads, decorative pillows, etc.)	Not Common	3–6%± Big Box/Mass Market 5%± Independent Retailers
Outer Bed (3-pc. ensemble: pillow shams, comforter face/duvet, bed skirt)	$0.00–10,000±	3–6%± Big Box/Mass Market 5%± Independent Retailers
Inner Bed (3-pc. ensemble: pillowcases, fitted and flat sheets)	$0.00–15,000±	3%± Big Box/Mass Market 5%± Independent Retailers
KITCHEN PRODUCTS		
Soft Goods: Countertop (textile ensemble: kitchen towels, dish cloths, potholders, oven mitts.)	$0.00–10,000±	3–6%± Big Box/Mass Market 5%± Independent Retailers
Soft Goods: Floor (single-design floor mats and kitchen rugs)	Not Common	3–5%± Big Box/Mass Market 5%± Independent Retailers
Hard Goods (canister sets, spoon holders, trivets, etc.)	$0.00–10,000±	3–6%± Big Box/Mass Market 5%± Independent Retailers

WALLCOVERING	Advance Against Royalties[2]	Royalty Percent[3]
Collection (# of pieces variable)	$1,000–5,000± per collection	2–5%± Mass Market 5%± for big name licensees like Disney®
Per Design	$800± per design	2–5%± Mass Market 5%± for big name licenses like Disney®

FLOOR COVERING	Advance Against Royalties[2]	Royalty Percent[3]
Single Designs (sizes variable)	Not Common	3–5%± Big Box/Mass Market 5%± Independent Retailers

TABLETOP PRODUCTS	Advance Against Royalties[2]	Royalty Percent[3]
Soft Goods (3–4 pc. textile ensemble: tablecloth, runner, placemat, and napkin)	$0.00–150± per design $0.00–1,500± per 3–4 pieces	3–6%± Big Box/Mass Market 5%± Independent Retailers
Hard Goods (3–6 pc. ensemble: dinner/salad plate, soup/cereal bowl, cup and saucer)	$0.00–1,500±	4–5%± Big Box/Mass Market 5%± Independent Retailers

PAPER PRODUCTS[6] (ranges reflect complexity)[7]	Advance Against Royalties[2]	Royalty Percent[3]
Single Images (non-specified use)	$0–250± per design	3–6% Big Box/Mass Market 5–8%± Independent Retailers
Gift Giving: Gift Bags (single image)	$100± each	2.5% Big Box/Mass Market 3–6%± Independent Retailers
Memory Keeping: Storage Boxes (set of 3)	$500± each	2.5% Big Box/Mass Market 3–6%± Independent Retailers
Collections: Groups of related designs that fall into a specific category. Number of designs will vary based on company needs.	$0.00–750± depending on number of pieces and complexity	2.5% Big Box/Mass Market 3–6%± Independent Retailers

1. **LICENSING**—the practice of a designer (licensor) giving a buyer (licensee) permission to use(rent) their work(s) for a specified product/ product line, length of time, geographic location and any other stipulations agreed upon by the designer and buyer or via the designer's licensing agent.

2. **ADVANCE AGAINST ROYALTIES** ranges in Figure 10-1 do not represent specific prices for particular jobs. The advance is often a payment deducted from future royalties. Once the advance amount is reached in sales, then royalties are collected by the designer, if part of the agreement. The designer and buyer are free to negotiate independently or via the designer's licensing agent. There is no "standard" contract across industries or even within a company.

3. **ROYALTY PERCENTS** are commonly based on a percent of net sales paid to the designer; in today's marketplace it is becoming more common for the buyer to pay only a royalty percentage. In some cases, the designer will receive a small up-front fee (advance against royalties) in addition to royalties.

4. **BIG BOX/MASS MARKET STORES** can be split into 2 categories: Target, Walmart, etc., are considered general merchandise, whereas Best Buy, Home Depot, etc., are considered specialty stores.

5. **INDEPENDENT RETAIL STORES** are privately owned businesses.

6. **PAPER PRODUCTS** often feature designs that range from a single image to several related images used for one or more of the products listed within the main categories below. In some instances, a design(s) could be used across categories.

* **Gift Giving** may include gift wrap, gift bags, tissue, gift tags, and enclosures.
* **Party Goods** may include invites/thank you cards, cups, plates, napkins, favor bags, table covers, centerpieces, etc.
* **Memory Keeping** may include albums, scrapbooks, journal covers, picture frames, scrapbook papers, storage boxes.

7. **COMPLEXITY:** A **simple design** could be defined as 2–6 flat colors, simple motifs (e.g., dots), open ground. A **complex design** could be defined as 7–12+ flat and tonal colors; detailed motifs (e.g., watercolor); fine line work; textures; packed layout, little ground; inclusion of special treatments, such as foil/glitter/flocking, embossing, laser cuts, etc.

10–2 Surface Pattern Design ✳ Hourly & Day Rates[1]

ORIGINAL HAND-RENDERED DESIGNS[3]	HOURLY RATE (based on experience)	DAY RATE (based on experience)
ON-SITE		
Apparel[2]	$40–80±	$320–640±
Home Fashions	$65–100±	$520–900±
Paper Products	$20–70±	$200–600±
OFF-SITE		
Apparel[2]	$50–80±	$400–800± per artwork
Home Fashions	$75–150±	Usually project-based fees
Paper Products	$50–75±	Usually project-based fees
CAD/PRODUCTION WORK[4]	HOURLY RATE (based on experience)	DAY RATE (based on experience)
ON-SITE		
Apparel[2]	$40–80±	$400–800±
Home Fashions (excludes floorcovering)	$75–100±	$600–800±
Home Fashions: Colorwork per design; based on complexity	$45–75±	$360–700±
Floor Covering: Rug Design	$40±	N/A
Floor Covering: Colorwork per design; based on complexity	$40–100±	N/A
Paper Products	$40–70±	$320–560±
OFF-SITE		
Apparel[2]	$35–85±	$400–800±
Home Fashions (based on client and experience; off-site CAD can be hourly and/or project-based)	$75–100±	Usually project-based fees
Paper Products	$35–80±	Usually project-based fees
MILL WORK[5]	HOURLY RATE (based on experience)	DAY RATE (based on experience)
Home Fashions	N/A (handled internally or via vendors)	$400 (8 hr. shift)
MARKET RESEARCH[6]	HOURLY RATE (based on experience)	DAY RATE (based on experience)
Apparel[2]	More likely to have in-house staff travel or purchase a package, service, or online subscription with professional forecasting companies/studios to meet this need.	
Home Fashions	$45–100±	Usually project-based fees
Paper Products	$25–70±	Usually project-based fees

10–2 Surface Pattern Design ✳ Hourly & Day Rates[1] *(continued)*

PRODUCT DEVELOPMENT[7]	HOURLY RATE (based on experience)	DAY RATE (based on experience)
Apparel[2]	Usually occurs as part of a consultant agreement covering a broad range of responsibility for an entire brand and is usually a project-based fee.	
Home Fashions	Usually occurs as part of a consultant agreement covering a broad range of responsibility for an entire brand and is more project-fee based	
Paper Products	$25–70±	

1. **HOURLY & DAY RATES:** *On- and off-site freelancer's roles and hourly/day rates are experience-based and typically all-encompassing. Responsibilities can range from hand, CAD, color, and trend work, etc. The content provided is also affected by the designer's education/degree, prior industry experience, company size, and geographic location.*

2. **APPAREL:** *Experience Levels may be defined as Assistant Freelancer = college graduate, entry-level, approx. $25 per hour; Junior Freelancer = 3–5 years, approx. $45 per hour; Senior Freelancer I = 5–8 years, approx. $65 per hour; Senior Freelancer II = 8–10 years, up to approx. $80 per hour.*

3. **ORIGINAL HAND-RENDERED DESIGNS:** *On-site work may include, but is not limited to, creating original hand-rendered designs; development of original designs, purchased designs, or company archives via CAD. Off-site work may include, but is not limited to, commissioned hand-rendered original designs via in-house instruction and further development via CAD based on company needs.*

4. **CAD/PRODUCTION WORK:** *On and off-site work may include, but is not limited to, color reduction and cleaning of original, purchased designs or company archives; color separations, development of repeats, coordinates and/or colorways, product mappings, and presentations. Based on the company's studio, other tasks may be assigned appropriate to skill level.*

5. **MILL WORK** *is based on an 8-hour day. Types of work may include, but are not limited to, approval of engraving, strike-offs, color. Usually involves international travel. Travel time is often billed in addition to the day rate.*

6. **MARKET RESEARCH:** *Trend and color research/reports; compilation of research into visuals, such as story/mood/trend boards. Trend boards are visual collages of conducted research to identify upcoming colors, themes, materials, textures, etc., to provide information to clients as inspiration and creative direction for upcoming lines. They communicate a wide range of information quickly and are commonly used within design fields. Trend boards are either physical or digital, but commonly both. Usually involves international travel. Travel time is often billed in addition to the day rate.*

7. **PRODUCT DEVELOPMENT** *usually refers to all stages involved in bringing a product from concept to consumer and can include product specifications, market analysis, design concept, financial considerations, production scheduling, and more.*

10–3 Comparative Flat Fees for Surface Pattern Design ✳ Apparel Textiles

Fees in Figure 10–3 do not reflect any specific trade practices and do not constitute specific prices for particular jobs. The buyer and seller are free to negotiate, with each designer independently or via the designer's agent/rep deciding how to price the work, after taking all factors into account. Reading the more detailed information about pricing factors provided in the text will help in pricing projects.

DESIGNS FOR PRINTED TEXTILES (Accessories: designs used for scarves, shawls, ties, handbags, etc.; Garments: designs used for clothing)	
Croquis[2]	**Hand-Rendered[1]/CAD[1]**
Speculative[3]	$200–400± each (per croquis, w/o repeat or colorway, based on complexity)
Developed[4]	$250–450± each (per croquis, w/o repeat or colorway, based on complexity)
Commissioned[5] (9 x 12")	$500–600± each (per croquis, w/ repeat and/or colorway, based on complexity)
Engineered[6]/Repetitive Designs[7]	**Hand-Rendered[1]/CAD[1]**
Speculative	$500–600± each (per croquis, w/ repeat and/or colorway, based on complexity)
Commissioned	$500–600± each (per croquis, w/ repeat and/or colorway, based on complexity)
DESIGNS FOR WOVEN TEXTILES (Accessories, Garments)	
Engineered/Repetitive Designs	**Hand-Woven Sample:** $150–$400± each (per sample, based on complexity)
DESIGNS FOR KNITTED TEXTILES (Garments)	
Engineered/Repetitive Designs	**Hand-Woven Sample:** $200–$550± each (per sample, based on complexity)
COLORWAYS[8] (commissioned)	
Engineered/Repetitive Designs	**CAD:** $150–$300± each (based on complexity)

1. **PRINTED TEXTILES: Hand-rendered designs** are created with traditional media and digitized in house or by the designer for an extra fee. **CAD designs** are created digitally using off-the shelf or proprietary software and delivered as a digital file. A **simple design** could be defined as 2–6 flat colors, simple motifs (e.g., dots), open ground. A **complex design** could be defined as 7–12+ flat and tonal colors, detailed motifs (e.g., watercolor), fine line work, textures, packed layout, little ground.

2. **CROQUIS:** Designs created as an original full-color rendered concept/sketch, sometimes with the suggestion of a repeat. Note: Some designers may charge an additional fee to put a croquis/sketch into a factory repeat.

3. **CROQUIS—SPECULATIVE:** Designs (may be in repeat or not) created for direct sale or licensing at trade shows, not created for a specific end-use or client and is further developed in-house or by the designer (for which an additional fee may be negotiated).

4. **CROQUIS DEVELOPED:** In-house or commissioned designer takes the client's purchased design(s) and develops into a factory repeat, rendering the engraving area and possibly creating coordinates and colorways.

5. **COMMISSIONED DESIGNS:** When a designer is hired by a company for a flat/hourly rate to provide specifics such as, but not limited to, market research; creating trend boards, hand-rendered croquis, creating repetitive or engineered lead designs; developing CAD coordinates and/or colorways, etc., while collaborating with the client to ensure the creative focus and production specs are met.

6. **ENGINEERED DESIGNS:** A full-color design created to fit a specific product's dimensions. Can be speculative or commissioned.

7. **REPETITIVE DESIGNS:** A full-color design in a factory repeat with the engraving area rendered.

8. **COLORWAYS:** Multiple color treatments for an approved design generated digitally; may include scanning and cleaning prior to creating the colorways. Price increases with number of colors and amount of editing; usually commissioned.

10–4 Comparative Flat Fees for Surface Pattern Design
✳ Home Fashions: Decorative Printed Textiles

Fees in Figure 10–4 do not reflect any specific trade practices and do not constitute specific prices for particular jobs. The buyer and seller are free to negotiate, with each designer independently or via the designer's agent/rep deciding how to price the work, after taking all factors into account. Reading the more detailed information about pricing factors provided in the text will help in pricing projects.

	HAND-RENDERED[1] (prices based on complexity)	CAD[1] (prices based on complexity)
DESIGNS FOR ACCESSORIES		
DECORATIVE THROW PILLOWS: ENGINEERED DESIGNS[2]		
Square: 16 x 16",18 x18", 20 x 20", 22 x 22", 24 x 24" **Rectangular:** 12 x 18", 12 x 20", 12 x 24", 16 x 26", 16 x 36"	$150–500± or hourly rate	$250–750± or hourly rate
COLORWAYS[3] (Commissioned)[4]		
Engineered Designs	NA	$100± each or hourly rate
DESIGNS FOR THROWS/COVERLETS		
Engineered/Repetitive Designs[5]	$400–800± each	$500–800± each
COLORWAYS (Commissioned)		
Engineered/Repetitive Designs	NA	$200± each or hourly rate
DESIGNS FOR WINDOW TREATMENTS: SOFT GOODS (Curtains/Sheers, Drapes, Swags, Valances, Roman Shades, etc.)		
Croquis[6]	$450–700± each	$500–750± each
Croquis Developed[7]	$450–800± each	$500–800± each
Engineered/Repetitive Designs	$500–1,000± each	$1000–1,200± each
REPETITIVE DESIGNS: MM SIZES[8]		
27"	$600–1,200± each	$1,200–2,500± each
25.25"	$500–1,000± each	$650–2,000± each
18"	$500–1,000± each	$550–1,500± each
13.5"	$300–900± each	$350–1,000± each
6.75 – 9"	$300–550± each	$450–500± each
COLORWAYS (Commissioned)		
27", 18", 13.5", 9", 6.75", 4.5", 3"	NA	$100–300± each
DESIGNS FOR UPHOLSTERY: MM SIZES		
27"	$700–2,000± each	$700–1,900± each
25.25"	$600–1,850± each	$600–1,800± each

10–4 Comparative Flat Fees for Surface Pattern Design
✳ Home Fashions: Decorative Printed Textiles *(continued)*

DESIGNS FOR UPHOLSTERY: MM SIZES		
18"	$500–1750± each	$500–750± each
13.5"	$350–700± each	$350–550± each
6.75–9"	$250–500± each	$250–900± each
COLORWAYS (Commissioned)[4]		
27", 18", 13.5"	NA	$200–400± each
9", 6.75", 4.5", 3"	NA	$25–50± each

1. **HAND-RENDERED DESIGNS** *are created with traditional media and digitized in house or by the designer for an extra fee.* **CAD designs** *are created digitally using off-the-shelf or proprietary software and delivered as a digital file. A* **simple design** *could be defined as 2–6 flat colors, simple motifs (e.g., dots), open ground. A* **complex design** *could be defined as 7–12+ flat and tonal colors, detailed motifs (e.g., watercolor), fine line work, textures, packed layout, little ground.*

2. **ENGINEERED DESIGNS:** *A full-color design created to fit a specific product's dimensions. Can be speculative or commissioned.*

3. **COLORWAYS:** *Multiple color treatments for an approved design generated digitally; may include scanning and cleaning prior to creating the colorways. Price increases with number of colors and amount of editing; usually commissioned.*

4. **COMMISSIONED DESIGNS:** *When a designer is hired by a company for a flat/hourly rate to provide specifics such as, but not limited to, market research; creating trend boards, hand-rendered croquis, creating repetitive or engineered lead designs; developing CAD coordinates and/or colorways, etc., while collaborating with the client to ensure the creative focus and production specs are met.*

5. **REPETITIVE DESIGNS:** *A full-color design in a factory repeat with the engraving area rendered.*

6. **CROQUIS:** *Design created as an original full-color rendered concept/ sketch, sometimes with the suggestion of a repeat. Note: Some designers may charge an additional fee to put a croquis/sketch into a factory repeat.*

7. **CROQUIS DEVELOPED:** *In-house or commissioned designer takes the client's purchased design(s) and develops into a factory repeat, rendering the engraving area and possibly creating coordinates and colorways.*

8. **MM (MAIN MODULE) SIZES:** *The height of the design to be put into repeat; widths vary depending on end-use and manufacturer.*

10-5 Comparative Flat Fees for Surface Pattern Design
✳ Home Fashion: Bath Products

Fees in Figure 10–5 do not reflect any specific trade practices and do not constitute specific prices for particular jobs. The buyer and seller are free to negotiate, with each designer independently or via the designer's agent/rep deciding how to price the work, after taking all factors into account. Reading the more detailed information about pricing factors provided in the text will help in pricing projects.

SOFT GOODS[1] (All prices based on complexity)[1]	
PRINTED TEXTILES	**Hand-Rendered[1]**
B&W Concept Sketches (wash cloth; hand, guest/face & bath towels)	Up to $250± per group
PRINTED TEXTILES	**Hand-Rendered/CAD[1]**
Single Full-Color Motif: Purchased for specific needs to assist with in-house studio development for wash cloth; hand, guest/face, and bath towel layouts.	$200–450± each
Single Engineered[2]/Repetitive Design[3] Purchased and developed via CAD in-house for wash cloths; hand, guest/face, and bath towels.	Engineered: Up to $750± each Repeated: Up to $1,200± each,
CROQUIS[4]	**Hand-Rendered/CAD[1]**
Wash cloth; hand, guest/face towels	$200–450± each
Bath Towel	$400–500± each
ENGINEERED/REPETITIVE DESIGNS	**Hand-Rendered/CAD[1]**
Wash cloth; hand, guest/face towels	$400–500± each
Bath Towel	$500–1,000± each
3-Piece Ensemble (Wash cloth, hand & bath towels)	$500–1,000± each
ENGINEERED/REPETITIVE DESIGNS	**CAD**
Colorways[5] (Commissioned)[6]	$300–400± each
SHOWER CURTAINS (FABRIC/VINYL)	**Hand-Rendered**
B&W Concept Sketches	Up to $250± each
SHOWER CURTAINS (FABRIC/VINYL)	**Hand-Rendered/CAD**
Croquis Developed[7] (Fabric 25 ¼" MM[8]/Vinyl 24" MM)	$400–1,000± each
Engineered	$750– 1,200± each
Repetitive Designs[3] (Fabric 25 ¼" MM/Vinyl 24" MM)	$800–1,200± each
SHOWER CURTAINS (FABRIC/VINYL)	**CAD**
Colorways (commissioned)	$100–200± each

10-5 Comparative Flat Fees for Surface Pattern Design
✳ Home Fashion: Bath Products *(continued)*

SOFT GOODS[1] (All prices based on complexity)[1]	
BATH MATS/RUGS	**Hand-Rendered**
B&W Concept Sketches	$150–250± each
BATH MATS/RUGS	**Hand-Rendered/CAD**
Croquis Developed	$200–450± each
Engineered	$300–800± each
WOVEN/TUFTED TEXTILES (+$50 if showing woven or tufted texture)	**Hand-Rendered/CAD**
Single Engineered/Repetitive Design	
Wash Cloth; Hand, Guest/Face Towels	$150–250± each
Bath Towel	$350–400± each
3-Piece Ensemble (Wash cloth, hand and bath towels)	$400–700± per ensemble
Bath Mats/Rugs	$300–450± per design
Embroidery (Color Concepts)	$150–350± per design
HARD GOODS[9] (All prices based on complexity)	
ACCESSORIES (Toothbrush holder, lotion dispenser, soap dish, tumbler, tissue cover, and wastebasket)	**Hand-Rendered[9]**
Single Pieces (B&W concepts, 2-D)	$100–150± each
B&W Shape Concepts (8 x 10" thumbnails)	$100–150 each
ACCESSORIES (Toothbrush holder, lotion dispenser, soap dish, tumbler, tissue cover, and wastebasket)	**Hand-Rendered/CAD[9]**
Croquis[4] (2-D)	$75–175± each
Mechanicals (3-D)	$150–500 each
Ensembles (Full-scale 2-D color renderings, with 3-D production-ready mechanicals)	
4-Piece: Toothbrush Holder, Lotion Dispenser, Soap Dish, Tumbler	$1,200–2,000± per ensemble
6-Piece: 4 Pieces above + Tissue Cover and Wastebasket	$1,300–2,500 per ensemble
Client (company) Concept: Full-color rendering (2-D)	$300–350 each
Designer Concept: Full-Color Rendering (2-D)	$600–700 each

10-5 Comparative Flat Fees for Surface Pattern Design
✳ **Home Fashion: Bath Products** (continued)

1. ***SOFT GOODS: PRINTED TEXTILES: Hand-rendered designs*** are created with traditional media and digitized in house or by the designer for an extra fee. **CAD designs** are created digitally using off-the-shelf or proprietary software and delivered as a digital file. A **simple design** could be defined as 2–6 flat colors, simple motifs (e.g., dots), open ground. A **complex design** could be defined as 7–12+ flat and tonal colors, detailed motifs (e.g., watercolor), fine line work, textures, packed layout, little ground.

2. ***ENGINEERED DESIGNS:*** A full-color design created to fit a specific product's dimensions. Can be speculative or commissioned.

3. ***REPETITIVE DESIGNS:*** A full-color design in a factory repeat, with the engraving area rendered.

4. ***CROQUIS:*** Designs created as an original full-color rendered concept/sketch, sometimes with the suggestion of a repeat. Note: Some designers may charge an additional fee to put a croquis/sketch into a factory repeat.

5. ***COLORWAYS:*** Multiple color treatments for an approved design generated digitally; may include scanning and cleaning prior to creating the colorways. Price increases with number of colors and amount of editing; usually commissioned.

6. ***COMMISSIONED DESIGNS:*** Designer is hired by a company for a flat/hourly rate to provide specifics such as, but not limited to, performing market research; creating trend boards, hand-rendered croquis, and repetitive or engineered lead designs; and developing CAD coordinates and/or colorways, etc., while collaborating with the client to ensure the creative focus and production specs are met.

7. ***CROQUIS DEVELOPED:*** In-house or commissioned designer takes the client's purchased design(s) and develops into a factory repeat, rendering the engraving area and possibly creating coordinates and colorways.

8. ***MM (MAIN MODULE) SIZES:*** The height of the design to be put into repeat; widths vary depending on end-use and manufacturer.

9. ***HARD GOODS: Hand-rendered*** designs are created with traditional media and digitized in house or by the designer for an extra fee. **CAD designs** are created digitally using off-the-shelf or proprietary software and delivered as a digital file. A **simple design** could be defined as 2–6 flat colors, simple motifs (e.g., dots), open ground. A **complex design** could be defined as 7–12+ flat and tonal colors, detailed motifs (e.g., watercolor), fine line work, textures; packed layout, little ground.

10–6 Comparative Flat Fees for Surface Pattern Design
✳ Home Fashions: Bedding Products

Fees in Figure 10–6 do not reflect any specific trade practices and do not constitute specific prices for particular jobs. The buyer and seller are free to negotiate, with each designer independently or via the designer's agent/rep deciding how to price the work, after taking all factors into account. Reading the more detailed information about pricing factors provided in the text will help in pricing projects.

PRINTED TEXTILES[1] (Prices based on complexity, unless noted otherwise)	
ACCESSORIES (Boudoir, breakfast pillows, neck roll)	Hand-Rendered[1]/CAD[1]
Croquis Developed[2]	$25–100± each
Engineered[3]/Repetitive Designs[4]	$100–250± each or project-based via invoices.
OUTER BED (Shams/comforter face/duvet)	Hand-Rendered[1]/CAD[1]
Croquis[5]	$250–600± each
Croquis Developed	$550–800± each
Repetitive Designs (36" MM[6])	$1,200–1,500± each
Repetitive Designs (Variable MM)	$1,200–2,000± each
OUTER BED (Shams/comforter face/duvet)	CAD
Colorways[7] (Commissioned[8])	$200–350± each
INNER BED *Standard Pillowcase*	Hand-Rendered/CAD
Croquis Developed	$200–550± each
Engineered[4]	$200–450± each
INNER BED *Flat w/o Hem Treatment/Fitted Sheet*	Hand-Rendered/CAD
Croquis Developed	$125–500± each
Repetitive Designs (36" MM)	$500–950± each
INNER BED	CAD
Colorways (Commissioned)	$75–650± each
CONCEPT DEVELOPMENT/EMBELLISHMENTS	HAND-RENDERED/CAD
Croquis (Mini samples, decorative pillows, pillowcases, shams)	$100–350± each
5-Piece Ensemble	$550± each
Straight Sewing Sample (Cut & sew of existing yardage)	$65± per hour (based on experience/expertise)
CONCEPT DEVELOPMENT/EMBELLISHMENTS	HAND SAMPLES
Technique Pieces (Quilted, embroidered, pleated, etc.)	$80–200± each

10–6 Comparative Flat Fees for Surface Pattern Design
✳ Home Fashions: Bedding Products *(continued)*

1. **PRINTED TEXTILES: HAND-RENDERED DESIGNS** *are created with traditional media and digitized in house or by the designer for an extra fee. CAD Designs are created digitally using off-the-shelf or proprietary software and delivered as a digital file. A* **simple design** *could be defined as 2–6 flat colors, simple motifs (e.g., dots), open ground. A* **complex design** *could be defined as 7–12+ flat and tonal colors, detailed motifs (e.g., watercolor), fine line work, textures, packed layout, little ground.*

2. **CROQUIS DEVELOPED:** *In-house or commissioned designer takes the client's purchased design(s) and develops into a factory repeat, rendering the engraving area and possibly creating coordinates and colorways.*

3. **ENGINEERED DESIGNS:** *A full-color design created to fit a specific product's dimensions. Can be speculative or commissioned.*

4. **REPETITIVE DESIGNS:** *A full-color design in a factory repeat with the engraving area rendered.*

5. **CROQUIS:** *Design created as an original full-color rendered concept/ sketch, sometimes with the suggestion of a repeat. Note: Some designers may charge an additional fee to put a croquis/sketch into a factory repeat.*

6. **MM (MAIN MODULE) SIZES:** *The height of the design to be put into repeat; widths vary depending on end-use and manufacturer.*

7. **COLORWAYS:** *Multiple color treatments for an approved design generated digitally; may include scanning and cleaning prior to creating the colorways. Price increases with number of colors and amount of editing; usually commissioned.*

8. **COMMISSIONED DESIGNS:** *When a designer is hired by a company at a flat/hourly rate to provide specifics such as, but not limited to, performing market research; creating trend boards, hand-rendered croquis, and repetitive or engineered lead designs; and developing CAD coordinates and/or colorways, etc., while collaborating with the client to ensure the creative focus and production specs are met.*

10–7 Comparative Flat Fees for Surface Pattern Design
✳ Home Fashions: Kitchen & Tabletop Products

Fees in Figure 10–7 do not reflect any specific trade practices and do not constitute specific prices for particular jobs. The buyer and seller are free to negotiate, with each designer independently or via the designer's agent/rep deciding how to price the work, after taking all factors into account. Reading the more detailed information about pricing factors provided in the text will help in pricing projects.

SOFT GOODS[1] (prices based on complexity, unless noted otherwise)	
KITCHEN TEXTILES (Designs purchased to be developed via CAD in-house, for printed or woven kitchen towels, dish cloths, potholders, or oven mitts)	**HAND-RENDERED[1]/CAD[1]**
Croquis[2]	$400–600± each
Croquis Developed[3]	$400–700± each
Engineered[4]	$100–500± each
Repetitive Designs[5]	$500–1,200± each
KITCHEN TEXTILES (Designs purchased to be developed via CAD in-house, for printed or woven kitchen towels, dish cloths, potholders, or oven mitts)	**CAD**
Colorways[6] (Commissioned[7])	$50–100± each
TABLETOP TEXTILES (Designs purchased to be developed via CAD in-house, for printed or woven tablecloths, table rounds or squares, runners, placemats, or napkins)	**HAND-RENDERED/CAD**
Croquis	$300–700± each
Croquis Developed	$400–900± each
TABLECLOTHS/RUNNERS (Engineered[4]/Repetitive Designs)	**HAND-RENDERED/CAD**
Prints	$500–1,200± each
Wovens	$900–1,000± each
PLACEMATS/NAPKINS (Engineered/Repetitive Designs)	**HAND-RENDERED/CAD**
Prints	$300–600± each
Wovens	$300–600± each
PLACEMATS/NAPKINS (Engineered/Repetitive Designs)	**CAD**
Colorways (Commissioned)	$70–150± each
HARD GOODS[8] (Prices based on complexity, unless noted otherwise)	
SERVEWARE[9] (Charger; dinner, luncheon, salad/dessert, bread/butter plates; soup/cereal bowls; cup and saucer)	**HAND-RENDERED/CAD**
Engineered: Single Design	$300–600± each
Repetitive Designs (2–3 pieces)	$650–700± (small scale); $700–800± (large scale)

10–7 Comparative Flat Fees for Surface Pattern Design
✳ Home Fashions: Kitchen & Tabletop Products *(continued)*

HARD GOODS[8] (Prices based on complexity, unless noted otherwise)	
ENGINEERED/CROQUIS DEVELOPED	**HAND-RENDERED/CAD**
5-Piece Place Setting (Dinner and salad plate; soup/cereal bowl; cup and saucer)	$1,000–5,000±
Serviceware[10] Tea/Coffee Set; Sugar Bowl; Creamer; Butter, Casserole, and Vegetable Dishes; Gravy Boat; Platters; Salt and Pepper, etc.	$300–1,500± (based on complexity and # of pieces)

1. **SOFT GOODS: Hand-rendered designs** *are created with traditional media and digitized in house or by the designer for an extra fee.* **CAD designs** *are created digitally using off-the shelf or proprietary software and delivered as a digital file. A* **simple design** *could be defined as 2–6 flat colors, simple motifs (e.g., dots), open ground. A* **complex design** *could be defined as 7–12+ flat and tonal colors, detailed motifs (e.g., watercolor), fine line work, textures, packed layout, little ground.*

2. **CROQUIS:** *Designs created as an original full-color rendered concept/sketch, sometimes with the suggestion of a repeat. Note: Some designers may charge an additional fee to put a croquis/sketch into a factory repeat.*

3. **CROQUIS DEVELOPED:** *In-house or commissioned designer takes the client's purchased design(s) and develops into a factory repeat, rendering the engraving area and possibly creating coordinates and colorways.*

4. **ENGINEERED DESIGNS:** *A full-color design created to fit a specific product's dimensions. Can be speculative or commissioned.*

5. **REPETITIVE DESIGNS:** *A full-color design in a factory repeat with the engraving area rendered.*

6. **COLORWAYS:** *Multiple color treatments for an approved design generated digitally; may include scanning and cleaning prior to creating the colorways. Price increases with number of colors and amount of editing; usually commissioned.*

7. **COMMISSIONED DESIGNS:** *When a designer is hired by a company for a flat/hourly rate to provide specifics such as, but not limited to, performing market research; creating trend boards, hand-rendered croquis, and repetitive or engineered lead designs; and developing CAD coordinates and/or colorways, etc., while collaborating with the client to ensure the creative focus and production specs are met.*

8. **HARD GOODS:** *A* **simple design** *could be defined as 2–3 flat colors, simple motifs (e.g., dots); open ground; no sculptured, embossed, or additional components. A* **complex design** *could be defined as 4+ flat and tonal colors, detailed motifs (e.g., watercolor), fine line work, textures, sculptured, embossed, or additional 3-D components; little ground.*

9. **SERVEWARE:** *An individual place setting.*

10. **SERVICEWARE:** *Components used to "service" an entire table.*

10–8 Comparative Flat Fees for Surface Pattern Design
✳ Home Fashions: Floor Covering

Fees in Figure 10–8 do not reflect any specific trade practices and do not constitute specific prices for particular jobs. The buyer and seller are free to negotiate, with each designer independently or via the designer's agent/rep deciding how to price the work, after taking all factors into account. Reading the more detailed information about pricing factors provided in the text will help in pricing projects.

FLOORCOVERING (CARPETS/AREA RUGS)	
2–3-COLOR DESIGN—SIMPLE DESIGNS (CAD)	
In repeat, no border or simple band border	$200± each
In repeat, with detailed border	$275± each
Colorways	$40± each
4–8-COLOR DESIGN—SIMPLE DESIGNS (CAD)	
In repeat, no border or simple band border	$375± each
In repeat, with detailed border	$400± each
Colorways	$60± each
9–20-COLOR DESIGN—COMPLICATED DESIGNS (CAD)	
In repeat, no border or simple band border	$600± each
In repeat, with detailed border	$730± each
Colorways	$80± each
21–30-COLOR DESIGN—COMPLICATED DESIGNS (CAD)	
In repeat, no order or simple band border	$840± each
In repeat, with detailed border	$980± each
Colorways	$100± each
COMPLICATED DESIGNS (Handmade)	
20+ Colors, Wall to Wall, Ballroom Size, with or without repeat	Estimated on a per design basis

10–9 Comparative Flat Fees for Surface Pattern Design
✳ Home Fashions: Wallcovering

Fees in Figure 10–9 do not reflect any specific trade practices and do not constitute specific prices for particular jobs. The buyer and seller are free to negotiate, with each designer independently or via the designer's agent/rep deciding how to price the work, after taking all factors into account. Reading the more detailed information about pricing factors provided in the text will help in pricing projects.

WALLCOVERING[1] (Designs in Repeat[2])		
RESIDENTIAL (Wallcovering used for personal spaces)		
Side Walls[3]	**Hand-Rendered**[1]	**CAD Designs**[1]
Small Scale	$600± each	$400± each
Medium Scale	$750± each	$600± each
Simple[1] Patterns (Textured)	$800–1,000± each	$800–900± each
Fine/Detailed Rendering	$1,100–1,500± each	$1,000–1,150± each
Complex[1]/Special Technique	$1,100–2,500± each	$1,000–1,500± each
Traditional Borders[4]	$900–1,100± each (based on complexity)	$900–1,100± each (based on complexity)
COMMERCIAL/CONTRACT (Wallcovering used for public spaces)		
Side Walls[3]	**Hand-Rendered**[1]	**CAD Designs**[1]
Small Scale	$600± each	$400± each
Medium Scale	$800± each	$600± each
Simple (Textured)	$800–1,000± each	$800–900± each
Fine/Detailed Rendering	$1,100–1,250± each	$1,000–1,150± each
Complex/Special Technique	$1,100–1,250± each	$1,000–1,150± each

1. **WALLCOVERING: Hand-rendered designs** are created with traditional media and digitized in house or by the designer for an extra fee. **CAD designs** are created digitally using off-the-shelf or proprietary software and delivered as a digital file. A **simple design** could be defined as 2–6 flat colors, simple motifs (e.g., dots); open ground. A **complex design** could be defined as 7–12+ flat and tonal colors, detailed motifs (e.g., watercolor), fine line work, textures, packed layout, little ground. Inclusion of colors for special treatments, such as flocking, embossing, beading, pearlescent, etc.
Note: CAD Designs: Additional fees may include disc(s) with completed design files ($25–50 per disc depending on source).

2. **DESIGNS IN REPEAT:** A full-color design in a factory repeat with the engraving area rendered.

3. **SIDE WALLS:** Usually the lead design(s) of a wallcovering group/collection with multiple-color motifs of varying scale with little ground. Intended to cover an entire wall or ½ wall.

4. **TRADITIONAL BORDERS:** Borders used at the ceiling and/or at the chair rail.

10–10 Comparative Flat Fees for Surface Pattern Design
✳ Paper & Novelty Products

Fees in Figure 10–10 do not reflect any specific trade practices and do not constitute specific prices for particular jobs. The buyer and seller are free to negotiate, with each designer independently or via the designer's agent/rep deciding how to price the work, after taking all factors into account. Reading the more detailed information about pricing factors provided in the text will help in pricing projects.

PAPER PRODUCTS[1]	CONCEPTS (based on complexity)[1]	HAND-RENDERED/CAD DESIGNS (based on complexity)[1]
GIFT GIVING		
Invitations/Thank You Cards	$150–250± each	$400–500± each
Gift Tags/Enclosures	$50–$100± each	—
Gift Wrap (roll, sheet)/Tissue	$250–800± each	$300–600± each
Gift Bags	$300–800± each	$300–1,000± each
Multiple Components (# Variable: could include gift wrap, coordinating bags with top lip and gusset designs, bag tags, stickers, and tissue)	—	$750–1,500± each (Also based on quantity purchased)
PARTY GOODS/CELEBRATION		
Paper Plate and Napkin	—	$500–700± each
Favor Bag (Usually a company will ask to include a Party Goods collection.)	—	$200–700± each (Also based on quantity purchased)
MEMORY KEEPING		
Album, Scrapbook, Journal Covers	—	$300–650± each
Picture Frames	—	$250± each
Scrapbook Papers	—	$150± each
SPECULATIVE[2]/COMMISSIONED[3] DESIGNS (Developed In-House)	**Hand-Rendered**	**CAD Designs**
Single Designs	$1,200± each	$550–1,500± each (Based on complexity and if there are coordinates)
Purchased Collections (# of components variable) (Speculative)	—	$500–2,000± each
Trend Boards[4] (Commissioned)	—	$1,000–1,150± each
NOVELTY PRODUCTS[5]	HAND-RENDERED (based on complexity)[5]	CAD DESIGNS (based on complexity)[5]
T-SHIRT GRAPHICS		
Single Image (non-specified use)	$650–1,000± each	$600–800± each
Placement Prints[6]	$250± each	$400–700± each
Engineered Designs[7]	$500± each	$500–800± each

10–10 Comparative Flat Fees for Surface Pattern Design
✳ Paper & Novelty Products (continued)

NOVELTY PRODUCTS[5]	HAND-RENDERED (based on complexity)[5]	CAD DESIGNS (based on complexity)[5]
BEACH TOWELS		
Print Designs	$650± each	—
Woven Designs	$600± each	—
Beach Blankets	$700± each	—
Beach Hoodies (Engineered Designs)	$650–750± each	—

1. **PAPER PRODUCTS:** Concept: In-house, speculative, or commissioned designer's original full-color rendered sketch. **Hand-rendered designs** are created with traditional media and digitized in house or by the designer for an extra fee. **CAD designs** are created digitally using off-the-shelf or proprietary software and delivered as a digital file. A **simple design** could be defined as 2–6 flat colors, simple motifs (e.g., dots), open ground. A **complex design** could be defined as 7–12+ flat and tonal colors, detailed motifs (e.g., watercolor), fine line work, textures, packed layout, little ground. Inclusion of colors for special treatments, such as foil/glitter/flocking, embossing, laser cuts, etc. Note: Companies may not buy individual pieces; they would likely purchase a design(s)/ illustration(s), with or without coordinates, and then translate that into a full matching collection in-house using imagery from the purchased works.

2. **SPECULATIVE:** Designer's original hand-rendered/CAD designs (may be in repeat or not) created for direct sale or licensing at trade shows; not created for a specific product or client and is further developed in-house or by the designer (an additional fee may be negotiated).

3. **COMMISSIONED DESIGNS:** When a designer is hired by a company for a flat/hourly rate to provide specifics such as, but not limited to, performing market research; creating trend boards, hand-rendered croquis, and repetitive or engineered lead designs; developing CAD coordinates and/or colorways, etc., while collaborating with the client to ensure the creative focus and production specs are met.

4. **TREND BOARDS** are visual collages of conducted research to identify upcoming colors, themes, materials, textures, etc. to provide information to clients as inspiration and creative direction for upcoming lines. They communicate a wide range of information quickly and are commonly used within design fields. Trend boards are either physical or digital but usually both; commissioned.

5. **NOVELTY PRODUCTS: Hand-rendered designs** are created with traditional media and digitized in house or by the designer for an extra fee. **CAD designs** are created digitally, using off-the-shelf or proprietary software and delivered as a digital file. A **simple design** could be defined as 2–6 flat colors, simple motifs (e.g., dots), open ground. A **complex design** could be defined as 7–12+ flat and tonal colors, detailed motifs (e.g., watercolor), fine line work, textures, packed layout, little ground.

6. **PLACEMENT PRINTS:** A design created to be "placed" in one position on a product, not intended to be developed into a repetitive design. Can be speculative or commissioned.

7. **ENGINEERED DESIGNS:** A full-color design created to fit a specific product's dimensions. Can be speculative or commissioned.

Protecting Your Business
& Intellectual Property

{ 11 }

Legal Rights & Issues

NOTE: The information contained in this chapter does not constitute legal advice; proper advice from a legal professional should be sought when necessary.

This chapter discusses the many legal aspects involved in doing business as a graphic artist. Of paramount concern are understanding and protecting copyright, both in the United States and internationally. Other issues, such as work made for hire, moral rights, and fair practices, are also included.

RECOGNIZING THE NEED to stimulate the spread of learning and the dissemination of ideas, our nation's founders provided protection for creators of intellectual property when they wrote the U.S. Constitution. Article I, Section 8, empowers Congress to "promote the progress of science and useful arts by securing for limited times to authors and inventors the exclusive right to their respective writings and discoveries." This established the foundation for our copyright laws, which acknowledge artwork as intellectual property that is traded in the marketplace as a valuable economic resource.

In today's visual world, the works created by graphic artists are among the most powerful vehicles for communicating ideas in our society. An enticing illustration can sell a product. A successful logo can evoke a company's goodwill in the public mind. A compelling poster can move an entire population to action.

Like other creative professionals—actors, musicians, dancers, writers, photographers—graphic artists occupy a special place in our society and economy. Their unique vision, skill, and style enable them to attract clients, sell their work, and earn their livelihood. Like other professionals, graphic artists provide their highly skilled services and creative input within a framework of professional standards and ethics. But the work of graphic artists is vulnerable and requires the maximum protection of our laws, not only to prevent unauthorized exploitation, but also to ensure that artists can continue to work without economic or competitive disadvantages.

The Graphic Artists Guild

The Graphic Artists Guild's constitution and membership mandate is to "promote and maintain high professional standards of ethics and practice, and to secure the conformance of all buyers, users, sellers, and employers to established standards." Further, the Guild seeks to "establish, implement, and enforce laws and policies... designed to accomplish these ends." The organization's legislative agenda, therefore, is based on the needs and desires expressed by its members and its constitutionally mandated goals.

One of the primary goals of the Graphic Artists Guild is to help buyers recognize the value of graphic art to their businesses and the importance of fair and ethical relationships with graphic artists. The Guild upholds the standard of a value-for-value exchange, recognizing that both client and artist contribute to a successful working relationship.

The Guild monitors and influences public policy developments, including legislative initiatives at the local, state, and federal levels, and regulatory actions by a range of agencies. Additionally, the Guild has advocated for state laws to encourage fair practices, to protect artists' authorship rights, and to create tax equity for artists, as well as federal legislation to strengthen protections against copyright infringement, to develop a national standard for artists' authorship rights, to establish a small-claims tribunal for copyright infringement actions, and to extend the copyright term to conform to the European standard, which is life plus 70 years. The Guild drafted model legislation and lobbied locally and nationally on these issues. Its early successes in California, Massachusetts, New York, and Oregon created a wave of interest in artists' rights legislation. The Guild continues to work with other professional organizations on common issues affecting graphic artists and other creators when they arise within the industry.

United States Copyright Law

Graphic artists' livelihoods depend on their ability to claim authorship of the works they create. They build their reputations—and thus their ability to attract clients and build a career—on the basis of past performance. Indeed, artists' careers succeed or fail because of their skill and style in communicating the ideas and messages society needs to disseminate. Artists' rights to control the use of their original creative art are defined primarily by copyright law, which also provides the basis for pricing and fair-trade practices.

U.S. copyright law was created to extend limited monopolies to provide economic rewards and protections to artists and other creators. This encourages the dissemination of creative works, thereby serving the public interest. The current copyright law (Copyright Act of 1976) became effective January 1, 1978.

In 1998 the Digital Millennium Copyright Act (DMCA) was enacted; it implemented two 1996 World Intellectual Property Organization copyright treaties. The DMCA's most significant feature is that it affirms that copyright applies in digital network environments as well as in print, film, and recording media. Therefore, copyright laws apply to digitally created art and design, as they do to any visual or audiovisual work. It is also possible to register copyright in computer source codes as a literary work, protecting the code as it is expressed in fundamental computer language.

Copyright protection occurs at the time the work is created and put in tangible form (including digital files). Copyright is vested in the creator except in certain limited cases. Copyright in works created by a salaried employee, or that are commissioned from a freelancer under certain limited circumstances, is vested in the employer or client as *work made for hire* (a more detailed discussion of work made for hire can be found later in this chapter).

If two or more artists create a work with the intention that their contributions be merged into inseparable or interdependent parts of a unitary whole, the result is a *joint work* according to copyright law. Joint authorship must be intended at the time the work is created and implies co-creation of the piece from conception to fulfillment. Modification by a second artist of a piece by a first artist does not constitute joint authorship; instead, it is considered a *derivative work* (see section on Derivative Works later in this chapter).

A Bundle of Rights

An artist's copyright is actually a bundle of individual rights. These broadly include the rights **to copy** (commonly known as the "right of reproduction"); **to publicly display**, **distribute**, and **perform**; and **to create a derivative work from an existing work**. Each specific use can be transferred outright or licensed separately for a specific length of time. Fees are determined primarily by the value agreed upon for the specific rights.

The ability to transfer or license limited usage, or limited rights, to a work of art for a fee is an issue of basic fairness. The true value of a work, however, is difficult to determine (particularly before the work has been executed), considering that the potential economic life of the work is the length of time granted by copyright law, which is currently the author's life plus 70 years. Therefore, negotiations over the price of a commissioned work are normally based on the initial rights the client wishes to purchase.

Transferring Rights

Copyright owners can "transfer" or "grant" to another party any portion or all of the bundled rights in each work. An agreement to give your client exclusive rights in one of the bundled rights under copyright, such as all reproduction rights, or to assign to your client all rights (meaning, you are giving the client the entire bundle of copyrights) must be done in writing, signed by the artist or the artist's agent. Those rights not specifically transferred in writing are retained by the artist. Nonexclusive rights, which can be granted to more than one client at a time, may be granted orally. However, it's in the best interest of both parties to grant even nonexclusive rights in writing.

For contributions to collective works, such as magazines, anthologies, and encyclopedias, where there is no signed agreement, the law presumes there has been a grant of only nonexclusive rights for use in that particular collective work. All other rights remain vested with the artist.

Copyright is separate from ownership of the physical art and is sold separately. State laws in New York and California require the transfer of the original, physical art to be in writing. These laws were passed after successful lobbying by artists to stop clients from insisting that transactions transferring reproduction rights also included the sale of the original art.

Licensing Rights

An artist can license non-exclusive rights of copyright to a client to use a work for a particular purpose, for a particular length of time, or in a particular geographic area. Such non-exclusive licenses mean the artist is still the owner of the copyright for any uses not licensed and regains ownership of the entire copyright after the term of the license has expired. For instance, an artist can license the right to make copies of a work, display it, and make derivative works from it. Each of these licenses has a value that may be much higher than the value of transferring all rights in the work, and thus assigning the entire copyright to the buyer. The market will determine those values; what has no particular value today may have great value tomorrow. If artists license limited rights rather than transfer all rights, they will be able to take advantage of any value the work may have in the future, or any uses that were not thought of when it was created.

For example, an artist creates an illustration for a magazine cover, but then the magazine wants to use it for a promotional poster. The magazine has to go back to the artist for another license to use it on the poster and pay the artist an additional fee for that use. If a graphic artist is hired to create an illustration for a company that wants widespread use of the illustration on all its products, packaging, and related collateral, the artist must be paid accordingly for assigning all the rights to the company so it can use the illustration in any way it wants. (The artist may want to stipulate in the agreement that he or she may use the illustration for self-promotional purposes.)

If an artist is only paid to create an illustration for a more limited purpose, such as for an annual report, then it should be spelled out in writing that the company cannot use the illustration on any other materials, such as brochures, advertisements, signage, websites, or a wall mural in the company's office building. Although the artist legally retains all rights not expressly granted, the best approach is to state explicitly in a written licensing contract/agreement what each party may or may not do with the work. Many clients are not educated about this aspect of copyright law and often assume that any time they pay for commissioned work, they have acquired all rights. A "silent" agreement invites misunderstandings.

Joint authors hold copyright as "tenants in common," unless there is an agreement between them to the contrary. Either creator can license any rights to the work without the other's permission, providing that the proceeds are shared equally.

Licensing is a business decision. Only the individual artist and client can decide what terms or length of time best suit the client and the situation. When in doubt, it is always good business to keep, control, and defend copyright rights. Examples of short- and long-term licensing agreements are provided in the Appendix: Contracts & Forms.

Discussed below are some issues involved with licensing the various types of rights covered under copyright law.

RIGHT OF REPRODUCTION

Reproduction rights give the copyright owner the exclusive right to reproduce or make copies of the image. Courts have held that digital scanning of a work constitutes making a reproduction. Grants of reproduction rights may be limited to the number of copies, length of time, geographic area, exclusivity, market, edition, and so on, as agreed by the rights purchaser and the copyright owner.

TASINI ET AL. V. THE NEW YORK TIMES

A landmark Supreme Court case in 2001 addressed the issue of electronic licensing as applied to freelance authors. As a result of this case, many clients are insisting that reproduction licenses include rights to reproduce the work in all media, including electronic and digital forms now known or developed in the future.

In *Tasini et al. v. The New York Times*, authors who owned copyrights to individual articles previously published in periodicals claimed infringement by their publishers who had made the articles available on electronic databases.

The authors based their copyright claim on the fact that they each owned the copyright to their individual articles and that these copyrights were infringed when the publishers, after printing the articles under their original licenses, included them in electronic databases without the authors' consent or additional payment. The publishers did not dispute that the authors owned the copyright to their individual works. Rather, the publishers asserted that they each owned the copyright in the "collective works" that they produced and were afforded the privilege, under Section 201(c), of "reproducing and distributing" the individual works in "any revision of that collective work." The issue was this: whether one or more of the electronic databases could be considered a "revision" of the individual periodicals from which the articles were taken.

Section 201(c) affords a privilege to authors of collective works: "In the absence of an express transfer of the copyright or of any rights under it, the owner of copyright in the collective work is presumed to have acquired only the privilege of reproducing and distributing the contribution as part of that particular collective work, any revision of that collective work, and any later collective work in the same series."

The Supreme Court found that the most natural reading of the "revision" of "that collective work" protects only later editions of a particular issue of a periodical, such as the final edition of a newspaper. It protects the use of an individual contribution in a collective work that is somewhat altered from the original in which the copyrighted article was first published, but that is not in any ordinary sense a "later" work in the "same series." Subsequent cases have made it clear, however, that Section 201(c) allows the "image-based" representation of complete pages included in CD-ROM compilations.

RIGHT OF DISTRIBUTION

The right to control distribution of a tangible copy of a work remains the right of the copyright holder, unless that particular tangible copy is sold or distributed with the copyright owner's authorization (for example, your client buys a limited-edition print). Once sold, under the "first sale" doctrine, that particular item may be resold, passed on, rented, and so on, though it may not be copied or used for derivative works.

Digital distribution is considered the same as distributing a tangible version of a work, unless the distribution is made under a limited license, such as a "shrink-wrap" license included with software, which says you are not purchasing the software itself but only a limited license to use it (typically the license terms forbid you to resell the software to someone else, or use it on more than one computer). The wording states that by opening the package (usually shrink-wrapped), you agree to the license terms. The online version of this type of license is sometimes referred to as a "click-wrap" license.

Digital reproduction rights should be specified separately. Technology can now be used to embed in any type of work—text, image, or computer source code—licensing terms and digital copyright management information that identifies rights holders, permitted uses, exclusions, and appropriate fees for a particular use. Digital delivery systems permit potential users to choose a work, indicate intended uses, and pay appropriate usage fees with the click of a mouse.

RIGHT OF PERFORMANCE

Works that are part of certain multimedia, such as video broadcasts or PowerPoint presentations, also involve performance rights, which may require explicit licensing. A court held in one case that a video game was "performed" (played) without authorization by the end-user in a public arcade.

RIGHT TO CREATE A DERIVATIVE WORK

A derivative work is one that is based on one or more preexisting works. It may be termed a modification, adaptation, or translation, and applies to a work that, according to copyright law, is "recast, transformed or adapted." Most substantial alterations of an image, including editorial revisions, probably constitute creation of a derivative work. A derivative work created with the permission of the original copyright holder is itself copyrightable. Created without permission, derivative works are infringing (unless the original work is not protected by copyright).

The creator of the derivative work owns rights to his or her contributions if they are original and copyrightable apart from the original work but does not gain any rights to the underlying work (whether it was copyrighted or copyright free). The standard for originality of the new contributions is relatively low, but some new artistic expression is required. For example, a photograph of an existing artwork for an exhibition catalog would not add new artistic expression because the photographer is using technical skills to faithfully depict the original artwork. Similarly, a retouched photograph, where the final image is not substantially different from the original, would probably not be considered a derivative work. Courts have found such changes to be primarily mechanical and thus not original.

One lawsuit that involved failure to pay for second-use rights may also help define what constitutes a derivative work. Eighteen plaintiffs in *Teri J. McDermott, CMI, et al. v. Advanstar Communications, Inc.*, sued the largest U.S. publisher of medical and trade magazines for allowing their illustrations, in which they had granted only first North American print rights, to be reprinted in at least 27 countries over a period of more than 20 years. Not only was the geographic term of the licenses violated, but the artists also were able to document instances of cropped signatures, intentionally dropped attributions, and cases where the images were intentionally changed, cropped, flopped, and recolored. Because the modifications were primarily mechanical, the resulting images would not be considered derivative works.

On the other hand, the courts may view changes resulting from digital image manipulation as artistic, rather than mechanical, thereby creating sufficient originality for a copyrightable derivative work. An illustration based on a photograph would also add copyrightable artistic expression because the illustrator is contributing new artistic style. Andy Warhol's portraits are examples of copyrightable derivative works because of his extensive manipulation and additions to the underlying photographs.

In most cases, combining images in an electronic composite constitutes the creation of a derivative work of each of the contributing images. A derivative work in which both the original and the second artist have contributed creative input can be a joint work, with copyright held by both parties, only if both artists intended to create a joint work at the time of the work's creation.

Clients who receive unlimited "all rights" transfers to use graphic artwork are getting rights to create and exploit derivative works. When contracts are silent on the scope of rights, courts may determine that unlimited rights were granted. This makes it all the more important for graphic artists to specify grants of rights with regard to image manipulation up front and in writing. The dividing line between an unauthorized derivative work that infringes another copyright owner's rights and a non-infringing work that may make fair use of an existing image is still blurred. See the Fair Use section later in this chapter.

Termination of Rights Transfers

Under both the 1909 and the 1976 Acts, copyright owners have an opportunity to terminate transfers of copyright interests that were made many years ago. Under the 1976 Act, which applies to works created after 1977, the copyright owner (or their heirs) may terminate grants 40-45 years after the date of the grant or 35-40 years from the date of publication, whichever is earlier. Under the 1909 Act, transfers made prior to January 1, 1978, may also be subject to termination after 56 or 75 years, depending on when the work was originally copyrighted under the old copyright law. The mechanics and timing of such terminations are quite complex. The Supreme Court has held that an author's pre-1978 grant of renewal-term rights terminates automatically if the author does not survive into the start of the renewal term.

This "right of termination or reversion" feature of Copyright Law is particularly important when transfers or licenses are for exceptionally long periods of time and when artists who have since become successful wish to regain rights to their early work.

Under both Acts, any type of transfer, whether an assignment of all rights, license of exclusive rights, or license of nonexclusive rights, may be terminated. However, if the licensee has already created authorized derivative works, termination will not end the licensee's rights to continue exploiting those existing derivative works. Termination does not apply to works made for hire.

Artists or their heirs whose grants of rights are approaching 35 years should contact the Copyright Office for forms and procedures for serving notices of termination. The formalities of termination are detailed; the exact form of notice is specified by, and must be filed with, the Copyright Office. See https://www.copyright.gov/recordation/termination.html. Consultation with copyright counsel is highly recommended, as the rules are complex, and any mistakes will invalidate the attempted termination. Artists will lose the opportunity to reclaim rights to their creations if they fail to comply with the proper procedures.

Practices Governing Original Art

Well-known illustrators can command high prices for the sale of original art. Many graphic artists also sell their original works through galleries, to collectors, and to corporations. Original art may be valuable to the artist because it can be exhibited, used as portfolio pieces, given as gifts, or bequeathed as part of an estate. Concern for protecting ownership of an original work stems not only from artists' interests in obtaining additional income from the sale of the original, but also from their interest in protecting their reputations and careers.

Ownership of the physical art, while separate from ownership of copyright, is similarly vested with the artist from the moment it is created (unless it was created by an employee using employer's materials). Selling the artwork does not transfer any rights of copyright to the buyer, just as selling the copyright does not give a client any claim to the physical artwork.

Original art may be given to the client temporarily, so reproductions can be made, but the client must take reasonable care of it and return it undamaged to the artist. Of course, separate fees can be negotiated with a client or any other party who wishes to buy the physical artwork. The artist who wishes to sell original art should stipulate on the invoice or bill of sale the extent of copyright interest, if any, that is also being transferred with the original art. To prevent misconceptions, it is also wise to state affirmatively that no rights to reproduce the work are being granted (when that is more typically the case). To be able to license any copyright interest he or she has decided to keep, the artist should also keep a reproduction-quality transparency or a high-resolution digital file of the work.

Copyright Notice

Since 1989, U.S. copyright law no longer requires a copyright notice: original artwork is protected from the moment of its creation, whether or not it is inscribed with a copyright notice. It is best, however, for artists to have their copyright notice appear with their work whenever it is published, placed on public display, or distributed. Copyright notices help avoid certain risks of infringement and will also legally prevent copiers from claiming that their infringement was "innocent" (innocent infringers do not escape liability, but monetary damages assessed against them may be minimal, and they may be shielded from paying the artist's attorneys' fees). If a copyist intentionally removes your copyright notice, you may have additional remedies under the DMCA (see below).

The copyright notice can be placed on the back of a work of art or, when it is published, adjacent to the artwork. Other reasonable placements of the copyright notice for published works are specified by the Copyright Office in Circular 3, https://www.copyright.gov/circs/circo3.pdf and Compendium III, https://www.copyright.gov/comp3/chap2200/ch2200-notice.pdf. Pieces in an artist's portfolio should have copyright notices on them, including published pieces when the artist retains the copyright.

The elements that make up a copyright notice are "Copyright," the symbol ©, or "Copr."; the year of creation (or, if the work is published, of the first publication); and the name of the corporation or the artist's name, an abbreviation of the name, or an alternate designation by which the artist is known: © 2001 Jane Artist, for example. The form and placement of the notice should be understood by artist and client and should be reflected in a written agreement. When use of the art has been temporarily granted to a client, the notice should be in the artist's name; however, if the client holds an exclusive license, it may be placed in the client's name for the duration of the use

Removal of Copyright Management Information

The Digital Millennium Copyright Act of 1998 (DMCA) makes it a violation of U.S. law to circumvent any copyright protection mechanism in the digital environment and to intentionally remove any copyright management information (CMI) that owners of intellectual properties attach to their works, such as the title and other information identifying the work and the names of, and other identifying information about the author and the copyright owner of the work, including the information set forth in a notice of copyright.

Unfortunately, many social media sites use software that automatically removes metadata and other copyright management information from files that are uploaded by users.

While jurisprudence in this area is still developing, many courts have held that such automated practices do not meet the requirement for liability that such removal must be intentional. On the positive side, courts have routinely held that almost any form of information qualifies as copyright management information, and such information need not be embedded in the image file. For example, accreditation located immediately adjacent to the image is sufficient. Attempts by defendants to limit the definition of copyright management information to metadata or formal copyright notices have been rebuffed. Some courts have held that CMI protection applies not only to digital works, but also to CMI on any tangible media. To qualify for this protection, however, copyright notices or CMI must be clearly associated with the particular work. For example, copyright notices at the bottom of a web page, or in the title page of a book, will not be considered CMI for individual images.

DMCA Takedown Notices

In addition to the provisions setting liability for intentional removal of copyright management information (see above), the DMCA created tools for copyright owners to have infringing copies of their works removed from online platforms by giving online service providers a strong incentive to promptly take down reported infringements. Section 512 of the DMCA limits online service provider liability by preventing a service provider from incurring monetary liability for copyright infringements carried by its service in relation to the following four areas: e-mail, system caching, websites, and browsers.

RELEVANCE FOR GRAPHIC ARTISTS

Section 512 has important ramifications for graphic artists in two areas: the removal or blocking of infringing material, and the terms of service imposed by online service providers. The first area is of particular concern because of the *Kelly v. Arriba Soft Corporation* case. In April 1999, photographer Les Kelly sued Arriba Soft for vacuuming his images off the Internet and displaying them on its commercial search engine without his knowledge or permission. The U.S. district court in California ruled that the search engine's unauthorized copying and display of Kelly's copyrighted images falls under "fair use" and that Kelly's copyrights had not been violated. Because of the huge impact this decision could have on intellectual property rights on the Internet, Kelly appealed, and the Ninth Circuit held that only Arriba Soft's creation and display of low-resolution thumbnail images was fair use. While there was no final ruling on the full-size high-resolution images, this case is widely interpreted as indicating that such full-size copies constitute infringement.

PROTECTION FOR SERVICE PROVIDERS

Arriba Soft, Google, and other search engines are "information location tools" within the meaning of Section 512. Other examples of eligible service providers are sites that host listings or content by users (or "subscribers"), including sales sites like eBay and Amazon, print-on-demand sites like Cafe Press and DeviantArt, social media sites like Facebook and Instagram, and stock sites like The iSpot or Shutterstock.

A service provider will qualify for protection against infringement claims if it meets several conditions:

* First, the provider cannot have actual knowledge that the material or activity on its site is infringing; or
* Second, if the provider doesn't have such actual knowledge, it cannot be aware of facts or circumstances which make the specific infringing activity apparent; or

* Third, upon learning of the infringement, the provider acts expeditiously to remove, or disable access to, the material; and
* Fourth, the provider has the right and ability to control the infringing activity and does not receive a financial benefit directly attributable to the infringing activity.
* The provider must also adopt and reasonably implement a policy of terminating the accounts of subscribers who are repeat infringers.
* Finally, to avail themselves of the protections offered in Section 512, service providers must file the name and contact information for a designated agent with the Copyright Office to receive notification of claimed infringements and must also post such information on its own site.

Section 512 (c)(3) provides for a notice and takedown procedure, under which a copyright holder submits a notification to the provider's designated agent. The notification must comply with the formal requirements set forth in the statute by including

(i) A physical or electronic signature of a person authorized to act on behalf of the owner of an exclusive right that is allegedly infringed.

(ii) Identification of the copyrighted work claimed to have been infringed, or, if multiple copyrighted works at a single online site are covered by a single notification, a representative list of such works at that site.

(iii) Identification of the material that is claimed to be infringing or to be the subject of infringing activity and that is to be removed or access to which is to be disabled, and information reasonably sufficient to permit the service provider to locate the material.

(iv) Information reasonably sufficient to permit the service provider to contact the complaining party, such as an address, telephone number, and, if available, an electronic mail address at which the complaining party may be contacted.

(v) A statement that the complaining party has a good faith belief that use of the material in the manner complained of is not authorized by the copyright owner, its agent, or the law.; and

(vi) A statement that the information in the notification is accurate, and under penalty of perjury, that the complaining party is authorized to act on behalf of the owner of an exclusive right that is allegedly infringed.

Upon receiving a proper notice of infringement, the provider must expeditiously remove or block access to the infringing material and notify the subscriber that it has done so. The subscriber may serve a counter-notification, under penalty of perjury, that the material was wrongly removed. Unless the copyright holder files an action against the subscriber, the service provider must put the material back up within 10 to 14 business days after receiving the counter-notification.

This procedure is supposed to offer copyright holders rapid relief from online infringements pending resolution of a copyright dispute, rather than requiring a matter to be first adjudicated through the court system. Note, however, that to preserve blocking or disabling when a counter-notice is filed, the claimant must file a court action in a very short period of time. However, a completed copyright registration, meaning a certificate of registration has been issued, is necessary to embark on any court action. Given the long lead time that registration requires, or the alternative—the high cost of a "Special Handling" registration—it is clearly unwise to leave work unregistered and particularly unwise to post any unregistered work online.

ONLINE SERVICE PROVIDERS TERMS OF SERVICE

The requirements of Section 512 generally specify that the service provider must not have knowledge that the material is infringing and must not receive any financial benefit directly attributable to the infringing activity. This raises interesting issues regarding provider terms of service agreements. Many service providers claim for themselves a nonexclusive copyright interest in their subscribers' material as part of their terms of service. These have included claims of the right to alter the work, prepare derivative works, and make use of the works in various ways that potentially offer financial benefit. Others participate directly in making, selling, and deriving income from products bearing subscribers' works. The requirements of Section 512 call into question whether sites with such terms of service or profit-sharing are eligible for Section 512 protection. As of this writing, at least one court has determined that print-on-demand sites are protected under Section 512 only with respect to displaying infringing content. In *Greg Young Publishing, Inc. v. Zazzle, Inc.* (C.D. Cal. May 1, 2017), the court held that once such sites actually fulfill an order by making and shipping an infringing item, they are clearly benefiting financially from the infringement, and the Section 512 safe harbor from liability no longer applies.

The obvious conclusion is that all creators should register their work and familiarize themselves with the provisions of Section 512 so that they may be prepared to make use of the protections it offers. To learn more about Section 512 and other aspects of the DMCA, visit the Copyright Office website (www.copyright.gov/dmca-directory/).

ISSUES WITH THE TAKEDOWN NOTICE

Since the DMCA notice procedure was written into law, it's proven to be of limited effectiveness in combating copyright infringement online. Although the procedure creates an avenue for copyright holders to have their infringed work removed from a website, the procedure has come under fire from all sides.

The problem with the DMCA takedown notice is that it puts the burden on copyright holders to police the Internet for infringement. ISPs have no incentive to police content before receiving a takedown notice, since prior knowledge that content may be infringing would forfeit their safe harbor exemption.

In 2016, the U.S. Copyright Office conducted a panel discussion on issues with the DMCA takedown process, which solicited the experiences of the various stakeholders. The testimony was divided: those representing artists and authors described a system that is essentially broken, while technology companies (including ISPs) professed satisfaction with a process that serves them well.

A common complaint of rights holders was that as soon as their infringed work was removed in response to a DMCA notice, it would reappear; creators described spending several hours per day devoted to hunting down infringements and issuing takedown requests, often for the same infringing content. Rights holders were unanimous in stating that the law needs to be revised to "take down and stay down."

Another issue that rights holders described was the onerous takedown process that technology companies such as Facebook, Google, Amazon, and YouTube, as well as some other service providers, have devised. Their processes seem to be deliberate attempts to make it difficult for rights holders to issue notices—often the information for how to file a DMCA notice is not easily found, and in some cases, sites require complainants to sign up as a member to implement the DMCA process.

There needs to be a standardized form for takedown notices—perhaps created by the Copyright Office—to enable a clear, simpler procedure, and prevent ISPs and technology companies from piling on additional requirements. It remains to be seen what the Copyright Office will do with the findings from the panel discussion. Adjustments to the law would have to be made by Congress.

Copyright Duration

How long copyright lasts depends on when the work was created. Under the Copyright Act of 1909, which covers works created before January 1, 1978, copyright protection was obtained either through registration or publication with a formal copyright notice. Works were given an initial 28-year term. Copyrights that were set to expire after the initial 28-year term had to be renewed by submission of a specific renewal form to extend protections for another 28 years. Because of this onerous provision, many valuable works, such as the famous Frank Capra movie *It's a Wonderful Life,* fell into the public domain, to the detriment of their creators or the creators' heirs.

In 1992, the Automatic Renewal Act was passed to protect the "widows and orphans" of authors who did not, or could not, register the copyright's renewal. The law provides that copyrights secured prior to 1978 live out their 28-year first term and, if renewed, an additional 67-year second term. Although this renewal term is automatically provided for works first published or registered in 1964 or later, the Copyright Office does not issue a renewal certificate for these works unless a renewal application and fee are received and registered in the Copyright Office.

The Copyright Act of 1976 changed the rules for when a copyright is obtained and how long it lasts. Works created on or after January 1, 1978, are protected by copyright upon their creation, and they lasted for the life of the author plus 50 years.

COPYRIGHT EXTENSION

As a participating member in the former Coalition of Creators and Copyright Owners, the Graphic Artists Guild long advocated extending the term of U.S. copyright law from life plus 50 years to life plus 70 years, to bring U.S. law into harmony with most other Berne Convention signatories. The Copyright Term Extension Act, passed by the 105th Congress and signed into law by President Clinton in 1998, did just that. Approximately 20 organizations in the coalition supported extending the term of copyright for the following reasons, among others:

* Artists and other authors now live longer, and the term of copyright needs to reflect that. Further, currently created works now have greater value for longer periods of time.
* A longer term of copyright is good for American business. The International Intellectual Property Alliance reported that in 2017, the core copyright-based industries in the United States, which include the visual and graphic arts, were major contributors to the U.S. GDP, accounting for more than $1.3 trillion or 6.85% of the U.S. economy.
* Term extension allows the United States to continue to be a leader in international copyright. Intellectual property generally, and copyright in particular, are among the brightest spots in our balance of trade. Copyrighted works that the world wants are overwhelmingly those created in the United States.
* The primary reason for passage of this law was to bring U.S. copyright terms into harmony with other Berne Convention signatories so that European copyright owners would not have an unfair advantage over U.S. rights holders.
* Term extension discourages retaliatory legislation and trade policies by other countries. The European community extends protection to foreign copyrights under the "rule of the shorter term," which limits protection in the European community to the length of the term in the home country. Failure to extend the U.S. term would protect U.S. copyrights for the shorter term of life plus 50 only, while protecting European copyrights for the longer term. This would have placed U.S. copyright holders at a tremendous disadvantage in the global marketplace.
* Worldwide harmonization facilitates international trade and a greater exchange of copyrighted property between countries.

For reasons of simplification, the 20-year term extension was applied across the board to all copyrights, including works made for hire, which have been extended from 75 to 95 years after publication, or 120 years after creation if the work was not published. The Graphic Artists Guild strenuously opposed lengthening the copyright term of works made for hire, as it might provide an incentive for more work-made-for-hire agreements. More importantly, since work-made-for-hire agreements do not exist in most other countries that signed the Berne Convention, this extension creates disharmony with practices in other countries. The constitutionality of the term extension was challenged in the U.S. Supreme Court. The challenge was defeated when the court upheld the Copyright Term Extension Act in January 2003.

Copyright Limitations

Copyright owners have the exclusive right to reproduce or sell their work, prepare derivative works (such as an animation based on a painting), and publicly perform or display their work. Generally, anyone who violates these rights is infringing on the copyright and can be assessed monetary damages and prevented from continuing the infringement.

There are, however, some limitations on artists' exclusive control of their work.

Underlying Ideas or Concepts

Copyright protects only the artistic expression of an artwork; not the underlying idea or concept of the work. To be infringing, a work has to be "substantially similar" in artistic expression. For example, in a 1999 case called *Kerr v. The New Yorker Magazine*, illustrator Thomas Kerr alleged that a *New Yorker* cover illustration by Anita Kunz infringed his line drawing because both images depicted a person with a mohawk haircut in the shape of the New York City skyline. The court held that there was no copyright infringement because only Kerr's idea had been copied, not the specific artistic expression: Kunz's illustration was a full-color rendering in a completely different artistic style and depicted a person with different features.

Artistic Style

Generally, an artist's style is not protected unless the copyist also copied some particular content from another artist's work. For example, in a 2003 case called *Kroenke v. General Motors Corp.*, an advertising agency approached illustrator Anita Kroenke to create illustrations for promotional materials for General Motors. After Ms. Kroenke declined, the agency hired another illustrator to create illustrations imitating Kroenke's distinctive flat-color illustrative style. The New York court held that there was no copyright infringement, because the works differed in color, spatial orientation of figures, setting, mood, and themes, and that details allegedly copied from Kroenke's works did not bear substantial literal similarity to any specific details of Kroenke's illustrations.

Independent Creation

Copyright protects only against actual copying of another work. Thus, even if a work is very similar to someone else's work, there is no infringement if the second artist had never seen that other work. Since actual copying is often hard to prove, courts accept as proof of actual copying evidence that the defendant had access to the original work (for example, if it was widely available online) and that the second work is substantially similar in artistic expres-

sion. There is an exception to this rule for works that are so "strikingly similar" that it must have been copied; in such cases, proof of access is not required.

Fair Use

Another limitation allows for so-called "fair use" of a copyrighted work, including use for such purposes as news reporting, teaching, scholarship, or research.

Courts consider four statutory criteria to determine whether a work is fair use:

1. **The purpose and character of the use:**
   Is the new work being used for non-commercial purposes, such as news reporting or political speech? This does not mean any use by news organizations and educational or non-profit entities qualifies as non-commercial. If the new work is something such entities would normally obtain as clients of the artist or photographer, it will be considered commercial and thus this factor would weigh against fair use.

   Is the new work "transformative"? Courts are struggling with the concept of "transformative," which requires a subjective evaluation of whether the work "merely supersedes the objects of the original creation, or instead uses the original work as 'raw material'" and "adds something new, with a further purpose or different character, altering the first with new expression, meaning, or message." Works considered transformative are more likely to be held as fair use.

2. **The nature of the original work, such as whether it is more factual than fictional:**
   Is the original work a creative illustration or "art" photograph, or is it a factual documentation of something, like a product photo or a cityscape?

3. **How much of the original work was used:**
   Substance (importance of the borrowed content's quality):
   How much of the meaningful content of a work has been reproduced? This may be a very small portion of a work in terms of size, but still be the crucial nugget that delivers the main idea. Another measure of substantial content is whether the element taken is unique, recognizable, or identifiable.
   Extent of work copied:
   How much, literally, of a work has been reproduced? There is no percentage rule, e.g., that changing an image 20% (however that might be measurable) avoids infringement. Taking even a proportionately

small excerpt that is the "heart" of the copied work will weigh against fair use. The specific quantity or quality of permissible copying can only be determined in court, and that is a situation generally to be avoided.

4. **Whether the new use affects the potential market for the original work:**
Does the new work compete in the same market as the original work, including established or likely-to-be-developed licensing markets for the original work?

Fair use is a possible defense against an accusation of infringement that may be used both by an artist who incorporates someone else's copyrighted work into his or her own work and by someone using an artist's original work without permission. Under the above criteria, a magazine may use an artist's work to accompany or illustrate an article about the artist's life under the fair use defense. Fair use also permits artists to display a work executed for a client on a work-made-for-hire basis in their portfolio (provided the work does not otherwise violate the client's rights, for example, by revealing confidential information). Fair use protects quotations in commentaries and reviews and parody and caricature as forms of commentary on the copyrighted work. Because of this "free speech" aspect, fair use is often put forth as a justification for freely using copyrighted works in situations where use clearly should be compensated. One example is in academic settings, where works have been copied and distributed to a class rather than purchased. When this is done to the detriment of the market for the author's work, courts have rejected the fair use defense.

The free speech aspect of fair use is also cited by ideologues opposed to the concept of copyright protection, who wish to enjoy the benefit of others' creativity without being burdened by the necessity of paying for what they use. These "information-wants-to-be-free" advocates forget that all creative work comes at a price. Creators deserve to be compensated for their work; when their compensation is safeguarded, the public benefits, for the promise of compensation creates an atmosphere where creativity flourishes.

A few artists and designers who expect the copyright laws to protect their work sometimes abuse the rights of other artists and designers. For example, artists often copy photographs to create paintings or sculptures. Photographs are copyrightable works: all of the artistic aspects comprising a photograph, such as the point of view, lighting, and composition, are protected. Works that copy those aspects of a photograph will be

infringing derivative works, unless the new work adds sufficiently transformative elements to qualify as fair use. For example, Andy Warhol's portraits comprising highly contrasted versions of original photographs with unique color and graphic treatments, have been deemed fair use. Some agencies and design firms routinely use images without permission to develop comps for client presentations. If a different artist is hired to create new artwork based on such comps, this practice risks liability for two counts of copyright infringement. Courts have found that unauthorized comping is a separate instance of infringement, in addition to infringement based on a too-close copying of the imagery used in the comp for the final artwork. (In 1996, the Guild organized 16 industry organizations behind the "Ask First" campaign, which is a copyright awareness program intended to end unauthorized use of images in client presentations.)

Collage art and appropriation art genres also use pre-existing art as a basis for new imagery. This used to be considered a gray area. However, recent court decisions indicate that collages—providing that they combine copies of many different works in a complex new arrangement—are likely to be deemed transformative fair use rather than infringing derivative works. In 2006, in a case called *Blanch v. Koons*, the Second Circuit Court of Appeals in New York held that a Jeff Koons painting, which included an identical copy of an advertising photograph as part of a collage made up of many other images, was transformative. In 2013, the same court held that most works in a series of collages called *Canal Zone* by Richard Prince, which combined original photographs by Patrick Cariou with additional imagery, were also excused as transformative fair use. However, the court held that a few of the *Canal Zone* collages, which merely added a couple of images overlaid on Cariou's photographs, were not fair use as a matter of law. The case settled after that ruling; however, it is generally accepted that this case set standards for determining fair use with respect to collage art.

The Copyright Office keeps a database of fair use cases with a search feature which can be accessed here: https://www.copyright.gov/fair-use/. However, it is always advisable to consult a copyright attorney if you are uncertain whether your work will qualify as fair use.

Compulsory Licensing

A provision of copyright law dealing with compulsory licensing permits a noncommercial, educational broadcasting station to use certain published works without the artist's consent so long as the station pays the government-set royalty rate. (Some published works, such as dramatic ones, are not covered by this license.) If the broadcaster does not pay the license fee, or underpays it, the use will be considered an infringement.

Programs produced independently for airing on public stations are eligible for compulsory licenses, but the license does not extend to secondary (after broadcast) markets such as merchandising, toys, books, or DVD sales.

States' Liability for Copyright Infringement

The U.S. Copyright Act, in establishing remedies (monetary damages, injunctions, and in some cases, the ability to recover attorneys' fees) against infringement, intended these remedies to apply to "anyone who violates any of the exclusive rights of the copyright owner." According to the Copyright Office, "anyone" was meant to include states, state institutions, and state employees. But in 1985, the Supreme Court ruled in a five-to-four decision that the Eleventh Amendment to the Constitution, which generally grants states immunity from lawsuits and monetary judgments in federal courts, could not be negated by Congress except by explicit and unequivocal language. Subsequent courts decided that under this test, the Copyright Act's language was not specific enough and so opened the door for many state-funded institutions to use copyrighted materials without permission, without paying or giving credit, and without fear of reprisal from the copyright owner.

In 1990, Congress attempted to correct this inequity by passing the Copyright Remedy Clarification Act ("CRCA"), so that states and their agents would once again be subject to all penalties and sanctions for copyright infringement. Grassroots lobbying by the Guild and its members helped obtain passage of this new law. Unfortunately, some courts have struck down the CRCA as unconstitutional. As of this writing, the matter is before the Supreme Court in a case called *Allen v. Cooper*. In that case, the state of North Carolina copied registered copyrighted videos and images of the shipwreck of *Queen Anne's Revenge*, the flagship of the infamous pirate Blackbeard. After reaching a settlement in which it agreed not to further infringe these works, North Carolina continued to do so, and even passed a state law declaring the works to be a matter of public record. The Fourth Circuit held that the CRCA was unconstitutional. The Guild joined many other photographers' and artists organizations in an *amicus* brief to the Supreme Court, advocating for reversal of the Fourth Circuit's opinion so that the CRCA will be upheld and artists will be entitled to sue state actors for copyright infringement.

Work Made for Hire

While *work made for hire* is defined under U.S. Copyright Law, the term is so misunderstood by graphic artists and clients alike that it deserves its own section in this chapter.

Work made for hire is a provision of the U.S. Copyright Act intended to be a narrow exception to the general rule that the artist (known as the "author" in copyright parlance) who creates a work owns the copyright to it. The provision confers initial authorship and copyright ownership instead to the employer or other hiring party who commissions the work, leaving the artist with no rights whatsoever. While such a result may be justifiable in a traditional employment setting, a freelance artist, considered to be an independent contractor for all purposes except copyright, has no access to the usual employee benefits that may compensate for the loss of that copyright and the future earnings it may represent.

Under the law, a work made for hire can come into existence in two ways: an employee creating a copyrightable work within the scope of employment; or an independent contractor creating a specially ordered or commissioned work in one of several categories, verified by a written contract signed by both parties and expressly stating that it is a "work made for hire."

An employed artist is usually defined as one who works at the employer's office during regular business hours on a scheduled basis (although increasingly, remote working arrangements are recognized), is directed by the employer, and works with tools supplied by the employer. More importantly, an artist is considered an employee if he or she is entitled to employment benefits and has taxes withheld from his or her paycheck. (For further details, see the *CCNV v. Reid* section later in this chapter, and the Employment Issues section of Chapter 3, Professional Issues.)

Even as an employee, an artist may negotiate a separate written contract with the employer, apart from the employment agreement, that transfers copyright ownership to the artist in some or all of the work created in the regular course of employment. And it is also possible, though highly unusual, for an artist working under a work-made-for-hire agreement to receive royalties according to a written contract.

Work-Made-for-Hire Criteria

Work created by a freelance artist, by contrast, can be work made for hire only if *both* of the following two conditions are met: 1) the artist and the client sign an agreement stating that the work is "work made for hire," *and*

2) the work falls under one of the following nine categories as enumerated in the law:

1. A contribution to a collective work (such as a magazine, newspaper, encyclopedia, or anthology).
2. A contribution used as part of a motion picture or other audiovisual work.
3. A supplementary work, which includes pictorial illustrations, maps, and charts, done to supplement a work by another author.
4. A compilation (new arrangement of preexisting works or data).
5. A translation.
6. An atlas.
7. A test.
8. Answer material for a test.
9. An instructional text (defined as a literary, pictorial, or graphic work prepared for publication and with the purpose of use in systematic instructional activities).

Works that fall outside these categories are legally ineligible to be a work made for hire, even with a signed contract. Not so clear are works like comic books, print advertising, or websites. Some clients may add fallback language in a work-made-for-hire contract that provides for an assignment of all rights if a work is deemed not to be work made for hire. Creators should resist signing such contracts and should challenge them if a commissioned work does not fall within the specified categories. Ultimately, the courts may have to determine a particular work's eligibility.

These criteria apply only to work done on special order or commission by an independent contractor. If there is no written agreement, if the agreement does not specifically state that the work is "work made for hire," if such an agreement is not signed, or if the work does not fall into one of the above categories, then there is no work made for hire, and the artist automatically retains authorship and copyright ownership. (Nevertheless, many clients are uninformed about these legal requirements, and they may believe that because they paid for a freelancer's work, they "own" it. If it is not the artist's intention to transfer all rights, it is always better to have a written contract that clearly explains that copyright ownership remains with the artist, and articulates the specific usage rights being granted to the client.)

By signing a work-made-for-hire contract, a freelance artist becomes an "employee" only for the purposes of copyright law and for no other purpose. In addition to losing authorship status, the freelance artist receives no regular salary, unemployment, workers' compensation, or disability insurance benefits; nor does he/she receive health insurance, sick pay, vacation, pension, or profit-sharing opportunities that a company may provide to formal, salaried employees. When a freelance artist signs a work-made-for-hire contract, the artist has no further relationship with the work and cannot display, copy, or use it for other purposes such as in the artist's portfolio, except by relying on a claim of fair use. The client, now considered the legal author, may change the art and use it again without limitation or any additional compensation to the artist.

Some clients still attempt to gain windfall benefits from works made for hire where there was no signed agreement by claiming that extensive supervision, control, and direction made the artist a *de facto* employee, and therefore the work was legally work made for hire. The Supreme Court resolved the issue in *CCNV v. Reid* (see below), affirming that, in virtually all cases, commissioned works executed by independent contractors cannot be works made for hire unless the work falls into one of the nine specified categories listed above *and* a written agreement stating the work is a work made for hire has been signed by both parties.

The Graphic Artists Guild is opposed to the use of work-made-for-hire contracts. Work made for hire is an unfair practice that strips the artist of the moral right of paternity—the right to be recognized as a work's author (see section on Moral Rights later in this chapter). It gives clients economic benefits and recognition that belong to the creative artist. Such contracts devalue the integrity of artists and their work by empowering clients to alter the work without consulting the artist and by preventing artists from obtaining any payment for the future use of their work.

Work-Made-for-Hire Abuse

Clients who insist on a work-made-for-hire arrangement may resort to other means that, while unethical, are not prohibited under current copyright law. Some businesses coerce freelancers by denying assignments to artists who do not accept work made for hire. Some clients attempt to designate a work as work made for hire after the fact by requiring that the artist endorse a payment check or sign a purchase order on which work-made-for-hire terms appear (usually in fine print). Unless this confirms a previous oral agreement, artists who encounter this should request a new payment check (see *Playboy Enterprises, Inc. v. Dumas* below) or cross out the incorrect work-made-for-hire statement.

Some work-made-for-hire contracts understood by the artist to be for a single project may actually have work-made-for-hire language that covers all future work.

Artists just entering the industry are especially vulnerable to such blanket work-made-for-hire agreements; unfortunately, by the time they have the reputation to resist work made for hire, clients already have the artist's signed agreement on file.

LEGAL CLARIFICATION

The following two court cases illustrate ways in which clients have forced work-made-for-hire arrangements on artists in order to circumvent copyright law, resulting in artists losing control of their images. Although the final rulings in both cases favored the artists and severely limited the potential for work-made-for-hire abuses, the language of the decisions was not strong enough to eliminate abuses entirely.

CCNV V. REID

In 1989, the Supreme Court ruled unanimously that the employee clause in the Copyright Act's work-made-for-hire provision could not be applied to independent contractors unless the relationship between the artist and the hiring party was determined to be one of conventional employment based on the application of a rigorous test of 13 factors (based on English common law).

This landmark case involved freelance sculptor James Earl Reid versus homeless advocate Mitch Snyder and the Community for Creative Non-Violence (CCNV) over a commissioned sculpture created by Reid but conceived and partly directed by Snyder. Even though there was no written contract between the parties, and even though sculpture does not fall into any of the nine categories of specially ordered works, the district court found Reid to be an employee because he was under Snyder's "supervision and control" and awarded the copyright to CCNV. The Supreme Court reversed this ruling.

The factors the Supreme Court relied upon in deciding James Reid's employment status were

* The hiring party's right to control the manner and means by which the product was accomplished
* The skill required
* The source of the "instrumentalities" and tools
* The location of the work
* The duration of the relationship between the parties
* Whether the hiring party had the right to assign additional projects to the hired party
* The hired party's discretion over when and how long to work
* The method of payment
* The hired party's role in hiring and paying assistants

* Whether the work was part of the regular business of the hiring party
* Whether the hiring party was in business
* The provision of employee benefits
* The tax treatment of the hired party

The Court made it clear that no one of these factors is determinative, but that all factors must be examined. In applying them to the *Reid* case, the Court found Reid to be an independent contractor, not an employee.

The practical consequences of this landmark decision are that some clients have reexamined their policies of insisting on work made for hire from freelancers, determining that it is more desirable and economical to purchase only the specific rights needed. Those clients who insist on work made for hire must comply strictly with the requirement for written agreements that state expressly that a work is work made for hire *and* the work must also fall within the nine statutory categories.

Although the Supreme Court decision narrowed one loophole, others remain. Under the "joint authorship" provision of the Copyright Act, a work may be presumed to be a collaborative effort between the artist and the client, granting each party the right to exploit the work independently of the other without regard to the importance of their respective contributions—if each party's contribution is copyrightable—so long as profits are accounted for and divided equally. This can only result, however, if both parties intend the work to be jointly owned, a condition that is difficult to meet when credit and creative control are reserved to the artist. Note that both joint authors must have contributed copyrightable authorship to the final work product, meaning that mere art direction, which is conceptual rather than tangible artistic expression, does not meet this requirement.

PLAYBOY ENTERPRISES, INC. V. DUMAS

The practice of introducing back-of-check contract terms, used by some clients to force a work made for hire arrangement, was severely limited by a 1995 federal court decision in the case of *Playboy Enterprises, Inc. v. Dumas*. Let stand by the U.S. Supreme Court, the Second Circuit Court of Appeals unequivocally rejected declarations of a work-made-for-hire agreement after the contract was fulfilled. The Appeals Court did not agree, however, as the Graphic Artists Guild argued in its *amicus curiae* brief, that work-made-for-hire agreements must be established in writing before work begins.

The case resulted from an attempt by the widow of artist Patrick Nagle, Jennifer Dumas, to stop Playboy from selling new editions of her late husband's work that had been commissioned by Playboy. He had endorsed checks with work-made-for-hire language on the back; therefore, claimed Playboy, the company was the legal author of the work.

The Court decided that, at least when evaluating work-made-for-hire issues under the old 1909 Act (which was superseded by the 1976 Act, applicable to all works created after 1977), "the written requirement can be met by a writing executed after the work is created, if the writing confirms a prior agreement, either explicit or implicit, made before the creation of the work."

The Graphic Artists Guild strongly recommends that artists and clients confirm all assignments in writing *before* work begins, detailing the terms of the agreement and the specific rights licensed. This professional practice avoids any confusion, misunderstanding, or legal action concerning the rights transferred.

Artists confronted with incorrect work-made-for-hire language on the back of checks may consider crossing it out and writing "deposited without conditions" to mitigate the attempted rights grab.

State Laws Extending Copyright Protection

While they are not part of the federal U.S. Copyright Law, certain state laws have been passed that strengthen copyright protection.

The Fair Practices Act

The Fair Practices Act, signed into law in Oregon, California, Georgia, and New York State, clarifies who owns the original work of art when reproduction rights are sold. This legislation was drafted by the Guild's attorneys based on concerns raised by Guild members.

The Act provides that an original work of art can become the property of a client only if the sale is in writing. The passage of this act reinforces one of the premises of the copyright law: works of art have value beyond their reproduction for a specific purpose, and this value rightly belongs to the artist who created the art. The Fair Practices Act prevents clients from holding on to originals unless they have written sales agreements with the creator. In those states where it applies, this act solves problems that can arise when clients believe they have obtained ownership of the original art when in fact they have only purchased rights of reproduction, or when they believe they have obtained an original through an ambiguous oral agreement.

In Oregon and California, the law also provides that

any ambiguity about the ownership of reproduction rights shall be resolved in favor of the artist. For artists whose livelihoods depend on resale of reproduction rights and on sales of original works, the law is critical.

The Rights in Works of Fine Art Act

Another important piece of legislation that prevents unauthorized reproduction of artwork was enacted by the Georgia Rights in Works of Fine Art Act of 1990. This statute requires commercial printers to obtain written affidavits from their clients attesting that the artist has authorized the reproduction of the work when the printing of the art (painting, drawing, photograph, or work of graphic art) costs $2,000 or more. Echoing federal copyright law, the Georgia law separates the ownership of artwork from the right to reproduce it and puts clients on notice that bills of sale or purchase orders must state explicitly the extent of the rights purchased. Any client or printer who uses or reuses artwork without the written permission of the artist is subject to misdemeanor penalties. The former Atlanta Chapter of the Guild was instrumental in getting the law passed.

Copyright Registration

Current copyright law automatically "protects" original artwork from the moment it is created, even without a copyright notice, and even if the artist has not registered the work. This is an improvement over previous law, when copyrights could be lost permanently if a work was published without registration, without a copyright notice, or with an incorrect notice. Artworks created after 1977 are protected, whether or not they are published or registered. However, the bulk of the benefits that the copyright law offers to artists are available only through formally registering the art with the U.S. Copyright Office of the Library of Congress.

Benefits of Registration

Registration establishes a public record of the artist's claim to authorship. More importantly, having a registration certificate is a necessary prerequisite to asserting any copyright claim in court. As long as a work is registered any time from its creation to five years after first publication, then the court will consider the registration to be *prima facie* evidence of copyright ownership. *Prima facie* evidence means that the burden is on the infringer to disprove the copyright's validity, rather than on the artist to prove that the copyright is valid.

The timeliness of registration has become more important than ever. On March 4, 2019, the Supreme Court decided that copyright owners may not file infringement lawsuits until the Copyright Office has issued a registration certificate for the infringed work. Prior to the 2019 ruling, courts in some jurisdictions allowed copyright owners to sue for infringement as soon as they filed an application to register their copyrights. In other words, when you discovered an infringement, you could quickly file for registration and then use the threat of a lawsuit as bargaining power to stop the infringement, because once a copyright registration certificate was issued, it had an effective date retroactive to the date you filed the application.

The new ruling is a major setback for copyright owners because it can take a long time to receive your certificate after you register a copyright (4–7 months or longer). If you have not already registered your work when you discover an infringement, you must now wait several months before you can file a lawsuit. The alternative is to pay a very costly fee to expedite the processing of your application, which can still take several weeks (as of this writing, the extra fee is $800). If you have not done so already, it is highly recommended that you implement a system in your workflow of proactively registering copyrights.

The benefits of registration increase if a work is registered within three months of publication or prior to a particular infringement ("early registration"): in such cases, the successful artist is entitled to recover statutory damages for infringement. Additionally, such early registration allows the prevailing party to recoup attorney's fees at the judge's discretion. This is useful when evaluating whether an infringement is worth pursuing.

Damages are considered by a court only after infringement has been proven. If a work has been registered early as noted above, the artist can ask the court to determine recovery by multiplying the number of works infringed times an amount specified by the copyright statute: a sum between $750 and $30,000 that the court considers just (if the defendant can prove the infringement was "innocent," the minimum is lowered to $200). Because this range is determined by the statute, these are called "statutory damages." If the copyright owner can prove to the court that the infringement was willful (i.e., not inadvertent), the statutory damages may be increased to $150,000 per work infringed. Because damages are based on the number of works infringed, not on the number of infringements of a single work, in some situations it would be more advantageous to seek actual damages; for example, if a defendant copied one of your designs onto greeting cards, then put it on coffee mugs, then on T-shirts, and sold millions of each, the defendant is still only liable for one award of statutory damages. Obviously, in that situation you would go for actual damages instead, which would be higher.

Thus, there are many incentives, both positive and negative, for following the procedures and ensuring timely registration. If a work is not registered within five years of publication, registration will not be considered *prima facie* evidence by the court. Additionally, if an infringement occurs before early registration, the right to attorney's fees and statutory damages is lost. Recovery will be limited to the amount of actual damages that can be proved: essentially, whatever profits may be attributed to the infringement. That puts a major burden on the artist pursuing an infringement claim because he/she will have to prove the infringer's gross profits. After that, the infringer must prove what portions of the profits are not attributable to the copyrighted work. Since an artist never knows when an infringement may occur, it is prudent to register early. Not only are statutory damages easier to obtain than actual damages, they can run much higher.

Fortunately, registration is relatively easy.

Registration Methods, Forms, & Fees

An application for copyright registration contains three essential elements: a **completed application form**, a **nonrefundable filing fee**, and a **nonreturnable deposit**—that is, a copy or copies of the work being registered and "deposited" with the Copyright Office. The Office will not review your claim until it has received these three elements in compliance with its regulations and policies.

The fees in the following sections went into effect March 20, 2020. However, fees do change periodically. For up-to-date fees, as well as a complete list of fees, visit https://www.copyright.gov/about/fees.html.

ONLINE REGISTRATION

To serve the public more efficiently and effectively, the Copyright Office established its Electronic Copyright Office (eCO) in 2008. Currently, the following works can be registered online, using the **Standard Registration** option:

* **An individual work** (literary work, visual arts work, motion picture, musical work, sound recording, and other performing arts work)
* **A single serial issue**
* In certain situations, **multiple works** with one application

The **Single Application** is a simplified registration option, only available with online registration. It allows a single author to register a claim in one work that is solely owned by the same author and is not a work made for hire. Certain types of works are not eligible for the Single Application option, as they create a more complex application that takes additional time to examine.

As part of the online registration process, the form will ask you to identify the category of your works. The Visual Arts category covers a wide variety of pictorial, graphic, sculptural, and architectural works, including works originally created by computer. Some examples of visual arts works include advertisements, cartoons and comic books, fabric designs, wrapping paper, graphic design, greeting cards, illustrations, maps, paintings, photographs, product packaging, websites of predominantly visual content, and some logos. (Note: under current Copyright Office practices, purely typographic logos will not be registered, nor will logos which comprise common geographical shapes.) Any one work in this category can be registered as a single work. Requirements are very strict as to what "one work" means. For example, a page with two drawings on it is not eligible nor are multiple versions of a logo, a portfolio of photographs, or a set of matching jewelry because each of these things contain multiple units of work. For complete guidelines as to what is and is not eligible for Single Application registration, refer to Circular 11, available at https://www.copyright.gov/circs/circ11.pdf.

Online registration is the Office's preferred method of registration, which is given priority. The advantages of online registration over paper registration include the following:

* A lower filing fee, currently $45 for a Single Application (single author, same claimant, one work, not for hire) and $65 for a Standard Applications (all other filings) vs. $125 for paper forms
* Faster processing time (an average of 4 months vs. 7 months for paper forms if no correspondence is required)
* Online status tracking
* Secure payment by credit or debit card, electronic check, or Copyright Office deposit account
* Ability to upload certain categories of deposits (copies of artwork) into eCO as electronic files

Before using the online service, it is recommended that you review eCO FAQs and tutorials on the Office's website for important details and guidelines about the process. Tutorials, which will walk you through the process step-by-step, are available in video and PDF formats. Informa-

tional circulars may be accessed at https://www.copyright.gov/circs/. The circulars listed under the category "Visual Arts Works" are especially helpful for graphic arts.

PAPER REGISTRATION

Although the Copyright Office strongly encourages you to apply online whenever possible, you may still be able to register your work using one of the PDF forms available on the Office's website. The various forms and explanations for their use can be found here: https://www.copyright.gov/forms/; https://www.copyright.gov/registration/. However, as of this writing, the Copyright Office has made known its intention to eliminate the paper filing option for most situations.

Paper Form VA (visual arts) is used to register most works made by graphic artists (see above). Other registration forms may be needed at certain times by graphic artists. If audiovisual work is created, including motion pictures, animations, and video games, then Form PA is appropriate. When an artist creates both art and text in a work, and the text predominates, Form TX should be used, and the description should indicate "text with accompanying art." Generally, Form TX is also used to register computer software (including any graphics that are part of screen displays generated by the software), blogs, and databases. All forms come with line-by-line instructions.

SUBMITTING APPLICATIONS

ONLINE

Submitting an online application involves three simple steps, done in the following order:

1. Complete the application.
2. Pay the associated fee.
3. Submit a deposit copy of your work.

Payment options include paying with a credit/debit card or ACH transfer via Pay.gov or through a Copyright Office deposit account. Pay.gov is a secure, web-based application operated by the U.S. Treasury Department that allows users to make online payments to government agencies. The Office also maintains a system of deposit accounts for those who frequently use its services. An individual or a firm may establish a deposit account, make advance deposits into their account, and charge copyright fees against their balance via eCO.

If the artwork being registered meets the requirements for depositing with electronic files, then the entire application can be submitted online, or the registrant has the option of completing the forms and paying online but depositing artwork as hard copies sent by mail/courier. If the artwork does not qualify for electronic depositing, then the latter method must be used. Both unpublished works and works published only electronically can be deposited electronically. The eCO website provides a complete list of the classes of work that can be deposited electronically, as well as acceptable file formats and other specifications for electronic deposits (https://www.copyright.gov/eco/help-file-types.html).

Payment is required before the system will prompt you to upload copies of your work as an electronic file or print out a shipping slip if you intend to submit hard copies of your work. The shipping slip must accompany your hard copy deposit when it is shipped.

PAPER

The following are needed to submit a paper application for registration:

* The completed registration form,
* The required deposit, and
* A check or money order for the required registration fee.

Registrants should refer to the appropriate circulars for specific deposit requirements. Graphic artists will find Circular 40a, "Deposit Requirements for Registration of Claims to Visual Arts Material," the most helpful. Originals should never be sent to the Copyright Office for registration purposes. The artist should keep copies of all work submitted with each registration form for easy reference. (Note: under current Copyright Office practices, physical copies for published works are discarded after a few years.)

Once you complete your paper application, mail it with your filing fee and deposit, all in the same package, to the address on the final page of the application. To avoid damage to hard-copy deposits caused by security processing, package the following items in boxes rather than envelopes for mailing to the Copyright Office:

* Electronic media such as audiocassettes, videocassettes, CDs, and DVDs
* Microform
* Photographs
* Slick advertisements, color photocopies, and other print items

Applications should be sent by a service that provides an accurate record of delivery. It is essential to have an accurate record of the delivery date and proof of delivery, in the event that it is necessary to expedite a registration in progress for the purpose of filing a lawsuit or to trace an application in the rare instance that it is lost during processing.

Registration of Multiple Works

As a general rule, a copyright registration covers one work, and you must prepare a separate application and submit a separate filing fee and deposit for each work you want to register. There are, however, some limited exceptions to this rule, which allow registration of multiple works on one application form with one filing fee. These exceptions include

* Collective Works
* Group Registrations
* Works Packaged as a Single Unit

Artists can save money by registering a number of works on one application for a single fee if their work falls under one of these categories. Some of them apply only to published or unpublished works, so it helps to know the Copyright Office's definitions of each.

"Unpublished work" includes any work that has not been published at the time it is sent to the Copyright Office. Even if an artist knows that the work will be published the next week, if it is unpublished at the time a completed application is sent to the Copyright Office, it may be registered with other works as unpublished work.

"Published" means that copies of the work have been made available to the public by sale or other transfer of ownership, or by rental, lease, or lending. Offering to distribute copies to a group of persons for the purposes of further distribution, public performance, or public display also constitutes publication. A public performance or display of a work (for example, display in a gallery) does not in itself constitute publication.

The definition of "publication" in U.S. copyright law does not specifically address online displays. The Copyright Office asks the applicant, who knows the facts surrounding the distribution of a work, to decide whether posting work online makes it "published" or "unpublished" for purposes of registration. Thus, you can choose how you want to register such works. Logically, if a site offers downloads of the works, then copies are being offered to the public, and thus they are published. On the other hand, if the site does not authorize downloads, the works are arguably being displayed only, and thus are unpublished. However, some courts have assumed, without evaluation, that works shown online are published. Also, when determining whether to register online works as published or unpublished, it is important to remember that unpublished works do not receive the three-month grace period for early registration (see Benefits of Registration earlier in this chapter).

For registration purposes, a website is considered a web page or set of interconnected web pages, including a home page, located on the same computer or server and prepared and maintained as a collection of information by a person, group, or organization. Although a website may contain text, artwork, photographs, music, videos, or other copyrightable content, the Copyright Office does not typically consider a website itself to be a copyrightable work. However, you may be able to register a website or a specific web page if it satisfies the statutory requirements for a compilation or collective work (see below). To learn the specifics about registering online work, refer to *Circular 66: Copyright Registration of Websites and Website Content*, available on the Office's website. https://www.copyright.gov/circs/circ66.pdf.

COLLECTIVE WORKS

A *collective work* is a compilation of separate and independent contributions assembled into a collective whole. Published and unpublished works are eligible for registration as a collective work. Representative examples of collective works include newspapers, magazines, or other periodicals containing multiple articles, illustrations, and photographs. A collective work is *not* a single unified work that contains separate parts or elements (such as an illustrated children's book created by one person), a unified work created by multiple authors (such as a children's book created by a writer and an illustrator in collaboration with each other), or a single contribution to a collective work.

Under the Copyright Act, a collective work is considered one work for purposes of registration. A registration for a collective work covers the copyrightable authorship in the selection, coordination, or arrangement of the work. The arrangement must be somewhat creative: a simple grid arrangement will not be considered copyrightable. A registration for a collective work may also cover individual works contained in it only if (1) the collective work and the individual works are owned by the same party, (2) the individual works have not been previously published or previously registered, and (3) the individual works are not in the public domain.

By contrast, if the copyright owner of a magazine, for example, does not own the copyright in the illustrations or photographs, or if the images have been previously published, then those images must be registered separately as an individual contribution to the collective work.

Examples of separate and independent works within a collective work include an article within a periodical, a song included on an album, and separate articles and photographs that appear in a newspaper

A collective work is generally considered a single work for purposes of calculating statutory damages; therefore, registering a collective work together with the individual works contained in it may have important consequences in an infringement action. When you register a number of individual works as part of a collective work, you may be entitled to only one award of statutory damages for the collective work as a whole rather than a separate award for each individual work, even if the defendant infringed all of those works.

For more detailed information about what works can and cannot be registered as collective works, refer to the Copyright Office *Circular 34: Multiple Works*, available at https://www.copyright.gov/circs/circ34.pdf.

In the online registering process, you cannot register a Collective Work as a Single Application. Through a series of initial questions, you will be directed to the Standard Application instead.

GROUP REGISTRATION

There are several types of multiple works that may qualify as a *group registration* on one application for one fee. The Office currently offers group registration options for the following types of works:

* Unpublished works
* Serials
* Newspapers
* Newsletters
* Contributions to periodicals
* Published and unpublished photographs
* Database updates and revisions
* Questions, answers, and other items prepared for use in a secure test

UNPUBLISHED WORKS
Up to 10 unpublished artworks may be registered together for a single fee, currently $65, if the group meets the following requirements:

* All the works are by the same author or joint author,
* All the authors are named as copyright claimants, and
* Each work belongs to the same administration class (e.g. visual arts, performing arts, sound recording, text, etc.).

The last requirement means that you cannot register 2-D illustrations (visual arts) along with animations (performing arts). Photographs are subject to different rules, under which up to 750 photographs can be registered together.

Group registration of unpublished works can no longer be done using a paper form or the Standard Application. Applicants must use the new online application form titled "Group of Unpublished Works" and upload digital copies of their works to the electronic registration system. (Photographers must use the online application form GRUPH.)

Each work in the group must be titled, although the titles may be simple numbers. A registration for a group of unpublished works or a group of unpublished photographs will remain in effect even if the works included in the group are subsequently published, either separately or together. You can seek another registration for the first published edition of a work in the group; however, that is entirely optional and not necessary to secure the statutory benefits of registration. Each work within the group is considered a separately registered work, and the copyright owner may be entitled to claim a separate award of statutory damages for each work covered by a group.

It is more economical for an artist to register all images for a job, including rough sketches, as unpublished groups of 10, for one fee per group, as soon as finals are submitted to the client. Otherwise, once the final artwork is published, it has to be registered separately from the unpublished images that were created for the same job. To make sure that copyright registration occurs—and happens in a timely manner—submitting copyright applications should be a routine function scheduled in the artist's workflow for a project or assignment. Although registration fees should not be charged to the client as line items, they should be figured into the artist's cost of doing business when calculating rates.

PUBLISHED WORKS

The following published artworks may be submitted for registration as a "Group" for a single filing fee:

* Serials (Online or Form SE/Group) (per issue; min. 2 issues)
* Newspapers (Online only; refer to Circular 62a)
* Qualified newsletters (Form G/DN)
* Published Photographs (Online only) (up to 750)
* Contributions to Periodicals (Online only; refer to Circular 62c)
* Group Automated Database Updates (within a 3-month period) Photographic (Online or paper); Non-Photographic (Paper only)

Note that while some of the above forms allow group registration of work covering an entire year, the post-publication grace period for the strongest copyright protection is only three months. It would be wise for an artist who works for a great many periodicals and newspapers to submit group registration forms at least every four months to ensure the strongest copyright protection.

WORKS PACKAGED AS A SINGLE UNIT

The *unit of publication* registration option allows for published works to be registered on one application with one filing fee provided that the works were physically packaged or bundled together as a single unit and that they were first published in that integrated unit. A few examples of units of publication that may be registered on one application are

* A board game with playing pieces, game board, and written instructions
* A bound volume published with a dust jacket
* A book published with a CD-ROM
* A children's book with a set of stickers
* A compact disc containing multiple sound recordings packaged together with liner notes and cover artwork
* A package of greeting cards

The requirements for registering a number of works as a unit of publication are very specific, and most works, including online works, do not qualify for this option. You can use it only if it meets all of the following requirements:

* All of the copyrightable elements are recognizable as self-contained works,
* All of the works claimed in the application are first published as a single unit on the same date,
* The copyright claimant for all of the works claimed in the unit is the same,
* The unit, and all of the works within the unit, is distributed in a physical format,
* The unit contains an actual physical copy or phonorecord of all the works, and
* The unit is distributed to the general public.

Proof of Registration

The Copyright Office receives more than 500,000 registrations annually. Online applications are confirmed via e-mail, downloadable pending application forms are generated, and their process can be tracked through the eCO. Paper registrations are given lowest priority in the Copyright Office, and no receipt confirmation or tracking information is provided. The registration process for paper registrations is an average of 7 months, but it can take up to 18 months if there are complications. If there is any difficulty or question about the registration, the Copyright Office will contact the registrant during that interval.

There is also a "Special Handling" procedure that can result in a registration in ten to fifteen business days, but this is much more expensive (an additional $800 vs. the basic $45–$125 fee), and it can only be used in certain circumstances, such as when a lawsuit or business transaction requires immediate registration. If the application cannot be accepted, a letter will be sent explaining why it was rejected. Applicants generally have an opportunity to challenge such rejections. In such cases, it is wise to consult a copyright attorney.

After registration is granted, the registrant will receive a certificate from the Copyright Office that will have an effective date retroactive to the date the application (complete with fee and deposit) was received in acceptable form. An artist does not have to receive the certificate before publishing, copying, or displaying a registered work, nor does the artist need permission from the Copyright Office to place a notice of copyright on any work, whether registered or not. However, an artist cannot file a lawsuit for copyright infringement until the registration certificate is issued.

Additional Registration Information

To speak to a Copyright Office staff member, call 202-707-3000 or 1-877-476-0778 (toll free). Recorded information is available 24 hours a day. Order paper forms by calling 202-707-9100.

Access and download circulars, forms, tutorials, and other information from the Copyright Office website at www.copyright.gov.

Protecting Copyrights

In addition to registering their copyrights, graphic artists need to be proactive about protecting their copyrights, as well as those of other creators, before they begin work on a project.

Written Agreements

The best way to protect against violations of copyright by clients is through written agreements. Clients often assume that because they paid for the work, they own all rights. To avoid such misunderstandings, contracts should be in writing, and should clearly state the rights granted, usage, and duration of time for which a license is granted. All other rights should be explicitly reserved to the artist or copyright holder. (For additional information about contracts, see Chapter 12, Standard Contracts & Business Tools.)

USAGE RIGHTS

The importance of spelling out the usage rights the client is purchasing, in the graphic artist's estimate, and in the letter of confirmation or formal contract, cannot be overemphasized. Most legal problems between artist and client arise because the original terms and any later changes were not expressed clearly in writing. The invoice should not be the first time a client sees or hears about copyright. Clients must be equally careful to assess their usage needs in relation to their budget at the start of a project, as most artists adjust their fees according to the rights purchased.

Depending on the scope of the project and the needs of the client, limited rights of reproduction for digital art and design may be appropriate. Graphic artists should specify the number of copies permitted, the form in which they will be made, the degree of resolution, limitations on scaling up or down, and so forth. Other specified limitations usually include the number of appearances or length of time the rights are being licensed for, the market, the media, the geographic area, and the degree of exclusivity. Recent surveys show that payment may be by flat fee or by royalty on either a straight percentage basis or a sliding scale. Royalties may differ for uses of the same piece in different markets.

While typefaces are not copyrightable, the software that produces them is protected by copyright. Most type companies license their fonts for both personal and commercial use, which allows sales and distribution of designs and documents created using the font software, but it does not allow distribution of the software itself. Allowed uses may include printed materials, logos, and rendered content like photographs, film, video and bitmap graphics. If distributed, the design should not contain the original font, but can be converted to vector outlines, rasterized, or subsetted and embedded in an electronic document like a PDF or eBook. Artists are generally able to own copyright in works, such as logos, that they create using the fonts. Artists should check the specifics of their licensing agreement to ensure that such uses are allowed.

With the growth of technology, and as-yet-unimagined vistas opening in digital media, many clients have begun adding increasingly broad rights-ownership language to contracts. Artists should be alert to any clauses buying "all electronic rights" or "all rights in all media now in existence or invented in the future in perpetuity throughout the universe." These overly broad grants of rights effectively give the client indefinite and unspecified use of a creator's work without additional compensation or input into uses. Such clauses can be as damaging to artists as traditional work-made-for-hire arrangements; artists lose valuable sources of future income and control over their images and reputations. Historically, artists and other creators have been able to withstand such onslaughts by negotiating strenuously, both individually and collectively. (For more information on artists' negotiating options, see Chapter 1, Essential Business Practices.) If a client insists on such all rights language, artists should ensure they are getting appropriately higher fees.

QUALITY CONTROL

Quality control is a legitimate negotiating point that affects the artist's reputation and income. Contracts should specify whether alteration or modification will take place. A contract may specifically prohibit manipulation: for example:

This work may not be digitally manipulated, altered, or scanned without specific written permission from the artist. An alternative is: This license does not give [Buyer] the right to produce any derivative works and [Buyer] agrees not to manipulate the image except as we have agreed in writing.

Stock agencies can play a role in preventing and monitoring unauthorized use of art by using contracts stating that the image may not be manipulated without the artist's permission and that the artist must be given the first opportunity to make any desired changes. Requesting printed samples of all stock work also helps the artist monitor the image's appearance. Agencies can protect their own and their artists' interests by conducting random checks of the media to spot unauthorized uses.

DERIVATIVE WORKS

Written agreements should be used to grant or limit the right to create a derivative work from an existing image. Terms should specify whether derivative works will be permitted, or, if the art does not yet exist, whether the creators will collaborate equally to devise a new, original joint work with a shared copyright. Advance discussion of these issues can help avoid awkward and unpleasant situations.

By granting a general right to prepare a derivative work, an artist in effect permits the client to do anything to the artwork to create something new. Therefore, specifying how the work may be manipulated or adapted for other media will better protect one's rights. As with the license of any copyrighted image, intended markets, rights of reproduction, and so on, granted to any derivative work should be clearly specified.

As digital markets proliferate, publishers have new types of projects in which to use art. Many of these will be derivative works compiling text, image, and sound. An appropriate license should be negotiated that describes the product and specifies that the client is licensing the right to use the art in that product. A storyboard, outline, or comp may be attached to help explain the project.

Assigning the entire copyright, or all rights, or granting complete reproduction and derivative-work rights entitles the receiving party to manipulate the art or design at will. While some artists and designers are interested in granting broad-rights licenses, many artists and designers prefer to control their work tightly and restrict image manipulation subject to their approval. Each artist or designer determines what constitutes appropriate compensation for the scope of the licensing rights granted.

Diligent Recordkeeping

As always, creating a paper trail and keeping good records can help prove infringement. For example, it is good business practice to keep copies of all written agreements and date-stamped records of telephone conversations in which changes were discussed. Saving copies of work in stages may also help prove that an infringement has been made. And saving reference images with a record of their sources and rights agreements can protect against infringement claims by others.

Digital Defense

Be aware that unauthorized use of digital media may be particularly difficult to monitor. While contracts provide the clearest overall legal copyright protection, a preemptive line of defense may be taken digitally. For example, artwork intended for presentation but not for reproduction can be provided in a low-resolution form that is unsuitable for further use.

Technological approaches are developed continually to ensure protection and to monitor the appearance or alteration of a work. Encryption, or programming an invisible protective code into the body of a work, may be useful, though determined hackers can break most codes. Experts have also discussed embedding a self-destructing key in a digital image so that after a certain number of uses it can no longer be accessed. Digital pictures can also be labeled visibly so that notice of ownership and the terms of any license always accompany the image. Other types of "watermarking" can be as simple as embedding a copyright notice, in an image that will be visible if reproduced.

Discussion of intellectual property law with regard to the Internet is ongoing, but currently consists of more questions than answers. What goes online, and how it is used, mixes the copyright, commercial, and contractual interests of many parties. Online vendors, for example, may be more interested in getting out a lot of information to attract customers and be less motivated to monitor what happens afterwards. A publisher or original creator, though, wants to maintain control.

Ethical Practices & Artists' Liability

PERMISSIONS

The easiest way to avoid infringing the copyright of another creator is to confirm that permission has been obtained in advance, in writing, which specifies any intended use of copyrighted art, such as making a composite or other derivative work.

Copyrighted digital images require the same respect as any other copyrighted images—permission for use is required under federal copyright law. No one, for example, should make unauthorized or pirated copies of application software.

For online images, a Google reverse image search can be done to try to find the copyright owner. All copyrighted works, registered since 1978, can be searched online on the Copyright Office website at https://cocatalog.loc.gov/cgi-bin/Pwebrecon.cgi?DB=local&PAGE=First. Once a copyright owner has been found, contact the owner to ask for permission to use the image. It may be unavailable for use, available for use, or only available under certain circumstances.

If you can't find the copyright holder, assume the image is copyrighted. Rather than face a possible infringement claim, err on the safe side and don't use the image. For some works, referred to as "orphan works," it's impossible to find the copyright holder, but the copyright may still be in effect.

ORPHAN WORKS

An *orphan work* is generally understood to mean older works which are still technically protected by copyright, but whose owners have abandoned their rights or have gone out of business without transferring the rights. The U.S. Copyright Office defines orphan works as "copy-righted works whose owners are difficult or even impossible to locate." This definition is problematic, especially for visual works. Unlike literary works and others that are known by searchable titles, visual works are not easily searchable, and thus it may be impossible to locate the copyright owner even for current visual works.

There are two basic categories of orphan works:

* Works created by individual living authors who still own their copyright, or deceased authors whose copyright has passed to their heirs, and who are not able to be located either because they have not kept their contact information current with the U.S. Copyright Office, their names are not on their work, or they never registered their work at all. Such works are not true orphans as their copyright owners still exist.
* Works that were owned by a business, the business is defunct and its assets—including intellectual property rights—were not sold or assigned to anyone else. In these circumstances, the works are truly orphaned because there is no copyright owner.

An especially compelling argument for releasing the copyright on orphaned works, or allowing users to copy them with very limited infringement remedies, pertains to preserving artistic works in danger of being lost forever, such as the need to restore decomposing silent films made in the 1920s by Hollywood studios long defunct. A parallel situation exists for old books that are out of print.

The Guild's position on the orphan works issue is that it is too complicated to be resolved with an all-or-nothing rule. Instead, usage requests for orphaned works should be handled on a case-by-case basis, taking into consideration the inherent difficulty of searching for copyright owners of visual works.

Pressure from non-profit users, such as universities, libraries, archives, and museums, led to the request by Congress that the U.S. Copyright Office propose a solution to the problem at the beginning of 2006. In 2008, both the House and Senate introduced similar bills, S. 2913 and H.R. 5889, to remedy the problem. Although the Senate bill passed, the House bill was never passed, and there has not been any new legislation since.

The U.S. Copyright Office heard a variety of viewpoints on a wide range of issues impacting orphan works and mass digitization efforts in a series of public roundtables it held in 2014. The Office's final analysis and recommendation were released in a report in June 2015, entitled "Orphan Works and Mass Digitization: A Report of the Register of Copyrights" (www.copyright.gov/orphan/reports/orphan-works2015.pdf).

Editors and other artwork buyers may want to crop or otherwise manipulate an image, and digital retouching makes that incredibly easy. Clear contractual terms spelling out the artist's rights and a good relationship with an editor or art director ensure that the artist will be involved throughout the editorial process so the best aesthetic results can be obtained. All changes should be discussed with the artist, and the artist should be given the first opportunity to make them or to approve changes that the art director or client would like to make. The Guild's position is that no image manipulation should take place without the artist's knowledge and permission, and any changes should be made on a duplicate copy of the art. (See previous sections on Quality Control and Derivative Works.)

A traditional exception is for low-resolution images provided by sources such as stock houses. Many of these are used in presentations, with the expectation that rights to the image will be purchased if the concept is approved. The Graphic Artists Guild advocates always asking permission before using another artist's sample or portfolio images in presentations, regardless of the image resolution.

CELEBRITY, PRIVACY, & LIKENESS ISSUES

Artists are occasionally asked by clients to reproduce or imitate images of recognizable individuals. The potential for right of publicity infringement in such cases is serious and underscores the need for including indemnification clauses protecting artists in all contracts. (See the Right of Publicity section, later in this chapter.)

All illustration or design has the potential for invasion-of-privacy issues. For example, the advertising or trade use of a living (and in many states, even a deceased) person's name or likeness without permission is a violation of publicity rights and/or an invasion of privacy, and claims may be in the hundreds of thousands of dollars for an infringement. "Advertising or trade" means virtually all uses other than factual, editorial, or literary content of magazines, newspapers, books, television programs, and films; it includes print and TV ads, company brochures, packaging, and other commercial uses. Public and private figures are protected equally.

The test of "likeness" is whether an ordinary person would recognize the complainant as the person depicted or suggested in the illustration. It need not be a perfect likeness, or even a likeness at all. For example, race car drivers have successfully claimed publicity rights in their famous cars. The best protection in these cases is

a signed release from the person whose likeness is used (for a model release form, see the Appendix: Contracts & Forms), and any contract should provide for this if a problem is likely to arise.

PHOTOGRAPHIC REFERENCES

If an artist copies a person's likeness or other imagery from another work—a photograph, for example—in making an illustration, the photographer or copyright holder might have a claim for copyright infringement. The test of an infringement is whether an ordinary person would say that one work is copied from the other; the copying need not be exact.

Given the substantial amount of photography used as reference for illustration, as well as the frequent incorporation of photographs into designs, everyone, particularly freelance artists, should exercise extreme caution in this area. Of course, common themes and images, such as city skylines, are in the public domain and may be used freely. Infringement requires copying specific artistic expression in a work, so mere similarity in style or concept will not constitute an infringement.

WARRANTIES & INDEMNITIES

Because of privacy and infringement risks, many advertisers and publishers carry special liability insurance to cover these types of claims. That, however, may not provide complete protection, particularly for the freelance artist, who may be sued along with the client. Sometimes clients insist that artists incorporate images that might infringe on someone's right of privacy or copyright. Artists need to incorporate an indemnification clause in their agreements that hold the artist harmless in this situation. A sample indemnification clause reads as follows:

You [client] agree to indemnify and hold [artist] harmless against all claims, including but not limited to claims of copyright or trademark infringement, violations of the rights of privacy or publicity or defamation, arising out of use of [the work] or any source materials required or provided by you [client].

Many contracts today require an artist to warrant that the work does not infringe on any other work, and they demand that the artist hold the company harmless for any action arising from breach of this warranty. It is possible to rewrite and limit these clauses to minimize the artist's liability. For example, artists can rewrite the warranty clause so that they are not responsible for infringements arising from any reference or textual material provided by the client. Artists can also limit the warranty so that it does not infringe "to the best of the artist's knowledge and belief." And they can limit liability to "meritorious" claims arising from an actual breach of warranty.

Fighting Infringement

Infringement of work protected by copyright law is rampant on the Internet where users mistakenly believe that everything that they see is available for using, sharing, and reposting. Some of the infringement is due to ignorance about copyright, but in other cases, it is willful and deliberate. Even large, multi-million-dollar corporations that employ legal departments to protect their own intellectual property have been guilty of infringing the copyrights of others.

Illustrators and photographers are often victims of infringement. Unfortunately, the burden of fighting infringement rests with the copyright holder. Some artists have employed the practice of regularly searching the Internet for infringement as part of their business routine (see the interview, Art & Business: A Beautiful Partnership, in Part 4). One simple way to do this is by using Google's Image Search:

1. Go to the Google search page, click on *Images* in upper right corner.
2. Click on the camera icon on the far right of the search bar. This will bring up the "search by image" box.
3. You will be given three options: you can either drag the image into the box, paste the URL for the image you want to search for, or upload the image.
4. Click on *Search* and the results will show you every instance where someone has used that image.

CONTACTING INFRINGERS

Once an online infringement has been found, copyright holders should contact both the person who posted the work and the Internet Service Provider (ISP) that hosts the website where the infringed image is located. Both parties are part of the infringement—the ISP is considered to be enabling the infringement to be seen online.

First, send the ISP a DMCA takedown notice to remove the infringed image from the website it is hosting. You do not need to have a copyright registration to use the DMCA process. As discussed in detail in a previous section on the DMCA Takedown Notice, the takedown notice has limited effectiveness for copyright holders, but it's better than doing nothing, especially if the infringer is trying to resell your work. Most ISPs will honor a takedown notice rather than risk being sued for infringement. However,

some ISPs may not comply, especially if they are located outside the United States. The ISP is required to notify the website owner when it takes down an infringing image and give the owner a chance to file a counter-notice alleging that the image was not being infringed.

Second, immediately send the website owner a cease and desist letter to let the person know you are serious about protecting your rights and you want to ensure there are no repeat infringements. A copy of a Cease and Desist Letter that you can use is found in this handbook's Appendix: Contracts and Forms. If your work is being sold by the infringer, you will also want the contact info for any customers to make sure they do not use the work. The Cease and Desist Letter also asks for an accounting of any profits the infringer has made from the sale of your work. This will be useful information if you take legal action.

If your cease and desist letter is ignored, have your intellectual property attorney send a second letter, which may be more effective. Sometimes just the threat of legal action will be enough to get the infringer to stop using the image.

TAKING LEGAL ACTION

If notifying an infringer does not stop the infringement, copyright holders who have registered their copyright and received the Certificate of Registration have the option of taking the infringer to court. Unfortunately, taking a copyright infringement case to federal court is extremely expensive and is often out of the financial reach of self-employed artists and small businesses. For small copyright infringements, the legal costs often outstrip the potential award, and moreover, it is difficult to find an attorney who will take a small infringement case. The extent of the infringement, its potential effect on the livelihood of the artist, and the financial gain if the suit were to be successful must be weighed against the cost of representation and legal proceedings, especially if the suit were to prove unsuccessful. It is worth an initial meeting with an intellectual property attorney to give you an expert evaluation of what the cost could be and if your case is worth fighting in court.

THE CASE ACT

Due to the prohibitive cost of taking infringement cases to court for most copyright holders, they are left with few viable options to defend their copyrights, and in the case of small infringements, there is no viable option. The Graphic Artists Guild and other artist advocacy groups have been pursuing legislation for years that would provide an alternative to federal court for prosecuting small copyright infringement cases.

The introduction of the Copyright Alternative in Small Claims Enforcement Act (the CASE Act) proposed establishing a small copyright claims tribunal within the Copyright Office. Similar to the way a small-claims court handles disputes quickly and easily, the small copyright claims tribunal would expeditiously handle small copyright disputes in which the potential award is less than $15,000 for a single infringement, or $30,000 for multiple infringements (injunctive relief—requiring that the infringement stop—would be voluntary by the defendant). The system would be staffed by three full-time Copyright Claims Officers to be appointed by the Library of Congress.

The process would be inexpensive for copyright holders, as legal counsel would not be required. Claimants could represent themselves or seek the help of law students on a *pro bono* basis. Use of the small-claims tribunal would be entirely voluntary for both parties, since the Seventh Amendment guarantees the right to a trial by jury. Because the cost of litigation is so high, potential defendants have at least some incentive to opt in. Artists with a large copyright infringement could still opt to go to federal court.

On May 1, 2019, the latest iteration of the CASE Act was introduced—by both the House (H.R. 2426) and the Senate (S. 1273)—with bipartisan co-sponsorship by nine Representatives and four Senators. The CASE Act was passed by Congress on December 21, 2020, as part of an omnibus spending and COVID-19 relief bill and signed into law by the President on December 27, 2020.

An outpouring of grassroots support from Guild members and other artists is credited with raising awareness of the CASE Act among members of Congress and impressing upon them the need for a small copyright claims solution for individual artists.

Legal Rights Beyond U.S. Copyright Law

Right of Publicity

Unlike copyright, the right of publicity is not created by federal law but by the laws of each individual state. These laws vary greatly in their details, but most states recognize a general right for a person to control the commercial use of his or her name, likeness, and other aspects of "personal identity." Some states have enacted statutes to govern these rights, some rely on "common law" principles developed by the courts, and some, like California, recognize both.

Not surprisingly, these state laws are inconsistent. In New York, the right of publicity is written into the state civil rights statute, which provides that "any person whose name, portrait, picture, or voice is used within this state for advertising purposes or purposes of trade without the written consent" of the subject may be sued for injunctive and monetary relief. Significantly, this right extends to "any person" in New York, not merely to celebrities or people in the public eye. So, in New York, at least, it is illegal to market a sketch of the corner grocer as a poster for Boar's Head cold cuts, no matter how unknown he may be.

In California, the statute covers largely the same conduct as the New York law, but it can also protect the rights of the deceased, both famous and obscure. Under New York law, once a person is dead, they have no more right of publicity: witness throngs of vendors selling unauthorized John Lennon merchandise outside the Dakota apartment building where Lennon used to live. As long as those vendors sell their wares only in New York and do not otherwise violate the trademark laws (merchandise that suggests a false endorsement by the singer might be actionable under the federal Lanham Act, for example, even if it did not violate state law), they are doing nothing wrong because under New York law, Lennon's right of publicity died with him. Wisconsin law also limits coverage to living people.

Those same vendors could not operate legally in California. The California statute allows the heirs or survivors of a deceased "personality" to continue to control that person's right of publicity for 50 years after death, provided they register with the Secretary of State and pay a small fee. Indeed, even without filing the necessary paperwork, the heirs of a deceased person can enjoin unauthorized uses in California, but they cannot recover monetary damages until they have complied with the statutory formalities.

Other states go even further in granting postmortem rights of publicity, with Indiana and Oklahoma protecting the right for 100 years after death and Tennessee, home of the late Elvis Presley, recognizing it in perpetuity, so long as it continues to be used (by his estate or its authorized licensees) for commercial purposes. Other states, such as Washington, provide for a 10-year post-mortem right for ordinary people but offer 75 years of protection for those whose images have "commercial value." Accordingly, it is best to assume that even the long deceased may have enforceable rights of publicity somewhere.

There are several limitations and exceptions to the right of publicity, most importantly those involving First Amendment protection for "newsworthy" images. The same likeness of a celebrity that might be prohibited on a T-shirt may be permissible as an illustration for an article in a commercial publication if two conditions are met. First, the image must bear some reasonable relation to the content of the article. Second, the article must concern a matter of legitimate "public interest," a broad concept that encompasses everything from hard news to celebrity gossip. As the courts have defined it, virtually any story or article will qualify as a matter of public interest, so long as it is not merely an advertisement in disguise. Moreover, if the story itself is legitimate and the image is reasonably related to it, the likeness can also be used on posters and billboards advertising the publication, on the theory that the protected nature of the initial use extends to advertisements for the protected speech.

In addition, both California and New York recognize a "fine art" exception, also rooted in the First Amendment. The California statute exempts "single and original works of fine art." The Right of Publicity statute does not include any definition of the term "fine art." The statute clearly provides, however, that, as with newsworthy publications, advertisements for legitimate works of fine art, such as gallery posters, do not violate the statute.

In New York, there is no direct statutory language regarding fine art, but the courts have recently interpreted the statute to exempt two- and three-dimensional works of art from the law. In *Simeonov v. Tiegs*, the Civil Court held that an artist who created a plaster casting of model Cheryl Tiegs could "sell at least a limited number of copies" of the work without violating Tiegs's right of publicity because such activities did not amount to a use of her likeness "for purposes of trade." In this case, the New York statute was read to permit such sales to avoid creating a possible conflict between the state statute and the First Amendment. A recent case involving artist Barbara Kruger went further, finding no "purpose of trade" with respect to T-shirts, refrigerator magnets, and other items sold in the gift shop of the Whitney Museum. The ruling stated that those items were merely reproductions of a Kruger work being shown at the Whitney, and the Kruger work was itself clearly protected under the First Amendment.

In California, however, the standard is more subjective. In *Comedy III Productions, Inc. v. Gary Saderup, Inc.*, the California Supreme Court held that although limited edition prints were entitled to first amendment protection, those rights must be balanced against celebrities' rights of publicity. Rather than focusing on whether there is a "purpose of trade," California courts look at whether the artwork on the item is "transformative." Artwork is transformative if it is perceived as "primarily the artist's own expression rather than the subject's likeness." Under that standard, the courts have held that a realistic portrait of the Three Stooges, when reproduced on fine arts prints as well as T-shirts, was a commercial use in violation of the Stooges' rights of publicity. On the other hand, caricatures of Johnny and Edgar Winter in a comic book were held sufficiently transformative not to infringe the Winters' publicity rights.

In 1989, the Second Circuit Court of Appeals (New York), in a case called *Rogers v. Grimaldi*, created the "Rogers Test." Ginger Rogers unsuccessfully sued over distribution of the 1986 Federico Fellini film "Ginger and Fred," about two Italian cabaret performers who emulated the more famous pairing of Fred Astaire and Ginger Rogers. The court held that such use did not violate federal trademark law or New York's rights of publicity law. The Rogers test means that use of a celebrity's name or image in an artistic work that is at least minimally relevant to the content of the work is protected by the First Amendment, provided that the use does not explicitly denote authorship, sponsorship, or endorsement by the celebrity, or explicitly mislead as to content of the work. It has been followed in many other jurisdictions.

OBTAINING PERMISSION

If none of the exceptions apply to a particular project, and the subject has not been deceased for at least 100 years, a graphic artist may decide that permission is required. If possible, think about this issue sooner rather than later. Under both the New York and California statutes, the subject's written consent must be obtained before the use occurs. Also, it is necessary to obtain permission from all the proper parties.

In *Wendt v. Host International, Inc.*, a corporation licensed the rights to make life-size robotic replicas of the characters "Norm" and "Cliff" from the TV series *Cheers*. Even though the copyright owner of the show granted permission, George Wendt and John Ratzenberger, the actors who portrayed the characters, brought a successful action for violation of their rights of publicity under California law.

There has been some discussion in recent years about creating a single federal right of publicity statute that would eliminate the confusing inconsistencies in the various state laws, but no such change in the law is expected any time soon. Until it happens, the prudent graphic artist has only two choices: master the byzantine laws of all 50 states or get those model releases.

Moral Rights

Moral rights are derived from the French doctrine of *droit moral*, which recognizes certain inherent personal rights of creators in their works, even after the works have been sold or the copyright transferred. These rights stand above and distinct from copyright. The doctrine traditionally grants artists and writers four specific rights:

1. The right to protect the integrity of their work to prevent any modification, distortion, or mutilation that would be prejudicial to their honor or reputation.
2. The right of attribution (or paternity) to insist that their authorship be acknowledged properly and to prevent use of their names on works they did not create.
3. The right of disclosure to decide if, when, and how a work is presented to the public.
4. The right of recall to withdraw, destroy, or disavow a work if it is changed or no longer represents their views.

THE BERNE CONVENTION

Moral rights have long been an integral part of copyright protection laws in most European nations but were largely rejected and ignored in the United States. In 1886, the United States refused to join the Berne Convention, a worldwide multinational treaty for the protection of literary and artistic works that protects moral rights as a matter of course. Member nations participating in Berne are required to frame their copyright laws according to certain minimum standards, and to guarantee reciprocity to citizens of any other member.

After 100 years, economic realities and skyrocketing foreign piracy forced the United States to seek entry into the Berne Convention. By that time, the 1976 Copyright Act had brought the United States closer to other Berne standards. For example, duration of copyright was extended from a term of 28 years, renewable only once, to the life of the creator plus 50 years. Formalities, such as requiring publication with a copyright notice or registration to obtain U.S. copyright protection, were also eliminated.

Several states have enacted various forms of moral rights statutes, due in great part to the Guild's involvement. Certain moral rights elements have also been protected in state and federal courts, which saw them as questions of unfair competition, privacy, or defamation. The totality of the American legal system, therefore, persuaded Berne administrators that the United States qualified for membership.

In 1988, the United States became the eightieth country to sign the Berne Convention, thereby extending protection to American works in 24 nations with which the United States had no separate copyright agreements. This also succeeded in stemming the loss of billions of dollars in royalties to copyright owners. Although works are now protected the moment they are created, and the Berne Convention does not require copyright notice, it is still advisable to affix a copyright notice (© *2009 Jane Artist* or *Copyright 2009 Jane Artist*) because it bars the defense of innocent infringement in court and also because it affords international copyright protection in those countries that are members of another treaty, the Universal Copyright Convention (UCC), which still requires a copyright notice on a work. Although foreign works are currently exempt from the American registration requirements as a pre-condition for filing a lawsuit, American works still have to be registered with the U.S. Copyright Office before their creators can sue for infringement. Both foreign and U.S. authors must register early in order to be eligible for statutory damages and attorney's fees (see Benefits of Registration earlier in this chapter).

THE VISUAL ARTISTS RIGHTS ACT

Most of the cases that have brought moral rights problems to the public's attention revolve around mutilation of works of fine art. Some memorable cases include Pablo Picasso's *Trois Femmes*, which was cut into one-inch squares and sold as original Picassos by two entrepreneurs in 1986; the destruction and removal of an Isamu Noguchi sculpture from a New York office lobby; and the alteration by the Marriott Corporation of a historic William Smith mural in a landmark Maryland building.

Accreditation is another important moral rights issue. A case widely publicized in the graphic arts arena involved Alberto Vargas's series, *The Varga Girls*, which ran in *Esquire* magazine, under contracts that granted to *Esquire* all rights in his illustrations. After Vargas terminated his contract, the magazine continued to run the series under the name *The Esquire Girls* without giving Vargas credit. Vargas brought *Esquire* to court, alleging that *Esquire* had violated an implied agreement to give him credit for the works. The court rejected his argument, essentially finding that without an explicit contractual provision, artists have no moral rights in the United States to be credited for their work.

Moral rights legislation at both the state and federal levels has been proposed and supported vigorously by the Graphic Artists Guild since the late 1970s. Successes in California (1979), New York (1983), Maine and Massachusetts (1985), and other states, established the momentum to advance a federal version.

By presenting testimony about the problems that illustrators and designers face, the Graphic Artists Guild has been able to broaden state legislation. For instance, members of the Graphic Artists Guild have forcefully argued that the appearance of their artwork with unauthorized alterations or defacement can damage an otherwise vital career. The state bills that the Guild helped to pass recognize artists' ongoing relationships with the work they create.

The federal Visual Artists Rights Act (VARA), Section 106A of the Copyright Act, was finally enacted by Congress in 1990. Although the act is a positive first step toward comprehensive moral rights legislation, unfortunately, it has limited application and, ironically, may invalidate, through federal preemption (discussed below), many state statutes that may be far more protective.

The law covers only visual arts and only one-of-a-kind works that are defined as original paintings and drawings; and prints, photographs made solely for exhibition, and sculptures, existing in a single copy or in a limited edition of 200 or fewer copies, signed and numbered consecutively by the artist. Specifically excluded are any kind of commercial or applied arts (advertising, promotion, packaging); posters, maps, charts, and technical drawings; motion pictures and other audiovisual works; books, magazines, newspapers, and periodicals; electronically produced work; any work-made-for-hire; and any noncopyrightable work.

The moral rights protected are limited to those of attribution and integrity. To be actionable, a distortion, mutilation, or other modification of a work must be intentional. Mere natural deterioration is not actionable unless caused by gross negligence. In addition, the act places two burdens on the artist: to prove that a threatened action would be "prejudicial to his or her honor or reputation" and, if the goal is to prevent destruction of a work, to prove that it is "of recognized stature." Since no guidelines are provided for either standard, their meaning will have to be determined in the courts on a case-by-case basis.

The law stipulates that these rights exist exclusively with the artist during his or her lifetime and may not be transferred. They may be waived, but only by an expressly written and signed agreement. In the case of a joint work, each contributing artist may claim or waive the rights for all the others. The act also contains special provisions for works installed on buildings (murals or bas reliefs), which allow destruction of the art if it cannot be removed from the buildings.

A potential problem of the law is that it includes a preemption provision that can be read to supersede any existing state laws that protect equivalent rights. Among the questions that will probably have to be answered in the courts are whether the state statutes, many of which apply to other visual works or extend greater protections, are completely preempted or only partially so. So far, a lower court in New York has held that VARA does preempt state law regarding attribution rights. In 2016, a lower court in California held that VARA preempts state law regarding rights of integrity.

Resale Royalties

Another time-honored French doctrine, like moral rights, that transcends rights of copyright and ownership of the original work in most Berne signatory countries is *droit de suite*. It grants to creators a share in the value of their works by guaranteeing that the artist receives a certain percentage of the sale price every time a work is resold.

In the United States, such rights—known as resale royalties—existed only in California. In 2016, several artists, including Chuck Close, sued the major auction houses for failing to pay them resale royalties. California federal courts held that the Resale Royalties Act unconstitutionally regulated interstate commerce. In July 2018, the Ninth Circuit of the U.S. Appeals Court ruled that artists aren't entitled to royalties for artwork sold at auction because the federal Copyright Act pre-empts the California Resale Royalties Act.

Several pieces of legislation have been introduced since 2011 that would provide for a national resale royalty right. The most recent was the bi-partisan, bi-cameral American Royalties Too Act of 2018 (ART Act), introduced in both houses on September 25, 2018 (S.3488/H.6868) and referred to their respective Judiciary Committees. The Act would provide visual artists with a 5% royalty on their art when it is resold at auction. The royalty would only apply to sales at auction houses that sell over a million dollars of art per year. Private sales and exclusively online auctions would be exempted. All art sold for less than $5,000 would be exempted, and the 5% royalty would be capped at $35,000, no matter how high the sale price is.

Over 70 countries, including all the nations of the European Union and Australia, already have such a law. However, they do not compensate American artists for their considerable sales abroad because the United States does not have reciprocal resale royalty rights. If the ART Act were passed, it would finally allow American artists to get their fair share of sales at home, as well as overseas.

Trademarks

A *trademark* may be a word, symbol, design, or slogan, or a combination of words and designs, that identifies and distinguishes the goods of one party from those of another. Marks that identify the source of services rather than goods are typically referred to as *service marks*. A trademark for goods appears on the product or its packaging, while a service mark is usually used to identify the owner's services in advertising and business materials. The protection given to trademarks and service marks is identical, and "trademark" or "mark" is often used to refer to both.

While a copyright protects an artistic or literary work and a patent protects an invention, a trademark protects a business name or brand. For example, Adobe is used as the trademark for certain software products, Mickey Mouse is a trademarked character for Disney, and Amtrak is a service mark for railroad service. Product names and logos are the most traditional forms of trademarks. Sounds, such as jingles, can also be used as trademarks, as can product shapes or configurations such as Coca Cola's distinctive bottle shape. Although trademarks are often created by freelance designers, the trademark rights will be owned by the client, because the client will be using the design as its own brand. Graphic artists may own their own trademark rights in logos or designs that they use for their own businesses.

Trademark protection can last indefinitely if the mark continues to be used for source identification. A valid trademark gives the owner the right to prevent others from using a mark that might be confusingly similar to the owner's mark. If anyone else uses the identical or similar mark for similar goods or services, then the first user can prevent the latecomer from using the mark. The test for infringement is whether there would be a likelihood of confusion as to the source of the goods and services.

For maximum trademark protection, a party using a trademark in interstate commerce should register it with the U.S. Patent and Trademark Office (USPTO). The Office prefers electronic filing. You can access forms through the Trademark Electronic Application System (TEAS), at www.uspto.gov/teas/index.html.

For information about applying for a trademark, consult the USPTO website at www.uspto.gov.

Unlike copyrights, trademarks can be infringed without actual copying. It is recommended that a search be conducted to determine whether a confusingly similar mark is already in use by another party, since the application fee will not be refunded if the application is rejected. Trademark searches, preparation, and application filing or trademark registration can be done online; however, the best practice is to have a professional screening search performed. Designers should include provisions in their client contracts stating that the client is responsible for trademark searching, and that the designer is not warranting non-infringement of trademarks except in cases of actual copying.

The owner of a federal trademark or service mark registration may give notice of registration by using the ® symbol, which may be used only after the mark is registered (the Graphic Artists Guild logo, the Guild's service mark, appears in print with an ®). Trademark owners who do not have federal registration may only use the symbol TM for trademarks. The symbol SM is used for unregistered service marks.

While not mandatory, federal registration protects the trademark throughout the United States, even in geographical areas in which the mark is not used. Federal registration is legal evidence of trademark ownership and the exclusive right to use the mark in inter-state commerce. As in copyright, someone with a federal registration can be eligible for special remedies, including attorney's fees and enhanced damages, when willful infringement is proven. Unlike copyright, however, there is no requirement to register a trademark before suing for infringement. Also, unlike copyright, trademark registration only applies to a particular product or service, not to the entire universe of possible uses. Thus, different parties may each have valid registrations for the same or similar marks, such as "Cadillac" for automobiles and cat food, provided their areas of business are sufficiently unrelated that consumers would not be confused by the similarity.

Legal Cases Involving Artists

In the past three decades, there have been several legal cases involving the work of artists and photographers that have raised concerns for graphic artists and their clients about potential trademark infringement liability.

LANDMARK BUILDINGS

A relatively new application of trademark law has been attempted by the owners of landmark buildings, such as the Chrysler Building, Rockefeller Center, or the Flatiron Building in New York City, who are trying to monetize use of illustrations or photographs of their buildings on everything from advertising to note cards and textbooks. The problem is now affecting illustrators and graphic artists who work either on assignment for a client or are selling stock. Clients are increasingly reluctant to use these images in the face of demand letters by large corporate building owners. In many cases this simply results in another work being chosen for the job. No one wants to risk legal action or having to pull an advertisement after it has been created. Few creators can afford to be caught in a lawsuit over usage rights. For instance, the New York Stock Exchange, alleging trademark violation, sued a casino in Las Vegas for building a model of its facade on their gambling floor. The Stock Exchange ultimately lost the suit.

It is important to note that a 1999 ruling by the Federal District Court for the Northern District of Ohio held in favor of photographer Chuck Gentile against the Rock & Roll Hall of Fame. The court denied the museum's request to stop the sale of a poster with a night photograph taken by Gentile of the Rock & Roll Hall of Fame. The ruling stated that (1) the Rock & Roll Hall of Fame's building design was not used as a trademark, so the poster could not infringe trademark rights; (2) Gentile did not use the poster as a trademark, so he was not infringing any alleged trademark rights; and (3) the use of the identifying phrase "Rock & Roll Hall of Fame" under the photograph was fair use and did not infringe any trademark rights. This ruling was affirmed by the Sixth Circuit Court of Appeals.

While this decision cannot be construed to mean that no photograph or illustration of a building could ever violate a trademark, it seems very difficult after this decision for the owner of a building to convince a court that an image of a building infringed any trademark rights. This decision supports the position that, in most situations, a photograph or illustration of a building does not violate the building owner's trademark and additional permission is not legally required. Since trademark infringement turns on issues of confusion as to the origin of goods and services, it is still advisable to analyze each use on a case-by-case basis.

TRADEMARKS IN PAINTINGS

One 1995 case that threatened the artist's right to reproduce a trademark in a painting involved the use of celebrity animals and images associated with professional sports. Visual artist Jenness Cortez was sued by the New York Racing Association (NYRA) in July 1995 for her use of the Saratoga Race Track, including the use of the word "Saratoga," in her original paintings, etchings, and lithographs. NYRA claimed the right to a portion of the income derived from the sale of her work. In August 1996, a U.S. district court dismissed the case, saying Cortez's work was covered by the First Amendment. In a strongly worded decision affirming that artists can include trademarked images or symbols in their paintings, the judge noted, however, that the artist does not have the right to gratuitously include trademarks that are not already part of a particular scene. Although Cortez was subsequently sued by the owner and agents of the horse Cigar for trademark infringement and unauthorized use of the horse's image, that case was also settled in Cortez's favor in 1997.

In 2009, the University of Alabama sued artist Daniel A. Moore over his paintings depicting famous football scenes involving the University's teams. The paintings featured realistic portrayals of the University's team uniforms, including helmets, jerseys, and crimson and white colors. Moore has reproduced his paintings as prints and calendars, as well as on mugs and other articles. Moore contended that he did not need permission because the uniforms were being used to realistically portray historical events. Like the New York court, the Alabama courts held that it was not a trademark infringement to depict the University's team uniforms in paintings, prints, calendars, and other items such as mugs.

Trade Dress

Graphic artists need a way to protect against copycats who capitalize on successful projects by passing off work that is stylistically similar at a lower fee. Although an artist's style cannot be copyrighted, the concept of *trade dress*— that part of trademark law that protects an established look—has been used by artists to support their claims of imitation.

It is important for artists to understand the difference between what is protected under copyright law and what is protected under trademark law. Copyright protects the tangible expression of an idea fixed in some tangible, reproducible format (written word, music, or image). Trade dress is a subset of trademark law. Trade dress protects a product's overall appearance or packaging, but only to the extent that such trade dress functions as a brand. A single color can be protected under trade dress. For example, the color magenta is claimed by T-Mobile as a feature of its trademark. Using extremely broad definitions of trade dress, businesses have successfully won trade dress cases involving restaurant atmosphere, style of comedy, smell, and even sound.

Generally, the law governing trade dress is the same as for trademarks. A 1988 amendment to Section 43(a) of the Lanham Act (federal trademark law) permits civil actions against any person whose trade dress is likely to cause confusion "as to the origin, sponsorship, or approval of his or her goods, services, or commercial activities by another person."

Legal Cases Supporting Trade Dress

The Lanham Act was amended in 1988 to make it consistent with court decisions in trade dress cases. One that is of particular interest to designers is the 1986 Missouri case, *Hartford House, Ltd. v. Hallmark Cards, Inc.* Hartford House Ltd., one of the manufacturers of Blue Mountain Cards, claimed that Hallmark Cards' Personal Touch product line was confusingly similar to Blue Mountain's Airebrush Feelings and WaterColor Feelings lines of greeting cards. The district court determined that the trade dress—overall appearance or arrangement of features—of the two Blue Mountain lines of cards had acquired a "secondary meaning" and that there was a likelihood of confusion among card purchasers as to the source of the cards. "Secondary meaning" refers to the public's perception of the cards' appearance as a Blue Mountain brand, not just an aesthetically pleasing design. The U.S. Court of Appeals for the Tenth Circuit held that certain greeting cards in the Blue Mountain lines were protected under trade dress since they contained inherently distinctive and uniform features that combined in an overall look that consumers could recognize and attribute to Blue Mountain. Some of these distinguishing features included the following:

1. A two-fold card containing poetry on the first page and the third page
2. A deckle edge on the right side of the first page
3. A high-quality, uncoated and textured art paper for the cards
4. Lengthy poetry, written in free verse, typically with a personal message
5. Appearance of hand-lettered calligraphy on the first and third page with the first letter of the words often enlarged
6. The look of the cards primarily characterized by backgrounds of soft colors done with air brush blends or light watercolor strokes, usually depicting simple contrasting foreground scenes superimposed in the background

Hallmark was prohibited from marketing or advertising certain cards in its Personal Touch line that duplicated these features.

It is important to note that the ruling in the Blue Mountain case does not mean that artistic style on its own can be protected under trademark law. The court specified: "Blue Mountain has not been granted exclusive rights in an artistic style or in some concept, idea, or theme of expression. Rather, it is Blue Mountain's specific artistic expression, in combination with other features to produce an overall Blue Mountain look, that is being protected."

Given that unfair competition by imitators is one of the critical issues affecting the graphic arts industry today, it is vital for artists to understand trade dress law so that they can include it in their arsenal. However, in order to claim trademark or trade dress rights, an artist must prove that the look of their work performs the job of a "designation of origin" in the way that the Blue Mountain cards were found to have done. If it does not do this, then trade dress protection will not apply.

Thus, the challenge for graphic artists is to prove that their services are eligible for "branding," as in any other business that provides services or manufactures products, and to convince the courts that these "services" are distinctive and protectable as trade dress. The most encouraging development in this area was a 1992 New York decision, *Romm Art Creations v. Sincha International*, which found that an artist's style was "inherently distinctive" and thus protectable against "slavish imitations" by a competitor. The decision has been criticized, however, and artists continue to face judicial skepticism when asserting trade dress rights in style per se.

A Supreme Court case from 2003, *Dastar v. Twentieth Century Fox Film Corp.*, may limit the ability of graphic artists to claim trade dress infringement. In that case, the defendant marketed a video that copied a public domain television series without acknowledging the original authors of the series. The Court held that trademark protects only those who market tangible goods or services, and thus the failure to credit those who created the series content was not a false designation of origin under trademark law. Similarly, when graphic art is copied, claims of trade dress infringement will likely be available only to the graphic artist's client, the business that is using the artist's work for its goods or services (such as Hallmark or Blue Mountain in the above examples), unless the artist is using the artwork to sell her own products or services directly to the public.

One of the current arenas for trade dress jurisprudence is web design. Trade dress may be available to designers to protect their rights in their own websites. In 2007, in *Blue Nile, Inc. v. Ice.com, Inc.*, the plaintiff sued the defendant for copying the overall "look and feel" of the plaintiff's retail jewelry website, including the design of the plaintiff's search pages. Although the court requested more information before it could rule definitively, the court held that it was possible for the website's look and feel to merit trade dress protection if the plaintiff's copyright did not already cover the issue. This case addressed two important questions:

1. Whether "look and feel" infringements of a website qualify as trade dress infringements, and
2. Whether these infringements are preempted by existing copyright law.

More recently, courts in the United States have passed a number of judgments that affirm that a website's trade dress can be protected. Trade dress can protect copyright elements of a website, but only if they function independently as a brand. Thus, the written text, software code, and imagery may not be protected. Courts have recognized two components as falling under trade dress protection when considering the "look and feel" of a website—the visual design and the interface design. Together, these two incorporate static elements, interactive elements, and the overall style or impression. As in print media, the "look" of a website's design includes the colors, shapes, layouts, and typefaces. The "feel" corresponds to certain dynamic navigation elements, including buttons, boxes, menus, and hyperlinks.

For Further Reading…

An expert resource geared to graphic artists on U.S Copyright and related rights is *Legalities,* a column written by intellectual property Attorney Linda Joy Kattwinkel for AIGA/San Francisco. Attorney Kattwinkel is also a visual artist and a former graphic artist. You will find more specific information about many of the issues covered above, written in an easy-to-understand style. All of the *Legalities* issues can be accessed at www.owe.com/resources/legalities/.

International & Canadian Copyright

Any discussion of this subject begins with the proviso that there is no such thing as international copyright law. Each country has its own copyright laws; there is no single international copyright law. Artists are protected under each country's laws through the copyright relations their home country shares with other countries.

In practical terms, this means that a U.S. artist is protected by copyright in most other countries, although that protection may be to a different degree and scope than in the United States. At the time of writing, there are 177 (out of the total 195) countries that are members of the Berne Convention, the leading international copyright treaty. Berne member-countries protect the works by citizens of other member countries to the same extent as they protect works of their own citizens (except that, if copyright has expired under the copyright owner's home country, the member country does not have to apply a longer term of copyright under its own laws). Since countries protect others' works under their own copyright laws, an American may have a different degree of protection in the United States than when her works are used in France. For example, moral rights may be stronger or weaker and protect a narrower or wider variety of authors of works depending on each country's copyright act. In some countries, such as France, there is very strong perpetual moral rights protection for creators of all copyright-protected works. In other countries, such as Canada, moral rights protection is for creators of all works, but the rights are waivable and endure only for the length of the copyright protection (life plus 50 years). For example, if you live in the United States and your client is in Europe, you will have those strong moral rights when your work is used in Europe. As another example, Canadian clients may ask you to waive your moral rights in the work that you prepare for them.

Copyright laws around the world protect artists and provide them with negotiating power. All copyright laws are based on the same basic principles. Copyright laws establish a certain copyright culture within a country and help set industry standards in contractual relationships. For instance, because of the work-for-hire provision in the U.S. Copyright Act, it is common practice in certain industries, such as the film industry, to require writers and other creators to assign all their rights. In Canada, where there is no work-made-for-hire provision (though there is an "employment" provision as discussed later in this chapter), a screenwriter generally retains the copyright to his/her script and licenses the rights to a licensee/producer to make a film out of it.

Canadian and European artists often serve U.S. clients, and vice versa. Given the phenomenal expansion of the global economy, which can only continue to grow, it is in the Guild's interest to improve standards for all graphic artists around the world. Establishing a relationship and signing agreements with graphic arts unions or organizations in other countries will help ensure that all artists compete on talent and portfolio, not on rights and price.

Canadian versus United States Rights

The following section highlights and contrasts the important features of Canadian copyright law as it applies to the visual communications industries.[1]

REGISTERING COPYRIGHT

Copyright is automatic in Canada and always has been. There is a voluntary registration system but, unlike in the United States, no deposit system where artists send in a copy of their works. (If you do mail in a copy of your work with your copyright application in Canada, the copy will be returned to you.) Canadians will find much more space in U.S. contracts (than in Canadian contracts) devoted to copyright registration and documentation issues (and these are often standard clauses). Due to the lack of mandatory deposit requirements in Canada, many Canadians register and deposit a copy of their works with the U.S. Copyright Office as a way to establish a record of ownership and date of first creation of their work. The voluntary registration system in Canada is important for anyone exploiting a work in Canada, as there are certain advantages for those who register and then later sue to enforce their rights.

USING THE COPYRIGHT SYMBOL

There are no copyright symbol and notice requirements under Canadian or U.S. copyright law. Canadian creators and owners generally include a copyright notice to remind the public that copyright does exist in their works. Your notice can be as simple as including the copyright symbol ©, year of publication and name of the copyright owner. See the article, "The International Copyright Symbol," at https://www.copyrightlaws.com/copyright-symbol-notice-year/.

DURATION OF COPYRIGHT

There is no renewal of copyright in Canada, nor are there any works that fall into the public domain and are then at a later date protected by copyright. A literary or artistic work in Canada is generally protected for 50 years after the death of the author (the 50 years are determined from the end of the calendar year, rather than by the anniversary of the death). For example, all of a photographer's photographs would have the same duration of copyright: the copyright would last for 50 years following the end of the calendar year in which the photographer died. A work that is being exploited in both Canada and the United States may be licensed for a part of the duration of copyright or for its full term.

On September 30, 2018, Canada, the United States, and Mexico completed negotiations on a new trade agreement, the United States-Mexico-Canada Agreement (USMCA) to replace the North American Free Trade Agreement (NAFTA). The USMCA is not yet in effect, and NAFTA will continue in effect until the USMCA is ratified in each of the three countries. Under the USMCA, the minimum duration of copyright protection in the United States, Canada, and Mexico will be life-plus-seventy years. So, although the current duration of copyright protection in Canada is life-plus-fifty years, you should be aware that it will be changing to life-plus-seventy in the near future on a yet unknown date.

REVERSIONARY INTEREST PROVISO

In Canada, where the author of a work is the first owner of the copyright (if it is not a product of employment or a government work), any copyright acquired by contract becomes void 25 years after the author's death. This does not mean that the term of copyright is affected. It means that, if specific conditions apply, any subsequent owner of copyright will lose his or her rights 25 years after the author's death. At this time, the copyright becomes part of the author's estate, and only the estate has the right to deal with the copyright. Conditions affecting this reversion include when the author disposes of the copyright by will for the period following the 25-year limit. Thus, the reversion may be avoided by the author bequeathing copyright for the period between 25 and 50 years after his or her death.

The reversion does not apply when a work is part of a collective work or when a work or part thereof has been licensed to be published in a collective work such as a magazine or an encyclopedia.

COMMISSIONED WORKS

Since the 2012 amendments to the Canadian Copyright Act, a photographer, painter, or engraver owns the copyright in commissioned photographs, portraits, and engravings. However, a person who commissioned a photograph or portrait for personal purposes and for valuable consideration may use the photograph or portrait for pri-

---

1. The information on Canadian copyright law is as the law exists on 28 October 2019. Updates on Canadian and international copyright law can be found at www.copyrightlaws.com and more specifically at the Centre for Canadian Copyright Law at https://www.copyrightlaws.com/centre-for-canadian-copyright-law/.

vate or non-commercial purposes or permit the use of it for those purposes. This is true unless the photographer or painter have agreed otherwise.[2]

EMPLOYMENT WORK

In Canada, three criteria must be met in order for works made during employment to belong initially to the employer:

* The employee must be employed under a "contract of service."
* The work must be created in the course of performing the contract.
* There must not be any provision in a contract that states that the employee owns the copyright (such a contract need not be in writing).

One important distinction between the U.S. work-made-for-hire and the Canadian employment works provision is that in Canada, notwithstanding that the employee does not own the copyright, the employee continues to retain the moral rights. An employee can never license these moral rights, though he or she can waive them. Another distinction is that under U.S. work-made-for-hire, the employer is the author of the work, whereas in Canada, the creator of the work remains its author while the employer is the owner of the work. This also affects how duration of copyright is determined in the two countries. In Canada, duration of copyright in an employment situation remains determined by the life of the author of the work.

MORAL RIGHTS

Under Canadian law, there are three types of moral rights:

* The right of paternity.
* The right of integrity.
* The right of association.

These rights are discussed at length previously in this

chapter in the section on Moral Rights (especially The Berne Convention).

Even when an artist transfers copyright and even when the work is owned by an employer, the artist has moral rights unless they are waived. Moral rights in Canada last for 50 years from the end of the calendar year in which the creator died—this is the same duration of copyright protection in Canada. Upon death, moral rights can be passed to an artist's heirs, but not otherwise transferred. Artists can agree not to exercise one or more of their moral rights, that is, to waive some or all of their moral rights, and this is something artists working with a Canadian company should be aware of.[3]

The United States has moral rights for authors of limited works of visual art under the Visual Artists Rights Act, which is part of the U.S. Copyright Act (see section earlier in this chapter). The duration depends on when the work was created and/or transferred but generally lasts for 70 years after the death of the author. The moral rights are not transferable by license or assignment; however, they can be waived in writing. A waiver means that the author of the work will not exercise their moral rights.

FAIR USE/DEALING & EXCEPTIONS

Canada does not have a fair use provision but has a provision, often seen in Commonwealth countries, known as the *fair dealing provision*. Similar to fair use, fair dealing is intentionally drafted in an ambiguous manner to apply to a variety of situations that would be too long to list in the copyright act. For use of a work to be fair dealing, it must be for one of the following purposes: criticism, review, research, private study, education, parody, or satire. If the use falls under one of these purposes, then according to the Supreme Court of Canada, you must then examine the fairness of the use, including the purpose of the dealing, character of the dealing, nature of the work, amount of the dealing, effect of the dealing on the work, and available alternatives. The court has also said that there may be additional factors that help a court determine whether the dealing is fair. Fair dealing must be interpreted on a case-by-case basis to apply to the particular circumstances at hand and requires a judgment call.

The Canadian Copyright Act has exceptions in various situations, and for specific user groups such as schools, libraries, archives, and museums. Certain incidental uses

---

2. Prior to the amendments, a special rule applied to commissioned engravings, photographs, or portraits. For these works, the person ordering the work was deemed to be the first owner of the copyright if the following conditions were met:
   * The person ordering the work offered valuable consideration, such as money or services.
   * The work was created because of the order and was not created prior to the order being made.
   This held true provided there was no agreement between the commissioner and the creator stating that copyright subsists with the creator of the work.

---

3. See articles, "Moral Rights in Canadian Copyright Law," at https://www.copyrightlaws.com/moral-rights-in-canadian-copyright-law/, and "Moral Rights in U.S. Copyright Law" at https://www.copyrightlaws.com/moral-rights-in-u-s-copyright-law/

of copyright materials that are not deliberate may be considered an exception (and not an infringement) under Canadian copyright law. With the differences between the two laws, in certain circumstances a U.S. artist may find that certain free uses of work in the United States may be uses for which permission must be requested and paid for in Canada. The converse is also true. Canadian artists may find that there may be free uses of their work in the United States for which they would be paid in Canada. Although some situations can be reversed by mutual consent in contracts between the relevant parties, the exceptions will still apply if a third party is using the work outside the scope of the agreement, in which case the third party's behavior will be subject to the copyright act in the country in which the work is being used.

GOVERNMENT WORKS

In the United States, there is no copyright protection for works created by the federal government. However, the federal government can own copyright in works created for it by independent contractors (as opposed to government employees), e.g., postage stamp artwork. The U.S. federal government also can purchase a copyright in a work. In Canada, the government owns the copyright to works produced by its employees, and sometimes by independent contractors/consultants (this latter situation is governed by contracts), and use of government works may require permission from the government. Permission to reproduce Canadian government works "in part or in whole, and by any means, for personal or public noncommercial purposes, or for cost-recovery purposes, is not required, unless otherwise specified in the material you wish to reproduce" (see www.canada.ca/en/canadian-heritage/services/crown-copyright-request.html).

Thus, a Canadian artist whose work incorporates government works is more likely than his/her U.S. counterpart to have cleared copyright in that work before including it in his or her work. In this situation, although permission may not be required from the U.S. government for use of the work in the United States, permission may be required when the same work is used in Canada. Therefore, an American artist should be careful in making any warranties and representations regarding copyright clearance of works incorporating any government materials when those works are used in Canada.

GOVERNING LAW

Parties to an agreement are generally free to choose the state or province and country whose law will govern the agreement. That is usually settled by negotiation. The contract should state under which jurisdiction the contract is to be interpreted, especially when work is to be created, performed, or delivered in more than one jurisdiction. It is usually in the artist's best interests to have his/her own state/province's law govern the contract for ease of access to a lawyer in that jurisdiction, for knowledge of the law and local culture, as well as for convenience (especially when considering costs), should arbitration or court action be necessary.

Remember that an agreement on governing law does not in itself determine the jurisdiction where a suit may be physically filed and heard, only the law under which that suit will be decided. It is possible to agree (and negotiate) that a contract will be judged by U.S. law but adjudicated in Canada, or vice versa. It is also possible to agree upon the governing law without specifying a jurisdiction for adjudication, which leaves the aggrieved party with the freedom to file suit in the most convenient location.

More and more agreements are now subject to mediation and binding arbitration in a place halfway between the cities of the contracting parties. This can help limit costs and travel time. Governing law can have complicated consequences, so, if possible, you would want feedback from a lawyer who specializes in this area before including it in your agreements.

For Further Education...

Canadian Copyright Law, 4th Edition by Lesley Ellen Harris is an in-depth resource for more detailed information about copyright law in Canada.

The website, Copyrightlaws.com, offers understandable tutorials and comprehensive certificate courses in U.S. and Canadian copyright law and licensing. Of special interest is the course, *Certificate in Licensing Digital Content*. The site also features blog posts on various copyright-related topics.

{ 12 }

Standard Contracts & Business Tools

This chapter describes exactly why graphic artists need contracts to define and protect business relationships. Seven different types of contracts and their applications are explained, as well as what contracts should include. Also provided is advice on what to do when things go wrong. Both a Glossary of contract terms and an Appendix of sample contracts for various graphic art assignments can be found at the back of the book.

CONTRACTS INCREASINGLY DEFINE *the business side of graphic arts as the professional landscape of the graphic artist has changed dramatically over the last 20 years. Digital media, new technology, growing competition in the workplace, and the consolidation of publishing firms have all placed new demands on artists and on the companies that hire them. While clients routinely ask for more considerations, often without additional compensation, artists struggle to retain control and to bolster the value of their work.*

At first glance, contracts may instill you with dread, but they can make doing business much easier and prevent potential misunderstandings. When the basic concepts are understood, contracts can protect both the artist and the client. And contracts can provide a common working language by which each job can proceed. With a little time and patience, you can learn not only how to read your clients' contracts but also how to structure agreements that best represent your own interests.

The Importance of Contracts

As a graphic artist trying to make a living from your talents, you will find early on that there are two sides to your career—the creative side and the business side. Both are equally important to your success, whether you are a self-employed independent contractor or the owner of a studio that employs other creatives. The art that you create—whether illustration, design, or a combination of both—is your intellectual property or your assets. Like all valuable assets, it needs protecting.

You will be hired to work on projects that also require an investment of assets on the part of the client—namely the client's money in exchange for your services. The client will also want to protect its assets. In any business relationship, both parties are also risking something less tangible—their reputations. Contracts serve to protect the assets and reputations of both parties.

There are always two perspectives on an assignment. Clients may assume they own more rights than the artist's fee dictates. The graphic artist may expect to be paid immediately upon delivery, while the client routinely pays 30 days or more after publication. To avoid confusion and misunderstanding, a well-written contract defines the working relationship of the client and the artist, the use of the finished work, and how changes in the scope of the project are to be handled.

Most contracts for graphic artwork provide

* A definition of the project or assignment
* Limitations on the use of the work
* Terms for such professional issues as payment and artist's credit
* Protection in the event of a dispute

The most important fact to remember when reading a contract is that the person or business who drafts the contract is concerned with rights and controls that are advantageous to them. Their objective is to get the other party to agree to the protections laid out in the document. As independent contractors, artists should make every effort to present their own contracts. This may not always be possible, so having a clear understanding of contract language is important.

Graphic artists have the same advantages as clients when they read contracts. Although the legal language may seem daunting at first, every clause contains basic principles and concerns regarding the specific assignment and affecting general studio policy. With a little common sense and a knowledge of common contract terms (see the Glossary for definitions of terms introduced in this chapter), artists can learn to understand and negotiate many legal documents.

How Contracts Protect

A contract is an agreement, whether oral or written, that defines the obligations and responsibilities of each party. One party makes an offer, usually containing terms that benefit that party. The second party considers the offer and negotiates terms to reflect their needs. Ideally, each party should benefit equally from the contract. Once both parties agree to the terms of the contract and sign it, the agreement is legally binding.

In written contracts, obligations are defined in paragraphs (clauses), and all terms within a contract are potentially subject to negotiation before the agreement is finalized. Clauses in graphic art contracts typically set business standards for the following:

* Payment and kill fees;
* The number of roughs, comps, pages, or products;
* Alterations;
* Licensing and copyright transfers;
* Dispute resolution; and
* Limitations on unauthorized uses of the finished work.

Each party is notified that certain behavior is expected and that a breach of that behavior can result in legal proceedings. At times contract language may seem harsh, but the intent is to protect the signers from potential misunderstandings as the job proceeds.

It is important to understand and agree to terms *before* starting a job. Should an artist start a job after seeing a client's contract but without signing it, it could be argued that the artist has accepted the terms and that the contract is binding. By making sure all terms are agreed upon before starting, the graphic artist enjoys the protections of a binding contract.

Agreements that are straightforward, clearly written, and customized to the project provide a positive work environment for both client and artist. The content should reflect the best interests of all parties, or at least an agreeable compromise. One-sided documents that require a signature without possibility of negotiation are not advantageous to either party.

Importance of Contracts for Freelancers

The importance of contracts for freelancers was recognized by New York City with the passage of the ground-breaking Freelance Isn't Free Act. Introduced by New York City Councilman Brad Lander, championed by the Freelancers Union, and supported by the Graphic Artists Guild and other Freelancers Union partners, the act was signed into law by Mayor Bill de Blasio on November 16, 2016. This municipal law was the first of its kind in the nation. It redresses the growing trend of late- and non-payment experienced by freelancers, as documented in a nationwide survey conducted by the Freelancers Union in 2015, of over 5,000 freelancers. According to the respondents, 71% had encountered difficulty collecting payment in their careers, while 50% had experienced problems in the previous year. Of those who had difficulty collecting payment, 34% were never paid. According to the survey, freelancers lose an average of $6,000 annually in non-payment.

The Freelance Isn't Free law, which went into effect May 2017, requires that clients supply freelancers with a written contract for projects with a value of $800 or more over a three-month period and that they pay freelancers within 30 days of the submission of an invoice. The law prohibits clients from pressuring freelancers to accept payment lower than the agreed-upon fee in return for timely payment. Freelancers can file a complaint with the New York City Department of Consumer Affairs or bring a court action against delinquent clients. If the court rules in the freelancer's favor, the client may have to pay legal fees as well as fines up to double the amount owed. Repeat violators may be fined up to $25,000 by the City. The Freelancers Union plans to take the initiative nationally, encouraging freelancers to propose similar legislation in their municipalities.

Seven Basic Types of Contracts

Contracts can be as simple as an oral agreement or as complex as a multi-page document. Regardless of the scope of the project, a written contract is always advisable. Seldom will one standard contract be appropriate for every job, so flexibility and customization are key to drawing up contracts. Here are some of the more common types of contracts, ranging from the simplest to the more complex.

1. Oral Agreement

While written agreements are always preferred, circumstances do not always allow for them. Thus, many jobs are assigned over the phone, where usually just the bare essentials are discussed: the work needed, the timeline for the work, where the work will be used, how it will be reproduced, and the compensation. The graphic artist orally accepts the client's terms over the phone or in person with a simple handshake. An *oral agreement* is legally binding. If a dispute arises over the terms of the agreement, however, proving what was actually intended can be difficult. Often one party's memory contradicts another's, and there is no set rule to determine what evidence will be allowed for review by the courts. If there are no witnesses or documents to prove the specific terms of the agreement, either side could prevail.

If you have built a long-standing relationship with a client, an oral agreement may be adequate. Before accepting an oral agreement, ask yourself: "Am I dealing with the owner of the business or a representative of the owner? Who will be accountable if there is a dispute in the agreement? Am I willing to take a risk with this person?"

2. Letter of Agreement or Engagement

If an assignment is initiated by an oral agreement as described above, the artist will have more legal protection if he or she finalizes the deal with a one-page document defining the project. Called a *letter of agreement*, this document can be very simple and should include a project description, the deliverables, when they are due, usage and ownership rights, kill fees, and so on. It is advisable to have a standard letter of agreement on file in your computer, which you can tailor to the project and e-mail to the client if time is limited.

3. Purchase Order

Some companies use *purchase orders (POs)* to assign work to contributors or to track jobs from assignment to payment. POs often resemble invoice forms, with a tracking number and a statement of the assignment and terms, which often appears in small print on the back or the bottom of the order. Many POs now function as contracts, including assignment of rights and more general terms, and require the graphic artist's signature before the job starts or before the artist's invoice can be processed for payment.

Purchase orders, however, can present a problem for the graphic artist. Because they are often general boilerplate documents, automatically sent out by buyers with each assignment, they do not clearly state the expectations and obligations of both parties for a specific assignment. Should a dispute about terms arise, graphic artists run the risk of not being as well protected as they would be with a custom contract. If there are unacceptable terms on a PO, you should cross them out using the addendum procedure outlined later in this chapter under "Working with Client's Contracts."

4. Working Contract

A *working contract* is what everyone recognizes as a contract, complete with legal language and clauses. Regardless of its length, a working contract can be written in clear, concise language or convoluted, confusing terminology. Either way, artists are often intimidated by the appearance of a contract and for this reason do not properly review it before signing. It cannot be stressed enough how important it is to understand the meaning of each clause in a contract before signing it. If read with patience, even the most confusing contract can be understood.

Traditionally, detailed working contracts are usually used for more complex jobs that require periodic payments or royalties, such as books or other major commissions. As the digital marketplace grows and the nature of corporate business changes, graphic artists must expect to deal with clients' growing demands for greater rights and control over projects. Increasingly, longer, more complicated contracts are used for such seemingly simple jobs as editorial assignments that in the past were covered by simple letters of agreement.

One strategy for coping with such client demands is for you to create your own working contracts that reflect your studio policies and basic business standards. The standard contract can then be customized to suit particular projects. You need to be prepared to deal with client contracts—always considering a contract to be a first offer to be negotiated. A client's contract, when properly negotiated, protects both parties equally.

5. Post-Project "Contracts"

Terms in small type at the bottom or on the back of a graphic artist's invoice, on the back of a client's check, or even on a purchase order sent from the client after receiving the artist's invoice are all examples of *post-project contracts*. The legality of such after-the-fact documents is questionable and subject to varying interpretation in the courts. Usually they do not require two signatures, which erodes their authority as agreements between two parties.

Using post-project contracts is not a smart business

strategy for either you or the client. It is always best to promote open communication by using standard contracts and letters of agreement that can be easily customized, offered for discussion, and signed before the job begins. That way the job proceeds with all terms and expectations understood and agreed to by both parties. The time and expense invested in preparing them is minimal compared with the legal costs that may result if a dispute arises.

INVOICES

Invoice contracts are sometimes used by graphic artists and artists' representatives who do not want to alarm or intimidate clients with lengthy contracts. As with POs, the terms are usually preprinted and are not specific to the assignment at hand. It is important to point out that invoice contracts provide little legal protection, since no signatures are involved. To be legally binding, such forms must conform to an oral or written agreement made before the work was started.

CHECKS

Check contracts are the trickiest. Sometimes an artist receives a check for services rendered, but the amount represents less than the full, agreed-upon fee. Endorsing and cashing a check that states "payment in full" could possibly be considered acceptance by the artist of the lower payment for all the services rendered. In the 1995 federal case of *Playboy Enterprises, Inc. v. Dumas*, the court decided that payment in this form is not legal unless the check restates a "prior agreement, either explicit or implied, made before the creation of the work." (For a more detailed discussion of this case, see Chapter 11, Legal Rights & Issues.)

It is very important to note that in New York State this type of activity is legal and is considered payment in full. This could possibly hurt the artist. Before cashing any check that represents less than the agreed-upon amount, it is always advisable for the artist to verify that the check was not sent in lieu of full payment. Also, check your respective state's laws to see if signing a check has similar ramifications.

For a discussion of other problems associated with terms added to a client's check, see the Checks with Conditions section in Chapter 1, Essential Business Practices.

6. Boilerplate Contract

A *boilerplate contract* contains generic or formulaic language (standard terminology). There are two definitions of a boilerplate contract. One is a document used as a general template for a wide range of projects, with clauses and elements that are altered to fit a particular project before the contract is offered. As a matter of studio policy, graphic artists should design their own boilerplate letters of agreement and working contracts for ongoing use. Then the graphic artist has a basic contract that can be customized as needed for each assignment.

Although never clearly labeled as such, a boilerplate contract can also be used as a multiple-use contract, designed to cover a wide variety of projects with no customization. Multiple-use contracts, provided by both large and small companies, can be recognized by their obvious general clauses, especially in the assignment of rights and licensing. They must be carefully reviewed and negotiated because they typically request many more concessions than are realistic for the project at hand.

To deal effectively with noncustomized boilerplates, you need to establish your own studio policy (see the Using Contracts section later in this chapter) that defines general terms and expectations for various assignments. This sets a business standard that you can work from when negotiating all contracts, but especially standard contracts with general clauses.

7. Retainer Agreement

Although retainer agreements are most often used by attorneys and accountants, they are also used with increasing frequency by graphic designers and sometimes by illustrators.

When signing a retainer agreement, the graphic artist agrees to work for the client for a specific amount of time over a given period or on a particular project for a fee paid according to an agreed-upon schedule. Often the schedule includes an initial payment, which reduces the graphic artist's risk; otherwise the designer is virtually extending credit to a possibly unknown client. The payment also guarantees the designer's availability for the duration of the project.

Retainers may take several forms:

1. **Annual retainer:** Payment schedules vary, but the client usually agrees to pay a substantial fee upon signing—30% is recommended—and the graphic artist guarantees to be available to work for the client as needed. The agreement may include a specific number of hours or days devoted to the client's needs, with additional time billed as used. Payment for time not used is forfeited or can be accumulated throughout the year as credit.

2. **Project-based retainer:** This type also involves

a substantial fee upon signing—30% is recommended—to retain the graphic artist's services as a one-time deposit against future billings. Hourly rates are set, and the client is kept informed of the hours billed against the retainer. After the retainer hours are used, regular hourly billing continues. If the fee is not completely used, the remaining amount may or may not be refundable.

3. **Service retainer:** This agreement covers longer-term commitments of six months to a year, with payments made in monthly installments. Design services are billed against this retainer, which is very similar to a level billing program where annual project fees are set with a client, who pays the fees in equal installments.

The service retainer is different from the more traditional annual retainer, which is usually based on hourly billing. The problem with hourly billing is that the client may lose control over costs—especially if the clock keeps ticking. In a project-based agreement, both sides know exactly what fees will change hands.

The advantages to the graphic artist of working on retainer are guarantees of long-term artist/client relationships, multiple projects, and a steady cash flow. Among the disadvantages are clients calling too often about minor issues and expecting priority over nonretainer clients. Clients may also question whether they are getting all the services they are paying for. A retainer relationship may sometimes limit the graphic artist's ability to compete for other assignments.

Among the advantages of retainers for the client are cost savings, since retainer work is usually done at a 10-to-15% discount. (Additional billable hours may or may not be discounted.) A graphic artist who is on retainer is fully aware of the company's needs and products and gives preferential treatment to the company—two benefits that are increasingly valued in this age of tight deadlines. A sample Service Retainer Agreement can be found in the Appendix: Contracts & Forms.

What a Contract Should Include

Contracts in the visual communication industries usually cover four issues: copyright use, payment, legal, and working relationship.

Copyright Use Issues

In the graphic arts, the value of a particular work of art or design depends on its use. An illustration used for a small local magazine has one value; the same illustration used in a worldwide advertising campaign is worth far more. A logo designed for a local mom-and-pop store has much less value than a logo used by a global corporation. Use and value to the client determine price. (For more on use and value, see the Pricing Your Services section in Chapter 1 and the Copyright section in Chapter 11.)

Under copyright law, the exclusive use of a design or artwork licensed by a client must be transferred in writing. To avoid any future dispute between client and artist, it is always best to clearly specify which uses are agreed upon in a written contract. As important as it is to specify where and how a work is going to be used, it is equally important to stipulate where it cannot be used. A contract should describe in detail exactly where, how, and how long a work can be used, including the following issues:

Type of medium/product: Where will the finished work appear: in a magazine, in a newspaper ad, in a TV commercial, on a website, in software, on a DVD cover, on a billboard, or on a household product? Or in multiple media? In the age of multimedia, it is extremely important to be specific about each medium where the work will be used, since each use helps define the final value of the work.

Category of use: What is the intent of the use: advertising, editorial, corporate, institutional, entertainment, or educational? To understand the difference in value between a single magazine page and a multimarket campaign, it may help to study the many pricing charts based on survey results that appear in Chapters 5 and 7 of this book.

Geographic area of use: How widely will the work be used: North America, Europe, all over the world, on planets yet to be discovered? As the span of the marketplace increases, so does the work's exposure, which can increase its present and future value.

Duration of use: How long will the work be used: for one time, for one year, for two editions? Limitations on duration of use allow graphic artists to control the exposure of their work and to receive fair market value in each venue where their work appears.

All-rights terms: Such clauses allow clients unlimited use of a work, including in multiple markets and in any way the client may see fit. An all-rights clause (also called a "buyout," which is a misleading term and one to be avoided) is often used for logos, in advertising, or in other areas where a design appears so frequently that keeping track of usage is impossible. An artist who agrees to all-rights terms should always consider appropriate compensation.

Ownership of original art: Who retains the original? Giving a client the right to artwork or to a design for a specified use or a particular period of time is different from selling the client the physical artwork or sending the client a digital file. The sale of original art is often a secondary market for graphic artists and is, by law, a transaction separate from the transfer or sale of reproduction rights.

Licensing third parties: Many clients specify the right to resell or transfer their agreed-upon rights to others. This can be for resale purposes or to allow the work to flow through normal channels of manufacture and distribution. Keep in mind that transferring the right to license to a client may effectively remove the artist's control over the work and divert any potential resale revenue from the artist.

Exclusivity: Who has the right to license, use, or resell the artwork? *Exclusive rights* means that only the client can use the art for the agreed-upon purposes for the time specified and that the artist or designer cannot resell the art to, or adapt it for, any other person or concern within the same medium, category of use, or type of product for the time period stipulated in the contract. *Nonexclusive rights* means that while the client can use the art for the agreed purposes, the artist can also resell the work to other clients.

Many contracts, especially editorial ones, may combine exclusive and nonexclusive terms. For example, a magazine may ask for exclusive terms for 60 days from the date of publication. After 60 days, the contract stipulates nonexclusive terms, allowing the magazine to continue to use the image while the artist is free to resell the work to other clients. Nonexclusive rights can extend the use and value of artwork to clients; you should consider this added value when determining the price of your work.

Work made for hire: A *work-made-for-hire clause* vests authorship of art or design in the client. The graphic artist hands over all rights to the client, including copyright, all preliminary concepts, and even the original. It is strongly recommended that as an independent contractor you not sign a work-made-for-hire contract because you become, in effect, an employee of the client for copyright purposes only, but with none of the benefits or compensation usually associated with employment. Furthermore, by relinquishing your copyright, you are losing any potential future income from your art. Note that the contract must specifically include the language "work made for hire"

and be signed by both the client and artist to qualify as such. (For a thorough discussion of work made for hire, see Chapter 11, Legal Rights & Issues.)

Payment Issues

How much will be paid for a particular use or design? When is payment due? Are there penalties if it is not paid on time? All these issues fall under this category.

Fee/estimate: What is the monetary value of the final work? A variety of factors are used to estimate and set fees: media and geographic areas in which the work will appear, frequency of use, and allocation of a variety of rights.

Additional expenses: If the contract is part of an estimate, how much is estimated for expenses? If outside vendors are used, who will pay their costs and when? Are delivery fees and supplies paid for by the client or the graphic artist? Will the client be notified if expenses exceed the original estimate by a certain percentage? When is payment for the expenses carried by the graphic artist due from the client? Will those expenses be marked up?

Kill/cancellation fees: If a project is canceled for reasons beyond the control of the graphic artist, the project is considered "killed." Typical charges for services rendered can be 20 to 50% if the work is killed during the initial sketch stage, 50 to 100% if killed after completion of the sketch stage, and 100% if killed after the final design is completed.

"Rejection" is used when an assignment is canceled due to client dissatisfaction. Perhaps the final art deviates from the agreed-upon sketch or the style is different from the artist's portfolio or samples shown to obtain the job. Common cancellation fees are 25 to 50% of the total fee if canceled before completion of final art, and 50 to 100% after the final artwork is completed.

Determining whether a job is killed or rejected may become a matter of common sense and negotiation. Both the graphic artist and the client need to realistically evaluate the causes for terminating the project and negotiate payment accordingly. Contracts should provide a clear directive that the client, in killing or canceling the project, gives up any agreed-upon copyright transfer or license. Any future use is subject to renegotiation.

Payment schedule: When are payments due? For large projects, payment is often divided into scheduled segments, called "progress payments." An example is a percentage upon signing, a percentage due after approval of the initial designs, and the remainder, plus expenses, upon delivery of the final work. Smaller jobs may simply require payment at delivery or net 30 days after delivery of the artwork.

As with any schedule, specific deadlines can be crucial, and the graphic artist should consider whether the final payment plan is realistic. There is a big difference between 30 days after receipt of the invoice and 30 days after first use, which may be delayed for many reasons beyond the artist's control.

Late-payment fees: When is a payment late and subject to penalties? After 30 days? Some artists charge a penalty fee (such as 1 1/2% of the total), due every month that the balance remains unpaid. As an incentive for timely payment, some artists offer clients a small discount (such as 2%) if payment is received within a short period of time after the invoice date (for example, 15 days).

Client alterations: Any changes requested by the client that are integral to the original assignment are usually considered part of the process and not client (or author's) alterations. When changes go beyond the original, agreed-upon scope of a project, they are billable beyond the agreed-upon price. These changes can be billed by the hour (the artist's hourly rate is often stipulated in the contract) or by an additional fee agreed upon at the time of the change.

If the nature of the assignment changes in the middle of the project, the graphic artist may assume that the client is liable for an additional fee and increased expenses. It is important to specify such expectations in the initial contract. It is also important to discuss the change in the original assignment with the client so there is no misunderstanding at the time of completion and billing.

Taxes: What taxes are due, and who pays them? Some taxes to consider are state sales tax and transfer taxes. (See the Sales Tax section in Chapter 3, Professional Issues.)

Default/legal fees: How will the matter be settled should the client fail to pay the bill? If there is a dispute regarding rights or use, who will cover the expenses incurred in the resolution of the dispute? (See the Remedies section under Legal Issues, below.)

Legal Issues

Clauses in this category define responsibilities over such legal issues as questions of ownership, libel, and recourse in disputes.

WARRANTY

A *warranty* is an assurance by the creator that the work is original and unique, created solely by the artist or designer for the buyer. It protects the buyer from legal action based on the art or design supplied to them by the graphic artist.

A warranty may also guarantee that the graphic artist holds the exclusive rights to the artwork or design, has the authority to sell the agreed-upon rights, and that no one else may claim these rights. Typical warranties of this type may state that "to the best of the artist's knowledge," the artist has not infringed on any person's copyright in creating the artwork.

Some buyers want to be assured that nothing in a work is considered "obscene" or "indecent." This may be a matter of personal taste that is beyond the artist's control. If a client is adamant about certain issues, this language ("no explicit sexual references") should be clearly stated in the wording of the contract.

INDEMNITY

Indemnity is a common clause in contracts that seek to exempt or protect the client and/or the graphic artist from damages or liability in actions brought by third parties. Should someone other than the client or graphic artist sue one of the parties, this clause protects the other from also being brought into the lawsuit. Similarly, graphic artists should insert wording into any contract that will protect them if a client causes the work to be subject to any litigation.

An indemnity clause should be negotiated based on the scale and scope of the work. A typical indemnification clause reads: "Artist holds client harmless from and against any and all judgments and related costs and expenses arising out of, or concerning artist's rights in, the material provided."

REMEDIES

Remedy clauses map out agreed-upon courses of action by which a disagreement or breach of contract can be resolved. Solutions in remedy clauses include negotiation, mediation, arbitration, and court action. Several points should be considered:

TYPES OF REMEDIES
Will the claim be taken to an arbitrator or mediator agreed upon by both parties or appointed by only one party, or will the dispute be settled in court? It is important to note the difference between arbitration and mediation.

Arbitration by a neutral party results in a binding decision, enforced by a court. In *mediation*, an impartial mediator seeks to facilitate an agreement between the two parties. A mediator can be appointed by a judge or another third party, such as an arts mediation service, but the resolution is binding upon the parties only if the parties agree to it in writing. Does agreement to use arbitration or mediation waive all rights to otherwise pursue additional settlement in court? (It may or may not; see the When Things Go Wrong section later in this chapter.)

GEOGRAPHIC AREA

Where will resolution of the dispute be pursued? Individual cities, counties, and states all have different laws and codes that govern and affect a final ruling in a dispute. If the client and the graphic artist do business in different locales, a remedy clause should specify where arbitration or court action will take place.

LEGAL EXPENSES

Who will pay legal costs, such as lawyers and research, should a dispute arise? Clients often try to establish that the graphic artist bears full financial responsibility regarding expenses incurred in the settlement of a dispute. This responsibility often extends beyond the client/graphic artist relationship to actions by third parties who feel the work has somehow infringed on their rights.

CURE PROVISION

A *cure provision* is a clause in the contract that gives an infringing party a certain amount of time to "fix" a mistake before any legal action is taken. Such a provision is necessary for both parties because often circumstances beyond anyone's control create situations adverse to the agreement; for example, late delivery of supplies by a third party could cause the graphic artist to miss a deadline. The typical cure provision gives a party approximately 30 days to cure the breach.

Working Relationship Issues

This category describes areas in a contract that define the basic working elements of a project: the function and facets of the job, what is expected and when, who approves the work, and so on. The following is a standard list for any assignment:

Project description: The project description is one of the main considerations in setting compensation for the work. Be sure to include the project name, a thorough description of the project, uses, and copyright transfers. Both parties benefit when the scope of the project is described in as much detail as possible.

Work stages and scheduling: What is expected at the various stages and when? What is the responsibility of each party at each stage? How many ideas will be presented in the initial stages, and how many revisions are reasonable under the stated fee schedule? Is there a penalty for missed deadlines? Number of revisions, scheduled sign-offs, and time allowed for turnaround are important considerations governing the work. Both graphic artist and client should strive to set realistic expectations for each stage.

Approval process: Who accepts and approves the work, and when? How long does the client have to review and sign off on concepts, comps, or final art or design without upsetting the final delivery date? The contract may include language that specifies a monetary penalty for missed deadlines, especially at the final deliverable stage.

Final artwork and return of originals: What form should the final deliverable work take: reflective art, transparency, digital file? Is final art to be hand-deivered, mailed, express-mailed, or electronically delivered? When should the artist expect physical original artwork to be returned? What would be appropriate compensation in the event of damage or loss of the original? Does the artist receive tear sheets or finished samples? Delivery and care of the artwork as well as samples of the printed work are all concerns that should be governed by the contract.

Using Contracts

The more proactive you are in managing your business, the less intimidated you will be by unreasonable situations. By its nature, all creative work, which straddles the line between the personal and the practical, is not the average business transaction. The following three suggestions enable you to adopt a proactive stance.

Create a Boilerplate Contract

Start by drafting a basic studio contract based on the ones in the Appendix. Study contracts sent by clients and incorporate appropriate clauses into a boilerplate contract. Also compare notes with other professionals in the field about what clauses should be included.

Save the boilerplate contract as a template in your computer. Then customize the contract by changing, adding, or removing clauses to suit a particular job and print it out on studio letterhead. By designing your contract to look as professional as possible, you project businesslike authority, and your contract will be taken more seriously.

Follow the same procedure to draft your own letter of agreement for less complicated jobs and store it for future use.

Establish a Studio Policy

Being proactive means anticipating the needs of your business as well as your client's before assignments come in. Setting a studio policy eliminates possible problems and conflicts before they arise.

Using an established policy depersonalizes the process of negotiation. Policies can be quoted whenever something unpleasant arises, such as: "Our policy is no returns without receipt." So, the artist is not saying "no"; the studio is saying "no." In reality, the artist and the studio are one and the same, but clients are less likely to question a business policy than to badger an individual.

As a businessperson, it is easy to establish a list of policies that support your work. Prepare a written statement, and then practice stating the studio policy aloud. Try saying: "I'm sorry, but we have a studio policy of not signing work-made-for-hire contracts." With practice, the phrase will sound natural and convincing.

In addition to establishing priorities, studio policies help pinpoint difficult or problem clients. Should a job sound confusing or the client undependable, the artist can simply say, "This job sounds terrific. Let me send you our standard letter of agreement so that you are aware of our studio policy. When you are ready, just sign and return the letter, and I'll get started on the work." The letter communicates to the client the terms under which you will and will not consider a job.

The following are some recommended studio policies:

* Do not ever work on projects without a signed agreement.
* Do not accept work-made-for-hire terms.
* Do not accept all-rights terms (or buyouts).
* Do not do work on speculation.
* Refuse contracts that deny the artist the opportunity to negotiate terms.
* Establish a studio minimum for work.
* Do not quote estimates on the spot; allow time for reflection.
* Establish a policy of delaying before signing a contract. No matter how exciting the prospect of the job, set aside an hour to read over the contract, remembering that any agreement must benefit both parties, not just one.

Working with Clients' Contracts

When a client says, "I have a contract to send you," do not automatically assume it is unfavorable to you. But, on the other hand, do not assume it incorporates your best interests. Every contract offers an opportunity to work out an agreement. Tell the client you are looking forward to seeing the contract. Then follow these steps:

Get acquainted: Make a copy of the contract. Then read through it carefully without interruption, using a pen to make notes and a highlighter to mark problem areas.

Isolate problem areas: After the first read-through, pause and read it again, noting any areas you do not understand and repetitive clauses. Occasionally a client's legal department may try to establish a right in several clauses spread throughout a document or insert a clause under an inappropriate heading. Write additional notes in the margin.

Compare notes: Does the contract reflect what the client said when assigning the job? Is the client saying one thing and the contract another? Does the contract ask for more rights or terms than initially discussed? Does the stated fee support what the contract requests? If not, make notes about the items that are beyond the scope of the assignment and estimate what is needed to cover the additional work.

Start the rewrite process: Methodically cross out sentences and rewrite passages that are unreasonable. (Remember, negotiation takes place between two parties.) Be aware of the client's concerns, as well as your own. Although the client may have submitted a one-sided contract, it is important to alter the contract so that it reflects a reasonable agreement. An invaluable skill in client negotiations is understanding both sides of the transaction and working in good faith toward a common understanding. The goal is for both parties to sign an agreement that supports an ongoing working relationship. Keep that in mind during the rewrite.

Alter the original: Now copy your changes neatly onto the original contract, using a ruler and a thin black pen (do not obliterate the original). Put your initials in the margin next to each change. Should changes to a clause be so extensive that an addendum is required, cross out the entire clause and write "See addendum" next to the section. Compile all the addenda on separate sheets; title each one with the clause number, the name of the clause, and the title "Addendum" so the client can easily locate the original clause in the contract. For instance: "Section 4. Grant of License Addendum," followed by the rewritten clause. Then attach the addenda to the contract.

Send it to the client: Mail or e-mail the altered contract with a cover letter thanking the client for sending it. Be sure to alert the client to any alterations by stating something like: "Please note that I have made substantial changes in the contract sent. The changes occur in Sections 3, 5, and 8. Please feel free to contact me should you have any questions regarding these changes." Then conclude with a positive statement and a polite request: "I am looking forward to starting the project as soon as I receive the signed contract."

Prepare for a reaction: Arriving at an appropriate contract often involves a series of back-and-forth compromises. Expect questions about the reasons behind the revisions and deletions. Be prepared to explain why alterations were made. If the client insists on reinserting a deleted clause, try to negotiate additional compensation for it. As in all business transactions, but especially phone conversations, remain calm, businesslike, and personally removed from the issues.

Determine, in advance, your minimum requirements: Be prepared to turn down the job if they are not met. Remember that not all negotiations result in projects.

Negotiation

Negotiation is discussed in depth in Chapter 1, Essential Business Practices. Some of the more important points are summarized below.

When negotiating a contract, position yourself as an expert: you have a skill or talent that the client needs but does not have. Act as professionally as possible and strive for a win-win solution. Create a document that lists standard points you want to cover or an agenda that outlines topics to be covered, and refer to the document whenever negotiating, particularly over the phone. Whether a project is interesting purely for the money, because it is a valuable showcase, or because it will help establish a working relationship with a new client, using a standard agenda may influence what you agree to during negotiations.

In addition, you may want to develop a "position paper" with several questions that will help evaluate any negotiation:

1. What value—monetary or otherwise—will I derive from this job?
2. Is the compensation sufficient to cover my time and expenses?
3. What payment would I like for the job?
4. What payment am I willing to accept?
5. What is the lowest acceptable price?
6. Can I afford not to do the job?
7. What will I do with the time if I turn it down?

Determine the Client's Real Goals

When clients try to insert work-made-for-hire clauses in contracts or demand all rights to artwork, an effort should be made to determine the client's real goals. Such terms may have been put in a contract by a zealous lawyer trying to anticipate every possible contingency. However, such terms usually are excessive and, if priced accordingly, make the work too expensive.

Most art directors and creative service personnel who commission art and design have little or no understanding of contract and copyright issues. They are too busy managing a number of creative projects in unusually hectic, high-pressure surroundings, and, like artists, most of them would prefer to spend their time in creative pursuits rather than administering legal details. So, if the artist has a clear understanding of what contract amendments should be added and how to word them, some problems will be avoided.

Keep Written Records

Keep thorough written records of every negotiation, including the initial checklist that should include

* A job description
* Due dates
* Fees and expenses
* Notes on the person representing the client
* Records of follow-up meetings and phone calls
* Hours on the job
* Sketches or layouts
* Contracts
* Invoices
* Records of verbal communication (follow-up meetings and phone calls)
* All written correspondence (e-mail, memos, and business letters)

This is the "job packet" that provides a paper trail in the event that a disagreement or misunderstanding interferes with completing the project and receiving payment.

Discuss Money Last

* Discussion of money is where most disagreements occur; focus first on areas where agreement can be reached.
* The price of a project cannot be determined until all the factors that define the project are thoroughly discussed and agreed upon by both parties.
* Deferring discussion of money gives time for both parties to develop a relationship based on working toward a common goal.
* Negotiating on price before reaching agreement on services, deliverables, and usage is premature and can prove to be costly.

Stay Calm & Professional

Tactical problems may occur, especially if emotions become involved, so try to stay calm, cool, and collected at all times, even if the client does not. If the person you are negotiating with claims to lack decision-making authority on terms, talk about the project as a joint venture and solicit the person as your newfound "partner." That may inspire the person to negotiate with his or her boss to defend your needs. If a contract states that it is a "standard contract" and cannot be changed, remember that contracts are working documents that should protect both parties. Do not agree to sign a standard contract if it does not protect you. Do not be afraid to strike out unfavorable sections or terms. If necessary, the defense "My attorney has instructed me not to sign contracts with these conditions" may be used to suggest alterations.

Think It Over

Do not ever feel obligated to respond immediately, especially if a client starts a negotiation with "I only have $500, but I think you'd be great for the job." You can acknowledge the figure and still find creative ways to ask for more money. For instance, try selling the client usage of an existing piece of art (stock). (See Chapter 4, Maximizing Income.)

It is always best to tell the client you will call back after you've had a chance to think about the project. Then take time to review the terms and note any points you want to change. If a project has many variables, you might consider discussing it with an associate or if you are a Guild member, consulting the Guild's Legal Referral Network (see Professional Resources on the Guild website at www.graphicartistsguild.org/member-benefits/).

It is important to note that negotiation will not lead to a good contract in every situation. In some relationships the balance of power is so skewed that one party must either yield to unfavorable conditions or give up the opportunity, but it is possible to maximize assets and protect yourself from an agreement that may be detrimental to you.

Remember that not every negotiation is destined to end in an agreement. Two parties can "agree to disagree" amicably and part ways, possibly trying again in the future. The ability to approach negotiation with levelheaded objectivity, keeping it in perspective, gives a skilled negotiator the attitude necessary to obtain the most favorable agreement.

Seeking Legal Advice
Before Calling a Lawyer

Though some contracts may appear incomprehensible at first glance, the more contracts you read, the more you will understand. In most circumstances, consulting with a lawyer is not necessary. For smaller projects, the cost of a lawyer could easily be more than the assignment fee! Sometimes, especially in the beginning, you just need help with a particular clause. Below are some less expensive ways to come to terms with contracts:

Network: Call fellow graphic artists, talk openly about contracts, and ask their opinions. Establish a network or support group with other artists in your discipline to share information about contracts and companies. Join graphic artist communities and forums on the Internet. The Graphic Artists Guild has active Facebook and LinkedIn communities that discuss a variety of topics of interest to graphic artists. The Guild also offers a series of Creative Professional Webinars, open to the graphic arts community at a nominal fee (free for members).

Read and grow wiser: In addition to this book, many other books educate artists about contracts and business matters (see those listed in Chapter 15, Resources & References). The Internet has many websites and blogs that provide business support to graphic artists; a number of them are hosted by artists. The Guild's website (www.graphicartistsguild.org) has a resource section that might have an answer to your question.

When to Call a Lawyer

When writing or negotiating a contract, there are situations when you should consult a lawyer:

* For large and/or complicated projects involving complex royalty or licensing issues
* For projects requiring lengthy schedules and/or penalties
* For licensing work in multinational markets

When Things Go Wrong

At the other end of a legal negotiation is the question of what to do when things go wrong after a contract has been signed. The fact that the contract exists at all is usually a deterrent to a violation of terms, but when an agreed-upon clause is violated, it becomes a breach of contract.

There are many ways to address a contract breach, most of them without incurring great expense. No matter what method you use, once you know things are going wrong, it is essential to maintain a thorough paper trail to document your side of the case.

Establish a Paper Trail

* Keep copies of all letters sent to the client, including e-mails.
* Reflect on your memory of key conversations and oral agreements before the job, during the job, and after the job is completed. Write notes for future reference.
* Record all telephone calls made regarding the dispute, including the date and year of the call. Take notes about the content of each call, the people involved in the conversation, and what was agreed/not agreed to. If necessary, follow up each conversation with a brief letter recording your understanding of the conversation. That allows clients to respond if they feel the facts are inaccurate. Keep the telephone log as a separate file, and do not write on the contract.
* Set up specific dates when you expect an agreed-upon action to be taken. Send all correspondence by certified mail, return receipt requested, and file the receipt with a copy of the letter for future reference.
* Keep a folder with all receipts, notes, and papers regarding the problem.

Take Action to Resolve the Problem

There will be times when the client has no intention of solving the problem. Like any other businessperson, the graphic artist has a wide range of available options, depending on the scope and severity of the problem. The following list of actions is scaled from minor to major breaches of a contract (refer back to the Getting Paid section of Chapter 1, Essential Business Practices for a more in-depth explanation of these actions):

Write to the offending client, asking for a remedy to the problem. Mention that you plan to use the contract to prove your point, if needed, in court. Spell out specifics. This is your first brick when laying a foundation for action if going to court.

Negotiate one-on-one: Try to avoid potentially expensive arbitration or legal fees by offering to sit down and negotiate a resolution. Even in extreme circumstances, it is always better to attempt to negotiate before entering the legal system. (Review the Negotiation section in Chapter 1, Essential Business Practices.)

Mediate: Mediation is an informally structured but more aggressive style of negotiation in which an impartial third party is brought in to facilitate the discussion between disputing parties. If the parties are able to resolve their differences with the mediator's assistance, the resolution is written up as a Memorandum of Agreement, which is then signed by both parties and the mediator. Such a memorandum constitutes an enforceable contract between the parties. The Volunteer Lawyers for the Arts (VLA) organization provides low-cost or free mediation services for artists, with fees based on a sliding scale. (For a list, see Part 5, Resources & References.)

Consider Small-Claims court: If the breach is payment-related and the fee is within the allowable range, small-claims court is often an inexpensive way to recover damages. States vary as to maximum amounts allowed in Small-Claims cases. Many books exist to help you navigate through Small-Claims court.

Call arts organizations for referrals: Check with local arts organizations for legal groups that specialize in the arts, such as Volunteer Lawyers for the Arts and other non-profit organizations. Often these organizations can also refer you to local mediators and arbitrators. Chapter 1, Essential Business Practices also has valuable information regarding negotiation strategies.

Be Confident

Although this chapter won't prepare you for a legal career, you should now feel more confident in reading, negotiating, and even drafting simple contracts for your business. By making these business practices an integral part of your studio policy, you will protect your business and minimize disputes. You also will project a professionalism that clients appreciate and respect. Refer to the Glossary for definitions of important legal terms. Samples of a variety of contracts and business forms are found in the Appendix: Contracts & Forms.

Now that you are armed with the business essentials from Part 1, the pricing guidelines and trade customs for your discipline found in Part 2, and ways to protect your intellectual property and legal rights from Part 3, you have the knowledge for the business side of what it takes to become a self-employed graphic artist. Combine it with your creative skills and go forth and prosper.

If you still need some inspiration, read in Part 4 the interviews with eleven graphic artists who have utilized many of the practices in this handbook to create sustainable careers as self-employed graphic artists.

4

Successfully
Applying Practices

Meet 11 self-employed graphic artists from various disciplines who have been able to earn a successful living, some in rather unique ways. As they share their experiences, you will discover that they are successful not only because of their talent, creative skills, and hard work, but because they utilize many of the business practices promoted in this handbook. You will also notice they share several of the same attributes—adaptability, flexibility, determination, generosity, and resourcefulness—traits that have enabled them to survive the ups and downs of self-employment over the long haul. They are professionals who understand the value of their work and its potential to produce future income—and price and protect it accordingly.

May their experiences inspire you, whether you are considering self-employment or have already taken the plunge. Or, perhaps you need to breathe new life into your existing freelance career.

BIL DONOVAN
Fashioning a Career with Passion & Perseverance

PHOTO COURTESY OF DARIO CALMESE

Bil Donovan is one of the most prolific and esteemed fashion and lifestyle illustrators working today. As an artist, author, educator and spokesperson, he is a true champion of the art form. His client list currently includes Christian Dior, where he has served as artist-in-residence since 2009, Neiman Marcus, The Metropolitan Museum of Art, *Vogue*, St. Regis Hotels, Kim Crawford Vineyards, Saks, *New York Magazine*, *Elle*, and L'Occitane, to name a few.

Bil is the author of *Advanced Fashion Drawing: Lifestyle Illustration* and has illustrated several other fashion books. In addition to client work, he currently teaches illustration at the Fashion Institute of Technology (FIT) and at the School of Visual Arts (SVA) in New York City. He has spoken on the subject of fashion and lifestyle illustration at the L'Oréal Melbourne Fashion Festival and the ICON6 and ICON10 Illustration Conferences, and he has led workshops in several countries and at The Society of Illustrators in New York City, where he is a member and active volunteer. Bil continues to facilitate panels, lectures, and workshops with other prominent artists to promote the art of fashion illustration and share his passion with a wider audience.

You grew up in South Philly, an Irish/Italian blue-collar working-class neighborhood, a far cry from the glamorous fashion worlds of New York, Milan, and Paris. What was your inspiration for becoming an illustrator—specifically a fashion illustrator?

I loved to draw as a child—there was something magical about creating an image from your imagination with a crayon and paper. South Philly was not a bastion of high fashion, yet I was attracted and exposed to the glamour and élan of fashion through the cinema. I loved seeing iconic beauties such as Grace Kelly, Elizabeth Taylor, and my favorite, Audrey Hepburn, fill the screen with style, grace, and glamour. That world was a stark departure from the reality of my neighborhood, and I was captivated by those moments and recreated them though my passion of drawing. I began to think of pursuing a career as a commercial artist. I was unaware that there was a genre of work called fashion illustration.

Out of high school, my brother-in-law got me a job at a bank during the graveyard shift. During the day when all my friends were in college, I began drawing more earnestly and enrolled in continuing education classes at the Philadelphia College of Art. In a drawing foundations class, one artist did a scene of a glass bottle and fruit for a still life assignment. I was enthralled by her ability to create translucency and reflections in her rendering of the bottle. Reality crashed into my romantic ideal of being an artist. I realized that pursuit was more than taking a few drawing classes. It was a long journey and a commitment I questioned whether I had the determination and talent to pursue. A career as an artist was considered an anomaly in my neighborhood, which heightened my anxiety, and combined with my inadequate skill set, led me to believe I was wasting my time. I took a Color and Design class which explored color theory, design, and creativity. We were given a series of assignments not involving drawing or draftsmanship but thinking creatively to find visual solutions to the given assignment. I loved that class. And the instructor loved my work—she remarked that I was extremely creative. That was it, I had something, and I held onto that validation to continue taking classes.

When people see an artist who is working successfully in the world of the rich and famous, they often believe that either the person is so incredibly talented that they were an instant success or that they must have connections in that world. Using your own experience as an example, please dispel that myth.

I am not an overnight success. I am where I am in my career due to a strong work ethic and a desire to be the best. I am a bit modest to a fault, and I have never relied on networking to find work. I was the boy from South Philadelphia, so I was intimidated by the social circles in New York. Plus, I wanted to earn work on merit, not on who I knew. Of course, it happens, but I never solicited those I knew to garner work. I pursued my passion for fashion illustration by enrolling in the Fashion Institute of Technology, where dreams of being a fashion illustrator were dashed in my first semester. A respected professor informed me that I did not have the skill set to be a fashion illustrator and that I should change my major to textile design.

Hearing an instructor tell you that you had no natural talent for something you dreamed of doing could have ended your fashion career right then. How did you deal with it and how has that criticism influenced your career?

I may not have had the skill set, but I had passion. When I informed my professor that this was my dream, fueled by my passion of drawing and fashion,

© BIL DONOVAN

she offered this advice, "Well then you need to draw, a lot!" and I did. I filled my sketchbook with multiple drawings of everything and anything in my immediate vision. I drew my cat, my hat, my friends, my toothpaste, and doing laundry. I began to see an improvement—slow but steady—and I developed a thirst for knowledge. I was driven by a desire to be the best artist I could, and that involved being in a competitive studio setting with fellow artists. Aside from dropping into any available drawing class at FIT, I also began taking evening classes at SVA. I studied with the legendary Jack Potter for six years and took additional classes in Graphic Design, Comics, Color, Acrylic, Oil, Watercolor, Sculpture—any class I thought would nurture my skill sets and put me on a path to achieve my goal of being a fashion illustrator.

How did you break into a career as a fashion illustrator?

I would peruse ads in the back of *Women's Wear Daily*. Occasionally they would post an ad for a fashion illustrator. I was determined to work. My first job was to create 70 illustrations for a trend report for Lord and Taylor. It did not pay much, but the opportunity to work for a reputable company had a certain allure. The work was terrible. I was just out of FIT and not experienced, so the images were not perfect, but they served the purpose and the client was happy. I took on small jobs—spots, storyboards, stamp-size ads for a clothing store on Madison Avenue. And I kept taking classes and refining my work and exploring media. That is essential advice to any perspective illustrator: you will need a job to earn money, but it's essential that you block out time to make work, to develop your style, and explore your vision.

After six years of fulfilling a lifelong dream of working in Milan, you came back to the U.S. and discovered that fashion illustration was being pushed out by photography and that the creative world was being decimated by AIDS. You couldn't find work, so it was a very dark period in your life. How did you rise from the ashes and rebuild your fashion illustration career?

It was a difficult period. I was doing very well in Milan, and I assumed that I would continue that success in the States. But there was not a market for fashion illustration, and I was devastated by the AIDS crisis. My friends and acquaintances were dying, and the government did not care. I was angry and wanted to paint my frustration and what was happening. I couldn't do a fashion illustration, so I began to do paintings influenced by David La Salle. I created diptychs of homoerotic male figures with a flower in full bloom. The work was graphically beautiful but empty of content.

I wanted to find a way to communicate my voice, and I thought, "Well if I am going to be broke, I may as well be a broke fine artist. So, I started taking evening classes at SVA in the fine art departments. I began teaching at the same time at FIT, and it was great to be back in school studying new territory to relate to my students. I found my voice and enrolled full-time for studio arts.

I divorced myself from fashion art and focused on my fine art. Sometimes when you let go of something, it comes back, and that is what happened. I began to get more and more work in fashion, and I realized that I still loved it. I was approached by *Vogue* to do live drawings at a PR event. During the event, a young lady asked me to do a portrait of her, and to make her look beautiful. So, I did, and I made her look a bit like Bridget Bardot. After her fashion portrait, I had 20 women in line and *Vogue* booked me for another event—a Christian Dior event in December 2008. After this event, I was offered an exclusive contract as Dior's first artist in residence.

What do you do as artist-in-residence at Dior?

I travel the country doing personal appearances at Saks, Neiman Marcus, and Bergdorf's, creating live fashion portraits of Dior's Beauty and Couture clientele. I also have created images for Dior for tote bags, charities, and notecards to promote the brand.

You started working in watercolor, then experimented with different media and came back to watercolor. It seems to be a very unforgiving medium for the quick work you often have to do.

Watercolor and inks are magical media— they have a spirit that is free and unique. You have to allow them to breathe and do what they want to do, nurture them a bit, and take chances. Sometimes it does not work out, but when it does, it's fantastic. That is what I love about the media— they're unpredictable, and not knowing what will show up is much more exciting than the expected.

You've been quoted as saying, "I never say 'no' to an opportunity, as you never know where it will lead." Using an example from your career, explain how this philosophy has added to your success.

I was commissioned to create an illustration for a shoe company. When the manager pulled a clunky shoe to illustrate, I suggested he use a more fluid shoe for the invite. He commented "Well, what do you know? Have you ever designed shoes?" I replied, "I have." It was a white lie. I did do some drawings of shoes in Milan for a friend, and I would put my spin on those just a bit, but I had never designed shoes. He told me to show him some designs. I did 48, and I was hired on the spot as a designer for Albert Nippon Shoes.

I traveled all over Italy to factories and showrooms as a designer for two years, continuing with my freelance. However, I resigned, as it was interfering with my illustration work. My friends thought it was a huge mistake to leave the security of a job, but in my heart, I was not fulfilled.

You were later invited to teach at FIT, the same school where you were told you had no natural talent. That must have been a satisfying moment in your career. You also teach illustration at SVA. What are some important concepts you want your students to come away with?

Teaching is an incredible privilege. One is not a born teacher—you learn and earn it. I consider it an honor. I like to push the students out of their comfort zone, to take risks and be BOLD. I would rather see a bold, strong drawing that is off than one that is safe and perfect. That's boring to me. And I share that idea with my students. I give them a series of exercises to make them think before they draw—to observe, analyze the figure through a given premise, then communicate that premise through line, shape, texture, etc. I mix it up. I throw in accident and chance to throw them off—to look at possibilities beyond their process and as a means to further explore possibilities to create work that is unique and of their voice. In order to succeed, you have to be willing to fail.

Digital work can be flat and devoid of content. The work that shines is art that has a solid foundation in traditional skills. Filters and digital technology allow anyone to make a digital piece of work, but it's the artists who have that foundation who make a difference. Look at Marcos Chin and Yumiko Shumizo as examples. I do everything by hand, but I may at times incorporate Photoshop to enhance or play with an image.

I speak about the business side in every class. I explain about everything from storyboards to illustrating a book to communicating with clients and soliciting work. I don't teach fashion specifically, but I do teach those techniques and processes associated with fashion illustration—stylization, exaggeration, selectivity, repetition, and scale—but applied to general illustration.

How important have multiple streams of revenue been in making a sustainable living as a self-employed illustrator?

The nature of business for an illustrator has evolved. I am fortunate to have the ability and opportunity to work in many markets. It just evolved. Illustrators today have an opportunity to brand their work and what the work represents. I love sharing information, and my years of study brought about an opportunity to write a textbook and to now lecture doing live master classes. That is something I enjoy, sharing my viewpoint and challenging fellow artists to reconsider preconceived notions of making work. The giclée prints I sell on my website just came out of a demand for prints of my artwork, and the scarves followed the prints. I have two wonderful friends with a silk mill in Como who asked if I was

interested, and as I mentioned before, I never say "no" to an opportunity. I have a contract with Dior, and I freelance. My main sources of income are from freelance and Dior. The other venues I participate in substantiate that income.

What words of encouragement can you give to self-employed graphic artists who encounter stumbling blocks in their careers, whether it's negative criticism, a personal setback, lack of work, changes in the industry, etc.?

FOLLOW YOUR PASSION. Remember why you became an artist. Criticism—positive and negative—forces you to defend your choices and allows you to be confident in those choices. Personal setbacks are a fact of life—acknowledge them, but don't allow them to become baggage—move beyond and continue on your path. I always found solace during rough times by focusing on my art.

CREATE OPPORTUNITIES. Use social media to promote your work and create a series of work that can be prints or printed on merchandise and set up an account for sales. Look to trade magazines, which will more likely commission a new illustrator than a seasoned one for work.

STAY ATTUNED AND TAKE CLASSES. The world of illustration is organic. When I was contemplating going back to SVA for a degree in Fine Art, I said to my partner, "Do you know how old I will be when I get my degree?" and he replied, "The same age as if you don't."

www.bildonovanlimited.com

DONOVAN

© BIL DONOVAN

ELLEN BYRNE
It's Never Too Late to Follow Your Dreams

Ellen Byrne, a self-employed illustrator living in Frederick, MD, didn't start her career until she was in her 40s. Despite a late start and some initial rejection, Ellen feels being a freelance illustrator is "the best job in the world—getting to know all kinds of people from many sides of life, the excitement of discovering the challenges the next e-mail or call will bring. Developing a strategy and efficient solution to making a client's project come alive with the right visuals are challenges I enjoy daily."

Ellen's clients include several national and regional publications, book publishers, universities, foundations, professional associations, arts organizations, and national and international corporations. She has won several gold and silver local and district Addy Awards, as well as the coveted National Gold Addy Award for Illustration.

BOSTON POSTER (COMMISSIONED BY JAPANESE COMPANY, SATO) © ELLEN BYRNE

BOSTON SAILBOATS (PRIVATE PROJECT) © ELLEN BYRNE

You started your own business in 2003 and won a local Gold Addy Award just a year later, with several subsequent Gold and Silver Addy Awards since. How did that make you feel in terms of the negative reception you had received originally?

Amazing—I always had confidence, but the awards were validation and recognition from professional industry judges. This was important as far as getting future work. Nothing succeeds like success!

How many years did it take before your freelance business was sustainable?

About four years before I got steady assignments. Joining the iSpot on the advice of a colleague was a tremendous boost. Almost immediately, I got an assignment for a national magazine cover.

Did you always work digitally? Describe your creative process.

Originally, I painted and drew using old-school technology because computers weren't around, then once they were, I couldn't afford the technology or the software. In the late 90s, I learned Adobe Illustrator at a community college and started some personal projects.

As for my process, it depends on the client—some provide their own images and source materials for what they want; others expect me to do the research. In Adobe Illustrator I put the photos and references on a layer and then draw on a layer above.

You said your grandfather taught you art techniques when you were a child. Was he also an artist?

Yes, he was an oil painter who did work for friends and family. He encouraged and motivated me. Art was appreciated in the family, so this gave me confidence.

You started your career in your 40s, after raising four children. How difficult was that?

Fortunately for me, we settled in a small city 40 miles from Washington, D.C., with many design and arts communities. Meeting people with similar passions was essential to learning of local commercial art opportunities.

When a job coach told you that your goal was unrealistic and a prospective employer laughed at you, you must have been devastated. What did you do?

Nothing could have deterred me. I like a challenge, so I set out to prove them wrong.

Do you think that besides their ignorance, they were reacting with age bias?

They may have assumed I wouldn't have fresh ideas or artwork.

What would you tell other artists who have faced negative feedback from professionals similar to what you received?

Feel bad for a few minutes and then get on with it and prove them wrong.

How did you actually break into the industry? What was your first commission?

I entered paintings in poster art contests, joined the American Advertising Federation (Ad Club), and purchased my first *Graphic Artist Guild Handbook: Pricing & Ethical Guidelines* at Borders. Then I exhibited my paintings and drawings at art festivals. It was at one of these festivals that my work was noticed by the president of a design company in a neighboring county. She gave me my first assignment, cover art for a national association brochure, which led to other jobs in the D.C. area.

BOSTON POSTER (VARIATION SOLD ON ETSY) © ELLEN BYRNE

people respond to and purchase. My two styles are dorky and "modern realism." When people put money where their mouth is, it guides my direction in future projects.

Do you have any other streams of revenue?

Aside from commissioned projects, I sell framed prints in a retail setting locally, in Baltimore, and at the American Visionary Art Museum's gift shop. I've taught sophomore Illustration 1 at the Maryland Institute College of Art (MICA) where I used the *Guild Handbook* with my students. I also get quarterly income from licensing on products.

You said that everything that's happened to you in your career is the result of a personal project. What is the best example of that?

Several years ago, I illustrated the Boston skyline as a gift for a cousin. Two years later, I was contacted by a Japanese photo and licensing agency that does work for corporations. They were looking for someone to illustrate four seasonal posters of four different global cities for a Japanese pharmaceutical company.

Seeing the pleasure this gave people also taught me early that it wasn't just about money.

Your style is very colorful and imaginative. Where do you get your ideas from?

Observing everyday life on walks and people watching.

As an adult, you moved around a lot and couldn't finish a degree program because your husband was in the Army. Many of your works are maps and illustrations in a travel poster style. Where have you lived, and do you think your style is influenced by moving frequently?

Hawaii; D.C.; Nuremberg, Germany; Massachusetts; Denver; and San Francisco. The travel posters are mostly personal projects. I don't think moving frequently influenced me as far as style goes. I just always loved travel posters.

You have an Etsy shop where you sell prints of your illustrations. Has that been an additional revenue stream for you?

It has, but more than that, it's been an excellent way to get feedback on a concept or style, to see what individual

THE PARENT TRAP (TWO-PAGE SPREAD FOR *BETHESDA MAGAZINE*) © ELLEN BYRNE

TWO BOOK COVERS (FOR DUTCH COMPANY, ATLAS PUBLISHING) © ELLEN BYRNE

The president of the corporation had attended school in Boston, so he wanted to start with Boston. The agency found my Boston image on Pinterest. Currently, I am working on a third series for them—this time with international festivals as the theme. It was my personal project—my cousin's gift—that launched this collaboration.

Amazing—it just shows that you never know where a job will come from or why your art resonates with a prospective client. What advice would you give graphic artists just starting their careers, especially those who want to be self-employed?

GET SEEN. Because of the Internet, opportunities have never been as accessible as they are today. The field of illustrators has grown equally, however, so strategize how to get your work seen. Short on a budget? Pinterest is free—you don't need Pinterest Business. It's a visual search engine, and your pins can link directly to your website or e-mail, which makes Pinterest great for bringing potential clients to you. Use your titles and keywords wisely. Sharing is the point of Pinterest, so fresh eyes are always looking. Several art directors and clients have found me via Pinterest. The key is getting seen by the right people.

KNOW YOUR RIGHTS. Pick up a recent edition of the *Graphic Artists Guild Handbook: Pricing & Ethical Guidelines*. It's a one-stop resource and full of answers about copyright, other legal rights, and everything about the graphic arts business.

ASK A SEASONED ILLUSTRATOR about their avenues for finding "leads" to commercial work. I'm constantly impressed with how generously creative people share their knowledge and experience. A well-known illustrator told me of several portfolio sites where art directors look for talent.

DEVELOP A REALLY THICK SKIN. Rejection happens on an everyday basis, even to established professionals. Don't take rejection personally. Move on.

PRESERVE YOUR NATIVE FILES. You may need them for future projects. Here's an example: I illustrated an article, "The Parent Trap," about the sandwich generation for *Bethesda Magazine*. *Kaiser Health News* also paid me for usage of the same image. Then several years later, out of the blue, I was contacted by Atlas Publishing in the Netherlands. They were publishing two books, *Sandwich Woman* and *I Don't Know How She Does It* and had come across the Bethesda article and wanted to use the heart of the image, but with tweaking, on both book covers.

It's also a good example of why artists should retain the rights to their work—you were able to sell four usages from one piece of art.

www.ellenbyrne.com

DAN MALL

Proving a Business Model Can Be Both Friendly and Profitable

Dan Mall is an award-winning designer, creative director, and advisor from Philadelphia. He is the founder and CEO of SuperFriendly, a successful design collective where he collaborates with a group of trusted, well-known "superfriends," which are hand-picked for each project, rather than having a staff of full-time employees. SuperFriendly's diverse clients have included Harvard University, *Smashing Magazine*, ExxonMobil, O'Reilly Media, Google, and *Entertainment Weekly*, among others. Dan is also the co-founder of SuperBooked, a service that helps creative professionals find work with a little help from their friends, and the author of the book, *Pricing Design*.

Dan takes pride in his ability to articulate and communicate ideas. He's written for publications like *A List Apart* and *.NET Magazine*. At home in front of audiences, he's led client meetings, training sessions, and workshops, as well as presentations at conferences, such as SXSW, An Event Apart, and Future of Web Design. He has also taught advertising at the Miami Ad School, web and graphic design at the University of the Arts, and Flash at the School of Visual Arts.

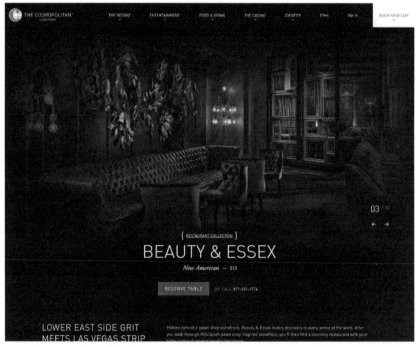

EXPECT THE UNEXPECTED ON THE NEW SITE FOR THE COSMOPOLITAN OF LAS VEGAS, A LUXURY HOTEL AND CASINO © SUPERFRIENDLY

You designed your business, SuperFriendly, as a collaborative model that you refer to as The SuperFriend Model. Rather than hiring a staff, you custom-build teams of freelancers with the skills best suited for each specific job. What was your inspiration for this model and how does it work?

I certainly didn't invent this—the SuperFriend Model is based on the Hollywood model, which is the way that Hollywood has been making movies forever. It's funny to think about this, but the world's greatest actors are 1099 contractors, not W2 employees, and that has nothing to do with their ability to make excellent movies.

The SuperFriend model has really proven out for us through a combination of both positive and negative reinforcement. For most of my career, I've been lucky to work with some very talented generalists, but we've all felt the pain of not having a specialist where we could have used one. Also, I've been in many a pitch where just mentioning the bio of a particular specialist caused the prospective client to choose our team, right on the spot. Unfortunately, having a host of specific specialists on the bench is untenable for most agencies... and that's where the SuperFriend model shines.

How does your agency name translate to how you and your teams work with clients?

It's layered! First of all, with a name like "SuperFriendly," we can't just be a bunch of grumps. At the very least, clients expect some amount of good-naturedness from us.

The "Super" part is trickier. One of the core tenets of every SuperFriendly project is making something that only this team could make. That keeps the focus on what each SuperFriend brings to the table and how to best use their combined set of skills.

You've said that because you sell "good work" to clients, you mainly choose people and their work that you know to form your teams. You must need a fairly large pool of SuperFriends for those times when certain specialists are not available. How do you go about expanding the pool?

Most agencies hire when they have a specific need, which is too late. At that stage, the interview process is under duress, and I've seen many of the wrong people get hired because the need to fill the role seems greater than the need to fill it well. For SuperFriendly, I'm always on the lookout for great specialists, and I'll interview them long before we have a particular need on a project. We'll work out logistics and even go so far as to putting service agreements in place without a work order so that when the right project comes along, we'll already know how we're going to work together. Said differently, talented people become SuperFriends before they work on a SuperFriendly project.

Organizing and managing a different team for each project must take a lot of time and coordination on your part. How do you manage this without any full-time employees?

I have a lot of help! Back to the Hollywood model, every good movie has a good director and a good producer. All SuperFriendly projects have a director and a producer. I've been either director or producer on some projects, but most projects have their own team. It's important that each SuperFriendly team have the ability to make its own decisions and follow the vision set by that project's director.

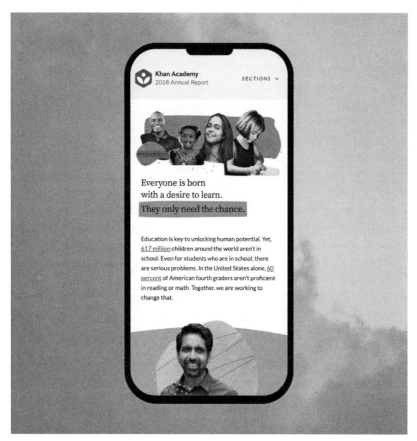

LATEST ANNUAL REPORT FOR KHAN ACADEMY © SUPERFRIENDLY

could make together with that trust already earned.

On the SuperFriendly website's contact page, you are very upfront about what kind of projects you love to work with as well as those you don't like to get involved with. Has this helped to discourage clients who are just shopping around for the lowest price or those who have unrealistic demands and schedules?

Not as much as I'd like! On the contrary, though, the contact language isn't really designed to discourage the wrong kind of client; it's intended to encourage the right kind! We find that the prospective clients that use our template are the ones we tend to have the best collaborations with. They come in humbly willing to speak our language in the sales process, which makes us way more apt to try and speak theirs during the project.

You've been in business for yourself for 8 years. How successful has The SuperFriend Model been?

Pretty good so far! SuperFriendly's been profitable since day 1, clients are happy with the results, and SuperFriends have been growing in their careers as a result of the work we do. I'd say that's success!

Many small businesses experience growing pains at some point. What have you done to keep on top of that?

I'm lucky to have realized early on that it's wise to hire people to do the things that I'm not good at and have no desire or business trying to get better at. From day 1, SuperFriendly has had a CPA, a producer, and an executive assistant. We've since added a lawyer and a salesperson to that mix. Even though I'm a designer by trade, we really saw a boost in work quality and output once I removed myself from project work. The projects themselves have been better for it, and it's freed me up to actually

With team members located in different geographic areas and working remotely, how do the teams "meet" and work together?

The most successful SuperFriends are ones that are pros at working in a distributed way, one of the main traits of which is the natural desire to overcommunicate—to communicate decisions and plans redundantly. My friend Mandy Brown describes this in more detail in her article, "Making Remote Teams Work" (http://stet. editorially.com/articles/making-remote-teams-work/).

But we also try to make time to work together in person as much as we can. Most projects have at least one or two times when the team and I get together in person and develop strong bonds that carry them through tough times on projects.

Much has been written about the lack of communication between the design team and the development team on a project, both feeling left out of important decisions. You started your career as a developer, then moved to design, and then finally to sales to be more involved in the decision process. Why is the sales process such an important part of the way SuperFriendly does business and how much time is spent on it?

The sales process is where alignment between customers and the team begins. It's where agreements are formed, both implicitly and explicitly. Perhaps most importantly, it's where trust should be formed. If we wait until the project starts, to try and build trust, it's often too late. Great projects are built on a foundation of trust, and the sales process is where that happens. Otherwise, you spend valuable project time trying to earn trust, instead of seeing what you be a CEO and focus on bigger picture challenges like growing the network of SuperFriends and incubating new product and service offerings.

How does your model affect pricing a project for a client? You've already said you work out each prospective SuperFriend's pricing fees and terms ahead of time, before they are hired for a project. So, do you estimate the price of the project first and then choose members of the team based on the cost of the project and the client's budget?

The very first sales conversations tend to focus on what value can be created for the client. Once we can determine what that value is, then we try and figure out if we can be profitable in delivering that value. Part of that equation is certainly knowing whether the SuperFriends who have the skills to create that value can do it in a way that's profitable for us.

We shoot for at least a 50% margin on every project. For example, if we determine that the value of a project to a particular client is $100k, we give ourselves up to $50k to spend on all subcontractors on the project. That means we can't hire a $75k art director; that'd be a terrible business decision, not to mention not leaving any room for other subcontractors. Because value drives cost—and not cost driving price—we'd be smarter to get a $20k or $30k art director. They might not be able to do what the $75k art director can, but it does make for a profitable project.

Having a large pool of SuperFriends makes this possible. Without that flexibility, we'd be stuck turning the project away or doing the work unprofitably.

This brings us to the book you wrote, Pricing Design, which promotes value pricing. What is the advantage of value pricing? Do you recommend that all freelancers use value pricing?

I always recommend that people price in the way that makes them most comfortable. If you're uncomfortable with any form of pricing, you won't do a great job selling it. If pricing hourly is working for you, keep on trucking!

The biggest advantage I've seen to value pricing is that a value price should always be one that the client can afford. (I wrote about that in my article, "Break-Even Points for Value Pricing.") By focusing on what value can be created—a focus toward a return on the client's investment—you'd be remiss to recommend that your client should spend more than they'd get in return.

You are also the co-founder of SuperBooked, which helps creative freelancers forge formidable team-ups. It seems to be built around making connections and sharing work. How does it work?

At every level, from beginner to seasoned professional, everyone has at least a small number of people who would trust them to do great work. SuperBooked intends to make it easier for people to use their existing connections to get work.

You are extremely creative and prolific—also speaking at conferences, teaching, blogging, and appearing on podcasts. How do you make time to do all of these things without burning out?

I accept the firehose. I accept that there are things I'll miss; I'm content with that. There are tweets I'll miss, e-mails I'll miss, opportunities I'll miss. Accepting that early on made me realize that I can choose what things I miss, which means I can choose which things

I can take part in. I try not to say the passive phrase, "I don't have time;" instead, I prefer taking ownership of it by choosing that it's not a priority.

It's different for everyone, and priorities change daily, hourly. But thinking about it this way puts me in the driver's seat and makes me conscious of how I'm shaping my own life. We all have the same amount of time and can't make more of it, but we can be active about how we use the time we have. Ironically, the more things I say "no" to, the more I'm somehow able to accomplish.

If you could condense the most important things you've learned from the SuperFriendly experience into a few gold nuggets of advice for other self-employed creatives, what would they be?

SuperFriendly's values are to

1. Work together
2. Play together
3. Eat together
4. Win together

Those four things have been the basis of every great project I've worked on.

http://superfriend.ly/ and **https://danmall.me**

ALAN & BEAU DANIELS
Art & Business

A BEAUTIFUL PARTNERSHIP

The married duo, Beau and Alan Daniels, have grown a very financially successful illustration business for almost 40 years, which has supported them and their four children. Originally from England and now based in Portland, OR, the couple came to Los Angeles to work on the original *Blade Runner* film. Their business specializes in highly detailed technical illustration, maps, and infographics, with clients from major companies in a variety of industries—automotive, aviation, nautical, entertainment, industrial, medical, publishing, and retail products.

You both went to college in England. Alan, you studied fine art, sculpture, and interactive electronic environments; and Beau studied science. How did your paths cross?

When I was first at sculpture college, I was staying in a house of a friend of Beau's mother. One day in walks this absolute brat wearing a huge velvet cape. She was and still is my true love, though. We fell in love, moved in together—that was it. As she always has said—I never stood a chance. Best thing that ever happened for me.

Alan, in college, you studied under some quite famous artists (David Hockney, Roland Piche, David Hall, Phillip Glass, Billy Apple). What did you learn from them?

Perseverance. We had weekly critiques of our work, always on a Friday just before the pubs opened. It was often highly destructive, the idea was to destroy all preconceptions and make you start from scratch. You learnt to get over the critique and move forward. A major philosophy of the school was to think conceptually, without any thought as to how you were going to proceed, then solve the problem as to how to make the concept real. After all, this was sculpture and you had to have a physical solution at the end of each assignment. The school taught us not to create just within our comfort zone: get out and learn new things.

Beau, you studied science, yet you became an illustrator. How did that happen?

Eventually Alan was getting so much work that he needed help to complete the projects. I had been pretty good with drawing for science classes, I have a great eye for design, so I helped out more and more. Illustration is not my first love. I like dealing with people and the finance of the work.

Beau, from the look of your work, you'd never know illustration is not your first love. You like what most people dislike! You've been in business together for almost 40 years. Alan, there are many people who would not want to work with their spouse. Why do you think your partnership has been so successful?

We still find each other interesting. We are best friends, lovers, and partners in life. Without each other, I don't think each of us feels whole. Beau is very good at dealing with clients—me, not so much. I have a short fuse. I am okay if they want to talk technical, but I don't like to talk money. I have never had a need to worry about that side as Beau takes care of it.

You are very fortunate. How do you divide up the rest of the responsibilities of the business side—marketing, client communications, contracts, licensing, etc.?

Beau is the business side of the work—client relations, work creation. She loves hunting down new work. I think that is where she gets the most pleasure out of illustration. I take care of web presence but need to improve my social media skills.

So, you both have experience doing the illustration. Do you work collaboratively on client projects, or do you divide them up according to your individual skill sets?

We both do our own illustration projects, collaborating in thought, but seldom physically, on the same piece. Beau is always the calming influence on the project, if it is complex. Sometimes we could be working on several hundred pieces for the automotive or energy sectors at the same time, but she just has this wonderful way of making everything orderly and logical. Our skill sets are pretty much entwined with each other; one of us could take over from the other if it is needed, but we also jealously guard our individual creative.

How were you able to break into technical illustration?

After college and spending several years doing performance art throughout Europe, we returned to England and decided to raise a family. We needed to make sure we had a regular stable income, or at least as much as one can hope for in the arts. I had always drawn

and painted as well as the sculpture thing. People seemed to like what we did, so we set out to market it.

We were and always have been very lucky. We met John Spencer, a rep for London's Young Artists Agency, now Quantum art agency. John made my art marketable in about 12 months. We ended up doing mostly science fiction book covers and my airbrush pinup paintings. We soon got galleries interested and started doing commission work. Through my airbrush work, we had developed a relationship with Paper Moon Graphics in California and decided we should go take a look at L.A. We fell in love with California, returned to the UK, and went about the process of immigration.

Again, we were lucky—one of the people who regularly bought our work was an immigration attorney with offices in London and Los Angeles. We traded paintings for our green cards. While we were on holiday in California, we took our portfolio with us, always looking for new work. We showed it around a bit and received some good reaction. One of the Art Directors I showed our work to sent the portfolio to an artist's rep, Elise Rosenthal. She got in touch with us when we were back in the UK, and we started to develop a business relationship. One of the collectors of our work, Richard Lobel of Museum Galleries in London, bought our entire collection of commercial work that we had done with Young Artists to help finance our move to Los Angeles, although he hated the idea. When we arrived in L.A., we were immediately put to work on movie posters. The first one was for *The Wiz Kid*. It was a very strange environment to be in—husband, wife, two children, hotel room compressors, and the ever-present offer of stimulants to get you through the work. We hated it.

We had contact with Ridley Scott through the Young Artist Agency, and we started to work on the first *Blade Runner* movie doing some of the matt work. After several other movie projects, we got tired of the movie environment

and started to look for another field that had less ego attached to it. One avenue we pursued was character generation for DIC studios, where we freelanced on the *Bigs and Littles* and *Inspector Gadget*. We could have continued, but the pressure of work was too much—we would have burnt out in a few short years. We started to extend our portfolio, which Beau calls "Following the Money."

We met an artist's rep, John Steinberg, who liked what we were doing and asked if we would like to work alongside David Kimble—our introduction to the technical side of illustration. We did technical illustrations with David for a few years, until it came time to move on. After John Steinberg's death, we found a new rep, Nancy George. Through Nancy, we started to work on major automotive accounts, and we were inundated with work. It was long hours, seven days a week, but the pressure now was always from us, not the clients. When Nancy died, we did not look for a new rep as the illustration business was restructuring. It was easier now to self-promote through *Workbook*. Then later on, we stopped using *Workbook* and started web marketing. It was an easy transition as we had already built a good client roster and reputation. We tended to always be lucky and have major clients with long extended workloads.

What was your first technical commission?

Our first technical illustration was a cutaway engine for Honda Motorcycles. It scared me to death! I had to succeed at this. Beau said, "Just one nut at a time"—that's what got me through.

What in your background helped you become experts at technical illustration?

The thing that helped us the most in technical illustration work is that we both love looking and searching for new knowledge. We had technical projects

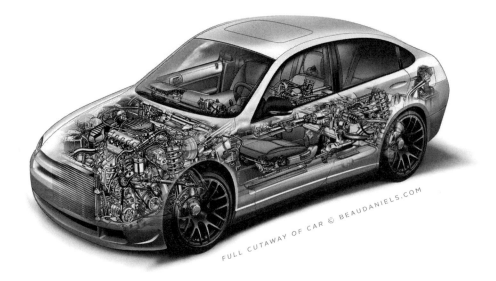

FULL CUTAWAY OF CAR © BEAUDANIELS.COM

that initially we would know nothing about, but that is what is exciting. You get to learn about things that you probably would not look out for. Beau's science background is an incredible resource; my love of building cars doesn't hurt on the technical side. Sculpture helps as it teaches you to commit. Unlike working on the computer, there is no undo, or "what ifs." I think the biggest problem with illustration today is the ability to forever change your mind. There is nothing that cannot be undone, so decisions are not made. We now create all illustrations knowing that it is inevitable that changes will be made because nobody needs to think it through beforehand. Content decisions seem to be made in an ongoing process, because everybody knows anything can be changed.

You are also known for your infographics. Explain what makes yours unique.

Infographics—the best learning experience ever! Trying to explain something to a general populace that maybe has little or no understanding of the content is a great challenge. It can't be too simplistic, or you will alienate a

large portion of the audience. Equally, it can't be too sophisticated for the same reason. We have had the great fortune to have been asked by Cisco, Motorola, and Exxon Mobile to revamp all of their illustration and infographics. We learned so much about industries we did not understand—that for us is the greater pleasure. Because it is two of us working on the infographic concept, we have to split the interest between two people with differing views. This, I think, is why our infographics work, as it is not a singular approach.

Please explain your work process.

Research, lots of it, the more the better! "Please, clients, shower us with everything you have. We don't care if it seems irrelevant to you, we just need to pick through." We do make client meetings when needed, but most of the time it can be done via telephone and e-mail. Blueprints, drawings, sketches, written ideas, anything that the client has, we want. Physical product, even better. We love taking stuff apart, but you will get it back in a body bag.

What is the most complex and time-consuming work you do, and how long does it take to complete?

Most complex without a doubt is a cutaway cruise ship. In creating a cutaway ship, often without blueprints, we rely on a photographer going onboard to do a shoot around, although this is seldom possible because of the ship security arrangements. Again, anything the client has will help, and the best is if the ship is already built. It is searching for holiday snaps taken by people onboard—a lot of times in the background is the very item you are having a problem solving. The ship illustrations are just a 900-hour jigsaw puzzle, but at the end of each one you are exhausted. We also take cruises ourselves to help visualize with the cruise ship industry, take photographs, orientation sketches, etc.

You have many major companies from various industries as clients. Are there jobs you refuse to do?

We do refuse a considerable amount of work, if we don't consider it ethical. We will not do work for hire, but often we can talk our way around the work for hire

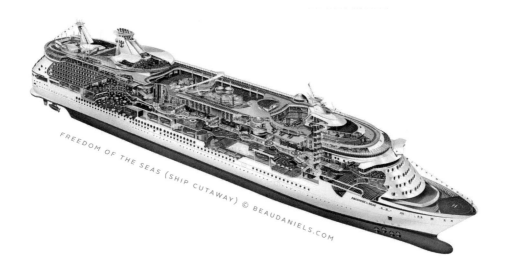

FREEDOM OF THE SEAS (SHIP CUTAWAY) © BEAUDANIELS.COM

because most times, they don't know what they are asking for. Budgets have stagnated, so we will not do cheap jobs. They are the most trouble—it's almost as if because you work cheap, you have undervalued yourself and don't deserve the respect of the client. Recently we have been asked by another cruise line to do five cutaway ships in only three months. They never objected to the budget. We only wish it could have been done.

In 2003, you sued Honda and its ad agency, Rubin Postaer & Associates (RPA), for copyright infringement and won. Many graphic artists would be intimidated by such a large company. Can you briefly describe how your work was infringed, how you discovered the infringements, and why you decided to sue them?

We had no choice but to sue RPA and Honda. They had taken our livelihood away from us. The way we worked on Honda illustrations with RPA was we licensed the images instead of direct sale. When you are looking at maybe 300 illustrations for a car company, if you charged what would be the ideal amount, you probably would not get the work, so

we worked out a way of charging so much the first year and a sliding scale of pricing for subsequent years. This for us was a gamble but one we were pretty sure of. A technical illustration of a cutaway engine will have a shelf life of X number of years. If we can spread that cost, then we would stand a better chance of getting the work, even on a cutaway car. If the body changes, most of the engineering stays the same, so we would charge a license fee plus the cost of any additional changes. This worked well for many years until the bean counters decided that there was a better way of reducing the costs.

It was decided at RPA to get another illustrator or illustrators to copy our work and purchase it from them on a buyout basis. We don't do buyout, work for hire, or ever sell copyright—it's basically all we have. They made a mistake—when we work on that number of illustrations and have been down to the R and D to do a photo shoot, we inevitably will end up missing something. If it were a full cutaway car, for instance, I might have forgotten to shoot the latch on the cupholders. So, we would fake what we thought it should look like in the illustrations. This happens a lot in technical illustration, usually

with insignificant parts. If it were a suspension or engine part, that would be a different story. Anyhow, they copied our mistakes—that was a gotcha moment! RPA did not do due diligence to their client.

How ironic that you could prove they stole your work because they copied your mistakes!

It was a horrible process—one that made me sick. I became obsessed by it, and we fought it tooth and nail. It was not pleasant, but we were not going to let them get away with it. Then we met Greg Victoroff, who became and still is our copyright lawyer. He is tenacious, understanding, and above all a gentleman. Beau calls him our "pet gorilla." I doubt we could have gotten through it without him. That fact alone is frightening—that in order to do battle with these agencies, you have to fight with your money against clients that have in-house lawyers who deal with intellectual property issues all the time. For an individual illustrator, this is a considerable expense. You have to be pretty sure of your facts before embarking on that route.

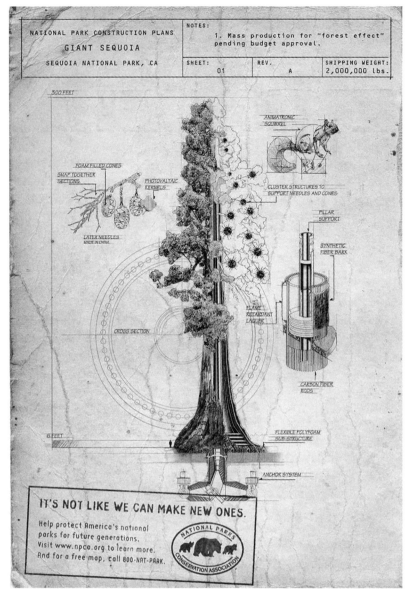

NATIONAL PARK CONSTRUCTION PLANS

GIANT SEQUOIA

SEQUOIA NATIONAL PARK, CA

NOTES:
1. Mass production for "forest effect" pending budget approval.

SHEET: 01 REV. A SHIPPING WEIGHT: 2,000,000 lbs.

300 FEET

ANIMATRONIC SQUIRREL

FOAM FILLED CONES

SNAP TOGETHER SECTIONS

PHOTOVOLTAIC KERNELS

CLUSTER STRUCTURES TO SUPPORT NEEDLES AND CONES

LATEX NEEDLES MADE IN CHINA

PILLAR SUPPORT

SYNTHETIC FIBER BARK

CROSS SECTION

FLAME RETARDANT LACQUER

6 FEET

CARBON FIBER RODS

FLEXIBLE POLYFOAM SUB-STRUCTURE

ANCHOR SYSTEM

IT'S NOT LIKE WE CAN MAKE NEW ONES.

Help protect America's national parks for future generations. Visit www.npca.org to learn more. And for a free map, call 800-NAT-PARK.

NATIONAL PARKS CONSERVATION ASSOCIATION

GIANT SEQUOIA © BEAUDANIELS.COM

Your lawyer credits your meticulous recordkeeping as one of the reasons why your case was successful. What did you learn from this experience?

Here is where Beau steps in. Every conversation with a client and our studio is noted and date-stamped by Beau. She keeps incredible records of everything and can at any instant pull up information relating to the case. Beau always kept records even before catching people stealing our work. Secretly, I think she loves the investigative process—it's just a game to her. It drives me crazy and gives me ulcers.

Does copyright infringement continue to be a big problem for your business?

Copyright issues are a huge problem! We search daily for infringing usages, usually through Google's image search, sometimes TinEye. We will contact the infringers. If they play nice, all is good; if they piss Beau off, then they have a problem. She will not let go. DMCA take-down notices don't seem to do much good. Google will take stuff down, but you have to jump through hoops. Flickr, etc., [are] just about the same. Companies and dodgy web designers don't seem to grasp that it is not a free-for-all out there and that stealing work will have consequences. Their excuses are many, their apologies, if they give them, are worthless, and the attitude upon being caught tends to be belligerent.

Finally, what advice would you give other graphic artists about protecting their intellectual property and making a sustainable living?

REGISTER YOUR COPYRIGHTS.
Registering copyright is very important for us. It's not so bad for us as our work is very expensive, so we can factor that into the cost. For editorial work, it's no less important, but I don't know how the

cost of registration would be absorbed. You just have to be very careful with the form-filling as any mistake will be used against you. Don't expect to get lawyer fees awarded to you. It will most likely not happen—we have filed numerous cases and have never had lawyer fees added. Should you continue to fight? Absolutely! Even just bringing it to the attention of the client may make them think twice in the future.

TAKE A BUSINESS COURSE. It should be mandatory in college. This is a business, not a hobby. A lot of clients will treat you like it's your hobby, and some get exasperated at what you have to charge, but there are a lot of expenses a freelancer has to support that somebody employed does not. I would say follow your passion, but to survive, we followed the money.

THERE ARE NO GUARANTEES. Would I recommend getting into technical illustration in this economic environment, NO. If you have something very individual to express or a very unique style, then give it a shot. You would have to be as lucky as we were, and I think the time for being lucky has run out.

www.beaudaniels.com

STEVEN NOBLE
Carving out a Successful Career
Line by Line

Steven Noble, whose studio is in Petaluma, CA, is internationally recognized as a master of the scratch-board medium. A graduate of the University of California, Davis, Steve has become equally adept in woodcut, pen and ink, traditional engraving, and steel engraving styles. Over the course of his 30-year career, he has created many nationally recognized logos and ad campaigns for a large list of prestigious and high caliber clients, such as Coors, ExxonMobil, JP Morgan, and Mercedes-Benz. In 2008, he was commissioned to create the official logo of the White House. His highly disciplined, precise, and complex line work encompasses a large volume of diverse subject matter that includes food, portraits, animals, maps, architecture, and corporate conceptual images.

In 2016, Steve was recognized by a panel of judges from amongst his peers as one of the 200 Best Illustrators Worldwide. Many of his works have won awards for best logo mark, packaging, and branding. Steve continues to strive for excellence in his work and is always up for the next challenge.

LOGO FOR SLS HOTEL, LAS VEGAS. HAND-CARVED FROM CLAYBOARD © NOBLE ILLUSTRATIONS, INC.

You majored in economics in college, not art. How did you end up with a career in illustration?

My father passed away at the very same time I graduated from college, and I had a change of heart as far as the direction I wanted to take with my career. I met someone who was a commercial artist and he became my mentor.

With your scratchboard illustrations, you have mastered very niche styles that are evocative of the past and simpler times—woodcuts and engraving. How did you get interested in these handcrafted traditional mediums?

I've always loved woodcuts and engravings, since they've remained in style over the ages. I also follow history, and a lot of these mediums have been used by artists in prints going back 500 years, such as the works of Albrecht Dürer.

Please explain the scratchboard process and how you've perfected it.

The scratchboard process begins with a traditional scratchboard—a board covered in a thin coating of fine, white clay and then sprayed with black ink. Handcrafted illustrations are created using a sharp tool to scratch lines through the black ink to reveal white in a negative removal process. Using precision X-acto knives, I'm able to create very fine line strokes, which allow for versatility in the details. Over the years, I've perfected my scratchboard skills so that I can create styles that are evocative of traditional mediums by varying the size and complexity of the lines—from bold cuts that have the rustic feel of a woodcut to the highly detailed and intricate steel engraving technique found on paper currency that simulates old copper plate etching. I also offer etching, line art, and graphic styles.

DISTRÖYA SPIRIT LABEL ILLUSTRATION. HAND-CARVED FROM CLAYBOARD.
© NOBLE ILLUSTRATIONS, INC.

There are self-employed illustrators who say they can't make a living from their art, yet you've been successfully self-employed for 30 years. Besides your incredible talent, what do you attribute your success to?

Having a strong head for business and working both sides of the brain—the fantasy versus the analytical side. I think you either have it or you don't. I've made sure I had financial protection and a buffer for the down times—rental income, investments, stock market, etc. I also circulate passive income back into my business.

Do you think being an economics major helped contribute to your success as an illustrator?

Very little. Most of what I've learned about the business of illustration has come from the real world. Doing everything on the spot and learning the ropes the hard way—trial and error.

An additional revenue stream for you is the sale of stock illustration from your own website. How much of your total revenue comes from selling stock? And, what made you decide to sell your own stock as opposed to going through an agent or a stock house?

It's probably 15–25% of my total income, depending on the year. I've been selling my own stock since the very beginning of my business. I prefer to retain control over my art and not give away 50% to an agency.

You have a separate, easy-to-use website for selling stock. In addition to selling usage licenses of your existing illustrations, you sell what you refer to as "semi-stock." Please explain what that is.

Semi-stock falls halfway between custom illustration and stock illustration. It offers clients the option to license one of my existing illustrations with slight alterations to meet the client's specific needs, without having to create a whole new illustration, and therefore saving money, as opposed to doing a full custom illustration. Because I am doing the alterations or additions to my own illustration, I can create a "new" illustration while keeping the integrity of the original illustration without it looking like a collaged or pasted illustration. The changes are seamless.

CREATING AN UPDATED VERSION OF THE AMERICAN EXPRESS CENTURION USING SCRATCHBOARD FOR A CLASSIC ENGRAVED LOOK.
© NOBLE ILLUSTRATIONS, INC.

Has semi-stock been popular with clients? What do they like about it?

Yes. It gives them an easy process and they don't have to pay as much as they would for a custom illustration. Also, the turnaround time is quicker, so it's a good option if they have a tight deadline.

How difficult has it been to keep track of stock licenses?

It's all done through the stock price quote form process. When clients fill out the quote form on my website, they are asked very specific questions about how they are going to use the illustration. Their responses generate the usage rights they need, which in turn determines price.

Therefore, licenses are easy to track because they are documented right from the very beginning.

Why are the lines in a contract or written agreement just as important as the beautifully executed lines in your illustrations?

Because your intellectual property is your livelihood, you need to stipulate exactly which usage rights you are licensing to a client—including territorial rights, media application, and duration. These are the three basic pieces of information needed to determine costs. Spelling out these usage rights also prevents future misunderstandings and protects

your interests in the event you need to bring legal action against a client for infringement.

Based on your own experience, what advice would you give other self-employed illustrators who are trying to make a sustainable living?

I would recommend that they be completely focused on their career, since it takes a lot of energy, commitment, and perseverance to maintain a consistent and sustainable career.

www.stevennoble.com or **www.scratchboardstock.net**

FINISHED LOGO ON AMERICAN EXPRESS CREDIT CARD. © NOBLE ILLUSTRATIONS, INC.

THE CELEBRATION. ONE OF SIX AWARD-WINNING LABEL ILLUSTRATIONS FOR ESPOLÓN TEQUILA. HAND-CARVED WITH X-ACTO KNIFE ON BLACK-INKED CLAYBOARD. © NOBLE ILLUSTRATIONS, INC.

LAUREN HOM
The Queen of Passion Projects

Lauren Hom is a designer and letterer based in Detroit, schooled in New York, and raised in Los Angeles. She is known for her bright color palettes, playful letterforms, and quirky copywriting. She is also a blogger, author, and workshop presenter. Passionate about side projects and food, Lauren has lettered for lunch and worn bread on her head.

Lauren's clients have included Starbucks, Google, AT&T, YouTube, and *Time* magazine. Her work has been recognized by *Communication Arts*, the Type Directors Club, and the Webby Awards.

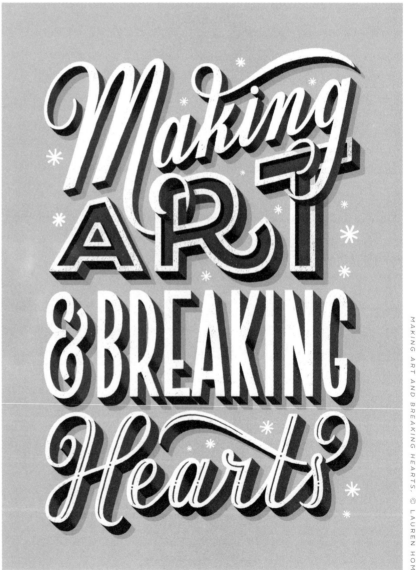

MAKING ART AND BREAKING HEARTS. © LAUREN HOM

What inspires and drives you to do passion projects?

Honestly, I mostly do passion projects for fun. In college, I was inspired by a communication design class taught by Gail Anderson. It was the first class I had where the projects we got were open-ended. Instead of saying, "design a book cover for this specific title," she would give us prompts like, "design a deck of cards about any topic of your choosing," or "design a brand identity for your favorite neighborhood in New York City." That was really interesting to me because I saw people take it in so many different directions, and those open-ended projects were the very first time I started to see my creative voice emerge. I didn't even realize it, but now that I look back, that's where it all began.

All the projects I chose were either about humor, emotions, or food. That class got my brain thinking in a way that a lot of my other classes hadn't. I genuinely loved the creative freedom of making something just for fun. What also drives me with passion projects is having a creative outlet that is all my own, where I get to be the creative director *and* the designer—there are no revisions, and it's really liberating.

When you started your blog Daily Dishonesty *("the beautiful little lies we tell ourselves everyday"), did you have any idea it would jump start your career?*

I truly had no idea that it would jump-start my career. I started *Daily Dishonesty* at the beginning of my senior year of college just for fun to make my girlfriends (and me) laugh, and to have something to do that wasn't advertising. I really loved lettering and drawing. Because I was so immersed in the advertising program, I felt like I wanted a little variety, a break from doing the same kind of ad stuff over and over again. My motivation was, again, to always have something that was entirely mine, that was a creative escape,

that just felt fun to work on. And little white lies that 20-something-year-olds tell themselves was all of those things.

Daily Dishonesty was really light-hearted. I put it on the Internet to have a place where I could send my friends to go check out this collection I was making. With my ad brain, I gave it a catchy name—*Daily Dishonesty*—and bundled it up in a nice little package. Strangers started finding and sharing it, and I didn't expect that. After that experience I realized how powerful a passion project could be. At the very least, if it didn't launch my next thing, I had fun with it. That's why I always operate from a place of fun because then I'm not too upset if it doesn't take off on a marketing or PR level—that's part of my strategy, too.

It would be very enlightening for other graphic artists to see all the opportunities that resulted from that single passion project.

When *Daily Dishonesty* first started spreading, I only posted a dozen or so of them, and they started trending on Tumblr from people re-blogging and sharing them. In the first three months of it being online, my blog gained about 10,000 followers, and that was the very first time that I felt the responsibility of having an audience. I was like, "Oh, wow! People are actually here for this and they're paying attention and I want to keep this updated now because they're expecting new things."

This gave me a great sense of motivation. It was re-blogged enough that people started pinning it to Pinterest and sharing it on design blogs. This momentum started circulating outside of the original platform I hosted it on. Being featured on those design blogs and lifestyle websites gave me a lot of credibility.

From there, a literary agent sent me an e-mail saying, basically, "I found your work on Pinterest and think that this project could be a blog-to-book." I worked with her to put together a pitch

FOODIE WITH A BOOTY © LAUREN HOM

and we ended up selling it as a book with Abrams, a publisher in New York City.

Working on *Daily Dishonesty* for so long also gave me a really solid piece of work to add to my portfolio. Prior to that, I had only been doing odd jobs with freelance work: business cards, wedding invitations, whatever came my way. But having such a large series of lettering work positioned me as a letterer kind of by accident. It wasn't necessarily intentional, but when people see a large volume of work in a certain style on your site or blog, they assume that's what you're specialized in.

People were starting to reach out specifically for lettering projects—and I said "yes" to all of them. They started off as very small projects, and then slightly bigger ones, and then larger clients started finding me. These baby steps definitely got the ball rolling for the bigger projects I do now. The reason that I book bigger work now is because I built up that credibility all the way from the start, six or seven years ago.

Daily Dishonestly also was directly responsible for landing me my very first big editorial project, which was illustrating the headline in a feature article spread in *Los Angeles Magazine*. The creative director found me while he was browsing on a popular type blog called Type Everything. He reached out with, "Hey, I saw one of your pieces on this blog and I think it's perfect for our feature spread. I'm putting you through to my boss right now and I'd like to hire you." He specifically referenced this one piece to pitch me to the editor-in-chief that said, "I'm not scared of the dark." It was swirly and on a navy background with gold embellishments.

After that issue hit newsstands, about a dozen other editorial projects lined up within the following year. One little insider tip is that the creative departments at regional and city magazines oftentimes subscribe to other regional and city magazines, and because of that, I got exposure with a lot of publications outside of Los Angeles. This led to a bunch of covers and interior spreads—and similar to my other earlier projects, things slowly built up from there. So, in addition to all the freelance work I was getting, this domino effect also marked the start of this particular avenue of my career.

Daily Dishonesty also won me a lot of credibility through design awards. Due to the positive feedback I was receiving from followers, how it went viral online, and the amount of freelance work I was getting from it, I gained the confidence to pay the fee to enter it into these competitions. I ended up walking away with a handful of really powerful industry awards that I could now link to in my portfolio, which gave me even more credibility.

Essentially, most of the work I'm doing now is directly tied to *Daily Dishonesty*, even though it was almost seven years ago. And I'm really, really grateful for that. It was also the catalyst for a lot of people to start following my work. Whenever I go to events or conferences, I am always particularly charmed when people come up to me and say they've been following me since my Tumblr days. It's really sweet and proof of the power of a really authentic passion project—something that you make from your heart that you find amusing or powerful, and it connects you with the

right people. When someone sees your work and they connect with it, they might become a lifelong follower or fan and maybe even a potential client.

You said you didn't want to become a "one trick pony" and needed to build your lettering portfolio, so you came up with Will Letter for Lunch. ***How did restaurants react to your offer to letter their daily specials in exchange for food?***

Because most restaurants had chalkboards already, it wasn't like I was an alien coming in and offering some completely foreign service. I assumed someone at the restaurant had to be doing the chalkboard. So, there was at least that connection that made pitching a little bit easier. Within a week and a half or so of pitching my idea, I had an e-mail from someone who was interested.

Did you get any commissions as a result of this project?

I ended up getting a lot of commissions as a result of this project, too. I originally started the project to build my chalkboard skills, expand my lettering portfolio, and try something new. Again, my goal was to package it up as a nice bite-sized idea. The commissions that I first received were mostly repeat clients from the restaurants I had worked with for *Will Letter for Lunch*. I would go in and offer to do their chalkboards, but I only did one per week and one per restaurant. If I originally agreed to do a restaurant's chalkboard for barter and then a month later, they e-mailed me saying, "Hey, we really loved the chalkboard you did for us. Can you come back and do another one?" I would say something like, "As a rule, I only ever do one barter per restaurant. However, if you had a budget for something like this, I'd be happy to come in." And that's how it started.

Then I'd get bigger requests from restaurants that wanted something larger

than an A-frame chalkboard. If they wanted anything that was significantly larger than the menu special I was offering, I would say something like, "I usually limit these to just the A-frames, but if you wanted something bigger, we can do a partial barter, part cash." I started negotiating up from there. And by setting those parameters for myself, I was able to start charging for that work.

Now my portfolio had a lot of restaurant chalkboards as well as some slightly bigger restaurant menu boards and projects to show. From there, I started doing chalk projects for bigger clients who weren't even necessarily in the restaurant industry. I got hired by Chobani and Linkedin to do chalkboard murals in their headquarters in New York City. You'll see a trend here—it honestly just snowballed from there. I started getting inquiries from more and more businesses.

I was hired to do a chalk lettering mural for The Culinary Institute of America, but they had me do it digitally, and then printed it out, and put it on the wall of their Student Center. That was successful, so I started doing digital chalk projects where I wasn't physically going in and doing the work. I was just creating from my Wacom tablet with a chalk-like Photoshop brush. After The Culinary Institute mural, I got a big commercial job with Samuel Adams.

What happened with *Will Letter for Lunch* was the same thing that happened with *Daily Dishonesty*, where the project started small, got a little bit bigger, and then it built upon itself more and more. Once I had the confirmation that, "Okay, I did both of these projects and had similar results," I realized how powerful these types of projects were, and that there was a process to them. That experience definitely got the gears turning about using passion projects as a strategic tool that I could use whenever I needed or wanted something in my career or had a specific goal in mind. From that point on, I knew I had this tool in my back pocket to explore future avenues for growth.

Your Flour Crowns (bread on your head) passion project looks so professionally produced that it could be an ad campaign for companies that sell bakery products. Later, you revealed in your blog just how inexpensive the production side really was. Did the food cost more than the production expenses?

I'd say that the cost of all of the food probably totaled just as much as the other stuff I used like lighting, background, additional products, and the headbands. My takeaway here is that you don't necessarily need a lot to make a passion project. I used a digital camera that I already had, a Canon G7 X, which is a middle-range digital camera. I opted for natural lighting, either early in the morning or when the sun wasn't super high in the sky. I would shoot in the backyard at my grandma's house—so fancy, I know. For the backdrops, I bought these 48-inch wide paper rolls from Amazon. For the materials, I found some cheap headbands and wire, a glue gun, and then bought the food—that was really it.

My setup wasn't very glamorous, but I've always been resourceful, so I knew that I could achieve the look I wanted without spending a ton of money. One problem that a lot of creatives run into is that you get an idea for a passion project, but you're hesitant to spend a lot of money on it because you're just betting on the results. There's no guarantee that this passion project is going to pay off in any way or get you more projects or get you featured anywhere. It's totally understandable. I felt this way and started thinking, "What's the lowest production cost I could have for this project while still getting my idea across?" And that's the formula I tend to use with my projects because I'm a big believer in the possibility of ideas being executed well without having to be wildly expensive. The hardest part of this project was achieving a high fashion look. Figuring out how to pose and get the right

look was challenging because I knew that the juxtaposition of me in full makeup and a nice dress with this crown of bread on my head would be more impactful with more contrast and would be funnier if I nailed the high fashion feel.

One thing that I've always believed to be true is that good ideas are more important than good production value. It's still important to have your project look nice and presented well, but it's not as important as a lot of people might think. If production value and cost are the thing holding you back from a passion project, I highly recommend reconsidering your approach or getting creative with how you can make it happen within your budget constraints.

I believe that, whether you're a student or you're working full-time or funds are tight, you can find a way to use what you have and still create something that will pack a punch. Figure out how to simplify the artwork so you can make it more manageable with your schedule. Because what you don't want to do is dream too big and make every piece take 25 hours to complete. If you come out of the gate guns blazing but your project isn't manageable, you'll find yourself three weeks in, completely burnt out, and unable to keep up with it.

I always err on the side of setting realistic expectations and parameters because I know I'm so much more likely to stick with something if it's manageable. I'm conservative when it comes to how intricate the project is and how much I can actually add to my plate, which has allowed me to produce a consistent stream of work over time.

Have you received any work as a result of Flour Crowns?

I haven't received any client work from the *Flour Crowns* project. However, I did have Wix (the website builder) reach out wanting to sponsor the passion project's website. So, I did a sponsorship with them, a couple of social media posts, and a blog post. That was the only way *Flour*

Crowns has directly monetized itself. But indirectly, I got a bunch of press for it and was written up in a number of creative blogs, so if anything, it's helped me stand out from the crowd and build rapport with my audience. It was a fun opportunity to show off my personality. After all, I don't know how many other lettering artists out there have a silly series of photographs of bread on their heads! It makes me chuckle every single time I see it, and people bring it up all the time. I'd say one out of every four or five clients will mention something like, "Oh, by the way, I love your *Flour Crowns* project."

You've been quoted when asked about finding an audience for your side projects that you design for your own demographic. Why does that make sense?

I have a saying that "I like to design for me and my friends," aka my own demographic, because I know myself best. The Internet connects us in ways that humans have never been connected before, so there are definitely people out there who are like you, who like what you like, who are going through the same things, or who have the same sense of humor as you do, even if they're not geographically close to you. I believe that I am my best marketer because I am also my own target audience. Anything that I find funny, people like me are going to find funny, too. So, I use myself and my girlfriends as my target audience.

It's also more fun to make stuff that you like, instead of agonizing over trying to find the perfect audience fit for your work. People who are like you will eventually stumble across it and gravitate towards it.

It's also important to design for universal experiences like emotions and everyday things. This belief came from something they taught us in ad school— to always consider human truths, or things that most humans do. I always tell people that they're probably sitting on a gold mine of ideas that are right out of their daily lives and they just haven't uncovered them yet.

With *Daily Dishonesty*, for instance, I picked up on the fact that my friends and I all lied about these little things. I thought it was just a silly commonality among my friends and me, but it also resonated with tens of thousands of other people on the Internet who also lied about little mundane things, like, "I'm not drinking this weekend." Or, "I'll just have one bite." It struck a universal chord because humans, no matter where we're from or how we were brought up, experience a lot of the same emotions.

Another example is a project I did in 2013, after I went through a really bad breakup. I was hurting and because I was feeling snarky and sassy, I lettered the phrase "Ex Boyfriend Tears" on a flask and a cup, and I started selling them online. It turned out that couples break up all the time (unfortunately), so there were other people out there who thought the flask was funny and relatable. I sold about $10,000 worth of them, much to my surprise! The demand was so high that I kept making more and more. It was definitely a validating experience of navigating this painful breakup and trying to make light of it in a way that resonated with so many other people.

You have several revenue streams, in addition to client work—online workshops and courses, speaking engagements, and sale of products. What revenue stream has been most lucrative?

Surprisingly, the most lucrative revenue stream has been online classes. I had no idea how successful these could be! I earned money teaching a Skillshare class and a Brit+Co class, which are third-party online class platforms where they produce the class for you, but it wasn't what I would consider super lucrative. However, I had fun doing them. So, I started teaching in-person workshops and realized that I really loved

connecting with people, sharing what I know, and answering questions. But I also realized that in-person workshops couldn't scale because there is a very real maximum number of people you can teach at one time.

Then, at the suggestion of a woman that I met while traveling (who would later end up being my business coach), I started to produce and teach my own online classes in marketing, passion projects, and lettering. I created my very first online course called Passion to Paid, where I basically took the formula that worked for me personally and taught people how to apply it to their own ideas, and how to use that to market themselves.

At the time I put it online, I had an audience of maybe 60,000 people, which was a decent size, but not big enough to really gauge what would come of it. The course ended up selling like crazy, and I made more money in those two weeks the class launched than I had from any singular client project, ever!

Previously, client work was the thing that was the main revenue generator, but then I realized the power of online courses because of the scalability. I can only teach about 20 to 30 people at a time with an in-person workshop, but with pre-recorded online courses, I was able to take in 250 students at once, which was a very exciting and powerful reality of the online platform.

It's still worth teaching in person because not everyone wants to learn lettering online, even though a decent amount of people do. Online courses also appeal to certain people—maybe you have social anxiety and you don't want to go into a workshop environment or be around other people. If you can learn from the comfort of your own home, that's really enticing as well.

At first, one of my hesitations about teaching online was I questioned if I had the credibility to teach online. I didn't realize that three years leading up to my online teaching had been full of answering e-mails from students who

were interested in my work and doing interviews on design blogs. I was always really generous with my knowledge via my Instagram page and through tutorials because I liked answering people's questions and they were fun. By doing all of these things, I was unknowingly priming myself to teach and be recognized as an expert in the field. So, when I launched my very first classes, I was blown away by the response and I know it was directly tied to me being so generous with my audience in the years prior.

Now, I would say that about 40% of my income is from teaching online and in-person, another 40% is client work, and the remaining 20% is speaking engagements and social media influencer opportunities. Teaching completely changed my business model. I originally thought I was going to just freelance 100% of the time, maybe sell some posters on the side, and that would be it. But I've realized that things can change really quickly, and I had to pivot. I started in advertising and then I moved to freelance lettering, and now I'm doing lettering and teaching. I have made all these pivots in just seven years, which makes me excited and curious for what the next seven years will hold.

I think that's the mindset that a lot of freelancers, especially creative freelancers, need to have now. What works today might not work in a year, or two or three years down the road. But if you use your creativity and are up for a challenge, you'll figure out how to adapt to the moving digital landscape and what people want, and you'll be able to figure out a path for yourself.

You did not major in art or design in college. Instead, you majored in advertising. Did your education turn out to be an asset or a hindrance to your career as a self-employed creative?

When I quit my advertising job, I had a lot of anxiety and stress around the feeling that I had wasted four years of school and almost a year of my professional life in advertising. I thought that I had to completely start over from scratch and was going to be five years behind everybody else. But in reality, it ended up being an asset because of the skills that I learned in advertising, like creative problem solving, conceptual thinking, and working on deadlines with briefs. All of that came in handy as a self-employed creative because it's helped with getting my work shared online, branding myself, and working with clients.

When I was on my own doing passion projects, I realized that this whole time, I was selling myself, using the same skills I learned to sell a product. But now the product was myself.

You should be excited about yourself, too, and believe in your skills and the product you sell, along with the value you bring. When you think of yourself in a higher regard and believe that you are valuable, it's a lot easier to promote yourself and sell yourself in an authentic (non-cheesy) way. Confidence plays a big role in your success. Willingness to put yourself out there and make the thing you want to make requires being true to yourself.

Do you have any pearls of wisdom to pass along to other creatives about the importance or benefits of doing passion projects?

THINK OF PASSION PROJECTS AS A NECESSARY THING TO DO IF YOU WANT TO BE A SUCCESSFUL FREELANCER—NOT JUST A NICE-TO-HAVE. Personal work is necessary for satisfaction, motivation, and for growing your business.

PASSION PROJECTS HELP ESTABLISH YOUR VOICE AND BRAND. If you only put client work in your portfolio, then you're building your portfolio only based on other people's projects and what they think your work is good for. This will then begin to dictate your voice instead

of you dictating your own voice. Passion projects establish your presence, so people know who you are, what you're all about, and what to hire you for.

PASSION PROJECTS CAN BE REALLY POWERFUL BECAUSE WORKING ON A SERIES IS MORE IMPACTFUL THAN WORKING ON A ONE-OFF PIECE. There's nothing wrong with making individual pieces of work, but when you work in a series like _Flour Crowns_ where there are 20–40 pieces under one umbrella concept, it gives you a foundation for talking about your work over and over again. It gives people something to follow along with, and it is more ownable because it differentiates you.

PERSONAL WORK IS A GREAT WAY TO STAY IN CONTROL OF YOUR CAREER. One thing I've been telling myself a lot this year is "you are always in the driver's seat." If something's not going your way or something isn't satisfying you, you are in control of figuring out a way to fix that—and for me, passion projects are the way that I shift the gears of my self-employed creative career. They provide a way to steer your career in whatever direction you want to go. It's important as a freelancer to regularly self-evaluate and figure out what you want, and in what direction you want to head in.

IF YOU MAKE PASSION PROJECTS THAT ARE ABOUT THINGS THAT YOU'RE EXCITED ABOUT, IT MAKES PEOPLE EXCITED ABOUT YOU. People who work with me now will oftentimes bring up _Flour Crowns_ or _Daily Dishonesty_. They're excited to work with me because I created these projects that excited them, too, even though they're hiring me for something completely different.

I am just one of tens of thousands of lettering artists. Even though I've done work for big clients, people don't necessarily associate me with those projects right away. When I meet people, they associate me as the designer who did _Daily Dishonesty_ or _Will Letter for Lunch_. People remember my passion

WORK HARD SNACK OFTEN MURAL
© LAUREN HOM

project the most because they have the most of my personality tied to them, and they're completely unique to me. When I do passion projects, it makes me feel like I have this one special thing—even if it's just one thing that makes me different than everybody else, and I love that.

DO PERSONAL WORK BECAUSE EVEN IF IT'S JUST FOR YOU, EVEN IF IT'S JUST FOR FUN, ACTION LEADS TO MORE ACTION. No matter how good things are going right now, no matter how much you want a change from your current situation, you should be working on passion projects. And I intend to do the exact same thing, hopefully for the very lengthy span of my creative career.

www.homsweethom.com

SEAN KANE
Hitting a Home Run with a Niche Project

Sean Kane is an illustrator raised in the Chicago area, with stops around the Pacific Northwest, who now calls Ontario, Canada, home. A professional artist for 25 years, he has created illustrations for clients in the publishing and corporate worlds, including *The New York Times*, Amazon.com, *The Wall Street Journal*, Charles Schwab, and Target stores, among others. In 2011, Sean teamed his illustration skills with his passion for baseball to create a niche market for unique, hand-painted baseball gloves.

ESPN.com, NBC Sports.com, and MLB Network Radio have featured Sean's baseball glove artwork, and in January 2016, he was named "Artist of the Month" by the National Art Museum of Sport. His custom baseball gloves have been commissioned by baseball organizations, Hall of Fame players, and fans as well as purchased by collectors. The gloves have been featured in several exhibits and are in the collections of the National Baseball Hall of Fame & Museum, Cooperstown, and the Negro Leagues Baseball Museum, Kansas City.

ANDRE DAWSON © 2019 SEAN KANE

Where did you get the idea for painting custom baseball gloves?

Between illustration projects in early 2001, leading up to a trip to Arizona to watch Spring Training, I grabbed an old glove that was in my studio and started painting a cartoonish baseball design on it—a player eating a hot dog, a pennant, the words, "Play Ball," etc. I wanted something fun to have as a conversation starter with other fans. Even better, Tony Gwynn, a Hall-of-Fame player with the Padres, said he liked it and autographed it.

Ten years later, as the market for editorial illustration shifted and my efforts at licensing art for products were limping along, the glove hung on my studio wall and generated more interest from visitors than anything else I had on display! With gentle nudging from a business coach, I began imagining how the glove idea could evolve into a new art form and possible side project incorporating my personal interests and art and design skills.

How important was baseball to you growing up? What player did you choose to paint on a glove first?

Baseball was a big part of growing up—watching baseball in the afternoons at my grandparents' house, playing Little League and neighborhood Wiffleball games, and going to Cubs and White Sox games—not to mention collecting cards and newspaper clippings and writing to teams requesting stickers and anything else they'd send me. Baseball took up a large portion of my time and imagination. I even painted my batting helmets to match favorite team logos at the time!

Babe Ruth was the first player I painted when I revisited the glove idea in 2011 and began experimenting with the whole concept, designs, and materials.

What was your first attempt at marketing the idea?

The first baby steps were e-mails and photos to a few sports blogs, which didn't lead to much. Then in the fall of 2012, I cold contacted (via LinkedIn!) a former L.A. Dodgers General Manager, who also had Chicago roots. To my surprise, he responded with great enthusiasm and encouragement.

With his positive response, I decided to unofficially invite myself to the Baseball Winter Meetings in Nashville a few weeks later! It was time to see what I could learn about the industry and get feedback about the viability of my art within the baseball world.

I researched who else I might be able to meet while lingering around the lobby and wandering the baseball industry trade show. I ordered a clear carrying bag which, when slung over my shoulder, became a walking art gallery for two gloves and I carried a third in my hand with a notebook and newly printed postcards. It was a great way for busy baseball folks to quickly glimpse the gloves. I met the former Dodgers GM, who then kindly, unexpectedly, invited journalist friends to stop and take a look at my creations on the vintage gloves.

You really put a lot of thought into that marketing opportunity.

The whole experience—sharing the work on the sidelines of the event and meeting people in baseball—was simultaneously scary and fun (and exhausting). It was also a confidence booster, receiving the input I had hoped for while putting myself and my work out there in a very unorthodox way—at least compared to the way I had marketed myself as an illustrator via direct mail or exhibiting at an art licensing show.

When did you realize there was a viable market for your gloves?

Within hours of being introduced to a few baseball media people at the Winter Meetings—even before I got back to my hotel room—there was an article about my work on the NBC Sports.com website. I was up until the early hours of the morning answering e-mails and talking to prospective buyers on the West Coast who were interested in a Jackie Robinson painted glove. My wife was getting calls at home. A couple of days later there was the top mention in an ESPN holiday gift guide, and I was interviewed on MLB Network Radio. It was an intense and exciting time, and it confirmed for me that I might really be onto something good with this very niche idea.

Who are your customers and how does your love of the game resonate with them?

My customers include a wide range of baseball people, including Major League teams, baseball-related institutions/charities, former and current players, including Hall of Famers, and their friends and families, and individual collectors who buy for themselves or to give as gifts. Each project or request is unique, which certainly keeps things interesting—from retirement gifts given as on-field presentations and 40th birthday presents to auction items and private keepsakes.

I've been told by collectors that they appreciate the way I display the history of the game and how I'm able to bring a player's story alive, which is music to my ears and exactly what I strive for.

Andre Dawson, a Hall of Famer who played for the Cubs when I was growing up, called me to create a glove for him. I nearly fell out of my chair! He had seen my work at an event we were both at. Once I delivered the glove, he said he liked it so much that he decided to keep it for himself instead of giving it as a gift, which was his initial intention. This is my version of hitting a home run!

You promote your gloves on your website and you've received a lot of press. Do you have to do any additional marketing?

Yes. The other marketing I do includes attending a couple of baseball-related events each year, as an exhibitor or guest, which gives me a chance to share my work in face-to-face settings. Also, I participate in at least one exhibit each year, usually a group show of sports art or baseball art. Lastly, I send a quarterly newsletter to my mailing list with updates on projects, upcoming events, or other items they may find interesting. Posting on social media occasionally, too.

Your passion for baseball also shows in every detail of your paintings and even in the gloves themselves. Explain how much research you do before starting a painting and why it's important to you that it be as authentic as possible.

At least half of the time for a glove project is usually spent learning about the player(s) to be featured and their career, including photo references to base a portrait on. This research is usually happening in tandem with my effort to source a glove from their playing era, relevant to the position they played and what hand they caught with. Sometimes gloves from the 1980s are harder to locate than 100-year-old gloves. I pour over graphics from the era in which the player played—everything from movie posters and ticket stubs to stadium signs and baseball uniform databases.

The inputs from the research and finding the right "canvas" are important so that I have as good a chance as possible to create an object that will transport, in a way, the viewer to the time and place related to the player and help to capture

their story. The glove art isn't meant to be a historical artifact, necessarily, but more of a concise visual story bringing all the elements together into an orderly, hopefully beautiful, design. It's still illustration in that way, I feel!

Where do you find the vintage gloves?

Primarily from specialty sports antiques dealers. Sometimes on eBay. Other times directly from teams and glove manufacturers when I'm working on something for a current or recent player. Collectors also send me their own gloves to be painted, which is an honor and thrill!

Once I was sent a new Gold Glove from Rawlings for a special project for Cal Ripken Jr.'s foundation. And for personal projects, I've waited five years to find just the right antique glove.

I'm careful not to use mitts that are inherently valuable on their own; I prefer the neglected ones that I can bring back

to life. I wouldn't want to paint on Babe Ruth's actual glove, for instance!

On average, how much time does one glove take to complete and how much does a commissioned glove cost?

I typically spend 100–120 hours on a painted glove, including all of the research, glove sourcing, design time, hand-lettering and, finally, painting. Plus, the half-day it usually takes to package a glove to ship and photograph it before it leaves the studio.

Currently (late 2019) custom commissioned gloves start at $4000 and go up, depending on design complexity, multiple portraits, glove sourcing, framing requests, etc.

You still do your regular illustration work for clients as well as the gloves, and you also sell associated baseball products, such as a book, greeting cards, and postcards of the glove art.

BUCK O'NEIL © 2019 SEAN KANE

THURMAN MUNSON (TOP), JEFF BAGWELL (MIDDLE), LOU GEHRIG (BOTTOM) © 2019 SEAN KANE

What percent of your total annual revenue comes from the baseball niche market versus your other client illustration work?

The baseball-related work comprises about three-quarters of my art business revenue now.

That's amazing! The glove art seems to be more than just a niche market for you—it's more like a passion project preserving the history of baseball. For example, explain what you are doing for the 2020 exhibit at your alma mater, Butler University in Indianapolis.

The exhibit at Butler will present baseball glove art I've painted over the last decade and will highlight the game's history and Indiana connections. These Hoosier-inspired pieces will touch on the Negro Leagues (which had its first league game in Indianapolis), the Federal League, Women in Baseball (two *A League of Their Own* teams were in Indiana), Integration, and Music in the Game ("Take Me Out to The Ballgame" was composed by an Indianapolis native!). It'll be exciting if the work can introduce some of the local connections to baseball's history or refresh memories of them.

You donate one glove each year to a charity. Why do you believe in giving back?

Basically, it's fun and feels right. I like knowing that my skills, the thing that comes easiest to me, can be used for good and to help someone or a group. Money raised via my donated work over the years has been part of funding for inner-city youth baseball, mental health services, etc. I'm not sure how else to apply my skills to helping real-world problems, so this seems like one small way and I need to do more.

In 2019, one of your gloves, featuring pitcher "Dizzy Dean," was voted into the National Baseball Hall of Fame and Museum collection joining "works of art that contribute to the museum's mission of preserving history, honoring excellence, and connecting generations." How did you feel when you heard your work was accepted?

I was thrilled, of course! I wasn't going to be represented in the Hall of Fame as a ball player, that's for sure, so knowing my art is in the collection for fans to enjoy is pretty exciting. A proud moment, definitely.

If you were to coach other graphic artists who are considering creating a niche market for their work, what tips would you give them?

CUT OUT THE GUESSWORK AND ASSUMPTIONS. As early as possible, get direct input from people working in the niche or those who you think would be customers. Online input could work, but I found that getting out of my studio for in-person meetings and "show and tell" were the most productive for getting solid, usable feedback.

GO DEEP—GET INVOLVED IN THE INDUSTRY, GO TO EVENTS, JOIN TRADE GROUPS, ETC. I can't over-emphasize how meaningful it has been to be present, in real life. Friendship possibilities aside, it makes business sense, and it's surprising how quickly one can become recognized in a niche or industry.

ESTABLISH CREDIBILITY EARLY WITHIN THE NICHE. Without being too much of a self-promoter, it doesn't hurt to get a few personal endorsements, quotes, or recognized publications on your bio. It will help prospective customers in your niche to gain trust with your product or service.

SAY "YES" OFTEN. I said "Yes" a lot when I was starting this work, probably more than I should have if looking at things from a work/life balance and dollars and cents point of view. But, "yes" allowed me to stretch in many ways—to realize what works and what doesn't, what clients or events or pricing solutions worked, what was going to suck all the life and time out of my art practice, and, over time, what to ultimately narrow my focus on.

www.seankane.com

JAMES & JON SHOLLY
A Brotherly Contribution to Preserving Design History

PHOTOS COURTESY OF POLINA OSHEROV

Brothers James and Jon Sholly are the talent behind the Indianapolis-based design studio known as Commercial Artisan, founded in 1990. Their work for a diverse group of clients—foundations, arts institutions, corporations, universities, and friends—is rooted in a belief that there is a creative opportunity to be found in every assignment. In addition to their client work, the brothers publish *Commercial Article*, which explores under-documented design figures from Indiana.

Commercial Artisan's work has appeared in many publications including design journals *Emigré* and *Metropolis*. They have been honored by *Print Magazine*, *Communication Arts*, American Center for Design, and AIGA, among others. Their projects have been included in major exhibitions at the Cooper-Hewitt, Smithsonian Design Museum, the Walker Art Center, and their alma mater, the Herron School of Art and Design. In 2018, James was honored by Herron with its Distinguished Alumnus Award. James and Jon were also the interior book designers for the 13th and 14th editions of this handbook.

What influenced each of you to study graphic design?

JAMES: Although we probably didn't think about it at the time, we grew up surrounded by the Scandinavian design that our parents favored and brought into our house. I think that this instilled an appreciation for simplicity that we frequently employ in our own work. Once I realized that designing album covers was a job, I was hooked!

JON: As a kid I watched Jim progress through a design education and the creation of a design practice, so this was naturally a huge influence. Outside of that, I was attracted to alternative comic books, punk and underground music, and the 1980s DIY culture. While in high school I started making flyers for local bands, and I see that as my entry into life as a graphic designer.

You moved around a lot growing up. What made you decide to settle in Indianapolis?

JAMES: Jon and I are Army brats and grew up moving all over the country. I was in my third year of art school when my dad received his orders to relocate to Kansas. I wanted to finish my education and was a little tired of always being uprooted, so I decided to stick around. I began making connections and little by little became established here. Indianapolis is a really nice place to live. It's also generally perceived as a design underdog, which makes upending people's expectations extremely satisfying.

JON: My parents decided to return to Indianapolis after our dad retired from the military. Initially, I stayed behind in Kansas, but a general lack of focus led me to eventually follow them. It took me a while to acclimate, but the city is filled with numerous tiny surprises and

POSTER FOR CONCERT AT LUNA MUSIC, FEATURING SINGER/SONGWRITER MARK KOZELEK OF SUN KIL MOON. © COMMERCIAL ARTISAN 2019

handle most of our client meetings, billing, and general office stuff.

JON: I've found that working on the technical aspects of the job has been where my strengths lie and I derive a lot of satisfaction in that area.

How do you approach jobs—do you collaborate on each project or do you divide up the jobs?

JAMES: It's ideal to be able to collaborate on every project, but it doesn't always happen. More times than not, one of us—usually me—will begin chasing an idea, and the other one will join in when it makes sense. I always say that I'm the big brother, so Jon's used to me bossing him around!

JON: While I'd say it's true that I'm used to being "bossed around," the way we work together has evolved quite naturally, and I don't think either of us thinks much about it. No matter what the project is, we'll always bounce ideas off each other, and I personally will ask him for some of that "Jim magic" when my idea well runs dry.

Do you ever disagree about the design direction of a project, and if so, how do you deal with disagreements?

JAMES: People always say that if they worked with their sibling, it would either be the greatest thing ever, or they would kill each other. Fortunately, we're in the former category. We rarely disagree about a project's direction, but we're typically able to work through disagreements when they happen. In the end, I never feel like it's one person's direction, and we're both able to bring what we want to the project.

JON: Of course we disagree at times, but we don't have too much difficulty resolving them. We've been like that our whole lives, so it makes sense that's how we work together. Hopefully, this won't sound too precious, but Jim's a pretty brilliant design thinker, so it's not hard to get on board with his ideas if I'm not feeling particularly confident in mine.

continues to evolve in mostly positive ways. It hasn't been difficult to stay here.

It's somewhat unusual to find brothers working together in a design business. How did that happen?

JAMES: I had been working on my own when Jon decided to attend the Herron School of Art + Design. When he had time, he began to help me when I had small tasks or projects that required assistance. It was really great to have him around, so as graduation drew nearer, we started talking about the possibility of him joining me.

JON: I admired Jim and the work he was doing, so it was a given that I wanted to try to work with him at some point. I had no idea if I'd actually be *good enough* to work with him when I graduated, but I applied myself very hard in school and thankfully made the cut!

Do you each have your own specialties or skill sets?

JAMES: It used to be that we were both involved in the design of every project, but as the years have gone by, my role has become more Art Director and Jon is more of the hands-on designer. I also

As self-employed designers, how do you deal with the feast or famine nature of the business? What have you done to protect yourselves financially during the downtimes?

JAMES: I think one of the reasons we've been around as long as we have is that the terror of slow times never really goes away. Our history will show that work always picks back up again, but I can never remember that fact when we're in the middle it. That fear is a great motivating factor to make new calls, update our website, find time for lunch with a vendor, or any of the other things we should be doing when we're busy. We've always kept a low overhead—our studio is in my house—and tried to be reasonable about spending, so times aren't as tough when work slows down.

A large side project for you is working to preserve regional design history through the publication of Commercial Article, each issue exploring the work of an Indiana design figure whose life and work you feel has been under-documented. What was the inspiration behind this project?

JAMES: Around 2005 we began to create a self-promotion for the studio but couldn't arrive at an approach that didn't seem embarrassing. We joked about it being much easier and interesting if we could create a self-promotion that instead talked about how great some other designer was. It was a silly idea, but it resonated with us, so we started thinking about our local design heroes whose work and lives had never been properly documented. It took a few issues to hit our stride, but we're now working on our 13th issue and have had the opportunity to profile little known or forgotten Indiana figures from graphic, architectural, industrial, fashion, environmental, and consumer design disciplines.

How much research do you have to do and what are your sources?

JAMES: A lot of time goes into research. We work with a writer who helps develop the focus of the story and does most of the legwork to track down sources, while Jon and I attempt to track down examples of the subject's work or other important visual material. Throughout the process, we communicate closely with the writer and exchange information, which typically comes from family members, friends, archives, historical societies, and eBay. This part can take up to six months before we even begin considering the design. Then another four to five months to design, proof, and produce the printed publication. Part of the reason it takes so long is that most of the work is done outside of our regular studio and client-based work.

You've published 12 issues so far. What subject was the most interesting or perhaps the most surprising?

JAMES: They're all fascinating and fun to immerse yourself in as they're happening, but there are a few that stand out.

Leslie Ayres was a Fred Astaire-like architect who worked primarily from the 1930s to the 1950s and whose work was barely known in Indianapolis, despite his many achievements in the city. During the course of investigating his life and work, obscure and surprising connections led us to a distant relative who was in possession of a large number of Ayres's renderings that hadn't seen the light of day for more than 60 years. We were able to connect the relative to a local architectural archive where the drawings will now be cared for, so future researchers will have access to them.

Xenia Miller was a really surprising figure. We knew that she was a patron of art and architecture throughout central Indiana, but we had no idea what a significant contribution she made—particularly in her vision for the Miller

House, the masterpiece credited to Eero Saarinen.

JON: Every issue's been enlightening, and it really is difficult to determine who was the most interesting. I personally found the experience of working on *Commercial Article 04: Marshall Studios* to be where the potential for this ongoing project really took off.

We had been somewhat aware of Marshall Studios (Jane & Gordon Martz) ceramics and felt this would be a good subject to focus on. In our initial research, Jim found a website outlining the history of Marshall Studios. The man who created and maintained this site lived only a few miles from us. He had located the abandoned and deteriorating Marshall Studios factory and showroom in Veedersburg, IN, where he discovered and saved a treasure trove of documents, photographs, catalogs, and other ephemera. This literal garbage became the bulk of reference and visual materials for the issue. We also decided to play with the format of this issue, and rather than producing a saddle stitched booklet, we printed a single large sheet that folded down to the same dimensions as the previous issues. One side of this sheet was a "newspaper" laid out with all the text and supplemental images; the other side was a poster featuring a life-sized image of one of the beautiful Marshall Studios lamps.

After this issue, I felt that our creative opportunities with *Commercial Article* were huge.

You sell copies of Commercial Article from your website, and it was included in a touring graphic design exhibition at major museums. Besides being a labor of love, has it had other benefits for you, such as being an additional revenue stream or promoting your business?

JAMES: Sales, with a few exceptions, have always been modest. So, it's not really a revenue stream—maybe an expense stream!!! We learned early on that the act of documenting this history and encountering the people that care about it is what makes the process so rewarding. It's been helpful in connecting us to other people concerned with design history and has probably become the one project that we're most associated with.

So, it sounds as if Commercial Article is most beneficial for preserving regional design history. Why is this important to you, and what are your plans for the future of the project?

JAMES: Preserving and recording Indiana's design history has become a mission for us. Our efforts are modest and meant to be an introduction to our subjects. In some instances, if we hadn't documented certain designers, their stories and the remarkable work would be lost. This would be tragic. So many important designs disappear when the designer passes away, or they languish under beds or in closets until they're thrown out. Our recent issue about Stupid, Inc. is a perfect example. An Internet search for this Mad Men-era producer of novelty stationery will yield zero results, except for our publication. It's only because one person saved examples of this very funny work that we have the content to record and share with our readers.

COMMERCIAL ARTICLE 12

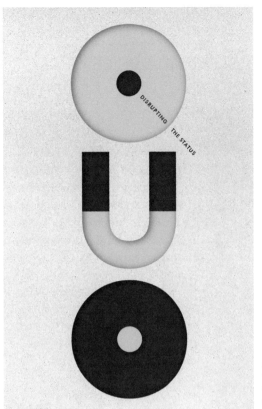

AIA INDIANAPOLIS 2018
YEAR IN REVIEW /
DISRUPTING THE STATUS
QUO. © COMMERCIAL
ARTISAN 2019

What do you think is the key to your success as collaborators?

JAMES: As I think back over the 15+ years that we've worked together, I'm amazed at all of the fun we've had and all of the work we've done that I'm so proud of. It's such a privilege to get to work with Jon and I feel incredibly lucky. I think we're attuned to each other's sensibilities and—because of our history of growing up together—compatible in ways that we wouldn't be with other people.

JON: Outside of genuinely liking and caring for one another, we have compatible personalities, enjoy the work we do, still find the work challenging and inspiring, and are proud of our achievements. As far as I'm concerned, this is the very definition of "success."

COVER FOR 12TH ISSUE OF COMMERCIAL
ARTICLE, SELF-PUBLISHED DESIGN
HISTORY JOURNAL. © COMMERCIAL
ARTISAN 2019. ILLUSTRATION BY
DANE LOVE, ONE OF THREE FOUNDING
MEMBERS OF STUPID, INC.

You've maintained an independent, successful business for 30 years. What advice would you give other graphic artists who are considering self-employment?

JAMES: When I began working as an independent designer, I had no business experience and didn't know very much about how a design studio operated. I would encourage anybody considering self-employment to learn as much as they can, but not to let inexperience deter them from trying it. I believe that a self-motivated designer can figure it out. I see people all around me who unexpectedly lose their jobs or face extremely daunting circumstances in their careers, and I have always felt that there may be more security in having no security. In other words, relying on yourself to make things happen may be a more secure strategy than waiting for somebody else to do it.

www.commercialartisan.com

FREDERICK H. CARLSON
A Successful Illustration Career

ADJUSTING TO THE CYCLES

PHOTOGRAPH COURTESY OF
NANCY FLURY CARLSON, ©2019.

Illustrator Fred Carlson grew up in rural Connecticut. After earning a degree in design at Carnegie Mellon University, he stayed in the Pittsburgh area, where he has been self-employed for 40 years. He is one of the most well-known artist/illustrators in the mid-Atlantic market having completed works as large as room-sized murals and as small as one of his 400 music packaging covers.

Fred's awards have included two acceptances into the New York Society of Illustrators Annual Exhibition. Recent nationally recognized assignments have included a DVD cover series for Guitar Workshop of famous blues guitarists. Other clients have included major newspapers and magazines, music recording companies, national corporations, foundations, and several universities. Fred's nature illustration is permanently installed at the Smithsonian/National Zoo in Washington DC, Cleveland Metroparks Zoo, and Moraine State Park Jennings Education Center.

Actively involved in his profession, Fred taught Advanced Illustration at Carnegie Mellon for 14 years. He has lectured widely on his work, both as an independent artist and in his roles as Graphic Artists Guild President (1991-1993) and as Pittsburgh Society of Illustrators (PSI) President (2000 to 2004). In 2003, Fred was a Speaker at the ICON3 National Illustration Conference. He currently serves PSI as Treasurer and New Member Contact.

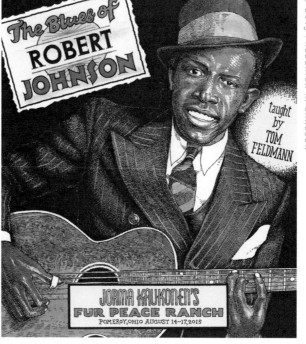

© 2015 FREDERICK H. CARLSON / *THE BLUES OF ROBERT JOHNSON* (BINDER COVER AND EVENT POSTER)

What were your early influences that made you want to pursue design and illustration as a career?

My desire to constantly draw is still remembered by friends of mine who have known me since the early 1960s. They remind me about this all-consuming activity all the time! Marvel Comics, Norman Rockwell, NC Wyeth, *Mad Magazine*, sci-fi paperback artists like Frank Frazetta, and rock album covers all gave me a varied set of influences, to say the least! Focusing on fundamentals, I had a high-school art teacher, Pat DiCosimo, a terrific printmaker who got me to think about my artwork and reproductions. I decided to pursue graphic design and illustration rather than fine arts by the time I was applying for college.

In the Design Department at Carnegie Mellon University, I focused on the Pushpin aesthetic and problem-solving ability, and the way their group and the successful freelancers who split off from their group, handled illustration and design projects without apologizing for their own influences from the pre-TV era. In the early to mid-70s, design education at Carnegie Mellon stressed print production technology, Swiss graphic design philosophy, and fundamentals of drawing and painting and problem solving. I specialized in illustration at Carnegie Mellon because I wanted to be responsible for the creative end-product, and I felt graphic designers were limited by being the hub, or center point, of the spokes in the wheel that put the varied parts together. I wanted to point to my work and say, "I illustrated that!"

Being exposed to speakers like Milton Glaser, Alan E. Cober, Dick Hess, Paul Davis, and Brad Holland gave me the confidence to complete a fairly strong graduate portfolio and get hired by a top studio—Pitt Studios—in business since WWI days, right after college. My basic drawing skills, especially with people and portraits, gave me the entrée to jump into studio life and absorb everything there

was to know about production, various painting/technique methods, and design sensibility. I was raw but unceasing about getting better and getting work.

There are illustrators who say they cannot make a sustainable living from their art, yet you've been self-employed for 40 years. How have you managed to do that?

You have to be able to adjust to the up and down cycles: hold on to the people who use you for a long period of time, if possible. Being self-employed is more about saving than spending... you have to do both and saving is less sexy, but it is an absolute imperative. It used to be "plan, work hard, and save for three or four good years to get through an inevitable bad year." Nowadays it's more like "plan and save two good years to get through a third bad year!"

Keep marketing your work to clients known as "the steadies"—art directors who move from job to job but they trust someone like me who is known as reliable; or a client who has used you for a magazine for 15 years because you continually give them your best work. At the same time, challenge yourself on the side to flavor it up, change, and bring in other twists to your work—clients love to see evolution if they trust your basic reliability! Reinvest in marketing in a discerning manner—so many ways to promote, and many are dirt cheap, but make sure you save!

You also have other revenue streams besides the commissioned client work—teaching and selling giclée prints of posters in your online shop. Has selling giclée prints been profitable?

Teaching a single illustration class to senior advanced students was a great experience at Carnegie Mellon from 1981 to 1994. Regarding the online retail poster business selling my giclées, yes, it is now profitable. I started selling them

in 2015. By January 2018 (2 ½ years later), revenue from prints surpassed revenue from commissions that month. These things take time, but if you are diligent, success will follow.

Since you started your career before the digital age, how would you say advances in technology have affected your career? Was it difficult adjusting to the changes in technology?

I have come to the realization, as I looked at what I was taught from 1973–1977, that the technology I was exposed to, and the print production methods of those years, were all pushed aside within a few years after I started freelancing. Technology is always a moving system within the design profession. It's no better and no worse today or in 1995, than it was in the late 1970s. Every couple of years I discover that some watercolor stock I like is no longer produced, or a pencil line has been discontinued, frame suppliers are out of business, computer programs no longer are in synch with my computer, scanners no longer want to work—it's all a challenge.

You have to rely on your own foundations and not blame success or failure on the tools around you. My biggest challenge was servicing my music business clients after computer design programs fell into everyone's hands around 1993 and I had been shipping mechanicals for a decade and a half. You buy, you learn, you get aggravated, and finally things work out and you can compete with everyone else again! Being involved in your local or regional graphic arts organizations is a huge teaching/learning benefit to navigate these technical waters—people are generous in their helping mode regarding sharing ideas about new tech.

You have very diverse illustration styles, from realistic nature illustration to your bold and colorful DVD covers and posters of blues musicians. What came first?

From 1980 to around 1998 my editorial and corporate jobs featured my graphite and watercolor look that I always found refreshingly fast and impactful. When I started doing the large natural science educational commissions, that style stayed; the assignments were coming from big design and architectural firms who wanted a natural look. Some of the finishes started tightening up as realism was always desired. I had long strings of assignments from the *Wall Street Journal* and *National Review* and those ADs liked the watercolor look. After 9/11, subtlety wasn't selling, and my lighter coloration seemed to fall into the background, so I consciously began changing my palette to stronger colors. I also found that I could manipulate color in Photoshop after scanning my work, so I felt more freedom to experiment with color choices.

Changing your palette is definitely another example of adjusting to cycles to survive. The DVD covers and posters of famous blues musicians are very evocative of the poster art of their time period, including your hand-lettering. How did you get involved in illustrating recordings of blues musicians?

Since 1984, I was getting commissions for music packaging jobs from many labels, combining my research, illustration, hand lettering, and production knowledge to serve hundreds of projects. After 1994 when digital took over, I still got a lot of jobs because of my illustration skills and my vast research library of musicians related to roots music. I continued building this large inventory of music-related images and the copyright for all these projects was mine, so I decided I wanted to find a secondary market for these images! I started selling them retail as giclée music posters in 2015, and I generated a huge amount of international interest in my work through social media strategy. The buzz

generated from exposing these posters through social media create a feedback loop where my assignments follow along as ADs see the poster imagery.

I have always been a huge fan of collecting Americana. Ad graphics and signage are a huge part of that collection, so those influences percolated up into my projects. Like some of my earlier Pushpin influences, combining the overall graphic package with my illustrations created a look that my clients really enjoy and most importantly, the graphics DO boost sales and people collect projects where my work appears, I find out!

You've been a long-time member of both the Graphic Artists Guild and the Pittsburgh Society of Illustrators, and you've held offices in both organizations. How important has this involvement been to your career?

Professional organizations are absolutely crucial to career longevity. More importantly, being committed as an officer leads to the vast increase of "on the ground" knowledge of the business that is so valuable. I counsel young illustrators all the time not to just join, sit on the sidelines, and listen, but to get in the middle of the action. It always pays off in the long run. Serving others always cycles back to the server being the receiver of reward.

How are you going to get the most out of your client budgets unless you know how to price? This is one among many obvious examples. There is always more professional development and marketing that all of us need to be doing. Professional organizations are where you will get the most knowledge, which leads to professional credibility, which leads to clients listening to you with an open ear. As a leader in professional organizations, one also learns the people skills and management skills that improve your own business process.

BULLFROG (PROMOTIONAL ARTWORK FOR NATURAL SCIENCE CLIENTS) ©2015 FREDERICK H. CARLSON

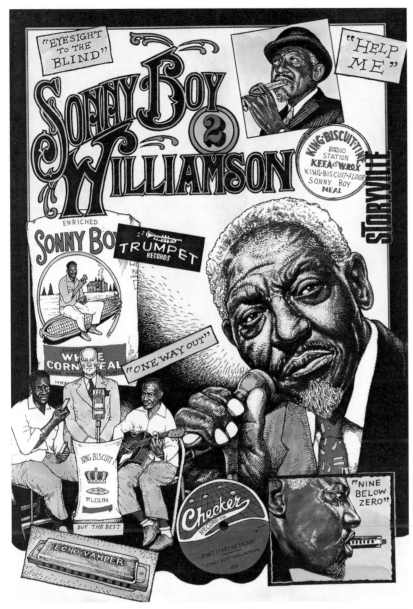

SONNY BOY WILLIAMSON II (PRIVATE COMMISSION) © 2018 FREDERICK H. CARLSON

ways to make images—who speaks for the profession of illustration and design if it were not for ASIP, the Guild, AIGA, and my own local Pittsburgh Society of Illustrators?

Based on your experience of being successfully self-employed for four decades, what advice would you give to graphic artists—those just starting their career or who have a staff job—who want to work for themselves?

Ask yourself these questions: **CAN YOU WAKE UP AND GO TO YOUR STUDIO SPACE AND UNCEASINGLY WORK, PROMOTE, AND PAY ATTENTION TO THE DETAILS OF BUSINESS MANAGEMENT? EVERY DAY? WITH VIGOR AND EXCITEMENT?** There are a lot of distractions at home. Do not spend money like studio rent, cars, or exorbitant sourcebook expenses, unless you already have it saved away. I tell young illustrators that this is the Creative Survival Fund that is only for the growth and care and feeding of your own company.
CAN YOU COMMUNICATE YOUR PERSONALITY AND RELIABILITY AND YOUR IMAGERY IN YOUR PROMOTIONS? There are a lot of easier ways to make a living.
ARE YOU A SELF-LEARNER AND DO YOU KNOW WHERE TO GO TO GET BUSINESS AND CREATIVE QUESTIONS ANSWERED? Do you own your own copy of the Guild's *Pricing & Ethical Guidelines*—not a borrowed one?
ARE YOU READY FOR THE CHALLENGE OF ADJUSTING TO THE CYCLES?

www.carlsonstudio.com

Graphic artists just starting their careers today seem to be very connected through social media and know how to use it to promote their work. Do you think it's still important for them to join professional organizations?

Absolutely. Social media tends to be too fragmented—participating only in social media for promotion does not equate with learning everything about the broader market. Remember, knowing the broader market gives you more options in your career planning. Hence, a longer career! As creative businesspeople, we also need a sense of challenge to DO better work, and sharing with other professionals leads to constant inspiration provided by the environments of professional organizations. And, very importantly, creative professionals *NEED* organizations to speak on behalf of their profession on larger issues that affect everyone. The communications marketplace is packed with ideas, strategies, techniques, and different

Resources
& References

Part 5 lists many of the valuable resources and references—books, publications, directories, related organizations, conferences, trade shows, merchandise markets, and websites—that graphic arts professionals have found helpful.

ACCESS *to a wide range of resources helps graphic artists keep up with the demands of their profession. The Graphic Artists Guild has collected the information in this part over the course of its five decades and offers it as a service to the visual communications industry. Though every effort has been made to provide the most up-to-date contact information, some listings will have changed. The Guild is always looking to add useful resources and encourages readers to notify the Guild of additional ones that should be included in the next edition.*

Recommended Books

Albers, Josef
The Interaction of Color: 50th Anniversary Edition.
YALE UNIVERSITY PRESS, 2013.

Auman, Megan
The Purpose of Profit: Why Making Money Is the Key to Creating Your Best Work.
SELF-PUBLISHED: https://designinganmba.com

Baker, Ronald J.
Pricing on Purpose: Creating and Capturing Value, 1st Edition.
HOBOKEN, NJ: JOHN WILEY & SONS, INC., 2006.

Benun, Ilise
The Creative Professional's Guide to Money: How to Think About It, How to Talk About it, How to Manage It.
CINCINNATI, OH: F&W MEDIA, INC., 2011.

Berger, Craig
Wayfinding: Designing and Implementing Graphic Navigational Systems.
SWITZERLAND: ROTOVISION, 2009.

Brewer, Robert Lee
Children's Writer's & Illustrator's Market, 2019.
BLUE ASH, OH: WRITER'S DIGEST BOOKS, 2018.
(published annually)

Brewer, Robert Lee
Writer's Market, 2020.
BLUE ASH, OH: WRITER'S DIGEST BOOKS, 2019.
(published annually)

Brophy, Maria.
Art Money & Success. A complete and easy-to-follow system for the artist who wasn't born with a business mind.
SAN CLEMENTE, CA: SON OF THE SEA, INC., 2017.

Calori, Chris, and David Vanden-Eynden
Signage and Wayfinding Design: A Complete Guide to Creating Environmental Graphic Design Systems, 2nd Edition.
HOBOKEN, NJ: JOHN WILEY & SONS, INC., 2015.

Cameron, Julia
The Artist's Way: A Spiritual Path to Higher Creativity, 25th Anniversary Edition.
NEW YORK: TARCHERPERIGEE, 2016.

Chapin, Kari
Grow Your Handmade Business: How to Envision, Develop, and Sustain a Successful Creative Business
NORTH ADAMS, MA: STOREY PUBLISHING, 2012.

Chapin, Kari
The Handmade Marketplace, 2nd Edition: How to Sell Your Crafts Locally, Globally, and Online.
NORTH ADAMS, MA: STOREY PUBLISHING, 2014.

Cho, Joy Deangdeelert, and Meg Mateo Ilasco
Creative, Inc.: The Ultimate Guide to Running a Successful Freelance Business.
SAN FRANCISCO: CHRONICLE BOOKS, LLC, 2010.

Congdon, Lisa, and Meg Mateo Ilasco
Art, Inc.: The Essential Guide for Building Your Career as an Artist.
SAN FRANCISCO: CHRONICLE BOOKS, LLC, 2014.

Cooke, Andy
Graphic Design for Art, Fashion, Film, Architecture, Photography, Product Design and Everything in Between.
NEW YORK: PRESTEL, 2018.

Craig, James, William Bevington, and Irene Korol Scala
Designing with Type: The Essential Guide to Typography, 5th ed.
NEW YORK: WATSON-GUPTILL, 2006.

Crawford, Tad, and Eva Doman Bruck
Business & Legal Forms for Graphic Designers, 4th ed.
NEW YORK: ALLWORTH PRESS, 2013.

Crawford, Tad
Business & Legal Forms for Illustrators, 4th ed.
NEW YORK: ALLWORTH PRESS, 2016.

Crawford, Tad
Legal Guide for the Visual Artist, 5th ed.
NEW YORK: ALLWORTH PRESS, 2010.

Cruz, Andy, Rich Roat, Ken Barber, and J.J. Abrams
House Industries: The Process Is the Inspiration.
NEW YORK: WATSON-GUPTILL, 2017.

Cusack, Margaret
Picture Your World in Appliqué: Creating Unique Images with Fabric.
NEW YORK: WATSON-GUPTILL, 2005.

D'Agnese, Joseph, and Denise Kiernan
The Money Book for Freelancers, Part-Timers, and the Self-Employed: The Only Personal Finance System for People with Not-So-Regular Jobs.
NEW YORK: THREE RIVERS PRESS, 2010.

Davis, Douglas
Creative Strategy and the Business of Design.
BLUE ASH, OH: HOW BOOKS, 2016.

Donovan, Bil
Advanced Fashion Drawing; Lifestyle Illustration.
LONDON: LAURENCE KING PUBLISHING LTD., 2010.

Dougherty, Brian
Green Graphic Design.
NEW YORK: ALLWORTH PRESS, 2008.

Enns, Blair.
Pricing Creativity: A Guide to Profit Beyond the Billable Hour
HTTPS://WWW.WINWITHOUTPITCHING.COM/PRICING-CREATIVITY/ (AVAILABLE FROM AUTHOR AS BINDER, VIDEOS, E-BOOK, OR PACKAGE)

Enns, Blair.
The Win without Pitching Manifesto.
NASHVILLE, TN: ROCKBENCH PUBLISHING CORP., 2010, 2014.
(hardcover, Kindle editions)

Evamy, Michael.
Logo: The Reference Guide to Symbols and Logotypes.
LONDON: LAURENCE KING PUBLISHING LTD., 2015.

Evans, Poppy, Aaris Sherin, and Irina Lee
The Graphic Design Reference & Specification Book: Everything Graphic Designers Need to Know Every Day.
BEVERLY, MA: ROCKPORT PUBLISHERS, 2013.

Faulkner, Andrew, and Conrad Chavez
Adobe Photoshop CC Classroom in a Book
ADOBE PRESS, 2018.

Foote, Cameron S.
The Business Side of Creativity: The Comprehensive Guide to Starting and Running a Small Graphic Design or Communication Business, 4th Updated Edition.
NEW YORK: W.W. NORTON & COMPANY, 2014.

Gibson, David
The Wayfinding Handbook: Information Design for Public Places.
NEW YORK: PRINCETON ARCHITECTURAL PRESS, 2009.

Gilkey, Charlie
How to Go from Idea to Done.
LOUISVILLE, CO: SOUNDS TRUE, 2019.

Godbout, Mario
How to Succeed as a Graphic Designer, Revised Second Edition. (Kindle)
QUEBEC: DESIGNERS INSIGHTS, A DIVISION OF MGD INC., 2017.

Guillebeau, Chris
100 Side Hustles.
EMERYVILLE, CA: TEN SPEED PRESS, 2019.

Harris, Lesley Ellen
Canadian Copyright Law, 4th ed.
HOBOKEN, NJ: JOHN WILEY AND SONS, INC., 2013.

Heller, Steven, and Gail Anderson
The Graphic Design Idea Book: Inspiration from 50 Masters.
LONDON: LAURENCE KING PUBLISHING, 2016.

Hennessy, Brittany.
Influencer: Building Your Personal Brand in the Age of Social Media.
NEW YORK: CITADEL PRESS BOOKS, 2018.

Hirst, Tom
Pricing Freelance Projects: Using value realistically to know what to charge and get paid what you're worth.
SELF-PUBLISHED: HTTPS://GUMROAD.COM/L/PCULZ, 2020.

Hische, Jessica
In Progress: See Inside a Lettering Artist's Sketchbook and Process, from Pencil to Vector.
SAN FRANCISCO, CA: CHRONICLE BOOKS LLC, 2015.

Hodges, Elaine R.S., ed.
The Guild Handbook of Scientific Illustration, 2nd ed.
NEW YORK: JOHN WILEY & SONS, 2003.

Hora, Mies, and Nick Sienty
Official Signs & Icons 3.
STONY POINT, NY: ULTIMATE SYMBOL, INC., 2017.

Horowitz, Sara.
The Freelancer's Bible: Everything You Need to Know to Have the Career of Your Dreams—On Your Terms.
NEW YORK: WORKMAN PUBLISHING COMPANY, INC., 2012.

Hyndman, Sarah
Why Fonts Matter.
BERKELEY, CA: GINGKO PRESS, 2016.

Janda, Michael
Burn Your Portfolio: Stuff They Don't Teach You in Design School, but Should.
NEW RIDERS, 2013.

Janda, Michael
The Psychology of Graphic Design Pricing: Price Creative Work with Confidence. Win More Bids. Make More Money.
SELF-PUBLISHED, 2019.

Jenkins, Sue
Web Design All-in-One For Dummies, 2nd ed.
HOBOKEN, NJ: JOHN WILEY & SONS, INC., 2013.

Kleon, Austin
Keep Going: 10 Ways to Stay Creative in Good Times and Bad.
NEW YORK: WORKMAN PUBLISHING COMPANY, 2019.

Kleon, Austin
Show Your Work!
NEW YORK: WORKMAN PUBLISHING COMPANY, 2014.

Krysa, Danielle
Your Inner Critic Is a Big Jerk: And Other Truths About Being Creative.
SAN FRANCISCO: CHRONICLE BOOKS LLC, 2016.

Kurtz, Adam J.
Things Are What You Make of Them: Life Advice for Creatives.
NEW YORK: TARCHERPERIGEE, 2017.

Lawlor, Veronica.
The Urban Sketching Handbook: Reportage and Documentary Drawing: Tips and Techniques for Drawing on Location (Urban Sketching Handbooks).
BLOOMINGTON, IN: QUARRY BOOKS, 2015.

Lee, Marshall
Bookmaking: Editing, Design, Production, 3rd ed.
NEW YORK: W.W. NORTON & CO., 2009.

Leland, Caryn R.
Licensing Art & Design: A Professional's Guide to Licensing and Royalty Agreements, revised edition.
NEW YORK: ALLWORTH PRESS, 1995.
(content is still very relevant today)

Levine, Mark L.
Negotiating a Book Contract: A Guide for Authors, Agents and Lawyers.
HUBBARDSTON, MA: ASPHODEL PRESS, 2009.

Lorenc, Jan, and Lee Skolnick, and Craig Berger
What Is Exhibition Design?
SWITZERLAND: ROTOVISION, 2010.

Malinic, Radim
The Book of Ideas: A Journal of Creative Direction and Graphic Design, Vols. 1 & 2.
LONDON: BRAND NU LIMITED, 2016, 2018.

Mall, Dan
Pricing Design.
NEW YORK: A BOOK APART, 2016.

Marcotte, Ethan
Responsive Web Design.
NEW YORK: A BOOK APART, 2011.

McCann, Michael, and Angela Babin
Health Hazards Manual for Artists, 6th ed.
GUILFORD, CT: THE LYONS PRESS, 2008.

Melton, Brittany.
Dear Freelancer: Words of Wisdom to Help You Thrive in the World of Freelancing.
SELF-PUBLISHED, 2018.

Michalowicz, Mike
Profit First: Transform Your Business from a Cash-Eating Monster to a Money-Making Machine.
NEW YORK: PORTFOLIO, 2017.

Michels, Caroll
How to Survive and Prosper as an Artist: Selling Yourself without Selling Your Soul, 7th ed.
NEW YORK: ALLWORTH PRESS, 2018.

Mohammed, Rafi
The 1% Windfall: How Successful Companies Use Price to Profit and Grow.
NEW YORK: HARPERCOLLINS, 2010.

Norman, Donald A.
The Design of Everyday Things, Revised and Expanded Edition.
NEW YORK: BASIC BOOKS, 2013.

Rees, Darrell
How to Be an Illustrator, 2nd ed.
LONDON: LAURENCE KING PUBLISHING, 2014.

Rixford, Ellen S.
Figures in the Fourth Dimension: Mechanical Movement for Puppets and Automata.
NEW YORK: SELF-PUBLISHED, 2015.
www.figuresinthefourthdimension.com

Rixford, Ellen S.
3-Dimensional Illustration: Designing with Paper, Clay, Casts, Wood, Assemblage, Plastics, Fabric, Metal, and Food.
NEW YORK: WATSON-GUPTILL, 1992.

Rossol, Monona
The Artist's Complete Health & Safety Guide, 4th ed.
NEW YORK: ALLWORTH PRESS, 2019.

Shaughnessy, Adrian.
How to Be a Graphic Designer without Losing Your Soul. (Expanded Edition)
HUDSON, NY: PRINCETON ARCHITECTURAL PRESS, 2010.

Sher, Barbara, and Annie Gottlieb
Wishcraft: How to Get What You Really Want, 30th Anniversary Edition.
NEW YORK: BALLANTINE BOOKS, 2004

Sherin, Aaris, and Poppy Evans
Forms, Folds and Sizes, Second Edition: All the Details Graphic Designers Need to Know but Can Never Find.
BEVERLY, MA: ROCKPORT PUBLISHERS, 2009.

Sinek, Simon
Start with Why: How Great Leaders Inspire Everyone to Take Action.
NEW YORK: PORTFOLIO/PENGUIN GROUP, 2009.

Tholenaar, Jan, Alston W. Purvis, and Cees De Jong

Type: A Visual History of Fonts and Graphic Styles,
Volume 1: 1628–1900.
LOS ANGELES: TASCHEN AMERICA, 2009.

Vangool, Janine
Uppercase Compendium of Craft & Creativity.
ALBERTA, CANADA: UPPERCASE PUBLISHING, INC, 2015.

Vaynerchuk, Gary
Jab, Jab, Jab, Right Hook: How to Tell Your Story in a
Noisy Social World.
NEW YORK: HARPER BUSINESS, 2013.

Wheeler, Alina.
Designing Brand Identity: An Essential Guide for the
Whole Branding Team, 5th ed.
HOBOKEN, NJ: JOHN WILEY & SONS, INC., 2018.

Wilde, Judith, and Richard Wilde
Visual Literacy: A Conceptual Approach to Graphic
Problem Solving.
NEW YORK: WATSON-GUPTILL, 2000.

Wilson, Lee
The Pocket Legal Companion to Copyright: A User-
Friendly Handbook for Protecting and Profiting from
Copyrights.
NEW YORK: ALLWORTH PRESS, 2012.

Woodward, Michael.
Licensing Art, 101, Third Edition Updated: Publishing
and Licensing Your Artwork for Profit.
ARTNETWORK PRESS, 2007.

Wroblewski, Luke
Mobile First.
NEW YORK: A BOOK APART, 2011.

Relevant Publications

Graphic Arts & Communication

3 x 3, The Magazine of Contemporary Illustration
www.3x3mag.com

Adobe Create Magazine
https://create.adobe.com/

Advertising Age
www.adage.com

Adweek
www.adweek.com

Airbrush Action
www.airbrushaction.com

American Printer
www.americanprinter.com

Animation Magazine
www.animationmagazine.net

Applied Arts
www.appliedartsmag.com

The Artist's Magazine
www.artistsnetwork.com/subscribe/

Before & After
www.bamagazine.com

CGarchitect
www.cgarchitect.com

Communication Arts
www.commarts.com

Creative Business
www.creativebusiness.com

DART (Design Arts Daily)
www.ai-ap.com/publications/dart

Digital Camera World
www.digitalcameraworld.com

Folio
www.foliomag.com

Graphic Design USA
www.gdusa.com

Graphis
www.graphis.com

Imagine FX
www.creativebloq.com/imaginefx

Layers Magazine
www.layersmagazine.com

Letter Arts Review
www.johnnealbooks.com/prod_detail_list/Letter-Arts-Review

Macworld
www.macworld.com

Motionographer
www.motionographer.com

net: The voice of web design
www.medium.com/net-magazine

Packaging Digest
www.packagingdigest.com

PC Magazine
www.pcmag.com

PC World
www.pcworld.com

pdn: Photo District News
www.pdnonline.com

Printing News
www.myprintresource.com

PW: Publishers Weekly
www.publishersweekly.com

Sign & Digital Graphics
www.sdgmag.com

Smashing Magazine
www.smashingmagazine.com

Starting your Own Communication Design Business.
Free downloadable booklet on setting up your creative
business, by Lara Kisielewska:
https://graphicartistsguild.org/starting-your-own-communication-design-business/
Also see three-part webinar on the same topic:
https://graphicartistsguild.org/product/start-run-grow-your-design-business/

Surface Design Journal
www.surfacedesign.org/journal/about-the-journal

Surface Magazine
www.surfacemag.com

T3 Smarter Living
www.t3.com

UPPERCASE Magazine
www.uppercasemagazine.com

WWD
www.wwd.com

Wired Magazine
www.wired.com

Trade Publications of Interest

ART/WALL DÉCOR

Art Business News
www.artbusinessnews.com

DÉCOR Magazine
www.artbusinessnews.com/category/decor-magazine

CRAFTS & HOBBIES

Somerset Studio
The Art of Paper and Mixed-Media
www.somersetstudio.com

GIFT & STATIONERY INDUSTRY

Giftbeat
www.giftbeat.com

Giftware News
www.giftwarenews.com

Museums & More
www.museumsandmore.com

Party & Halloween Retailer
www.partypaper.com

Souvenirs, Gifts & Novelties
www.sgnmag.com

HOME ACCENTS

Home Accents Today
www.homeaccentstoday.com

Home Textiles Today
www.homeandtextilestoday.com

Furniture, Lighting & Decor
www.furniturelightingdecor.com

LICENSING

Art Buyer
The magazine of licensed art and images
www.artbuyermag.com

License Global
www.licenseglobal.com

Licensing Today Worldwide
www.ltwmag.com

The Licensing Letter
www.thelicensingletter.com

The Pop Insider
www.thepopinsider.com

PET INDUSTRY

Pet Age
www.petage.com

Pet Business
www.petbusiness.com

Pet Product News Magazine
www.petproductnews.com

Industry Directories

Artist's & Graphic Designer's Market
www.artistsmarketonline.com

Gale Directory of Publications and Broadcast Media
www.gale.com

National Association of Schools of Art & Design Directory Lists
www.nasad.arts-accredit.org/directory-lists

O'Dwyer's Directory of Public Relations Firms Database
www.odwyerpr.com/pr_firms_database

Standard Periodical Directory
www.gale.com

ThomasNet.com
(Find Suppliers. Source Products.)
www.thomasnet.com

Promotion & Marketing Resources
Buyer Databases & List Services

Agency Access
www.agencyaccess.com
Agency Access provides cutting-edge marketing services allowing photographers, illustrators, reps, and stock agencies to showcase their work to top industry creative professionals, through highly targeted and customized list memberships services, e-mail marketing and design, direct mail services and consulting services. Agency Access provides tools that can assist in communicating creative talent and expanding business.

Animation Industry Database (aidb)
www.aidb.com
The ultimate resource for the professional animation, visual effects, and gaming-related communities. Includes free downloadable directories to find animation, visual effects, and related companies located worldwide. Covers almost 5,000 companies and schools. Useful as a buyer's guide, a way to find clients, get work, and obtain products and services.

Creative Access
www.creativeaccess.com | 800-422-2377
Graphic design firms, corporations, ad agencies, publishers, magazines, and printers.

REDBOOKS Agency and Advertising Database
www.redbooks.com
The premier advertising database, with the most comprehensive, up-to-date info on the top advertisers and agencies.

Talent Source Books & Annuals

The Alternative Pick / Altpick.com
www.altpick.com

American Illustration
American Photography
www.ai-ap.com

Communication Arts Annuals
www.commarts.com

Directory of Illustration
www.directoryofillustration.com/browse-the-book.aspx

Graphis Annuals
www.graphis.com

Medical Illustration & Animation
(Print & online: biomedical, medical-legal, life science
& natural science)
www.medillsb.com

PRINT Regional Design Annual
www.printmag.com/design-competitions/regional-
design-annual

Society of Illustrators Annual
www.societyillustrators.org/shop/product-type/si-
publications

Workbook
www.workbook.com

Portfolio Websites

Altpick
www.altpick.com
(Design, fine art, illustration, photography)

Behance
www.behance.net
(Visual, package, motion, interactive, game, sound)

Carbonmade
www.carbonmade.com
(All creative disciplines)

Coroflot
www.coroflot.com
(Design, including graphic, exhibit, packaging,
industrial, product, UI/UX)

Creative Talent Network, Inc. (CTN)
www.creativetalentnetwork.com
(Animation, visual EFX, video game industries)

DeviantArt
www.deviantart.com
(All art)

Directory of Illustration
www.directoryofillustration.com
(Illustration, motion, animation)

Folioplanet
www.folioplanet.com
(A directory of illustration links, portfolios, and stock
images)

The ispot
www.theispot.com
(Illustration)

Webtoon
www.webtoons.com

Online Outlets for Selling Art

Online outlets (platforms) vary greatly as to the services
and options they offer, the products they accept, and
their pricing structures and fees. Before you choose an
online outlet to sell your art, it is in your best interest to
research and compare several outlets to find the one that
best matches your needs, your particular art, and your
income expectations. You should not enter into an agreement until you have read the outlet's Terms of Service very
carefully.

Art of Where
www.artofwhere.com
(Publish and sell art on retail products)

ArtPal
www.artpal.com
(Sell both original art—all kinds, including sculpture and
ceramics, and print-on-demand art (prints and products); no membership fees or commissions on profits;
artists can choose whether to do fulfillment themselves
or have ArtPal do it.)

Café Press
www.cafepress.com
(Sell your designs on retail products)

Comixology
www.comixology.com
(Self-publish comics and graphic novels)

Creative Market
www.creativemarket.com
(A platform where designers can open a shop to sell their work; set own prices; keep 70% of sales.)

DeviantART
www.deviantart.com
(Sell prints and digital downloads of your work in all genres, as well as all types of artisan crafts; pre-determined base prices and royalty paid on sales (can change maximum price and royalty percentage with Core Membership at an annual cost.)

Etsy
www.etsy.com
(Sell art and crafts you create)

Pixels
www.pixels.com
(Sell your photos on custom wall art and retail products)

Redbubble
www.redbubble.com
(Sell art on a variety of products. Choose your own markup. Redbubble manufactures and provides fulfillment.)

Society6
www.society6.com
(Sell art on a wide variety of products. Society6 manufactures and provides fulfillment and pays artists a royalty.)

Zazzle
www.zazzle.com
(Publish and sell your art and photographs on retail products; Zazzle provides fulfillment; determine your own royalty/retail price.)

Juried Art Fairs & Festivals

Art Fair Calendar
www.artfaircalendar.com
(Lists juried fine art and crafts fairs and arts festivals nationwide by state; updated annually; lists calls for entries; ranks best fairs; includes artists' blog.)

Fairs & Festivals
www.fairsandfestivals.net/
(Lists festivals, craft shows, art fairs, and events by state; can use advance search on site to find juried shows.)

FestivalNet
www.festivalnet.com
(Most extensive and comprehensive searchable online database of festivals and fairs in North America; can search for juried art fairs and festivals, as well as crafts fairs.)

Employment & Freelance Opportunities
Creative Staffing Agencies

24 Seven
www.24seventalent.com/
(Staffing agency for digital marketing, creative services, content and copywriting, development and tech, and e-commerce. Includes freelance.)

Creative Circle
www.creativecircle.com
(Staffing agency for digital creatives, including freelance.)

Onward Search
www.onwardsearch.com/
(Recruitment and staffing agency for digital, creative, and marketing professionals; job listings.)

Paladin
www.paladinstaff.com/
(Recruitment and staffing agency for creative, marketing, communications, and digital fields, including freelance opportunities.)

The Creative Group (TCG)
www.roberthalf.com/creativegroup
(Staffing agency for creative jobs, including full-time, project-based, freelance.)

Vitamin T (Aquent)
https://vitamintalent.com/
(Staffing agency for creative talent, including freelancers.)

Job Boards & Sites

Dice
www.dice.com
(Technical careers)

FreeeUp
www.freeeup.com
(Opportunities for freelancers who go through pre-vetting process and are approved)

Indeed
www.indeed.com
(All careers)

Graphic Artists Guild Career Board
https://graphicartistsguild.org/member-benefits/
career-listing/

Guru
www.guru.com
(Freelance opportunities, including design, art, multimedia, and web)

Upwork
www.upwork.com
(Freelance opportunities in all fields)

Organizations
Artists' Health and Safety

Arts, Craft and Theater Safety (A.C.T.S.)
212-777-0062 | www.artscraftstheatersafety.org
Publishes newsletter and books about artists' health hazards and safe working conditions.

Communication Workers of America (CWA)
Occupational Safety & Health Department
202-434-1160
www.cwa-union.org/national-issues/health-and-safety
Publishes "Computer Workplace Ergonomics" and other health and safety fact sheets.

New York Committee for Occupational Safety and Health (NYCOSH)
212-227-6440 | www.nycosh.org
NYCOSH is one of 26 COSH coalitions around the country that provide information on workplace hazards.

Occupational Safety and Health Administration (OSHA)
U.S. Department of Labor
800-321-6742 | www.osha.gov

Graphic Arts & Related Occupations

AIGA, the professional association for design
212-807-1990 | www.aiga.org

American Photographic Artists (APA)
800-272-6264 ext. 12 | www.apanational.com

American Society of Architectural Illustrators (ASAI)
207-966-2062 | www.asai.org

American Society of Media Photographers (ASMP)
877-771-2767 | www.asmp.org

Association of Registered Graphic Designers (RGD)
1-888-274-3668 | www.rgd.ca

Association of Science Fiction & Fantasy Artists (ASFA)
www.asfa-art.org

Creative Talent Network, Inc. (CTN)
(818) 827-7138 | www.creativetalentnetwork.com

Freelancers Union
www.freelancersunion.org

Graphic Artists Guild
212-791-3400 | www.graphicartistsguild.org

Guild of Natural Science Illustrators
Tel/Fax: 301.309.1514 | www.gnsi.org

International Council of Design (ico-D)
+1-514-875-7545 | www.ico-d.org

National Cartoonists Society
407-994-6703 | www.nationalcartoonists.com

National Endowment for the Arts (NEA)
202-682-5400 | www.arts.gov

National Press Photographers Association (NPPA)
706-542-2506 | www.nppa.org

New York Foundation for the Arts (NYFA)
212-366-6900 | www.nyfa.org

North America Nature Photography Association (NANPA)
618-547-7616 | www.nanpa.org

Professional Photographers of America, Inc. (PPA)
800-786-6277| www.ppa.com

Society for Experiential Graphic Design (SEGD)
202-638-5555 | www.segd.org

Society for News Design (SND)
407-420-7748 | www.snd.org

Society of Children's Book Writers & Illustrators
(SCBWI)
323-782-1010 | www.scbwi.org

Society of Illustrators (SI)
212-838-2560 | www.societyillustrators.org

Society of Typographic Aficionados (SoTA)
www.typesociety.org | info@typesociety.org

SoDA: the digital society
http://sodaspeaks.com

Surface Design Association (SDA)
707-829-3110 | www.surfacedesign.org

The Animation Guild, IATSE Local 839 (TAG)
818-845-7500 | www.animationguild.org

The NewsGuild - CWA
202-434-7177 | www.newsguild.org

The One Club for Creativity
(A merger of the former Art Directors Club and
The One Club)
212-979-1900 | www.oneclub.org

The Society of Publication Designers (SPD)
212-223-3332 | www.spd.org

The Software & Information Industry Association
(SIIA)
202-289-7442 | www.siia.net

The Type Directors Club (TDC)
212-633-8943 | www.tdc.org

WebProfessionals.org
662-493-2776 | www.webprofessionals.org

Intellectual Property

Authors Coalition of America, LLC (ACA)
www.authorscoalition.org
The Coalition is an organization of U.S.-based authors
and creators united to receive and distribute non-
title-specific reprographic royalties to Member
Organizations.

Copyright Alliance
www.copyrightalliance.org
The Copyright Alliance is committed to promoting the
cultural and economic benefits of copyright, providing
information and resources on the contributions
of copyright, and upholding the contributions of
copyright to the fiscal health of this nation and for the
good of creators, owners, and consumers around the
world. Their site includes videos from creators on why
copyright is important, copyright FAQs, and Copyright
Explained, an easy-to-understand explanation of the
basics of U.S. copyright law.

The Copyright Society of the USA (CSUSA)
www.csusa.org
The Society is a not-for-profit corporation dedicated to
advancing the study and understanding of copyright
law and related rights in literature, music, art, theater,
motion pictures, television, computer software,
architecture, and other works of authorship; and their
distribution via both traditional and new media. CSUSA
is also sponsor of Copyright Awareness Week. Site
contains curricula for teaching copyright awareness in
schools, including history and interesting facts.

International Federation of Reproduction Rights
Organizations (IFRRO)
www.ifrro.org
The Federation's purpose is to facilitate, on an
international basis, the collective management of
reproduction and other rights relevant to copyrighted
works through the co-operation of its member
Reproduction Rights Organizations (RROs).

Picture Licensing Universal System
(PLUS Coalition)
www.useplus.com
PLUS is a cooperative, multi-industry initiative,
operating as a three-part system that clearly defines
and categorizes image usage around the world, from
granting and acquiring licenses to tracking and
managing them well into the future.

U.S. Copyright Office
877-476-0778 (toll free), 202-707-3000
www.copyright.gov
Maintains an up-to-date website with basic copyright
information and everything artists need for registering,
including online registration, forms and circulars, a
useful FAQ on copyrights, the Fair Use Index, and a
searchable database of fair use decisions.

U.S. Patent and Trademark Office (USPTO)
800-786-9199 (M-F, 8:30 a.m.–8:00 p.m. ET), 800-877-
8339 (TTY customer assistance)
www.uspto.gov
Source of information, support, and forms for
registering patents and trademarks. Maintains up-to-
date website, featuring online trademark searches and
application filing for trademark registration. Includes
basic information and FAQs about trademarks and
step-by-step directions for filing. Forms available for
downloading and printing.

Related Trade Organizations

Association for Creative Industries (AFCI)
312-321-6811
www.craftandhobby.org

Color Association of the United States (CAUS)
212-947-7774 | www.colorassociation.com

Color Marketing Group
703.329.8500 | www.colormarketing.org

Data & Marketing Association (DMA)
212-768-7277 | www.thedma.org

Greeting Card Association
202-216-9627 | www.greetingcard.org

Licensing International
212-244-1944 | www.licensinginternational.org
The leading trade organization for the global licensing
industry. Its mission is to foster the growth and
expansion of licensing around the world, raise the level
of professionalism for licensing practitioners, and
create greater awareness of the benefits of licensing to
the business community at large.

National Association for the Self-Employed (NASE)
1-800-649-6273 (continental U.S.), 1-800-232-6273
(AK & HI)
www.nase.org

Legal Services for the Arts

COMIC BOOK LEGAL DEFENSE FUND (CBLDF)

www.cbldf.org
The Comic Book Legal Defense Fund is a non-profit
organization dedicated to protecting the First
Amendment rights of the comics medium.

VOLUNTEER LAWYERS FOR THE ARTS

*The following listings were updated as of August 2019.
However, the contact information changes frequently,
so readers are advised to visit the websites given for the
most up-to-date information. Availability of the VLA
program by state also changes from time to time. If
you do not see your state in the following list, try doing
an online search. The program may be part of a local
arts organization or sponsored by a law school or an
individual law office.*

ARIZONA
Volunteer Legal Assistance for Artists (VLAA)
www.artsadvocacy.org

AUSTRALIA
Arts Law Centre of Australia
1-800-221-457 (toll-free from Australia)
Local: 02- 9356-2566
www.artslaw.com.au

CANADA
CARFAC
866-344-6161 | www.carfac.ca

CALIFORNIA
California Lawyers for the Arts (CLA)
(Statewide)
888-775-8995 | www.calawyersforthearts.org

California Lawyers for the Arts
(Berkeley)
888-775-8995 | Iris@calawyersforthearts.org

California Lawyers for the Arts
(Greater Los Angeles Area)
310-207-0001 | losangeles@calawyersforthearts.org

California Lawyers for the Arts
(Greater Sacramento Area)
916-442-6210 | sacramento@calawyersforthearts.org

California Lawyers for the Arts
(Greater San Diego Area)
888-775-8995 | sandiego@calawyersforthearts.org

California Lawyers for the Arts
(San Francisco)
415-775-7200 | cla@calawyersforthearts.org

COLORADO
Colorado Attorneys for the Arts (CAFTA)
720-428-6720 | main@cbca.org
www.cbca.org/colorado-attorneys-for-the-arts

DISTRICT OF COLUMBIA
Washington Area Lawyers for the Arts (WALA)
202.289.4440 | www.waladc.org

FLORIDA
Florida Lawyers for the Arts, Inc. (FLA)
727-823-5809 | www.artslawfl.org

GEORGIA
Georgia Lawyers for the Arts
404-873-3911 | www.glarts.org

ILLINOIS
Lawyers for the Creative Arts
(Chicago area)
312-649-4111 | www.law-arts.org

Volunteer Lawyers & Accountants for the Arts (VLAA)
(Madison & St. Clair Counties)
314-863-6930 | www.vlaa.org

KANSAS
Kansas City Volunteer Lawyers & Accountants for the
Arts (KCVLAA)
816-974-8522 | www.kcvlaa.org

LOUISIANA
Arts Council of New Orleans
504-523-1465 | www.artsneworleans.org

MARYLAND
Maryland Volunteer Lawyers for the Arts (MDVLA)
410-752-1633 | www.mdvla.org

MASSACHUSETTS
Arts & Business Council of Greater Boston
617-350-7600 | www.artsandbusinesscouncil.org

MINNESOTA
Springboard for the Arts
(Lowertown St. Paul)
651-292-4381 | www.springboardforthearts.org

Springboard for the Arts
(Fergus Falls)
218-998-4037 | www.springboardforthearts.org

MISSOURI
Kansas City Volunteer Lawyers & Accountants for the
Arts (KCVLAA)
816-974-8522 | www.kcvlaa.org

Volunteer Lawyers & Accountants for the Arts (VLAA)
(St. Louis)
314-863-6930 | www.vlaa.org

NEW YORK
Volunteer Lawyers for the Arts (VLA)
212-319-2787 Ext. 1 | www.vlany.org

OHIO
Volunteer Lawyers for the Arts
c/o The Cleveland Metropolitan Bar Association
216-696-3525 | www.clemetrobar.org/VLA

OREGON
Oregon Volunteer Lawyers for the Arts
www.oregonvla.org | legalhelp@oregonvla.org

PENNSYLVANIA
Philadelphia Volunteer Lawyers for the Arts
c/o Arts & Business Council of Greater Philadelphia
215-790-3836 x1
www.artsbusinessphl.org/philadelphia-volunteer-
lawyers-arts

Pittsburgh Volunteer Lawyers for the Arts
c/o Greater Pittsburgh Arts Council
412-391-2060 | www.pittsburghartscouncil.org/vla

RHODE ISLAND
Ocean State Lawyers for the Arts (OSLA)
401-789-5686 | www.artslaw.org

Volunteer Lawyers & Professionals for the Arts
c/o Arts & Business Council of Greater Nashville
(615) 460–8274 | www.abcnashville.org

TEXAS
Texas Accountants & Lawyers for the Arts (TALA)
512-459-8252 | Toll Free: 800-526-8252
www.talarts.org | info@talarts.org

UTAH
Utah Lawyers for the Arts
www.utahlawyersforthearts.org

WASHINGTON
Washington Lawyers for the Arts (WLA)
206-328-7053 | www.thewla.org

Conferences, Trade Shows & Merchandise Markets

NOTE: Information is subject to change.

AmericasMart Atlanta
800.ATL-MART | www.americasmart.com

Arts Business Summit
https://clarkhulingsfund.org/events/art-business-summit/

Awwwards Digital Thinkers Conference
https://conference.awwwards.com/

Blueprint
(Surface Design & Print Show)
www.blueprintshows.com

Comic-Con International
San Diego, CA
WonderCon
Anaheim, CA
www.comic-con.org

CreativePro Week
www.CreativeProWeek.com

CTN Animation Expo
(Creative Talent Network)
www.ctnanimationexpo.com

Design To Festival
http://designto.org/the-dx-presents-edit-expo-for-design-innovation-technology/

Emerald Expositions
949-226-5700 | www.emeraldexpositions.com

Dallas Market Center (DMC)
214-655-6100 | www.dallasmarketcenter.com

Fancy Food Shows
New York, NY and San Francisco, CA
www.specialtyfood.com/fancy-food-show

Game Developers Conference (GDC)
www.gdconf.com

Gift Shop
Calendar of Gift Trade Shows & Expositions
www.giftshopmag.com/tradeshows

HOW Design Live Conference
www.howdesignlive.com

ICON: The Illustration Conference
www.theillustrationconference.org

L.A. Design Festival
www.ladesignfestival.org

L.A. Mart
213-763-5800

LetterWest
www.conference.letterwest.com
(Annual conference specific to hand-lettering)

Licensing Expo
www.licensingexpo.com

MoCCA Arts Festival
www.societyillustrators.org/mocca-arts-festival

National Stationery Show (NSS)*
www.nationalstationeryshow.com

NY NOW*
www.nynow.com

San Francisco Design Week
www.sfdesignweek.org

Self-Employment in the Arts (SEA)
www.selfemploymentinthearts.com/annual-conference

SIGGRAPH
(Computer graphics & interactive techniques)
www.siggraph.org

Society of Children's Book Writers
& Illustrators Conferences
323-782-1010 | www.scbwi.org

Spectrum Fantastic Art Live
408-206-2346 | www.spectrumfantasticartlive.com

Surface Design Association Conference
707-829-3110
www.surfacedesign.org/events-exhibits/conferences

Surtex Show*
www.surtex.com

The Toy Association Toy Fair
212-675-1141 | www.toyassociation.org

TypeCon
www.typecon.com

Typographics
A Design Festival for People Who Use Type
type@cooper.edu
See: Emerald Expositions for contact information.

Useful Software & Tools
Business

BlinkBid
www.blinkbid.com
Cloud-based estimating, production, invoicing software
for creative professionals.

FreshBooks Cloud Accounting
www.freshbooks.com
Small business online accounting software.

GoDaddy Online Bookkeeping
www.godaddy.com/bookkeeping
Includes tax tools, invoicing, reports and more.

Harvest
www.getharvest.com
Time and expense tracking software.

Wave Accounting
www.waveapps.com
Free financial software for small businesses; low
subscription for additional services.

Online Image Tracking

Digimarc
www.digimarc.com
Tracks images by embedded metadata.

Google Reverse Image Search
https://support.google.com/websearch/
answer/1325808?co=GENIE.
Platform%3DDesktop&hl=en
Free catch-all, via Google search, to see where your
images are being used.

TinEye
www.tineye.com
Free reverse image search, plus paid apps for tracking
images.

Online Classes & Courses

Brit & Co
www.brit.co/shop/classes/
Short online classes in categories of lettering,
illustration, photography, business, design, fiber arts.

CGschool
www.vimeo.com/ondemand/cgschoolmasterclass
Architectural Viz Training Master Classes.

CourseCraft
www.coursecraft.net
Create and sell your own e-course or online course.

Coursera
www.coursera.org
Online courses from the top universities. Paid courses
include graded assignments and a certificate of
completion. You can also explore lectures and non-
graded material for free.

Creative Bug
www.creativebug.com
Online video arts and crafts workshops and techniques. Learn how to paint, knit, crochet, sew, screen print, and more.

CreativeLive
www.creativelive.com
Curated creative classes, inspiration, and tips by the world's top experts. Subject matter includes art and design, photo and video, and craft and maker. There are also business-related classes for freelancers and entrepreneurs in the money and life category.

Envatotuts+
http://code.tutsplus.com
Tutorials, video courses, and learning guides for learning creative skills in code, design, illustration, photography, video, web design, game development, business, and more.

HOW Design University (HOW U)
www.howdesignuniversity.com/
Online courses, workshops, and certification programs (graphic design, SEO for designers, marketing, in-house management, animation, branding, infographic design, UX design, web development, creative business entrepreneurship)
Includes interactive course content, discussion boards, optional instructor feedback

Learning Revolution
www.learningrevolution.net
A comprehensive website of resources for creating online courses. Includes online course platforms, course creation tools, screen recording software, video and podcasting equipment, as well as blog and newsletter.

LinkedInLearning (formerly Lynda.com)
www.lynda.com
Online subscription courses in software development, web design and development, graphic design, digital photography, and business, etc. All major software represented. Free video tutorials to preview training courses. Subscriptions available by month or year.

Make Art that Sells
www.makeartthatsells.com/online-courses/
Online courses from art agent Lilla Rogers and self-help author Beth Kempton with an emphasis on marketing illustration, including illustrating children's books. Also free mini-courses and a blog.

School of Motion
www.schoolofmotion.com
Online courses and tutorials for those who want to pursue motion design or improve their mograph and animation skills. Also includes a blog and podcasts.

Skillshare
www.skillshare.com
An online learning community with classes taught by expert practitioners, including animation, graphic design, illustration, business, entrepreneurship, mobile and web development, photography, film, crafts, and writing. Also an opportunity to create income by teaching your skills on the site.

Sitepoint
www.sitepoint.com
A community for web professionals, including courses, tutorials, books, forums, podcasts, and more.

Teachable
www.teachable.com
Share your knowledge and be rewarded for it by creating and selling your own online courses. Teachable includes guides and tools for building a course website. Tiered pricing plans.

Thinkific
www.thinkific.com
An all-in-one platform to create and sell online courses under your own brand. Tiered pricing plans, but you get to keep all revenue from your courses.

Udemy
www.udemy.com
Online courses from the world's experts, including design, development, photography, marketing, business, IT, and software.

Vimeo
www.vimeo.com
Ad-free video sharing platform, with tiered levels of pricing. With upgraded membership, you can also rent or sell your videos on the platform.

W3Schools
www.w3schools.com
Web development tutorials for beginners and experts.

Informative Websites & Blogs

Adobe
www.adobe.com
Tutorials, blogs, free newsletters, and free technical announcements via e-mail.

Adobe Labs
www.labs.adobe.com
Opportunities to experience and evaluate new and emerging innovations, technologies, and products from Adobe.

All About Vision
www.allaboutvision.com
Everything you'd want to know about eye conditions and diseases and how to take care of your eyes. Specific sections on digital eye strain and dry eye disease.

All Art Licensing
www.allartlicensing.com
Offers mini courses, coaching, and consulting, and a great blog on licensing.

Alphabettes.org
www.alphabettes.org
This blog *is* an international showcase for work, commentary, and research on lettering, typography, and type design. The loose network supports and promotes the work of all women in these disciplines.

Animation World Network (AWN)
https://awn.com/
The largest animation-related publishing group on the Internet, providing a wide range of interesting, relevant, and helpful info pertaining to all aspects of animation. It covers areas as diverse as animator profiles, independent film distribution, commercial studio activities, licensing, CGI and other animation technologies, as well as in-depth coverage of current events in all fields of animation.

Artfixed
www.artfixed.com
Artfixed is about bringing a useful new perspective to the visual arts world through science, case studies, and hard data, so creative craftspeople can make informed decisions about their careers.

Association of Registered Graphic Designers (RGD)
www.rgd.ca
Through RGD, Canadian designers exchange ideas, educate, and inspire; set professional standards; and build a strong, supportive community dedicated to advocating for the value of design.

Blue Light Exposed
www.bluelightexposed.com
University of Montreal, School of Optometry website with in-depth explanation of what blue light is and why it is dangerous. Also provides suggestions for protecting yourself against its harmful effects. Related blog.

Can I use...
www.caniuse.com
Compatibility tables for the support of the individual features in HTML5, CSS3, SVG, JS API, and more in desktop and mobile browsers.

Copyrightlaws.com
www.copyrightlaws.com
A portal for copyright and licensing information for creators, owners, distributors, and consumers of copyright-protected materials, which was created by attorney Lesley Ellen Harris, a consultant on U.S., Canadian, and international copyright and licensing issues. The site provides free resources including articles and an e-letter on copyright. Questions about copyright and licensing asked through the blog will be promptly answered.

Creative Bloq
www.creativebloq.com
A daily mix of advice and inspiration for digital and traditional artists, web designers, graphic designers, 3D and VFX artists, illustrators, and more.

Creative Market
www.creativemarket.com
Creative Market is an online marketplace that sells ready-to-use and customizable design content in a variety of different categories including photos, graphics, templates, themes, fonts, etc. that are created by independent makers. Join and receive 6 free assets per week. Also includes a blog with inspiration and tutorials.

Creative Pro
www.creativepro.com
Tutorials and tips on creative topics and business practices.

CSS-Tricks
www.css-tricks.com
Much more than CSS, the blog is about building websites and all that it entails, mostly from a front-end perspective. Also includes videos, a newsletter, and job board.

DesignBolts
www.designbolts.com
Design freebies, tech, tutorials, and articles.

Double Your Freelancing
www.doubleyourfreelancing.com
Articles, guides, and courses designed to help you build a successful and profitable freelance business.

Dynamic Drive
www.dynamicdrive.com
Free, original DHTML and JavaScripts to enhance your website.

Fleen
www.fleen.com
A blog about webcomics.

Gamasutra
www.gamasutra.com
A website and blog devoted to the art and business of making games. Includes newsletters, a job board, and the *Game Career Guide*.

Game Industry Career Guide
www.gameindustrycareerguide.com
Practical, real-world advice on getting educated for and landing a job in the video game industry. Includes schools, job descriptions, a job board, and annual salary guide.

Graphic Artists Guild
www.graphicartistsguild.org
Numerous resources for graphic artists and art buyers: copyright and contract information; updates on the latest legislation affecting creative professionals; access to professional webinars and monthly virtual chats; a job board; archived issues of Guild newsletters and publications; a portfolio section, organized by artistic discipline; and a members-only section that includes free archived webinars for downloading, and professional discounts.

Inker Linker
www.inkerlinker.com
Whether you want a printer who is as much of a perfectionist as you are, have a very small press run, or require a special printing or finishing technique (e.g., die-cutting, embossing, edge painting, foil stamping, etc.), this website (by letterer and illustrator Jessica Hische) is worth checking out. Graphic artists who have worked with any of the printers listed can add comments and ratings about their experiences. You can also search printers by the types of printing they offer (offset, letterpress, digital, engraving, or screen).

Interactive Advertising Bureau (IAB)
www.iab.net
IAB is composed of more than 650 leading media and technology companies that are responsible for selling online advertising in the United States. The IAB evaluates and recommends standards and practices, and fields critical research on interactive advertising. Of particular value to graphic artists designing and illustrating interactive advertising are IAB's descriptions, examples, dimensions, and creative guidelines for various types of interactive ads, as well as a glossary of terms used in the industry.

Library of Congress/Copyright Office
www.loc.gov | www.loc.gov/copyright
Home of the U.S. Copyright Office as well as online exhibitions and access to several digital collections.

Living Wage Calculator
https://livingwage.mit.edu/
Developed by the Massachusetts Institute of Technology, this wage calculator is a useful tool for self-employed graphic artists trying to figure out pricing. It calculates the hourly living wage by state and county— what a resident in a locality would need to earn to meet a minimum standard of living. It shows the living wage (compared to the minimum wage) by the number of adults and dependents in a household. It also breaks down typical annual expenses for each combination of adults and dependents.

Loomier
www.loomier.co
A website for artists who mean business. Resources and tools to help you monetize your art to create a successful and sustainable business, including coaching, e-courses, articles, an extensive free resource library, and a community Facebook group.

Louise Myer's Visual Social Media
www.louisem.com
An award-winning blog full of tips for succeeding at visual social media marketing. Geared to small businesses, it includes information about image sizes, photo optimization, how to use hashtags, copyright issues, etc., and lists of additional resources. Also available are both free and for-purchase guides.

MacInTouch
www.macintouch.com
Independent news site, providing news, information, and analysis about Apple Macintosh and iPhone/iOS.

Morguefile
www.morguefile.com
A public image archive for creatives by creatives. Free photos for inspiration, reference, and use (even commercial). Very flexible usage terms and no licensing fees.

MyFonts
www.myfonts.com
World's largest collection of fonts: find fonts for a project, identify fonts that you've seen, try fonts before buying. Site also includes the newsletter Rising Stars featuring popular new fonts.

Neenah Paper
www.neenahpaper.com/resources
Resource center contains great information on paper, postal requirements (size standards, business reply mail, etc.), and glossary of paper terms. Design resources include Adobe Swatch Exchange Files and downloadable dielines and templates.

Notes on Design (NoD)
www.sessions.edu/notes-on-design
NoD is a curated online design magazine that brings graphic designers sophisticated content daily. Its panel of guest authors includes professional designers, writers, educators, and business owners, each of whom write to inspire creativity, improve the quality of your work, and promote engaged thinking about today's most pressing design topics.

Oozled
www.oozled.com
Curated feed of resources for everything creative for designers, web developers, and visual artists. Includes productivity and business tools.

Patreon
www.patreon.com
An online platform where artists can get "patrons" to help them achieve sustainable income to keep on creating. Support can be project-based or ongoing. Patrons (fans) pledge a monthly fee on a tiered subscription system in return for such things as sneak peeks, behind-the-scenes access, bonus materials, and online classes—the larger the pledge, the more perks the fan receives. Patreon takes a 5% commission from pledges, and the artist receives the remainder.

Princeton University Office of Environmental Health & Safety (EHS)
https://ehs.princeton.edu/health-safety-the-campus-community/art-theater-safety/art-safety
EHS provides leadership, technical support, information and training, consultation, and periodic audits of environmental, health and safety practices, and regulatory compliance. Of special interest to artists is a comprehensive section devoted to Art Safety, including common safety concerns and precautions and hazardous substances listed by specific discipline.

Productive Flourishing
www.productiveflourishing.com
A community for the doers with the vision to see how the world could be, the smarts to figure out how to make it happen, and the grit to do the work. Free planners and worksheets for creatives and entrepreneurs. Also publishes digital planner packs and books. Website includes a free content library and a blog and podcast of business advice.

SciArtNOW
www.sciartnow.com
A resource devoted to the business of medical illustration. Tips, tricks, and hands-on advice for medical and scientific illustrators. Includes podcasts, tutorials, and international job postings.

Search Engine Roundtable
www.seroundtable.com
Provides a single source for the most interesting threads covered at the Search Engine Marketing forums.

Search Engine Watch
www.searchenginewatch.com
Search Engine Watch provides tips and information about searching the Web, analysis of the search engine industry, and help to site owners trying to improve their ability to be found in search engines.

Self-Employment in the Arts (SEA)
www.selfemploymentinthearts.com
Housed at North Central College in Naperville, IL, SEA is a program geared towards helping emerging visual, performing, literary, and media artists gain the resources and connections they need to be successful self-employed artists. Programming includes an annual conference, regional workshops, panel discussions, webinars, competitions and more.

Shopify's Business and Domain Name Generator
www.shopify.com/tools/business-name-generator
Enter in your desired business name, find out if other businesses are using it, and see available domain names.

Sprout Social
www.sproutsocial.com
In-depth articles for small businesses trying to use social media as part of marketing.

Tax, Accounting, and Payroll Sites Directory
www.taxsites.com
One-stop shopping for all types of tax information, this is an extremely easy-to-use site with direct links to international, federal, state, and local tax websites, organized in chart form. It includes tax law and regulations, rates and tables, forms and publications, news, and updates. Also has sections relating to accounting and payroll. A service of Accountants World, LLC.

Technical Illustrators.org
www.technicalillustrators.org
A blog and community for technical illustrators by technical illustrators. Includes a freelance hourly rate calculator and list of resources.

TED
www.ted.com
Ideas worth spreading (technology, entertainment, design, etc.). Riveting and inspirational talks by remarkable people.

The Business of Art Licensing
www.art-licensing.biz/the-dos-and-donts-of-art-licensing-1-ten-secrets-to-success-in-art-licensing/
From the blog of Porterfield's Fine Art Licensing, the article, "Do's and Don't's of Art Licensing #1," provides artists with 10 valuable secrets for success in licensing their art, from choice of subject matter that sells to how to prepare submissions.

The Clark Hulings Fund for Visual Artists
www.clarkhulingsfund.org
The Clark Hulings Fund for Visual Artists (CHF) is a 501(c)(3) nonprofit organization that equips professional visual artists to be self-sustaining entrepreneurs.

The 11 Second Club
www.11secondclub.com
Sponsored by animationmentor.com, The 11 Second Club conducts monthly character animation challenges open to everyone. It provides a free platform to train and test animation skills.

The Most Comprehensive Free Directory for Artists
www.ghenadiesontu.com/blog/2018/8/4/the-most-comprehensive-free-directory-for-artists
An indispensable resource, curated by artist Ghenadie Sontu, for artists who want to promote and sell their work. It lists website providers; online gallery, auction, marketplace, social media, and referral sites; as well as print-on-demand resources, sites offering commissions, and miscellaneous resources for artists.

Web Design Group (WDG)
www.htmlhelp.com
The Web Design Group was founded to promote the creation of non-browser-specific, non-resolution-specific, creative and informative sites that are accessible to all users worldwide.

Webdesigner Depot
www.webdesignerdepot.com
Blog site featuring posts on web and mobile design/development, code, usability issues, etc., as well as sources for freebies.communications Commission website, with answers to frequently-asked questions at https://crtc.gc.ca/eng/com500/faq500.htm.

Appendix: Contracts & Forms

This Appendix contains standard Graphic Artists Guild contracts and other useful forms for doing business. The forms appear in order from general (all purpose or for use by most graphic artists) to specific (by discipline).

How to Use These Forms

It should be noted that while these forms are as comprehensive as possible, some terms might not be suited to a given assignment. However, these forms can be used as starting points for your own customized contracts. Be aware that legal language is written to be precise, and attempts to simplify contract terms into "plain English" or delete contract terms altogether may leave the artist exposed to misinterpretation and misunderstanding of important aspects of an agreement.

Digital versions of all the forms in this section are also available for download at https:// graphicartistsguild.org/dpegs-contract-downloads. For additional information, e-mail membership@graphicartistsguild.org.

[Date]

FOR SETTLEMENT PURPOSES ONLY
FED. R. EVID. 408

[First and Last Name][Address]
RE: *[List project or issue]*

Dear *[Name]*:

It has come to my attention that you have made an unauthorized use of my copyrighted work entitled *[name of work]* ("the Work"). I own all rights, including copyright, in the Work, [first published in *[date]*], [and have registered copyright therein]. Your work entitled *[name of infringing work]* is essentially identical to the Work [or clearly copies certain portions of the Work]. *[Give a few examples that illustrate direct copying.]*

As you neither asked for nor received permission to use the Work as the basis for *[name of infringing work]* nor to make or distribute copies, including electronic copies, of same, I believe you have willfully infringed my rights under 17 U.S.C. Section 101 et seq. [and could be liable for statutory damages as high as $150,000 as set forth in Section 504(c) (2) therein].*

I demand that you immediately cease the use and distribution of *[name of infringing work]* and all other infringing works derived from the Work, and that you delete or remove from circulation all copies, including electronic copies, of same; that you deliver to me, if applicable, all unused, undistributed copies of same, or destroy such copies immediately; and that you desist from this or any other infringement of my rights in the future. I also require an accounting of all profits you have made to date from sales or other exploitation of *[name of infringing work]*. If I have not received an affirmative response from you by *[date–give them about 2 weeks]* indicating that you have fully complied with these requirements, I shall take further action against you. This letter is written without prejudice to my rights, all of which are hereby expressly reserved.

Very truly yours,

*Text in brackets only applies if the copyright for the infringed work has been registered.

ARTIST-AGENT AGREEMENT (Front)

[Artist's Letterhead]

Remove all language in italics before using this form.

Agreement, this day of   *[date]*   between
_____

(hereinafter referred to as the "Artist"), residing at
_____

and   (hereinafter referred to as the "Agent"),
_____

residing at
_____

WHEREAS, the Artist is an established artist of proven talents; and

WHEREAS, the Artist wishes to have an agent represent him or her in marketing certain rights enumerated herein; and

WHEREAS, the Agent is capable of marketing the artwork produced by the Artist; and

WHEREAS, the Agent wishes to represent the Artist;

Now, THEREFORE, in consideration of the foregoing premises and the mutual covenants hereinafter set forth and other valuable consideration, the parties hereto agree as follows:

1. AGENCY
The Artist appoints the Agent to act as his or her [non-] exclusive representative: **(A)** in the following geographical area:

_____

_____

_____

(B) for the markets listed here *[specify publishing, advertising, etc.]*:

_____

_____

_____

The Agent agrees to use his or her best efforts in submitting the Artist's work for the purpose of securing assignments for the Artist. The Agent shall negotiate the terms of any assignment that is offered, but the Artist shall have the right to reject any assignment if he or she finds the terms thereof unacceptable.

2. PROMOTION
The Artist shall provide the Agent with such samples of work as are from time to time necessary for the purpose of securing assignments. These samples shall remain the property of the Artist and all samples and copies thereof shall be returned to Artist, and digital copies in Agent's possession shall be permanently deleted, within 30 days of termination of this Agreement. The Agent shall take reasonable efforts to protect the work from loss or damage, but shall be liable for such loss or damage only if caused by the Agent's negligence. Promotional expenses, including but not limited to promotional mailings and paid advertising, shall be paid _____% by the Agent and _____% by the Artist. The Agent shall bear the expenses of shipping, insurance, and similar marketing expenses.

3. TERM
This Agreement shall take effect on the day of _____*[date]*_____ and remain in full force and effect for a term of *[number of years]*, unless terminated as provided in Paragraph 9.

4. COMMISSIONS
The Agent shall be entitled to the following commissions: **(A)** On assignments secured by the Agent during the term of this Agreement, 25% of the billing. **(B)** On house accounts, 10% of the billing. For purposes of this Agreement, house accounts are defined as accounts obtained by the Artist at any time or obtained by another agent representing the Artist prior to the commencement of this Agreement and are listed in Schedule A attached to this Agreement. It is understood by both parties that no commission shall be paid on assignments rejected by the Artist or for which the Artist fails to receive payment, regardless of the reason payment is not made. Further, no commissions shall be payable in either **(A)** or **(B)** above, for any part of the billing that is due to expenses incurred by the Artists in performing the assignment, whether or not such expenses are reimbursed by the Client. In the event that a flat fee is paid by the Client, it shall be reduced by the amount of expenses incurred by the Artist in performing the assignment, and the Agent's commission shall be payable only on the fee as reduced for expenses.

5. BILLING
The [ ] Artist [ ] Agent shall be responsible for all billings.

6. PAYMENTS
The party responsible for billing (the "Billing Party") agrees to hold all funds due to the other party as trust funds in an account separate from the Billing Party's funds prior to making payment to the other party. The Billing Party shall make all payments due within 10 days of receipt of any fees covered by this Agreement. Late payments shall be accompanied by interest calculated at the rate of _____% per month thereafter.

7. ACCOUNTINGS
The Billing Party shall send copies of invoices to the other party when rendered. If requested, that party shall also provide the other party with semiannual accountings showing all assignments for the period, the Clients' names, the fees paid, expenses incurred by the Artist, the dates of payment, the amounts on which the Agent's commissions are to be calculated, and the sums due less those amounts already paid.

ARTIST-AGENT AGREEMENT (Back)

8. INSPECTION OF THE BOOKS AND RECORDS

The Billing Party shall keep the books and records with respect to commissions due at his or her place of business and permit the other party to inspect these books and records during normal business hours on the giving of reasonable notice.

8. TERMINATION

This Agreement may be terminated by either party by giving 30 days written notice to the other party. If the Artist receives assignments after the termination date from Clients originally obtained by the Agent during the term of this Agreement, the commission specified in Paragraph 4 **(A)** shall be payable to the Agent under the following circumstances: If the Agent has represented the Artist for 6 months or less, the Agent shall receive a commission on such assignments received by the Artist within 90 days of the date of termination. This period shall increase by 30 days for each additional 6 months that the Agent has represented the Artist, but in no event shall such period exceed 180 days.

9. ASSIGNMENT

This Agreement shall not be assigned by either of the parties hereto. It shall be binding on and inure to the benefit of the successors, administrators, executors, or heirs of the Agent and Artist.

10.   DISPUTE RESOLUTION

Any disputes in excess of $ _____ *[maximum limit for small-claims court]* arising out of this Agreement shall be submitted to mediation in accordance with the rules of

_____ *[name of local lawyers for the arts mediation program]*. The prevailing party in any dispute resolved by litigation shall be entitled to recover its attorney's fees and costs, provided that party initiated or participated in mediation as set forth herein.

12. NOTICES

All notices shall be given to the parties at their respective addresses set forth above.

13. INDEPENDENT CONTRACTOR STATUS

Both parties agree that the Agent is acting as an independent contractor. This Agreement is not an employment agreement, nor does it constitute a joint venture or partnership between the Artist and Agent.

14. AMENDMENTS AND MERGER

All amendments to this Agreement must be written. This Agreement incorporates the entire understanding of the parties.

15. GOVERNING LAW

This Agreement shall be governed by the laws of the State of _____.

IN WITNESS WHEREOF, the parties have signed this Agreement as of the date set forth above.

SCHEDULE A: HOUSE ACCOUNTS

Date _____

1. *[Name and address of Client]* _____

2. _____

3. _____

4. _____

5. _____

6. _____

7. _____

8. _____

9. _____

10. _____

11. _____

12. _____

Artist _____   **Agent** _____

ARTWORK INVENTORY FORM

[Artist's Letterhead]

Remove all language in italics before using this form.

ID#

Final or Rough

Name of Publication

Date Sent

Date Accepted

Date Final Due *[if applicable]*

Fee Negotiated

Date Rejected

Date Artwork Returned

ALL-PURPOSE PURCHASE ORDER (Front)

[Art Buyer's Letterhead]

Remove all language in italics before using this form.

TO

Commissioned by

Date

Purchase Order Number

Job Number

ASSIGNMENT DESCRIPTION *[Indicate any preliminary presentations required by the buyer.]*

Delivery Date

Fee

BUYER SHALL REIMBURSE ARTIST FOR THE FOLLOWING EXPENSES

Messengers

Travel

Software

Models

Telephone

Transparencies

Props

Proofs

Film Output

Other

RIGHTS GRANTED. BUYER PURCHASES THE FOLLOWING EXCLUSIVE RIGHTS FOR USAGE OF FINAL ART DELIVERED TO BUYER:

Title or Product *[name]*

Category or Use *[advertising, corporate, promotional, editorial, etc.]*

Medium of Use *[consumer or trade magazine, annual report, TV, book, website, online publications, device apps, etc.]*

Edition (if book) *[hardcover, mass-market paperback, quality paperback, e-book, etc.]*

Geographic Area *[if applicable]*

Time Period *[if applicable]*

Artist reserves any usage rights not expressly granted. Any usage beyond that granted to buyer herein shall require the payment of Artist's standard licensing rate for such usage. All usage rights are conditioned upon receipt of full payment. Upon receipt of full payment, Artist shall deliver digital files necessary to enable Client's usage rights granted herein. Artist retains the rights to display all work created by Artist for this project, including preliminary designs and final deliverables, in Artist's portfolios, including in print and online, and to submit such work to design periodicals and competitions, provided that no confidential information is revealed thereby.

ALL-PURPOSE PURCHASE ORDER (Back)

TERMS

1. Time for Payment
All invoices shall be paid within 30 days of receipt. The grant of any license or right of copyright is conditioned on receipt of full payment.

2. Default in Payment
The Buyer shall assume responsibility for all collection of legal fees necessitated by default in payment.

3. Changes
Buyer shall make additional payments for changes requested beyond original assignment. However, no additional payment shall be made for changes required to conform to the original assignment description. The Buyer shall offer the Artist first opportunity to make any changes.

4. Expenses
Buyer shall reimburse Artist for all expenses arising from this assignment, including the payment of any sales taxes due on this assignment. Buyer's approval shall be obtained for any increases in fees or expenses that exceed the original estimate by 10% or more.

5. Cancellation
In the event of cancellation of this assignment, ownership of all copyrights and the original artwork shall be retained by the Artist; Buyer shall return originals and all copies thereof to Artist, and permanently delete all digital copies thereof; and a cancellation fee for work completed, based on the contract price and expenses already incurred, shall be paid by the Buyer.

6. Ownership of Artwork
The Artist retains ownership of all original artwork, whether preliminary or final, and the Buyer shall return such artwork, and all copies thereof, and shall permanently delete all digital copies thereof, within 30 days of the expiration of Buyer's usage rights.

7. Credit Lines
The Buyer shall give Artist and any other creators a credit line with any editorial usage. If similar credit lines are to be given with other types of usage, it must be so indicated here:

_____

_____

☐ If this box is checked, the credit line shall be in the form:

© [date] _____ .

8. Releases
Buyer shall indemnify Artist against all claims and expenses, including reasonable attorney's fees, due to uses for which no release was requested in writing, or for uses that exceed authority granted by a release.

9. Modifications
Modification of the Agreement must be written, except that the invoice may include, and Buyer shall pay, fees or expenses that were orally authorized in order to progress promptly with the work.

10. Warranty of Originality
The Artist warrants and represents that, to the best of his/her knowledge, the work assigned hereunder is original and has not been previously published, or that consent to use has been obtained consistent with the rights granted to Buyer herein; that all work or portions thereof obtained through the undersigned from third parties is original and that consent to use has been obtained consistent with the rights granted to Buyer herein; that the Artist has full authority to make this Agreement; and that the work prepared by the Artist does not contain any scandalous, libelous, or unlawful matter. This warranty does not extend to any uses that the Buyer or others may make of the Artist's product that may infringe on the rights of others. Buyer expressly agrees that it will hold the Artist harmless for all liability caused by the Buyer's use of the Artist's product to the extent such use infringes on the rights of others.

10. Limitation of Liability
Buyer agrees that it shall not hold Artist or his/her agents or employees liable for any incidental or consequential damages that arise from Artist's failure to perform any aspect of the Project in a timely manner, regardless of whether such failure was caused by intentional or negligent acts or omissions of Artist or a third party. Furthermore, Artist disclaims all implied warranties, including the warranty of merchantability and fitness for a particular purpose. Buyer shall be responsible for all compliance with laws or government rules or regulations applicable to Buyer's final product(s).

To the extent the Deliverables include any word, symbol, logo, or other content used to designate Buyer as the source of goods or services ("Trademarks"), Buyer shall have sole responsibility for ensuring that Trademarks do not infringe the rights of third parties, and Buyer shall indemnify, save, and hold harmless Artist from any and all damages, liabilities, costs, losses, or expenses arising out of any claim, demand, or action by a third party alleging trademark infringement, or arising out of Buyer's failure to obtain trademark clearance or permissions, for use of Trademarks.

The maximum liability of Artist to Buyer for damages for any and all causes whatsoever, and Buyer's maximum remedy, regardless of the form of action, shall be limited to an amount equal to the total fees paid by Buyer to Artist hereunder. In no event shall Artist be liable for any indirect, incidental, special, consequential, exemplary, or punitive damages arising out of or related to the Services, even if Artist has been advised of the possibility of such damages.

12. Dispute Resolution
Any disputes in excess of $_____ [maximum limit for small-claims court] arising out of this Agreement shall be submitted to mediation in accordance with the rules of _____
[name of local lawyers for the arts mediation program]. The prevailing party in any dispute resolved by litigation shall be entitled to recover its attorney's fees and costs, provided that party initiated or participated in mediation as set forth herein.

12. Acceptance of Terms
The signature of both parties shall evidence acceptance of these terms.

CONSENTED AND AGREED TO:

_____   _____   _____
Artist's signature/date   Authorized signature/date   Buyer's name and title

NONDISCLOSURE AGREEMENT FOR SUBMITTING IDEAS *[Illustrator's or Designer's Letterhead]*

Remove all language in italics before using this form.

Agreement, this day of _____ *[date]* _____ between _____

(hereinafter referred to as the "Illustrator" or "Designer"), located at _____

and _____ (hereinafter referred to as the "Recipient"), located at _____

WHEREAS, the Illustrator [or Designer] has developed certain valuable information, concepts, ideas, or designs, which the Illustrator [or Designer] deems confidential (hereinafter referred to as the "Information"); and

WHEREAS, the Recipient is in the business of using such Information for its projects and wishes to review the Information; and

WHEREAS, the Illustrator [or Designer] wishes to disclose this Information to the Recipient; and

WHEREAS, the Recipient is willing not to disclose this Information, as provided in this Agreement;

Now, THEREFORE, in consideration of the foregoing premises and the mutual covenants hereinafter set forth and other valuable considerations, the parties hereto agree as follows:

1. DISCLOSURE
Illustrator [or Designer] shall disclose to the Recipient the Information, which concerns

_____

_____

_____

2. PROMOTION
Recipient agrees that this disclosure is only for the purpose of the Recipient's evaluation to determine its interest in the commercial exploitation of the Information.

3. LIMITATION ON USE
Recipient agrees not to copy, manufacture, sell, deal in, or otherwise use or appropriate the disclosed Information in any way whatsoever, including but not limited to adaptation, imitation, redesign, or modification. Nothing contained in this Agreement shall be deemed to give Recipient any rights whatsoever in and to the Information.

4. CONFIDENTIALITY
Recipient understands and agrees that the unauthorized disclosure of the Information by the Recipient to others would irreparably damage the Illustrator [or Designer]. As consideration and in return for the disclosure of this Information, the Recipient shall keep secret and hold in confidence all such Information and treat the Information as if it were the Recipient's own property by not disclosing it to any person or entity.

5. GOOD-FAITH NEGOTIATIONS
If, on the basis of the evaluation of the Information, Recipient wishes to pursue the exploitation thereof, Recipient agrees to enter into good-faith negotiations to arrive at a mutually satisfactory agreement for these purposes. Until and unless such an agreement is entered into, this nondisclosure Agreement shall remain in force.

6. MISCELLANY
This Agreement shall be binding upon and shall inure to the benefit of the parties and their respective legal representatives, successors, and assigns.

© Tad Crawford 1990

In witness whereof, the parties have signed this Agreement as of the date first set forth above.

Illustrator [or Designer] _____

Recipient _____

Company Name _____

By _____

Authorized signatory, title _____

WORK CHANGE ORDER FORM

[Designer's Letterhead]

Remove all language in italics before using this form.

CLIENT

Change Order Number _____

Project _____

Date _____

Work Change Requested By _____

Job Number _____

PHASE

☐ Concept Development   ☐ Production   ☐ Other

☐ Design Development   ☐ Project Implementation

WORK CHANGE DESCRIPTION	COST CHANGE	SCHEDULE CHANGE
_____	_____	_____
_____	_____	_____
_____	_____	_____
_____	_____	_____
_____	_____	_____
_____	_____	_____

This is not an invoice. Revised specifications on work in progress represents information that is either different from that which the original project budget and schedule were based upon, or follows after client's approval to the stage of work in which this (these) item(s) appear(s). Changes in time and cost quoted here may be approximate, unless otherwise noted. Your signature below will constitute authorization to proceed with the change(s) and your agreement to pay additional charges noted above. Kindly return a signed and dated copy of this form to: _____ . The information contained in this work change order is assumed to be correct and acceptable to client unless designer is otherwise notified in writing _____ days of the date of this document.

Authorized Signature _____

Print Name _____

Date _____

Reprinted with permission from *Business and Legal Forms for Graphic Designers, 3rd Edition* by Tad Crawford and Eva Doman Bruck, 2003

LICENSING AGREEMENT (Short Form)

[Licensor's Letterhead]

Remove all language in italics before using this form.

1. _____ (The "Licensor")

hereby grants to_____(the "Licensee") a

nonexclusive license to use the image entitled "_____

_____" attached hereto (the "Image") created and owned

by Licensor on _____ ("Licensed Products") and to distribute and sell

these Licensed Products in_____ *[territory]*

for a term of _____ years commencing_____ *[date]*,

in accordance with the terms and conditions of this Agreement.

2. Licensor shall retain all copyrights in and to the Image. Licensee shall identify the Licensor as the artist on the Licensed Products and shall reproduce thereon the following copyright notice:
© *[Licensor's name and date]*.

3. Licensee agrees to pay the Licensor a nonrefundable royalty of $_____ [or] (_____%) percent of the net sales of the Licensed Products. "Net Sales" as used herein shall mean sales to customers less pre-paid freight and credits for lawful and customary volume rebates, actual returns, and allowances. Royalties shall be deemed to accrue when the Licensed Products are sold, shipped, or invoiced, whichever first occurs.

4. Licensee shall pay Licensor a nonrefundable advance in the amount of $_____ upon signing of this Agreement. Licensee further agrees to pay Licensor a guaranteed nonrefundable minimum royalty of $_____ every month.

5. Royalty payments shall be paid on the first day of each month commencing _____ *[date]*, and Licensee shall furnish Licensor with monthly statements of account showing the kinds and quantities of all Licensed Products sold, the prices received therefore, and all deductions for freight, volume rebates, returns, and allowances. The first royalty statement shall be sent on _____ *[date]*.

6. Licensor shall have the right to terminate this Agreement upon 30 days' notice if Licensee fails to make any payment required of it and does not cure this default within said 30 days, whereupon all rights granted herein shall revert immediately to the Licensor.

7. Licensee agrees to keep complete and accurate books and records relating to the sale of the Licensed Products. Licensor shall have the right to inspect Licensee's books and records concerning sales of the Licensed Products upon prior written notice.

8. Licensee shall give Licensor, free of charge, _____ *[number]* samples of each of the Licensed Products for Licensor's personal use. Licensor shall have the right to purchase additional samples of the Licensed Products at the Licensee's manufacturing cost. "Manufacturing cost" shall be $_____ per Licensed Product.

9. Licensor shall have the right to approve the quality of the reproduction of the Image on the Licensed Products and on any advertising or promotional materials, and Licensor shall not unreasonably withhold approval.

10. Licensee shall use its best efforts to promote, distribute, and sell the Licensed Products, and said Products shall be of the highest commercial quality.

11. All rights not specifically transferred by this Agreement are reserved to the Licensor. Any transfer of rights is conditional upon receipt of full payment.

12. The Licensee shall hold the Licensor harmless from and against any loss, expense, or damage occasioned by any claim, demand, suit, or recovery against the Licensor arising out of the use of the Image or the manufacture and/or sale of the Licensed Products.

13. Nothing herein shall be construed to constitute the parties hereto joint ventures, nor shall any similar relationship be deemed to exist between them. This Agreement shall not be assigned in whole or in part without the prior written consent of the Licensor.

14. This Agreement shall be governed by and construed in accordance with the laws of the State of _____ *[state in which Licensor resides]* as applied to transactions entered into and to be performed wholly within said state between said state's residents without regard to principles of conflict of laws. The parties submit exclusively to the personal jurisdiction of the federal district court for the _____ District of _____ *[district in which Licensor resides]* and the courts of said state. Licensee waives all defenses of lack of personal jurisdiction and forum non conveniens.

15. All notices, demands, payments, royalty payments and statements shall be sent to the Licensor at the following address: _____and to the Licensee at: _____
_____.

16. This Agreement constitutes the entire agreement between the parties hereto and shall not be modified, amended, or changed in any way except by written agreement signed by both parties hereto. This Agreement supersedes all prior or simultaneous representations, discussions, negotiations, and agreements, whether written or oral, between the parties concerning the Image.

17. This Agreement shall be binding upon and shall inure to the benefit of the parties, their successors, and assigns. Licensee shall not assign its rights under this Agreement, in whole or in part, without the prior written approval of Licensor.

In witness whereof, the parties have executed this Licensing Agreement on _____ *[date]*

Licensee *[company name]* _____

Authorized by *[name, position]* _____

Licensor *[name]* _____

© Caryn R. Leland 2012

LICENSING AGREEMENT (Long Form – Front)

[Licensor's Letterhead]

Remove all language in italics before using this form.

1. Grant of License

Agreement made this _____ day of _____, 20_____,

between _____ (the "Licensor"), having an

address at _____ , and

_____ (the "Licensee"),

having an address at _____ whereby Licensor grants to Licensee a license to use the designs listed on the attached Schedules A and B (the "Designs") in accordance with the terms and conditions of this Agreement and only for the production, sale, advertising, and promotion of certain articles (the "Licensed Products") described in Schedule A for the Term and in the Territory set forth in said Schedule. Licensee shall have the right to affix the Trademarks:

_____ and _____ on or to the Licensed Products and on packaging, advertising, and promotional materials sold, used, or distributed in connection with the Licensed Products.

2. Licensor's Representation and Credits

A. Licensor warrants that Licensor has the right to grant to the Licensee all of the rights conveyed in this Agreement. The Licensee shall have no right, license, or permission except as herein expressly granted. All rights not specifically transferred by the Agreement are reserved to the Licensor.

B. The Licensee prominently shall display and identify the Licensor as the designer on each Licensed Product and on all packaging, advertising, and display, and in all publicity therefore, and shall have reproduced thereon (or on an approved tag or label) the following notices:

"© _____ *[Licensor's name and date]* All rights reserved." The Licensed Products shall be marketed under the name:

_____ for

_____ *[if applicable].* The name shall not be co-joined with any third party's name without the Licensor's express written permission.

C. The Licensee shall have the right to use the Licensor's name, portrait, or picture, in a dignified manner consistent with the Licensor's reputation, in advertising or other promotional materials associated with the sale of the Licensed Products.

3. Royalties and Statements of Account

A. Licensee agrees to pay Licensor a nonrefundable royalty of $ _____

[or] (_____ %) of the net sales of all of the Licensed Products incorporating and embodying the Designs. "Net sales" is defined as sales direct to customers less prepaid freight and credits for lawful and customary volume rebates, actual returns, and allowances; the aggregate of said deductions and credits shall not exceed 3% of accrued royalties in any year. No costs incurred in the manufacture, sale, distribution, or exploitation of the Licensed Products shall be deducted from any royalties due to Licensor. Royalties shall be deemed to accrue when the Licensed Products are sold, shipped, or invoiced, whichever first occurs.

B. Royalty payments for all sales shall be due on the 15th day after the end of each calendar quarter. At that time and regardless if any Licensed Products were sold during the preceding time period, Licensee shall furnish Licensor an itemized statement categorized by Design, showing the kinds and quantities of all Licensed Products sold and the prices received therefor, and all deductions for freight, volume rebates, returns, and allowances. The first royalty

statement shall commence on: _____ *[date].*

C. If Licensor has not received the royalty payment as required by the foregoing paragraph 3B within 21 days following the end of each calendar quarter, a monthly service charge of 1 1/2% shall accrue thereon and become due and owing from the date on which such royalty payment became due and owing.

4. Advances and Minimum Royalties

A. In each year of this Agreement, Licensee agrees to pay Licensor a Guaranteed Minimum Royalty in the amount of $_____ , of which

$_____ shall be deemed a Nonrefundable Advance against royalties. The difference, if any, between the Advance and the Guaranteed Minimum Royalty shall be divided equally and paid quarterly over the term of this Agreement commencing with the quarter beginning

_____ *[date].*

B. The Nonrefundable Advance shall be paid on the signing of this Agreement. No part of the Guaranteed Minimum Royalty or the Nonrefundable Advance shall be repayable to Licensee.

C. On signing of this Agreement, Licensee shall pay Licensor a nonrefundable design fee in the amount of $_____ per Design. This fee shall not be applied against royalties.

D. Licensor has the right to terminate this Agreement upon the giving of 30 days' notice to Licensee if the Licensee fails to pay any portion of the Guaranteed Minimum Royalty when due.

5. Books and Records

Licensee agrees to keep complete and accurate books and records relating to the sale and other distribution of each of the Licensed Products. Licensor or its representative shall have the right to inspect Licensee's books and records relating to the sales of the Licensed Products upon 30 days' prior written notice. Any discrepancies over 5% between the royalties received and the royalties due will be subject to the royalty payment set forth herein and paid immediately. If the audit discloses such an underpayment of 5% or more, Licensee shall reimburse the Licensor for all the costs of said audit.

6. Quality of Licensed Products, Approval, and Advertising

A. Licensee agrees that the Licensed Products shall be of the highest standard and quality and of such style and appearance as to be best suited to their exploitation to the best advantage and to the protection and enhancement of the Licensed Products and the good will pertaining thereto. The Licensed Products shall be manufactured, sold, and distributed in accordance with all applicable national, state, and local laws.

B. In order to ensure that the development, manufacture, appearance, quality, and distribution of each Licensed Product is consonant with the Licensor's good will associated with its reputation, copyrights, and trademark, Licensor shall have the right to approve, in advance, the quality of the Licensed Products (including, without limitation, concepts and preliminary prototypes, layouts, or camera-ready art prior to production of first sample and revised production sample, if any), all packaging, advertising, promotional and publicity materials, and displays for the Licensed Products.

C. On signing this Agreement, Licensee shall be responsible for delivering all items requiring prior approval pursuant to Paragraph 6B without cost to the Licensor. Licensor agrees not to withhold approval unreasonably.

D. Licensee shall not release or distribute any Licensed Product without securing each of the prior approvals provided for in Paragraph 6B. Licensee shall not depart from any approval secured in accordance with Paragraph 6B without Licensor's prior written consent.

E. Licensee agrees to expend at least _____ % percent of anticipated gross sales of the Licensed Products annually to promote and advertise sales of the Licensed Products.

7. Nonexclusive Rights

Nothing in this Agreement shall be construed to prevent Licensor from granting other licenses for the use of the Designs or from utilizing the Designs in any manner whatsoever, except that the Licensor shall not grant other Licenses for the use of the Designs in connection with the sale of the Licensed Products in the Territory to which this License extends during the term of this Agreement.

8. Non-acquisition of Rights

The Licensee's use of the Designs and Trademarks shall inure to the benefit of the Licensor. If Licensee acquires any trade rights, trademarks, equities, titles, or other rights in and to the Designs or in the Trademark, by operation of law, usage, or otherwise during the term of this Agreement or any extension thereof, Licensee shall forthwith upon the expiration of this Agreement or any extension thereof or sooner termination, assign and transfer the same to Licensor without any consideration other than the consideration of this Agreement.

9. Licensee's Representations

The Licensee warrants and represents that during the term of this License and for any time thereafter, it, or any of its affiliated, associated, or subsidiary companies will not copy, imitate, or authorize the imitation or copying of the Designs, Trade names, and Trademarks, or any distinctive feature of the fore-going or other designs submitted to the Licensee by Licensor. Without prejudice to any other remedies the Licensor may have, royalties as provided herein shall accrue and be paid by Licensee on all items embodying and incorporating imitated or copied Designs.

10. Registrations and Infringements

A. The Licensor has the right but not the obligation to obtain, at its own cost, appropriate copyright, trademark, and patent protection for the Designs and the Trademarks. At Licensor's request and at Licensee's sole cost and expense, Licensee shall make all necessary and appropriate registrations in the name of Licensor to protect the copyrights, trademarks, and patents in and to the Licensed Products and the advertising, promotional, and packaging material in the Territory in which the Licensed Products are sold. Copies of all applications shall be submitted for approval to Licensor prior to filing. The Licensee and Licensor agree to cooperate with each other to assist in the filing of said registrations.

B. Licensee shall not at any time apply for or abet any third party to apply for copyright, trademark, or patent protection that would affect Licensor's ownership of any rights in the Designs or the Trademarks.

C. Licensee shall notify Licensor in writing immediately upon discovery of any infringements or imitations by others of the Designs, Trade names, or Trademarks. Licensor in its sole discretion may bring any suit, action, or proceeding Licensor deems appropriate to protect Licensor's rights in the Designs, Trade names, and Trademarks, including, without limitation, for copyright and trademark infringement and for unfair competition. If for any reason Licensor does not institute any such suit or take any such action or proceeding, upon written notice to the Licensor, Licensee may institute

such appropriate suit, action, or proceeding in Licensee's and Licensor's names. In any event, Licensee and Licensor shall cooperate fully with each other in the prosecution of such suit, action, or proceeding. Licensor reserves the right, at Licensor's cost and expense, to join in any pending suit, action, or proceeding. The instituting party shall pay all costs and expenses, including legal fees, incurred by the instituting party. All recoveries and awards, including settlements received, after payments of costs and legal fees, shall be divided 75% percent to the instituting party and 25% percent to the other party

11. Indemnification and Insurance

A. The Licensee hereby agrees to indemnify and hold the Licensor harmless against all liability, cost, loss, expense (including reasonable attorney's fees), or damages paid, incurred, or occasioned by any claim, demand, suit, settlement, or recovery against the Licensor, without limitation, arising out of the breach or claim of breach of this Agreement; the use of the Designs by it or any third party the manufacture, distribution, and sale of the Licensed Products; and for any alleged defects in the Licensed Products. Licensee hereby consents to submit to the personal jurisdiction of any court, tribunal, or forum in which an action or proceeding is brought involving a claim to which this foregoing indemnification shall apply.

B. Licensee shall obtain at its sole cost and expense product liability insurance in an amount providing sufficient and adequate coverage, but not less than $1 million combined single limit coverage protecting the Licensor against any claims or lawsuits arising from alleged defects in the Licensed Product.

12. Grounds for and Consequences of Termination

A. Licensor shall have the right to terminate this Agreement by written notice, and all the rights granted to the Licensee shall revert forthwith to the Licensor and all royalties or other payments shall become due and payable immediately if:

i. Licensee fails to comply with or fulfill any of the terms or conditions of this Agreement;

ii. The Licensed Products have not been offered or made available for sale by

Licensee _____ months from the date hereof;

iii. Licensee ceases to manufacture and sell the Licensed Products in commercially reasonable quantities; or

iv. The Licensee is adjudicated as bankrupt, makes an assignment for the benefit of creditors, or liquidates its business.

B. Licensee, as quickly as possible, but in no event later than 30 days after such termination, shall submit to Licensor the statements required in Paragraph 3 for all sales and distributions through the date of termination. Licensor shall have the right to conduct an actual inventory on the date of termination or thereafter to verify the accuracy of said statements.

C. In the event of termination, all payments theretofore made to the Licensor shall belong to the Licensor without prejudice to any other remedies the Licensor may have.

13. Sell-off Right

Provided Licensee is not in default of any term or condition of this Agreement, Licensee shall have the right for a period of _____ months from the expiration of this Agreement or any extension thereof to sell inventory on hand subject to the terms and conditions of this Agreement, including the payment of royalties and guaranteed minimum royalties on sales that continue during this additional period.

14. Purchase at Cost

A. Licensor shall have the right to purchase from Licensee, at Licensee's man-ufacturing cost, such number of Licensed Products as Licensor may specify in writing to Licensee, but not to exceed _____ for any Licensed Product. For purposes of this Paragraph, "manufacturing cost" shall mean $_____ per Licensed Product. Any amounts due to Licensee pursuant to this Paragraph shall not be deducted from any royalties, including any minimum royalties, owed to Licensor.

B. Licensee agrees to give the Licensor, without charge, _____ [number] of each of the Licensed Products.

15. Miscellaneous Provisions

A. Nothing herein shall be construed to constitute the parties hereto partners or joint ventures, nor shall any similar relationship be deemed to exist between them.

B. The rights herein granted are personal to the Licensee and shall not be transferred or assigned, in whole or in part, without the prior written consent of the Licensor.

C. No waiver of any condition or covenant of this Agreement by either party hereto shall be deemed to imply or constitute a further waiver by such party of the same or any other condition. This Agreement shall be binding upon and shall inure to the benefit of the parties, their successors, and assigns.

D. Whatever claim Licensor may have against Licensee hereunder for royalties or for damages shall become a first lien upon all of the items produced under this Agreement in the possession or under the control of the Licensee upon the expiration or termination of this Agreement.

E. This Agreement shall be construed in accordance with the laws of

_____ [state]. The Licensee hereby consents to submit

to the personal jurisdiction of the _____ Court,

_____ County, and Federal Court of the District of

_____ [federal court district in which Licensor resides] for all purposes in connection with this Agreement.

F. All notices and demands shall be sent in writing by certified mail, return receipt requested, at the addresses above first written; royalty statements, payments, and samples of Licensed Products and related materials shall be sent by regular mail.

G. This Agreement constitutes the entire agreement between the parties hereto and shall not be modified, amended, or changed in any way except by written agreement signed by both parties hereto. This Agreement supersedes all prior or simultaneous representations, discussions, negotiations, and agreements, whether written or oral, between the parties hereto concerning the Designs. Licensee shall not assign this Agreement.

In witness whereof, the parties have executed this Licensing Agreement as of the date first set forth above.

Licensee [company name] _____

By [name, position] _____

Licensor _____

© Caryn R. Leland 2012

GRAPHIC DESIGNER'S ESTIMATE & CONFIRMATION FORM (Front) *[Designer's Letterhead]*

Remove all language in italics before using this form.

TO

Date _____

Commissioned by _____

Assignment Number _____

Client's Purchase Order Number _____

ASSIGNMENT DESCRIPTION

Delivery Date *[predicated on receipt of all materials to be supplied by Client]* _____

Materials Supplied by _____

Assignment Number _____

Fee _____

FEE PAYMENT SCHEDULE

_____

_____

_____

_____

BUYER SHALL REIMBURSE ARTIST FOR THE FOLLOWING EXPENSES

Illustration	Toll Telephone Calls	Copies
Printing *[if brokered by Designer]*	Materials & Supplies	Other Expenses
Photography	Transportation & Travel	SUBTOTAL
Client's Alterations	Messengers	SALES TAX
Models & Props	Shipping & Insurance	TOTAL

RIGHTS GRANTED (Check one box only):

☐ **Usage Rights Granted:** Buyer purchases the following exclusive rights for usage of final art delivered to Buyer:

Title or Product *[name]* _____

Category or Use
[advertising, corporate, promotional, editorial, etc.] _____

Medium of Use
*[consumer or trade magazine, annual report, TV,
book, website, online publications, device apps, etc.]* _____

Edition (if book) *[hardcover, mass-market paperback,
quality paperback, e-book, etc.]* _____

Geographic Area *[if applicable]* _____

Time Period *[if applicable]* _____

Any usage rights not exclusively granted are reserved to the Designer. Usage beyond that granted to the Client herein shall require payment of an additional fee in the amount of Designer's standard licensing fee for such usage, subject to all terms. Any grant of rights is conditional upon receipt of full payment. Upon receipt of full payment, Designer shall deliver digital files necessary to enable Client's usage rights granted herein. Designer retains the rights to display all work created by Designer for this Project, including preliminary designs and final Deliverables, in Designer's portfolios, including in print and online, and to submit such work to design periodicals and competitions.

OR

☐ **Ownership Transferred**

Upon Designer's receipt of all payments due, Designer hereby assigns to Client all rights, title, and interest, including copyright, in and to the final Deliverables and, if requested, Designer shall provide digital files comprising the Deliverables. Designer retains all rights, including copyrights, in and to preliminary sketches and alternative designs not selected by Client. Designer retains the rights to display all work created by Designer for this Project, including preliminary designs and final Deliverables, in Designer's portfolios, including in print and online, and to submit such work to design periodicals and competitions.

GRAPHIC DESIGNER'S ESTIMATE & CONFIRMATION FORM (Back)

TERMS

1. Time for Payment
All invoices are payable within 30 days of receipt. A 1 1/2% monthly service charge is payable on all overdue balances. The grant of any license or right of copyright is conditioned on receipt of full payment.

2. Default in Payment
The Client shall assume responsibility for all collection of legal fees necessitated by default in payment.

3. Estimates
The fees and expenses shown are minimum estimates only. Final fees and expenses shall be shown when invoice is rendered. The Client's approval shall be obtained for any increases in fees or expenses that exceed the original estimate by 10% or more.

4. Changes
The Client shall be responsible for making additional payments for changes requested by the Client beyond the original assignment. However, no additional payment shall be made for changes required to conform to the original assignment description. The Client shall offer the Designer the first opportunity to make any changes.

5. Expenses
The Client shall reimburse the Designer for all expenses arising from this assignment, including the payment of any sales taxes due on this assignment, and shall advance $_____ to the Designer for payment of said expenses.

6. Cancellation
In the event of cancellation of this assignment, ownership of all copyrights and the original artwork shall be retained by the Designer, and a cancellation fee for work completed, based on the contract price and expenses already incurred, shall be paid by the Client.

7. Ownership and Return of Artwork
The Designer retains ownership of all originals and copies of the artwork, whether preliminary or final, and the Client shall return such artwork, including digital media, and shall permanently delete all digital copies thereof, within 30 days of use unless indicated otherwise below:

8. Credit Lines
The Designer and any other creators shall receive a credit line with any editorial usage. If similar credit lines are to be given with other types of usage, it must be so indicated here:

9. Releases
The Client shall indemnify the Designer against all claims and expenses, including reasonable attorney's fees, due to uses for which no release was requested in writing or for uses that exceed authority granted by a release.

10. Modifications
Modification of the Agreement must be written, except that the invoice may include, and the Client shall pay, fees or expenses that were orally authorized in order to progress promptly with the work.

11. Alterations
Any electronic alteration of artwork or graphic design comprising the Designer's work products (color shift, mirroring, flopping, combination cut and paste, deletion) is prohibited without the express permission of the Designer. The Designer will be given first opportunity to make any alterations required. Unauthorized alterations shall constitute additional use and will be billed accordingly.

12. Warranty of Originality
The Designer warrants and represents that, to the best of his/her knowledge, the final work products delivered hereunder are original and have not been previously published, or that consent to use has been obtained consistent with the rights granted to Client herein; that all work or portions thereof obtained through the undersigned from third parties is original or, if previously published, that consent to use has been obtained consistent with the rights granted to Client herein; that the Designer has full authority to make this Agreement; and that the final work products prepared by the Designer do not contain any scandalous, libelous, or unlawful matter. This warranty does not extend to any uses that the Client or others may make of the Designer's work products that may infringe on the rights of others. Client expressly agrees that it will hold the Designer harmless for all liability caused by the Client's unauthorized use of the Designer's work products to the extent such use infringes on the rights of others.

13. Limitation of Liability
Client agrees that it shall not hold the Designer or his/her agents or employees liable for any incidental or consequential damages that arise from the Designer's failure to perform any aspect of the Project in a timely manner, regardless of whether such failure was caused by intentional or negligent acts or omissions of the Designer or a third party. Furthermore, the Designer disclaims all implied warranties, including the warranty of merchantability and fitness for a particular purpose. Client shall be responsible for all compliance with laws or government rules or regulations applicable to Client's final product(s).

To the extent the final work products include any word, symbols, logos or other content used to designate Client as the source of goods or services ("Trademarks"), Client shall have sole responsibility for ensuring that Trademarks do not infringe the rights of third parties, and Client shall indemnify, save, and hold harmless Designer from any and all damages, liabilities, costs, losses, or expenses arising out of any claim, demand, or action by a third party alleging trademark infringement, or arising out of Client's failure to obtain trademark clearance or permissions, for use of Trademarks.

The maximum liability of Designer to Client for damages for any and all causes whatsoever, and Client's maximum remedy, regardless of the form of action, shall be limited to an amount equal to the total fees paid by Client to Designer hereunder. In no event shall Designer be liable for any indirect, incidental, special, consequential, exemplary, or punitive damages arising out of or related to the Services, even if Designer has been advised of the possibility of such damages.

14. Dispute Resolution
Any disputes in excess of $——————— *[maximum limit for small-claims court]* arising out of this Agreement shall be submitted to mediation in accordance with the rules of——————
[name of local lawyers for the arts mediation program]. The prevailing party in any dispute resolved by litigation shall be entitled to recover its attorney's fees and costs, provided that party initiated or participated in mediation as set forth herein.

15. Acceptance of Terms
The signature of both parties shall evidence acceptance of these terms.

CONSENTED AND AGREED TO:

_____   _____   _____
Designer's signature/date   Authorized signature/date   Client's name and title

NONCOMPETITION CLAUSE

Remove all language in italics before using this form.

This clause and its explanatory text have been supplied by Tad Crawford, the author of Legal Guide for the Visual Artist and Business and Legal Forms for Graphic Designers *(Allworth Press), and are used here by permission.*

Often a designer working with an illustrator, photographer, or even another designer will place that supplier in direct contact with a client. In such a case, the normal expectation would be that the supplier would not then go directly to the client seeking business that the original designer might have been able to handle for the client. However, this expectation may not always be realized and sometimes it becomes wise to include the expectation as a clause in the contract with the supplier. Such a clause might read as follows:

> Supplier understands that in the course of working for the Designer, the Supplier may sometimes have direct contact with the clients of the Designer or access to confidential information such as lists of the Designer's clients. The Supplier agrees not to seek work from such clients of the Designer without the Designer's express, written permission. This clause shall include but not be limited to the following clients of the Designer:

> _____

> _____

> _____

> _____

> In the event of any breach of this clause, the Supplier shall pay the Designer_____ as liquidated damages and shall also be responsible for the Designer's reasonable attorneys' fees and court costs. The parties have considered and agree that this amount of liquidated damages represents a reasonable estimated fair average compensation for losses Designer might sustain as a result of a violation of this paragraph.

The amount of the liquidated damages might be two or three times the fee paid to the supplier if the supplier is doing an assignment for the designer. If the supplier is not working for the designer but gains access to confidential client lists, the liquidated damages might be an amount per client contacted. The clause should serve as a warning to any supplier that the designer considers clients to be proprietary and will not tolerate any attempts by suppliers to compete for the designer's clients.

GRAPHIC DESIGNER'S INVOICE (Front)

[Designer's Letterhead]

Remove all language in italics before using this form.

TO

Date _____

Commissioned by _____

Assignment Number _____

Invoice Number _____

Client's Purchase Order Number _____

ASSIGNMENT DESCRIPTION

_____

FEE PAYMENT SCHEDULE

_____

ITEMIZED EXPENSES (OTHER BILLABLE EXPENSES)

Illustration _____	Toll Telephone Calls _____	Copies _____
Printing *[if brokered by Designer]* _____	Materials & Supplies _____	Other Expenses _____
Photography _____	Transportation & Travel _____	SUBTOTAL _____
Client's Alterations _____	Messengers _____	SALES TAX _____
Models & Props _____	Shipping & Insurance _____	TOTAL _____

RIGHTS GRANTED (Check one box only):

☐ **Usage Rights Granted**

Title or Product *[name]*

Category or Use *[advertising, corporate, promotional, editorial, etc.]*

Medium of Use *[consumer or trade magazine, annual report, TV, book, website, online publications, device apps, etc.]*

Edition (if book) *[hardcover, mass-market paperback, quality paperback, e-book, etc.]*

Geographic Area *[if applicable]*

Time Period *[if applicable]*

Any usage rights not exclusively transferred are reserved to the Designer. Usage beyond that granted to the Client herein shall require payment of an additional fee in the amount of Designer's standard licensing fee for such usage, subject to all terms. Any grant of right is conditional upon receipt of full payment. Upon receipt of full payment, Designer shall deliver digital files necessary to enable Client's usage rights granted herein. Designer retains the rights to display all work created by Designer for this Project, including preliminary designs and final Deliverables, in Designer's portfolios, including in print and online, and to submit such work to design periodicals and competitions.

OR

☐ **Ownership Transferred**

Upon Designer's receipt of all payments due, Designer hereby assigns to Client all rights, title and interest, including copyright, in and to the final Deliverables and, if requested, Designer shall provide digital files comprising the Deliverables. Designer retains all rights, including copyrights, in and to preliminary sketches and alternative designs not selected by Client. Designer retains the rights to display all work created by Designer for this Project, including preliminary designs and final Deliverables, in Designer's portfolios, including in print and online, and to submit such work to design periodicals and competitions.

GRAPHIC DESIGNER'S INVOICE (Back)

TERMS

1. Time for Payment
All invoices are payable within 30 days of receipt. A 1 1/2% monthly service charge is payable on all overdue balances. The grant of any license or right of copyright is conditioned on receipt of full payment.

2. Default in Payment
The Client shall assume responsibility for all collection of legal fees necessitated by default in payment.

3. Expenses
The Client shall reimburse the Designer for all expenses arising from this assignment, including the payment of any sales taxes due on this assignment.

4. Changes
The Client shall be responsible for making additional payments for changes requested by the Client beyond the original assignment. However, no additional payment shall be made for changes required to conform to the original assignment description. The Client shall offer the Designer the first opportunity to make any changes.

5. Cancellation
In the event of cancellation of this assignment, ownership of all copyrights and the original artwork shall be retained by the Designer, and a cancellation fee for work completed, based on the contract price and expenses already incurred, shall be paid by the Client.

6. Ownership of Artwork
The Designer retains ownership of all originals and copies of the artwork, whether preliminary or final, and the Client shall return such artwork, including digital media, and shall permanently delete all digital copies thereof, within 30 days of use unless indicated otherwise below:

_____

_____

7. Credit Lines
The Designer and any other creators shall receive a credit line with any editorial usage. If similar credit lines are to be given with other types of usage, it must be so indicated here:

_____

_____

8. Releases
The Client shall indemnify the Designer against all claims and expenses, including reasonable attorney's fees, due to uses for which no release was requested in writing or for uses that exceed authority granted by a release.

9. Modifications
Modification of the Agreement must be written, except that the invoice may include, and the Client shall pay, fees or expenses that were orally authorized in order to progress promptly with the work.

10. Alterations
Any electronic alteration of artwork or graphic design comprising the Designer's work products (color shift, mirroring, flopping, combination cut and paste, deletion) is prohibited without the express permission of the Designer. The Designer will be given first opportunity to make any alterations required. Unauthorized alterations shall constitute additional use and will be billed accordingly.

11. Warranty of Originality
The Designer warrants and represents that, to the best of his/her knowledge, the work assigned hereunder is original and has not been previously published, or that consent to use has been obtained consistent with the rights granted to Client herein; that all work or portions thereof obtained through the undersigned from third parties is original and that the consent to use has been obtained consistent with the rights granted to Client herein; that the Designer has full authority to make this agreement; and that the work prepared by the Designer does not contain any scandal-ous, libelous, or unlawful matter. This warranty does not extend to any uses that the Client or others may make of the Designer's product that may in-fringe on the rights of others. Client expressly agrees that it will hold the Designer harmless for all liability caused by the Client's unauthorized use of the Designer's product to the extent such use infringes on the rights of others.

12. Limitation of Liability
Client agrees that it shall not hold the Designer or his/her agents or employees liable for any incidental or consequential damages that arise from the Designer's failure to perform any aspect of the Project in a timely manner, regardless of whether such failure was caused by intentional or negligent acts or omissions of the Designer or a third party. Furthermore, the Designer disclaims all implied warranties, including the warranty of merchantability and fitness for a particular purpose. Client shall be responsible for all compliance with laws or government rules or regulations applicable to Client's final product(s).

To the extent the Deliverables include any word, symbol, logo, or other content used to designate Client as the source of goods or services ("Trademarks"), Client shall have sole responsibility for ensuring that Trademarks do not infringe the rights of third parties, and Client shall indemnify, save, and hold harmless Designer from any and all damages, liabilities, costs, losses, or expenses arising out of any claim, demand, or action by a third party alleging trademark infringement, or arising out of Client's failure to obtain trademark clearance or permissions, for use of Trademarks.

The maximum liability of Designer to Client for damages for any and all causes whatsoever, and Client's maximum remedy, regardless of the form of action, shall be limited to an amount equal to the total fees paid by Client to Designer hereunder. In no event shall Designer be liable for any indirect, incidental, special, consequential, exemplary, or punitive damages arising out of or related to the Services, even if Designer has been advised of the possibility of such damages.

13. Dispute Resolution
Any disputes in excess of $ _____ *[maximum limit for small-claims court]* arising out of this Agreement shall be submitted to mediation in accordance with the rules of _____
[name of local lawyers for the arts mediation program]. The prevailing party in any dispute resolved by litigation shall be entitled to recover its attorney's fees and costs, provided that party initiated or participated in mediation as set forth herein.

CONSENTED AND AGREED TO:

_____   _____   _____
Designer's signature/date   Authorized signature/date   Client's name and title

SERVICE RETAINER AGREEMENT (front)

Remove all language in italics before using this form.

This Service Retainer Agreement ("Agreement") is entered into by and between _____ ("Client")

and _____ ("Designer"), is effective as of the last date of signature below, and

shall continue in effect until cancelled pursuant to paragraph 5 below ("Term").

Client requires ongoing services such as those provided by Designer, and wishes to engage Designer to perform such services as a subcontractor on an ongoing basis; and Designer agrees to provide such services as set forth herein. For good and valuable consideration, the parties agree as follows:

1. Services

1.1 *Services.* Designer agrees to provide to Client the design services and deliverables set forth in the attached Statement of Work ("SOW") (the "Services"). The Services are estimated to require _____ hours of Designer's time per month.

1.2 *Revisions/Changes.* The SOW reflects the scope of work initially required by Client and Designer's time to complete such work. If Client requests additional revisions, changes, or services in any particular month, Designer will advise Client of the additional time required, and shall invoice Client for such additional Services on a time and materials basis, at the hourly rate of $_____ per hour. Upon mutual agreement, additional SOWs may be attached hereto to modify the Services on an ongoing basis. If additional SOWs increase the time needed to perform the Services per month, the parties shall adjust the Retainer accordingly.

1.3 *Independent Contractor.* Designer is an independent contractor, not an employee of Client. Designer shall perform the Services under the general direction of Client, but Designer shall determine, in Designer's sole discretion, the manner and means by which the Services are accomplished. Designer may engage third-party subcontractors to perform any of the Services ("Design Agents").

1.4 *No Exclusivity.* This Agreement does not create an exclusive relationship between the parties. Client may engage others to perform services of the same or similar nature to those provided by Designer, and Designer may offer and provide design services to others, solicit work from third parties and otherwise advertise the services offered by Designer.

2. Compensation

2.1 *Retainer.* During the Term of this Agreement Client shall pay to Designer an advance monthly Retainer in the amount of $_____.

2.2 *Expenses.* Client shall reimburse Designer for out-of-pocket expenses incurred in performance of the Services for licenses to use Third-Party Materials, photocopies, travel expenses, postage, courier, and the like.

2.3. *Invoices.* Client shall pay the first Retainer upon execution of this Agreement. Thereafter, Designer shall invoice Client for the Retainer in advance for each month, which shall be paid within five (5) days of receipt. Designer shall invoice Client for additional fees and expenses on a monthly basis, which Client shall pay within thirty (30) days of receipt. Designer may invoice Client in advance for substantial expenses, for example, licenses for Third-Party Materials, and Client shall pay such advance invoices within the time frame requested by Designer.

3. Intellectual Property

3.1 *Final Works.* Upon completion of the Services each month, and expressly conditioned upon full payment of all fees and costs due therefore, Designer assigns to Client all rights, title and interest, including copyright, in and to the final deliverables comprising the finished works approved for implementation by Client ("Final Works"). Designer warrants and represents that, to the best of its knowledge, the Final Works are original to Designer and/or its Design Agents; and that Designer has procured from its Design Agents appropriate agreements as necessary to grant the ownership rights assigned to Client herein. Designer shall cooperate with Client and shall execute any additional documents reasonably requested by Client to evidence such assignment. Client hereby grants to Designer the nonexclusive right to reproduce, publish and display the Final Works in its portfolios in all media including print and online, and in galleries, design periodicals and other media or exhibits for the purposes of recognition of creative excellence or professional advancement in the field of design, and Designer retains the right to be credited with authorship therein.

3.2 *Preliminary Works.* Designer retains intellectual property ownership of all other work product and deliverables, including but not limited to explorations, alternate or preliminary designs not selected for implementation by Client, interim refinements, and proof of concept deliverables ("Preliminary Works"), and Client shall return all Preliminary Works to Designer within thirty (30) days of Designer's request.

3.3 *Third-Party Materials.* Designer shall inform Client of any need to license, at Client's expense, materials owned by third parties to be incorporated into the Final Works (for example, photography, illustration, font licenses, text), and Client shall obtain the license(s) necessary to permit Client's use of such materials. Client acknowledges that no rights are granted to Client for use of third-party materials in Preliminary Works, including proof of concept deliverables. In the event Client fails to properly secure or otherwise arrange for any necessary licenses for use of third-party materials, or instructs Designer to incorporate third-party materials into deliverables, Client hereby indemnifies, saves and holds harmless Designer from any and all damages, liabilities, costs, losses or expenses arising out of any claim, demand, or action by a third party arising out of such use.

4. Warranties:

Designer warrants and represents that the Services shall be performed and completed in a professional manner, and that the Work Product is original to Designer and, to the best of Designer's knowledge, shall not infringe the copyright, trademark, trade secret, publicity or privacy rights, or other intellectual property or proprietary rights of third parties. This warranty does not extend to any unauthorized use of Preliminary Works or adaptations made to the Final Works by Client.

5. Cancellation/Delays

5.1 *Cancellation.* Either party may cancel this Agreement upon thirty (30) days written notice for convenience, or upon thirty (30) days notice for material breach of this Agreement, if the other party fails to cure the breach within that thirty-day period. In the event of such cancellation, Designer retains ownership of all rights, including copyrights, in and to all deliverables except Final Works for which Client has already made full payment (retainer and any additional hourly fees and expenses).

5.2 *Delays.* Client acknowledges and agrees that Designer's ability to meet schedules is dependent upon Client's prompt performance of its obligations to provide materials, approvals and instructions, and that any delays in Client's performance or requests for changes to the scope of work as set forth in the SOW may delay the Services. Any such delay caused by Client shall not constitute a breach by Designer of this Agreement.

5.3 *Kill Fee.* Client acknowledges that Designer has reserved time to perform the Services for each month, and Designer was not able to accept other work for that month. Accordingly, in the event Client cancels or delays the Services, Client shall pay to Designer, in addition to the retainer and expenses already incurred through the date of such cancellation or delay, a kill fee equal to a pro rata portion of the retainer amount for the period ending thirty (30) days following the date of termination , unless Designer is able to secure new work for that time for the same or greater compensation.

5.4 *Force Majeure.* Designer shall notify Client if Designer is unable to timely complete the Services or any portion thereof by reason of fire, earthquake, labor dispute, act of God or public enemy, death, illness or incapacity of Designer or any local, state, federal, national or international law, governmental order or regulation, or any other event beyond Designer's control, and the parties will then discuss in good faith revisions to the schedule for completion of the Services. Designer shall not be deemed in breach of this Agreement in such circumstances.

6. Confidential Information

Each party acknowledges that in connection with the Proposal it may receive certain confidential or proprietary technical and business information and materials of the other party ("Confidential Information"). Each party, its agents and employees shall hold and maintain in strict confidence all Confidential Information, shall not disclose Confidential Information to any third party; and shall not use any Confidential Information except as may be necessary to perform its obligations under the Proposal. Notwithstanding the foregoing, Confidential Information will not include any information that is or becomes generally publicly known through no fault of the receiving party, or is rightfully received from a third party. Client shall not solicit services directly from Designer's employees or Design Agents without Designer's prior written consent.

7. Limitation of Liability

Client shall be responsible for all compliance with laws or government rules or regulations applicable to Client's final products. Client shall have sole responsibility for ensuring that any deliverables comprising trade names, words, symbols, designs, logos or other devices or designs used by Client to designate the origin or source of goods or services ("Trademarks") are available for use in commerce and federal registration and do not otherwise infringe the rights of any third party. Client hereby indemnifies, saves and holds harmless Designer from any and all damages, liabilities, costs, losses or expenses arising out of any claim, demand, or action by any third party alleging any infringement arising out of Client's use of Trademarks. The maximum liability of Designer to Client for damages for any and all causes whatsoever, and Client's maximum remedy, regardless of the form of action, shall be limited to an amount equal to the total fees paid by Client to Designer hereunder. In no event shall Designer be liable for any indirect, incidental, special, consequential, exemplary or punitive damages arising out of or related to the Services, even if Designer has been advised of the possibility of such damages.

8. General

Any modifications of this Agreement must be in writing signed by both parties. This Agreement shall be construed and enforced under the laws of the United States and the State of _____ without reference to or application of conflict of law rules. In the event of a dispute arising out of this Agreement, the parties agree to attempt to resolve any dispute by negotiation between the parties. If they are unable to resolve the dispute, either party may commence mediation and/or binding arbitration through _____ ___ *[name of local mediation/arbitration program]*, or other forum mutually agreed to by the parties. The prevailing party in any dispute resolved by binding arbitration or litigation shall be entitled to recover its attorneys' fees and costs. Litigation arising from this Agreement shall be brought in state or federal court, as appropriate, within _____ *[state, local district court].* This Agreement, together with the SOW(s), comprises the entire understanding of the parties hereto on the subject matter herein contained, and supersedes and merges all prior and contemporaneous agreements, understandings and discussions between the parties relating to the Services. All notices shall be delivered in writing to the parties' respective addresses provided below, or as subsequently updated.

Designer:

Name:_____

Address: _____

Designer Contact Name: _____

Signed: _____ Date: _____

Client:

Name:_____

Address: _____

Client Officer Name: _____

Title: _____

Signed: _____ Date: _____

DIGITAL MEDIA INVOICE (Front)

CLIENT

Date

Commissioned by

Purchase Order Number

Job Number

DESCRIPTION OF ASSIGNMENT

Primary Use *[describe primary venue or device(s) for which designer's work will be used, e.g., website, blog site, mobile phones/devices, tablets, online advertising, original e-books]*

Additional Uses *[describe any additional allowed uses, e.g., promotional materials in print and online]*

Deliverables *[describe scope of project / digital files to be delivered]*

Description of Source Materials to Be Supplied by Client

Date Due

Client acknowledges that the date due is an approximation only, and any delays caused by Client's failure to timely sign this document or deliver materials or approvals shall extend the final due date and shall not be considered a material breach by Designer.

Deliverable(s) may be used only for the purposes stated below. All other use(s) and modification(s) is (are) prohibited. Deliverable(s) may not be copied without the Designer's permission except as required for the Uses set forth above.

USAGE RIGHTS GRANTED

Any grant of rights is conditional upon receipt of full payment.

Distribution/Geographical Area

System Applications *[for use on specific machine, or compiled into other operation languages]*

PRODUCTION SCHEDULE

(Including milestones, dates due, and appropriate fees.)

Milestone	Due Date	Payment upon Acceptance
Contract Signing		$
Delivery of Preliminary Designs		$
Delivery of Fully-Developed Selected Design for approval		$
Delivery of Final Deliverables		$
Acceptance of Final Deliverables		$
Total		$

Bonus: Client agrees to pay Designer a bonus of $ _____ payable to the Designer in the event acceptable Final Deliverables are delivered to the Client prior to *[date]* _____ .

TERMS

1. Time for Payment

Each milestone is payable upon the Client's acceptance of the Deliverables. All invoices are payable within 30 days of receipt. A 1 1/2% monthly service charge is payable on all overdue balances. The grant of any license or right of copyright is conditioned on receipt of full payment.

2. Default in Payment

The Client shall assume responsibility for all collection of legal fees necessitated by default in payment.

3. Estimates

If this form is used for an estimate or assignment confirmation, the fees and expenses shown are minimum estimates only. Final fees and expenses shall be shown when invoice is rendered. The Client's approval shall be obtained for any increases in fees or expenses that exceed the original estimate by 10% or more.

4. Expenses

The Client shall reimburse the Designer for all expenses arising from this assignment, including payment on any sales taxes due on this assignment and shall advance $_____ to the Designer for payment of said expenses.

5. Technology Access

Access to Internet or other technology platforms will be provided by a separate Internet Service Provider (ISP) or other provider to be contracted by the Client and who will not be party to this Agreement.

6. Progress Reports

The Designer shall contact or meet with the Client on a mutually acceptable schedule to report all tasks completed, problems encountered, and recommended changes relating to the development and testing of the Deliverables. The Designer shall inform the Client promptly by telephone upon discovery of any event or problem that may significantly delay the development of the work.

7. Third Party Materials

The Designer shall notify the Client of any licensing and/or permissions required for content or programming to be included in or support Client's use of the Deliverables. Client shall be responsible for paying all license fees for such third party materials.

8. Changes

The Client shall be responsible for making additional payments for changes requested by the Client beyond the scope of the original assignment. However, no additional payment shall be made for changes required to conform to the original assignment description. The Client shall offer the Designer the first opportunity to make any changes.

9. Testing and Acceptance Procedures

The Designer will make every good-faith effort to thoroughly test all Deliverables and make all necessary corrections as a result of such testing prior to handing over the Deliverables to the Client. Upon receipt of each Deliverable, the Client shall either accept the Deliverable and make the milestone payment set forth or provide the Designer with written notice of any corrections to be made and a suggested date for completion, which should be mutually acceptable to both the Designer and the Client. The Designer shall designate *[name]* _____ and the Client shall designate *[name]* _____ as the only designated persons who will send and accept all Deliverables, and receive and make all communications between the Designer and the Client. Neither party shall have any obligation to consider for approval or respond to materials submitted other than through the designated person listed above. Each party has the right to change its designated person upon _____ day(s) notice to the other.

10. Maintenance

The Designer agrees to provide the Client with reasonable technical support and assistance to maintain and update the Deliverables on the Internet or applicable wireless service(s) ("Maintenance Services") during the Warranty Period of *[dates]*_____ at no cost to the Client. Such assistance shall not exceed _____ hours per calendar month. After the expiration of the Warranty Period, the developer agrees to provide the Client with Maintenance Services an annual fee of $_____ for a period of _____ years after the last day of the Warranty Period ("Maintenance Period"), payable 30 days prior to the commencement date of each year of the Maintenance Period. Such Maintenance Services shall include correcting any errors or any failure of the Deliverables to conform to the specifications. Maintenance Services shall not include the development of enhancements to the originally contracted project.

11. Enhancements

If the Client wishes to modify the Deliverables, the Designer shall be given first option to provide a bid to perform such enhancements.

12. Confidential Information

The Designer acknowledges and agrees that the source materials and technical and marketing plans or other sensitive business information, including all materials containing said information, that are supplied by the Client to the Designer, or are incorporated into the Deliverables shall be considered confidential information and shall not be disclosed to the public by Designer without the Client's prior written permission. Information shall not be considered confidential if it is already publicly known through no act of the Designer. Designer retains the rights to display all work created by Designer for this Project, including preliminary designs and final Deliverables, in Designer's portfolios, including in print and online, and to submit such work to design periodicals and competitions, provided that no confidential information is revealed thereby.

13. Return of Source Information

Upon the Client's acceptance of the Final Deliverables, or upon the cancellation of the Project, the Designer shall return to the Client all copies and originals of the Client's source materials.

14. Cancellation

In the event of cancellation of this assignment, ownership of all rights in Designer's work products shall be retained by the Designer, and Client shall have no rights to use or adapt the work products. A cancellation fee for work completed, based on the pro-rated portion of the next payment and expenses already incurred, shall be paid by the Client, and Client shall promptly return to Designer all copies of Designer's work products and shall permanently delete all digital copies thereof.

15. Ownership of Copyright

Client acknowledges and agrees that the Designer retains all rights of copyright in all work created by Designer for this Project, including preliminary designs and Final Deliverables.

16. Ownership and Return of Work Products

Upon receipt of full payment, Designer shall deliver digital files necessary to enable Client's usage rights granted herein. Designer retains ownership of all original work products, in any media, including digital files, whether preliminary or final. Client will return all work products, and permanently delete all digital files, within 30 days after expiration of Client's usage rights hereunder.

17. Ownership of Designer's Tools

All design tools developed and utilized by Designer in creating or supporting Client's use of the Deliverables, including without limitation preexisting and newly developed application tools and other software, and general non-copyrightable concepts such as interactive structures, layout, navigational, and functional elements (collectively, "Designer Tools"), shall be owned solely by Designer. Designer hereby grants to Client a nonexclusive, nontransferable (other than the right to sublicense such uses to Client's web hosting, Internet, or wireless service providers), perpetual, worldwide license to use the Designer Tools solely with the Final Deliverables.

18. Copy-Protection

The Client must copy-protect all Final Deliverables against duplication or alteration.

19. Credit Lines

The Designer shall be given credit as the creator of the Deliverables in close proximity to the Deliverables as they appear in print, and on the first page or screen of broadcast, electronic, and digital media.

☐ If this box is checked, the credit line shall be in the form:

© *[date]*   .

20. Alterations

Any electronic alteration of artwork or graphic design comprising the Deliverables (color shift, mirroring, flopping, combination cut and paste, deletion) is prohibited without the express permission of the Designer. The Designer will be given first opportunity to make any alterations required. Unauthorized alterations shall constitute additional use and will be billed accordingly.

21. Other Operating Systems Conversion

The Designer shall be given first option at compiling the work for operating systems beyond the original use.

22. Unauthorized Use and Program Licenses

The Client will indemnify the Designer against all claims and expenses arising from uses of third party content or property for which the Client does not have rights to or authority to use. The Client will be responsible for payment of any special licensing or royalty fees resulting from such use.

23. Warranty of Originality

The Designer warrants and represents that, to the best of his/her knowledge, the Deliverables are original and have not been previously published, or that consent to use has been obtained consistent with the rights granted to Client herein; that all work or portions thereof obtained through the undersigned from third parties is original and that consent to use has been obtained consistent with the rights granted to Client herein; that the Designer has full authority to make this Agreement; and that the work prepared by the Designer does not contain any scandalous, libelous, or un-lawful matter. This warranty does not extend to any uses that the Client or others may make of the Designer's work products that may infringe on the rights of others. Client expressly agrees that it will hold the Designer harmless for all liability caused by the Client's unauthorized use of the Designer's work products to the extent such use infringes on the rights of others.

24. Limitation of Liability

Client agrees that it shall not hold the Designer or his/her agents or employees liable for any incidental or consequential damages that arise from the Designer's failure to perform any aspect of the Project in a timely manner, regardless of whether such failure was caused by intentional or negligent acts or omissions of the Designer or a third party. Furthermore, the Designer disclaims all implied warranties, including the warranty of merchantability and fitness for a particular purpose. Client shall be responsible for all compliance with laws or government rules or regulations applicable to Client's final product(s).

To the extent the Deliverables include any word, symbol, logo, or other content used to designate Client as the source of goods or services ("Trademarks"), Client shall have sole responsibility for ensuring that Trademarks do not infringe the rights of third parties, and Client shall indemnify, save, and hold harmless Designer from any and all damages, liabilities, costs, losses, or expenses arising out of any claim, demand, or action by a third party alleging trademark infringement, or arising out of Client's failure to obtain trademark clearance or permissions, for use of Trademarks.

The maximum liability of Designer to Client for damages for any and all causes whatsoever, and Client's maximum remedy, regardless of the form of action, shall be limited to an amount equal to the total fees paid by Client to Designer hereunder. In no event shall Designer be liable for any indirect, incidental, special, consequential, exemplary, or punitive damages arising out of or related to the Services, even if Designer has been advised of the possibility of such damages.

25. Dispute Resolution

Any disputes in excess of $_____ *[maximum limit for small-claims court]* arising out of this Agreement shall be submitted to mediation in accordance with the rules of _____*[name of local lawyers for the arts mediation program]*. The prevailing party in any dispute resolved by litigation shall be entitled to recover its attorney's fees and costs, provided that party initiated or participated in mediation as set forth herein.

25. Acceptance of Terms

The signature of both parties shall evidence acceptance of these terms.

CONSENTED AND AGREED TO:

_____   _____   _____
Designer's signature/date   Authorized signature/date   Client's name and title

WEBSITE DESIGN & MAINTENANCE ORDER FORM (Front)

[Designer's Letterhead]

This job order form is a sample of a possible contract for website development and maintenance. Since the field is changing very rapidly, artists should view this as a model and amend it to fit their particular circumstances. Remove all language in italics before using this form.

CLIENT

Date

Commissioned by

Purchase Order Number

Job Number

DESCRIPTION OF ASSIGNMENT

Services: Designer shall design a website for Client consisting of the following components (the "Deliverables"):

Timing: Designer will promptly give written notice in the event that Designer reasonably expects any delay in completing any aspect of the Project. Client acknowledges and agrees that Designer's ability to meet deadlines depends upon Client's prompt performance of its obligations to provide materials and approvals and that any delays in Client's performance or changes in the Services requested by Client may delay delivery of the Deliverables. Any such delays caused by Client shall not constitute a breach of Designer's obligations under this Agreement.

Unless otherwise agreed in writing, Designer shall deliver all Deliverables to Client electronically.

Description of Materials to Be Supplied by Client:

Date Due:

RIGHTS GRANTED

Client Content: All proprietary information and all creative content provided by Client to Designer for incorporation in the Deliverables ("Client Content") shall remain the sole property of Client and its assigns, and Client and its assigns shall be the sole owner of all trade secrets, patents, copyrights, and other rights in connection therewith. Client hereby grants to Designer a nonexclusive, nontransferable license to use, reproduce, modify, display, and publish the Client Content solely in connection with Designer's performance of the Services.

Designer Creative Content: For the purposes of this Agreement, "Designer Creative Content" shall mean all creative content developed by Designer, or commissioned by Designer exclusively for the Project, and incorporated in the Deliverables, including without limitation all visual elements, graphic design, illustration, photography, animation, sounds, typographic treatments and text, and all modifications to Client Content developed by Designer. Designer hereby grants to Client the exclusive, perpetual, and worldwide right to use, reproduce, modify, and display the Designer Creative Content solely in connection with the Project. As defined and used herein and throughout this Agreement, Designer Creative Content specifically excludes all Designer Tools (defined below).

Third Party Materials: Third party materials that are incorporated into the Deliverables, including without limitation standardized application tools, web authoring tools and other software, and stock photography (collectively, "Third Party Materials") shall be owned by the respective third parties.

Designer Tools: All design tools developed and utilized by Designer in performing the Services, including without limitation pre-existing and newly developed web authoring tools, application tools and other software, and general non-copyrightable concepts such as website architecture, layout, navigational and functional elements (collectively, "Designer Tools"), shall be owned solely by Designer. Designer hereby grants to Client a nonexclusive, nontransferable (other than the right to sublicense such uses to Client's web hosting or Internet service providers), perpetual, worldwide license to use, display, and modify the Designer Tools solely in connection with the Client's web site.

Any grant of rights is conditional upon receipt of full payment. Upon receipt of full payment, Designer shall deliver digital files necessary to enable Client's usage rights granted herein. Designer retains the rights to display all work created by Designer for this project, including preliminary designs and final Deliverables, in Designer's portfolios, including in print and online, and to submit such work to design periodicals and competitions, provided that no confidential information is revealed thereby.

WEBSITE DESIGN & MAINTENANCE ORDER FORM (Back)

PRODUCTION SCHEDULE
(Including milestones, dates due, and appropriate fees.)

Milestone	Due Date	Payment upon Acceptance
Contract Signing		$
Delivery of Website Design		$
Delivery of Beta Version		$
Delivery of Final Version (includes return of source materials to Client)		$
Acceptance of Final Version		$
Total		$

Bonus: Client agrees to pay Designer a bonus of $_____ payable to the Designer in the event an acceptable Final Version of the Website is delivered to the Client prior to *[date]* _____.

TERMS

1. Time for Payment
Payment is due at each milestone upon the Client's acceptance of the Deliverables. All invoices are payable within 30 days of receipt. A 1 1/2% monthly service charge is payable on all overdue balances. The grant of any license or right of copyright is conditioned on receipt of full payment.

2. Default in Payment
The Client shall assume responsibility for all collection of legal fees necessitated by default in payment.

3. Estimates
If this form is used for an estimate or assignment confirmation, the fees and expenses shown are minimum estimates only. Final fees and expenses shall be shown when invoice is rendered. The Client's approval shall be obtained for any increases in fees or expenses that exceed the original estimate by 10% or more.

4. Expenses
The Client shall reimburse the Designer for all expenses arising from this assignment, including the payment of any sales taxes due on this assignment, and shall advance $_____ to the Designer for payment of said expenses.

5. Internet Access
Access to Internet will be provided by a separate Internet Service Provider (ISP) to be contracted by the Client and who will not be party to this Agreement.

6. Progress Reports
The Designer shall contact or meet with the Client on a mutually acceptable schedule to report all tasks completed, problems encountered, and recommended changes relating to the development and testing of the website. The Designer shall inform the Client promptly by telephone upon discovery of any event or problem that may delay the development of the work significantly.

7. Third Party Licenses
Designer shall inform Client of all Third Party Materials that Client may need to license at Client's own expense, and unless otherwise arranged by Client, Designer shall obtain a license for Client to use the Third Party Materials. Client shall be responsible for executing and paying for such licenses.

8. Changes
The Client shall be responsible for making additional payments for changes beyond the original assignment requested by the Client. However, no additional payment shall be made for changes required to conform to the original assignment description. The Client shall offer the Designer the first opportunity to make any changes.

9. Testing and Acceptance Procedures
The Designer will make every good-faith effort to test all Deliverables thoroughly and make all necessary corrections as a result of such testing prior to handing over the Deliverables to the Client. Upon receipt of the Deliverables, the Client shall either accept the Deliverable and make the milestone payment set forth herein or provide the Designer with written notice of any corrections to be made and a suggested date for completion, which should be mutually acceptable to both the Designer and the Client. The Designer shall designate *[name]* _____ and the Client shall designate *[name]* _____ as the only designated persons who will send and accept all Deliverables and receive and make all communications between the Designer and the Client. Neither party shall have any obligation to consider for approval or respond to materials submitted other than through the designated persons listed above. Each party has the right to change its designated person upon _____ day(s) notice to the other.

10. Website Maintenance
The Designer agrees to provide the Client with reasonable technical support and assistance to maintain and update the website on the Internet during the Warranty Period of *[dates]* _____ at no cost to the Client. Such assistance shall not exceed _____ hours per calendar month. After the expiration of the Warranty Period, the Designer agrees to provide the Client with reasonable technical support and assistance to maintain and update the website on the Internet for an annual fee of $_____ for a period of _____ years after the last day of the Warranty Period payable 30 days prior to the commencement date of each year of the Maintenance Period. Such maintenance shall include correcting any errors or any failure of the website to conform to the specifications. Maintenance shall not include the development of enhancements to the originally contracted project.

11. Enhancements
Under the maintenance agreement, if the Client wishes to modify the website, the Designer shall be given first option to provide a bid to perform such enhancements.

12. Confidential Information
The Designer acknowledges and agrees that the source materials and technical and marketing plans or other sensitive business information, as specified by the Client, including all materials containing said information, that are supplied by the Client to the Designer or developed by the Designer in the

course of developing the website are to be considered confidential information and shall not be disclosed to the public by Designer without the Client's prior written permission. Information shall not be considered confidential if it is already publicly known through no act of the Designer.

13. Warranties and Representations.

By Client. Client represents, warrants, and covenants to Designer that **(i)** Client owns all right, title, and interest in, or has full and sufficient authority to use in the manner contemplated in this Agreement, all of the Client Content, **(ii)** to the best of Client's knowledge, the Client Content does not infringe the rights of any party, and use of the Client Content in connection with the Project does not and will not violate the rights of any third parties, including without limitation trade secrets, trademarks, publicity, privacy, copyright, and patents, **(iii)** Client shall comply with the terms and conditions of any licensing agreements which govern the use of Third Party Materials, **(iv)** Client shall comply with all applicable foreign, federal, state, and local laws and regulations as they relate to the Services and Deliverables, including but not limited to, all advertising laws and regulations, consumer protection laws, and any laws or regulations relating to web sites and electronic commerce.

By Designer. Designer represents, warrants, and covenants to Client that: **(i)** Designer shall perform the Services in a professional and workmanlike manner and in accordance with all reasonable professional standards for similar services, and **(ii)** the Deliverables will be free from Deficiencies. "Deficiency" shall mean a failure to comply with the Specifications in any material respect, but shall not include any problems caused by Client Content, modifications, alterations or changes made to Deliverables by Client or any third party after delivery by Designer, or the interaction of Deliverables with third party applications such as web browsers other than those specified in the Project Proposal. The parties acknowledge that Client's sole remedy and Designer's sole liability for a breach of this Section 13 **(ii)** is for Designer to correct any Deficiency identified within thirty (30) days of Client's receipt of the final Deliverables. In the event that a Deficiency is caused by Third Party Materials, Designer's sole obligation shall be to substitute alternative Third Party Materials.

Designer further represents, warrants, and covenants to Client that **(i)** except for Third Party Materials and Client Content, the Deliverables shall be the original work of Designer or its independent contractors, **(ii)** if the Deliverables include the work of independent contractors commissioned for the Project by Designer, Designer shall have agreements in place with such independent contractors which contain provisions assigning all necessary rights, title, and interest in and to the Deliverables sufficient for Designer to grant the ownership interests and licenses provided in this Agreement, and **(iii)** to the best of Designer's knowledge, the Designer Creative Content and the Designer Tools do not infringe the rights of any party, and use of same in connection with the Project will not violate the rights of any third parties, including without limitation trade secrets, trademarks, publicity, privacy, copyright, and patents, except to the extent that such violations are caused by Client Content, or the modification of, or use of the Deliverables in combination with materials or equipment outside the scope of the applicable Specifications, by Client or third parties.

Except for the express warranties stated above, Designer makes no warranties whatsoever. Designer explicitly disclaims any other warranties or any kind, either express or implied, including but not limited to warranties of merchantability or fitness for a particular purpose.

By Client. Client agrees to indemnify, save, and hold harmless Designer from any and all damages, liabilities, costs, losses, or expenses arising out of any claim, demand, or action by a third party which is inconsistent with Client's representations made herein, except to the extent such damages, liabilities, costs, losses, or expenses arise directly as a result of gross negligence or willful misconduct of Designer; provided that **(i)** Designer promptly notifies Client in writing of the claim; **(ii)** Client has sole control of the defense and all related settlement negotiations; and **(iii)** Designer provides Client with the assistance, information, and authority necessary to perform Client's obligations under this section. Client will reimburse the reasonable out-of-pocket expenses incurred by Designer in providing such assistance.

By Designer. Subject to the limitations on warranties and liability provided herein, Designer agrees to indemnify, save, and hold harmless Client from any and all damages, liabilities, costs, losses, or expenses arising out of any claim, demand, or action by a third party which is inconsistent with Designer's representations made herein, except to the extent such damages, liabilities, costs, losses or expenses arise directly as a result of gross negligence or willful misconduct of Client; provided that **(i)** Client promptly notifies Designer in writing of the claim; **(ii)** Designer has sole control of the defense and all related settlement negotiations; and **(iii)** Client provides Designer with the assistance, information, and authority necessary to perform Designer's obligations under this section. Designer will reimburse the reasonable out-of-pocket expenses incurred by Client in providing such assistance. Notwithstanding the foregoing, Designer shall have no obligation to defend or indemnify Client for any infringement claim of any kind to the extent such claim is based on unauthorized modification of the Deliverables, arises from Client's failure to use updated or modified Deliverables provided by Designer, or arises from Designer's inclusion or use of Client Content.

15. Limitation of Liability

Client agrees that it shall not hold the Designer or his/her agents or employees liable for any incidental or consequential damages that arise from the Designer's failure to perform any aspect of the project in a timely manner, regardless of whether such failure was caused by intentional or negligent acts or omissions of the Designer or a third party. Furthermore, the Designer disclaims all implied warranties, including the warranty of merchantability and fitness for a particular purpose. Client shall be responsible for all compliance with laws or government rules or regulations applicable to Client's final product(s).

To the extent the Deliverables include any word, symbols, logos, or other content used to designate Client as the source of goods or services ("Trademarks"), Client shall have sole responsibility for ensuring that Trademarks do not infringe the rights of third parties, and Client shall indemnify, save, and hold harmless Designer from any and all damages, liabilities, costs, losses, or expenses arising out of any claim, demand, or action by a third party alleging trademark infringement, or arising out of Client's failure to obtain trademark clearance or permissions, for use of Trademarks.

The maximum liability of Designer to Client for damages for any and all causes whatsoever, and Client's maximum remedy, regardless of the form of action, shall be limited to an amount equal to the total fees paid by Client to Designer hereunder. In no event shall Designer be liable for any indirect, incidental, special, consequential, exemplary, or punitive damages arising out of or related to the Services, even if Designer has been advised of the possibility of such damages.

16. Dispute Resolution

Any disputes in excess of $_____ *[maximum limit for small-claims court]* arising out of this Agreement shall be submitted to mediation in accordance with the rules of _____*[name of local lawyers for the arts mediation program]*. The prevailing party in any dispute resolved by litigation shall be entitled to recover its attorney's fees and costs, provided that party initiated or participated in mediation as set forth herein.

17. Acceptance of Terms

The signature of both parties shall evidence acceptance of these terms.

CONSENTED AND AGREED TO:

_____

Designer's signature/date

_____

Authorized signature/date

_____

Client's name and title

MAGAZINE PURCHASE ORDER FOR COMMISSIONED ILLUSTRATION *[Magazine's Letterhead]*

Remove all language in italics before using this form.

This letter is to serve as our contract for you to create certain illustrations for us under the terms described herein.

1. Job Description
We, *[the Magazine name]*, retain you, the Illustrator, to create _____ illustration(s) described as follows *[indicate if sketches are required]*:

_____

_____

to be delivered to the Magazine by _____ *[date]* for

publication in our magazine titled *[name]* _____ .

2. Grant of Rights
The Illustrator hereby grants to the Magazine first North American magazine rights in the illustration(s) for publication in one print edition, and one online display of that same edition, but not including any display or reproduction in additional editions, adaptations, compilations, retrospectives, or other new works. All rights not expressly granted to the Magazine hereunder are reserved to the Illustrator. Upon receipt of full payment, Illustrator shall deliver digital files necessary to enable the usage rights granted to Magazine herein.

3. Price
The Magazine agrees to pay the Illustrator the following license fee:

$_____ in full consideration for the Illustrator's grant of rights to the Magazine. Any grant of rights is conditional upon receipt of full payment.

4. Changes
The Illustrator shall be given the first option to make any changes in the work that the Magazine may deem necessary. However, no additional compensation shall be paid unless such changes are necessitated by error on the Magazine's part, in which case a new contract between us shall be entered into on mutually agreeable terms to cover changes to be done by the Illustrator.

5. Cancellation
If, prior to the Illustrator's completion of finishes, the Magazine cancels the assignment, either because the illustrations are unsatisfactory to the Magazine or for any other reason, the Magazine agrees to pay the Illustrator a cancellation fee of 50% of the purchase price. If, after the Illustrator's completion of the art, the Magazine cancels the assignment, the Magazine agrees to pay 50% of the purchase price if cancellation is due to the illustrations not being reasonably satisfactory and 100% of the purchase price if cancellation is due to any other cause. In the event of cancellation, the Illustrator shall retain ownership of all artwork and rights of copyright, but the Illustrator agrees to show the Magazine the artwork if the Magazine so requests so that the Magazine may make its own evaluation as to the degree of completion of the artwork.

6. Copyright Notice and Authorship Credit
Copyright notice shall appear in the Illustrator's name in close proximity to the illustration(s). The Illustrator shall have the right to receive authorship credit for the illustration and to have such credit removed if the Illustrator so desires due to changes made by the Magazine that are unsatisfactory to the Illustrator.

7. Payments
Payment shall be made within 30 days of the billing date.

8. Ownership of Artwork
The Illustrator shall retain ownership of all original artwork and the Magazine shall return such artwork, and all copies thereof, to the Illustrator, and shall permanently delete all digital copies thereof, within 30 days of expiration or termination of the license granted herein.

9. Acceptance of Terms
To constitute this as a binding agreement between us, please sign both copies of this letter beneath the words "consented and agreed to" and return one copy to the Magazine for its files.

CONSENTED AND AGREED TO:

_____
Artist's signature/date

_____
Magazine

_____
Authorized signature/date

_____
Name and title

ILLUSTRATOR'S ESTIMATE & CONFIRMATION FORM (Front)

[Illustrator's Letterhead]

Remove all language in italics before using this form.

CLIENT

Date _____

Commissioned by _____

Illustrator's Job Number _____

Client's Job Number _____

ASSIGNMENT DESCRIPTION

_____

_____

DELIVERY SCHEDULE

_____

_____

FEE PAYMENT SCHEDULE

_____

_____

ESTIMATED EXPENSES (OTHER BILLABLE EXPENSES)

Toll Telephone Calls	Messengers	After Sketches
Shipping & Insurance	Other Expenses	After Finish
Transit & Travel	Cancellation Fee (percentage of fee)	Sale of Original Art
Client's Alterations	Before Sketches	

RIGHTS GRANTED

Any usage rights not exclusively transferred are reserved to the Illustrator. Usage beyond that granted to the Client herein shall require payment of an additional fee at Illustrator's standard license fees, subject to all terms.

For use in magazines and newspapers, first North American reproduction rights unless specified otherwise here:

_____

For all other uses, the Client acquires only the following rights:

_____

Title or Product *[name]* _____

Category or Use *[advertising, corporate, promotional, editorial, etc.]* _____

Medium of Use *[consumer or trade magazine, annual report, TV, book, website, online publications, device apps, etc.]* _____

Geographic Area *[if applicable]* _____

Time Period *[if applicable]* _____

Number of Uses *[if applicable]* _____

Other *[if applicable]* _____

Original artwork, including sketches and any other preliminary material, and all copyrights therein, remains the property of the Illustrator unless purchased by a payment of a separate fee. Any grant of rights is conditional upon receipt of full payment. Upon receipt of full payment, Illustrator shall deliver digital files necessary to enable Client's usage rights granted herein. Illustrator retains the rights to display all work created by Illustrator for this Project, including preliminary materials and final art, in Illustrator's portfolios, including in print and online, and to submit such work to design periodicals and competitions.

ILLUSTRATOR'S ESTIMATE & CONFIRMATION FORM (Back)

TERMS

1. Time for Payment
Payment is due within 30 days of receipt of invoice. A 1 1/2% monthly service charge will be billed for late payment. Any advances or partial payments shall be indicated under Payment Schedule on front.

2. Default in Payment
The Client shall assume responsibility for all collection of legal fees necessitated by default in payment.

3. Grant of Rights
The grant of rights is conditioned on receipt of full payment.

4. Expenses
The Client shall reimburse the Illustrator for all expenses arising from the assignment.

5. Estimates
The fees and expenses shown are minimum estimates only. Final fees and expenses shall be shown when invoice is rendered. The Client's approval shall be obtained for any increases in fees or expenses that exceed the original estimate by 10% or more.

6. Sales Tax
The Client shall be responsible for the payment of sales tax, if any such tax is due.

7. Cancellation
In the event of cancellation or breach by the Client, the Illustrator shall retain ownership of all rights of copyright and the original artwork, including sketches and any other preliminary materials, and Client shall return all copies and permanently delete all digital copies thereof. The Client shall pay the Illustrator according to the following schedule: 50% of original fee if canceled after preliminary sketches are completed, 100% if canceled after completion of finished art.

8. Alterations
Alteration to artwork shall not be made without consulting the Illustrator, and the Illustrator shall be allowed the first option to make alterations when possible. After acceptance of artwork, if alterations are required, a pay-ment shall be charged over the original amount. Alterations not due to the fault of the Illustrator shall be billed separately.

9. Credit Lines
On any contribution for magazine or book use, the Illustrator shall receive name credit in print. If name credit is to be given with other types of use, it must be specified here:

_____

_____

☐ If this box is checked, the credit line shall be in the form:

© [date]_____

10. Return of Artwork
The Client assumes responsibility for the return of the artwork in undamaged condition within 30 days of first reproduction. Client shall return all copies and permanently delete all digital copies of the artwork, including sketches and any other preliminary materials, within 30 days after expiration of Client's usage rights.

11. Loss or Damage to Artwork
The value of lost or damaged artwork is placed at no less than $_____ per piece.

12. Unauthorized Use
The Client will indemnify the Illustrator against all claims and expenses, including reasonable attorney's fees, arising from uses for which no release was requested in writing or for uses exceeding the authority granted by a release or the license granted herein.

13. Warranty of Originality
The Illustrator warrants and represents that, to the best of his/her knowledge, the work assigned hereunder is original and has not been previously published, or that consent to use has been obtained consistent with the rights granted to Client herein.; that all work or portions thereof obtained through the undersigned from third parties is original and that consent to use has been obtained consistent with the rights granted to Client herein; that the Illustrator has full authority to make this Agreement; and that the work prepared by the Illustrator does not contain any scandalous, libelous, or unlawful matter. This warranty does not extend to any uses that the Client or others may make of the Artist's product that may infringe on the rights of others. Client expressly agrees that it will hold the Illustrator harmless for all liability caused by the Client's unauthorized use of the Illustrator's product to the extent such use infringes on the rights of others.

14. Limitation of Liability
Client agrees that it shall not hold the Illustrator or his/her agents or employees liable for any incidental or consequential damages that arise from the Illustrator's failure to perform any aspect of the Project in a timely manner, regardless of whether such failure was caused by intentional or negligent acts or omissions of the Illustrator or a third party.

15. Dispute Resolution
Any disputes in excess of $ _____ *[maximum limit for small-claims court]* arising out of this Agreement shall be submitted to mediation in accordance with the rules of _____
[name of local lawyers for the arts mediation program]. The prevailing party in any dispute resolved by litigation shall be entitled to recover its attorneys' fees and costs, provided that party initiated or participated in mediation as set forth herein.

16. Acceptance of Terms
The signature of both parties shall evidence acceptance of these terms.

CONSENTED AND AGREED TO:

_____   _____   _____
Illustrator's signature/date   Authorized signature/date   Client's name and title

ALL-PURPOSE ILLUSTRATOR'S LETTER OF AGREEMENT (Front) *[Illustrator's Letterhead]*

This letter of agreement is a model, which should be amended to fit the artist's particular circumstances. Remove all language in italics before using this form.

CLIENT

Commissioned by _____

Date _____

Job/Invoice Number _____

Shipping Number _____

Illustrator's Tax ID (Social Security) Number _____

THIS AGREEMENT MUST BE SIGNED AND RETURNED BEFORE ARTIST CAN SCHEDULE OR BEGIN THIS JOB.

Project Title *[if any]* _____

Client's Purchase Order Number *[if available]* _____

DESCRIPTION

Subject Matter _____

Size _____

Color or Black & White _____

Media *[specify any electronic/digital media]* _____

Any Relevant Production Information _____

DUE DATES

Sketch _____

Final _____

USAGE RIGHTS GRANTED IN FINAL ART

Duration of Usage _____

Limitations on Media in Which Used *[e.g., print rights only, no electronic usage]* _____

Limitations on Number of Insertions *[if appropriate]* _____

Limitations on Geographical Use *[North American, English editions]* _____

Owner of Original Art *[only if different from Credits below]* _____

Fee for Rights Granted _____

ALL-PURPOSE ILLUSTRATOR'S LETTER OF AGREEMENT (Back)

TERMS

1. Reservation of Rights

All rights not expressly granted above are retained by the Artist, including any electronic rights or usage unless specified above and including, but not limited to, all rights in sketches, comps, or other preliminary materials. Any grant of rights is conditional upon receipt of full payment. Upon receipt of full payment, Artist shall deliver digital files necessary to enable Client's usage rights granted herein. Any use additional to that expressly granted above requires arrangement for payment of a separate fee. Artist retains the rights to display all work created by Artist for this Project, including preliminary materials and final art, in Artist's portfolios, including in print and online, and to submit such work to design periodicals and competitions.

2. Revisions

(**A**) Preliminary Work/Sketches: Artist agrees to submit _____ *[insert studio standard]* rough sketches and/or _____ *[insert studio standard]* finished sketches for Client's approval. Additional fees will be charged to Client for revisions made after such sketches and for all revisions that reflect a new direction for the assignment or new conceptual input.

(**B**) Finished Art: Client agrees to pay Artist an additional fee, to be negotiated separately, for changes requested to final art where Client asked Artist to proceed directly to final art.

No additional fee shall be billed for changes required to bring final artwork up to original specifications or assignment description. Client agrees to offer Artist the first opportunity to make any changes to final artwork.

3. Cancellation Fees

Fifty percent (50%) of the final fee is due within 30 days of notification that for any reason the job is canceled or postponed before the final stage. One hundred percent (100%) of the total fee is due despite cancellation or postponement of the job if the art has been completed. Upon cancellation, Artist retains all rights to the art, and all original art and copies thereof must be returned, including sketches, comps, or other preliminary materials, and Client shall permanently delete all digital copies thereof.

4. Credits and Copies

A credit line suitable to the design of the page or context will be used. Client agrees to pay an additional 50% of the total fee, excluding expenses, for failure to include credit line. Credit line is required independent of Artist's signature, which shall be included at Artist's discretion unless otherwise agreed in writing above. Client agrees to provide Artist with *[insert studio standard]* sample copies of any printed material.

5. Payment

Payment for finished work is due upon acceptance, net 30 days. The Client's right to use the work is conditioned upon receipt of payment within 30 days of acceptance and upon Client's compliance with the terms of this Agreement. A 1 1/2% monthly service charge will be billed against late payment.

6. Original Art

Original art remains the property of the Artist unless expressed otherwise in the Agreement. Client is responsible for return of original art in undamaged condition within 30 days of first reproduction. Client shall also return all copies of the art, and permanently delete all digital copies thereof, within 30 days after expiration of Client's usage rights.

7. Additional Expenses

If Client does not provide a courier/shipping number in the space provided above, shipping charges will be added to the final invoice. Client agrees to reimburse Artist for the following expenses:

Research _____
Messengers _____
Models _____
Props _____
Travel _____
Telephone _____
Proofs _____
Software _____
Transparencies _____
Other _____

8. Permissions and Releases

The Client agrees to indemnify and hold the Artist harmless against any and all claims, costs, and expenses, including attorney's fees, due to materials included in the Work at the request of the Client for which no copyright permission or privacy release was requested or for which uses exceed the uses allowed pursuant to a permission or release or the scope of the license granted hereunder.

9. Miscellany

This Agreement shall be binding upon the parties, their heirs, successors, assigns, and personal representatives. This Agreement constitutes the entire understanding of the parties. Its terms can be modified only by an instrument in writing signed by both parties, except that the Client may authorize expenses or revisions orally. No terms attached to any check for payment under this Agreement can modify the Agreement except under an independent instrument in writing signed by both parties. Any disputes in excess of $_____ *[maximum limit for small-claims court]* arising out of this Agreement shall be submitted to mediation in accordance with the rules of _____ *[name of local lawyers for the arts mediation program]*. The prevailing party in any dispute resolved by litigation shall be entitled to recover its attorney's fees and costs, provided that party initiated or participated in mediation as set forth herein. A waiver of a breach of any of the provisions of this Agreement shall not be construed as a continuing waiver of other breaches of the same or other provisions. This Agreement shall be governed by the laws of the State of _____*[name of your state]* and courts of such State shall have exclusive jurisdiction and venue.

CONSENTED AND AGREED TO:

_____
Artist's signature/date

_____
Authorized signature/date

_____
Buyer's name and title

_____
Accounts payable contact name/phone

ILLUSTRATOR'S RELEASE FORM FOR MODELS

[Illustrator's Letterhead]

Remove all language in italics before using this form.

In consideration of _____ dollars ($_____), receipt of which is acknowledged,

I, _____ , do hereby give _____ , his or

her assigns, licenses, and legal representatives the irrevocable right to use my name (or any fictional name), picture, portrait, or

photograph in all forms and media and in all manners, including composite or distorted representations, for advertising, trade,

or any other lawful purposes, and I waive any right to inspect or approve the finished version(s), including written copy that may

be created in connection therewith. I am of full age.* I have read this release and am fully familiar with its contents.

_____
Witness

_____
Model

_____
Address

_____
Address

_____
Date

CONSENT (if applicable)

I am the parent or guardian of the minor named above and have the legal authority to execute the above release. I approve the foregoing and waive any rights in the premises.

_____
Witness

_____
Parent or Guardian

_____
Address

_____
Address

_____
Date

* *[Delete this sentence if the subject is a minor. The parent or guardian must then sign the consent.]*

Reproduced with permission from *Business and Legal Forms for Illustrators* by Tad Crawford (Allworth Press).

ILLUSTRATOR'S INVOICE (Front)

[Illustrator's Letterhead]

Remove all language in italics before using this form.

CLIENT

Date

Commissioned by

Illustrator's Job Number

Client's Job Number

ASSIGNMENT DESCRIPTION

FEE PAYMENT SCHEDULE

ITEMIZED EXPENSES (OTHER BILLABLE EXPENSES)

Toll Telephone Calls	Messengers	SUBTOTAL
Client's Alterations	Cancellation Fee	SALES TAX
Transportation & Travel	Shipping & Insurance	PAYMENTS ON ACCOUNT
Sale of Original Art	Miscellaneous	BALANCE DUE

RIGHTS GRANTED IN FINAL ART

Any usage rights not granted are reserved to the Illustrator. Usage beyond that granted to the Client herein shall require payment of an additional fee in the amount of Illustrator's standard fee for such usage, subject to all terms. For use in magazines and newspapers, first North American reproduction rights unless specified otherwise here: _____

For all other uses, the Client acquires only the following rights: _____

Title or Product *[name]*

Category or Use *[advertising, corporate, promotional, editorial, etc.]*

Medium of Use *[consumer or trade magazine, annual report, TV, book, website, online publications, device apps, etc.]*

Geographic Area *[if applicable]*

Time Period *[if applicable]*

Number of Uses *[if applicable]*

Other *[if applicable]*

Original artwork, including sketches and any other preliminary materials, and all copyrights therein, remains the property of the Illustrator unless purchased by payment of a separate fee subject to all terms.

Any grant of rights is conditional upon receipt of full payment.

Upon receipt of full payment, Illustrator shall deliver digital files necessary to enable Client's usage rights granted herein. Illustrator retains the rights to display all work created by Illustrator for this Project, including preliminary materials and final art, in Illustrator's portfolios, including in print and online, and to submit such work to design periodicals and competitions.

TERMS

1. Time for Payment
Payment is due within 30 days of receipt of invoice. A 1 1/2% monthly service charge will be billed for late payment.

2. Default in Payment
The Client shall assume responsibility for all collection of legal fees necessitated by default in payment.

3. Expenses
The Client shall reimburse the Illustrator for all expenses arising from the assignment.

4. Sales Tax
The Client shall be responsible for the payment of sales tax, if any such tax is due.

5. Grant of Rights
The grant of rights is conditioned on receipt of payment.

6. Credit Lines
On any contribution for magazine or book use, the Illustrator shall receive name credit in print. If name credit is to be given with other types of use, it must be specified here:

_____

_____

☐ If this box is checked, the credit line shall be in the form:

© [*date*]_____

7. Additional Limitations
If the Illustrator and the Client have agreed to additional limitations as to either the duration or geographical extent of the permitted use, specify here:

_____

_____

_____

8. Return of Artwork
The Client assumes responsibility for the return of the artwork in undamaged condition within 30 days of first reproduction. Client shall return all copies and permanently delete all digital copies of the artwork, including sketches and any other preliminary materials, within 30 days after expiration of Client's usage rights.

9. Loss or Damage to Artwork
The value of lost or damaged artwork is placed at no less than $ _____ per piece.

10. Alterations
Alteration to artwork shall not be made without consulting the initial Illustrator, and the Illustrator shall be allowed the first option to make alterations when possible. After acceptance of artwork, if alterations are required, a payment shall be charged over the original amount.

11. Unauthorized Use
The Client will indemnify the Illustrator against all claims and expenses, including reasonable attorney's fees, arising from uses for which no release was requested in writing or for uses exceeding the authority granted by a release or the license granted herein.

12. Warranty of Originality
The Illustrator warrants and represents that, to the best of his/her knowledge, the work assigned hereunder is original and has not been previously published, or that consent to use has been obtained consistent with the rights granted to Client herein; that all work or portions thereof obtained through the undersigned from third parties is original and that consent to use has been obtained consistent with the rights granted to Client herein; that the Illustrator has full authority to make this Agreement; and that the work prepared by the Illustrator does not contain any scandalous, libelous, or unlawful matter. This warranty does not extend to any uses that the Client or others may make of the Illustrator's product that may infringe on the rights of others. Client expressly agrees that it will hold the Illustrator harmless for all liability caused by the Client's unauthorized use of the Illustrator's product to the extent such use infringes on the rights of others.

9. Limitation of Liability
Client agrees that it shall not hold the Illustrator or his/her agents or employees liable for any incidental or consequential damages that arise from the Illustrator's failure to perform any aspect of the Project in a timely manner, regardless of whether such failure was caused by intentional or negligent acts or omissions of the Illustrator or a third party.

10. Dispute Resolution
Any disputes in excess of $_____ [*maximum limit for small-claims court*] arising out of this Agreement shall be submitted to mediation in accordance with the rules of_____ [*name of local lawyers for the arts mediation program*]. The prevailing party in any dispute resolved by litigation shall be entitled to recover its attorney's fees and costs, provided that party initiated or participated in mediation as set forth herein.

SURFACE PATTERN DESIGNER–AGENT AGREEMENT (FRONT) *Designer's Letterhead]*

Remove all language in italics before using this form.

Agreement, this day of	*[date]*	**between**

(Hereinafter referred to as the "designer"), **residing at**

and (hereinafter referred to as the "agent"), **residing at**

Whereas, the Designer is a professional surface pattern designer; and

Whereas, the Designer wishes to have an Agent represent him or her in marketing certain rights enumerated herein; and

Whereas, the Agent is capable of marketing the artwork produced by the Designer; and

Whereas, the Agent wishes to represent the Designer;

Now, therefore, in consideration of the foregoing premises and the mutual covenants hereinafter set forth and other valuable consideration, the parties hereto agree as follows:

1. AGENCY
The Designer appoints the Agent to act as his or her representative for:

☐ **Speculative** - Direct sale of designs to buyers in varying

markets, on-site via tradeshows or buyer/agent meetings.

☐ **Commissioned Work** - Securing exclusive creative work, such

as market research for CAD and/or physical trend boards; original hand-rendered croquis; engineered designs, placement print, or repetitive designs; development of CAD coordinates, colorways, etc., from clients in varying markets, via agents' collaboration with the client to ensure the creative focus and production specs are met by the designer, as provided in Paragraph 6.

☐ **Off-Site Service Work** - Securing of service work from clients

in varying markets. Service work is defined to include, but is not limited to, repeat, coordinate, and colorway development for designs originated by the Designer, other designers, or company archives.

☐ **Other** _____

The Agent agrees to use his/her best efforts in submitting the Designer's creative work for the purpose of making sales or securing assignments for the Designer. For the purposes of this Agreement, the term "creative work" shall be defined to include designs, repeats, colorways, and any other product of the Designer's effort. The Agent shall negotiate the terms of any assignment that is offered, but the Designer shall have the right to reject any assignment if he or she finds the terms unacceptable. Nothing contained herein shall prevent the Designer from making sales or securing work for his or her own account without liability for commissions except for accounts that have been secured for the Designer by the Agent during the period of time that the Agent represents the Designer. Further, the Designer agrees, when selling his or her creative work or taking orders, not to accept a price that is below the price structure of his or her Agent. After a period of _____ months, the Designer may remove his or her unsold creative work from the Agent's portfolio to do with as the Designer wishes.

2. CREATIVE WORK AND RISK OF LOSS, THEFT, OR DAMAGE
All creative work in any media including digital media submitted to the Agent for sale or for the purpose of securing work shall remain the property of the Designer. The Agent shall issue a receipt to the Designer for all creative work that the Designer submits to the Agent. If creative work is lost, stolen, or damaged while in the Agent's possession due to the Agent's failure to exercise reasonable care, the Agent will be held liable for the value of the creative work. Proof of any loss, theft, or damage must be furnished by the Agent to the Designer upon request. When selling creative work, taking an order, or allowing a client to hold artwork (See 7. Holding Policy) for consideration, the Agent agrees to use invoice, order, or holding forms that provide that the client may not make or retain copies of the creative work, and shall be responsible for loss, theft, or damage to creative work while being held by the client, and to require the client's signature on such forms. The Agent agrees to enforce these provisions, including taking legal action as necessary. If the Agent undertakes legal action, any recovery shall first be used to reimburse the amount of attorney's fees and other expenses incurred and the balance of the recovery shall be divided between Agent and Designer in the respective percentages set forth in Paragraph 5. If the Agent chooses not to require the client to be responsible as described herein, then the Agent agrees to assume these responsibilities. If the Agent receives insurance proceeds due to loss, theft, or damage of artwork while in the Agent's or client's possession, the Designer shall receive no less than that portion of the proceeds that have been paid for the Designer's creative work.

3. TERM
This Agreement shall take effect on the _____ *[day]* of

_____ *[year]*, and remain in full force and effect until terminated by the Designer or Agent as provided in Paragraph 10.

4. FEES
At this time, the minimum base fees charged to clients by the Agent for speculative sales and commissioned creative work are as follows:

SPECULATIVE SALES - Based on complexity, scale, etc.

Croquis/Concepts	$_____	ea.
Single Design in Repeat	$_____	ea.
Coordinates #_____@	$_____	ea.

COMMISSIONED WORK - Based on complexity, scale, etc.

Croquis/Concepts: 8.5 x 11" Hand Rendered/CAD

Lead Design $_____

Coordinates #_____@	$_____	ea.

SURFACE PATTERN DESIGNER–AGENT AGREEMENT (BACK)

B&W Design Development *(Upon approval of above as applicable.)*

Repeat Development: Lead Design: Hand $_____ CAD $_____

                         Coordinate 1:   Hand $_____ CAD $_____

                         Coordinate 2:   Hand $_____ CAD $_____

                         Coordinate 3:   Hand $_____ CAD $_____

Engineered Design: Hand $_____ CAD $_____

Placement Print: Hand $_____ CAD $_____

Design Completion *(Upon approval of B&W Repeat & Full-Color, Hand-Rendered / CAD Technique Sample as applicable per above. Full-Color, Hand-Rendered/CAD Engraving Area.)*

Lead Design $_____

Coordinate 1 $_____

Coordinate 2 $_____

Coordinate 3 $_____

Engineered Design $_____

Colorways / CAD: Lead Design $_____

Coordinate 1 $_____

Coordinate 2 $_____

Coordinate 3 $_____

Engineered Design $_____

OFF-SITE SERVICE WORK

Repeat Development: Lead Design: Hand $_____ CAD $_____

                         Coordinate 1:   Hand $_____ CAD $_____

                         Coordinate 2:   Hand $_____ CAD $_____

                         Coordinate 3:   Hand $_____ CAD $_____

Engineered Design: Hand $_____ CAD $_____

Placement Print: Hand $_____ CAD $_____

The Agent agrees that these prices are minimum prices only and shall be increased whenever possible (i.e., when the work is a rush job or becomes larger or more complicated than agreed upon). The Designer may increase minimum prices to reflect current market rates and/or inflation, and the Agent shall honor such increases upon notice thereof. The Agent shall obtain the Designer's written consent prior to entering into any contract for payment by royalty. No discounts shall be offered to clients by the Agent without first consulting the Designer. When leaving a design with the Agent for possible sale, the Designer shall agree with the Agent as to the price to be charged if the design should bring more than the Agent's base price.

5. AGENT'S COMMISSIONS

The rate of commission for all creative work, speculative or commissioned, shall be _____%. It is mutually agreed by both parties that no commissions shall be paid on assignments rejected by the Designer or for which the Designer does not receive payment, regardless of the reasons payment is not made. On commissioned originals and service work, expenses incurred in the execution of a job, such as phone calls, shipping, etc., shall be billed to the client in addition to the fee. No Agent's commission shall be paid on these amounts. In the event that a flat fee is paid by the client, it shall be reduced by the amount of expenses incurred by the Designer in performing the assignment, and the Agent's commission shall be payable only on the fee after reduction for expenses. It is mutually agreed that if the Agent offers a client a discount for multiple creative services including creative work performed on other designers' work or clients' archives, then that discount will come out of the Agent's commission since the Agent is the party who benefits from this volume.

6. COMMISSIONED WORK

Commissioned work refers to all creative work done on a non-speculative basis. The Agent shall provide the Designer with a copy of the completed order form that the client has signed. The order form shall set forth the responsibilities of the client in ordering and purchasing artwork. To this the Agent shall add the date by which the artwork must be completed and any additional instructions that the Agent feels are necessary to complete the job to the client's satisfaction. The Agent will sign these instructions. Any changes in the original instructions must be in writing, signed by the Agent, and contain a revised completion date. It is mutually agreed that all commissioned work generated by the Designer's work shall be offered first to the Designer. Under no circumstances may a Client be authorized to engage a different designer to create works based on Designer's work. The Designer has the right to refuse such work. The Agent agrees to use the order confirmation form of the Graphic Artists Guild, or a form that protects the interests of the Designer in the same manner as that form. The order form shall provide that the Designer will be paid for all changes of original instructions arising through no fault of the Designer. The order form shall also provide that if a job is canceled through no fault of the Designer, a kill fee shall be paid by the client based on the amount of work already done and the creative work and copyrights therein will remain the property of the Designer. In a case in which the job being canceled is based on creative work owned by the client, such as a previously purchased or archived design a labor fee will be charged as outlined above and the Designers' creative work will be destroyed. If the creative work is already completed in a satisfactory manner at the time the job is canceled, the client must pay the full fee.

7. HOLDING POLICY

In the event that a client wishes to hold the Designer's work for consideration, the Agent shall establish a maximum holding time with the client. This holding time shall not exceed 5 working days. Any other arrangements must first be discussed with the Designer. The Agent agrees to use the holding form of the Graphic Artists Guild, or a form that protects the interests of the Designer in the same manner as that form. All holding forms shall be available for the Designer to see at any time.

8. BILLINGS AND PAYMENTS

The Agent shall be responsible for all billings. The Agent agrees to use the invoice form of the Graphic Artists Guild, or a form that protects the interests of the Designer in the same manner as that form. The Agent agrees to provide the Designer with a copy of all bills to clients pertaining to the work of the Designer. The Designer will provide the Agent with a bill for his or her work for the particular job. The Designer's bill shall be paid by the Agent within 1 week after the delivery of the creative work(s) or, if the Agent finds it necessary, within 10 working days after receipt of payment from the client. The terms of all bills issued by the Agent shall require payment within 30 calendar days or less. If the client does not pay within that time, the Agent must immediately pursue payment and, upon request, inform the Designer that this has been done. The Agent agrees to take all necessary steps to collect payment, including taking legal action if necessary. If either the Agent or Designer undertakes legal action, any recovery shall first be used to reimburse the amount of attorney's fees and other expenses incurred, and the balance of the recovery shall be divided between the Agent and Designer in the respective percentages set forth in Paragraph 5. The Agent agrees, whenever possible, to bill in such a way that no single bill exceeds the maximum that can be sued for in small-claims court. Under no circumstances shall the Agent withhold payment to the Designer after the Agent has been paid. Late payments by the Agent to the Designer shall be accompanied by interest calculated at the rate of 1 1/2% monthly.

9. INSPECTION OF THE BOOKS AND RECORDS

The Designer shall have the right to inspect the Agent's books and records with respect to proceeds due the Designer. The Agent shall keep the books and records at the Agent's place of business and the Designer may make such an inspection during normal business hours after providing reasonable notice.

10. TERMINATION

This Agreement may be terminated by either party by giving 30 days' written notice by registered mail to the other party. All creative work executed by the Designer not sold by the Agent must be returned to the Designer within those 30 days, and Agent shall permanently delete all copies of digital creative work. In the event of termination, the Agent shall receive commissions for all sales made or assignments obtained by the Agent prior to the termination date, regardless of when payment is received. No commissions shall be payable for sales made or assignments obtained by the Designer after the termination date.

11. ASSIGNMENT

This Agreement shall not be assigned by either of the parties hereto. It shall be binding on and inure to the benefit of the successors, administrators, executors, or heirs of the Agent and Designer.

12. DISPUTE RESOLUTION

Any disputes in excess of $_____ [maximum limit for small-claims court] arising out of this Agreement shall be submitted to mediation in accordance with the rules of _____ [name of local lawyers for the arts mediation program]. The prevailing party in any dispute resolved by litigation shall be entitled to recover its attorney's fees and costs, provided that party initiated or participated in mediation as set forth herein.

13. NOTICES

All notices shall be given to the parties at their respective addresses set forth above.

14. INDEPENDENT CONTRACTOR STATUS

Both parties agree that the Agent is acting as an independent contractor. This Agreement is not an employment agreement, nor does it constitute a joint venture or partnership between the Designer and Agent.

15. AMENDMENTS AND MERGER

All amendments to this Agreement must be written. This Agreement incorporates the entire understanding of the parties.

16. OTHER PROVISIONS

_____

_____

_____

_____

_____

_____

_____

_____

_____

_____

17. GOVERNING LAW

This Agreement shall be governed by the laws of the State of

_____

18. ACCEPTANCE OF TERMS

The signature of both parties shall evidence acceptance of these terms.

In witness whereof, the parties have signed this agreement as of the date set forth above.

Designer: _____

Agent: _____

SURFACE PATTERN DESIGNER'S
ESTIMATE & CONFIRMATION FORM (FRONT)

[Designer's Letterhead]

Remove all language in italics before using this form.

CLIENT / COMPANY CONTACT NAME: _____ **DATE:** _____

_____

Address: _____ **City:** _____ **State:** _____ **Zip Code:** _____

Client / Company Contact Info: Work Phone: (_____)_____ Fax: (_____)_____ Cell: (_____)_____

E-mail Address: _____

_____

Description of design services Commissioned

Collection / Design Title: _____

End-Use(s) & Brief Description(s): _____

Lead Repetitive Design: Repeat Type | Size: _____|_____

Coordinate Design #1: Repeat Type | Size: _____|_____   **Coordinate Design #2: Repeat Type | Size:** _____|_____

Coordinate Design #3: Repeat Type | Size: _____|_____   **Coordinate Design #4: Repeat Type | Size:** _____|_____

Lead Engineered Design: Size(s): _____   **Lead Placement Print: Size(s):** _____

_____

ESTIMATED FEES

Croquis / Concepts: 8.5" x 11" / Hand Rendered / CAD   Lead Design: $ _____   Coordinates: Qty.: _____ @ $ _____ each

B&W Development (Upon approval of above croquis/concept as applicable):

Repeat Development: Lead Design: $ _____ **Coordinate #1: $** _____ **Coordinate #2: $** _____ **Coordinate #3: $** _____

Engineered Design: _____   **Placement Print:** _____

Design Completion (Upon approval of B&W Repeat & Full-Color, Hand-Rendered / CAD Technique Sample as applicable per above. Full-Color, Hand- Rendered/ CAD Engraving Area):

Repeat Development: Lead Repetitive Design: $ _____ **Coordinate #1: $** _____ **Coordinate #2: $** _____ **Coordinate #3: $** _____ **Coordinate #4: $** _____

Lead Engineered Design: _____   **Lead Placement Print:** _____

Colorways / CAD: Lead Repetitive Design: $ _____ **Coordinate #1: $** _____ **Coordinate #2: $** _____ **Coordinate #3: $** _____ **Coordinate #4: $** _____

Lead Engineered Design: _____   **Lead Placement Print:** _____

Other: _____

_____

Special Instructions / Comments: _____

_____

_____

_____

Due Date(s): _____

SURFACE PATTERN DESIGNER'S
ESTIMATE & CONFIRMATION FORM (BACK)

TERMS

1. Time for Payment
Because the major portion of the above work (the "Project") represents labor, all invoices are payable 15 days net. A 1 1/2% monthly service charge is payable on all unpaid balances after this period.

2. Default of Payment
The Client shall pay all costs, including attorneys' fees, incurred by the Designer and/or Designer's Agent necessitated by default in payment.

3. Estimated Prices
Prices shown above are minimum estimates only. Final prices shall be shown on the invoice.

4. Payment for Changes
Client shall be responsible for making additional payments for changes requested by Client in original assignment.

5. Expenses
Client shall be responsible for payment of all out-of-pocket expenses rising from assignment, including but not limited to mailings, messengers, shipping charges, and shipping insurance.

6. Sales Tax
Client shall assume responsibility for all sales taxes, if any, due on this Project.

7. Ownership
Upon completion of the Project and on condition of the Designer's receipt of all payments due, Designer hereby assigns to Client all rights, title, and interest, including copyright, in and to the final creative work, and, if requested, Designer shall provide to Client originals of the final creative work and/or digital files comprising the final creative work.

Once creative work has entered the marketplace, Designer retains the right to display all work created by Designer for this project, including preliminary designs and final creative work, in Designer's portfolio, including print and digital versions, provided the client is appropriately identified therewith. Designer retains all rights, including copyrights, in and to preliminary sketches and alternative designs not selected by Client.

8. Cancellation Fees
Work canceled by the Client while in progress shall be compensated for on the basis of completed work at the time of cancellation, and Designer shall retain all rights, including copyrights, in the creative work, whatever its stage of completion. Where Designer creates other derivative works based on Client's pre-purchased designs and/or company archives, a labor fee will be charged, and Client shall destroy all copies and/or permanently delete all digital copies of such derivative works.

9. insuring artwork
The Client agrees when shipping creative work to provide insurance covering the fair market value of the artwork.

10. Warranty of Originality
The Designer warrants and represents that to the best of Designer's knowledge, except with respect to content provided by Client, the creative work assigned to Client hereunder is original and has not been previously published, or that consent has been obtained through the undersigned from third parties for use of the creative work by Client on an unlimited basis; that the Designer has full authority to make this Agreement; and that the creative work prepared by the Designer does not contain any scandalous, libelous, or unlawful content. This warranty is limited to the creative work in the form created by the Designer and does not extend to any changes, derivatives, or other adaptations made to the work by the Client or third parties.

11. Limitation of Liability
Client agrees that it shall not hold the Designer or his/her agents or employees liable for any incidental or consequential damages that arise from the Designer's failure to perform any aspect of the Project in a timely manner, regardless of whether such failure was caused by intentional or negligent acts or omissions of the Designer or a third party.

12. Dispute Resolution
Any disputes in excess of $_____ [maximum limit for small-claims court] arising out of this Agreement shall be submitted to mediation in accordance with the rules of _____ [name of local lawyers for the arts mediation program]. The prevailing party in any dispute resolved by litigation shall be entitled to recover its attorney's fees and costs, provided that party initiated or participated in mediation as set forth herein.

13. ACCEPTANCE OF TERMS
The signature of both parties shall evidence acceptance of these terms.

Consented and agreed to:

Client / Company Contact Authorized Signature: _____

Title: _____ Date: _____

Agent / Representative Name: _____ Date: _____

Designer's Signature : _____ Date: _____

SURFACE PATTERN DESIGNER'S HOLDING FORM

[Designer's Letterhead]

Remove all language in italics before using this form.

CLIENT / COMPANY CONTACT NAME: _____ DATE: _____

_____

Address: _____ City: _____ State: _____ Zip Code: _____

Client / Company Contact Info: Work Phone: (_____)_____ Fax: (_____)_____ Cell: (_____)_____

E-mail Address: _____

NUMBER OF DESIGNS HELD

Design #: _____

Title / Description: _____

_____

_____

Price: _____

Design #: _____

Title / Description: _____

_____

_____

Price: _____

Design #: _____

Title / Description: _____

_____

_____

Price: _____

Design #: _____

Title / Description: _____

_____

_____

Price: _____

Design #: _____

Title / Description: _____

_____

_____

Price: _____

Design #: _____

Title / Description: _____

_____

_____

Price: _____

Design #: _____

Title / Description: _____

_____

_____

Price: _____

Design #: _____

Title / Description: _____

_____

_____

Price: _____

The submitted designs are original and protected under the copyright laws of the United States, Title 17 United States Code. These designs are submitted to you in confidence and on the following terms:

1. Ownership and Copyrights

You agree not to copy, including digitally or photographically, or modify directly or indirectly any of the creative work held by you, nor permit any third party to do any of the foregoing.

All creative work, digital media, and photographs developed from these designs, including the copyrights therein, remain my property and must be returned to me unless the creative works are purchased by you. Any transfer of rights is conditional upon receipt of full payment.

2. Responsibility for Creative Work

You agree to assume responsibility for loss, theft, or any damage to the designs while they are being held by you. It is agreed that the fair market value for each design is the price specified above.

3. Holding of Creative Work

You agree to hold these designs for a period not to exceed _____ working days from the above date. Any holding of creative work, including digital media, beyond that period shall constitute a binding purchase of a nonexclusive license to reproduce the work at the price specified above. You further agree not to allow any third party to hold any creative work unless specifically approved by me.

4. Dispute Resolution

Any disputes in excess of $_____ *[maximum limit for small-claims court]* arising out of this Agreement shall be submitted to mediation in accordance with the rules of _____ *[name of local lawyers for the arts mediation program]*. The prevailing party in any dispute resolved by litigation shall be entitled to recover its attorney's fees and costs, provided that party initiated or participated in mediation as set forth herein.

5. ACCEPTANCE OF TERMS

The signature of both parties shall evidence acceptance of these terms.

Consented and agreed to:

_____

Client / Company Name   Client / Company Contact Authorized Signature   Date

_____

Designer's Signature   Date

SURFACE PATTERN DESIGNER'S INVOICE

[Designer's Letterhead]

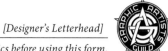

Remove all language in italics before using this form.

CLIENT / COMPANY CONTACT NAME: _____ DATE: _____

_____

Address: _____ City: _____ State: _____ Zip Code: _____

Client / Company Contact Info: Work Phone: (_____)_____ Fax: (_____)_____ Cell: (_____)_____

E-mail Address: _____

DESIGNER: _____

Address: _____ City: _____ State: _____ Zip Code: _____

INVOICE NUMBER: _____ PURCHASE ORDER NUMBER: _____

DescriptION OF SERVICES	ITEMIZED EXPENSES

Design / Collection #: _____ Price: _____   _____ Cost: _____

Creative Services: _____   _____ Cost: _____

_____   _____ Cost: _____

Design / Collection #: _____ Price: _____   _____ Cost: _____

Creative Services: _____   _____ Cost: _____

_____   _____ Cost: _____

Design / Collection #: _____ Price: _____   _____ Cost: _____

Creative Services: _____   _____ Cost: _____

_____   _____ Cost: _____

Subtotal: _____   Subtotal: _____

Taxes: _____

TOTAL: _____

Payments on Account: _____   Balance Due: _____

TERMS

1. Receipt of Artwork
Client acknowledges receipt of the creative work specified above.

2. Time for Payment
Because the major portion of the above work represents labor, all invoices are payable 15 days net. A 1 1/2% monthly service charge is payable on unpaid balance after expiration of period for payment.

3. Default in Payment
The Client shall assume responsibility for all collection of legal fees necessitated by default in payment.

4. Adjustments to Invoice
Client agrees to request any adjustments of accounts, terms, or other invoice data within 10 days of receipt of the invoice.

5. Ownership
Upon Designer's receipt of all payments due, Designer hereby assigns to Client all rights, title, and interest, including copyright, in and to the finished creative work and, if requested, Designer shall provide digital files comprising the creative work.

Once the creative work has entered the marketplace, Designer retains the right to display all work created by Designer for this project, including print and digital versions of preliminary designs and final creative work, in Designer's portfolio, provided that the Client is appropriately identified therewith. Designer retains all rights, including copyrights, in and to preliminary sketches and alternative designs not selected by Client.

6. Dispute Resolution
Any disputes in excess of $_____ *[maximum limit for small-claims court]* arising out of this Agreement shall be submitted to mediation in accordance with the rules of _____ *[name of local lawyers for the arts mediation program]*. The prevailing party in any dispute resolved by litigation shall be entitled to recover its attorney's fees and costs, provided that party initiated or participated in mediation as set forth herein.

7. ACCEPTANCE OF TERMS
The signature of both parties shall evidence acceptance of these terms.

Consented and agreed to:

Client / Company Contact Authorized Signature: _____ Date: _____

Agent / Representative Name: _____ Title: _____ Date: _____

Designer's Signature : _____ Date: _____

Glossary

2-D animation: Any hand-drawn graphic created for TV, film, etc., using either pen and ink or computer-generated imagery.

3-D animation: Use of modeling and/or digitizing to create objects that not only have shape and dimension but also can be viewed from any angle.

A

Account executive: Representative of an advertising agency who handles specific accounts and acts as a client liaison to the art director, creative director, and others creating advertising for the account.

Advance: Amount of money paid prior to the commencement of work or in the course of work. It may be intended to cover expenses, or it may be partial payment of the total fee. An advance as partial payment is common for a time-consuming project.

Advance on royalties or **advance payment against royalties:** Amount paid prior to actual sales of the commissioned item or work; sometimes paid in installments. Advances are generally not expected to be returned, even if unearned in sales. Both the terms and the size of the advance are negotiable.

Agreement: See *contract.*

All-Media rights: A contract term that asks the graphic artist, in essence, to allow the buyer to distribute work in all media (often it includes the clause "now known or invented in the future"). Media that convey art or design can take many forms: print media are books or magazines; electronic media includes portable media, such as DVDs, flash drives, etc., or multimedia presentations; other media are television, radio, and the Internet.

All-Rights contract: A contract that purchases all rights of usage for reproduction of an artwork forever. All-rights contracts are different from work-made-for-hire contracts, which strip away not only the graphic artist's rights but the graphic artist's authorship. Under an all-rights contract, the artist still retains statutory termination right. See also *perpetuity, termination rights,* and *work made for hire.*

Arbitration: Negotiation in a legal dispute by a neutral party that results in a binding decision, enforced by a court.

Art director: Usually an employee of an advertising agency, publishing house, magazine, or other user of a graphic artist's work. Some organizations hire freelance art directors to perform these duties. Responsibilities include selection of talent, purchase of visual work, and supervision of the quality and character of visual work.

Art staff: Group of artists working under an art director's supervision for a company such as an advertising agency, publisher, magazine, or large design studio.

Artists collective. A specific type of cooperative in which a group of artists work together to achieve a common goal that defines the collective. Everyone who is part of the collective jointly shares ownership, status, costs, benefits, and risks.

Artists cooperative: A legal entity owned and democratically governed by its members that provides benefits specific to the needs of its members. Each member owns one voting share and has one vote on major decisions, as outlined in its bylaws. Artists cooperatives are commonly formed to share marketing expenses, resources, or studio and gallery space.

Artwork: Any finished work of a graphic artist.

Assigning (transferring): Term commonly used for reselling or relicensing signed-over rights to artwork.

Attribution: Basic artist's right whereby the artist retains authorship of a work and is acknowledged properly for its creation. Attribution ensures that an artist's name not be used on works he or she did not create. Also called *paternity*.

Author's alterations (AA): Any changes requested by the client in service or responsibility beyond the scope outlined in the design proposal; these are billable expenses.

B

Backend: In website development, the backend delivers the content that populates the front end and provides the functionality not visible to the website visitor. It is the software and database that support a site, including advanced search mechanisms, built-in security, payment processing, audio and video streaming, etc.

Bailment: Obligation on the part of the individual(s) with whom art is left, to take reasonable care of it. This is a legal requirement and applies to situations such as a portfolio left for review.

Berne Convention: Worldwide multinational treaty for the protection of literary and artistic works that accepts moral rights as a matter of course. Member nations participating in Berne are required to frame their copyright laws according to certain minimum standards and to guarantee reciprocity to citizens of any other member nation.

Bid: To offer an amount as the price one will pay or accept.

Blanket contract: Contract kept on file by a publishing firm covering all future, and sometimes past, assignments.

Bleed (in printing): Any image or element on a page that touches the edge of the page and extends beyond the trim edge, leaving no margin, is said to bleed. It may bleed or extend off one or more sides. Photos, rules, clip art and decorative text elements can all bleed off the page.

Blog (a contraction of **web log):** A website or web page, usually maintained by an individual, that allows users to reflect, share opinions, and discuss various topics in the form of an online journal; readers may comment on posts written by others.

Blueline proofs: Nonreproducible photographic prints made from negatives, used in platemaking, which enable an editor to verify that all art and text are in proper position and that pages are in sequence. The term is still used in the digital workflow; however, the digital blueline is not blue, and it is made from the imposed electronic files that will be burned to the printing plates or sent directly to the press. Like traditional bluelines, the quality of the proof is not print quality or color accurate, but it is used for the same purpose.

Boilerplate: Contract or document containing formulaic language that can be used for a number of purposes or similar circumstances, requiring only minor alterations.

Book packagers: Independent suppliers who take over some or all of the functions for publishers of preparing a book. Functions include initiating projects, finding writers and illustrators, arranging for whatever extras may be involved, and striking deals with publishers.

Broker: Agent or representative.

Buyout: Imprecise term for an *all-rights transfer*.

C

Cancellation fee: A fee paid as compensation for the artist's or studio's effort in developing an illustration or design when a project is terminated or not used by the client for reasons outside the artist's control. See also *kill fee*.

Cartoonist: Professional artist who works in a humorous and satirical style, including political commentary.

Cast off: In publishing, to estimate the typeset number of pages based on the manuscript length.

CGI (Common Gateway Interface): A standard for running external programs from an Internet HTTP server. CGI specifies how to pass arguments to the executing program as part of the HTTP request. It also defines a set of environment variables.

Check with conditions: Attempt to add terms to contract or change terms after the work is completed by listing conditions on the check.

Claymation: Three-dimensional animation using clay figures or puppets.

Client accommodation: To work at fees below the normal rate in order to accommodate budgetary restrictions and to preserve a long-term working relationship.

Clip art: Public domain line art specifically designed for royalty-free reuse.

Code of Fair Practice: A code, drafted in 1948, to uphold existing laws and traditions and to help define an ethical standard for business practices and professional conduct in the graphic communications industry. The code has been used successfully since its formulation by thousands of industry professionals to create equitable business relationships.

Collage: (from the French: *coller*, "to glue") An artistic composition made of various materials, such as paper, cloth, or wood, glued on a surface.

Collateral: Materials created to support or reinforce a design or promotional concept.

Color proofs: First full-color printed pieces pulled off the press for approval before the press is considered ready to roll for the entire press run. Sometimes called *simple colored proofs*, these proofs are useful for making on-press corrections, particularly for problems resulting from improper registration and the effects of over-printing. Progressive proofs are the preferred method of accurately checking color.

Color separation: A photographic process that breaks up colors into basic components or separate pieces of film, which are later recombined to recreate the original image.

Colorways: In surface pattern design, the computer development of different color treatments for an approved design.

Commission: (n) Percentage of a fee paid by an artist to an artist's agent or gallery for service provided or business transacted. (v) The act of giving an artist an assignment to create a work of art.

Comprehensive/comp: Visualization of the idea for an illustration or a design, usually created for the client and artist to use as a guide for the finished work. "Tight comps" and "loose comps" refer to the degree of detail, rendering, and general accuracy used to create the comprehensive.

Confidentiality: Standard clause in contracts that prevents disclosure of company secrets and information concerning the job; may include a clause to prevent discussion of the contract terms.

Confirmation form: Contract used by an artist when no purchase order has been given or when the purchase order is incomplete with respect to important terms of the contract, such as amount of fee, rights transferred, and so on.

Contingency fee: Fee dependent on or conditioned by other circumstances.

Contract: Agreement, whether oral or written, whereby two parties bind themselves to perform certain obligations. Synonyms: *agreement* or *letter of agreement* if the contract takes the form of a letter.

Copy: Text of an advertisement, editorial content of a magazine or newspaper, or the text of a book.

Copyright: Authorship of a creative work that provides the exclusive legal right to reproduce, publish, and sell that work. Any artist creating artwork automatically owns the copyright to that work unless provisions have been made prior to the start of the project to transfer authorship to the buyer (see *work made for hire*).

Copyright registration: The establishment of a public record of the artist's claim to authorship and a necessary prerequisite to asserting any copyright claim in court.

Copywriter: Writer of advertising or publicity copy.

Copyright Royalty Tribunal Reform Act: Passed by Congress on December 17, 1993, the act established copyright arbitration royalty panels (CARPs) that set rates of compensation for the use of musical, graphic, sculptural, and pictorial works by noncommercial educational broadcasting stations. Also allows interested parties to negotiate voluntary agreements instead of invoking a CARP.

Co-working space: A membership-based workspace where diverse groups of freelancers, remote workers, startups, and other independent professionals work together in a shared communal setting. A more affordable alternative to renting an office space. Fees vary by size and configuration of space and by amenities offered.

Creative director: Usually an employee or officer of an advertising agency; his or her responsibilities include supervision of all aspects of the character and quality of the agency's work for its clients.

Croquis: 1) In fashion illustration, a rough sketch made by an artist. 2) In textile design for the apparel industry, a full-color design concept or sketch that is developed into repeats to meet the technical specifications of the manufacturer.

Cure provision: Clause in a contract that gives an infringing party a certain amount of time to "fix" a mistake before any legal action is taken.

D

De-escalation: A clause in a contact that allows for a decrease in extent, volume, or scope.

Derivative work: One based on one or more preexisting works; may be a modification, adaptation, or translation, and applies to a work that, according to copyright law, is "recast, transformed or adapted."

Design brief: Analysis of a project prepared by either the client or the designer. When the designer assumes this responsibility, it should be reflected in the design fee. The design brief for the design of a book, for example, may include (1) a copy of the manuscript, with a selection of representative copy for sample pages and a summary of all typographical problems, copy areas, code marks, and so on; (2) an outline of the publisher's manufacturing program for the book: compositor and composition method, printer and paper stock, binder and method of binding; (3) a description of the proposed physical characteristics of the book, such as trim size, page length, list price, quantity of first printing, and whether the book will print in one color or more than one. The publisher should also indicate whether any particular visual style is expected.

Director: In animation, the person who oversees an animated picture from conception to finish and has complete control over all phases: character design (usually supplied by an agency), layout, sound, and so on.

Distribution right: The right to control distribution of a work that is held by the copyright holder, unless sold.

Documentary design: Design adapted from a historical document or plate, usually in public domain because of its age, such as Art Deco, Art Nouveau, and Egyptian.

Droit de suite: A provision that grants creators a share in the value of their works by guaranteeing a certain percentage of the sale price every time a work is resold. In the United States, also known as *resale royalties.*

Dummy: 1) In book design and production, first-pass pages. 2) Book, brochure, or catalog idea in a roughly drawn form, usually made up to contain the proper number of pages and used as a reference for positioning and pagination.

Dynamic website: A website that contains information that changes, depending on the viewer of the site, the time of the day, the time zone, the native language of the country the viewer is in, or many other factors.

A dynamic site can contain client-side scripting or server-side scripting to generate the changing content, or a combination of both scripting types.

E

E-book: An electronic book or a book-length publication in digital form, consisting of text, images, or both, and produced on, published through, and readable on computers or other electronic devices. See also *fixed layout e-book* and *reflowable e-book.*

Electronic rights: Rights specified in a contract to control electronic publication and distribution. Graphic artists should make every effort to retain them if not needed by the client or negotiate a higher usage fee, using same criteria as for print rights.

E-mercial: A marketing tool that delivers its commercial message within a client's e-mail and often employs e-mail's ability to play animation and sound. Sophistication may range from the simple, such as a static business card, to an animated cartoon.

Engineered design: In surface pattern design, the designer's full-color design created to fit a specific product's dimensions; may be hand-rendered or CAD design.

Exclusive unlimited rights: Usage rights granted by an artist in which the artist may not sell any use to anyone else. The artist retains authorship rights and may reclaim these rights after 35 years. The artist may display the work or use it for self-promotion. Sale of the original art is a separate transaction.

Exclusive use: A usage right by which no one except the purchaser of the image may use the image without permission of the purchaser.

F

Fair use: A use of a copyrighted work not specifically defined, but resolved by courts by examining the purpose and character of the use; the nature of the copyrighted work; the amount and substantiality of the portion used in relation to the copyrighted work as a whole; and the effect of the use on the potential market for, or value of, the copyrighted work.

Finished art: Usually an illustration, photograph, or layout that is prepared and ready for the printer.

First North American serial rights: The right to be the first magazine to publish art for use in one specific issue to be distributed in North America.

First right: The right to be the first user of art for a one-time use; frequently describes the right to publish art in a magazine serial or drawn from a book in which the art will appear.

Fixed layout e-book: An e-book that can keep the same layout and design as its print book counterpart and can sometimes contain enhancements that make it more interesting and interactive, such as moving elements, animation, video, audio, touch interaction, etc.

Font: A variation in the weight, style, size, or level of condensation within a typeface. In common speech, *font* is often used interchangeably with *typeface*. The term also refers to the delivery mechanism of a typeface design. In traditional or manual typesetting, the font is made from metal or wood. Today, the font is a digital file. See also *variable font*.

Format: Arrangement of type and illustration that is used for many layouts; arrangement used in a series.

Fortune 500 company: *Fortune* magazine's annual listing of the 500 largest corporations in the United States, as measured by their gross revenues.

Freelance employee: An employee whose work hours are determined by the assignment and who uses his/her own workspace and materials; freelancers generally provide their own benefits. The freelancer often collects state sales tax from clients and pays his/her own income taxes.

Front end: In website development, the front end refers to the visual interface the website visitor experiences: the overall aesthetics, the navigation, and the interface layout.

G

Gams: Color chips used in surface pattern design consisting of each color in the design. Gams are created in different manners, depending on the media used and the production method. Designs for woven or knitted textiles may be accompanied by yarn samples for color matching.

Generic work: Art that has the potential for wide application in a variety of markets.

Graphic artist: Visual artist doing commercial work.

Graphic designer: Graphic artist and professional problem solver who works with the elements of typography, illustration, photography, and printing to create commercial communications tools such as brochures, advertising, signage, posters, electronic presentations and displays, book jackets, and other forms of printed, electronic, or graphic communications.

Graphic film artist: One skilled in creating special effects on film by use of computerized stands and/or adding computerized movement to artwork, such as television logos with glows and set movement.

Graphics: Visual communications.

Group head: Some advertising agencies organize their clients into groups under a group head who supervises the work of art directors on the various accounts.

H – I

House accounts: Clients that an artist contacted and developed before signing with a rep. Most artists do not pay commissions on house accounts that they service themselves, and they generally pay a lower commission on house accounts that the rep services.

Hybrid app: A mobile application that combines the common web-based development environment with the power of native applications. Like native apps, hybrid apps run on the device, but like mobile web apps, they are written with web technologies but use a native host.

Illustrator: Professional graphic artist who communicates an idea pictorially by creating a visual image for a specific purpose, using paint, pencil, pen, collage, computer, or any other graphic technique except photography.

Image: Pictorial idea.

Image processing: Manipulation of an image, usually digitally scanned, such as enhancement, colorizing, or distortions.

Indemnity: Common clause in contracts that seeks to exempt or protect the client and/or the graphic artist from damages or liability in actions brought by third parties.

Invoice: Statement given to a client showing the amount due in payment for an assignment. Usually submitted after work has been completed. If advance payments have been made, the invoice reflects these and shows the balance due.

J – K

Job ledger: A ledger or journal that contains standard columns for information such as job description, rights granted, fees and expenses, and billing information.

Kickback: Sum of money or a large figure paid to an artist by a supplier for the artist's part in passing on work such as printing. May be demanded by art buyers from artists in exchange for awarding commissions. Kickbacks are illegal. Often the supplier's kickback costs are hidden in invoices submitted to the client.

Kill fee: Payment by the client to the graphic artist when the client does not use a commissioned work. Includes two types of payments: *cancellation fee* and *rejection fee*.

L

Layout: The arrangement of all the design, visual, and text elements of an advertisement, magazine or book page, or any other graphic work (such as brochures and catalogs) intended for reproduction. Usually executed by an art director or graphic designer to be used as a guide in discussions with the client.

Layout artist: In animation, one who lays out and arranges backgrounds.

Letter of agreement: See *contract*.

Licensee: The entity that acquires the rights to use the design or property.

License: Right to sell or rent artwork or design for a specific use and period of time. It is in the graphic artist's interest to license use of work, rather than sign all-rights or work-made-for-hire contracts. See also *sublicensing rights*.

Licensing agent: An agent who usually handles marketing, contract negotiation, billing, and paperwork concerned with licensing art. An effective licensing agent has contacts at a number of companies.

Licensor: The artist or owner/creator of a design or property.

Ligatures: Letter combinations used in type design.

Limited rights: Specific usage rights that may range from one-time to extensive use, with details such as market, medium, time period, and geographic region spelled out in agreements.

Limited-edition print: A print made by lithography or serigraphy in a limited quantity, numbered and signed by the artist. May be created independently by a graphic artist or under contract with a gallery or publisher; payment made on commission or royalty basis.

Logo: Mark or symbol created for an individual, company, or product that translates its use, function, or essence into a graphic image.

Logotype: Any alphabetical configuration that is designed to identify by name a producer, company, publication, or individual.

M

Main module sizes (MM): In surface pattern design, the height of the design to be put into repeat; widths vary depending on manufacturer.

Markup (n) / **mark up** (v): (n) Service charge added to an expense account to reimburse the artist for the time needed to process the billing of items to the client and the cost of advancing the money to pay such expenses; (v) the process of adding such a charge.

Mechanical: Layout created by a production artist for the printer to use in the printing process.

Mediation: Negotiation in a legal dispute where an impartial person seeks to facilitate an agreement between the two parties. A mediator can be appointed by a judge or another third party, such as an arts mediation service, but the resolution is binding upon the parties only if the parties agree to it in writing.

Mobile app: A compact application software program that performs specific tasks for the mobile device user. See also *native app*, *mobile web app*, and *hybrid app*.

Mobile First: A method of website design used when designing for multiple devices in which the site for mobile devices is designed first and includes only those features and tasks that website visitors use the most. Then, for devices with larger screen sizes, the designer adds in other features and tasks as needed, based on user priority.

Mobile web app: A server-side application, accessed from the Internet. The software is written as web pages in HTML and CSS, with the interactive parts in HTML5 or server-side technology. The same app can be used by most devices that can surf the Web, regardless of brand.

Montage (in art): A composite image made by bringing together into a single composition a number of different images or parts of images and arranging them (such as by superimposing one on another or by overlapping them) so that they form a blended whole while remaining distinct. A *photomontage* is a montage made of photographic images.

Mood board: A tool used by a designer at the early stages of a project to convey to the client the overall feel, or emotional and contextual aspects, of a design concept. The board is composed of images and objects that inspire, target desires, and facilitate creativity and innovation.

Moonlighting: A situation in which a freelance commission is taken by a salaried person to be completed in the person's spare time.

Moral rights: Personal rights of creators in their original (not reproduced) works, regardless of the sale or transfer of copyrights. Specifically, right of identification of authorship, and right of approval, restriction, or limitation on use or subsequent modifications.

Motion graphics: Graphics that use video and/or animation technology to create the illusion of motion or a transforming appearance.

Multiple rights: Usage rights for artwork on high-exposure products that may need numerous rights over longer periods and more media, regions, and markets, with fees adjusted accordingly.

N – O

Native app: A mobile application installed on a device, either pre-installed or downloaded for free or for a small fee, from websites ("app stores").

No-assertion-of-rights clause: Contract item that clarifies that the rights licensed to the client are only the ones specified in the contract and that the artist retains all other rights. This clause should be included in every graphic artist's contract.

Noncompeting rights: Uses other than the original commission that do not conflict or compete with the commissioning party's business or market.

Nonexclusive use: A usage right in which the purchaser, along with the graphic artist, is allowed to reuse (or resell) a work in specified regions and situations. To avoid any future conflict of interest, all uses are specified and clarified in a written agreement.

Novelties: General term for gift or boutique-type items or for a wide variety of clever decorative or functional items. Some novelties can overlap as home accessories.

Optimization tools: Tools that fine tune a program so that it runs more quickly or takes up less space, or that configure a device or application so that it performs better.

Overhead: Nonbillable expenses such as rent, phone, insurance, secretarial and accounting services, and salaries.

Ownership of artwork: The copyright is separate and distinct from the material work in which it is embodied. For example, original artwork is owned by the creator even if rights of reproduction are transferred. Likewise, the artist can sell the original and retain rights of reproduction.

P

Packagers: Companies that coordinate all the components of a book publishing project and either present the fin-

ished concepts to publishers for execution or manufacture the books themselves and deliver bound volumes to the publisher.

Page makeup: Assembling in sequence all the typographic and/or illustrative elements of a brochure, catalog, book, or similar item.

Pass-through clause: Contract term that takes effect when an illustrator's share of a subsidiary sale exceeds a predetermined amount, and for which payment is usually received within 30 days of receipt.

Patent: Provision of intellectual property law that protects an invention rather than an image or a name.

Per diem: Day rate of pay given to a professional by a client to complete an assignment.

Perpetuity: Term meaning "forever" that is increasingly used in contracts to define length of usage. It is recommended that graphic artists negotiate rights for a limited time period rather than in perpetuity. See also *termination right.*

Plagiarism: Act of stealing and passing off the ideas or words of another as one's own; or the use of a created production without crediting the source.

Platform: Set of hardware components, operating system, and delivery media that provides specific functions and capabilities for the production or playback of digital programming.

Podcast: A series of audio or video digital media files that are released episodically and are downloadable, usually via an automated feed with computer software.

Point-of-purchase: A term used for collateral that includes all point-of-sale materials, such as signs, leaflets, shopping cart posters, catalogs, brochures, counter displays, etc.

Pom: A yarn sample used in knitted textile design for color matching.

Portfolio/artist's book: Reproductions and/or originals that represent the body of an artist's work.

Post-project contracts: Terms introduced after receiving the artist's invoice, listed at the bottom or on the back of invoices, checks, or even purchase orders.

Presentation boards: Any preliminary design mounted on boards that the graphic designer shows a client. In the fashion industry, color illustrations of a grouping of styles from the design collection that a manufacturer wishes to feature during market week sales.

Printer's error (PE): Mistake made in the film negatives, platemaking, or printing that is not due to the client's error, addition, or deletion. The cost of correction is normally absorbed by the printer.

Product definition statement: In app design, a concise explanation describing the app's main purpose and intended audience. The statement includes three parts: the differentiator, the solution, and the intended audience.

Production artist: Professional artist who works with a designer to take a layout from conception through the printing process.

Production coordinator: In animation, one responsible for making sure that everything is in order before it goes under the camera.

Profit: The difference remaining (net income) after overhead, expenses, and taxes are subtracted from income received (gross income).

Proposal/estimate: Graphic artist's detailed analysis of the cost and components of a project. Used to firm up an agreement before commencing work on a client's project.

Public domain: Status of works that have no copyright encumbrances and may be used freely for any purpose.

Purchase order (PO): Form given by a client to an artist describing the details of an assignment and, when signed by an authorized person, permitting work to commence.

R

Reference file: Clippings compiled by an illustrator or designer from newspapers, magazines, and other printed pieces that are referred to for ideas and inspiration as well as technical information. Digital images compiled from electronic sources or scanned from print sources and kept in a digital file or folder for the same purpose.

Reflowable e-book: An e-book format that employs real-time flowable text so it can be read on any e-reader and readers can adjust the font size and style to fit their reading preferences. There is no set pagination with a reflowable e-book because the number of words displayed per page can change based on user settings and the screen size of the particular device.

Rejection fee: Payment made by client to artist when the artwork does not satisfy the client's stated requirements. See also *kill fee.*

Remedies: Clauses that map out agreed-upon courses of action by which a disagreement or breach of contract can be resolved.

Representative/Rep: Professional agent who promotes specific talent in illustration, photography, or surface design and negotiates contracts for fees and commissions. Usually receives a percentage of the negotiated fee as payment for services provided to the talent.

Reprint right: Right to print something that has been published elsewhere.

Request for proposal (RFP): A design brief created by a client that contains all the background information, objectives, and specifications for a project that a design firm needs for creating and submitting a proposal.

Residuals: Payments received in addition to the original fee, usually for extended usage of a work. See also *royalty.*

Responsive Web Design: A fluidly constructed web page layout that scales from handheld device displays to large, high-resolution computer displays using flexible typography, flexible images, fluid grids, and CSS3 media queries.

Retainer agreement: An arrangement by which an artist agrees to work for a client for a specific length of time or on a particular project, for a fee paid according to an agreed-upon schedule. Can take several forms: annual, project-based, or service.

Return of artwork: The responsibility of a client to return original artwork undamaged to the graphic artist after using it during a project.

Reuse: Sale of additional rights to existing artwork; an opportunity for all illustrators and an important area of income for many.

Reversion right: 1) A book publishing contract provision that states that certain rights revert back to the artist in the event the publisher fails to publish within a specific period of time; and 2) a right under U.S. Copyright Law (see *Termination right*).

Right to modify (alteration): Purchaser of rights to use artwork in a collective work, such as a newspaper or magazine, holds the copyright only in the collective work, not in the underlying contribution (the art) itself. Since altered artwork is a derivative work of an original, if the artist does not grant the right to create a derivative work, the client has no right to alter the image. This holds true for non-collective works as well. Any alterations to artwork should be made in consultation with the initial artist.

Rights-managed stock art: Rights-managed stock refers to a copyright license which, if purchased by a user, allows the one-time use of the image as specified by the license. Rights can be granted on either a nonexclusive or exclusive basis.

Roughs: Loosely drawn ideas, often done in pencil on tracing paper, by an illustrator or designer. Usually several roughs are sketched before a comprehensive is developed from them.

Royalty: Payment to the artist that is based on a percentage of the revenue generated through the quantity of items sold, such as books, cards, or calendars. See also *Advance on royalties.*

Royalty-free distribution: Art inventories sold on CDs or DVDs, or as digital downloads, royalty free. Artist earns royalties on sales of the CDs or DVDs but are not paid royalties for additional use, and rights are sold outright.

Royalty-free stock art: In royalty-free licensing, the user is granted a determined set of rights to use the image in a variety of ways, for a one-time, flat fee. The artist owns the copyright. Also referred to as *microstock*.

S

Sales tax: The rate of taxation on items sold, established by each state government; in states that charge sales tax, the rate varies (in 2020, between 2.9 and 7.25%), and the types of products and services for which sales tax should be billed to the client also vary by state. The freelance graphic artist is often required to be licensed to charge, collect, and remit sales tax to the state on a quarterly basis.

Secondary right: Right to use art that has appeared elsewhere. Frequently applied to magazine use of art that has appeared previously in a book or another magazine.

Serveware: In surface pattern and retail product design, an individual place setting for the table (including plates, bowls, saucer, and cup).

Service mark: Provision of trademark law that identifies and protects the source of services rather than goods, indicated by the letters SM or in superscript (SM). Once a **service mark** has been federally registered, the standard registration **symbol** ® may be used—the same symbol used for registered trademarks.

Serviceware: In surface pattern and retail product design, the components used to "service" an entire table (e.g., platters, sugar bowl and creamer, salt and pepper shaker, casserole dishes, etc.).

Simultaneous right: Right to publish art at the same time as another publication. Normally used when two publications have markets that do not overlap.

Speculation: Accepting assignments without any guarantee of payment after work has been completed. Payment upon publication is also speculation.

Spine: Area between the front and back book bindings, on which the author, title, and publisher are indicate

Static website: A website that has web pages stored on the server in the format that is sent to a client web browser. It is primarily coded in Hypertext Markup Language (HTML).

Storyboard: (1) A visual presentation, drawn to scale, of a proposed television commercial or program or a feature film, using sequential frames to indicate camera angles, type of shot (close-up, extreme close-up), and backgrounds. It's essentially a plan for shooting a TV commercial, often accompanied by the announcer's script and the actor's lines. (2) Sketches of action for animation. Synonyms: *story* or *story sketches*.

Style: Particular artist's unique form of expression; also referred to as *look*. In surface design referred to as *hand*.

Stylists: Creative and managerial heads of departments, sometimes referred to as *style directors* or *art buyers*.

Sublicensing right: The right of the publisher to sell any of the rights granted to it to third parties. All such terms must be thoroughly spelled out in the contract so that the third party is under the same copyright limitations as any other client and so that the artist receives the same fee as any other client.

Subsidiary rights: In publishing, those rights not granted to the publisher but which the publisher has the right to sell to third parties. Proceeds of such sales are shared with the artist.

Surface pattern designer: Professional artist who creates art to be used in repeat on such surfaces as fabric, wallpaper, woven material, or ceramics.

Syndication: The act of selling artwork or another creative work for publication or broadcast to multiple newspapers, periodicals, websites, stations, etc. Often refers to sales of cartoons or comic strips.

T

Talent: Group of artists represented by an agent or gallery.

Tear sheet: Sample of finished work as it was reproduced, usually in print media.

Technique: Refers to the way a graphic artist uses a particular medium.

Termination right: Refers to (1) right provided under U.S. Copyright Law that gives the creator the unalienable right to terminate a grant of copyright 35 years after the grant was made, with the rights conveyed in the original grant reverting back to the grantor/creator; and (2) right to end a contract, most often with agent or broker.

Test Market: (v) To subject (a product) to trial in a limited market. Artwork has been historically purchased at low rates for use in a limited number of markets with additional fees stipulated if use is expanded.

Textbook: Any book used for educational purposes.

Thumbnail or thumbnail sketch: Very small, often sketchy visualization of an illustration or design. Usually several thumbnails are created together to show different approaches to the visual problem being solved.

Trade book: Any book sold in bookstores to the general public.

Trade dress: Part of trademark law that protects a product's total image and overall appearance. Trade dress is defined by a work's overall composition and design, including size, shape, color, texture, and graphics.

Trademark (™): Word, symbol, design, slogan, or a combination of words and designs that identifies and distinguishes the goods or services of one party from those of another.

Transparency/chrome: Full-color translucent photographic film positive. Also called *color slide*.

Trend boards: Visual collages of conducted research to identify upcoming colors, themes, materials, textures, etc., to provide information to clients and inspiration and creative direction for designers.

Typeface: The appearance and design of a system of characters (letters, numbers, symbols, etc.) as a whole.

Typography: A repeatable system of characters in which the letters, numbers, symbols, etc. always look the same in any combination. Typography also refers to the art of arranging letters and text in a way that makes the copy legible, clear, and visually appealing to the reader.

U – W

Unlimited rights: The purchase of all usage rights connected with a product for all media in all markets for an unlimited time. Longstanding trade custom provides that the artwork may be reproduced by the artist for self-promotion, and the artist may display the work. The artist also retains the copyright.

Variable font: A font file giving the user the capability to use a slider or some other means to specify any number of multiple weights and styles of a typeface, as opposed to a font file with a discrete weight or style.

Viral marketing: A self-propagating marketing technique aimed at replicating "word of mouth" on the Internet or via e-mail by facilitating and encouraging people to pass along a marketing message.

W3C (World Wide Web Consortium): International organization founded in 1994 that standardizes HTML used by most leading browsers. Its purpose is to develop open standards, so the Web evolves in a single direction rather than splintering into different factions.

Warranty/Indemnification clause: Clause in a contract in which a graphic artist guarantees that the work created will not violate the copyright of any party.

Web content management system (WCMS or Web CMS): Software implemented as a web application for creating and managing HTML content. The software provides authoring tools designed to allow users with little knowledge of programming or markup languages to create and manage content with relative ease.

Wireframe: In website design, the visual guide that represents the skeletal framework of a website. Also known as *page schematics* or *screen blueprints*, wireframes are created by user-experience professionals called *interaction designers*.

Work made for hire: For copyright purposes, "work made for hire," or similar terms such as "done for hire" or "for hire," signifies that the commissioning party owns the copyright of the artwork as if the commissioning party had, in fact, been the artist. *Work made for hire* (noun) and *work-made-for-hire* (adj.) are legal terms.

Working contract: Term referring to a document that everyone recognizes as a contract, complete with legal language and clauses.

Wraparound: Book jacket design and/or illustration that encompasses front and back covers, sometimes including book flaps.

Index

Note: Page numbers in italics indicate figures and tables.

MEMBERSHIP APPLICATION

GRAPHIC ARTISTS GUILD

31 West 34th Street, 8th Floor, New York, NY 10001
212-791-3400 | membership@graphicartistsguild.com | www.graphicartistsguild.com

You can also use this QR code to apply online.

The Graphic Artists Guild is a national organization comprising five (5) Regions. When you join the Guild, you join the National Organization and are assigned to a Region based on where you live.

Please complete all portions of this application, sign it, and return it with your application fee and dues payment to the address above, or use the QR code above to access a digital application.

☐ New Membership   ☐ Renew Membership   Referred By: _____

Please print legibly and provide a shipping address for UPS deliveries.

Name _____

Company _____

Position/Title _____

Street Address _____

City _____ State _____ Zip Code _____

Country _____

Phone (Include area code) _____

E-mail _____ Website _____

Has your work been published, e.g., print, web, etc?
☐ Yes   ☐ No

How did you learn about the Guild?
☐ Digital Ad
☐ Direct Mail
☐ Friend/Associate
☐ Guild Event/Webinar
☐ *Handbook: Pricing & Ethical Guidelines*
☐ Online Search
☐ School/Instructor
☐ Social Media
☐ Trade Show – Which show?: _____
☐ Other: _____

Discipline
In order of importance, please indicate no more than 3 disciplines. Please mark "1" for your primary discipline, "2" for your secondary discipline, and "3" for your tertiary discipline.

____ Animation/Motion Graphics
____ Art Direction
____ Artists' Representative
____ Broadcast Design
____ Cartooning
____ Dimensional Illustration/Model Making
____ Fashion Illustration
____ Graphic Design
____ Illustration
____ Pre-production (comps, storyboards, animatics)
____ Surface/Textile Design
____ Teaching Professional
____ Web/Interactive Design/Development
____ Website Design
____ Other: _____

Markets
In order of importance, please indicate no more than 3 markets in which you work. Please mark "1" for your primary market, "2" for your secondary market, and "3" for your tertiary market.

____ Advertising/Collateral
____ Architecture
____ Books
____ Charts/Maps
____ Consumer
____ Corporate
____ Displays/Exhibits
____ E-Commerce
____ Editorial
____ Educational
____ Entertainment
____ Fashion
____ Licensing/Merchandising
____ Online/Mobile Services
____ Packaging
____ Publishing
____ Social Media
____ Syndication
____ Other: _____

Employment Status
☐ Freelance
☐ Staff
☐ Freelance and Staff
☐ Student – Expected Graduation Year: _____
☐ Retired Graphic Artist
☐ Business Owner
☐ Other: _____

Please read and complete the 2nd page of this application.

Volunteer Opportunities

Volunteering is the quickest way to get the most out of your membership. Please select the volunteer opportunities you would be most interested in helping with from time to time or as time allows:

- ☐ Find contacts at colleges/maintain that list
- ☐ Publicize regional events
- ☐ Identify candidates and interview members for written spotlights
- ☐ Create graphics for use in ads (Facebook/banner)
- ☐ Create 30-second selfie videos ("Why I love the Guild," a studio tour, or a client case study)
- ☐ Share Guild resources over personal social media

- ☐ Assist with hosting tables at trade shows
- ☐ Share fun imagery for social media
- ☐ Be part of speaker's bureau
- ☐ Present a webinar (area of expertise _____)
- ☐ Phone banking (as needed)
- ☐ Write articles for *Guild E-News*
- ☐ Host a portfolio review in your area
- ☐ Other: _____

Membership Status

There are two types of membership, Professional and Associate. Associate also includes the Student and Lifetime categories of membership.

Professional Member (full voting rights) — Only working graphic artists who derive more than 50% of their income from their graphic art can be Professional Members. Professional Members are eligible to vote on Guild business and may hold elected office.

Associate Member (no voting rights) — All other interested persons in related fields who support the goals and purposes of the Guild are welcome to join as Associate Members, as are graphic arts students and retired artists. Associate Members may participate in all Guild activities and serve on committees but may not vote or hold office.

Dues (select one)

Voting Membership (select one payment option)
☐ Professional ○ Monthly ($19.95/mo.) ○ Annually ($200/yr.)

Non-voting Memberships (select one payment option)
☐ Associate ○ Monthly ($17.50/mo.) ○ Annually ($170/yr.)
☐ Student* Annually ($75/yr.)
☐ Lifetime** Annually ($75/yr.)

*The Student category is available to full-time students carrying at least 12 credit hours and is valid for one year beyond graduation. A photocopy of the current student ID is required.

**The Lifetime category is available to Guild members who have been members for 10+ years and who have since retired.

Application Fee

Guild dues are based upon your membership category. To offset the administrative expense of processing new or reinstated memberships, the Guild collects a $30 fee with each membership application. Please note that membership dues and application fees are not refundable.

Method of Payment

☐ Visa ☐ American Express ☐ Check
☐ MasterCard ☐ Discover ☐ Money Order

Card Number

Expiration Date (Ex., 08/23)   CVV Code

Name on Card

Dues Enclosed	$
Initiation/Reinstatement Fee*	$30.00
Total Payment	$

*A one-time fee. However, a reinstatement fee of $30 is charged for memberships renewed past 60 days of expiration.

To pay by credit card, either mail completed application to address below or apply online using QR code at top of application.

Makes checks payable to "Graphic Artists Guild, Inc." and send to 31 West 34th Street, 8th Floor, New York, NY 10001.

Returned checks are subject to a $25 service charge.

Membership Statement (signature required)

Please read and sign the following. Application will not be entered without acceptance.

For Professional Members Only — I derive more income from my own work as a graphic artist than I do as the owner or manager of any business that profits from the buying and/or selling of graphic artwork. I agree to abide by the Constitution and Bylaws* of the Graphic Artists Guild.

I further understand that my membership in the Graphic Artists Guild is continuous and that I will be billed annually (on the anniversary of my join date) or monthly for dues, as selected in the Dues area. If I wish to resign from the Graphic Artists Guild, I understand that I must do so in writing and that I will be responsible for the payment of any dues owed prior to the date of my resignation.

☐ Accept

Your Signature

For Associate Members Only — I agree to abide by the Constitution and Bylaws* of the Graphic Artists Guild. I understand that my membership in the Graphic Artists Guild is continuous and that I will be billed annually (on the anniversary of my join date) or monthly for dues, as selected in the Dues area. If I wish to resign from the Graphic Artists Guild, I understand that I must do so in writing and that I will be responsible for the payment of any dues owed prior to the date of my resignation.

☐ Accept

Your Signature

* A copy of the Guild's Constitution and Bylaws may be requested from the National office. Your membership is effective upon our receipt of this completed and signed application, the application fee, and the appropriate dues amount.

Privacy Policy

The Graphic Artists Guild will not divulge any information provided to it to any outside entity. All communications you receive will be within the Guild's normal course of business. Any offerings bearing the Guild logo reflect authorized member services and benefits.

Please allow 3-4 weeks to receive membership material.

For office use only

☐ PEGs_____   ☐ CARD_____

☐ DB_____   ☐ CODE_____